Teacher, Preacher, Soldier, Spy

Teacher, Preacher, Soldier, Spy

The Civil Wars of John R. Kelso

CHRISTOPHER GRASSO

OXFORD
UNIVERSITY PRESS

OXFORD
UNIVERSITY PRESS

Oxford University Press is a department of the University of Oxford. It furthers
the University's objective of excellence in research, scholarship, and education
by publishing worldwide. Oxford is a registered trade mark of Oxford University
Press in the UK and certain other countries.

Published in the United States of America by Oxford University Press
198 Madison Avenue, New York, NY 10016, United States of America.

Library of Congress Cataloging-in-Publication Data
Names: Grasso, Christopher, author.
Title: Teacher, preacher, soldier, spy : the civil wars of John R. Kelso / Christopher Grasso.
Description: New York, NY, United States of America : Oxford University Press, 2021. |
Includes bibliographical references.
Identifiers: LCCN 2021010043 (print) | LCCN 2021010044 (ebook) |
ISBN 9780197547328 (hardback ; alk. paper) | ISBN 9780197547342 (epub) |
ISBN 9780197547335 (updf)
Subjects: LCSH: Kelso, John R. (John Russell), 1831–1891. | Soldiers—Missouri—Biography. |
Legislators—United States—Biography.
Classification: LCC E467.1.K295 G73 2021 (print) | LCC E467.1.K295 (ebook) |
DDC 328.73/092 [B]—dc23
LC record available at https://lccn.loc.gov/2021010043
LC ebook record available at https://lccn.loc.gov/2021010044

DOI: 10.1093/oso/9780197547328.001.0001

1 3 5 7 9 8 6 4 2

Printed by Sheridan Books, Inc., United States of America

For
Erwin ("Joe") Dieu
Martin Dieu and Holly Elwood
Angela Goldin
Kris Stoever
Trudie Sheffield
John and Rhiannon Kelso

Contents

Teacher, Preacher, Soldier, Spy

Introduction

JOHN R. KELSO AND AMERICAN MANHOOD

I am large, I contain multitudes.
—WALT WHITMAN, Leaves of Grass, 1855

TEACHER, PREACHER, SOLDIER, spy; congressman, scholar, lecturer, author; Methodist, atheist, spiritualist, anarchist. John R. Kelso was also a strong-willed son, a passionate husband, and a loving and grieving father. He was many things. At the center of his life were the thrill and the trauma of the Civil War, which challenged his notions of manhood and honor, his ideals of liberty and equality, and his beliefs about politics, religion, morality, and human nature. Throughout his life, too, he fought private wars—not only against former friends and alienated family members, rebellious students and disaffected church congregations, political opponents and religious critics, but also against the warring impulses in his own complex character. His "checkered career," moreover, offers a unique vantage upon dimensions of nineteenth-century American culture that in the twenty-first are usually treated separately: religious revivalism and political anarchism; sex, divorce, and Civil War battles; freethinking and the Wild West. Over a century ago, a publisher of radical literature, who may have been one of the few people outside the family to have read his life story, wrote that John R. Kelso was "a remarkable man . . . the history of whose life reads more like romance than reality." Kelso's story, however, is not colorful fiction but an account of an ex-traordinary nineteenth-century American life.[1]

THE SMALL NOTICE appeared in the May 8, 1872, edition of the *Sacramento Daily Union*. At 7:30 on Friday evening, May 10, at Hamilton Hall, "Colonel John R. Kelso, the great guerrilla fighter of Missouri, will lecture . . . on the subject of his personal adventures." Admittance was twenty-five cents, or the cost of a meal at the Western Hotel, a block farther down on K Street.[2]

Newspaper readers in Sacramento might have heard of Kelso from the publicity he received immediately after his Civil War exploits in Missouri. Elected to Congress for the term beginning in 1865, Kelso became known in widely circulated press accounts as the guerrilla fighter who during the war had vowed "that he would not cut his hair and beard until he had killed twenty-five bushwhackers with his own hand. He recently passed through St. Louis for Washington, close-cropped, and boasts that his vow is fulfilled."[3] Sacramento readers probably did not see the description of Congressman Kelso first published in the *New York Herald-Tribune*, which multiplied the body count: "In another part of the House stands a little, small person, barely beyond boyhood, with eyes and hair of midnight black, yet looking and moving like a tiger. This is John R. Kelso of extreme Southern Missouri, who is said to have killed more than 60 Rebels with his own hand. He is scarred and shot from sole to crown, and in the border episodes of the war holds a strange wild prominence, where in the bitterness of the fight he retorted upon individual Rebels the violence they inaugurated, and hunted them, alone and persistently, like one in a *vendetta*. Here he is quiet, amiable, grave; but this studded roof, with its soft emblematic medallions, are in odd consonance with the dark and bloody vistas he has haunted."[4] A Missouri newspaper pointed out some of the "palpable errors": standing over 6 feet, 1 inch, the thirty-five-year-old Kelso was neither small nor "very youthful." But even the Missouri press, which laughed when Eastern tenderfoots romanticized and exaggerated the daring deeds of Missouri heroes, helped burnish the legend of John R. Kelso. The *Springfield Patriot* snorted derisively at an article on "Wild Bill" Hickok in *Harper's Monthly*, which claimed that Bill had personally dispatched several hundred rebels with his own hands. "We dare say that Captain Kelso, our present member of Congress, did double the execution 'with his own hands' on the Johnnies, during the war, that Bill did." Whether by the name "Kelso" or just with the generic tag "great guerrilla fighter of Missouri," the *Daily Union*'s ad enticed Sacramento's citizens to the lecture hall to hear true tales from the brutal border wars.[5]

Perhaps Kelso told about the time in the fall of 1862 when he was the hero of a raid on "a large band of rebel thieves and cut-throats led by two Medlock brothers," one called "Captain" and the other "Lieutenant." He had not intended to charge one of the Medlock's hideouts alone, but his men had fallen behind, and Kelso, running on a hog path through dense hazel bushes, suddenly burst out right into the yard in front of Captain Medlock's house.[6]

About a dozen men had been sleeping around a campfire in the yard. They were just waking and starting to get dressed. A man wearing only a shirt and holding his pants in his hand was just appearing in the open doorway. "The Captain, whom I knew from the description given of him by our guide, was just taking a seat on the outside of the house near the door to put on a pair of shoes which he held in his hands." The men looked up to see Kelso bound out of the bushes only about 30 yards away. They gaped at him in astonishment.[7]

Kelso rushed right up toward the campfire and the house and, quick as a flash, decided to yell, "Close in, boys, we'll get every one of them!" Imagining that Kelso's troops were right behind him in the hazel bushes, the man in the doorway darted out and fled in the opposite direction, running with his pants in his hands. Other semi-dressed men bolted out of the doorway and followed him. In the yard, men bounded up from their blankets. Some of them tried to grab their boots or their pants or their guns as they scattered. Most just ran. "I had never before seen such a fluttering of shirt-tails in the morning twilight," Kelso said, delighted. Captain Medlock, too, a large, heavy man, started to run. But as he reached the end of the house, he stopped and glanced around. No other soldiers had emerged from the woods. Still only a single man, running toward him. Medlock turned back toward the doorway and rushed to get his gun. Kelso was right behind him. Several "coarse-looking women" appeared in the doorway and began to scream: "Run, he'll get you!" Medlock pushed past the women and lunged for his gun at the far side of the room. Just as his hand touched the gun, Kelso stuck his revolver into Medlock's back and fired. "He fell like an ox, his fall shaking the whole house."[8]

Kelso whirled around, dashed back outside, and saw the other men fleeing across an open field. The closest one was already 60 yards away, running with his rifle in one hand and boots in another. Kelso yelled after him: "You infernal son of a bitch, come back!" The man quickly stopped, turned, threw his rifle to his shoulder, and fired. The bullet grazed the left side of Kelso's neck. Kelso, taking as careful aim as he could, fired back. The man didn't fall, and resumed running, so Kelso thought he had missed. Later the man's body would be found in the woods.[9]

Kelso rejoined his men. They had won a hard fight at another of the Medlocks' houses, though several had been badly wounded. The bodies of a half dozen dead rebels were laid out in the yard. Kelso's men marveled, though, at the successful attack he had undertaken, by himself, on Captain Medlock's men. With a few soldiers, Kelso went inside the house to find Lieutenant Medlock's body laid out on a cooling board and covered in a white cloth. A lovely woman, apparently the lieutenant's wife, stood by. This

Medlock, like his older brother, whom Kelso had just killed, and like the other men lying dead in the yard, had been a thief and a murderer. It was known that the lieutenant had gunned down several unarmed Union men. Kelso pulled the cloth away from the dead man's face, only to discover, upon close inspection, that Lieutenant Medlock was in fact alive and conscious. Kelso looked up at Mrs. Medlock. "She did not speak, but, with a look far more eloquent than any words could have been, she plead for the life of her wounded husband."[10]

Kelso ordered the other soldiers to leave the house, mount their horses, and rejoin the rest of the men. He would join them shortly, he said. When they were gone, he bent down and spoke into the lieutenant's ear: "You are not dead, and you know it, and you know that I know it. And now let me give you a little good advice. If you recover from your present wounds, quit this robbing business, and go south and fight like a man for your cause. And when you are gone, remember that it was *Kelso* that saved you."[11]

What kind of a man would charge into a den of thieves and shoot down one Medlock brother, only to spare the life of the other?

In Sacramento in 1872, three days after the announcement of the lecture about the "personal adventures" of the "great guerrilla fighter of Missouri," another notice appeared in the *Daily Union*. For twenty-five cents, townspeople could hear another lecture by John R. Kelso, with more to come. "God Is Gone!—What Has Become of Him? Prof. John R. Kelso, the crazy School Teacher, will tell you all about it. . . . This Lecture will be followed by others of equal interest." Although the advertisement did not list future topics, if atheism were not enough to shock the lecture-going population of Sacramento, Kelso could also deliver his talk on "Marriage," which likened matrimony to slavery and prostitution.[12]

Readers of the *Sacramento Daily Union*, however, might have associated Kelso's name with a different sort of personal trauma. A year and a half before the newspaper had printed the lecture announcements, it had carried on its front page a story from the Missouri press about the suicide of his fourteen-year-old son. "Yesterday about two o'clock P.M., the eldest son of John R. Kelso, living about three and a half miles southeast of town, was found dead in a ravine near his father's house." The article drew details from the coroner's report: death "was produced by the discharge of a pistol which was found in the clenched hand of the deceased. The muzzle of the pistol had been placed on or near the forehead while the deceased lay upon his back, the thumb of his right hand pressing the trigger. The ball penetrated to the brain, producing almost instant death. The deceased . . . was about 14 years old, a boy of remarkably fine scholarly attainments, prudent habits, and was industrious and thoughtful beyond his years."[13]

This tragedy was probably not one of the "personal adventures" that the famous guerrilla fighter, the former congressman, or the "crazy School Teacher" was willing to recount. But the man ready to argue that God was a myth and the Bible a book of fictions was also open to the idea that empirical evidence could demonstrate the existence of the afterlife—that the spirits of the dead, like his lost son, could speak to and comfort the living.

So who was John R. Kelso? Kelso himself seemed to ponder the question as he tried to start a new life in California. In 1873 he began to fill the eight hundred pages of a folio ledger book with copies of his congressional speeches, poetry, and public lectures. The calligraphic title page, decorated by the author's own hand, described the volume as "The Works of John R. Kelso," dedicated to his surviving son and posterity. On June 6, 1882, in his fifty-second year, on page 668 of this ledger book, he began his "Auto-Biography," dedicated to his three children. "Knowing that the sun of my life is now nearing its setting, and believing that a brief account of my eventful career will be of interest, and probably of some benefit to yourselves and your posterity, I have concluded to give you such an account," he wrote.[14]

Kelso then filled the remaining pages of the ledger with a vivid account of what he called his "checkered career." The early chapters portray a boy growing up in a rough log cabin in backwoods Ohio and Missouri and becoming ashamed of his patched trousers and dirty bare feet. Kelso describes his religious conversion, a traumatic experience mingled with his feelings for a local minister's pretty daughter. He educates himself by the light of the fireplace and becomes a schoolteacher and Methodist preacher, successful in everything but wedded life. The torment of his first marriage ends as his young, unhappy wife, seemingly on the verge of a breakdown, confesses her secrets. After his congregation turns against him, Kelso leaves his church in a spectacular fashion, publicly renouncing the central tenets of the faith and nearly going after slanderous opponents with a pistol.

By the time the shots are fired at Fort Sumter in April 1861, Kelso has rebuilt his life, graduating from college, marrying again, and opening his own school. His Missouri town is rabidly pro-Southern. Still, during a secessionists' rally, he leaps in front of the crowd and, risking getting shot down in front of a crowd of armed men, denounces his fellow townsmen as traitors. After rallying Union sentiment to his side, he becomes a major in the Missouri Home Guards, fights as a private with the 24th Infantry Regiment, and then joins the 14th (later the 8th) Cavalry Regiment of the Missouri State Militia.

Promoted from lieutenant to captain, Kelso is made a brevet colonel before being mustered out in April 1865. His narrative includes stirring descriptions of battles and gruesome depictions of bloody battlefields.

But his is not a conventional story of Civil War service. Kelso was also a spy for the Union, traveling alone, on foot, and in disguise deep into Confederate territory. When secessionist neighbors drive his family from their home and burn his house to the ground, he sneaks back to his hometown at night and, standing on the ashes of his home beneath the light of the midnight moon, vows revenge. Sleeping in the woods outside of town, he hunts down his offending neighbors after dark, appearing and disappearing like a ghost and terrorizing the whole community. On his way back to his regiment, he is captured by Confederate troops and is quickly tried and condemned to death. Before he can be led to the gallows, he makes an audacious escape. He then helps lead a series of daring raids into enemy territory, destroying enemy supplies, attacking outlaw hideouts, and capturing or killing guerrilla fighters. Mixed in with amusing and sometimes bizarre anecdotes from life in camp or on the march are also stories detailing corrupt Union officers who lead expeditions merely for plunder.

Kelso's autobiographical narrative in the "Works of John R. Kelso" ends abruptly after his gripping description of the Battle of Springfield, Missouri, in January 1863, where, as he describes it, a depleted force of 800 men held off an attack by a much larger Confederate army. His story of his personal life, too, stops with his suspicions about his wife at home being seduced by a former friend.

The remainder of his war career can be pieced together from regimental records and from the work of Wiley Britton, who wrote a late-nineteenth-century history based on diaries Britton kept during his service in the border lands with the Union army and on "several thousand" post-war interviews he conducted for the War Department to investigate pension and property claims. Britton preserved impressions of and stories about Kelso that testify to his renown as a fearless fighter in the brutal guerrilla battles of the Missouri Ozarks. Remembered as a polite and scholarly man, Kelso was always pacing about camp with a book in his hands. A courageous fighter, he also had the "eccentric" habit of entering small camps of Confederate raiders or bandits alone, by stealth or in disguise, catching the enemy off guard, and then gunning them down. He was celebrated by Union people for his extraordinary "individual heroism" and hated by his enemies as a "fanatical monster." His supporters and admirers elected him to Congress, and his manuscript "Works" preserves two revealing political speeches that define his version of

Radical Republicanism, and a third, published one on Reconstruction, was delivered in the House of Representatives on February 7, 1866. In the House, he was one of the first to call for the impeachment of President Andrew Johnson.[15]

Kelso returned to Missouri and school teaching, but his life's path turned sharply again, this time because of the deaths of two of his sons and the failure of his second marriage. Devastated, Kelso moved to California. He became involved in the civic life of Modesto, a railroad boom town that sprang up in 1870 and grew on the wealth of the surrounding wheat fields. Modesto was controlled by the men who ran its many saloons, brothels, and gambling houses—except on the dramatic occasions when citizens covered their faces and rode at night as vigilantes to try to clean up the town. In the 1870s, too, he would continue to pursue the studies that led him from Christianity to atheism, delivering the lectures that would constitute the five books he published in the next decade, including *The Real Blasphemers* (1883) and *Deity Analyzed* (1890). He also became an outspoken critic of conventional attitudes about sex and marriage, and a promoter of spiritualism.[16]

In Kelso's final years, his political radicalism intensified. In 1885 he moved to Longmont, Colorado. He declared himself to be an anarchist at a Colorado rally in 1889 and tried to explain what he meant in his final book, *Government Analyzed*, a work his third wife, Etta Dunbar, completed after his death and published in 1892. In that book he also reflected upon the misguided patriotic "blindness" that had caused him to slaughter his fellow men in the war, realizing that he had merely substituted a sacralized Nation for the God that he had left behind when he abandoned Christianity. Nearly done writing his chapter on "War," at the end of a discussion of the American Civil War and slavery, and in the middle of a sentence, John R. Kelso, in early January 1891, suffering, he thought, from the lingering effects of an old war wound, put down his pen. He died on January 26.

In the twentieth century, Kelso was quickly forgotten. His autobiography, never published, disappeared from sight. His folio ledger, the handwritten, eight-hundred-page "Works of John R. Kelso," reappeared at a book auction in the late 1990s. Purchased by the Huntington Library in San Marino California, the "Works" became available to scholars for the first time in the early twenty-first century but remained little known until 2017, when my annotated edition of the twelve wartime chapters from the "Works'" (incomplete) version of Kelso's autobiography were published as *Bloody Engagements: John R. Kelso's Civil War.*

The second half of Kelso's autobiography, covering the period after January 1863, if it had ever been completed, was presumed lost.[17]

But it was not. When *Bloody Engagements* was in press in the fall of 2016, I received a call from Erwin (Joe) Dieu, who identified himself as the great-great-grandson of John R. Kelso. "And," Mr. Dieu said, "I have some manuscripts." Those manuscripts turned out to be the complete "Autobiography of John R. Kelso," containing (and expanding upon) the "Works" version and continuing the story up to July 1885. Kelso had begun writing this version, in fourteen school composition books, in the spring of 1884. The complete narrative is over a quarter of a million words long. Then a cousin, Angela Goldin, came forward with a collection of poems, speeches, lectures, and essays that Kelso had prepared (but never published) in 1887. It is a remarkable archive documenting a rich and multifaceted life.

KELSO HIMSELF RECOGNIZED his Whitmanesque multiplicity and contradictions. In the preface to his "Miscellaneous Writings" in 1887, he noted the range of belief and sentiment that forty years of writing had expressed, "from the strictest Methodism to the rankest Atheism, and from the semi-monarchical doctrines of the old Whig Party to the most radical doctrines of Autonomy or Anarchism." A through-line in his work and his life, though, is his commitment to manhood. Manhood was the overarching ideal shaping his behavior when, as a teenager, he stood up to his father and left home; when, as a young schoolteacher, he confronted a gang of knife-wielding students in his schoolhouse; and when, as a minister, he rejected his church. It was the primary motivation for his stand against his secessionist neighbors in 1861. "I would rather die," he said then, than not "prove myself a man."[18]

"Manhood" in nineteenth-century America was about more than the gendered distinctions between the masculine and the feminine. It was what distinguished the man from the beast, or from people who lived like beasts, maturing passively rather than being self-consciously driven by moral purpose. It was what distinguished the man from the child, the former being in full self-possession of all his fully developed faculties. Bodily (and mental) health and vigor were necessary but not sufficient foundations for what was described as true manhood. Manhood had political characteristics: antislavery Northerners lamented that male slaves were prevented from achieving or expressing true manhood, but Northern Whites, too, were said to have had their manhood stunted by the Slave Power's infringements of their rights. Manhood also had economic characteristics: the link to economic independence, rooted in artisan and yeoman farmer ideals, lingered into the age of industrial capitalism.[19]

Kelso's early months of experience as a soldier also refined his understanding of manhood, especially as he compared himself to his neighbor and fellow officer, Dr. Eleazar Hovey, a man who would come to play an important role in Kelso's life. As Kelso had told his students on the day he closed his school in the spring of 1861, "I should stand by the Union. . . . I could not do otherwise and be true to my own conscience and my own manhood." Conscience was the moral instinct that allowed him to know right from wrong. Manhood allowed—demanded—that he take aggressive action based upon that knowledge, standing up and fighting, if necessary, for what was right and against what was wrong. But manhood was more complicated than that. How boys understood what it meant to become men, beyond a general aspiration to virtuous fortitude, differed for the sons of Alabama patriarchs and New York bankers, Boston clerks and Iowa farmers, Baltimore street sweepers and California miners. Even among men of the same race, class, ethnicity, and region, there were different and often competing dialects of manliness—competitive or fraternal, passionate or stoic, explosively violent or piously persevering. In the versions Kelso had absorbed in Ohio and Missouri, manhood was at once an expectation for all adult males (or at least all White ones), a quality of character to be developed and expressed, and a prized achievement to be earned from and recognized by different and sometimes conflicting social groups: a man's peers, his social superiors, and, perhaps most problematically, women.[20]

Dr. Hovey possessed nearly "every quality of gracious manhood." The doctor, forty-four years old and the father of five children, "was a remarkably handsome middle-aged man, highly educated and very intelligent. He was always kind, obliging and generous." A fine musician, he was also masterfully skilled in the art of conversation. "He was always cheerful and always sparkling with wit and humor." Kelso was proud of himself for the hard work he had done plowing fields, splitting rails, and making grindstones, but he was also a college graduate trying to conduct himself with "gentlemanly deportment." He marveled at Hovey's "gracefulness" and "the inimitable polish of his manners." Women loved Dr. Hovey, and he knew it. Men, though jealous of his effect on women, could not help liking and admiring him. Kelso could not help liking and admiring him too, although standing next to the luminescent doctor's smooth charm and debonair wit, especially around women, made him self-conscious, made him feel like the lesser man. "In the presence of this magnificent man . . . I felt as awkward and uncouth as the rudest rustic would feel in the presence of the grandest emperor. . . . In almost every thing that charms the average woman, he was undeniably far my superior."[21]

Yet if Kelso had learned somewhat different lessons about manliness in lumberyards and on riverboats than he did when studying Cicero, the war quickly clarified what being true to his own manhood really meant. When Hovey resigned from the militia and scurried off to Illinois for safety after the Battle of Wilson's Creek, he showed that he "was not the stuff of which true soldiers are made." Kelso came to see that "[i]n only two things was I decidedly his superior. These two things were *honor* and *courage*; and with many women, these things have less power to charm than have a well-fitting coat, an oily tongue, a silken moustache, and graceful movements." It wasn't really that there were two sorts of manhood—one for the parlor, and one for the battlefield. Honor and courage, he believed, were essential elements of "true Manhood."[22]

The war, not surprisingly, emphasized martial manhood. Northern soldiers' tracts during the war and memorial speeches immediately after its end spoke of how the crisis called forth courage and the defense of personal and national honor. Courage was hailed as an "essential ingredient of true manliness." It was not the courage of brutal ferocity or passionate impulse; it was "calm, cool, [and] self-reliant" because regulated by both a "sensitive conscience" and an "enlightened judgment," as one writer put it. The manhood awakened and developed by the war, it was said, was qualitatively different from that of peacetime. "The ambition to be a good businessman is nowise akin to the ambition of a good soldier," one newspaper writer argued in 1863. The experience of war, wrote Taylor Lewis in *The Heroic Periods in a Nation's History* (1866), lifted up Americans from the "false manhood" shaped by "the selfishness of ordinary life" to "the fullest stature of the most heroic humanity." One orator quoted Addison to say that "no man is glorious until he has had an opportunity of dying." In 1866, Major General Joshua L. Chamberlain, hero of Gettysburg, proclaimed that "There is something grand in overcoming the primal instincts—to be superior to hunger, cold, fatigue—to rise above the care of self, and the fear of death—the soul subduing the sense; it is a sort of regeneration; it is the transfiguration of human nature." Oliver Wendell Holmes thought Civil War veterans had been "touched by fire" and forever set apart from civilians by their experience of battle. The fire of war certainly touched Kelso, profoundly shaping his understanding of manhood and of himself.[23]

Through the lens of manhood, Kelso's marriage and family life cannot be seen as peripheral to his experience as a guerrilla fighter. He had two ambitions linking his public and private lives. He had long wanted a loving companion, a soul mate by the fireside, and he dreamed of making some grand mark upon history. He shared, in short, what has been called "the male project in its elemental form" for educated White men in mid-nineteenth-century America: the quests for love and glory. The war seemed to make the latter quest possible. His wife at home with the children could be the emotional bedrock supporting his military endeavors. This too was part of that male project: "The woman, once acquired, would sustain and bear witness to the male becoming; the man would in turn reconceive his becoming as a tribute to her love." "O Susie!" Kelso would write to his wife from camp, "I mean to be such a man as you will be proud of."[24]

The emotional nexus of battlefield and home is also present in the same soldiers' tracts and war literature praising the warrior's stoic courage. "Under the iron armor of the true man beats a soft, warm heart," wrote one observer. "I believe a great many soldiers are like September chestnuts," said another. "The outside is hard, and sharp, and shut up, but the inside is soft, and sweet, and good." Men in camp feel "the need of the kindly presence of home influences." They kept cherished tokens in their knapsacks from mothers, sisters, wives, and sweethearts. They were told that home, figured as a woman, admired their heroic deeds: "She approves your patience, amid the hardships of the field, but she clasps you to her heart for your endurance of sickness and wound." When the emotional support of wife and home failed, as it did for Kelso, the soldier had to look elsewhere. Some looked to God, but from the horrors he witnessed Kelso concluded that such a Being did not exist. He turned instead to look first to the approval of his commanding officers and then to the admiration of the men who served under him.[25]

After the war, some commentators worried that martial manhood might not be suitable for civilian life. For Kelso, however, Reconstruction-era politics was just the war continued through other means. His manly bravery as a soldier, too, was the foundation of his political career, and he often addressed voters as if they were all former comrades in arms. In the 1870s and '80s, his notion of true manhood also propelled his campaign against Christian hegemony and his stance against government corruption and corporate greed. Self-help manuals still preached the gospel of individualism, self-made manhood, and the cultivation of character, denying that the larger social forces and structures of the industrial age had much to do with a man's chances of success. The labor movement, however, stressed solidarity rather than individuality. Eugene Debs said the railroad strikers "stood up as one man and asserted their manhood." Although Kelso carried an individualistic, martial sense of manhood into his career as a freethinker and then as an anarchist, in his last years he also embraced the socialist critique of the structural problems in American society, wrestling with the tension between individualism and communalism in his last book, *Government Analyzed*. However individuality and fraternity might be reconciled, he became convinced that "all governments unman men."[26]

At the same time, his ideal of true manhood dictated his sense of himself as a sexual being, a husband, and a father, and it shaped his hopes for a historical legacy. As his second marriage collapsed, he complained that infrequent sex with his wife was a detriment to healthy manhood. In his last conversation with his son before the boy's suicide, he said he put his trust in "your own honor and your own manhood." Continuing to mourn the loss years later, and sensing the boy's spirit draw close, Kelso decided that his new belief in spiritualism was making him a "better man." In his later years, his perceived decline of manliness due to his physical ailments was the secret center of his despair as a disabled veteran. Still, in one of his last lectures, physical decline could not diminish the intensity of his convictions: "In nearly a hundred engagements, I fought for the preservation of the Union and the overthrow of chattel slavery in the South. And now, as the result of nearly a score of wounds, my life is slowly ebbing away. The balance of it I give to liberty. Let the enemies of liberty, then, take it as soon as they please. I am ready. And, as I have lived so will I die—a *man*."[27]

In self-help manuals and medical literature, speeches and sermons, memoirs and eulogies, manhood was held up as the perfection of self-disciplined virtues and the quintessence of admirable character, which transcended any crass measurement of success like the accumulation of material wealth. Through the lens of manhood as ideal and practice the many dimensions of Kelso's life—husband and father as well as teacher and preacher or soldier and politician—cannot be seen as separate. Manhood provides the cultural logic connecting sentiment and reason, compassion and competition, self-interest and self-sacrifice for Kelso and for many other nineteenth-century American men, especially middling White men in the borderlands of North and South in the Civil War era. This theme helps us see, not just in an individual life, but in a set of powerful prescriptive norms, how aspects of nineteenth-century American culture that might seem worlds apart were in fact experientially connected.

RICH AS THEY are, Kelso's writings narrate his life from his own particular perspective in the 1880s. He left some things unsaid and others were unseen.

Immersed in the flow of events, he was not—and could not have been—fully aware of the broader social, cultural, and political forces shaping his experience. Once, in California, walking alone, he tried to cross a mountain range at night in stormy weather. By the summit he was exhausted, and as the rain turned to snow, he knew he didn't have the strength to make the descent or the luxury of stopping without freezing to death. So he slipped into the cold dark waters of a rushing mountain stream, knowing that it would flow down into larger streams and eventually empty into the valley below. He let the torrent take him down, rushing blindly into the night. He listened for the roar of waterfalls ahead, and when he heard it he groped his way out of the water over slippery rocks and around dripping bushes, made his way to the bottom of the falls, and then reentered the rushing stream. When he finally pulled himself from the water at the base of the mountain and knocked on a farmer's door, the family who let him come in from the storm looked frightened as he explained what he had just done and were astonished that he had survived. Kelso's life was like that trip down the mountain. With brave—or reckless—determination, he plunged into the rushing stream of events, avoiding the worst dangers only by skill, fortitude, and luck. At the end, he had quite a story to tell, but only from the perspective of a desperate yet determined man, up to his neck in the churning waters, plunging down through the darkness.

The manuscripts in Kelso's own hand help us follow him into the stream; hindsight and historical scholarship offer a broader view. From the log cabins of backwoods Ohio, to the bloody battlefields of Civil War Missouri, to the corridors of power in Washington, D.C., during Reconstruction, to the new frontiers in California and Colorado; from conventional notions of marriage to an apparent endorsement of free love and of Mormon polygamy; from evangelicalism to atheism and spiritualism; from patriotic military and government service to an anarchistic critique of American corruption: the fuller story of Kelso's life not only further illuminates his complicated character but also the broader nineteenth-century American landscape through which he moved and found his way.

I

I Will Rule

HIS FIRST MEMORY was of the cry of wolves. As twilight deepened, the family gathered around a single dim tallow candle in their unfinished log cabin—his older sisters Ursula and Hannah, his mother holding baby Huldah Annie, and Johnny, nearly three. His father was away, having taken the two-horse wagon back to their former home for another load of their belongings. Their dog, Old Lion, who was supposed to be protecting them, had broken free to follow the wagon. First a lone wolf howled in the distance. Then the cry repeated, each time coming closer. It was answered by another, and then another, a pack gathering, approaching through the dense and darkening forest. His mother and Ursula began shoving their furniture—a few chairs and bedsteads—toward the cabin door. They pulled up the floorboards lain across half the dirt floor and reinforced the barricade. "[T]he forest around our cabin resounded with cries so terrible that, when once heard, they could never be forgotten."[1]

In the late fall of 1833, the Kelsos had moved 50 miles north from Franklin County, Ohio, to the dense forests stretching between the towns of Delaware and Mount Vernon, in the center of the state. They had probably traveled over the rutted Columbus to Mount Vernon Road, which had been cut through the forest twenty years before. As bad as the road was, an ever-increasing number of horse and oxen-drawn wagons like theirs had been sharing the route with the four-horse carriages of a regular stage line for at least a decade. Twelve miles south of their destination, in the village of Sunbury, the Kelsos would have seen a new brick schoolhouse and a framed house serving as a hotel, signs of progress in a cluster of log cabins. Seven miles farther and they would have crossed the county line into the township of Bennington. Four years later another family arriving here would find the forest so dense "that they could not see forty rods from the house" and could only find their way "by following a path that was marked by blazed trees." The land that would be the Kelsos' homestead bordered on one side a swamp that was covered with a knotted snarl of water bushes. "Almost impenetrable," Kelso remembered. Nearby, too, was a swath that a tornado had cut through the forest some years before, tearing down trees and piling the trunks and limbs and branches on top of one another, a chaotic jumble further tangled by matted vines and briars that had woven through the storm's debris. "Nearly impenetrable," Kelso repeated. But he was thinking of men and horses and not of the wolves approaching his family's new dwelling—the two-room cabin with the partial floor, space for a fireplace not yet built, and a single window covered only by a blanket to keep out the night air.[2]

And then the wolves charged the front door. His mother and sister fell back at the terrible and desperate sound the attackers made as they tried to get in. Retreating across the two rooms, Ursula and his mother grabbed more floorboards, more furniture—anything they could reach—and hurriedly barricaded the single window. The wolves circled, howling at the window. Frustrated there, they returned to the door, then back to the window, as the woman and the girl moved back and forth across the floor, trying to strengthen first one barricade and then the other. Finally, the cabin seemed secure and the wolves stopped their circling. Kelso's mother stayed up all night watching the blocked door and window, her baby on her lap and her three other children asleep at her feet.

Another attack from the wilderness was less terrifying but still posed a threat to the Kelsos. The "army of squirrels" came near harvest time in 1835. The little field of corn that the family had planted had ears ready to be picked, shucked, and roasted. But then the squirrels came. Legions of squirrels, weak and starving, descended on a single day and the family had to battle them from dawn until darkness to protect their crop. Kelso's father spent the day with his gun and his mother swung a maul to knock them out of the small trees in the cornfield. "Some of the squirrels were so weak from starvation that they could be killed with sticks held in the hand." Five-year-old Johnny spent the day piling dead squirrels in heaps.[3]

Although she had been frightened by the wolves and made anxious by the squirrels, Kelso's mother Anna loved the wilderness. She had grown up in the wilds of Ohio in the early nineteenth century. Kelso wrote: "Her father was a great hunter and here in a rude log cabin, beyond what were then the bounds of civilization, with no childish companions but little Indians, with no food but venison and wild turkeys, etc., and with no clothing but dressed deer-skins, she formed a love for the wild scenes of frontier life which clung to her till the day of her death." During their first spring in the cabin, the Kelsos had captured a little fawn, which became something of a family pet. Anna, still nursing Huldah Annie but producing, she thought, more milk than the baby could drink, would let the tame little deer jump in her lap and suckle from her breasts. Writing almost twenty years since his mother's death, Kelso remembered her with tenderness and affection. In her, too, he recognized aspects of himself. "From her, I inherited my form and my temperament as well as my love of the beautiful, my poetic talent, and my predisposition to melancholy."[4]

But Kelso was more than just his mother's son. He saw himself—and he saw his children, to whom he wrote—as bearing traits that had been passed down through the Kelso family for generations. Citing family tradition, and some fanciful etymology, Kelso thought his last name derived from the Greek verb "koso," meaning "I will rule," though his family was Scottish. He had been taught that one of his ancestors had been "the chieftain of a warlike clan in the south-eastern part of Scotland," and the word had been a family motto for generations, eventually being adopted as a surname with the decline of feudalism. Kelso thought the motto well chosen. "The family has always been noted for the pride, the energy, the bravery, the integrity, the intelligence, and the ambition of its members," he told his children. The family produced leaders, men—and here the autobiographer seemed to be thinking only of the men—who each had "a marked individuality and force of character." They were energetic and aggressive, with a high sense of honor and more than a little haughtiness. These character traits tended to surround Kelso men with warm friends and bitter enemies, but few people could look upon them with indifference. Kelso saw himself as epitomizing a family tradition of individualism.[5]

Marking one's own independent course may have been a family trait, but it also could create friction with the rest of the family. Kelso clearly saw his own experience during the Civil War, when he was ostracized by his pro-Southern extended family for supporting the Union, foreshadowed in the experience of his great-grandfather during the American Revolution. The Revolutionary patriot's father, "a man of wealth and distinction," had emigrated from Scotland to Ireland in the early eighteenth century. Robert Kelso, born in Ireland and educated at the University of Edinburgh, came to America and "cast his lot with that of the colonists." As the War of American Independence began, Robert returned to Ireland for an unpleasant visit—a stay made disagreeable because all his family and friends, except his father, quarreled with him over his support for the rebels. Sailing back to America, he served as assistant quartermaster in the 1st New Jersey Regiment. After the war he worked for two years in the War Department and then as inspector of the port of New York. John R. saw his great-grandfather's army uniform at his grandfather's house in Ohio, preserved as a family relic. According to family lore, Robert was in later years "an intimate friend of Thomas Paine, Thomas Jefferson, and Benjamin Franklin." What family tradition remembered as friendships may instead have been markers of Robert's political and religious sensibilities—signifiers important to the great-grandson writing a century later. Like Jefferson, Paine, and Franklin, Robert Kelso "was an unbeliever in the Christian Religion."[6]

Family tradition made few claims about prominent friends for intervening generations. Robert's only son, John, moved to New Jersey and married the daughter of a Revolutionary soldier named Sylvester. She bore four sons and a daughter; the eldest son was Robert Sylvester Kelso, the autobiographer's father. Robert Sylvester grew up on small farms in Kentucky, where he "graduated from a low log school-house," and in central Ohio, 12 miles east of Columbus, where he married Anna Rose in 1825 and began his own family. John R. Kelso's character sketch of his father assesses the older man with admiration, but also reveals a critical distance and the difference in temperament that separated father and son: "He was a remarkably well-formed man, of great strength and activity. . . . and was possessed of fine intellectual powers. As a financier, however, he was not at all successful. He was brimful of wit, was a fine debater, and was one of the best conversationists that I ever knew. No truer friend ever lived. He never quarreled, but in defense of the weak, or, when imposed upon himself, he was a terrific fighter. In a score or more of contests, he never met his match." He was overly optimistic, his son thought. "He trusted every body and was, of course, often imposed upon by those who were unworthy of trust." Robert's political views would conflict with John's: "In politics, he was a Whig, so long as the Whig party remained in existence. After the dissolution of that party, he became a Democrat and remained true to the Democratic Party during the balance of his life. He was intensely pro-slavery in his views, and warmly sympathized with the slave-holders of the South in their great rebellion."[7]

Robert Sylvester Kelso's wife, Anna, daughter of Philip and Ruth Rose, was, according to her son, less attractive and more melancholic, but a smart and sociable woman: "Her hair was straight and black. Her eyes were black, her complexion dark. . . . Although she was not by any means a beautiful woman, she was very pre-possessing in appearance, and often, when she warmed up in conversation upon any subject of interest, she became really fascinating. . . . In her political views, she was intensely pro-slavery, and she

wrote the best defense that I ever read of the 'divine institution of slavery.'"
From either or both of his parents, John R. Kelso could have acquired his
ability to talk his way out of difficult situations—or into them.[8]

He grew up with six siblings, all crowded into a small cabin. Ursula,
the eldest, was a "second edition" of their mother. Hannah, a year older
than John, was his first playmate. Huldah Annie, born in 1833, was, when
young, gregarious and ever-hopeful like their father, but years of affliction—
childlessness and a husband killed in a steam mill explosion—wore her down.
Robert Sylvester Kelso Jr., four years younger than John, would become
the autobiographer's closest friend and college classmate, though their lives
would then drift apart. Ruth Rose, born in 1838, was John's favorite sister. The
youngest child, Ellen (Ella), was born in 1840, the family's final year in Ohio.[9]

Robert Kelso bought 80 acres in the southeast quarter of Bennington
Township, Delaware County, Ohio, paying $100 in cash to the U.S. govern-
ment. This section of the Old Northwest Territory, secured by the government after treaties with the Delaware Indians, had been set aside by Congress
in 1796 to pay Continental soldiers who had served in the Revolutionary War.
Four-thousand-acre tracts had been taken up by officers and speculators like
Jonathan Dayton, who claimed the western half of Bennington and offered
those acres for sale shortly before the War of 1812. John Rosecrans, the only
White settler in the 5-mile-square township in that year, when it was still
being used as a Delaware hunting ground, lived in a cabin with his wife about
5 miles west of where the Kelsos would settle. Long gone by the time they
arrived, Rosecrans was still remembered as a great hunter who had worn a fur
cap made from the wildcat he had shot out of a tree. As settlers from Delaware
County began to follow Rosecrans into Bennington from the west, others
from Knox County entered the adjacent Bloomfield Township from the east.
The first, following Indian trails, were three hunters, including Enoch Harris,
a "mulatto" who was "jovial, good-natured," and "built like Hercules," as the
locals remembered, and who was living in a cabin with his wife and child by
1814. Bennington got its first sawmill in 1817, its first tavern in 1816, and had a
corn mill (supplying a distillery) by 1823. In 1830 Dr. A. W. Swetland opened
a double log cabin store in Bloomfield and stocked it with $4,000 worth of
goods; Swetland would exchange goods for ashes to supply his ashery (to make
pearl-ash for glass or ceramics). The cluster of houses built around Swetland's
store would become a local trading center named Sparta in 1837 (population
50 by 1840), on the Columbus to Mount Vernon road.[10]

For new settlers like the Kelsos, work began with clearing the heavy timber
from the land. Without cross-cutting saws, and to reduce the hard labor of

chopping with an axe, settlers built small fires and burned fallen trunks and limbs into sections, logs they could more easily haul. Log-rollings, like cabin raisings, were communal events, lubricated by whiskey, that brought neighboring settlers together. A family could get established in a cabin and clear between 5 and 10 acres of timber during the first year, although it would take another four years of clearing and planting before the land could fully support them. They plowed around the tree stumps, "sprouting" them by cutting off new green shoots when they appeared. Their plows had wooden mold boards—cast iron plows not appearing in the county until 1849—and they stirred the dirt with a one-horse shovel plow. They cast oats and sometimes wheat or rye by hand, covering the seeds with a triangular wooden or iron-toothed harrow and using a mattock to dig around the stumps of the trees. They planted corn, their most reliable crop, by hand, too, and children were sent to the fields to cover the seeds and then later to cultivate the soil between rows with a hoe. The men cut grass with a hand scythe, raked it, and stacked it in a clearing for the livestock. At the fall harvest, neighboring men—anyone within 10 to 15 miles was considered a neighbor—gathered to cut oats and buckwheat with a scythe and wheat or rye with a sickle on each other's fields. Children brought the men water and rye coffee, and an old man designated the "commisary" would dole out the whiskey. At the midday break, women provided the food from the iron skillets and Dutch ovens on the open fire and boys sharpened the scythes on a grindstone. Grains were threshed with a wooden flail and cleaned with a sheet and hand riddle. It could take a lone farmer all winter to thresh out and clean the crop from a 10-acre field, but some men specialized in the task, going around to neighboring farms and doing it for an agreed-upon price per bushel.[11]

Bennington and Bloomfield drew men like Allen Dwinell, a mill owner, investor, and lawyer, or Roswell Clark, an ambitious farmer who set up a profitable lime kiln, but also like Joshua Harris, a man from a family of drinkers and brawlers who transgressed the understood rules of fighting by hacking at his neighbor's arm with a hatchet, and Jacob Hess, who cracked his opponent's skull open with a shovel as they fought in a charcoal pit. There were the sturdy farm families and pious churchgoers that later local historians liked to memorialize, but also "several families" that those disapproving chroniclers said "were of a different type, and were sadly lacking in some moral and essential qualities that make up good citizens." A group of these Euro-American settlers a couple miles to the south of the Kelsos, "given to frolic and pleasurable indulgence," were nicknamed the "Tawaya," as if they were the remnants of an Indian tribe. Most of the frolics in the region involved whiskey, whether it was the boys who rolled drunks in a barrel until they vomited or the Bennington teacher who secretly spiked his schoolchildren's Christmas cider in 1837 and laughed as they stumbled or had to be carried home.[12]

By the age of six Johnny Kelso was spending much of his time in the forest hunting "raccoons, opossums, ground hogs, hares, minks, musk-rats, squirrels, etc." with his dog, Lion. With a little axe he opened hollow logs or cut down small trees in pursuit of his game. He climbed up larger trees to force his prey to jump to the ground where Lion waited to pounce. He fished in streams and reconnoitered the woods, Lion always leading the way home. The landscape he described decades later in his autobiography would have been familiar to other settlers in Delaware and Knox counties in the 1830s. The thick stands of timber—half beech, and the rest maple, elm, oak, and hickory—had not yet been cut down, and in their shade the swamps around Walnut Creek and its tributaries had not yet dried up. For the young boy hunting in the wilderness, "[t]hese were happy days."[13]

Kelso recalled that his interest in teaching began when he was very young—an interest, he reflected, connected to grander ambitions that were already beginning to appear at the age of five. "I began . . . to exhibit a de-cided taste, if not a decided talent for teaching. . . . I also had an ambition to win fame,—to become a hero or some other kind of important personage in the eyes of my parents, my playmates and others." His first pupils were some goslings his mother was raising. Little Johnny decided that he would teach the goslings to swim underwater like fish. He took one of the birds in his hands and waded into a nearby pond. He then held the gosling underwater and moved it along with his hand for a time sufficient enough to demonstrate the art of swimming and enable the bird to manage on its own.[14]

When he let it go, the gosling did little but float motionless in the water. Kelso determined that the bird must have expired from "natural causes," and tried again. Though getting the same result, he kept trying through a half dozen or more attempts. "I would doubtless have thus taught the entire lot of goslings, had not my mother appeared upon the scene." He thought she was going to shower him with praise but instead she scolded him severely and beat his backside with a beech limb until he wailed. The disappointment was crushing. He felt that he was "a martyr to a good cause."[15]

Kelso had better success with a young dog, though less with an old horse. When Old Lion, the family's watch dog, died after tangling with a porcupine, Johnny was determined that the new puppy, also called Lion to honor the old dog, would be a worthy successor. Young Lion learned many tricks—walking backward, or playing dead, for example—but also useful work around the farm and was Johnny's constant companion on hunting expeditions into the forest. The old, gentle horse that six-year-old Johnny was allowed to ride on his own, however, was a different challenge. Could the horse learn to walk backward, as Lion had? Because the horse walked forward when Johnny faced forward, the boy reasoned, it would be prompted to go backward if the rider on its back sat facing its tail. Johnny tried the experiment. He thought he could hold on by tightly grabbing a fold of skin on the horse's rump. This made the horse buck and pitch his rider over his head and over the fence. "I picked myself up and limped off to the house greatly disgusted with the bad conduct of that ungrateful old horse."[16]

Other serious childhood injuries involved his sister Hannah. One morning when they were small, and their parents were out of the house, Hannah and Johnny decided to grab some maple sugar, climb to the top of the bureau, and watch themselves enjoy their treat in the mirror. They sat up high, sugary faces to the looking glass and backs to the abyss, when Hannah somehow managed to shove Johnny, and he fell backward. He remembered beginning to fall, but not his head hitting the floorboards. He regained consciousness by sunset, vomiting, and confused about where the day had gone. Worse was another time he was sitting alone with Hannah. He was about three years old, and she about five. Johnny, holding a two-tined table fork, was spearing bugs and caterpillars that wandered by on the ground—"transfixing" them—for a bug collection. "Seeing a very small image of myself reflected in my sister's eye, and mistaking this image for a real living object, I undertook to transfix it as I would have transfixed a bug or a caterpillar. I made a skillful thrust and transfixed my sister's eye. I let go the fork and it hung in her eye till she pulled it out herself. The eye did not shrink away, and she was only slightly disfigured by the injury, but the sight in that eye was gone for ever." Kelso, writing his autobiography, winced at the memory. "It is now fifty years since this occurred, and my poor dear sister has long since gone where her loss can not affect her, and yet I grieve when I think of the great and irreparable harm I then so unintentionally inflicted upon her."[17]

When Johnny was about six years old, his mother decided it was time for him to be baptized. He had been taught to say his prayers every night. He had learned that God in Heaven had created him; he knew the Bible stories about Adam in the Garden, Noah in the ark, and Jonah in the belly of a whale. He had already decided to become a preacher, but not for the motives that would have pleased his mother. Recording memories that on this topic seem especially shaded by his mature views, Kelso described his younger self as recognizing preachers as skillful storytellers who could manipulate others and enhance their own power and wealth. As a six-year-old, the autobiographer wrote, he had already associated preaching with the idea of obtaining delicacies like roasted chicken. He saw how Moses would "go off by himself and talk to his god, and then come back and scare his people into complying with his wishes." Young Kelso, determined to—benevolently—rule his playmates, decided that he would invent a god, whom he named Dadle, and claim that he had private conversations with him. Dadle's revelations always seemed to enforce a single, central commandment: that Johnny's younger sister Huldah Annie and their other little friends "should obey me in all things and give me most of their apples, cakes and other good things." For a while, at least, the children obeyed the will of Dadle. "Some times my little flock became rebellious" but "I had simply to begin calling, in solemn tones, Dadle! Dadle! Dadle! This never failed to bring them into more complete subjection than ever." In writing this account years later, Kelso enjoyed telling the story but also thought that he was making a larger point about the psychological dynamics at work in organized religion. Just as parents invented stories of the "bugga-man" to encourage children to behave, ancient priests invented gods, and modern preachers threatened the fires of a hell, young Johnny believed that he "was doing a righteous act."[18]

This was not the sort of righteousness that Anna Kelso had in mind when she decided to take her son Johnny to church to get him baptized. Her husband Robert was a Universalist when she met him, hardly a Christian at all, in her view, and in a family line of deists and religious skeptics going back at least to the "friend" of Franklin, Jefferson, and Paine, but Anna was a fervent, shouting Methodist, and she encouraged Robert to become one too. The first religious society in Bennington had been organized in the southern part of the township by Methodists in 1818. Elders Tivis and Swarmstead visited from farther west in Delaware County to hold revival meetings, and soon neighbors were meeting in their cabins on the Sabbath to worship and pray. In 1828, Dr. Alfred Butters built a small log church on his property north of Morton's Corners, a few miles west of where the Kelsos would locate five years later. When the minister was serving congregations elsewhere, Dr. Butters himself would preach, dressed in his finest deerskin. The construction of Butters's cabin church in 1828 had coincided with camp meetings being held in the surrounding woods by "New Light" Christians, or "Disciples of Christ," followers of Alexander Campbell who competed with the Methodists for adherents. In 1838, the Bennington Methodists built the Methodist Episcopal Church to replace Butters's cabin. But when the Kelsos climbed into their wagon in 1839 to take Johnny to his baptism, they headed east rather than west, toward Sparta in Bloomfield.[19]

Methodists had organized the first religious society in Bloomfield, too, in 1818. Elder Thomas conducted a revival the following year that swept whole families into the church. In the midst of this religious enthusiasm, one man— tavern-keeper Seth Knowles—"held aloof from their meetings in scornful disdain." A later local historian described Knowles's sentiments as akin to those of the eighteenth-century satirical deist Voltaire or the later nineteenth-century crusading secularist Robert J. Ingersoll. The grown-up John R. Kelso would have appreciated Knowles's perspective, but not his manners. Knowles, according to the local history, "was a profane man, and took especial delight in annoying the worshippers on their way to meeting by the use of irreverent expletives." The Bloomfield Methodists built a log cabin for their meetings in 1823, used a larger one near Dr. Swetland's store in 1830, and then erected the Bloomfield Methodist Episcopal Church in 1839. But this last building may not have been finished at the time of Kelso's baptism, for the autobiographer mentions the meeting being held only in "the dwelling house of one of our neighbors."[20]

Getting Johnny to his baptism was an ordeal in itself. The boy misunderstood the purpose of the ritual. "After having several times threatened to whip me for some of my pranks, my mother told me that she was going to take me to church and have me baptized. I mistook this information for a threat, and imagined that baptism was a punishment far more terrible than whipping." What was going to happen to him? At the end of the meeting, he understood from his sisters, the preacher was going to inflict this "baptism" upon him in front of the whole congregation. "Fear gave place in my mind to indignation. . . . I would rebel. I would not submit to so monstrous an outrage." On the appointed Sunday morning, as the rest of the family prepared for church, Johnny ran and tried to hide. He climbed inside a barrel at the top of a grassy slope behind the cabin, and then rolled off down the hill. He hoped his family would just go off to church, leaving him behind. But his mother marched up to the barrel, the terrible beech limb in her hand. She dragged him out, and applied the rod to his backside in "a very businesslike manner, and yet with a great deal of solemnity, as was her wont on the 'Lord's Holy Day.'" The family then all rode off to church.[21]

At the church meeting, after the minister began preaching, Johnny slipped out the door and hid in "a thick mass of large jimson weeds." He heard the preacher droning on and on. He hoped that the meeting would end, the worshippers would disperse, and he would be able to come out of hiding and ride home with his parents. Instead, the whole congregation was organized to perform a search. Johnny knew he would be found. "At the word of command from the preacher, the whole line moved slowly forward, the men parting the high weeds with sticks as they advanced." The honor of discovery would fall to Archibald Throckmorton, a prominent member of the church and the son of a man who had been converted by John Wesley himself. Throckmorton parted the weeds over Johnny. "'Ah ha!" said he, 'here you are!' . . . He then seized me and drew me along by main force to the house, I pulling back all the time with all my might."[22]

The congregation reassembled and the boy was handed over to the minister. The preacher held him with both hands. Johnny thought this "baptism," this unimaginable punishment, would be even worse because he had tried to escape. Then the clergyman let go with one hand to reach for the glass of water. Johnny dropped down and bit the man on the leg with all his might. The minister grabbed the boy's head, pulled him loose, splashed some water on him, and then asked the Lord to "'bless and save the child.' He spoke in so angry a tone that I suspect he meant exactly the reverse of what he said . . . . In this way I was made fit to enter in at the pearly gates into the New Jerusalem."[23]

KELSO REMEMBERED THESE years in Ohio as the happiest he would ever know. His chief delight had been hunting and fishing with his constant companion, his dog, Lion. As he grew, he was given more responsibilities on the farm. At age seven he was feeding the animals, weeding the garden and cornfield, and chopping firewood. By age nine, he was driving the two-horse team in the fields. His mother used the beech limb less and praised him more.

When the family packed up their things for the move to Missouri in the late fall of 1840, a trip that would take them four weeks, nine-year-old Johnny was ready for an adventure. Before leaving his happy home in Ohio, he took a last look at his reflection in the water of a small brook near the cabin. If he ever returned, he resolved, he would look again at his reflection "and observe the change that time had wrought in the image reflected there."[24]

A quarter-century later, Kelso returned to the Ohio homestead. He got out of his one-horse hack into a light, dreary rain. The place had not been inhabited for twenty years. No new land had been cleared, and the fences were all where they had been. The barn was gone, but the old cabin still stood. Some of the trees around the house looked just as he remembered them—trees he had climbed as a young boy, with Lion waiting beneath. Others were much changed, like the sapling he and the other children had bent as "a te[e]ter": the trunk, now as thick as his body, still had a bend in it near the ground, "but the top had turned up and grown straight till it was now fifty feet or more in height." In the summers the children had loved playing in the shade beneath the old acorn tree, but that had been cut down. Kelso bent down and took a piece of its decayed stump as a "relic." The orchard was flourishing—the trees larger—and Kelso took a bite of one apple and slipped another into his pocket. There was little trace of the garden he had once weeded, and what the children "used to call the 'big field' had dwindled to a good sized potato patch." The old log cabin seemed much the same, "except wonderfully low and small." He touched the log wall and peeled away a small piece of bark, putting that, too, in his pocket as another relic. And then he went inside, driving out a few sheep that had taken shelter there from the rain.[25]

Holes in the old clapboard roof let water drip in in several places, and the ceiling that had once seemed so high was so low that he could not stand straight under the joists. But everything else looked nearly as it had a quarter century before. He could still see his father's axe marks on the old wooden mantle; the ladder, now wet and rotten, still led up to the loft. "There was my mother's corner by the old fireplace, and there were the very boards in the rough old floor upon which I used to kneel at the time of family prayer. I kneeled in that same spot on those same boards. I covered my face with my hands and wept as I recalled the family circle of long ago and thought where and what that family circle was now." He thought of his mother, young and proud and happy, as she put her hand lovingly on his head while he said his prayers—and then he imagined his mother's "lonely grave, in the far away wilds of the Rocky Mountains." Kelso, the boy who had learned to pray on that very spot, and the man who had lost the last glimmers of his religious faith on a bitter winter night in the midst of a brutal Civil War, was on his knees, weeping. He felt his "full heart burst out in prayer: 'Oh! God!—if there *is* any God—look upon me once more in compassion.'" Then he stood up. In his autobiography eighteen years after this final farewell to the Ohio homestead, he wrote: "That was the spot on which I had bowed to say my *first* prayer, and that was the spot on which I bowed to say my *last*."[26]

Before leaving the farm, he made his way to the brook. He looked, and "instead of the image of a chubby little boy, there now appeared the bearded and sad face of a middle-aged man." Then he climbed back into his one-horse hack and drove off into the rain.[27]

2

Hauntings

"[M]Y MENTAL SUFFERINGS became so great," Kelso later wrote, "that, at one time, I left my work to take my own life. An accidental meeting with a neighbor prevented me from executing this design." It was the summer of 1848, and Kelso was seventeen. As he wrote years later, the suicide of his own teenage son haunted the page. Had the boy in 1848 left home with a gun, like the boy in 1870, seeking a lonely place to end his misery? Kelso seemed to want to say to his other children that he understood—he had felt—that kind of pain. In his own life, the causes of his misery seemed clear: religious despair, first and foremost, he thought, but also his melancholic character, overwork, and a potent adolescent brew of sexual longing for a pretty girl and frustration with a domineering father.[1]

The Kelsos had moved from Ohio to northwestern Missouri in the fall of 1840, settling on the southern edge of a prairie in Daviess county, about 7 miles southwest of Gallatin, where Robert's brother Edgar and his family had moved in the mid-1830s. Young Johnny, then nine years old, thought the trip was a lark. But as the family settled in to their one-room cabin in the midst of winter, stuffing hay in the gaps in the log walls to keep out the cold and snow, he realized that his childhood was over. In Missouri, he would have to do a man's work. His father had hurt his leg badly with an axe. John, the oldest boy, would have to haul wood through all that hard winter—fuel for the fire, logs for building, rails for fencing. Young Lion, his companion on so many rambles through the Ohio woods, had died before the family made the trip west. In Missouri, Kelso knew, "[m]y days of play were gone forever."[2]

Like so many others on the American frontier, the Kelsos had gone west to find better, cheaper land. By 1830, when White settlers first began moving into the area of northwest Missouri that would become Daviess County, the Indians—the Iowa, Potawtomi, Sac (Sauk) and Fox—had already been forced farther west. Most of the early White settlers knew Indians only from the bands of hunters who occasionally traveled through the region. The Whites traded their animal skins for the powder and lead the Indians had received as part of their annual government annuity.[3]

Mormons, not Indians, haunted the landscape. Daviess and neighboring Caldwell counties were the epicenter of Missouri's Mormon War in 1838, in which sometimes bloody conflicts between Latter Day Saints and non-Mormon Missourians had prompted Governor Lilburn Boggs to issue an order to expel or exterminate the religious group. Kelso's family and neighbors spoke of a Mormon grave in the woods between Robert's and Uncle Edgar's farms—a grave some said was haunted. Whether or not a Saint had been buried in those woods, Edgar's property did abut land first cleared by a Mormon, James Bingham, the head of one of a dozen Mormon families in the Marrowbone Creek settlement. One of Robert's parcels had been owned by John Wilhite, who may have been the Wilhite named in later testimony as one of the perpetrators of the massacre at Haun's Mill, in which eighteen Mormons, including two children, were killed.[4]

Joseph Smith, a former treasure hunter in Palmyra, New York, reported revelations from God and produced a new scripture, the *Book of Mormon*, which he said he had translated from golden plates lent him by an angel. He organized the Church of Jesus Christ of Latter Day Saints in 1830. The church grew quickly, and Smith's ambitions grew with it. Latter Day Saints began arriving in Missouri in 1831, first settling in Jackson County, which borders the Missouri River in the northwestern part of the state. But the Mormons were forced out of Jackson by Missouri vigilantes in 1833. A sympathetic state legislator proposed that the one of the two new adjacent counties created in December, 1836—Daviess and Caldwell—be thought of as a place for Mormon settlement. Mormons began moving into Caldwell, as expected, but also north into Daviess. Proclaiming a revelation that God's chosen people would build their New Jerusalem in the West, and commanding Saints to come to the Missouri Zion, the Prophet Joseph Smith himself arrived in March 1838, and within two months was scouting land for Mormon settlements in Daviess. He planned a town on the Grand River in the center of Daviess, a few miles north of the tiny non-Mormon settlements of Millport and Gallatin. Smith named his new town "Adam-ondi-Ahman" (colloquially called "Diahman") because (it had been revealed to him) it was the place where Adam and Eve had settled after being expelled from the Garden of Eden (Jackson County, Missouri). Diahman would also be the site, Smith prophesied, where Old Adam would return in about a half century to usher in the Second Coming of Christ. For the Mormons, therefore, Daviess County became endowed with enormous theological significance.[5]

For non-theological reasons, Daviess was especially attractive to Mormons of lesser means. Like other settlers, they could take advantage of federal pre-emption laws that gave squatters who settled on government land a right to purchase once the lands were officially surveyed and put up for sale. In this way they could work the land for months or even years to earn the $1.25 per acre purchase price. The southwest corner of the county, however, where the Kelsos would settle, was surveyed early and government lands started being sold in 1836. James Bingham bought his 80 acres in 1837. His neighbor John Wilhite, who may have occupied his land in 1838, paid for it the following year.

Saints flooded into Daviess and Caldwell counties in the summer and fall of 1838, nearly 10,000 of them. In Caldwell, almost all the settlers were Mormon. By August in Daviess, Mormons made up half the population and a third of the voters, and a mile-long wagon train of Saints was making its way there from Ohio. By November, Mormons outnumbered non-Mormons in Daviess two to one.

Mormons and Missourians had some friendly relations early on. But Missourians thought the Mormons were a bunch of clannish, suspiciously Northern religious fanatics, and the Saints saw most Missourians as igno-rant and wicked country bumpkins who needed to convert or get out of the way. Mistrust and overreactions on both sides escalated tensions and led to violence. The rapid growth of the LDS Church in the two counties meant increased economic and political power, even as hostility from outside and dissension within the Church fueled a growing militancy. The Mormons pooled their resources, formed cooperatives, and shunned commercial re-lations with "Gentiles" (non-Mormons). They formed a militia called the Danites that drilled and marched, intending to keep dissenting Saints in line and to put hostile outsiders on notice. Church leader Sidney Rigdon threatened dissenters in a June speech, and in a Fourth of July address warned that if Gentiles harassed them there would be "a war of extermination." In Caldwell on Election Day in August, Danites handed out printed ballots to ensure that Saints voted as the Church desired. In Gallatin, the Daviess County seat, anti-Mormon Whig candidate William Peniston provoked a bloody brawl that chased the Saints from the polls.[6]

From August through October 1838, the situation devolved into what cit-izens described as a "civil war." Joseph Smith rode with 150 armed men of the Danite militia to Diahman and, with a hundred of them, visited the homes of a judge and other prominent Daviess citizens to force them to sign oaths promising not to bother Mormons. Armed anti-Mormon vigilantes rode to DeWitt, in Carroll County, threatening Saints and burning down a Mormon's house. The governor called out militia regiments to restore the peace, but they proved mostly ineffectual because their members sympathized with the anti-Mormon vigilantes. The Mormons then attacked Gallatin, Millport, and other settlements in Daviess, burning, plundering, and driving nearly all the Gentiles from the county. In mid-October, Mormon troops and Missouri militiamen clashed at Crooked River in Caldwell County, leaving three Saints and one Missourian dead. Responding to somewhat exaggerated reports of the conflict, Governor Boggs issued his October 27 order that the Mormons be "exterminated or driven from the state." Three days later (though they did not seem to have yet heard about the governor's order), 200 to 250 Missouri troops from Livingston, Carroll, and Daviess counties—probably including John Wilhite, the man who first started clearing the land that Robert Kelso would buy a few years later —swept down upon the Haun's Mill settlement of thirty-five to forty Mormon families in Caldwell county. Fifteen men and three boys tried to make a stand in a blacksmith's shop, but the Missourians easily poured in fire through the gaps in the log walls. The Saints, trapped, were slaughtered. One Mormon who tried to surrender was shot in the chest with his own gun. A ten-year-old boy, trying to hide under a bellows, begged for his life when discovered, but the militiaman blew the top of his head off, explaining later that "Nits will make lice, and if he had lived he would have become a Mormon." Seventeen other Saints died with him, and fifteen were wounded.[7]

Two days later, Joseph Smith and the Mormons at the Far West settlement in Caldwell, surrounded by 2,500 militiamen and outnumbered more the three to one, surrendered. In another two days, the Mormons at Diahman in Daviess surrendered too. Missouri's courts charged a few dozen Mormons with arson, burglary, and riot (Marrowbone Creek's James Bingham, who seems to have been part of the Mormon militia, was charged with the last two crimes). The LDS leadership, including the Prophet, was also charged with treason. Squatting Saints with preemptive claims to Daviess County land, hoping to buy the acres they had been clearing and improving, were unable to do so at the announced November 12 sale, so Gentiles were able to snatch up the land at bargain prices. In February, 1839, Mormons organized and began leaving the state. Prophet Smith and four others, awaiting trial, escaped in April and joined their brethren in Illinois. James Bingham, fined $1,000 in absentia, had his property sold at public auction by the Daviess County sheriff for five dollars.[8]

The memory of the brief "civil war" with the Mormons, where neighbors shot at each other, burned down each other's houses, and drove each other's barefoot children from their homes into the snow, lingered in Daviess County. But there was work to be done—land to be cleared, crops to be planted and harvested, money to be made. Kelso's Uncle Edgar, who had been in the region since 1834, started buying county land six months after the Mormon exodus. Robert bought three 40-acre parcels, including the tract originally purchased from the government by John Wilhite, from Edgar and another owner in early 1841.[9]

Folks said that Mormon ghosts still haunted the landscape. One night, when Kelso was about eleven, he stayed overnight at his Uncle Edgar's house. Other neighbors and friends were there too. On that rainy evening, as they sat around the fire, conversation turned to tales of ghosts and haunted houses, and finally to the grave that was said to be haunted in their own neighborhood. It was in the middle of the woods, just off the footpath connecting the brothers' farms. "It was the last resting place of a Mormon who had been murdered on that spot and buried where he lay," Kelso wrote. "Rumor, however, had it that his restless ghost was wont to perambulate the forest at night in the vicinity of his mortal remains." At this, young John, skeptical of such superstitions, spoke up and asserted that he would be brave enough to visit the grave at night. The others laughed and mocked him, but this only made him more determined. In the darkness and drizzle, the boy made his way across the field next to Edgar's house, and then into the forest. It was nearly midnight. "As I neared the grave, my courage began to decline, and I began to ask myself what proofs I had after all that there were no ghosts. I found myself fast becoming a believer in them. I looked toward the spot where I supposed the grave was. There was sure enough a ghost or at least a strange white object which I had never before seen." His first thought was to turn and run. But then he thought of how his retreat would be ridiculed. "I would go for the ghost. With a yell, I charged upon it and seized hold of it." His hands grasped a tall, old, rotten tree stump. Woodpeckers had pecked away the bark, and the decaying wood, bleached white by many days in the sun, reflected what little light there was that night in the dark forest. That "face of white old wood" was all Kelso ever saw of the ghost of the murdered Mormon.[10]

Whether the Kelsos' cabin had been built by an anti-Mormon vigilante, an anonymous Mormon squatter, or some other unknown settler who had thrown up the shelter and briefly cleared some land before moving on, it was barely more than a crude barn. The family of nine squeezed into a single windowless 16-by-16-foot room with a loft. It was built of oak logs with the bark still on them, covered by a clapboard roof held in place by weight poles, and inadequately warmed by a fireplace with a chimney made of sticks and clay. That first winter, in 1840–41, they slept on the puncheon floor and lived mostly on cornbread, or, when they could not get their corn ground, on parched corn and hominy. John helped his father build two more windowless rooms in the next two years, and once they got a gun he helped add meat to a diet that would also expand to include vegetables from the garden, coffee brewed from burnt corn, and tea made from crabapple tree bark.[11]

The farmers in Daviess carved their farms out of the timbered land along the Grand River and along the county's many creeks and streams rather than taking their plows to the prairies to try to cut through the roots of the wild grasses. And nine out of every ten men were farmers. A few householders pursued other occupations—carpenters, blacksmiths, shoemakers—but most of these were in Gallatin, several miles to the northeast of the Kelsos' cabin. The Kelsos and the other farmers along Marrowbone Creek ground their corn at the Reverend Jeremiah Lenhart's horse-powered mill (built in 1842) and then had to travel two days south to their principal trading towns along the Missouri River: Richmond in Ray County or Liberty in Clay County.[12]

Robert was a smart, strong, hard-working man, but he had no head for business. He was too trusting, his son later thought, and people took advantage of him. Though hale and hearty himself, illness in the family burdened Robert with medical bills. He tried to breed horses, but more than once he lost them all to disease. While his younger brother Edgar was one of the dozen richest men in the county and was already dubbed "Squire Kelso" by the mid-1840s, the worth of Robert's real estate placed him in the bottom third of his landowning peers. He had to sell 80 acres back to Edgar in 1847. He mortgaged his farm and almost lost it. The 60 improved acres on the 120-acre farm produced wheat, corn, oats, and honey; its pastures held, in 1850, twenty-three cows, twelve sheep, and three horses. John worked hard for his father—clearing land and building fences in the winter, plowing and planting in the spring, weeding in the summer, harvesting in the fall, taking care of the animals year round—and didn't complain. He was proud of the reputation he earned in the neighborhood as a young man of "indomitable energy, great industry, and careful management." But the teenager was also mortified by the poverty that kept him shoeless and clothed in coarse, patched homespun.[13]

John measured his physical and intellectual development at every birthday. By fourteen, he had "attained full puberty." At fifteen he weighed 160 pounds, and at sixteen 176. By eighteen he weighed 196 pounds and had reached his full height of 6 feet, 1-1/2 inches. He thought the growth of his mind was even more important. By the age of fifteen, "I was a man in size, strength, and labor; I suppose, too, for that time and condition of society, I was also a man in general intelligence."[14]

He had barely been to school back in Ohio. When he was seven, he begged his mother to teach him to read, and she began to do so while she worked around the cabin by tracing out letters with a piece of charcoal on a large kettle lid. His parents then saved pennies here and there and eventually had enough to buy John a copy of Noah Webster's *Elementary Spelling Book*. "To me, this book was an inestimable treasure." Eventually, he could spell every one of the thousands of words in the book's 150 lessons. In Missouri, Kelso's neighbors built a log school house in 1846, but with all his farm labor he had little time to attend and found little benefit when he did. Instead, each night he built a bright brush fire in the fireplace, laid a board across his lap to serve as a desk, and studied from the few books he could get his hands on or practiced writing on paper scraps with his goose quill pen and maple bark ink. During the day, he always had a book with him as he did his farm work. "While my team was resting or eating, I was learning, and while eating my own meals, I often placed my book beside my plate and studied while I ate." In this way, Kelso was able to puzzle over math problems and recite Samuel Kirkham's *English Grammar* eighteen times verbatim while behind the plow.[15]

Other books opened him to a wider world. He "thoroughly mastered" Olney's *Practical System of Modern Geography*, a textbook that had as its frontispiece the four varieties of mankind (European, Asiatic, African, and [Native] American). It asked the student, "To which race do *you* belong? Why?" This was something of a trick question, Kelso learned, for although the illustration had four the text added the Malay and spoke of five "varieties" (or "races") of the human "species" (or "race"). It then quickly noted that they blended imperceptibly together and that the scriptures taught that all men were brothers descended from the same parents. He would also have learned that there were four classes of society (savage, half-civilized, civilized, and enlightened), and that each ethnic group had its own particular character-istics. The British, for example, were intelligent and enterprising, but also too proud; the Chinese were courteous and industrious but also timid and jealous; Arabs were treacherous and ferocious, Tartars ignorant but brave, and Hottentots stupid and filthy, but Ethiopians were skilled in agriculture and manufacturing. The United States was distinguished, the book taught, for its excellent republican government, religious liberty, rapidly growing popula-tion, and intelligent and enterprising citizens. Woodcuts illustrated defining characteristics of different parts of the country: commerce and manufacturing in New England, flour mills in the mid-Atlantic, rice and cotton fields in the south. Kelso's own Missouri was illustrated by a wagon train.[16]

Some of his favorite books fired dreams of someday making his own heroic mark upon history. In Charles Rollin's popular *Ancient History* Kelso saw the rise and fall of Egypt, Babylon, Greece, and Rome. The pious Rollin was careful to remind readers that God was always orchestrating historical events for his purposes, and the author counseled that admiration for military heroes like Alexander the Great always needed to be tempered by reverence for the far greater Christian virtues. In Sir Walter Scott's *Life of Napoleon*, Kelso saw a man of great talent and tenacity—and also of enormous egotism—freed by the collapse of traditional society to rise to power in the one institution revolutionary France had left—the army. Napoleon's insatiable ambition for himself and France, in Scott's telling, brought order out of chaos but also bloodshed and misery. For young Kelso, reading by the flickering fireplace in his log cabin, the stories of daring men making history were more compelling than Rollin's or Scott's cautions about glory or ego. "The reading of these, and of other similar works," Kelso remembered, "aroused within me an undying ambition to do something and be something in the world."[17]

Kelso's troubles began with God and a girl. He encountered both at a neighbor's house. Jeremiah Lenhart, a Methodist preacher who owned the local gristmill, had gathered the township's first (non-Mormon) church in 1844. Joining the Lenharts in their home to hear the Word preached, to sing hymns and pray, and to weep over sin and rejoice at God's glory were a dozen or so neighbors, including Kelso's parents and his Aunt Nancy (but not his Uncle Edgar). John in the latter part of his fourteenth year underwent the powerful emotional experience that Methodists and other evangelicals called "getting religion," "regeneration," "conversion," and "the second birth." After an extended period of brooding about sin and praying for salvation, he suddenly felt flooded with an intense, rapturous joy—an experience he was taught to interpret as an upwelling love for God in a heart transformed by grace.

He also fell in love with the Reverend Lenhart's pretty daughter Sina (Francina), who was "as modest, gentle, generous, and affectionate as she was beautiful." But Sina, like God, though stirring his deepest and most powerful affections, was forever beyond his reach. She was three years older than Kelso and, at age seventeen, was already entertaining marriage proposals. He knew he did not have a chance. So he tried to avoid her, and when thrown into her company tried to conceal his adoration with a cold politeness. As he strove to master his yearning for Sina, he also struggled to rekindle his loving relationship with God. The rapturous joy had faded, replaced by religious despair. If

God's love had once touched his heart, it now seemed to withdraw, leaving him empty and alone.[18]

He stopped going to church. Sina would be there. And he was embarrassed by his tattered clothes and bare, dirty feet. He desperately wanted to join other earnest Christians and feel religion again. But to go, to listen to the sermon, and to sing and pray next to his family and friends and yet feel nothing—or, worse than nothing, to feel an empty despair, to feel a million miles away from God—this was unendurable. What had he done to lose God's love? He started to fear that he had somehow committed the unforgivable sin. Methodists taught that even someone who had been born again could fall from grace and get right back on the road to hell—a very real hell of unending torment in everlasting fire. "My sleep was disturbed by horrible visions of hell," Kelso later wrote. "Sometimes I waked with a cry so terrible that it made even myself shudder, as it rang in my own ears." A horrible accident must have made these nightmares very vivid. At the very time that Kelso was enduring all of this, Lenhart's five-year-old granddaughter Sarah had gotten too close to the fireplace. Her clothes burst into flame and she burned to death. Lenhart, or one of the other Methodists preachers who passed through the neighborhood, did not need to use this tragedy explicitly to add realism to their hell-fire sermons (though preachers were known to do this). The incident itself preached a sermon to the sinners in the hands of a sovereign God, and offered young Sarah's charred body as an image to trouble their dreams.[19]

Kelso prayed many times a day and read religious books, but found no comfort. And he worked. When in the summer of 1846, his father got a job teaching school about 10 miles away, John and his nine-year-old brother Robert did all the heavy farm labor. He threw himself into the work, sleeping as little as he could manage and trying to do nearly twice as much each day as would be expected of an adult farm laborer. He studied every night and did extra things, too, like training his father's horses and planting trees to beautify the farm. By harvest time he could proudly report that the Kelso farm had never been so productive.

After working so hard and so successfully, John was stunned to hear his father announce that John would spend the next year, 1847, as a laborer on the Mallory farm, 10 miles away from home. The boy did as he was told, but was soon homesick as well as still lovesick and soul-sick. He did housework as well as farm labor and earned double wages—$11 a month—although every cent went straight to Robert. Kelso missed his own farm, family, and friends. In the evenings, making little progress in his studies, he began writing poetry. In the one poem surviving from this period, "The Dream," the Devil appears and grabs the speaker by the neck, claiming his soul. Kelso, wrestling with the demons of religious despair, never felt more miserable. "I seemed to be vainly struggling against an adverse and inexorable fate; and often, when others were sleeping, I went out in the night, threw myself upon the ground, and wept bitterly over my hard and apparently hopeless lot,—my early blighted life."[20]

The following year he was back at home, splitting his labor between his father's farm and his Uncle Edgar's. During the spring in which he turned seventeen, however, he came down with typhoid pneumonia. Bedridden for weeks, he got bedsores and lost so much weight he felt like a living skeleton. During the worst stretch, he developed the "death hiccough," seemingly a sign that the end was near. He recovered, however, and was at full strength again by the summer—physically at least. His "mental suffering," if anything, had only become more acute. Finally he went to see his minister to discuss his religious turmoil. The clergyman listened, asked many questions in order to diagnose Kelso's spiritual state, and decided that God was testing the young man and trying to press him into the ministry. Kelso's spiritual counselor determined that he should become a licensed exhorter in the Methodist Episcopal Church South. Before Kelso knew what was happening, a date was set. The day before he was to receive his license, his anguish became so deep, so debilitating, that he left work and walked away from his father's farm with thoughts of killing himself.[21]

Then he accidentally met his neighbor. Perhaps the two passed on the dirt road—they greeted, maybe, or exchanged pleasantries. The young man probably looked distracted. He may have been carrying something. A gun? A rope? Whatever his neighbor said or did not say, Kelso was diverted from his path. He returned to his farm and to his work. The next day, he received his license as an exhorter, and began standing up before sinners and saints and bringing them closer to Christ. Kelso soon began teaching school and was as successful in the classroom as he was at Methodist prayer meetings. The dark skies above John R. Kelso finally began to brighten.

3

Hell Town

THE OLDER BOYS of Hell Town looked forward to the summer school term in 1852. Their village, just north of Ridgely in Platte County, Missouri, took its name from the rough characters who had settled there a decade earlier. In 1845, a grocer named Brown and his accomplice John McDaniel were hanged for robbing a wagon train and killing a man. If not yet criminals like Brown and McDaniel, the young "ruffians" who wore bowie knives to school had successfully chased off several previous schoolmasters and eagerly anticipated the next battle for control of the schoolhouse.[1]

In rural schools of the mid-nineteenth century, rowdy teenaged boys frequently challenged their male schoolmasters, who were often not much older. In many communities, the tension between the "masters" demanding absolute obedience and the students reluctant to give it was ritualized and diffused during the annual "barring-out." On these occasions, usually near the holidays, students barricaded the schoolhouse, refusing the teacher entry until he signed articles of surrender and brought treats or gave his pupils the day off. The barring-out rituals could turn nasty: one teacher tried blocking the chimney to smoke the students out and then took an axe to the door. Other schoolmasters managing to break into their schoolhouses gave the rebels a whipping. Usually, though, the ritual was a playful inversion of an already-established authority. Older boys refusing to submit to the rule of a new teacher was another matter. Schoolmasters told stories of having to demonstrate their physical command of the classroom. Sometimes a wooden switch and threats of more serious thrashings were enough. One teacher, whose predecessor had been tossed out a window, threw a rebellious student to the floor and continued the lesson with his foot on the boy's neck and an iron poker in his hand. Another laid out an assailant with a punch, pouncing on the student and slapping his face to reinforce the point. The knife-wielding boys of Hell Town, however, were more dangerous than most. Their two leaders were "really dangerous young men" with "ferocious brute courage."[2]

On the first day of school, the Hell Town gang didn't show up until after the first recess. Then they crowded noisily into the room, pushing and shoving. Taking their seats, they assessed their new teacher. The dark-eyed twenty-one-year-old had a calm demeanor. He was tall, well-built, and seemed to be someone accustomed to hard labor as well as book learning. They would test him. When he called the students to their work, the gang didn't touch their books. Soon they started whispering to each other, and, when they weren't reprimanded, began talking aloud. Still nothing from the schoolmaster. Then they began horsing around, scuffling, leaving their seats. Finally they decided simply to leave the schoolhouse, each one long-jumping out the doorway. Instead of returning to their seats when the teacher rang the bell at the end of the noon recess, they marched down to a creek about a hundred yards away, and, in full view of the schoolhouse and people passing on the public road, undressed and went swimming. They splashed and yelled and made obscene gestures all afternoon. Dripping wet, they returned to the classroom at evening dismissal. At the bell they cheered and crowding out the door, causing a great commotion. In the schoolyard, they stole hats from the smaller boys, throwing them into the creek or into the high branches of a hawthorn tree. Then they roughed up two or three boys who refused to join their gang. Through it all, their new schoolmaster hadn't said a word.

Kelso had watched them, however. They had shown their hand. He knew who the two leaders were and thought that, if he could conquer those two, the rebellion would collapse.

When the gang crowded into the schoolhouse the next morning, they found the school furniture arranged differently. (Kelso had moved things around "so that in a deadly conflict, if it came to that," he "would have the advantage.") They also saw five dogwood switches, each about 5 feet long, propped up against the wall at the back of the classroom. When the students were in their seats, Kelso addressed them. He was there to teach them, he said, but to do that, maintaining good order in the classroom was essential. He would treat them all with kindness, but they would have to obey his reasonable rules and regulations. If they disobeyed, they would be whipped, no matter how old or how big they were.[3]

A schoolmaster's schoolroom was his castle, Kelso further explained. Any attempt to hurt a teacher there was like an attack on a man in his home: he could use any means necessary to defend himself. He could even kill an assailant, if need be. It was well known in Hell Town that some of the students were armed with deadly weapons. It was also clear, Kelso said, "that they were banded together for the openly avowed purpose of resisting my authority, intimidating me, and breaking up my school." He would be justified—it was in fact his "imperative duty"—to do whatever it took "to suppress this wholly unprovoked and utterly unjustified rebellion." It was a challenge both to manhood and to legitimate authority.[4]

As he spoke, Kelso thought that his words were having the desired effect. Although the two leaders gave him "insolent looks and made derisive grimaces," they seemed to understand the new threat to their power. Kelso had no sooner turned to the day's lessons when the gang leaders slyly began nudging their younger classmates and whispering. The schoolmaster calmly put down his book, walked over to one of the offenders, firmly grabbed him by the arm, and pulled him to his feet. Kelso tightened his grip, making sure the boy could feel his strength. He led him to the aisle and counted off ten lashes with a dogwood switch. This restored order for the rest of the morning. At the lunch recess, the gang met in the shade of some trees in the yard. Closer to the schoolhouse, one of the older girls tried to persuade her brother to stay out of trouble.[5]

"Charley, this teacher is not like the other teachers," she warned. "Somebody is going to get hurt." But Charley wasn't worried. The gang was twenty strong, and there was only one school teacher, he said. He liked the odds.[6]

In the afternoon, the gang again went for a swim, and again only returned to the classroom, raucous and dripping, shortly before the evening dismissal bell. "Their faces wore looks of defiance," Kelso later recalled, "and they were evidently prepared for the conflict, which was now bound to take place, and which was to determine who was to rule that school." The schoolmaster did not let them take their seats. He asked the gang's principal leader if he would be so kind as to step up and take twenty lashes. "He put his hand upon the hilt of his bowie knife, drew the knife partly from the scabbard, and held it there, giving me, at the same time, a really murderous look. I then thought that I would have to kill him; and I confess that, all at once, I began to feel like killing him." Kelso stared into the gang leader's eyes, "looking my deadly intention into his very soul." I will count to ten, the schoolmaster said. If by the time I say "ten" you haven't come forward to be whipped and handed me your knife handle foremost, it will be too late. None of the other students in the room seemed to breathe. Kelso began counting slowly. The gang leader's "face assumed an ashy paleness, his lips and chin quivered," and when Kelso pronounced the word "seven," the rebel "drew his knife quickly, presented it handle foremost, and stood waiting." Kelso gave him the twenty lashes.

Then he called up the other leader, asked for his knife, and gave him twenty lashes too. He repeated this with the other members of the gang. He then announced that a second offense would earn forty lashes, a third eighty, and so on, doubling every time. School was dismissed for the day.[7]

News of Kelso's conquest spread quickly. The gang members were jeered. The next day, desperate and exasperated, the two leaders with three others again challenged Kelso's authority and received forty lashes each. Then he turned to another weapon in the nineteenth-century schoolmaster's arsenal: humiliation. He called the main gang leader to the front of the room. Kelso split the end of a four-foot lath and affixed it to the young man's nose and mocked him, calling him an exhibition elephant. "And so cowardly did this bully become," Kelso wrote, "when he found himself fully mastered, that he tamely submitted to this intolerable humiliation." Kelso then expelled him from the school and warned him never to come near the schoolhouse again. This broke the rebellion. Kelso had no more trouble for the rest of the term and never again had to reach for a dogwood switch.[8]

KELSO HAD TAKEN his first teaching job four years earlier, in his own neighborhood school. Although public lands had been set aside in each Missouri township for the support of public schools, in most counties by the 1850s these funds were more theoretical than real. Missouri children, if they attended school at all, more often went to subscription schools organized by local communities or private schools staffed by entrepreneurial teachers. In 1846 the farm families in Kelso's neighborhood had built a log cabin to serve as a schoolhouse for their children, and in the fall of 1848 they hired Robert Kelso's studious eldest son, the hard-working farm boy with dirty bare feet, to teach a four-month term.[9]

Even in this school of twenty-some students, two-thirds of whom were Kelso's siblings and cousins, the schoolmaster's authority was enforced by "a large hickory whip." In school rooms across the country, discipline was considered the foundation of all learning. Often the first question parents and local school boards asked teaching candidates was about how they would maintain order in a room crowded with pupils ranging in age from five years to twenty. Advice from the experts hammered this theme home too. "The first step a teacher must take . . ." educator Jacob Abbott had lectured back in 1831, "is to obtain the entire unqualified submission of the school to his authority." A disciplined classroom also served a larger social purpose, as Boston schoolmasters noted in 1844: "Implicit obedience to rightful authority must be inculcated and enforced upon children as the very germ of all good order in future society." While it had once been common for incorrect answers to be punished by a thwack with a ruler, by mid-century physical punishments were usually reserved for misbehavior. Even reformers who wanted to reduce the frequency of corporal punishments expected students to learn the habits of self-government through a strict obedience to the master's rightful authority.[10]

In his first school, however, the hickory whip seemed to serve more as a warning or an occasional last resort than as a daily tool of instruction. Kelso would later recollect that first teaching experience with great fondness. Although his memories were no doubt tinged by nostalgia, the pleasures of that schoolhouse even at the time strongly suggested to him that teaching might be his true calling—or, at least, a path toward a more fulfilling life than one spent behind a plow.

The school was a low log house covered with clapboards. On one wall, a log had been cut out, making one long, narrow window, which, in bad weather, could be closed by pulling down a long plank held to the wall with leather fasteners. On the opposite wall was a huge fireplace, 10 feet wide and 4 feet deep, in which on cold days they built roaring fires, burning nearly half a cord of wood at a time. The only desk was a wide plank affixed to the wall beneath the window, where the students took turns. Split logs served as their seats. Throughout the morning, they had quails, squirrels, and prairie chickens broiling or roasting over the fire, and they feasted both at their morning recess and at lunchtime. Years later, after Kelso had dined at the president's table in the White House, he wrote that he had never more enjoyed a meal than his "hot-broiled quail, eaten as I sat on those rude log benches, before that great fire-place, surrounded by my happy romping pupils."[11]

Teaching—instruction in reading, writing, arithmetic, and perhaps geography—was driven by the textbooks the students used, most of which were written as catechisms in a question-and-answer format. Students went through their lessons at their seats and then went up to the teacher singly to do their recitations. They copied sentences in copy books or on slates, perfecting their handwriting. They memorized passages and poems and delivered them orally as the teacher scrutinized their oratorical performance. The teacher was an overseer, making sure that students were dutifully doing their work. He could also be a drillmaster, taking groups of students through exercises orally. Students were expected to memorize facts, master skills, and demonstrate what they had learned through public speaking and contests such as spelling bees. As they committed facts to memory and developed their ability to read, write, speak, and cipher, students were also expected to absorb the values that permeated their textbook exercises: cultivate good manners and morals, venerate God and country, respect private property and legitimate authority, and develop self-reliance without self-indulgence. Kelso would never know a happier school than his first, "or one that did better learning."[12]

As Kelso became known in the neighborhood as an able teacher, his profile also rose through his labors as a Methodist exhorter. Methodism, which began in the eighteenth century as a heart-centered religious movement within the Church of England, had been merely a small and suspect sect in America until after the Revolution. Then, as the older denominations—the Episcopalians, Congregationalists, Presbyterians, and Quakers—limped along in the late eighteenth century, the Methodists and the Baptists preached emotional sermons with a simple, straightforward message about sin and salvation to common folks who began joining their churches by the thousands and then tens of thousands. Like the Baptists, the Methodists offered laypeople opportunities to cultivate and share a faith centered on their own experiences. In small weekly classes and prayer meetings as well as Sunday services and week-long camp meeting revivals, they practiced a religion of joy and tears, singing hymns to heaven and telling their own tales of lives transformed. Like the Baptists, too, the Methodists offered ambitious young men like Kelso who felt the call to preach the opportunity to enter the ministry without the time and expense of college and divinity study. Such young men could, depending upon their talents and drive, move up the ladder quite quickly from exhorters (who could lead prayer meetings, Bible studies, and worship services but not deliver formal sermons) to itinerant ministers to settled pastors and church elders. To their populist rhetoric and strategies encouraging lay participation, Methodists added an efficient hierarchical structure in which bishops directed young itinerant ministers on preaching circuits through the countryside, a model brilliantly adapted to an expanding frontier society. By the time Kelso had joined the church in the early 1840s, Methodism had become the largest Protestant denomination in the United States. As a successful schoolteacher and Methodist preacher-in-training, Kelso was a young man on the rise.[13]

Kelso usually held Sunday religious services in the schoolhouse or in one of his neighbor's homes. On Wednesday evenings, he led a young people's prayer meeting. There he guided a group of teenagers and young adults through hymns and prayers until they shook and shouted, praising God's glory and having "such a good time" until after midnight. He led the services after dismissing his school and finishing his farm chores, usually having to run the 8 miles to get there in time. Then he walked back, reaching home in the middle of the night, often not bothering to get a few hours' sleep before sunrise brought morning chores and the start of a new school day. On other evenings, he prepared his school lessons and continued his own studies, which were then focused on scripture and theology. Too busy to worry quite so much about going to hell, Kelso hoped his "intensively earnest work," especially as an exhorter, would "induce God to relent and reverse the decree of eternal damnation."[14]

His piety propelled him to run those 8 miles each week. But there were also girls there. Having recovered from his love-sickness for Sina, Kelso started to notice other pretty faces. He began to "spark around a little" with some of the girls, but nothing so serious as to damage a girl's reputation or rouse a shotgun-wielding father. A certain "Miss D," a red-haired, freckle-faced older girl who had already "trained a dozen or more of the young men . . . in the delightful art of sparking," gave Kelso his first lessons. He was more interested, though, in sweet, blue-eyed Bettie Splawn. His interest in Mary Adelia Moore, another preacher's daughter, was of a different character. He did not feel any powerful sexual attraction to her—or, as he put it, "I never felt any strong desire to caress her, as I would, unavoidably, have felt if my love for her had been founded on nature." His sense of her was bound up with his quest to draw close to God once again. "I loved her simply because . . . God seemed to love her and to always be with her."[15]

Before he even began courting Adelia, Kelso discovered he had a jealous rival: a wealthy young man at the prayer meeting named Robert Cravens, whose father owned a valuable farm and nine slaves. Cravens, who in Kelso's view was conceited, overbearing, and endowed "with a very meager supply of inferior brains," sensed that Kelso would be his chief obstacle to winning Adelia's hand. Kelso shined at the Wednesday evening meetings, admired by everyone for his eloquent extemporaneous prayers. Cravens thought he could defeat Kelso by out-praying him. But Cravens was a horrible public speaker and couldn't even recite the Lord's Prayer without stumbling over his words. So he paid a young Gallatin lawyer five dollars to compose an impressive prayer for him, and he tried to memorize it for delivery at the Wednesday meeting by practicing portions of it daily while pacing in a grove near his home. Kelso learned of this and foiled Cravens' plans simply by calling on him to lead the first prayer of the evening, before he was ready. "[Cravens] waited a moment, and then, in a deep bass voice said: 'Ahem! ahem! (clearing his throat.) Oh! Lord God, we pray thee to—to—ahem!—ahem! (Then raising his voice to a nervous tenor). Oh! Lord God, we pray thee to—ahem! ahem! (Then raising his voice to a nervous treble). Oh! Lord God, we pray thee to—ahem!—ahem—pshaw! (In great disgust). Amen.'" The worshippers, knowing of Cravens's boasts and enjoying Kelso's triumph, shook with suppressed laughter.[16]

After the school term ended and Kelso turned eighteen in the spring of 1849, he went to live for a few months with another nearby uncle, John W. Kelso, who with his wife Phoebe had a small farm, six children, and a side business manufacturing grindstones. Young John learned how to cut a block of sandstone from a quarry, and then turn the block on its side and with wedges split it into smaller pieces along the grain. Then with hammer and chisel he would chip the corners of the stone off and pierce its center for the eye of the wheel. The final smoothing of the wheel's edges produced clouds of grit and fine dust—inhaling it, full-time "turners" were said to get "grit consumption" and be dead in five years. But John had learned a valuable skill, because everyone needed grindstones to sharpen their blades and tools. He returned home and set up a grindstone shop on his father's farm. His labor was now worth about $3.00 a day to Robert, or five times the value of a common farmhand's work. Every cent still went to Robert—just like all the money John had ever earned from farm labor or teaching.[17]

One morning, Kelso left his grindstones for about two hours. When he returned, his father, already in a bad mood from some other cause and angry that his eldest son had stepped away from his work, ripped into him before John could even explain. Being so severely and unjustly chastised was bad enough, but suffering such a bitter reprimand in front of his mother and sisters, as if he were a negligent child, was more than he could bear. He turned to face his father. He did not lose his temper, but he stood his ground. I've never been away from my work, John said, but this one time it was unavoidable. I've never disobeyed you. I've worked hard, winter and summer, as few boys ever have. I've never kept a penny of the money I've earned. Although I teach school and lead church in these miserable patched clothes, I've never complained. But this is too much. I'll finish the grindstones we have on order, but then I'm leaving. I won't return to your house again except as a visitor.[18]

Robert's anger cooled. He admitted that John had been a hard worker and a good son. But then he became legalistic, shifting a conflict between father and son into something more like a negotiation between a master and his indentured servant. He invoked his paternal right, by common law and custom, to his child's wages until the child turned twenty-one. That right was in fact allied to the legal understanding of apprenticeship. In both cases, the father/master and the son/servant were in a hierarchical but reciprocal relationship. Robert's rights to John's wages were tied to obligations to feed, clothe, and educate. John's remark about his shabby clothing was not just a grievance; it was a none-too-subtle suggestion that Robert had reneged on his part of the implicit bargain. John could also have noted that his father had never spent anything on John's education beyond the cost of Webster's *Spelling Book* a decade earlier. Moreover, by the middle of the nineteenth century a father's common law rights were under considerable stress as part of what has been called a "civil war" in household governance. Acknowledging a new economy in which minors increasingly labored outside the home for cash, courts "increasingly imagined young people as capable of judging their own interests and acting for themselves." A father's failures to meet his obligations could be legally taken to imply a son's early emancipation from paternal authority. Fathers and sons usually worked out agreements wherein the father gave or sold the remaining time, canceling the debt of future wages or allowing the son to pay off the debt ahead of schedule. Robert chose the latter course. John would finish the last few grindstones and leave home, paying Robert ten dollars a month (somewhat more than a laboring man's average wage).[19]

So, around the first of August, 1849, John R. Kelso left home. In his pocket he had a five-franc piece—the most money he had ever owned at one time—which his father had given him as a parting gift. It was worth about 93 cents. With that and one extra coarse shirt, he crossed the threshold from boyhood to manhood and set out on his own.[20]

Over the next six months, Kelso worked in a stone quarry, on a riverboat, and in a lumberyard. He first walked 60 miles south to Lexington, a market town on the Missouri River, where he worked in the quarry and boarded with drunken Irishmen, wharf rats, and mosquitoes that together kept him up at night. When the quarry owner cheated Kelso out of his first month's wage, he got a job on a lumber boat. One night the boat was swamped and sunk by a wave from a big steamboat. Thrown into dangerous currents in the darkness, the boatmen could have drowned, but all managed to swim to shore. Kelso then took his first steamboat trip, heading to St. Louis aboard the *Saint Ange*. During this trip, his steamer engaged in an exciting race with another boat, and such races always had the added thrill of risk, since steamboat engines sometimes exploded under the strain. The danger to Kelso came not from an explosion, but from his attempt to imitate the experienced boatmen and throw a bucket tied to a rope overboard to get some water. Hit by a wave, the bucket jerked the rope wrapped around his wrist so hard that it almost broke his arm and pulled him overboard. Fortunately, the rope, rather than his arm, snapped. When he reached St. Louis, he saw the sights of the big city, but not finding any work that interested him, he walked the 150 miles back across the state toward Lexington. At a friend's lumberyard across the river, he got a job chopping wood for 50 cents a cord, which he did for two months until a bout of malaria drove him back to his father's house and his mother's nursing.[21]

In the spring of 1850, he began his career as an itinerant schoolteacher. He taught a term a few miles east of Gallatin for fifteen dollars a month, then one for eighteen dollars a month farther from home in Caldwell County, then for twenty dollars a month still farther away in Ray County. This last school term was interrupted, however, when the Missouri River flooded. Arriving at his schoolhouse, he found 6 feet of water in the room, with more rushing in. He saw other houses torn from their foundations and taken by the river. "Many families took refuge in trees," he recalled. "Here some of them remained, several days, exposed to the pelting storms, before they were rescued. I can never forget the scenes of terror and of suffering that I then witnessed. Parents tied themselves and their little ones fast to trees lest they fall asleep and drop into the raging floods below." For eight days, he worked to help "save the lives of these poor people."[22]

While engaged to teach a six-month term about 10 miles from his old neighborhood, he married Mary Adelia Moore, age seventeen, on August 28, 1851. He had decided that if he could join his life to one who was so sweetly pious, so "nearly angelic," he could become a better Christian. "I felt that, on her account, God would be present every day, in my home, and that, on her account, he might probably be induced to bless me also." In a letter to his sister Ursula, Kelso described Adelia as steady, accomplished, pious, and kind. When she consented to marry him, and in nearly all their conversations leading up to the wedding day, she wept—and apparently they were not tears of joy.[23]

At first, Adelia continued to live with her parents, and Kelso visited her on weekends. When he got a job 20 miles away, he could only see her once a month. He would begin walking after he dismissed school on a Friday evening and usually reached "Father Moore's" farm by midnight. Once, though, he got caught in a winter storm and spent the whole night lost in a swamp, trudging through the snow and often breaking through the ice and falling into thick mud. When he finally reached Adelia, she greeted him with "the utmost indifference," which "grieved" him "sorely." Adelia, he decided, was suffering from some secret sorrow which his presence only seemed to make worse.[24]

When he went to the town of New Market in Platte County, on the Missouri River across from Kansas, he sent for Adelia, but she quarreled with the family they boarded with and their three months there were far from pleasant. Then they moved 15 miles east to Ridgely and rented a house while Kelso taught in Hell Town. His triumph over the gang there built on the success he had had in his previous teaching engagements. In the evenings he continued to write poetry and make good progress in his own studies, focusing now on algebra, geometry, anatomy, physiology, and hygiene. So his work was going well, but his domestic life was still blighted. Adelia refused to call their little house a home and pined to be back at her parents' place. She was irritable and snappish. She busied herself only with religion, and even that did not make her happy. Not only was it becoming obvious that she did not love him, but, he reflected, "it seemed to be only from a sense of duty and not from any feeling of affection that she ever treated me with any wifely consideration at all." Kelso did his best to be a model husband: "I tried to be so good to her that she could not help loving me." He prayed every night to God to help him win her affections.[25]

If he did not pray for children he at least hoped for them and was saddened when after two years of marriage Adelia had still not become pregnant. He was shocked, then, and deeply hurt when he happened to discover that Adelia "was persistently using effectual means to prevent conception." Since she knew how badly he wanted children, he saw this as an "extreme unkindness" to him. More damaging, though, was his sense that she had committed a terrible sin. From an angel, she had fallen to become "a kind of murderess." He felt a "strange revulsion of feeling" toward her and, confronting her, told her that he "could not live with a woman who would thus destroy, in her own womb, the life germs of her own children." Wringing her hands in agony, Adelia agreed with John's bitter reproof, begged for his pardon, promised never to do it again, and feared that even if her husband could forgive her wickedness God would not. The following spring, on April 27, 1854, their daughter Florella was born.[26]

In the next year, as Kelso later wrote, "Every thing succeeded that I touched, and every body was loud in my praise." He moved his young family to Buchanan County just to the north and taught in two happy schools. He was promoted from exhorter to minister in the Methodist Church and "preached every Sunday to good congregations and soon became a successful revivalist." He was also the superintendent of a large Sunday school and a "worthy chief" in a lodge of Good Templars, a fraternal society. In every spare moment, he continued his own studies, working through a college curriculum. Florella was a delightful child and a ray of sunshine in their dreary household. Even Adelia's mood improved—less from the joy of motherhood, Kelso thought, than because she enjoyed sharing in his growing popularity and prestige. But as the Kelsos moved back to Platte County in the spring of 1855, to spend the next year just north of Weston and across the river from Fort Leavenworth, Kansas, the war on the border between Kansas and Missouri—the Midwestern civil war that preceded the Civil War—intruded upon their lives.[27]

Weston—like the whole county, like the whole Missouri-Kansas border region—had turned into a Hell Town: a place where authority was breaking down and men reached for weapons and threatened violence to settle the issue at hand. But which party stood like the schoolmaster, teaching a lesson about law and order, and which was the gang of rebels, needing to be mastered or humiliated and driven out?

The issue at hand in the mid-1850s was slavery. Slavery had defined Missouri at its very beginning three and a half decades earlier. The Missouri Compromise in 1820 had carved it out of Louisiana Purchase land and created it as the northernmost and westernmost slave state. In the 1850s, with new territory acquired in the Mexican War, Missouri was again at the center of national conflict. The Kansas-Nebraska Act of 1854 had left the question of slavery in Kansas up to the people who settled there. Proslavery Missourians, eager to claim more land to their west and desperate that their state not be surrounded on three sides by free territory (which would encourage runaways), wanted to make sure Kansas became a slave state. Slavery's opponents in other states quickly formed emigrant aid societies to support settlers who would preserve Kansas for free labor. Political and business leaders in Platte County in July 1854 called a public meeting and resolved to establish a "Self-Defensive Association" that would scrutinize and report "all suspicious looking persons" and call out armed men to protect slave property and proslavery settlement across the river. Other border counties established similar associations, which evolved into semi-secret vigilante groups, sometimes called "Blue Lodges." Proslavery Missourians, who had previously thought of themselves as Western farmers in a region distinct from both the plantation South and the industrializing North, began identifying with the beleaguered South and asserting their own Southernness as their domestic institution came under attack. They thought of themselves as defending their constitutionally guaranteed property and their equality as citizens in a White man's democracy.[28]

A majority of Missouri's Whites were proslavery. Most emigrants to the region in the first third of the nineteenth century were from the upper or backcountry south. They held a few slaves or, more frequently, none at all, but most of them endorsed the institution as the social mechanism maintaining

White supremacy. Missouri was a land of small farms and diversified agriculture, with a concentration on corn and hogs. Slaves amounted to about
13 percent of the population in 1850. About 18 percent of the Whites held
slaves, and most slaveholders in most of the state owned fewer than ten. The
exception was the "Little Dixie" region in the western two thirds of the state
along the Missouri River, where some counties were over 30 percent Black.
Platte County had not even existed until the late 1830s, when a special purchase extinguished Indian title and pushed the state boundary to the river.
White settlers flooded in, and they made money supplying migrants to
Oregon, Mormons in Salt Lake, the U.S. Army in Mexico, and gold rushers
to California, but also with labor-intensive crops like tobacco and hemp as in
Little Dixie. Slave traders did a good business: one advertised a coffle of 25 in
1849 and another offered a hundred for sale a few months later. By 1856, Platte
County had 3,300 slaves in a population of 18,500. Most of Kelso's neighbors
"were nearly all slave owners of that haughty class who looked with contempt
on any man who did not own slaves and who had to earn his own livelihood."
This disposition was "greatly intensified" by the Kansas troubles.[29]

Weston's anxious town fathers, the network of neighborhood watches
and informants, and the armed men who exchanged passwords and patrolled
at night, all kept their eyes open for any suspicious characters. "Every non-
slaveowner," Kelso wrote, "on our side of the river . . . was ostracized, so-
cially and in his business relations, unless he were wont to loudly hurrah
for slavery, and just as loudly to curse the [damned] Abolitionists and
'Black Republicans,'" the new political party coalescing against the Kansas-
Nebraska Act. Ohio-born Kelso was not "a Southern man," born and bred,
as swaggering slaveholders in Missouri were more frequently claiming for
themselves. He should have gotten some cover from being a minister in the
Methodist Episcopal Church *South*, the proslavery portion of the church
that had separated from the General Conference just a decade earlier. But
most of the wealthier farmers in Platte County were "clannish" Campbellites
(Disciples of Christ) who distrusted Methodists for religious reasons.
Kelso's manners and habits, too, could have raised suspicions among Platte's
proslavery patriots. "An ignorant, brutish, non-slaveowner, who cursed, used
slang, smoked, chewed, drank whiskey, etc, . . . was generally regarded, and
justly so, as on the pro-slavery side of this all-absorbing question." Kelso
didn't drink, smoke, chew, or curse, and tried to conduct himself as "an educated man of gentlemanly deportment." Though he could claim a Missouri
upbringing, this young teacher and preacher might have had the air of a
Yankee reformer about him: speaking bookish sentences, refusing a stiff

drink, and maybe even smuggling in abolitionist pamphlets to rouse up the Black folks.[30]

Kelso saw what Platte's defenders did to such dangerous characters. In April 1855, in Parkville, 20 miles south of Weston, a hundred people destroyed the newspaper office of George Park's *Luminary* for publishing antislavery sentiments. A month later, on May 17, in Weston itself a suspected abolitionist suffered the wrath of the public. "I saw a man in Weston," Kelso remembered, "for the crime of being silent in regard to slavery, subjected to one of the greatest outrages ever inflicted upon any free man in any country. He was a well-dressed, well-educated, well-behaved stranger.... Becoming suspected of being an Abolitionist, he was taken by a mob, composed of nearly all the men in the city, tarred and feathered, ridden on a rail, and then sold for ten cents at a mock auction. He probably hurt somebody for this afterwards." The man's name was William Phillips, an antislavery lawyer from Fort Leavenworth who had been dragged across the river after having criticized proslavery fraud at a recent election. In its ritual of humiliation, the Weston mob also shaved half of Phillips's head and made sure that the auctioneer was a Black man. But Kelso was right, Phillips did hurt somebody afterwards. When another proslavery mob visited his home in Fort Leavenworth Phillips shot and killed two assailants before being gunned down on his veranda.[31]

Kelso came from a staunchly proslavery family. His mother could cite chapter and verse in the biblical defense of slavery, and while his father could never afford to own slaves, he strongly supported a White man's right to slave property. Uncle Edgar had once owned at least one slave, and the extended Kelso clan thought there was nothing at all wrong in his doing so. But John, on his own, had examined the matter carefully. "I had fully studied the subject of this divinely established institution, and had, in my own mind, just as fully condemned it."[32]

In a letter published many years later, he described what it was like to be a teacher in a slave state where it was illegal to teach enslaved children to read or write without their master's consent. He told of the anguish he felt when, after two "bright and lovely slave children" came to him, asking to be taught, he had to turn them away. In a 1880s lecture, too, he described seeing an enslaved woman on an auction block (though the scene seems like a set piece taken from abolitionist literature). "She was a modest and virtuous Christian woman, a good and loving mother," Kelso said. He knew her well— she had once nursed him through a severe illness. The auctioneer "bared her back to show that she had never been cut up with the lash. He made her lift her clothing and expose the lower portions of her body to show that she was well formed and had good muscles. While she stood there, holding up her clothing, in the presence of her children and that great crowd of people, she trembled violently and wept piteously." Her master, a member of her own church, described "the fine size and shape of her limbs just as he might have expatiated upon the similar points in the legs of a horse which he wished to sell." Kelso watched her wail as she was sold and torn from her husband and five children.[33]

He does not fully explain his thinking in the late 1850s, but seems to have been more of a Free Soiler than an abolitionist. Building on themes from the Free Soil Party in the late 1840s, antislavery opponents of the Kansas-Nebraska Act in the mid-1850s deemphasized the moral critique of slavery's dehumanizing effects on Black people and warned of the "Slave Power"—that is, the slaveholders' economic, political, and social power—that degraded White laborers and non-slaveholding White citizens. Antislavery politicians denounced slaveholders as a tyrannical aristocratic class that trampled on the rights of all people—White or Black—who worked by the sweat of their own brows. This language seemed to speak to Kelso's own experience, from the arrogant Robert Cravens who had competed for Adelia's affections to his haughty Platte County neighbors who considered calloused hands the sign of a lesser man. For poor Whites of Southern sympathies, race trumped class: they supported the slave regime, even if it had little to do with their own economic self-interest, because they felt they shared the benefits of Whiteness with the richest man in town. For Kelso, class trumped race: it was less an issue of Black and White than of men who worked hard to better themselves versus a class of privileged parasites, the high and mighty who maintained their positions by sucking the life and labor out of others.[34]

Free Soilers could be nearly as racist as their proslavery opponents, and Kelso would later admit that he had imbibed many of the racial prejudices of his proslavery parents and of White Missourians in general. Focusing on protecting the free labor of White men, Free Soilers were angry at the slaveholders' unfair economic advantages and outsized political power, but often showed little concern for the Black men and women who actually suffered directly under slavery's lash. They neither wanted to live near nor compete for jobs with free Blacks, and they thought emancipated slaves ought to be shipped out of the country and colonized elsewhere. The proposed Free Soil (Topeka) constitution offered to a divided Kansas at once outlawed slavery and prohibited the settlement of free Blacks. Free states Iowa, Illinois, and Indiana passed free Black exclusion bills by wide margins. Missouri's powerful Blair family, architects of the emerging Republican Party, framed a state party platform that endorsed colonization, denounced racial amalgamation and Black equality, and declared "Missouri for White men and White men for Missouri." But even moderate and conservative Republicans embracing a Free Soil position on the western territories rather than outright abolitionism were still usually willing to grant Blacks civil if not political rights and legal if not social equality.[35]

There were antislavery Whites in the Missouri countryside. The White population was becoming more diverse, with more people moving in from places without a slaveholding history. By 1860, 15 percent of Missouri's White population had been born in free states and 12 percent had been foreign born. Especially outside St. Louis, opponents of slavery, whatever their heritage, were still in 1855 a disorganized minority, bullied and silenced by wealthier slaveholding men and the political demagogues who did their bidding. Kelso, for the time being, kept silent as he and Adelia felt increasingly ostracized in Platte County and watched the border war accelerate. On March 29, 1855, Senator David Rice Atchison and future governor Claiborne Fox Jackson led a large body of armed men into Kansas to vote illegally in the next day's territorial election to ensure that the proslavery candidates won. After more maneuvers gave proslavery forces unanimous control of the Kansas legislature, Free Soil emigrants met late in the year in Topeka, framed their own constitution, and elected their own legislature in January 1856. Armed proslavery partisans, who came to be called "border ruffians," began terrorizing settlers they suspected of antislavery sentiments, using arson and robbery to drive them off the land. On May 21, 1856, a proslavery force, mostly from Missouri, sacked the antislavery town of Lawrence. Three nights later, in response, abolitionist John Brown led a small party to Pottawatomie Creek and hacked five proslavery settlers to death. In the same week, and a week after Senator Charles Sumner had delivered a series of speeches about the proslavery "Crime against Kansas," Congressman Preston Brooks of South Carolina took a cane and beat Sumner bloody and senseless on the floor of the U.S. Senate. The halls of Congress had become Hell Town too. For the time being, Kelso continued to read the newspapers and keep quiet. The schoolmaster was not yet ready to take a stand.[36]

4

Wanderer upon the Earth

KELSO'S LIFE BEGAN to unravel in the spring of 1855. Within a year, he would become, as he put it, "a wifeless, homeless, churchless, and almost friendless and moneyless wanderer upon the earth." As winter set in, the wanderer would set out, with the world before him, a book of German grammar in his hand, a loaf of bread tied up in a handkerchief, and twenty-five dollars in his pocket, heading in a southerly direction but with no particular destination in mind. When he came to the Missouri River, he brushed off warnings and began to cross the thin ice on foot. The people on the riverbank then watched, in horror, as the ice broke and he fell through.[1]

For five months the year before, Kelso had taught a family school for Edward Snyder in Rock House Prairie, 20 miles northeast of Hell Town. Snyder was "a man of great wealth, enterprise, and intelligence." He owned real estate worth $17,500, or seven times the value of Squire Edgar Kelso's property back in Daviess County. Kelso taught five of Snyder's children and one grandchild: two in their twenties, three teenagers, and a six-year-old. He admired the Snyders as a "model family." Jemima Francis (Mima) Snyder, nineteen years old, was an especially "wonderful" student, one of the best he ever taught. Charming, cheerful, and earnest, she was also, Kelso thought, brilliant. "Indeed, in the most lofty flights that my own intellect was capable of taking, hers was capable of accompanying it." After the Kelsos moved back to Platte County, Mima joined them for a few months, attending the school he taught and continuing to share his lofty flights in the evenings at home.[2]

In those intellectual journeys, he was beginning to roam beyond the memorization of facts and mastery of skills to think more critically and creatively. In religious matters, he strayed from the path of Methodist orthodoxy and "was beginning to tread on the out-skirts of the realm of Liberalism." Religious liberalism generally referred to a cluster of ideas and attitudes that included confidence in human nature, an emphasis on an individual's free inquiry over reverence for any creed, and the conviction that spiritual truths were not confined to any single tradition. Kelso did not record what books or pamphlets or periodicals he managed to get a hold of that might have exposed him to a wider range of theological perspectives. Had he encountered Thomas Paine's *The Age of Reason*, the late eighteenth-century deist classic that debunked the authority of Scripture and was still being read and discussed in the middle of the nineteenth century, especially among inquisitive men and women in the laboring classes? Did he come across the abundant Universalist literature challenging the idea of an eternal hell, or the Unitarian critique of the Trinity? What of the new German biblical criticism, such as David Strauss's *Life of Jesus*, that treated the New Testament merely like other ancient mythologies? He doesn't say.[3]

In later writings, though, Kelso described this period as the beginning of his emancipation from the bonds of religious superstition. In a preface to his 1873 "Devil's Defense," a poem satirizing Christian beliefs, he attributed this awakening to two things: a growing revulsion of his moral instincts for a capricious Christian God who would save some of his children and damn others; and the application of his intellectual powers to the dogmas he was supposed to believe. Writing in the third person, he said he had been "told that without *faith* he would certainly be *damned*," but also "that this faith, so essential to salvation, '*is the gift of God*,' and that he could not exercise it unless God gave it to him." After years of earnest prayer from "a hungry and despairing soul," he had not received such faith, and "peace of mind" still eluded him. "At last he began to feel that it was *cruel and unjust* in God to thus *withhold* faith from him, and then *damn* him for not having it." Kelso revolted against such a system of religion, and "determined to weigh all its doctrines in the balances of *reason*, of *science*, and of *common sense*, and ascertained for himself, whether they were, or were not, founded on *truth*." Such an investigation, he thought, could not make his condition any worse. If the Methodists were right, he would end up in hell either way: as a believer without saving faith or as a doubter questioning doctrine. "In the strength of despair, therefore, he went boldly forward and having once dared to use his reason, he soon emerged from the darkness of ignorance and superstition, and into the light and gladness of truth. His fetters were broken and he became a free man."[4]

Kelso explained what he meant by weighing Christian doctrines in the balances of reason, science, and common sense. Doubt was the beginning of the process. "Primitive men had no idea of any kind of agency except that of a will or a mind like their own," so they imagined gods as the cause of all sorts of phenomena. Modern people who inherited ancient religious beliefs often did not think to doubt that God was the grand cause operating behind the screen of the observable world. Questioning this presupposition allowed for a rigorous examination of the available evidence on, for example, whether the order found in nature really did reveal an intelligent designer. The preponderance of available evidence one way or another (rather than the unreflective acceptance of the faith one was born into) produced belief or disbelief.

Doctrines also stood or fell by the test of logic and the comparison to scientific fact. Kelso dismantled key Christian tenets concerning God's creation of the world, his incarnation as Christ, and Christ's atonement on the cross. He moved from "premises no sane man will deny" through "a series of logical arguments and deductions" that ultimately undermined central Christian doctrines. He also exposed key notions like ascending into heaven or suffering in an underground hell as being based on an ancient cosmology that had long been exploded by modern astronomy and physics. A personal God like the one carried over from ignorant paganism into the Bible, he concluded, could not be the creator of the infinite universe known to modern science. By the 1870s he had rejected the vague deity of religious liberalism too. The God of some modern liberal theology, stripped of all individuality and locality, becomes "an intangible, invisible, imponderable, incomprehensible, negation equivalent to empty space," he argued, no more able to be worshipped as a person than electricity or gravity. He would argue that a self-existent and self-sustaining universe made more sense than imagining an antecedent God of any sort. But this conclusion would have still shocked him in the 1850s, as he talked with Mima and first drifted away from Methodism.[5]

Religious faith was perpetuated, Kelso argued, because people were born into belief systems the way they were born into race and nationality. Most never paused to doubt and investigate, and their societies, with "vast armies of priests," tried to ensure that they did not. Absurd stories like the Virgin Birth or the Resurrection were believed because they were "*shrouded* in *mystery*," having occurred in a dim and distant past. To combat this, Kelso tried to collapse the distance between the ancient world of wonders and the commonsensical present. The Christians' God in the Old Testament encouraged polygamy, so why not condemn him for it just as we condemn the Mormons? Would nineteenth-century Americans believe Mary's story about being impregnated by the Holy Ghost if she had been Mary Smith or Mary Brown, a pregnant girl in the neighborhood? Jesus in the Gospels is an itinerant enthusiast with dirty hands and soiled clothes who wanders about encouraging his followers neither to sow, nor to reap, nor to show concern for their families.

Is this really supposed to be an exemplary life? And Christians were taught to constantly praise Christ for his sacrifice on the cross. But who would not endure a painful death if they were certain that everlasting bliss in heaven awaited, and that by this relatively brief suffering they could rescue even one of their children (to say nothing of all of humanity) from eternal torment? Such appeals to common sense joined reason and science in Kelso's argument. He suggested that his employment of the three, together with a natural history of religion and a close textual analysis of Scripture, were the "long and thorough *investigation*" that initially freed him from religious superstition in the 1850s.[6]

Kelso's autobiographical story in the preface to the "Devil's Defense" sketches a standard Enlightenment counter-narrative to the formula of Christian conversion. A young man, alone in his study, dares to use his reason and questions the sacred dogmas that have been bequeathed to him— suppositions upon which, up until that point, his understanding of life had rested. Doubt opens a space for rational inquiry, and he is able to hold beliefs at a critical distance for examination, rather than unconsciously drawing inspiration from a pervasive atmosphere of faith. Solitude, too, opens up a space, a critical distance from family, friends, and community. The secluded and self-aware thinker sees the idols of his tribe for what they are. The result is a passage from ignorance and superstition to truth, from darkness to light, from mental slavery to freedom. The reality of Kelso's intellectual wandering through the 1850s and 60s, however, seems much messier—and much more embedded in his daily social experience—than this story of intellectual enlightenment through reason.[7]

As he talked excitedly with Mima about new ideas and wandered into the outskirts of religious liberalism in the mid-1850s, he abandoned two key evangelical doctrines. He stopped believing in the reality of Satan and a fiery hell—"old uncle Split-foot" and his brimstone dominion, he could now joke. Shedding this belief had enormous consequences. The doctrine had been the root of his spiritual torment. Once the Devil in hell faded to mere metaphor, it ceased to have a hold on him, and his fear and anxiety vanished. He began to see that all the hellfire preaching that he had heard over the years—and some, probably, that he had done himself—was little more than a form of psychological terrorism.[8]

His escape from the Methodists' hell also led him to abandon evangelical understandings of regenerating grace. He had previously believed that the powerful emotions that swept over believers as they prayed, sang hymns, or listened to sermons were the effects of God's Spirit—convicting them of their sins, regenerating their hearts, sanctifying their souls. But now he began to embrace a different explanation for his weeping, swooning listeners and for his years of personal spiritual turmoil. He, like other evangelicals, had felt a religious rapture, a "joy unspeakable and full of glory." When that feeling dissipated, however, he had been plunged into despair and depression, interpreting those dark nights of the soul, as countless others had, as God's displeasure and withdrawal. As he read more widely, thought more deeply, and followed his new paths of inquiry with Mima, he started to see that the feeling of joyous rapture, rather than evidence of being bathed in God's love, "was simply a magnetic or psychological exaltation." The religious experiences displayed at revival meetings, where dozens of people, merely from hearing the Word preached, could be thrown to the ground, paralyzed, entranced, or jerked with fits resembling an epileptic seizure—these, too, could be explained: "revivals were gotten up, not by the operation of the spirit of God upon our congregations, but by the operations of our spirits,—of our own magnetism." Moreover, these experiences were not unique to Christianity and were not therefore special evidence in its favor. Such things happened, he learned, "in all countries and among all peoples." Most people interpreted these powerful emotions and their physical effects as acts of their various gods, but, Kelso came to see, there was nothing supernatural about them at all.[9]

His use of the term "magnetism" reveals his new explanatory key. In the late eighteenth century, physician Franz Mesmer caused a stir in France by demonstrating extraordinary healing effects through convulsions brought about by what would later be called hypnotism. Mesmer explained the phenomenon by positing an ethereal fluid or force field—an "animal magnetism" similar to a magnetic field or electric charge. The skilled magnetizer—or mesmerist—could manipulate this field and produce astounding effects in the body and mind of the patient. A royal commission in 1784, which included Benjamin Franklin, found no evidence for Mesmer's theory and explained the effects as products of the imagination, but Mesmer's disciples continued the work in France and Germany. They made even more extravagant claims, insisting that their magnetized subjects could see things happen across town (clairvoyance) or peer into bodies and diagnose hidden diseases. Broader interest was revived in 1831 when a second French commission assessed mesmerism much more favorably. When John Elliotson, a professor of medicine at the University of London, began promoting mesmerism in 1837, British intellectuals weighed in on both sides. At about the same time in the United States, lectures by Charles Poyen sparked interest in New England. As in Britain, the excitement over animal magnetism spread in America both through a flurry of publications and through public lectures and demonstrations. By 1845, animal magnetism had come to Missouri and proponents began publishing *The Saint Louis Magnet* to spread the word.[10]

Mesmerism's profile rose when it became allied with another controversial "science"—phrenology. Developed initially by German physicians Franz Joseph Gall and Johann Gaspar Spurzheim in the late eighteenth and early nineteenth centuries, and elaborated by Scottish writer George Combe in the 1820s and 1830s, phrenology was a materialistic psychology seeing mind as a product of the brain and the brain as being composed of more than two dozen different organs, each located in a particular place on the cranium and each responsible for different dimensions of personality. Phreno-magnetism emerged as practitioners thought they could manipulate the magnetic fluid or field of specific organs—a subject's organ of Veneration (for God), for example, or the part of his brain controlling his Amativeness (sexual love). A former Methodist revivalist named La Roy Sunderland began investigating the phenomena of religious experience with these conceptual tools and started publishing a journal called *The Magnet* in New York in 1842, a model for the later periodical in Missouri.[11]

By the time Kelso was excitedly talking about these new ideas with Mima in the mid-1850s, the intellectual prestige of both phrenology and mesmerism had dimmed. The very practices that had popularized mesmerism—entertaining demonstrations with mesmerists making their magnetized subjects do remarkable things—made it increasingly disreputable among the learned. The commercialization, the crassness, the ever-more-bizarre claims made by traveling magnetizers and mesmeric healers caused scientists and intellectuals to recoil. Still, the theory of animal magnetism and the language of mesmerism had seeped into popular culture, inspiring writers such as Charles Dickens, Edgar Allan Poe, Nathaniel Hawthorne, and Walt Whitman. It lingered on in self-help manuals, home health guides, and advice books on love and courtship.

Kelso would also use the language of magnetism to help him understand sexual passion and romantic love. Perhaps, he began to think, his marriage to Adelia had been doomed from the start. "In many respects, we were not adapted to each other at all," he later wrote. "There was but little magnetic attraction between us." Not so with Mima: "Magnetically, she was my exact opposite." Opposites attract. Like some of the courtship advice books, Kelso merged magnetic language with assumptions from physiognomy, another eighteenth-century "science" that lingered on into the nineteenth century, this one holding that character and temperament were expressed in body shape, facial features, and complexion. Mima "was rather under the medium size of women, was remarkably well formed, and was very active. Her eyes were a light hazel, her hair and her complexion light. . . . Her forehead was too prominent to be consistent with perfect beauty, but her modesty, her gracefulness, her sweetness of disposition, her never failing cheerfulness, her glowing earnestness, and her wonderful brilliancy of intellect, combined with her sympathetic and affectionate nature, rendered her, to me at least, the most charming woman that I ever met." Magnetically drawn together, their temperaments also nicely complemented each other: she was sanguine (light hair and eyes, fair complexion, cheerfulness) and he was bilious (dark, brooding, but strong-willed and energetic).[12]

Yet, at first, Kelso did not feel any romantic or sexual attraction toward Mima. "The thought of loving her would have shocked me as being something very wicked. In regard to such things, I was still thoroughly orthodox." It is not that he felt the magnetic attraction to Mima, but, knowing that such feelings were sinful for a married man, he exerted willpower to suppress them. Rather, his sense of himself, of personal honor, of marital obligation, of right and wrong, of the possible and the impossible—all these things were so strong, had built walls so high, that he was not even aware that he was being pulled toward Mima in ways that would be considered improper. For a long time, he thought of her "only as a perfect lady, a true friend, and an excellent and charming pupil."[13]

Before Mima had arrived, John and Adelia had become more miserable than ever. Their clannish, proslavery Campbellite neighbors shunned them, and they spent most of their time alone. Adelia ignored John, or lost her temper and snapped at him, and didn't seem to care about what he thought or felt about anything. When he was sick, she offered no sympathy. When he was absent, she didn't miss him. They must have played out scenes from the drama of a million other unhappy marriages: the husband comes home after a long day; the wife looks up from her work; their faces turn, their eyes meet, but there is no warm greeting, no flicker of affection. Yet there was something else going on here. Adelia frequently sat in her chair, or lay curled on the bed, sobbing, and John began to fear for her sanity. "At times, her memory seemed to be paralyzed. When speaking upon any subject, she would suddenly find herself at a loss for the most common words; and sometimes, for some moments, she could not even tell her own name." He was convinced that some secret sorrow, perhaps some terrible, unspeakable tragedy, preyed on her mind. He alternated between feeling sorry for her and then for himself. His love, "totally unnourished by any reciprocation on her part, was slowly but surely dying."[14]

He tried to conceal his marital troubles from the outside world—from his neighbors, his students, and his church. But once Mima moved in with them, she could see it all. She saw Adelia's quiet cruelties and watched John tread ever so lightly around her moods. He felt that Mima could read his very soul and that she sympathized with his sorrows. They didn't speak of it—they didn't have to. A glance, a tone, a small kindness from Mima, and he knew that she knew. On the topics they did discuss—the ever-widening world of history, science, literature, and religion—their "souls soon came to be so thoroughly *en rapport*" that the thoughts and feelings of one became fully transparent to the other. He was certain that what she felt for him was the mirror image of his own feelings for her. It was not romantic love, he thought, but deep friendship. She felt his pain and wanted him to be happy.[15]

When the school term ended for the harvest in 1855, Mima returned home. In the shorter days of autumn, as the air cooled and the leaves turned brown, the darkness descended on the Kelsos' little house, and the walls closed in. In January 1856, Adelia gave birth to a son, Florellus, but the new baby did not bring joy to their dismal home. Even with the spring thaw, when they moved back to Rock-House Prairie and the Snyders' happy neighborhood, where the surrounding families were so impressed with Kelso's teaching that they began building an academy for him, and where Methodists from miles around flocked to Jones's Chapel every Sunday to hear him preach—even here, his despair only deepened. He saw Mima each day in school again, "more radiant than ever in her glorious woman-hood." He felt his soul reach out to her "in one great cry for comfort." At home, Adelia seemed more hostile than ever, as if purposely trying to drive him away.[16]

But then a new realization washed over him. Worn out by Adelia's fretful temper and brought to the end of his endurance, he finally felt his love for her drain away, leaving him stranded on "rocks of despair." Yet as he stood there, he also felt a rush of awareness, which he described as a surging tide and a tornado, that he was in love with Mima and that she loved him.[17]

Adelia, sensing that she and John had reached a breaking point, finally confessed her secret sorrow. She sat him down and told him that she didn't love him. She had always respected him but had never loved him, and had in fact been trying to drive him away. When they were courting, she had been deeply in love with another man, but her father had commanded her to marry Kelso instead. Kelso, Father Moore had decided, had a better chance of rising in the world and making a name for himself. Don't worry, Moore had assured

Adelia, you'll grow to love him in time—marriage was like that. Instead, she pined for her lost love, thought of him incessantly, and was tormented by the grief that she had made the wrong choice. She didn't wish Kelso dead, but she had hoped he would become so miserable that he would leave her and give her cause to get a divorce. "She said that, in marrying me, she had done me a great and irreparable wrong," Kelso later recounted, "a wrong which she feared that God would never forgive."[18]

However painful, the conversation also must have been a relief. At least there could be honesty between them. In this spirit, John made a confession of his own—an admission he would come to regret. He told Adelia that he had fallen in love with Mima. He had not done anything wrong—he had not even spoken to Mima about his feelings—but his heart, like Adelia's, yearned for someone else. This smoothed the waters between them. "We determined to separate in a friendly manner, to become divorced as soon and as quietly as possible, and thus become free to unite respectively with the objects of our love. We drew up and signed an agreement in regard to the disposition of the children and of the little property which we had accumulated. Then, promising to remain friends, we kissed and parted."[19]

Nineteenth-century American divorce was not a "no-fault" affair with couples merely citing irreconcilable differences: it supposed an innocent and injured party seeking to dissolve the union because of a spouse's grievous fault. It was still rare, though becoming less so, in Missouri. Unlike some other states, Missouri offered relatively liberal grounds for divorce and had long allowed its citizens to seek that legal remedy through convenient circuit courts rather than through the legislature. The main grounds in such contests were adultery, desertion, and cruelty. Kelso wasn't sure how he could make his case. There had been no adultery or desertion, and according to the statute, cruelty related only to physical harm, not to mental anguish. When courts did pay attention to verbal cruelty, too, it was usually in reference to words uttered that damaged a spouse's public reputation or authority over subordinates within the household. Another part of the statute, however, opened the door to considerable judicial discretion, citing as a ground when a spouse "shall offer such indignities to the person of the other as shall render his or her condition intolerable." With a signed letter from Adelia describing their situation and absolving him of all blame, Kelso would have a good case.[20]

The Kelsos' divorce, however, did not proceed quickly and quietly—in part because of John's actions. With Adelia's permission, he met with Mima and told her everything. Mima responded just as he had hoped: yes, she loved him too, she said, with an "undying and unutterable love." She gave him a lock of her hair, and, even though Kelso warned her that his divorce would cause a scandal and advised her to forget about him, for the first time they dared to imagine a future together.[21]

Adelia took the children and went back to her father's house in Daviess County. The Sunday following her departure, Keslo went for the last time to conduct services at his church. At Jones's Chapel, the congregation was always "very large" with "fine shouters" who nearly shook the timbers of the building when worship or revival meetings heated up. The congregants idolized Kelso. "As yet, they knew nothing of my domestic infelicities. On this occasion, therefore, they welcomed me, as usual, with demonstrations of delight." In his pocket he had Adelia's letter absolving him from any blame. The meeting began with hymns and an opening prayer, as it always had. Instead of preaching a sermon from the pulpit, however, Kelso addressed his flock and told them he could not preach to them that day or ever again. He was separating from his wife, he explained, something Methodist preachers were not supposed to do. He read Adelia's letter aloud, dismissed the meeting, and walked out of the chapel. "Not a word was spoken to me as I left the church. All seemed speechless with amazement."[22]

"Soon the storm burst forth in all its fury," Kelso wrote. The impact of the scandal was far worse than he had imagined. Adelia's father, the Reverend Lytle W. Moore, "raved like a fiend" and vowed vengeance. He brought countercharges against Kelso, all of them false, according to the autobiographer, except the one true and damaging claim that Kelso had fallen in love with another woman. Mima was summoned to testify; Mima's father, in language suggesting insulted honor and pistols at dawn, said that if his daughter were dragged into this scandal, he and Kelso "could not both live." Kelso quickly wrote to Mima, "requesting her to regard my words of love as recalled—as never having been uttered." He had hoped that she would see this as a tactical, temporary move and not an expression of his real affections. He was also concerned that professing his love to her before he was divorced was a sin. Apparently taking Kelso to be a cad, a coward, or both, Mima never contacted him again and quickly married someone else: an old suitor, Evans Ray, whom Kelso knew she did not love, "who was intellectually far her inferior, but who was an honorable man of wealth and good family." Kelso would never see Mima again.[23]

As his hopes for a future with Mima crumbled, Kelso watched as "Old Moore" continually worked to destroy his reputation. "A thousand vague conjectures, generally more or less unfavorable to myself, soon grew into positive assertions of my guilt." Moore's version of the affair, "black with malicious falsehoods, was obtained and duly magnified. . . . Led by Moore, the church people almost unanimously took sides against me with the ferocity of blood-hounds." On the Sunday following his resignation he returned to the chapel to sit among the members of his congregation as another man preached from the pulpit. "Most of my former flock . . . shunned me as they would have shunned a ferocious beast."[24]

Why had his community so quickly and completely forsaken him? Had he abused his power as a minister, they would have forgiven him, he reflected bitterly. Had he seduced some young women—"the Lord's ewe lambs"—in the church, as he afterward claimed that his father-in-law Moore had done, they would have pardoned him. "But I had not been guilty of any thing of this kind. In their eyes, my offense was a far greater one. My offense was that of being crushed under a great—and undeserved misfortune. This offense is one in which the public, and especially the religionists thereof, rarely forgive. With them, it is far better to be *fortunate* in *sin* than to be *unfortunate* in *innocence*." Power, even when abused, is respected. Weakness is not. Or perhaps the faithful suspected that Kelso was not an innocent man suffering from the bad luck to have married a woman who could not love him; perhaps, instead, they thought his domestic infelicities were God's judgments upon a secret sinner.[25]

Not long after Kelso had left behind his stunned congregation in Jones's Chapel, an annual conference of Southern Methodists met in Plattsburg, 15 miles to the east. Kelso traveled there to cut his connection to the ministry and to the Methodist Church. He did not intend to go quietly. He resolved to publicly attack the church orthodoxy that, privately, he had already abandoned. He planned, he said, "to burst a bomb in the camp of the lord, and to leave that camp in consternation."[26]

The meeting he attended was an annual gathering of ministers, deacons, and lay stewards of the Methodist Episcopal Church South in northwest Missouri that had been recently instituted by the presiding elder of Kelso's Weston District, William Goss Caples. Known as one of Missouri's finest preachers, Caples also had entrepreneurial energy and a talent for organizing. He was a "constitutionally cheerful" man, always with a ready quip or an amusing story. A friend remembered similar conferences—the excited bustle about the Methodist Church, with men streaming in on foot, on horseback, and in buggies. "As these men come and go every here and there you will hear a voice, quivering with pleasure, say, 'Yonder's Caples,' 'Caples is here,' 'How are you, Caples?'" The elder strides among them, shaking every hand like an eager politician pressing the flesh, greeting everyone warmly: "Why," says he, "there's

Billy—*God bless you, old fellow*! . . . "Why, Ben, bless your soul, is this you?"[27]
Caples took a "fatherly interest" in the young preachers in his district, calling
them "his boys." He prodded them, teased them, and praised them extravagantly when they did well. At the opening of the 1856 Plattsburg conference,
it was Kelso's turn to be anointed by Caples's compliments. News of Kelso's
marital scandal had not yet traveled far from home, and most of the men at the
conference, including Caples, who lived 25 miles from Rock-House Prairie,
still hadn't heard. "When my name was called," Kelso later wrote, "the Rev.
Mr. Caples, President Elder of my district, responded in a pretty little speech
in which he bestowed upon me the highest praise that I ever heard bestowed
upon a young minister." Kelso rose to acknowledge the remarks. But instead
of expressing gratitude, he now threw his "bomb," launching into a critique
of Methodist doctrine. He attacked the idea of eternal punishment in hell—
of "burning forever the souls of men for being just what God, when making
them, foresaw that they inevitably would be;—for being, in fact, just what he
had made them to be." He attacked other key ideas too, which "constituted
our most valuable priestly stock in trade," including the belief that their religious revivals demonstrated God's supernatural grace.[28]

The affable Caples was also an uncompromising conservative. With little
formal education, he read few books besides the Bible and a collection of favorite sermons, and he had no tolerance for new-fangled ideas. Any religious
notions that strayed from the central truth of salvation gained through Christ's
sacrifice on the cross were no better than atheism. Any philosophy that did not
acknowledge the authority of Scripture was blasphemy. Abolitionism, which
denied plain biblical truth, "was the deadliest sin of modern society." After
a half dozen other young preachers stood up for Kelso—defending not his
heretical ideas but his right to hold and express them—"Elder Caples . . . finally threw himself boldly into the breach." Caples pronounced him "a very
powerful and dangerous enemy," warning that if the young heretic's influence
were not immediately squelched, he "would, within ten years, ruin the church
and demoralize society."[29]

Kelso's opponents eventually turned from challenging his arguments to
attacking his reputation. Some of Caples's lieutenants brought up Kelso's marital problems. Kelso believed that "by the laws of the M. E. Church South,
a minister is not permitted to separate from his wife for any cause, except
that of adultery; and, in my case, that cause did not exist." The Methodist
Discipline cited no such rule, although something like it may have operated
as an unwritten code guiding expectations for clerical behavior. Caples, for
one, thought the marriage contract unbreakable, no matter how miserable

the union, and that the option of divorce would lead to "the destruction of the family, the very cornerstone of civilization and virtue."[30]

If the mere fact of Kelso's broken marriage wasn't damning enough, his "enemies" eventually produced a letter, which they claimed was from Adelia, denigrating his character and laying all the blame at his feet. Kelso knew the letter was a forgery and said so. He suspected—a suspicion he later confirmed—that the letter had been written by Adelia's father and the Reverend Daniel H. Root, a pastor stationed at Gallatin that Kelso called "one of the Roots of evil." Kelso was furious. He may have become too angry to speak for himself, but his father was there and became his advocate. As the heated exchanges finally neared their end, Robert rose. "The Methodist Church dare not be just in this case," he concluded. "She is forced to defend herself by fraud, by injustice, and by forgery. But my son will live to be honored by the world long after his enemies have gone down."[31]

Kelso resigned from the ministry, renounced his membership in the Methodist Church, and left the conference enraged. "Being excited and angry, I armed myself to shoot those two godly forgers." In mid-century Missouri, men often resorted to violence to defend their honor. Politicians still challenged one another to duels. Missouri's leading Whig, Thomas Hart Benton, who was running for governor that year, had once killed a man on the dueling ground. Claiborne Fox Jackson, a Democrat who would be elected governor in 1860, had once challenged an opponent to a duel with rifles at seventy paces. Frank P. Blair Jr., a founder of the state's Republican Party, was fined one dollar and a minute in jail for challenging an opponent to a duel in 1849. Men with less gentility defended their honor by shooting at each other with less ceremony than that demanded by the old aristocratic dueling code. The Western gunfight—men with holstered revolvers facing each other, the quicker draw "getting the drop" on the slower one—would not become a familiar ritual until after the war. In the first such gunfight to become famous, Wild Bill Hickock killed Daniel Tutt on a street in Springfield, Missouri, on July 20, 1865.[32]

A decade earlier, however, as Kelso armed himself, Missouri men already knew how to avenge offended manhood without being convicted of murder in the aftermath. The first step was for the insulted party to make his grievance public, declaring that the offense could have a justifiably fatal consequence. (Mima's father had taken this step, though he hedged it with a condition: if Mima were dragged into the scandal, then he and Kelso "could not both live.") Such a public posting put the offender on notice: arm yourself, it said. If you don't, you'll be a coward; if you do, know what to expect when we meet; if there is a confrontation, any violence ought to be dismissed in court as an act of self-defense. And juries did uphold such defenses of honor, no matter what statutes said against dueling or what the common law indicated about malice aforethought.[33]

Kelso did not end up going after the godly forgers with a gun—his father and a few remaining friends talked him out of it. But Old Moore heard the rumors and feared for his life. Kelso hired a lawyer in St. Joseph who started divorce proceedings on the ground of Adelia's ill treatment. Moore tried to delay the trial as long as possible to punish Kelso with additional legal fees. Waiting for a court appearance, Kelso heard that the Reverend Moore would be preaching at Jones's Chapel, so he and his brother Robert decided to attend. When they were a few miles from the chapel, a member of the congregation overtook them. Learning that Kelso was headed to Moore's service, the man spurred his horse and raced ahead to warn the preacher and the rest of the flock. "Old Moore . . . was sadly frightened and told the people to get away as fast as they could, declaring that I was a desperate man, that I would shoot him down in the pulpit, and that I would also probably shoot a good many other persons and then take my own life." The members of the congregation "almost piled on top of one another" rushing out of the church. Children who saw Kelso on the road started fleeing into the woods. They had once been his students. He called to them kindly. A few cautiously approached him, and after he assured them that he hadn't become an "awful dangerous man" as they had been told, they described what had just happened in the chapel and said that Moore had retreated to the house of a nearby neighbor named Cobb.[34]

Kelso walked to Cobb's house and began pacing back and forth in front of it, hoping to see the "wily villain" Lytle Moore. He saw only Cobb, who stood in the doorway and eyed him defiantly as his ten-year-old daughter peeked anxiously from behind one of her father's legs. Kelso caught a last glimpse of Adelia in the backyard before she fled into the house. The Kelso brothers then left. They heard later that a dozen armed men had guarded Moore that night at Cobb's house, but by then John and Robert were 20 miles away, quietly studying algebra.[35]

And so John R. Kelso found himself, as he wrote, "a wifeless, homeless, churchless, and almost friendless and moneyless wanderer upon the earth. I was free, however, and the world was before me. But whither should I go and what should I do?" His life had come undone, and everything was shadowed by his sorrow for his lost love, Mima. He felt "reckless."[36]

He considered seeking battlefield glory by joining William Walker in Nicaragua. A small Tennessean with Napoleonic visions of Central American conquest, Walker and a few dozen American mercenaries had interjected themselves into the Nicaraguan Civil War. By the end of October 1855, he had led forces that conquered the enemy capital of Grenada and had become the commander-in-chief of the Nicaraguan military under a coalition government. By April 1856, Walker was fighting Costa Rica; by June, after eliminating his rivals and orchestrating a bogus election, he declared himself president. Propaganda in the United States recruiting more soldiers and colonists hailed him as an agent of Manifest Destiny who would bring American republicanism and "the superior activity and intelligence of the Anglo Saxon" to Central America. Free Soilers and abolitionists suspected Walker and other filibusters of being tools for the expansion of slavery. Indeed, some of the proslavery "border ruffians" who attacked Lawrence, Kansas, in the spring of 1856 joined Walker in Nicaragua later that year. But Walker also recruited in Northern cities, and until he issued a decree legalizing slavery in September 1856, his own position on that question was ambiguous. When Kelso pondered joining him in the summer of 1856, he, like many other young men across the country, was drawn less by ideological convictions than by other motives: some sought the wages being offered to the mercenaries; others fled legal troubles or relationships gone sour; many had romantic desires for glory in battle conjured by the "roar of cannon," as a Missouri college student put it.[37]

Feeling like a rootless wanderer, Kelso fell back upon his childhood dreams of military heroism. But he also recognized the darker side of those dreams. "I would gladly have thrown my life away on the battle-field," he later wrote, acknowledging that contemplating becoming a soldier was as much a death wish as an ambition for martial glory. Two desires kept him from Nicaragua. One was the determination to triumph over the "enemies"—Lytle Moore and the other Methodists—who had turned on him. The other was his sense of obligation to his two children—Florella and Florellus. So, long before Walker had been chased out of Nicaragua or died in front of a Honduran firing squad, Kelso shifted his focus to another childhood ambition: to become a scholar. Instead of going to war, Kelso went to college.[38]

Pleasant Ridge College, 3 miles outside of Weston, was one of nine colleges and academies established in Platte County in the dozen years before the Civil War. With a staff of four led by President Brice W. Vineyard, the co-educational school, founded in 1852 and incorporated by the state in 1855, had about 170 students, half women and half men. Although it awarded college degrees, it was more like an advanced high school and an academy for training school teachers than a rigorous university. But for Kelso, who had taught himself by a log cabin fireplace, the large, handsome brick building on the ridge above Weston, and the leadership of Professor Vineyard, who had a degree from the venerable College of William and Mary and who taught Latin, Greek, and mathematics, it was an impressive seat of higher learning. Kelso, however, was afraid that he would not be admitted. Weston was Caples's hometown, and the region had become "intensely excited" over Kelso's heresies, his scandal, and the rumors that he had become a dangerous man. Many of the college's patrons, he knew, were church people who had become his "relentless enemies." But Professor Vineyard ignored the rumors and the patron protests, greeting Kelso with courtesy and kindness. Kelso enrolled for the fall term of 1856.[39]

Vineyard told Kelso that "he would rather his college would give birth to *'one lion than to a dozen foxes,'*" but there wasn't much in the curriculum or the conservative textbooks to inspire intellectual boldness or encourage a student to wander too far off the beaten track of received wisdom. John Abercrombie's *Inquiries Concerning the Intellectual Powers and the Investigation of Truth* insisted that materialism was opposed to the first principles of philosophy. Samuel Whelpley's *Compend of History* assured students of the credibility of Mosaic history. Francis Wayland's *Elements of Moral Science* asserted that natural conscience only did so much and that Christianity was essential for full moral development. Although nondenominational, Pleasant Ridge College remained rooted in mainstream Protestantism by requiring boarders to attend church and Sunday School each week (only females boarded at the college, however, and it is unclear whether male students living in town had to abide by the same rule). Kelso was determined to be the best student in the school. As with all things, he turned college into a competition and vowed to work himself to exhaustion, if necessary, in order to win. Entering as a senior (a placement based on studies he had previously mastered on his own) he signed up for eight classes, each meeting an hour every day. This gave him ten hours of daily homework, too, leaving only six hours a day for eating, sleeping, and anything else. But he would do whatever it took to be "the lion of the college."[40]

At age twenty-six, Kelso was the oldest student at the school. This fact, along with his notoriety, prompted his fellow students to regard him with "unfriendly curiosity." He won them over, however. His unfailing courtesy eventually put them at ease, and his academic successes earned their respect. In math class, he was able to solve a problem that even a blushing Professor

Vineyard had been unable to solve. Vineyard also selected him to read a poem he had been assigned to write, "Truth Is in a Well," to a public assembly of the entire student body and three hundred local citizens. When he rose to speak, the sea of unfriendly faces made him anxious and the paper rattled in his hands until he caught a look of "sympathy, friendliness, and hopefulness" in fatherly Vineyard's eyes. Kelso finished the poem to enthusiastic applause, was crowded by his classmates offering congratulations, and afterwards received several gushing notes from girls asking him for copies of the poem. He had become both successful and popular, but with overwork his health broke down by the end of the term. He withdrew from the college after the Christmas holiday.[41]

He "again became a wanderer," but his wandering would have a strategic purpose in his battle against Old Moore. Kelso withdrew his divorce case from the court at St. Joseph, resolving to file it elsewhere in Missouri—far from Platte and Buchanan counties so Moore would not travel to contest it. In early January 1857, he set out into the snow, with his loaf of bread in his handkerchief, his twenty-five dollars in his pocket, and his German grammar in his hand, walking south. "Where I should stop, I had not the remotest idea."[42]

At the Missouri River, a small group of people milled around the ferry crossing when he approached. The boat had stopped running, they said, because of the ice. Anybody cross yet on foot, he asked? No, they told him, no one had yet ventured out to test it. He paced back and forth, growing impatient, and then decided to cross. The ice is thin, they warned. If you fall through, you're as good as dead. But the reckless wanderer had made up his mind, and he "walked boldly forward without sounding the ice."[43]

They watched anxiously. They saw him step quickly several times, as if the ice were giving way beneath his feet and he was trying to get firmer footing. Then they saw him drop through. He was gone—the quick, cold currents would rush him to his death, and there was nothing the spectators could do.

Bizarrely, his legs suddenly poked out of the hole. His torso then emerged, and finally his head as he pushed his body from the water and back onto the ice. He rose to his feet, and continued walking to the opposite bank. When he reached it, the spectators cheered loudly and waved their hats and handkerchiefs. They had a story to tell at home that night, about the reckless wanderer, the crazy man who crossed the thin Missouri River ice.

When Kelso fell through a snow-covered air hole and plunged into the water, he thought, for a moment, that he was a goner. The cold, mighty current seized hold of him and struggled to pull him under. "I kept my presence of mind, however, perfectly; I was not, just then, conscious of being very much frightened." Kelso had learned this about himself. In times of danger he could remain calm. It was how he had first learned to swim when he was a boy. He had been trying to wade a creek when a strong current swept him off his feet and into deep water. Instead of panicking, he thought: Wait, just hold your breath, keep your face in the water, move your arms and legs methodically. . . . The next thing he knew, he had made it safely to shore. Here, plunging through the river ice, in a similar response to a "call of death," Kelso reacted calmly. He threw out his arms and caught the lower side of the air hole. He then worked his feet up as quickly as possible, thrusting his legs and, little by little, his whole body out of the water and back onto the ice. He stood and finished crossing. It wasn't until he reached the riverbank that he suddenly felt weak, felt "conscious of a shock that I wish never to have repeated." When he heard cheers from the opposite bank, he waved his hat and tried to cheer back. His "voice gave forth only a little husky, scared squeak." His wet clothing quickly froze stiff as he trudged off through the snow.[44]

5

Words on Fire

THE EXCITEMENT IN the public square outside his classroom and the looming national crisis compelled Kelso to close his school early. It was May 7, 1861. Jubilant speakers addressed a large crowd in front of the courthouse. Two more states—Virginia and Arkansas—had seceded from the Union. The process had begun in December, when South Carolina seceded, followed by six other Southern states. In his January inaugural address, Governor Claiborne Fox Jackson had insisted that Missouri would stand with its sister slaveholding states. In St. Louis, site of a large federal arsenal, paramilitary organizations on both sides started organizing and drilling. Temporarily dashing the private hopes of Governor Jackson and a powerful group of pro-Southern legislators, the state constitutional convention, which met in March, rejected secession. Then on April 12, 1861, the South Carolina militia attacked the U.S. garrison at Fort Sumter in the Charleston harbor. Jackson quickly rejected President Lincoln's call on April 15 for 75,000 volunteers to put down the rebellion. Instead, on April 22, the governor called for a special session of the legislature to reorganize the militia, and on May 3 he called for the militia to assemble. Claiming in public to be assuming a defensive posture of "armed neutrality" in the conflict between North and South, behind the scenes the governor was trying to maneuver Missouri out of the Union, and he wrote to Confederate president Jefferson Davis requesting artillery. By May 6, nearly 900 militia men had established "Camp Jackson" on the eastern edge of St. Louis, flying secessionist flags and threatening, the Unionists thought, the federal arsenal there. With the latest news of two more states seceding, the public speakers in Kelso's southwestern Missouri town of Buffalo exulted that the old Union was virtually destroyed and the new Confederacy established. "The Union seemed to have no friends present," he thought darkly as he heard the speeches and cheers. "Treason seemed to be triumphant."[1]

These were extraordinary times. To Kelso, an electrified Missouri seemed to pervert human nature itself. Children wished they could trade their toys for guns, and women wanted to march off to battlefields. Farmers left their fields, merchants their shops, and artisans their tools to crowd the streets and public squares of the state's cities and towns. "At every corner, fiery orators, with burning words and wild gesticulations, heightened still the already morbidly inflamed passions of the multitude." No public speakers could enflame passions quite like the preachers, who raged from their pulpits. If public opinion over slavery and secession were divided in Missouri as a whole, in Buffalo it seemed all on one side. Kelso had remained publicly quiet on these questions, but his silence was about to end. As he walked toward the courthouse, he felt that he "was irresistibly drifting" to his destiny. He was boldly walking out alone again, without testing the ice; he was about to stand up alone again and declare his opposition to a hostile crowd.[2]

He had much to lose. In the four years since he had walked south from Platte County, he had rebuilt his life. He had wandered down to Springfield, in southwestern Missouri. Liking the looks of the prosperous town, he filed his divorce suit at the courthouse and began teaching in local schools. His brother Robert, who also enrolled at Pleasant Ridge College, moved nearby to teach, too, and in their spare time they happily studied Latin and math together. Robert married one of his teenaged students. John, waiting through more court delays for his divorce, became interested in another student, fifteen-year-old Martha Susan ("Susie") Barnes. She had a musical voice, a sweet disposition, and an obvious interest in him. Considering his "strong sex" drive, he knew that "the cold, barren life of a celibate" was not the life for him. His daughter Florella had come to live with him, and he was seeking custody of his son Florellus, too. His children needed a mother. "I concluded that Susie was about as suitable a matrimonial mate as I would be likely ever again to find." So on September 23, 1858, a few days after his divorce from Adelia was finalized, John and Susie were married.[3]

After returning to Pleasant Ridge College in May of 1859 for his final exams, Kelso received his degree and moved his family about 35 miles north of Springfield to Buffalo, the Dallas County seat. Susie gave birth to their daughter Iantha. John opened a private academy, and the school thrived. Growing from seven to eighty students in the first half year, it drew young men and women seeking training to become teachers. Kelso's sister Ella signed on as an assistant teacher. At the same time, Kelso became a notable citizen in town, serving as a "Worthy Chief" in the Buffalo Lodge of Good Templars and emerging as the leader of the town's Temperance party. In the spring of

1860, he and Susie bought "a beautiful little farm" about a mile and a half from Buffalo. "It began to seem," Kelso thought, "that, at last, the cry of my heart for a loving companion, for a happy fire-side, was about to be realized."[4]

A year later, as he crossed Buffalo's crowded town square, Kelso felt the force of the public crisis, of national and personal destiny, compelling him to take a stand, even though he knew it would tear him away from that happy fireside. When a speaker finished yet another secessionist harangue, Kelso climbed the courthouse steps and called the attention of the crowd. He then pulled a sheet of paper from his pocket and read a series of pro-Union resolutions. Secession was treason, he declared to his stunned neighbors. He and other loyal citizens would fight to the death against the rebellion and in support of the United States. Governor Jackson had proclaimed that such words constituted treason against the state of Missouri, a capital offense. But it was Jackson and the secessionist legislators, Kelso charged, who were traitors deserving death. This was more than a political dispute. It involved personal honor. So he called out the governor and declared that he and Jackson "could not both live." Then Kelso walked down the steps and stood silently amongst the crowd.[5]

At first there was only "a general but indistinct murmur of low voices." Taken "utterly by surprise," the crowd "seemed thunder-struck" by Kelso's "audacity." Some louder voices began denouncing him as a "traitor to the South" who "ought to be shot down like a . . . sheep-killing dog." As the crowd's fury built, Kelso suddenly felt a child's fingers clutching one of his hands. "Looking down, I saw the anxious face of one of my late pupils, a bright little boy of eight years." The boy tugged at him, pulling him away from the crowd, leading him "behind some store buildings and into an old ware-house, the doors and windows of which were all closed." Four men sat in the darkness. We believe everything you just said out there, they told Kelso. But by publicly declaring your principles, you are just throwing your life away, practically begging the crowd to tear you to pieces. They offered to help hide him until tempers cooled. Kelso, refusing to hide or keep quiet, asked to borrow a revolver.[6]

That evening at home, he wrote "a scathing satire upon the secessionists" entitled "The Devil's First Epistle to the Buffalonians." He made several copies and, for dramatic effect, scorched the papers in the fireplace to suggest that the letter had come straight from hell. He went out that night and posted the sheets around town. The Devil's epistle caused some excitement and curiosity. Although Kelso had tried to disguise his handwriting, most townspeople guessed its author.[7]

The Devil's proslavery, pro-secession position was quite popular in Missouri. Less than a fifth of White Missourians held slaves, but the dominant political culture was proslavery: 85 percent of the men elected to office in the 1850s were slaveholders. Still, six months earlier, most of slavery's supporters in the state had wanted to remain in the Union. They were conservative Unionists who thought both abolitionists and secessionists were dangerous radicals. In the presidential election of 1860, Missourians split 117,000 votes between the two candidates wishing to preserve the slaveholding republic: Northern Democrat Stephen A. Douglas and John Bell of the Constitutional Union Party. Missouri voters gave the uncompromising proslavery and pro-secessionist Southern Democrat John C. Breckinridge 31,300 votes and Republican Abraham Lincoln, who opposed slavery in the territories but promised not to interfere with it in the states, received slightly more than 17,000. Democrat Claiborne Fox Jackson was privately in favor of Missouri's secession, but in order to win the governor's race he had to endorse Douglas and voice proslavery Unionism. The events that quickly followed the November elections—from the secession of seven Southern states through Ft. Sumter and its aftermath—pushed many if not most proslavery Missourians into the secessionist camp.[8]

By the late spring of 1861, Dallas County's citizens—at least the loud ones—seemed eager for the state to leave the Union and join the Confederacy. The previous fall, about 70 percent of the voters had chosen either Douglas or Bell for president, though Breckinridge ran stronger and Lincoln weaker than in the state at large. Kelso's town of Buffalo had more of a pro-Southern tilt than either the county or the state, and Governor Jackson, the man Kelso called out as a traitor, had received 70 percent of the vote. Benton township, which included Buffalo, was on average wealthier (per capita) than the other five townships in the county and had a higher proportion of slaveholders: in Dallas County, slightly less than 4 percent of households had slaves; in Benton, 8 percent did. A much higher percentage, however, had grown up with slavery and remained comfortable with it. Eighty-four percent of the county's household heads had been born in slaveholding states. A majority in the county came from the upper South, especially Tennessee. Slavery, for many of the hardscrabble White farmers and Ozark Mountain folk who favored it even though they owned no slaves themselves, was valued less as a vital economic system than as an institution that maintained the racial order. According to a Missouri saying, it was easy to get " 'Secesh' . . . from brush country and bad whiskey." But in Buffalo by May of 1861, it wasn't looking like supporters of secession would even need much whiskey. Southern partisans were arguing, nearly unopposed, that the only way that Missouri could continue to ensure a White person's "right" to slave property was for the state to join the Confederacy. They could stoke the fire for their cause, too, by thumping their Bibles and demonizing outsiders—Black Republican Yankees and the damned Dutch (Germans)—who dared interfere with the lives of local men with Southern sentiments.[9]

Almost all of Kelso's students in Buffalo came from secessionist families. When he had explained to them as he closed his school that he would stand by the Union, they "seemed grieved," but they shook his hand on the way out the door, some with tears in their eyes. Kelso's relatives—his parents and dear brother Robert, his sisters, uncles, aunts, and cousins—remained ardently proslavery and supported the South's right to secede. His parents and three of his sisters had moved to Colorado the previous year. Before he had mounted the Buffalo courthouse steps to make his public declaration in early May, he had written to them to explain his position and his intentions. They expressed their indignation and then cut off communication.[10]

A week after Kelso's announcement in front of the courthouse, a great meeting was held in Buffalo. Peter Wilkes and other noted secessionist speakers arrived from Springfield with a Confederate flag to be flown from the courthouse roof, and they were processed into a town square crowded with people from throughout the county. A band was ready to play Dixie and secession songs after the speeches, and men were ready to fire their guns into the air. Wilkes had spoken at a similar rally a hundred miles to the southwest in Newtonia on April 24. Buffalo secessionists most likely hoped that their event, too, would conclude with public resolutions supporting Jackson and the Southern cause.[11]

Kelso stood near the speakers' stand as Wilkes delivered his address. But Kelso also saw a young Buffalo merchant named John McConnell and about a half dozen other secret Union sympathizers that he had met over the previous week. They knew what Kelso planned to do and had tried, unsuccessfully, to dissuade him. Here they were, as if by chance, heavily armed and stationed near him and the speaker's stand. The orator's remarks were cheered and loudly applauded. As Kelso scanned the crowd, he saw "many men with pale faces and earnest expressions who, with set teeth, watched the proceedings, but who did not join in the applause." He next observed "a rough-looking lot of customers," about thirty hunters from the Niangua hills, dressed in buckskin, carrying long rifles, and belted with revolvers and bowie knives. Their hard faces did not betray their intentions. "[T]hey had heard that I was to be killed that day, if I attempted to speak," they told Kelso afterward, and "they had come to see who killed me and how the killing was done."[12]

Wilkes concluded his eloquent speech urging the people to stand as one for secession and the South. He cited Genesis and the Book of Revelation to argue that the seven states that had first seceded "were typified by the seven stars, the seven churches, the seven candlesticks, the seven years of plenty, the seven angels, and other sevens of the Bible, all of a glorious, a heaven-approved character." As the crowd applauded Wilkes, Kelso leaped in front of the stand and waved his hand for attention. "Instantly a dead silence prevailed. No one in the audience seemed even to breathe. The very audacity of my act seemed to hold them all fixed as if by a kind of fascination." Kelso knew how to play Wilkes's game. He parried Wilkes's reference to Genesis 41:29 (years of plenty) by drawing from the verse following it, which supplied an opposite image (years of famine); he turned the speaker's invocation of the first three chapters of Revelation upside down, by citing later chapters in the same book. "I showed that the seven seceding states were typified by the seven lean kine [cattle], the seven years of famine, the seven plagues, the seven vials of wrath, the seven heads of the dragon, the seven devils, and many other sevens of the Bible, all of a damnable—a heaven abominated character. I showed that, as Satan had drawn away one third of the hosts of heaven, so the arch fiend of secession had drawn away one third of the hosts of our Union, our heaven on earth."[13]

When Kelso had read his pro-Union resolutions aloud a week earlier, he was defiantly expressing heretical political sentiments and severing his connection to the community, asserting honorable manhood and contemptuously tossing his words like a bomb into a hostile crowd. This speech was different. He still believed he stood alone and was again risking his life to speak out for his unpopular principles, but this time he seemed motivated by something grander than defiant self-assertion. Inspired not by God's grace but by what he portrayed as a self-sacrificing patriotic spirit, he spoke—he preached—not just to damn the rebels but to embolden timid Unionists and to convert the undecided. "My whole being seemed aglow with a strange inspiration. I seemed to see in great letters of flame the very words that I should speak. I forgot myself and my danger. . . . I thought only of the cause I was defending and of victory."[14]

After neutralizing Wilkes's biblical rhetoric he turned to a different proof text: "the inimitable words of our immortal Washington's Farewell Address." He invoked the Revolutionary "forefathers" and prophesied the carnage and desolation that would follow from the Southern rebellion. His words, at least according to his autobiography, had their effect, like a revival sermon making sinners weep and saints shout. "Tears—loyal tears rolled down the rough

cheeks of many a brave and honest man who came there believing himself to
be a secessionist. . . . A mighty revolution was being wrought in that great assembly. A tidal wave of loyalty was rising that could not now be turned back,
or resisted. When I closed, the pent up feelings of hundreds found vent in
loud and hearty hurrahs for the Union and our brave old flag." After Kelso
had finished, W. B. Edwards, one of the closet Unionists he had met in the
darkened warehouse a week before, an old veteran with a war wound, hobbled
on his crutches into Kelso's place. Although a slaveholder, Edwards was ardently opposed to secession; he "poured forth a torrent of burning patriotic
eloquence" that turned "the loyal fire" Kelso had kindled "into a resistless
flame."[15]

Then Kelso decided it was time to separate the sheep from the goats. He
asked Edwards to go to one side of the town square and encouraged those
who supported "Washington, the Union, and the glorious 'Star-spangled
Banner'" to stand with him. Wilkes, Kelso said, could walk to the other side to
represent "Benedict Arnold, treason, and the Confederate flag." As Edwards
"hobbled to his place, several hundred men waved their hats, hurrahed for the
Union, and formed in a long line by his side." Wilkes, the other Springfield
secessionists, and their local supporters, "thunder-struck and alarmed,"
conferred quickly, grabbed their flag, and clattered away in their wagons as
the Union men cheered. "We had won a great, though a bloodless victory."[16]

News from St. Louis heightened the tension. On May 10, Captain Nathaniel
Lyon, commander of the St. Louis Arsenal, surrounded Camp Jackson with
about 6,500 troops and forced Governor Jackson's militiamen to surrender
even before they had unpacked the four Confederate artillery pieces they had
smuggled into camp. As Lyon's men marched the militia through the streets
of St. Louis to the arsenal, enraged civilians began pelting the Federals with
rocks and debris. The raw troops fired into the crowd and soon twenty-eight
civilians (as well as four soldiers and three captive State Guard militiamen)
were dead—a bloodletting that struck Southern sympathizers and even some
moderates as a sure sign of Federal tyranny.[17]

Secessionists and Unionists began arming and mobilizing across the state,
the balance of power shifting from county to county. The words and actions of
a few people sometimes tipped that balance. In Hickory County, adjacent to
Dallas in the northwest, the pro-Southern forces organized around the words
of a few local orators and the military leadership of a former sheriff. In Newton
County, in the state's southwest corner, the secessionist rally and resolutions
passed at Newtonia helped solidify the region for the Confederacy. Kelso's
impassioned speech in Buffalo resembled one given by Robert Pinckney

Matthews, a young pro-Union orator 35 miles south in Springfield. "Meetings were being held night and day to discuss the state of the country," Matthews later recalled. At a debate in front of a large crowd, "[e]xcitement was at a white heat and a small spark was liable to make a mighty flame at a moment's notice." The secessionist speaker raised his supporters "to the highest pitch of enthusiasm." Matthews stood to speak for the Union, and "a feeling came over me I cannot define. The whole subject and the consequences of disunion and disruption seemed to open before me and burn like fire on my brain. A sensation of exaltation was over me. What I said I know not, but when I was done, men were crowding around me shouting 'Union once and forever.' I realized the field was won and immediately formed a [Union] League of over 50 men who swore with uplifted hand to defend the 'Stars and Stripes' with every drop of blood in their veins."[18]

The newspapers reported that blood was already being spilled in clashes between Union and Confederate troops in Virginia, first in a skirmish at Fairfax County Courthouse on June 1, and then in a larger engagement near Newport News nine days later in which 18 Union soldiers and one Confederate died. In St. Louis, Nathaniel Lyon, promoted to brigadier general while being called a murderer in the pro-Southern press, met with Governor Jackson on June 11. A stubborn Republican abolitionist from Connecticut, Lyon refused to compromise with what he considered to be treason. "This means war," he said, abruptly ending the meeting and walking out of the room. Lyon was authorized by the secretary of war to enlist loyal Missourians to defend themselves, the state, and the United States; they would receive federal pay when called into active service. The next day Jackson called for 50,000 state volunteers to enlist in the State Guard and resist Federal despotism. The day after that, Lyon led a force of about 2,500 from St. Louis to the state capital in Jefferson City, but by the time he got there Jackson and his State Guard force had already evacuated to the southwest. Lyon, leaving three companies to guard Jefferson City, followed with about 1,700 men. In Boonville, on the Missouri River, on June 17, Lyon's and Jackson's forces skirmished, leaving eight dead and over a dozen wounded, before the State Guard retreated toward the southwest.[19]

Throughout the state, men rallied behind Jackson and formed pro-Confederate State Guard militias and behind Lyon to form pro-Union Home Guard militias. In Dallas, the Unionists acted first, and Kelso was the first man to volunteer. The second was Milton Burch, a thirty-nine-year-old Buffalo merchant, lame from a wound received in the War with Mexico. Kelso was elected major and Burch chosen to be a captain. When county enlistments had reached eight hundred men and they had a full regiment,

Kelso was nominated to be a colonel. He declined in favor of his "brave old soldier friend" Edwards, and then to be a lieutenant colonel, but he deferred again in favor of Dr. Eleazar Hovey, a popular physician and dentist. In Kelso's Dallas County Home Guard regiment, about half of the men "were armed with the old-fashioned long-barrel rifles used by the hunters of that time. A few had good shot-guns, and many had revolvers." The men with military experience like Edwards and Burch started drilling the others, introducing the hastily organized group of farmers and townsfolk to military discipline. The Guard took possession of the courthouse, proclaimed martial law, established a system of code words and signals, and began raiding the homes of well-known rebels, confiscating their guns.[20]

Just to the north of Dallas County in Hickory County, the secessionists in Black Oak Point acted first. A group of local businessmen—"noise makers and agitators," as a county historian described them—organized a State Guard regiment, but they put a tough and respected former sheriff, John Mabary, at its head when there was fighting to be done. Just to the north of Hickory in Benton County, six pro-Southern State Guard companies formed at Warsaw, and 20 miles away in a town called Cole Camp the mostly German inhabitants formed nine companies for the Home Guard.[21]

Word spread quickly in south-central Missouri about the early morning massacre at Cole Camp on June 19. Governor Jackson's retreating forces were heading toward Benton County. About four hundred men of the German Home Guard regiment, asleep in barns at either end of their training ground, would be in the way. Two State Guard companies, about 350 infantry and 100 cavalry, marched from Warsaw in the night, flying an American flag to confuse their enemies if spotted. After quietly bayonetting the picket guards, the pro-Confederate forces surrounded one of the barns, opened the doors at both ends of the building, and poured in fire upon the sleeping soldiers. When it was over, sixty-one Unionists were wounded and thirty-six killed. The State Guard soldiers also caught a spy on the road, tied him to a tree, and shot him.[22]

News about Cole Camp and rumors about other atrocities traveled quickly south into Dallas County, and frightened citizens thought that Hickory County's Captain Mabary had been in on the killing. And Mabary was said to be not far from Buffalo, preparing for another attack. One day in early July, terrified Unionist refuges from Hickory County galloped into Kelso's camp. Their hats were gone, their tired horses were covered with dust and foam, "and, with white lips, [they] reported that Mabary was, at that moment, only a few miles away, rapidly advancing upon our own position, burning every

Union house that came in his way, and hanging every Union man that fell into his hands." Thrown into a "wonderful excitement," the green troops of the Dallas County Home Guard scrambled to prepare for the attack. Mabary was coming! They had all heard the "blood-curdling tales" of "the redoubtable Mabary and his band of rebels." The men got ready, manned their posts, gripped their guns, and watched the horizon.[23]

They waited. After a few hours, anxiety turned to impatience for "a taste of real war." They eventually determined that word of Mabary's advance had been a rumor, probably started by rebels who wanted to see the Home Guards scramble. As the likelihood of an attack receded, their confidence that Buffalo's Unionists could have "whipped the hell out of" Mabary and his rebels grew. "Indeed, so ferociously brave did we become that we determined to send out an expedition against Mabary." Major Edwards sent Kelso out in command of two companies—about seventy-five men. They had decent horses but were poorly armed, still dressed in civilian clothing, and almost completely lacking in military experience.[24]

They marched north and set up camp about 8 miles from Black Oak as a thunderstorm dumped rain upon them. Kelso, worried about a surprise attack, stayed up all night to keep watch, staring into the rain and the darkness. As the weather cleared in the morning, he sent out a reconnoitering party, led by Captain Burch, expecting to get word that Mabary's forces were ready to defend the town. But Mabary and the State Guard were gone. When Kelso and the Dallas troops marched unopposed into town, Burch had already rounded up the four remaining rebel soldiers and fifty armed citizens, confiscated their weapons, and locked them in a church. Kelso had the door unlocked, strode in, proclaimed martial law, and set himself up as a judge in "a high court from whose decision there was no appeal." He promptly pronounced the fifty-four prisoners guilty of treason. Keeping the four soldiers as prisoners, he released the rest if they took an oath of allegiance to the United States.[25]

The Dallas County Home Guard then moved 4 miles east of town, following Mabary's troops. The enemy was only a few miles away, according to the scouts, and Mabary had a larger, better-armed force that occupied a strong position. Kelso did not dare attack, so he ordered his men to stop and set up camp. He planned to lure Mabary into attacking—to trick the enemy into thinking he was ill-prepared, so that Mabary's men could sweep down upon vulnerable Home Guard troops the way the State Guard had slaughtered the soldiers at Cole Camp. Kelso's camp was protected on two sides by the high fences of a large pasture and open to the prairie on two other sides. He had his

men line up their blankets to sleep on the wrong side of the fence and let their
horses loose in the pasture to graze. The sleeping soldiers would look exposed
and vulnerable to a sudden attack from across the prairie. At the first signal
from lookouts, however, the men would scramble behind the fence and shoot
at their attackers.

When the men were set, the lookouts posted, and all the campfires
extinguished, Kelso set out alone, on foot, on a road that cut across the dark
prairie, to do a little reconnoitering. About 3 miles from camp, he began to see
by the moonlight small parties of horsemen riding toward what he took to be
Mabary's camp. At the sound of hooves on the road, he would hide in the tall
grass nearby, his cocked revolver in hand, until the travelers passed. He could
sometimes hear parts of conversations, enough to learn that most of these
horsemen were armed rebel citizens riding out to join Mabary.

Kelso hurried back to a high point in the road from which he could
see his whole camp—the double line of 70 soldiers sleeping on blankets,
and the 50 refugees off to the left. This was where Mabary would go, Kelso
thought, to scout the enemy and assess the battlefield terrain. Hiding in
the high grass, he waited. "In a few minutes, sure enough, two men rode
up and stopped within twenty feet of the muzzle of my gun. They sat so
in range between myself and the moonlit sky that I could easily have sent
a bullet through them both." He imagined one of them must be Mabary
himself. He was close enough to hear them mutter and catch their tone of
confidence. "They seemed to think that they were going to surprise us completely and utterly destroy us." They had taken the bait. As soon as the men
left the rise in the road to return to Mabary's camp, Kelso ran back toward
his own.[26]

He ordered his officers to begin waking the men quietly and have them
move behind the fence. Each soldier was to pull his blanket over his saddle
or bags and leave his hat arranged to make it look like there were still men
asleep upon the ground. Kelso then called in the guards on the side facing
Mabary. "The way was now open for the enemy to come swooping down into
our camp and to fire into our empty blankets, while we, sky-lighting them
from our position behind the fence, each with a good rest for his gun, should
pour our own deadly volleys. In advance, I enjoyed the astonishment and consternation of the enemy when he should find himself fatally caught in his own
trap."[27]

One of the Hickory County refugees who had joined Kelso's troops saw
the soldiers climbing over the fence and into the pasture. "They're getting
their horses to leave!" he shouted. All 50 refugees rushed to get their horses.

Soldiers who had not yet been quietly roused jumped up and joined them. Men chased horses and yelled; Kelso and the officers shouted to restore order, but could not be heard. With fear of an imminent attack and the confusion of men and horses, all military discipline collapsed. When the men finally caught their horses, they quickly mounted and galloped away, many racing for cover in a nearby forest. A few rode all the way back to Buffalo, spreading the word that Kelso's command was being annihilated by the fearsome Captain Mabary.[28]

In a matter of minutes, Kelso's plan had been ruined and he was left with only a dozen men at the fence. Frustrated beyond measure and desperate in the face of an attack that could come at any moment, Kelso told the remaining dozen to leave too. He would stay and fight, he said, preferring death to disgrace. So long as they heard firing, they would know that he was still at his post, doing his duty. The twelve said they would stay to fight by his side. So they all took their positions behind the fence and waited. In the distance, outlined against the sky, they could see a small party of men on that rise in the road.

In a little while, a few more of Kelso's men returned to the fence, "eager to atone by their valor for their recent bad conduct." Then others began rejoining the ranks, a few at a time, until finally all but about a dozen had returned. With a few refugees also taking guns and getting behind the fence, Kelso again had a decent force—79 men—to face Mabary's attack. Yet the sky lightened, and then the sun rose, but still nothing happened. Years later, as Kelso put words on paper telling this story, he wished he could give it a more exciting ending. "I was now really eager for the enemy to come. It spoils a good story for them not to come. Were I writing a novel, I would have them come anyway and have the very devil whipped out of them. As it is, however, I can not do this. They did not come." Kelso learned afterwards that Mabary had seen the commotion in Kelso's camp, thought the Home Guards were preparing for battle, and therefore, realizing that he would not have the element of surprise, called off the attack.[29]

Disappointed, Kelso marched his men back to Buffalo. It began to rain heavily again. Still, at the town's border they were met by the rest of their regiment, who greeted them with a hero's welcome: loud drums, three hearty cheers, and a rifle volley. "And thus ended my first military expedition," Kelso later wrote. "It was far fuller of instruction than of glory." He returned to his little farmhouse, in time to be there while Susie gave birth to their son Ianthus. Toward the end of the month, he would have heard the bad news from back East: on July 21, in the first major battle of the war, the United States had suffered an embarrassing defeat at Bull Run, with nearly 500 soldiers killed and more than twice that wounded.[30]

Duty soon called Kelso away again. After the mid-June skirmish at Boonville, Governor Jackson's State Guard forces, commanded by former Missouri Governor Sterling Price, retreated to Cowskin Prairie in the southwest corner of the state. Their numbers grew, and they would also be joined by Confederate forces from Arkansas led by Brigadier General Ben McCulloch. General Nathaniel Lyon's Federal command reached Springfield on July 13. In early August, Major Edwards sent Kelso to Springfield with a wagon, a small escort, and a request for ammunition to supply the Dallas County regiment. Springfield was a hive of activity, and the mood was tense. The word was that the enemy, confident with its vastly superior numbers, was advancing on the town.[31]

Kelso found General Lyon in his office, "very nervous from overwork and from anxiety," dictating orders to his subordinates. He faced a difficult situation. Temperatures had soared to well over 100 degrees. Lyon's troops were exhausted from marches and from being on alert. Supplies, especially of food, were low, as was morale. He was losing troops as the ninety-day enlistments of many expired. His new commander, John C. Frémont, had just arrived in St. Louis on July 25 and had told Lyon no reinforcements would be coming because troops were needed in New Madrid. As Kelso stood in the general's office on that sweltering August day, Lyon had fewer than 6,000 men in his command and was estimating that the enemy had 30,000 (they actually had about 13,500). The wise choice, critics at the time and since have said, would have been for Lyon to withdraw to Rolla, 90 miles to the northeast, and fight another day. But Lyon had concluded, he said, that "to abandon the Southwest without a struggle would be a sad blow to our cause, and would greatly encourage the Rebels." He was determined to "fight and hope for the best." Kelso, even in retrospect, agreed: "Such a retreat, however, would have been regarded, by both friends and foes, as a virtual abandonment of the cause of the Union in Southern Missouri." As Kelso watched, Lyon ordered that his troops be issued as much ammunition as possible. The battle would be fought soon.[32]

When Kelso asked for ammunition to take back to Buffalo, Lyon gave him more than he requested and waved off the formality of a receipt. But the general told Kelso not to cart it back—he, his men, and the ammunition wagon would surely be captured by the enemy. Instead, Lyon wanted the Dallas Home Guard to come to Springfield as quickly as possible to help him fight. He asked Kelso if a written order to Colonel Edwards was needed. "I replied that I thought not;—that I thought a letter from myself would be sufficient." Kelso dashed off a note and sent it on a fast horse back to Buffalo. Edwards, however, "justly regarding this as an inexcusably loose way of doing business," refused to move his regiment on the basis of a note from Kelso rather than a written order from higher up the chain of command. Edwards asked again for Kelso to return immediately with the ammunition wagon. So on August 9, Lyon let Kelso leave with the wagon but wrote directly to Edwards: "I am surprised that orders here to you given were not sufficient to cause your command to repair to this point. I therefore direct that you repair here as heretofore directed with all possible dispatch and bring all the available force at your command with all the provisions you can bring without causing unnecessary delay. Arms and due equipments in the hands of your men are of course indispensable." Knowing that the Home Guards were still dressed as civilians and would be indistinguishable from many fighting on the opposing side, the general added a postscript: "Cause your men to wear a strip of white cloth on their hats." Lyon's order, however, would come too late.[33]

The next day, on August 10, 1861, State Guard and Confederate forces of about 12,000 men defeated Lyon's army of 5,400 at the Battle of Wilson's Creek, 12 miles southwest of Springfield. It was the second major battle, and second Union defeat, of the Civil War. The Union's Army of the West had 258 killed, including Lyon, 873 wounded, and 186 missing, for a total 1,317 casualties; the Confederate and State Guard casualties were roughly the same, but they took the field. Lyon, the first Union general to die in battle, was hailed as a martyr in the Northern press. By the time Kelso and the Dallas Home Guard approached Springfield, they met the remnants of Lyon's command and refugees hurrying in the opposite direction, urging them to turn around. They had no choice but to return to Buffalo and, the next day, join the full Union retreat from southwest Missouri. The rebel army was already in Springfield and was said to be advancing, and guerrilla bands were already beginning to roam the countryside and prey upon Unionists, but the soldiers had to follow orders, leave their families behind, and retreat farther north to regroup.[34]

Retreat to where? was the question. The Dallas County Home Guard camped together on that first night for what would turn out to be the last time. The men were demoralized by the disastrous turn of events. They were frustrated and worried about their families; they were angry and undisciplined. Colonel Edwards left the regiment and headed for Jefferson City. Lieutenant Colonel Hovey left to move himself and his family to Illinois, out of harm's way. The remaining officers argued. Some wanted to go to Rolla, and others to Jefferson City. Kelso, disgusted by the bickering and tired of being a part of a ragtag local militia as he watched it dissolve before his eyes, resigned and headed for the state capital, determined to enlist in "the regular volunteer service of the United States."[35]

Kelso's time in the Home Guard, as he said of his expedition against Mabary, had been full of instruction if not of glory. The experience had driven home lessons about honor, ambition, and manhood—values central to his life and at the heart, it seemed to him, of what the Civil War was all about.

Honor could not be enforced by a form of words. He had paroled prisoners after they swore an oath of allegiance to the United States, only to hear of them supporting the rebellion again within days—sometimes within hours—of their release. "The utter folly of administering this oath soon became apparent. Few of those, if any, who took it, under such circumstances ever held it as binding upon them. Indeed, I have come to the conclusion that, under any circumstances, oaths are utterly useless if not absolutely pernicious." An honorable man did not need an oath to tell the truth or do the right thing. A dishonorable one would do right only if forced and lie if he could get away with it.[36]

Kelso also believed that patriotic service did not mean disinterestedness or self-abnegation. It was wrong to try to divorce a commitment to country or cause from a man's individual ambitions. "It is generally thought to be the proper thing to condemn enterprising men for ambition. For my own part, however, I have very little use for any man, and no use at all for a soldier, who has no ambition. Such a man has no object in life and accomplishes nothing. Ambition is the very essence of energy. . . . Let ambition, then, be encouraged as a virtue and not discouraged as a form of wickedness."[37]

Kelso's linked ambitions for love and glory—the loving companion by the fireside supporting his chance to do something heroic and historic—now seemed far more possible than when he had fantasized about fighting in Nicaragua after the collapse of his first marriage. As the war offered opportunities for virtuous exertion and accomplishment unlike anything in civilian life, Susie and the children at home would be his emotional anchor. His love for Susie deepened as he spent time away from her, and she became, he said, the "idol" of his soul.[38]

His experience in the Home Guard also refined his understanding of manhood. He had told his students when he closed his school that he had to stand by the Union to "be true to my own conscience and my own manhood." What that meant became clearer in contrast to his neighbor, the debonair Dr. Eleazar Hovey, a "magnificent" man who possessed nearly "every quality of gracious manhood." Kelso had deferred to Dr. Hovey when the Home Guard chose its lieutenant colonel. He had also stepped aside in favor of W. B. Edwards when the regiment elected its colonel, but that act of deference made more sense: Kelso was not just acknowledging Edwards's age and social status (Edwards was a well-to-do farmer), but also his military experience and the leadership the veteran had shown with his fiery words at the secession rally. In ceding his place to Hovey, however, Kelso deferred to the doctor's polish, manners, and popularity. But when Hovey hurried to safety in Illinois after the Battle of Wilson's Creek, he demonstrated that he lacked two essentials of true manhood: honor and courage. Kelso noted ruefully, though, that honor and courage seemed to have less appeal than looks and charm for many women—perhaps, he began to worry, even for Susie.[39]

6

Who the Devil Are You, Anyway?

HUDDLED IN THEIR coats, the picket guards watched the road into the Union army camp at Lebanon, Missouri. It was a cold morning in early February 1862, and 4 inches of snow covered the ground. In the distance, a figure stumbled from the woods onto the road and begin tramping through the snow. They mounted their horses, drew their revolvers, and galloped toward him. As they approached, the ragged, filthy man stopped and slowly raised his bare hands over his head into the cold wind, spreading his fingers to show he was unarmed. The horses circled, the guns pointed, and the guards beheld a strange, dilapidated character. His bearded face was so dirty that it was impossible to guess his age. He wore no hat, and his dusty, tangled hair had snagged bits of dried leaves. He lacked overcoat and vest, and his shirt and pants were tattered and torn. His snowy shoes were full of holes. "Who the devil *are* you, anyway?" one asked. The man answered that he "was a farmer, a wood-chopper, a stone-cutter, a teacher and a preacher."[1]

"Who the devil are you, anyway?" The question had been asked or implied many times over the past six months. To a rebel woman giving the stranger breakfast at her door, he had admitted he was a Federal soldier. He explained that he fought to preserve the Union, not to free the slaves—a lie that set her at ease. To the magnificently mounted Confederate officer who had encountered him on the bank of the Current River, he had politely introduced himself as "John Russell," an ardent secessionist. He proved it by joining the officer and delivering speeches supporting the Southern cause at recruiting stations. To a dirt-poor hunter who ranted to the stranger about Yankees wanting to steal "niggers" and "niggers" wanting to steal White women, he echoed the coarse sentiments of the Missourians some thought of as "white trash." To the Confederate soldiers who had finally captured him, recognized him as a spy, and built a gallows to hang him for it, he actually told the truth. Yes, he said, he was a spy. Yes, as "John Russell," he had delivered speeches at Confederate recruiting stations. Yes, he had "jay-hawked" rebels in Dallas County—stolen from secessionist neighbors after they had stolen from him. And yes, he had "bushwhacked" some of those neighbors—gunned them down after they had destroyed his farm, burned down his house, taken his land, and driven his family out into the snow.[2]

He had escaped the Confederates, and now the Federal picket guards had him at gunpoint. He could have just said that he was John Russell Kelso, and although his men still called him "Major," he was a private in the 24th Missouri Infantry, just back from a spy mission into enemy territory with a report for General Samuel R. Curtis. But he was a different man than the one who had set out on his first espionage assignment the previous autumn. No longer the sunshine patriot waving the star-spangled banner, Kelso had in the past few months lost his God and found a new motive to fight. Feeling his blood burn at the suffering inflicted upon his family and friends, he had vowed revenge. After weeks of spying in enemy territory playing his "dangerous game," quickly shaping his identity to suit each new situation, he was no longer accustomed to answering a straightforward question like "Who the devil are you, anyway?" unless doing so would give him an advantage.

SIX MONTHS EARLIER, after the Battle of Wilson's Creek and the disintegration of the Dallas County Home Guard, Kelso had made his way to Jefferson City to join a Union regiment. He found everything there "in confusion." So did Brigadier General Ulysses S. Grant, who arrived there at about the same time. "I visited the camps of the different commands about this city and selected locations for troops yet to arrive," Grant wrote in a letter dated August 22, 1861. "I find great deficiency in everything for the comfort and efficiency of the army. Most of the troops are without clothing, camp and garrison equipage. . . . There are no rations for issue . . . and a general looseness prevailing."[3]

Kelso and other recruits flooding into the city were housed on the fairgrounds as the new regiments were formed. Since the beginning of the war, the states had taken the initiative in recruiting and forming military units, grafting state militias onto the U.S. Army. By December 1861, the regular army had 20,000 men and the state volunteers 640,000. In Missouri, on August 24, after the new (Union) government had been formed, Governor Hamilton Gamble issued a call for a new Six-Month Militia of 42,000 men. Each company (64–82 men) would elect its own officers (a captain and two lieutenants), and then the officers of each regiment's ten companies would elect the regiment's field officers (colonels and majors). Most of the men elected in the Home Guard regiments wanted the new forces to absorb the Home Guard companies, keeping the officers in place. Ambitious men without positions in the Home Guard, however, called for new elections and reorganization. "The wrangling became very warm and the intriguing very active," Kelso recounted, "many of these patriots, so ambitious for shoulder straps, declaring that the Union might go to hell before they would enter the service without a certainty of an office." Kelso was caught between two poles. A major in the Dallas County Home Guard, he had resigned his office when the regiment fell apart on the retreat after Wilson's Creek. Declining a majorate in a new regiment, he declared heatedly that he "would volunteer as a private and thus show to the world that my patriotism was entirely above selfish personal motives." Kelso, his Buffalo friend John McConnell (who had been a sergeant in the Home Guard), and a few others then strode up to an officer recruiting for Colonel James A. Mulligan's "Irish Brigade" (the 23rd Illinois Volunteer Infantry Regiment), and signed up as privates.[4]

Back at the barracks, the men asked Kelso to make a speech. His rousing address denounced the scheming mercenaries, to hooting and applause. Major John K. Hall, who would lose his rank if new elections were held, charged that Kelso fomented mutiny and had him marched out of the fairgrounds in front of several bayonets. Although Hall locked the gates so Kelso's supporters could not follow him out, many jumped the wall and joined him at the camp for Mulligan's men.[5]

There was not much to do during the day besides drill and guard the camp, but soon Kelso was helping to run things and he was elected to be a lieutenant. Sometimes he would get a pass and go out exploring the countryside, returning with ripe paw-paws, peaches, and apples for his men, his uniform and gun persuading reluctant farmers to donate the fruit to the cause. One of the few amusements the soldiers had in camp was a bare-knuckle boxing match on the parade ground most evenings, usually between a Chicagoan and a non-Chicagoan.[6]

Kelso did not receive his lieutenant's commission. Soon after he had been elected, most of Mulligan's Irish Brigade marched 125 miles west to Lexington, on the bluffs of the Missouri River, to reinforce the garrison there. On September 12, General Sterling Price's 15,000 State Guards began an attack on Colonel Mulligan's 3,500 men. After an eight-day siege, Mulligan had to surrender. Kelso and his Dallas County men, however, had been taken to St. Louis by "a villainous looking Captain" who was probably stealing the recruits for his own benefit. Kelso and his friend McConnell wound up being transferred to Company F of the 24th Missouri Infantry, serving as privates.[7]

They were stationed at Benton Barracks, about 5 miles outside St. Louis. A chaplain with the Iowa Infantry was impressed when he saw it in late 1861: "Benton Barracks is situated upon a very flat piece of land. . . . The buildings, so far as comfortable quarters for the soldiers was taken into consideration, I think were well designed. Good cook houses, with suitable furnaces for cooking were conveniently arranged in the rear of the Barracks. . . . [Water was] carried into the camp by the means of pipes leading from a large reservoir

John R. Kelso, ca. 1861-2. Photo courtesy of Martin Dieu and Holly Elwood.

situated upon an elevated part of the city. . . . The camp was well drained, consequently it never remained muddy any length of time after heavy rains. . . . Upon the whole, I never saw any better in all my travels as a soldier." The Western Sanitary Commission, however, described conditions that decimated the nearly 20,000 troops that filled the camp by December: "The most prevalent diseases were measles, pneumonia, typhoid fever, and diarrhea. . . . The barracks being rough buildings, with many open cracks, and floors without any space beneath, were far from comfortable. . . . The consequence was that many of the measles patients were afterwards attacked with pneumonia, and died." When Kelso arrived, the men were already complaining about the water and suffering from diarrhea, malaria, and cholera.[8]

Popular among the enlisted men, who still called him "Major," Kelso also curried favor at headquarters. He found the commander-in-chief, Major General Samuel R. Curtis, to be "a grand and good old man." A West Point graduate, Mexican War veteran, and former congressman from Iowa, the general took a liking to the private. The regiment's commander was Colonel Sempronius H. "Pony" Boyd, a lawyer, slaveholder, and staunch Unionist who had served as mayor of Springfield in 1856. Boyd, recognizing Kelso's popularity, promised to make him a captain when they had enough recruits to form a new company, and Kelso, now regretting his rash decision to enlist as a private, recruited for Boyd. But the company command went to someone else. Kelso came to suspect that this was how Boyd built up his regiment: get influential men recruiting, and then betray most of them. "Boyd was constitutionally a great liar," Kelso concluded about the man. "He did not try to be honest, and he would have failed, if he had tried."[9]

Kelso got his first taste of battle in the middle of October, 1861. Meriweather Jeff Thompson, brigadier general in the Missouri State Guard, was nicknamed the Swamp Fox after Revolutionary War hero Francis Marion for his ability to move his forces quickly over difficult terrain, strike suddenly, and then disappear. Thompson and his two thousand men had advanced north on October 11, hoping to disrupt Federal forces, recruit for the Confederacy, and take supplies. A detachment of 500 dragoons on October 15 attacked the Federal force at Blackwell, less than 50 miles south of St. Louis, and burned the Iron Mountain Railroad bridge across Big River. "It was a large three-span bridge," Thompson reported, "and cannot be rebuilt in months." Kelso's regiment was hurriedly sent to the bridge by rail. Packed into open cars that rattled and swayed with the speed, the soldiers rushed through the night, plunging one moment through the dark forests and then bursting into the open beneath a bright, moonlit sky. The train slowed as they neared the town, and they could see the glow from farmhouses the rebels had torched. When they reached the bridge at Big River, Kelso saw his first battlefield. Union soldiers lay dead in a stone pen where they had made their last stand. "Most of them had been shot in the head as they stood on their knees firing over their low stone wall. They had fallen backward, and I shuddered as I gazed upon their ghostly upturned faces and their glassy eyes gleaming in the moonlight." Rebel troops had bled and fallen only a dozen yards away. The arriving Federals took up a defensive position, ready for another attack. But toward morning, Kelso and some others, sent to reconnoiter, followed the enemy's trail and determined that Thompson's men had departed.[10]

On his way back to the battlefield, Kelso left his scouting party on the road and cautiously cut through the woods. He froze at the sight of a man crouched in the bushes, watching the movements of the Union troops. "Stepping up to him as noiselessly as a ghost, I clapped the muzzle of my gun to his back," Kelso remembered, "and bawled out to him to drop his gun and be damned quick about or I would drop him into hell. . . . [H]e came very near dropping into hell anyway from sudden fright." Kelso took the man's gun, marched him back to camp, and turned the prisoner over to his commanding officer. "Later in the war," Kelso reflected years afterward, "after my blood had become hot, I would have killed this man instead of capturing him."[11]

A few nights later the enemy returned. Lying low in the rifle pits they had dug, the Federals felt the bullets fly over their heads. Hats held up on sticks to test this were quickly shot off. They fired into the dark woods, but, unable to see the enemy, they doubted that their shots did much damage. An hour or so after the shooting stopped, Kelso got permission to scout the enemy. He crept behind the position that the rebels had held. "I could hear my own heart thumping. I was expecting, every moment, to feel the bodies or hear the whisperings of enemies." He planned to shoot if he came across anyone, hoping that surprise and a fear of hitting one of their own would prevent them from immediately shooting back. He moved closer. "All was silent as the grave." Then he spotted, low to the ground, in a patch of moonlight, a man's head. "For a moment, I did not move a muscle. I held my breath, and listened." He crept closer, ready to shoot and then escape into the darkness. The rebel did not move. Kelso began to understand: a random shot in the dark from their rifle pits had, after all, found and killed at least one rebel soldier. Kelso nudged the body to make sure and returned to his men.[12]

The regiment then moved south to Iron Mountain. Kelso and McConnell were sent 40 miles farther to scout the enemy. They missed the Battle of Fredericktown where, on October 21, combined Federal forces totaling about

4,500 men beat Jeff Thompson's "Swamp Rats," forcing them to retreat farther south. Kelso regretted missing out on his share of the glory.[13]

KELSO HAD UNDERTAKEN his first spy mission before the trip to the
bridge at Big River, and he continued spying after the Battle of Fredericktown.
General Curtis had asked him to go secretly and alone to "ascertain the numbers, intentions, etc. of the rebel forces then lying at Springfield." Taking the
train from St. Louis to the end of the line in Rolla, Kelso set out on foot for
Springfield, 120 miles away, in a heavy rain. He spent the first night under
an old bridge, the blanket over his head providing scant comfort from the
dirty water constantly dripping down on him. At sunrise, he headed into the
cold rain, avoiding the road but keeping it in sight as he tramped through
the wet bushes of the bordering forest. At nightfall, soaked to the skin, he
huddled under a tree, ate his hardtack, and listened to the moaning wind and
pattering rain. Resting his face between his knees, he tried to sleep. "I did not
dare kindle a fire. . . . That dreary night seemed like the longest I ever knew.
But morning at last dawned."[14]

The second day was much like the first. Finally, on the third day, the rain
stopped, the sun broke through the clouds, and he slept in a hazel thicket
while his clothes and blanket dried. Feeling refreshed, he resumed his
journey, walking by night and sleeping in the woods during the day until
he reached Springfield. At a farmhouse on the outskirts of town, the family
of one of his comrades took him in, fed him, and gave him a warm bed for
a couple days while he gathered information. Springfield in late September,
1861, was occupied by about five hundred State Guard troops under the
command of Col. Theodore T. Taylor; more enemy troops were still farther
south.[15]

Having gotten what he had come for, Kelso headed back north, but on
the return trip he passed through Buffalo. It was nearly midnight when he
reached his home. Moving cautiously through the darkness, quietly through
the door, he gently roused Susie from her sleep. She was surprised—and
displeased. What are you doing here? she asked, annoyed at the risk he was
taking. If someone sees you, the whole family will be in trouble. The house
could be surrounded at any moment by the rebels who patrolled the town,
she warned. There was no welcoming embrace, no kiss, not a "single kind or
loving word." She gave him some blankets and sent him to sleep in the woods.
He left, hoping she might come out to visit him, but she did not. He sulked,
rehearsing the encounter in his mind, unable to sleep. "My love had received
a great wound."[16]

The next morning she did come, and they talked, but he still felt bitter. She sent the children out to visit him, too, which lightened his mood. The following day, the skies opened up again. He needed to visit a friend who lived a few miles past the opposite side of Buffalo, and thinking that the heavy rains would keep townspeople indoors, he took a shortcut on an open road for a half mile or so. As soon as he set out, though, the rain stopped and two groups of horsemen appeared, one a few hundred yards ahead of him and the other a few hundred behind. Then a third party began trotting out from the forest toward him. He had been seen, and he knew it. He casually stepped from the road and started picking persimmons from a small clump of trees loaded with the ripening fruit. When the closest group of horsemen rode into a gulley and momentarily passed from sight, he dashed away and hid nearby in some reeds growing on the banks of a stream. The sudden disappearance of the rainy day persimmon picker raised an alarm, so the men spurred their horses. They trampled around by the fruit trees and right next to the reeds by the stream where he lay concealed. "I could feel large drops of cold sweat trickling down my body, and my heart kept thumping and pounding on the inner wall of my ribs at such a rate that I almost feared the enemy could hear it."[17]

At last, they left and Kelso made it back to the shelter of the wet forest. Eventually, though, to avoid the cold wet bushes, he started following a path, but soon ran into a boy from a rebel family who recognized him and would surely report him. Kelso left the path and tried to stay on rocky ground so he would be harder to track. From a hill he spotted three horsemen still on his trail. But he made it to his friend's house, where he arranged to obtain letters he could deliver to soldiers in St. Louis. After dark, he wound his way back to his hiding place in the woods near his home.

The sky cleared by morning and Susie hung John's blanket on the fence to dry. It was covered in green burrs from his nights in the woods. Some little girls, daughters of a neighboring woman with strong Southern sentiments, came over to play with the Kelso children. How, they wondered, did all those burrs get on that blanket? They went home and reported the curiosity to their mother. She herself soon appeared, full of questions, just as Kelso's friend from across town arrived with the packet of letters. Florella, although only seven years old, understood the danger. Sneaking out to her father's hiding place, she warned him. He went to his house and detained his neighbor until after sunset, feigning friendliness and telling lots of humorous stories. Despite the smile she kept on her face, he knew she would inform the rebel patrols as soon as she left his house, and he wanted the cover of darkness to make his escape.

She left, and told. He left, and the horsemen pursued. But Kelso headed southeast at first, rather than north, and they never found him. Again he slept by day and traveled by night, eating ears of corn taken from a field and potatoes dug up from a garden along the way. One night he nearly stumbled into a rebel camp. The men had just looted the farm of Joseph W. McClurg, a wealthy Unionist merchant of Lynn Creek who became a Missouri congressman and then governor. Avoiding them, he traveled through canyons and forests tangled with vines and briars, waded through creeks and crossed rivers. Twice he stopped at farmhouses and persuaded the women to give him food or directions. Finally, he made it to Jefferson City and boarded the train to St. Louis. "Although I had not conquered any body, I was welcomed back as a hero. Gen. Curtis was well pleased with my report."[18]

After he rejoined his regiment following the Battle of Fredricktown, Kelso was immediately sent out spying again, this time by Colonel Boyd. His assignment was "to go out in disguise, and pass along the entire southern border of Missouri, to the south-west corner." He was to determine "if it would be practicable" for the regiment "to pass through that line" into Arkansas. Kelso set off alone again, on foot and in civilian clothes, on a spying expedition that would take him even deeper into rebel territory.[19]

Such off-the-books spy missions by soldiers on special assignment were not unusual. Civil War espionage left only a thin record in the archives because military commanders did not like to write about military intelligence in their official reports and tended to steer clear of the legally and ethically dubious undertakings in their postwar memoirs. (Kelso would later complain that he was never paid for his secret service because of the lack of documentation.) The U.S. Army did not have a formal spy agency. Commanders hired their own spies and recruited scouts from among the enlisted men. Generals assigned espionage missions and often supervised intelligence gathering themselves. Major General George McClellan, general-in-chief of all the Union armies and commander of the Army of the Potomac, hired Alan Pinkerton, who had run a well-known detective agency before the war. The five spies working behind the lines supported McClellan's gross overestimations of Confederate troop size, which the general used to justify the caution and inaction that would so frustrate President Lincoln. Major General Ambrose Burnside, who replaced McClellan, failed to replace the Pinkerton men with better spies and in general neglected military intelligence. Major General Joseph Hooker, however, who next commanded the Army of the Potomac, created a modern intelligence staff that gathered and analyzed information from all sources: embedded civilian spies and military scouts; cavalry reconnaissance; the interrogation of deserters, prisoners of war, and escaped slaves; intercepted enemy dispatches and stolen signals; and clues found in Confederate newspapers. Hooker himself even took a spyglass and went up in a hot air balloon.[20]

In the Western theater, no generals scouted the enemy from the clouds but there were plenty of spies on the ground. Major General John C. Frémont, who arrived in Missouri in July 1861 to command the Department of the West, created an intelligence unit he named the "Jessie Scouts" in honor of his wife. Frémont's subordinate, Brigadier General Ulysses S. Grant, tried to recruit his own local secret service. Major General Henry W. Halleck, who arrived in Missouri after Frémont's departure in November 1861 to command the new Department of Missouri, quickly organized his own intelligence service, using a few of Frémont's Jessie Scouts. Halleck, though, always felt a little queasy about espionage. A military scholar nicknamed "Old Brains" and the author of an 1861 treatise on war and international law, Halleck argued that since spying was widely recognized as a felony punishable by death, military commanders should not induce people to commit such crimes (although spies could receive and pay for information already gathered). Besides, Halleck like other officers was frustrated by unreliable information, finding more trustworthy the intelligence derived from the interrogation of deserters and the surveillance by detached cavalry units.[21]

Still, spies were sent out. Kelso's favorite commanding officer, Brigadier General Samuel R. Curtis, whom Halleck made the commander of the Army of the Southwest in December, 1861, received information about the Confederate and State Guard occupation of southwestern Missouri from multiple sources, including civilian spies and military scouts like Kelso operating under cover. Commanders knew that for every spy who successfully penetrated the enemy's camp there might be three or four captured and a dozen turned back at the picket lines. So the officers sent out multiple men, separately but with the same mission. Spies like Kelso traveled hundreds of miles alone, in difficult conditions and dangerous circumstances, but the built-in redundancy made them, ultimately, expendable. According to one account, ten of the thirty or so men spying for General Philip Sheridan in the Shenandoah Valley wound up dead, two of them found hanging from tree limbs by their own halter straps. Lorain Ruggles, a corporal in the 20th Ohio Infantry who spied for Grant and other officers, claimed that of the eighteen other spies he had known, fifteen had been killed by the war's end. But they all had understood the danger when they signed up.[22]

Commanders recruited men who had the skills to travel alone through hostile territory, the intelligence to know what to look for, and the inclination to take risks. Former Texas Ranger James Pike, who spied and scouted for Sheridan, said he had volunteered for the secret service because the occupation was suited to his nature, allowing him greater independence of action. The danger, of course, was getting caught. As General Halleck later wrote, explaining both the law and the common practice for the Union and Confederate armies, men in uniform and under arms who operated secretly behind enemy lines were not technically spies, and if captured they ought to be—and often were—treated as prisoners of war. Spies, by contrast, traveled under false pretenses and under assumed identities, in disguise as civilians or in the enemy's uniform, and if captured they could be—and sometimes were—summarily executed. They worked, as the spy Henry Bascom Smith said, constantly in the shadow of the hangman's noose. One of the first spies that Grant sent out in the summer of 1861, Lieutenant Henry Houts of the 6th Missouri Infantry, managed to infiltrate the enemy's camp but was caught and put to death. "Don't you know," Lorain Ruggles's commanding officer reminded him, "that when you go out as a spy, you go, as it were, with a rope around your neck, ready for any body to draw it tight?"[23]

Soldiers on spy missions, despite General Halleck's qualms, did indeed travel under false pretenses. James Pike passed as a Confederate Cavalry officer, a Texas Ranger, and a ship's carpenter. H. B. Smith pretended to be a smuggler running blockades. John Morford was able to pass through picket lines in Kentucky pretending to be a drunk. Ruggles disguised himself as a rebel soldier and as a Confederate major on parole, but usually just dressed as a civilian. Disguise was less a matter of clothing than the assumption of a different political character. Even when wearing his Union blues, Pike could persuade people he was a Confederate spy in disguise. The ruse relied upon performance. As another spy recalled: "Hanging, disguised, on the outskirts of a camp, mixing with its idlers, laughing at their jokes, examining their arms, counting their numbers, endeavoring to discover the plans of their leaders . . . joining in the chorus of a rebel song, betting on rebel success, cursing abolitionism, despising northern fighters . . . praising the beauty of Southern belles and decrying that of Northern . . . is but a small portion of the practice of my profession as a spy."[24]

As the Union scout and spy Ruggles noted, "The very business [of spying] itself is an evasion of what you really are, or assuming to be what you are not. . . . To be successful as a spy, it is absolutely necessary to act as an assumed character." The disguise depended on a "ready address"—on verbal dexterity.

The spy that Ruggles described and Kelso became resembled the "confidence man," a familiar figure in antebellum America: a frontier trickster or a fast-talking city sharper. Journalists detailed the exploits of confidence men and made them symbols betraying anxieties about the slipperiness of identity and the vulnerabilities of trust in a turbulent democracy. In fiction, the confidence man was often a comic character. Johnson Jones Hooper's popular stories in the 1840s featured Capt. Simon Suggs, who duped his victims by quickly shaping his identity to meet their expectations and exploiting their gullibility. Kelso himself would later refer to a similar character, Sut Lovingood, a score-settling southwestern prankster in stories by George Washington Harris in the 1850s and 60s. Herman Melville's *The Confidence-Man* (1857) gave the figure poetic, political, and metaphysical depth, but few read that book; many more read self-help manuals that offered dark warnings of chameleon-like swindlers. In both fiction and fact, the confidence man was a quick-witted, smooth-talking master of the art of deceptive persuasion. He could, on the spot, assume a false identity, discern his mark's weaknesses, and weave a story that gained his listeners' trust and opened them to manipulation. Unlike most confidence men, Civil War spies were not trying to con their victims out of money, but to extract information. As the spy Ruggles wrote, the "essential qualification" of a good spy was being "an accomplished liar."[25]

The artful liar does not simply spin falsehoods: he balances lies and truths in the pursuit of plausibility; he modulates fact and fiction according to his immediate needs to persuade and manipulate. Ruggles had worked for many years in Arkansas before the war, and his detailed knowledge of people and places there helped reinforce his claims to Southernness. Pike had been a Texas Ranger in Waco and could similarly exploit assumptions linking place and politics. John Russell Kelso, worried that he might be recognized as the Buffalo Unionist, gave his name as "John Russell" and shaped that identity to meet the needs of the moment.

In his various encounters with people as "John Russell," Kelso veered toward or away from the truth as the situation warranted. On his first mission, after he had assessed the strength of the enemy occupying Springfield, he had stopped twice at farmhouses for directions and food. Each house was occupied by a woman whose husband, he learned, was away in the army. But which army? Through friendly conversation he had to elicit the allegiance of each woman before revealing his own. Chatting with the first farmwife as she milked her cow, he learned to his relief that she was married to a Federal officer. He got both useful directions and a good breakfast. A few days later, though, he accepted the hospitality of a woman who turned out to be a rebel soldier's wife. She asked many questions, but something about her earnest manner prompted him to mix some honesty in with his deception. Though traveling in civilian dress, he admitted that he had enlisted in the Union army. She asked if he even knew what he was fighting for. He truthfully answered that he fought to uphold the U.S. Constitution. The woman eyed him carefully and said he had "an honest look." But she explained that the real object of the North's war "was to free the 'niggers.'" If that were true, Kelso lied, he would put down his gun and leave the army at once. The woman seemed to pity him: "I have no doubt but that lots and lots of poor ignorant but well-meaning young men like you have been gulled into the Union army in this same way."[26]

At the beginning of his second expedition, he stopped at a log hut near the road for breakfast and tried to convey his Southern sympathies by the questions he asked his host. The half-dozen well-armed men at the table with him, however, seemed suspicious. But he worried even more about "the woman of the house, sharper than any of the men, [who] seemed to read me at once." As he sat awaiting breakfast, feeling her eyes upon him, he realized that he had made a stupid mistake. Disguised as a civilian, he had nonetheless crammed his coat pockets with hardtack, the distinctive cracker issued to Union soldiers. She glanced at his bulging pockets, then pulled her husband aside to whisper. He too scrutinized Kelso's pockets. After bolting a few mouthfuls of breakfast, Kelso excused himself and continued on his way. They were watching him as he went back out to the road. Because he walked south rather than north, they did not immediately stop him, but he imagined the woman telling the men to pursue him. He left the road for the forest, dumped the hardtack, and hid his revolvers more carefully under his coat.[27]

The sharp woman had read him even before she spotted the hardtack. As he traveled along the Arkansas border and met people, he would need to do a better job performing the "John Russell" they needed to see. His next encounter was with "a large and active-looking young man" headed in the same direction down an obscure country road. As they walked along together, Kelso tried to engage the man in conversation, but he was "reticent and non-committal." Kelso decided to make the first move: "I concluded to break the ice at once by letting him know that I was a southern man, and that I was neither afraid nor ashamed to own my principles. Without exhibiting the least expression of surprise or of pleasure, he gave me a strange look that I did not like, and simply replied, 'That's *my* ticket.'" Kelso still felt the man's unfriendly suspicion, and John Russell became a more virulent secessionist, pouring out "a tirade of abuse against the abolition Yankee government" and the damned Missouri Germans—"the lop-eared Dutch"—who supported it. Yet as he talked and the two walked down the lonely road cutting through a dense forest, the man's "keen black eyes" only darkened. As Kelso's anxiety heightened, John Russell's denunciations of the Union intensified.[28]

Suddenly, the man had heard enough. "All at once, with remarkable dexterity, he whipped out his revolver and held it cocked uncomfortably close to my head, exclaiming: 'I'll let you know that I'm a Union man. Now what have you got to say?'" Kelso knew it was too late to tell the truth. He could only plead that he was just expressing his political opinions. "'Well,' said he, 'you might express your honest sentiments without so much uncalled for abuse, and without telling so many damned lies.'" The cocked revolver remained at Kelso's forehead. Kelso could not draw his own gun, could not do anything but look the fellow steadily in the eye and, finally, keep quiet. The man hesitated, then dropped his gun, though he still kept it cocked and in his hand, and began walking onward. Kelso walked on too, silently. When they came to a fork in the road, the dark-eyed man—perhaps a Union spy too?— went left, Kelso went right, and they parted without a word.[29]

John Russell's career as a Confederate recruiter began a few days later on the banks of the Current River. Kelso had just waded across through 4 feet of cold water and was putting his shoes back on when a handsome Confederate officer rode up on a "magnificent charger." Kelso asked the officer if he knew where a hungry man might get a bite to eat. The gentleman offered the stranger a ride to his uncle's house nearby, where, he promised, they would be entertained with true Southern hospitality. While they rode, Kelso gave the "brave, honest, and unsuspicious man" his cover story as John Russell and "easily gained his confidence." The officer said that after resting a few days at his uncle's house, he planned to ride 30 miles toward Missouri's southwest corner and recruit for the Confederate army. Would Russell like to join him? Russell said that yes, he would.[30]

The uncle, a vigorous, genial, well-to-do farmer of fifty-five, kept their table well-supplied with fat wild turkeys. His wife, "a fine motherly woman" and "a first-class cook," roasted and dressed those turkeys to perfection. They feasted and talked politics. "She told me that she had five good manly sons in the southern army, and that she was now preparing her sixth son, her baby-boy, a fine lad of sixteen years, to go to his brothers." The boy was eager to go. "This good mother said that, dear as her noble sons were to her, she would, without a murmur, give them all up to the cause of the South, if that cause should need them;—that, with her own hands, she would make their burial clothes as she had made their soldier clothes."[31]

After a couple days with these "good people," Kelso and the officer rode 15 miles to the first recruiting station. Kelso's "new friend" had come to know John Russell "as an earnest southern man, who was well posted in regards to the affairs of the war, and who was a remarkably good talker." He insisted that Russell make a speech. So he did. Russell cited chapter and verse to show that the Bible supported slavery: passages in the Old Testament where God endorsed the institution, and passages in the New Testament where Paul urged slaves to obey their masters. Russell showed how the Constitution, too, propped up slavery: it had prevented Congress from interfering in the international slave trade before 1808, counted slaves as three-fifths of a person, provided for the return of fugitive slaves, and promised that the federal government would help states suppress slave rebellions. (In all of this, Russell was merely saying what Kelso knew to be true, though Kelso, unlike Russell, ardently believed that the North, not the South, was fighting for a moral cause.) The Northerners, Russell concluded, by opposing slavery "were defying God and trampling the Bible under their feet," and by denying the constitutional right to enslave, they had destroyed the Union. "I showed them, that the people of the North, by their un-Christian and their unconstitutional aggressions upon us, had absolved us from all allegiance to the United States, and, by making war upon us, had rendered it our duty to defend ourselves with all the means that God had placed within our power." He finished the speech by predicting that General Sterling Price would occupy St. Louis by winter. They applauded him enthusiastically, and several came forward to volunteer for Confederate service.[32]

Russell repeated the performance at the next recruiting station the following day. When he had finished speaking, and the men crowded around him to shake his hand and slap him on the back, a fine-looking elderly gentleman approached. "I always knew that we were in the right," he exclaimed. "I always knew that our cause was a just one. But I never before heard the facts so connected and the case made so plain." The man insisted that Russell come home with him for dinner and talk to his wife. So he did and enjoyed more Southern hospitality.[33]

Over a finely set table, they talked about morality and justice, politics and war. "The wife proved to be a highly educated and very intelligent lady. Free from the prevailing prejudices of the South, she held far more nearly correct views of the situation than were held by her husband and her neighbors." She thought secession was a grave mistake, and her husband had not been able to convince her otherwise. After dinner they "sat for some hours before the bright fire, eating apples, cracking nuts, drinking cider, and talking." Russell and the elderly woman conducted a long, friendly debate about secession. Her husband watched, his eyes sparkling in the firelight. He was delighted when Russell gained a point for his beloved Confederacy and equally delighted when his beloved wife gained one, showing her skill as a debater. They argued to a draw, neither persuading the other. But at the end of the evening the woman did say that, despite her reservations, she would do her best to support "her people of the South" since the war had begun and there was no turning back. The next morning, as the charming couple bid him goodbye, the good woman sent him off with God's blessing, an expression of warm friendship, and an enormous packed lunch that included "choice biscuits, a baked chicken, a cup of preserves, and some other delicacies."[34]

He left the elderly couple, as he had left the genial uncle and his wife, and then the Confederate officer, with powerfully mixed feelings. He liked them all. The two couples could not have been better hosts and seemed to have model marriages; the officer, with "his frank, open and manly countenance," struck him as "one of nature's true noblemen." He deeply regretted having to play a false character and deceive them. Still, there was something thrilling about this "battle of deception." Similarly, he knew that by standing up and giving speeches at Confederate recruiting stations he was "playing a very dangerous game." He was not so very far from Springfield and Buffalo, after all. It would not have been at all surprising if someone from back home had been at one of those stations, able to unmask the Confederate recruiter John Russell as the Federal soldier John Russell Kelso. In a snap the men would have stopped applauding and started looking for a rope and a tree limb. He felt "a kind of wild and romantic fascination" in facing this danger, but also a "long nervous tension" that seemed to tighten its grip with each passing day.[35]

Kelso again tried to avoid the roads and travel through the forests, but bad storms and hunger eventually drove him back to knocking on farmhouse doors—and back to his dangerous game. He stopped at a hunter's cabin, and it did not take him long to figure out how John Russell would gain the man's confidence. Kelso had met many like him. He was, in Kelso's view, "a sample of a large portion of the men of the South,—of that portion who did most of the fighting." The hunter exemplified "the gross unreasoning ignorance and the absurd prejudices that prevailed among the lower classes of the South." For them, the war was not about the constitutional principles he had debated with the elderly woman. It was not about losing the property rights that Southerners extended to human chattel, because "they *had* no *such property* to *lose.*" Men like the hunter furiously defended slavery even though they hadn't the money to even buy a horse, never mind a slave. The War of Northern

Aggression was a direct attack on White male privilege. Their rage was fueled by a tangle of anxieties about race, sex, and manhood. The hunter angrily argued that "should these abolition *nigger thieves* succeed in this hellish undertaking, the freed *buck niggers* would at once marry off all the white girls and thus force us to do without any wives at all, or else to put up with *she-niggers for wives*." For poor White men in the South, "the great fear that made them so willing to fight was the fear of *nigger equality*;—the fear that, if once freed, the *buck niggers* would be more than a match for us in the courting and the marrying of white girls. About the only arguments ever advanced by these men on this subject were: 'How would *you* like for a *big buck nigger* to step up to the side of *your sister* or *your daughter* and *ask her for her company*? How would *you* like for a *big buck nigger* to *marry your sister* or *your daughter*, etc.?' These arguments were always supposed to be, and generally actually were, unanswerable."[36]

All of this would have struck the genteel couple Kelso had dined with—or any in "the higher classes of the South who were generally well educated and intelligent"—as absurd. "These classes felt themselves too far above the negroes, and too far above the 'poor white trash,' also, to fear equality with either of them." But just as Kelso had given John Russell his best parlor manners for the elderly couple, Russell became a different character for the hunter. "By adapting my conversation to all of the easily-perceived prejudices of my host, I readily won his confidence and his admiration."[37]

At another stop, he used a similar kind of mirroring. He had been staggering through the darkness in cold rain and deep mud. He knocked on a farmhouse door, desperate for a warm fire and some food. A woman let him in and offered a seat by the fire but was not sure that she could let him stay the night. She was suspicious. As it became clear that she was married to an absent rebel captain, it also became clear that John Russell was a good Southern man. As she mentioned God frequently, Russell "became very religious, and had a great deal to say of the Lord, and of what he would do for us." Pleased with his politics and his godliness, she let him stay the night. At breakfast the next morning, she asked him to say grace. "I did so in fine Methodistic style, this being the last time I ever enacted that superstitious farce."[38]

Kelso finally neared Missouri's southwest corner. As he approached McDonald County, with Arkansas to the south and Indian Territory to the west, he was stopped twice by rebel parties and interrogated by their officers. "For me, these were critical moments. The least hesitation or faltering on my part would have cost me my life, and I was well aware of this fact. My perfect self-possession, however, and my very plausible story, from which I never varied, carried me safely through." Then Kelso did what he had come all that way to do: he scouted the strength and disposition of the enemy's troops. General Sterling Price, after his victory over Union forces (Mulligan's Irish Brigade) at the Battle of Lexington on the Missouri River (September 18–20, 1861), had withdrawn to the southwest corner to amass his forces. The string of victories beginning at Wilson's Creek in July had bolstered recruiting for the Southern cause, and Kelso could have learned that Price's Missouri State Guard had grown by half, totaling over 18,000 men. Forces with Confederate brigadier general Ben McCulloch, who had also been stationed at Springfield, had pulled back to northwest Arkansas. As Kelso had already guessed, Price was dreaming about consolidating his hold on southwestern Missouri and then taking St. Louis to extend the northern border of the Confederacy— although in Price's plan, it would be Confederate general Albert Sidney Johnston in the southeast, rather than Price himself, who would occupy the city. Meanwhile, Governor Jackson's rump legislature was meeting at Neosho, and would pass a secession bill on October 28. A month later, the Confederate Congress would welcome Missouri as the twelfth state of the Confederate States of America.[39]

Having learned what he could, Kelso headed back the 200 miles to Rolla, the closest Federal post. Spies coming in from the cold were always in danger of getting shot at by their own picket guards. When Kelso approached a guard on the outskirts of Rolla, however, the soldier had absent-mindedly left his rifle hanging from the bow of his saddle and wandered 20 yards away to pick grapes. Kelso was determined to teach him a lesson. He slipped up to the guard's horse, took the soldier's gun, and let out a war whoop. The soldier, spun, saw Kelso drawing a bead on him, and turned pale. "Ah ha!" Kelso said, "I've got you at last." "Yes," the soldier admitted miserably, "I reckon you have." Kelso ordered the man to step forward and he quizzed him about the Federal troops at Rolla, "threatening him with instant death if he did not promptly tell the truth." When the guard answer truthfully, Kelso offered to give him his gun back and explained that he, too, was a Federal soldier. "But do not forget this lesson! The next bush-whacker that comes along may be a real one and may not let you off so easily." The guard took his gun, looking relieved and "serenely happy."[40]

KELSO'S REGIMENT WAS at Rolla, having been sent ahead of the report- edly huge army commanded by General John C. Frémont that had begun its diagonal march across the state with the promise to clear the rebels from the southwest corner once and for all. Frémont's five divisions had left St. Louis on September 27, and then slowly moved southwest. The press inflated the size of his force to twenty thousand, forty thousand, (which is what Price and Kelso believed he had), or even sixty thousand troops. Frémont claimed only sixty-eight hundred were on the rolls in St. Louis, but men joined the ranks as he moved south, and when he reached Springfield he would have eighteen thousand. When Frémont had arrived in Missouri and taken command of the Department of the West three months earlier, he had faced a difficult situation, and it had only become worse. The enemy controlled southwestern Missouri and also threatened from the east. His own troops were poorly trained, disorganized, and meagerly supplied. Compounding these challenges, Frémont, never having been in charge of more than a few hundred men, was in over his head. He spent extravagantly and unwisely, secluded himself behind a bloated staff, and seemed more concerned with the pomp of his Body Guard than with decisive action. He quickly alienated the politically powerful Blair family (Congressman Frank and his brother Montgomery, in Lincoln's cabinet), and developed a grandiose plan to drive the enemy all the way to New Orleans, convincing his generals—including Kelso's admired General Curtis—that Frémont was incompetent. On August 30, without consulting Washington, Frémont had issued a proclamation authorizing his army to shoot anyone found with arms north of Union lines and to emancipate slaves held by rebels. The first provision would have invited Confederates to kill prisoners of war; the second leaped ahead of what Lincoln, anxious about keeping slaveholding Border States in the Union, was ready to do about slavery. Together with the string of Confederate and State Guard successes on the battlefield, these misjudgments put Frémont's command in jeopardy even before he left St. Louis. As Frémont and his troops plodded across the state, Lincoln and his advisors feared disaster. But Missouri Unionists like Kelso could see only the Pathfinder of the West, marching with his Body Guard in their plumed hats, astride magnificent chestnut horses, rallying thousands to the flag—a hero beginning a campaign to conquer.[41]

Kelso rested for a few days in camp at Rolla, but since his regiment had not received orders to join Frémont on the march to Springfield, he was given permission to return to Buffalo to secretly watch rebels and quietly recruit for the Union. Walking to Buffalo on a public road, he suddenly saw a large body of rebel cavalry approaching and only had time to dive behind a roadside log before being seen. He listened, heart pounding, as they chatted while trotting past within feet of him. They were "Freeman's regiment of semi-robber cavalry"—some of the seven hundred men under the command Colonel Thomas Roe Freeman camping about 30 miles south of Rolla. Freeman, a former judge from Phelps County, had helped organize the first regiment of pro-Southern State Guards in southeast Missouri. He would become known to the Federals as the "notorious" Freeman by allying with "guerrillas and horse thieves" and sending out small squads of bushwhackers to rob stagecoaches. Kelso knew, as he listened, that this squad contained a number of Buffalo and Dallas County men. "Many of the men would have known me and would have made short work of me if they had discovered me. . . . They seemed to understand that Frémont's army was to be permitted to reach Springfield unmolested; that it was to be there cut off and captured; and that the rebel army was to then go into winter quarters in Saint Louis."[42]

That night, slipping into a friend's house after dark, Kelso learned the terrible news. Shortly after his last visit home, rebel neighbors had burned his house to the ground. Nothing had been saved from the flames—everything he owned, including his library, writings, and family photographs—had been destroyed. His wife and children had been driven out, and the rebels threatened to burn down anyone else's house who took them in. He found his family in a shack that stood in the woods on a corner of his farm, trying to stay warm in clothes and blankets that some friendly neighbors had given them. Susie was managing everything with "cheerful fortitude," which, he wrote, made him proud of her and made her dearer to him than she had ever been before.[43]

The attack on his home and his family stunned him. It "had been inflicted in a cruel and malicious manner by men whom I had never injured." He felt something start to change inside of him. "Hitherto, I had been making war from motives of pure patriotism alone. I now felt, however, that from this time forward, a new, less noble, but a no less powerful motive would be added to my motives of patriotism to control my conduct. This new motive was *revenge*, an intense desire for blood, which, intensified by additional wrongs inflicted upon myself and my loved ones farther on, became at last with me an all-absorbing passion which nothing but the blood of my enemies could ever appease."[44]

Two days later, a division of Frémont's army poured through town, headed for Springfield. Jubilant Unionists cheered the soldiers as they marched and rode past. Kelso could live with his family openly and move about town freely, and Confederate sympathizers were the ones who had to stay in the shadows. Not surprisingly, some "of those who had been afflicted with the secession mania, now, all at once, began to exhibit symptoms of loyalty." Unionists who had suffered at the hands of their rebel neighbors sought retribution. Not far from Buffalo, on his way toward Springfield with Frémont, Major William

Dorsheimer saw a crowd, with the help of some Union soldiers, take revenge on the house of a local secessionist who had killed his Unionist neighbor when the region had been controlled by rebel forces. In Buffalo itself, "[s]everal Union men, who had been plundered by the rebels, now proceeded to collect the value, real or imaginary, of their several losses, from the wealthy secessionists of the county." Kelso "helped make some of these collections. In other words, we *robbed* those whose friends had robbed us. We had no doubt that Fremont, with his magnificent army, would sweep all the rebel forces west of the Mississippi River before him to the Gulf of Mexico."[45]

On October 25, the Federals made their first strike at Springfield. Major Charles Zagonyi, a fiery Hungarian who led Frémont's elaborately dressed Body Guard—three companies of elite cavalry, about 150 men—along with another 150 Prairie Scouts, advanced 50 miles ahead of Frémont's camp and engaged the enemy on the western side of town. Springfield had been reinforced since Kelso's surveillance, and the rebel camp held about twelve hundred men (Zagonyi thought nineteen hundred). The State Guard had advance warning and good position, on high ground at the edge of a dense woods. Sharpshooters opened fire on Zagonyi's men, picking them off their horses. But when Zagonyi and the Body Guards led a charge right at the rebel line, holding their sabers high and yelling "Frémont and the Union," the green and poorly armed State Guard troops broke and ran. The Federals pursued the fleeing infantry into the woods, where hand-to-hand fighting became vicious and deadly, and chased the cavalry into town, flushing the rebels from the streets of Springfield. Zagonyi took possession of the town square and raised an American flag at the courthouse. Having suffered nearly a hundred casualties (perhaps a couple dozen killed), the major knew he could not hold the town for long, so after a few hours he headed back to Frémont's camp with the report of his symbolic, if not strategic, victory.[46]

Frémont and the rest of the army entered Springfield two days later, after the rebel forces had withdrawn—which, as Kelso had overheard, they had planned to do anyway, with or without Zagonyi's charge. "It was a gala day in Springfield," Frémont's aide-de-camp William Dorsheimer recalled. "The Stars and Stripes were flying from windows and house-tops, and ladies and children, with little flags in their hands, stood on the door-steps to welcome us." Unionists came out of hiding, escaped slaves volunteered to help the Federal troops, and refugees began returning to town, even though there were rumors that rebel forces were gathering just 10 miles southwest of town at Wilson's Creek.[47]

Frémont's Body Guard, Springfield Public Square, 1861. From *Harper's Magazine*. History Museum on the Square, Springfield, Missouri.

But then came more bad news—two shocking blows, one after the other. First, after midnight on November 2–3, a courier handed Frémont an order from President Lincoln, relieving the general of command. The soldiers, like Kelso, who admired the general and the loyal citizens who had cheered him could hardly believe it. Kelso was convinced, even as he wrote about the episode two decades later, that Frémont's removal at this key moment was more than a "fatal mistake," it was "an atrocious crime," and he thought political scheming was at its root. He did not know whom to blame, but he intimated that Lincoln himself, or at least the president's political cronies, were looking ahead to the presidential campaign of 1864. He thought the whole thing was "a wicked conspiracy, concocted by ambitious men high in authority at Washington, to crush Fremont, of whose rising prestige they stood in fear. These men knew that Fremont was an ambitious man and that he had his eyes upon the presidency of three years ahead." Political machinations did help bring down Frémont, but these had to do with power in Missouri and Washington in 1861 and not primarily with the next presidential election. Yet Frémont was popular with his troops and had, with his emancipation proclamation, become a hero to Radicals. At the news of his removal, according to a reporter, his camp was briefly "in a semi-mutinous condition. . . . [S]everal regiments threw down their arms and refused to serve under any other commander."[48]

Worse than Frémont's removal was what came next: on November 8, interim commander David Hunter ordered a retreat to central Missouri. Hunter was worried about his supply lines southwest of the railheads at Rolla and Sedalia. And, on the eastern side of the state, as Ulysses Grant was attacking the Confederate garrison at Belmont, Southern forces were massing across the Mississippi River at Columbus, Kentucky. Hunter perceived the danger of being caught between two Confederate armies—one coming from the east and the other from the southwest—precisely Price's plan. So Hunter did what General Nathaniel Lyon had failed to do a few months earlier: he withdrew his troops from southwest Missouri in order to fight another day under more favorable circumstances. Southwestern Missouri Unionists like Kelso, however, saw the retreat as a disgrace and a betrayal. It crushed the hopes of the loyal citizens of the region and abandoned them to "an infuriated and relentless foe," surrendering their homes to plunder and flame and sacrificing many civilian lives to the rebels' vengeance.[49]

When the news reached Buffalo, everything changed. Men who a week before had been seizing rebel property, meekly and apologetically returned it. Some who had waved flags for Frémont now cursed the Union and saluted the Confederacy. Kelso ran into his neighbor, Harvey White. They had always been friendly. Yet White said, with a chuckle, "You abolitionists will now have to get out of this part of the country and stay out. Your property will be confiscated. I have therefore determined to have the first claim upon your farm, Mr. Kelso, by seizing upon it at once." As soon as Kelso left, White did indeed take Kelso's chickens, potatoes, corn, and farm tools. He let his sheep into Kelso's orchard and they destroyed the fruit trees. "To my shame," Kelso later reflected, "I did not kill him upon the spot."[50]

Thinking he had several days before rebel soldiers reached Buffalo, Kelso got on a fast horse and rode hard to catch up to his regiment, 75 miles away, retreating to Rolla. Colonel Boyd, however, told him to return to Dallas County to help loyal civilians evacuate. Kelso raced back, his exhausted horse collapsing 6 miles before he reached town. Frightened women and children on the roadside questioned the last stragglers of the retreating Federal army. Boyd had suggested that he confiscate teams and wagons from rebels if he needed to, so Kelso stole a light wagon and a yoke of small oxen from a wealthy farmer who was serving as an officer in the State Guard. Kelso then led a wagon train of Unionists out of town, heading northeast. They made 20 miles by nightfall. On the second day, they lost time by taking a road that proved impassable. On the morning of the third, as they headed toward the small town of Lebanon in Laclede County, a strange, excited man on horseback raced up to them, warning them to turn back. A rebel flag, he said, had been hoisted upon the Lebanon courthouse. He galloped away and suddenly a rebel cavalry swept out of the forest and surrounded them. Kelso, in his uniform, was caught standing helplessly beside his wagon, away from his guns. If these are local men, he thought, they'll know I've been taking rebel property and they'll shoot me. But it was a detachment from a Texas regiment. They took all the guns from the wagon train, or almost all: they claimed Kelso's old musket from the wagon but missed the new one Susie and her sister concealed by sitting on it. They tried to take the Kelsos' blankets, too, but his sister-in-law pleaded that their house had been burnt down and the blankets were all they had against the cold. The Texans relented, sending the train on its way. They kept the one soldier, Kelso, under arrest.[51]

The Texans told Kelso that they would soon be joined by Missourians, and he began to worry. He disguised his unease, however, by chatting affably and jesting with the soldiers. After several hours, they released him on parole—none too soon, he later learned, because the officer who owned the wagon and oxen Kelso had commandeered arrived in Lebanon not long afterward, hunting for the thief and intending to kill him.[52]

Snow fell heavily as Kelso reached the wagon train. By morning it was a foot deep. During the day, the temperature dropped, and as a strong wind swept over the open countryside it "hurled upon us great billows of drifting snow that almost blinded and stifled us." As the sun set, the wagon train, pushing through the snow drifts, came upon two "large and splendid" houses. Kelso tramped up to the first door and knocked. From the lady of the house, he "begged shelter for our sick and for our women who had young babies." I will not inconvenience myself, she haughtily replied, to save "black abolitionists from the sufferings which they had brought upon themselves." He tried again with the lady at the second house. He explained that he wasn't asking for beds—the women and children could sleep on the floor. They just needed shelter from the storm. But she refused him too.

"All my späh rooms have Tuhkey cähpets upon their floors," she said, "and I could not receive *such* company on my Tuhkey cähpets."

Kelso responded, sarcastically imitating her affected manner of speaking: "And are your 'Tuhkey cähpets' dearer to you . . . than our wives and our babes, who are perishing in this terrible storm, are to us?"

"I am not responsible," she replied, "for your being out in the storm."

"Well," Kelso said, "I hope the day will come when you will suffer just as our loved ones are now suffering."

"That," the lady huffed, "is not a Christian wish."

"That may be," said Kelso, "and yet hell is full of such Christians as you are."
He went back to his friends and said that they should just force their way into
both houses, but they refused, fearing some rebel band would then hunt them
down and murder them. "We struggled on, therefore, through the dense darkness, the drifting snows, and the dreadful cold."[53]

The wagon train finally stopped several hours after sundown, and they
tried to make camp in an open field covered with small post-oak trees. With
the few axes they had, they cut down some trees, but with the green wood,
covered with snow, it took them two more hours to kindle fires, and the fires
burned poorly, producing more smoke and sparks than heat. Some of the
women and children in the wagons were already frostbitten. "I placed our few
old blankets upon the snow, on the side of my fire opposite the wind, under
the canopy of smoke and sparks. Here I put my family to sleep." Susie tried to
care for their four-month-old baby, Ianthus. John took two-year-old Iantha
in his arms, opened his coat and shirt, and tried to warm her against his body.
She felt ice cold as she shivered and clung to him for warmth. She was also suffering from diarrhea, and several times he had to take her out into the drifting
snow so she could relieve herself. Finally, Susie and the children drifted off to
sleep, "moaning in their sad dreams."[54]

Kelso could not sleep. "I lay there thinking;—thinking thoughts of unutterable bitterness. What had I done that my life should be hunted as it
had been? What had my poor young wife and my little babes done that they
should be thus driven from their home to perish in the storms of winter?"
The blood in his veins felt "strangely hot." He sensed that his whole nature
was changing. All that was gentle in him was dying; all that was fierce was
strengthening. He blamed the rebels for all the suffering—not just the particular ones who had driven his family from his home, but all of them. He
blamed them and wanted blood. "I vowed to slay with my own hand *twenty-
five* rebels before I cut my hair." Years later he would see this vow as a kind
of "madness," but he also knew that it made "the *facts* of my subsequent war
career . . . more wonderful than almost any *fiction*."[55]

He got up from his blanket in the snow and wandered around the camp,
wanting "to see all that there was to be seen of suffering," as if to fuel his rage.
Some of the women were still up, caring for sick or frostbitten children and
weeping softly. At a distant fire he found a young couple, strangers who had
just joined the refugees the day before. "Here, a young wife, scarcely more
than a child herself, was confined in child-birth. Her bed was upon the snow,
upon the windward side of the fire. Her young husband and a few women
were trying to so hang up blankets about her upon sticks as to protect her

from the terrible blasts of wind and the billows of drifting snow." Kelso tried
to help them, but every few minutes a gust of wind blew the blankets down
and blew snow onto the suffering woman. The others helping her in her labor
tried to warm their numb hands by the fire. "And there, amid the howlings of
that fearful winter storm, by the dim and fitful light of that smoky log fire, her
child was born." When she heard the baby's faint cry, the mother muttered a
prayer, asking God "to spare *its life* for *her sake*, to spare *her life* for *its sake*,—to
spare *both lives* for *Christ's sake*." And then they both died.[56]

God did not hear her prayer, Kelso thought. "He was not out in that storm.
Is he ever out in such a storm? Is he ever present where he is really needed?
Does he ever hear the cries of the poor and perishing?" Why did he only listen
to the wealthy, with their well-fed priests and fancy churches? Why did he
never listen to Kelso's own prayers? "I have no use, no love, no respect for any
such god," Kelso decided. But there was no point being angry at God. Several
years before, as he renounced Methodism, Kelso had dismissed the biblical
God as a papier-mâché idol. But if he had still tended a small flame of religious faith, had still warmed himself by the soft, vague glow of Liberalism's
Benevolent Deity, that faith, too, was extinguished on that cold night. His
heart now confirmed where his intellectual travels had taken him, and after
that night he would say, "I have no belief in the existence of any such being."[57]

The next day, after wrapping the bodies of the young mother and her baby
in a single blanket and burying them in a shallow grave, the refugees moved
on. The storm had ceased, though they still suffered from the cold, especially
Kelso's five-year-old son Florellus, who since the house fire had neither pants
nor shoes and had to walk barefoot in the snow with a shawl wrapped around
his legs. After several more days, they finally reached St. Louis. The Kelsos
crossed the Mississippi River, and John left his family in Collinsville, Illinois,
with old friends from Buffalo including Dr. Hovey, who had fled there after
the Battle of Wilson's Creek. Kelso then returned to his regiment.[58]

He found the 24th Missouri Infantry at Rolla, camped "upon a bleak naked
hill exposed to the full force of the winter winds" and suffering from sickness,
with some men dying nearly every day. (General Curtis took command in
December and immediately ordered them to move to timbered valleys "for
the purpose of better providing against cold.") Kelso occupied his time by
studying German: he would be long remembered as the soldier who paced
around camps with a book in his hands. Sometimes he would help enter-
tain the men by debating religious questions with Sergeant Harvey Garrison,
who would later become a noted preacher for the Disciples of Christ. Since
his arrest by the Texans outside Lebanon, Kelso had been a prisoner of war

on parole, but in midwinter he was duly exchanged for a Confederate prisoner and could return to active duty. He and his friend Milton Burch were
permitted to return to Dallas County to scout the enemy. They stayed with
an elderly couple in the relatively safe northwest corner of the county. While
Burch, who was lame in one leg from an old war wound, remained at the
house and ate heartily, Kelso went on rambles through the hills and woods
and did some spying.[59]

One night, he visited Buffalo. At around midnight, he crept from the
darkness of the forest and onto his own property. He took a drink from his
own spring and then "stood upon the ashes of my dear old home." There, in
the moonlight, was the little playhouse his children had enjoyed; beyond was
the orchard he had tended, ruined by his neighbor's sheep. "As I stood there,
among those scenes, once so loved, now so desolate,—as I stood there in the
light of the moon, in the deep silence of the midnight hour, a feeling of unutterable loneliness came over me, and thoughts of unutterable bitterness
came crowding into my mind. I took off my hat, called the moon to witness,
and then repeated my vow of vengeance. In every one's life, there are certain
moments that never fade from memory, and, in my own life, this was one of
those moments." Then he returned to the dark woods.[60]

Several days later, Kelso returned to Buffalo and hid in the woods outside
of town. He watched the roads. Occasionally he would appear at night at a
friendly house to get food, but mostly he lived on raw corn. He slept a few
hours a day, never in the same place twice, with his face between his knees.
Ignoring hunger, cold, exhaustion, and the danger of getting caught, he focused on revenge. He had learned the names of several of the men who had
burned down his house. Most were men he knew, men he had never harmed
or offended. He would meet them, as he put it, to "transact some *very important business,—the most important business of their lives.*"[61]

He terrorized the town for nearly three weeks. Fear "spread like the wind."
Someone would anxiously report seeing Kelso's tracks in the snow near this
or that house, even at places he never actually visited. Another would imagine
seeing Kelso himself—perhaps a menacing figure at the tree line, glimpsed
at dusk from a window. Rumors reverberated through the town. "Like an
evil spirit that knew no rest, I appeared and disappeared leaving them all
wondering whence I came and whither I went." For one of his last "business transactions," he paid a call to Harvey White, the "Christian neighbor"
who had seized his farm. He slipped into White's house. Harvey might have
been at his table, or even in bed, enjoying the comforts of home, his familiar
four walls, the warmth of his hearth. And then suddenly there he was, a dark

figure from the woods, the firelight flickering in his eyes and along his gun
barrel: Kelso, come for a reckoning. Kelso wanted White to make a move—
some "war-like demonstration"—so he could justifiably shoot him. But White
stood stock still: "he turned deadly pale, shook like a leaf, and, for a time,
was utterly speechless." Finally, recovering himself a little, he spoke. I know
what you're here for, he said. I'm sick anyway—not long for this world. You
won't shorten my life by much. Then, beginning to blubber "like a whipped
schoolboy," he opened his shirt, exposed the white skin of his bosom, and told
Kelso to shoot. He was so wretched, such a mean, groveling "thing" rather
than a man, that Kelso lowered his gun in disgust and left. White would survive until the end of the war, when vigilantes hanged him and his eldest son
for theft. "Thus my vengeance came," Kelso thought when he heard the news,
"but not, as it should have come, by my own hand."[62]

He did not pull the trigger when he confronted White. But what about his
other "business transactions" during his three weeks haunting Buffalo? How
many of the twenty-five rebels he vowed to slay with his own hands did he
claim in his hometown? He would admit generally to "bushwhacking" there,
but in his memoirs he declined to give specifics: "For reasons of my own, I will
not now, and, perhaps, never will describe these business transactions in detail." When he left Buffalo, however, it was clear that he was gratified to have
begun his quest for revenge.[63]

FROM BUFFALO, KELSO headed south. Springfield had regained its strategic importance in Missouri's Civil War, and General Curtis had asked
him to do some more spying there. When the Federals withdrew from the
southwest, Price's State Guard had moved north to Oceola, recruiting in the
central part of the state. In December, though, the Union scored victories
in the northeast: a cavalry brigade captured thirteen hundred rebels at the
Blackwater River and another regiment broke up a camp of nine hundred near
Columbia. These developments prompted Price to move back to Springfield.
As the battlefield map shifted, loyal civilians in the southwest suffered. A petition from citizens in that region to General Halleck complained of rebels
"laying waste to the whole country and subjecting women and children to
destitution and starvation." Noting "[t]hat the recent retrograde movement
of our army from Springfield has been the cause of from 3,000 to 5,000 men,
women, and children leaving their homes, without money and many in a suffering condition," the citizens pleaded for fifteen thousand troops for protection. In a letter to General Price, Halleck charged that "you subsist your
troops by robbing and plundering the non-combatant Union inhabitants

of the southwestern counties of this State. They say that your troops robbed them of their provisions and clothing, carrying away their shoes and bedding, and even cutting cloth from their looms, and that you have driven women and children from their homes to starve and perish in the cold." By mid-January 1862, as part of Halleck's reorganization of Federal troops in Missouri, General Curtis was building up his Army of the Southwest at Rolla with the intention of striking Price. Kelso gathered what information he could from Springfield, where Price had his combined State Guard and Confederate force of eight thousand men. Then Kelso turned his steps northeast, back to Curtis and his regiment at Rolla.[64]

The cavalry caught Kelso when he was risking the roads in a snowstorm. This time there were no persimmon trees to pretend to pick, no roadside log to hide behind. A large rebel squad quickly surrounded him, disarmed him, and brought him to their camp. It was a mixed group from Texas, Arkansas, and Missouri, and some of the Missourians recognized him. He recognized one of them: the soldier who had shared his tent at Iron Mountain in the fall, apparently a rebel spy. As they fed their horses and ate dinner, Kelso tried to ingratiate himself with the men by telling a string of "ludicrous anecdotes" that kept them laughing. "Knowing that I was talking for my life,—making my captors feel kindly toward me, I threw my who[le] soul into my anecdotes, and never talked better." The Texans guarding him tried to get him to switch sides. Kelso lied and said that if the United States upheld Frémont's emancipation policy, he would join them—that he fought to preserve the Union, not to free the slaves. "The latter part of this statement was not true. I really did propose to fight for the utter wiping out of slavery, but I thought it good policy to talk as I did."[65]

In everything else, Kelso opted for candor. Union spies were generally instructed to tell the truth if captured: getting caught in a lie would only make their situation worse. Kelso also knew that honesty would earn him points for bravery. At the quick court-martial the rebels organized, he readily admitted that he had "jay-hawked" some Southern men in Dallas County and had "bush-whacked" some of the others who had burned down his house and driven out his family. But, he asked them, wouldn't any of you have done the same thing in those circumstances? As for spying, he acknowledged that he had done that, too, and, under cover, had even made some speeches at Confederate recruiting stations. But they had their own spies, and they knew, he argued, "that only the bravest and most faithful men on either side ever undertake this necessary service so full of danger." He had known the risks: "I volunteered with my eyes open. I knew that, by the cruel and unjust laws of war, I would, if captured, be condemned to death. At your hands, I expect to die. . . . You shall see, however, that I can die as I have lived—a man."[66]

Kelso was not, however, actually resigned to that fate, even as a detail was assigned to build a gallows from fence rails. The four Texans guarding him moved beyond earshot and began arguing his case. He overheard one of them say it was "a damned pity for so brave a man to be strung up like a damned dog." The officers who had tried and convicted him were still discussing his fate, too, and he could tell that his words and manner had affected at least one of them, a Texas captain who was arguing to spare his life. When they finished their consultation, the captain brought Kelso some blankets to sit on. Kelso asked him what they had decided. Although the officer was evasive, the prisoner could see by the man's expression that he "was doomed." The captain then whispered something to one of Kelso's guards and left.[67]

Kelso looked across the open field and watched men erect the tripod of fence rails that would serve as a gallows. Am I really going to die here, now, at the end of a rope, he asked himself? His own "inner consciousness" answered "*no*!" A powerful conviction assured him not only that he would escape this hangman's noose but that he was destined "to live to perform an important work after the close of the war."[68]

The guard who had received the whispered message from the captain, a soldier with "strangely expressive" eyes, wordlessly signaled to Kelso that he was a friend and would help him escape. Kelso silently conveyed that he understood. The soldier glanced at the brush thicket behind him. Seeing that the man was wearing a watch, Kelso asked him for the time. The man pulled out the pocket watch and held it open so Kelso could see, but with his thumbnail marked the spot on the dial ten minutes ahead of the minute hand—the time, Kelso understood, set for his execution. The soldier, complaining to his comrades that he was too hot so close to the fire, then switched places with another guard. The friend was now the only obstacle between Kelso and the thicket.[69]

The minutes ticked by. The gallows were ready. "My heart seemed to cease beating." Then a soldier to his left, who had been quietly talking with another guard, called his comrade a damned liar, and the man responded by throwing a punch. Kelso knew that was the signal—a distraction staged for his sake. He darted toward the brush. The friendly guard then happened to stumble out of his way and into the path of two pursuers. Kelso plunged into the thicket, stooping to protect his face from the sticks and thorns, and ran for his life. Four guns fired behind him. Bugles sounded and soldiers mounted their horses, but the escaping prisoner could only be followed through the dense thicket on foot.[70]

Kelso ran, plowing through the briars and brush, and then had to force himself to stop running, for it was better to stay in the thicket than venture out onto the open ground beyond it. He hid in the snow beneath the bushes, hat gone, clothes "torn to tatters," chest heaving, blood and sweat tricking over dozens of scratches, and feeling "a wild joy hard to describe." He listened, straining to hear any sound of pursuit, yet "heard nothing but the howlings of the winter winds among the leafless branches of the trees." As he lay there quietly, not moving a muscle, it began to snow again and he soon felt chilled to the bone. The rebels would not expect him to have stayed so close to their camp, however, and would probably not devote more than a day to hunting for him, so he decided to gather some fallen branches for a makeshift shelter and stay in the thicket. Despite the numbing cold, he slept through the night. He stayed there the next day and did not resume his journey north until the following night.[71]

He was underdressed in tattered old clothes, hungry, tired, and cold. "Avoiding as much as possible, all settlements, I stumbled along in the darkness, through snow about four inches deep. My course was devious and my progress was slow." After fifty hours with no more food than the few kernels of corn that had spilled from a passing cart, and unsure of where exactly he was, he decided he had to risk stopping at a house. To his delight, the people there told him that he was only 3 miles from Lebanon, where General Curtis's regiments were camping. Look, they said, you can see the smoke from their nearest picket station from here. He thanked them, and went toward the smoke.[72]

Once on the snowy road toward Lebanon, he soon saw the station ahead, and the guards saw him. They mounted their horses and galloped toward him with pistols in their hands. They searched him, turning his pockets inside out, and wondered at his dilapidated appearance. "Who the devil *are* you, anyway?" the sergeant asked. Kelso answered that he was a farmer, a wood-chopper, a stone-cutter, a teacher, and a preacher. As they took him into custody and brought him to the house where they stayed, the sergeant said that they didn't have need for any farming, wood-chopping, stone-cutting, or teaching, but they might be entertained by a good sermon. They offered to give him a chicken dinner if he would preach one. Kelso accepted the proposal.[73]

Most Union spies returning to Federal lines learned not to divulge their information to picket guards or even subordinate officers, preferring to report directly to the commander who sent them on the mission so their reports would not be garbled as they made their way up the chain of command. Kelso pushed this reluctance further than most by refusing even to divulge his identity to anyone but General Curtis. The guards made it clear that they would roast him a chicken, listen to him preach, and take him to see the general in the morning, but that if he tried to escape before then they'd put a bullet in his head. This suited the bedraggled preacher just fine; he mounted a table in the center of the room and began his sermon.[74]

He toyed with his audience. At first he seemed to suggest, by the verses he chose and the doctrines he extracted from them, that God supported the rebellion, and the soldiers started to scowl. But then he shifted, and his Bible stories and lessons all seemed to support the Union, and this made them smile. Finally, he concluded with a humorous exhortation that left them laughing heartily. Rewarded with roast chicken, sausages, and bread, he stuffed himself and then, for the first time in many nights, slept, well-fed and happy, by a warm fire.[75]

The next morning, the picket guards took him to Curtis's headquarters, where the general was meeting with his officers. Curtis did not have to ask who the devil this ragged man was: "the General recognized me at once. Rising and advancing to meet me, he took both of my hands in his, and, holding them thus while he expressed his joy at my return, gazing, meanwhile, into my eyes with a look such as a fond old father might bestow upon a beloved son who had returned to him after having been given up as lost." With great courtesy and compliments, Curtis introduced Kelso to the officers. After the meeting, Kelso and the general had a private conversation. He gave Curtis the intelligence he had gathered about the rebel forces near Springfield. As Kelso years later recalled the conversation, General Curtis seemed greatly pleased with the report. "He said that, upon my information he would prepare at once to act,—that he would march against Springfield just as soon as possible." Kelso may have told Curtis what the general reported a few days later, on Feb. 10, 1862 as his Army of the Southwest set out for Springfield: "Latest news from Springfield: [General Sterling] Price was still there. General [Daniel M.] Frost arrived Friday or Saturday with a few men, and his battery, with about 400 men, was expected within four days." Or it may have been the information that Curtis relayed to Capt. J. C. Kelton later the same day: "[General Earl] Van Dorn is moving up [from Arkansas] to join Price. . . . Van Dorn has promised 30,000 or 40,000 at Springfield very soon. Expects to be there with 10,000 by the 15th. These are the hopes and expectations of the enemy." But Curtis had other sources. "I see men every day direct from Springfield," he

General Samuel R. Curtis, ca. 1861–1865. Library of Congress, Washington, D.C.

wrote. "Of course I interrogate scouts, deserters, and all kinds of witnesses."
The general's son and aide-de-camp Lieutenant Samuel Prentis Curtis wrote
in 1866 that Lt. Col. Clark Wright, a resident of southwestern Missouri,
had "established a system of scouts and spies to ascertain the movements
and condition of the enemy. He reported to Curtis that he had six different
lines of communication direct from Springfield. . . . There were additional
means of receiving information from Springfield, through Colonel [John S.]
Phelps, through spies who reported directly to the commanding General, and
through other sources." Kelso, however warmly received, may not have been
as crucial as he imagined.[76]

When Kelso gave Curtis a fuller narrative of his adventures, the general's "grand old face lighted up with pleasure and approbation." But he was also concerned. He admired Kelso's "desperate daring," but the young man had risked too much. The general urged Kelso not to mention anything about his capture and conviction, even to his family. He had been condemned to death as a spy. "He said that a general knowledge of that fact, even in our own army could do no possible good and might greatly endanger my life." Now that the rebels knew him, he would be fighting "as it were, with a halter around my neck,—denied, in case of capture, the rights of a prisoner of war."[77]

The most important thing Kelso got from the conversation, however, was not the acknowledgment that his information was valuable or the advice about the danger he faced. It was Curtis's recognition and validation. The general treated him with affection and respect in front of his officers. When they were alone, they "conversed as friends—as equals,—he the magnificently uniformed Major general, I the tattered and half-naked weather-beaten private. He forgot his rank and his splendor. I forgot my rank and my rags." Many years later, Kelso wrote that "it does me good to recall the father[ly] pride and kindliness with which he then regarded me." The spy considered this his reward for all his effort and suffering.[78]

7

My Dear Susie, the Bullets Began to Scream

"MY DEAR SUSIE," Kelso wrote to his wife near the end of the Army of the Southwest's winter campaign in 1862. "Of course, you have learned through the news-papers something of the chase we made;—a chase scarce equaled on any other occasion in American history. . . . It would have done you good to see our boys sometimes. After a long day's march, they would be so weary that many seemed scarce able to drag themselves along; but, when the roar of cannons was heard in advance, all would spring forward, at double quick, seeming strong as ever, while loud cheers echoed along our ranks." The men always responded to the call of battle: "At such times, we plunged through creeks, tore through bush, all regardless of consequences, our only feeling being one of wild gladness at the prospect of getting a fight. At night, our trains would be behind, and, without food or blankets, we would drop down upon the frozen ground and sleep sweetly."[1]

In Collinsville, Illinois, Susie would have been able to follow the news of Kelso's regiment in the St. Louis newspapers from across the river. Throughout January 1862, Rolla correspondents to the *Missouri Republican* and the *Missouri Democrat* reported the buildup of General Curtis's forces. The newspapers also printed frustratingly contradictory reports and rumors about what General Price and the State Guard were up to in Springfield. Had Price's army dwindled to a despairing mob of 8,000 men, harnessed up and ready to flee farther south at the first sign of a Federal attack? Or had Price been reinforced with men, artillery, and provisions from Arkansas, and was now, with 15,000 or 20,000 troops, confidently picking out a battlefield or ready to make a stand? In early February, the *Republican* reported the Federal move to Lebanon, 60 miles southwest, or more than halfway to Springfield.

Curtis himself arrived on January 29, wrapped in a buffalo robe and pitching his tent in the snow. The main body of the army left Lebanon on the morning of February 10. By 5:00 p.m. they were camping at Copley, 18 miles closer, and by the end of the day they were at Marshfield (another 10 miles). The newspapers reported this four days later. A big battle seemed imminent, the correspondents added, warning that there would be a great loss of life on both sides.[2]

Commentary in the *Republican* put the campaign in the larger context of the war. A writer in early January explained that secessionists regarded the subjugation of Missouri as crucial to the Confederacy: it would help pressure Kentucky, make Kansas, New Mexico, and Indian Territory "easy prey," and enable control of the Missouri, Mississippi, and Ohio Rivers. Missouri's rebels, too weak to conquer the state on their own, needed men and provisions from the Confederacy. The corridor for that aid would be the southwest corner. The under-manned Lyon had known this, but had been defeated; the disorganized Frémont had known this, but had been withdrawn. In February, though, with the Army of the Southwest on the move, *Republican* editorials saw Curtis's campaign as part of a larger "continental" strategy that was finally emerging after months of Federal foot-dragging and fecklessness. With a line stretching from General Burnside's maneuvers in North Carolina, to Buell at Nashville, to Grant on the Tennessee River, and to Curtis on the western flank, the aim seemed to be to cut the Confederacy in half. The "principal theater of conflict" would be the "southwestern States," not Virginia. The paper rejoiced with Grant's great victories at Fort Henry (February 6) and Fort Donelson (February 16). If Curtis could destroy Price, the victory might not only save Missouri for the Union but also free up 30,000 to 50,000 men for service farther east and perhaps change the course of the war.[3]

The Army of the Southwest that marched to Springfield in February over terrible roads, alternately iced over or thick with mud, was initially composed of 12,100 men (9,600 infantry and 2,500 cavalry) and fifty guns. The nature of the enemy was less clear. Susie Kelso would have read conflicting reports and rumors in the newspapers. The men who marched had little better information. As a correspondent said when the army was still back in Rolla, to maintain secrecy, Curtis kept his troops in "utter ignorance." Curtis and Kelso may have had a good idea of what was happening at Springfield, but the average soldier did not. Infantry private Robert Pinckney Matthews, who marched with Curtis's army from Lebanon, recalled the rumors that changed every day: "One day there would be a report in camps that Price had 50,000 men concentrated at Springfield awaiting to give us battle. The next day, we

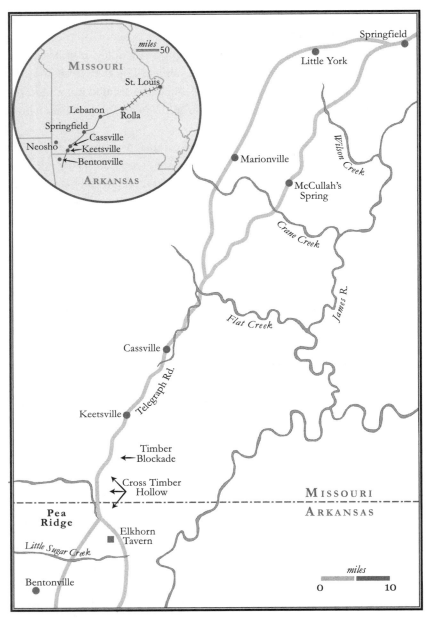

The March to Pea Ridge, Arkansas, February 1862. Drawn by Rebecca Wrenn. Map source: William Shea and Earl J. Hess, *Pea Ridge: Civil War Campaign in the West* (Chapel Hill: University of North Carolina Press, 1992), 31, map 2.1.

would hear that the rebels had fortified that place on every side, that forts and rifle pits extended five miles out from the town, and to take the place we would have to assault a strong line of earthworks every few hundred yards, this whole distance. The next day we would probably hear something else."[4]

Despite the roads, the Army of the Southwest moved with remarkable speed. Halleck, the bureaucrat sitting at his desk in St. Louis and coordinating the complicated logistics, had made the campaign possible; Curtis, the talented field commander, was making it happen. During the troop buildup, newspaper correspondents watching the long mule trains moving wagonloads of supplies noted the improvements from the chaos and corruption of the Frémont era. But Curtis ordered his troops to pack lightly and expected them to manage even if they got out ahead of their supply line, which, as Kelso's letter to Susie noted, often happened. Curtis ordered that they carry six days of light rations for the forced march. He reduced their ration of salt pork because it was expensive but doubled their ration of fresh beef and pork, which he said was "abundant in the country" and would be supplied through the commissary. He was wrong about the abundance: the men foraged constantly, but in a region that had been feeding enemy troops for months, the pickings were slim. One soldier wrote that "what beef we get it takes two men to hold up while one knocks them down," and he worried that "it looks like starving if we do not save rations." The men were already complaining in camp on their second night about "unmasticatable" cartilage being called beef, so to lighten the mood Kelso preached a humorous funeral sermon for the ancient, emaciated bull that had been slaughtered for their dinner.[5]

Will Price fight—or retreat? That was the question that newspapers—and, no doubt, their readers—kept asking. At 7:00 a.m. on February 12, the main body of Curtis's army marched to Pearson's Creek (8 miles from Springfield). At 10:30 a.m., rebel scouts fired upon their advance cavalry. Curtis answered with his howitzers. The front guards received sporadic fire through the afternoon. At nightfall 1,500 Confederate cavalry lined up across the road behind sharpshooters and attacked Curtis's outer picket. Federal troops returned fire again, killing two and wounding several, the general thought, though another soldier estimated eight or ten killed and ten wounded. The Confederates then pulled back to Springfield. On his way back from the skirmish to camp around midnight, Kelso "made the acquaintance of a chicken near a farm house, and persuaded it to accompany me to my camp." He was hungry and did not feel guilty about taking the "rebel chicken"—probably from the farm of E. R. Danforth, a wealthy slaveholder.[6]

It happened the next day, February 13, though Susie Kelso would not have learned the news until she got the paper printed two days later and read General Halleck's telegram: "The flag of the Union floats over the Court House in Springfield." Price and his troops had evacuated during the night, and the Army of the Southwest marched into town at 10:00 in the morning. It was an emotional moment for soldiers from southwest Missouri. An infantry private described the scene: "It was an hour of joy. . . . There is a language of the heart which speaks when all words fail to convey the thought. So with the members of our regiments whose homes and friends were here." Kelso was reminded of a powerful dream he had had during a spy mission in the fall, which now struck him as a premonition. He had been asleep, with his revolver in his hand, in a pine forest on a hill above the Current River: "I dreamed that I was standing on one of the corners formed by the public square and Saint Louis Street, in the city of Springfield, watching an army coming in and listening to the cheerings of the men." Here he was, at the edge of Springfield's public square, at the head of St. Louis Street, living what he had dreamed—but instead of being an observer on a street corner, he was one of the soldiers marching in. After a night camped in the southern part of town, the troops hurried southwest, on the Fayetteville Road, in pursuit of Price and his rebel army.[7]

The chase was on—a running battle down through Missouri's southwest corner and across the line into Arkansas. On most evenings, the head of Curtis's army would skirmish with the tail of Price's, sometimes for a few minutes and sometimes for an hour or more, and then the Confederates would withdraw farther south and the Federals would occupy the camp their enemy had just abandoned. By the evening of February 14, the Army of the Southwest was about 30 miles southwest of Springfield at McCullah's Spring. The advance cavalry was attacked at Crane Creek and made a stand until other forces joined them and the enemy retreated. When Curtis reported on the evening of February 15, he was at Flat Creek, nearing Cassville (60 miles southwest of Springfield). They had engaged the enemy again, driving them from their entrenchments at 3:00 p.m. The army moved out early on the morning of February 16.[8]

After each evening's skirmish, the Federal troops took over their enemy's abandoned camp, the fires still burning, the coffee still warm in pots left behind. They helped themselves to bushels and bushels of rebel corn. "Most of our provisions for the last ten days have been taken from the enemy," General Curtis happily reported. A correspondent for the St. Louis *Republican* found the entire road south strewn with supplies left by the hastily retreating rebels—wagons, blankets, guns. One evening, Kelso recalled, his comrades found twenty skinned cattle carcasses, but these the Federals wisely avoided. Two days after noting that he was pleased with the haul of rebel provisions, Curtis reported that forty-two of his men had been poisoned at Mud Town from eating food the enemy had left behind. Several men died and the others suffered terribly, according to a report three days later. In his diary, Henry Perrin Mann, who rode with Curtis as a member of the 15th Illinois Cavalry, attributed the deaths to poisoned whiskey.[9]

As they retreated, the Confederate and State Guard soldiers terrified the local population with warnings about the horrors that the Federals were about to unleash upon them. A newspaper correspondent writing from Cross Hollows found civilians "almost frightened out of their wits by tales told by Price's army." The country folk were warned that "all the men would be slayed, their wives and daughters turned over to the soldiers for the gratification of their lusts." Kelso heard other versions: "It was said that we were killing all the male rebels from ten years old up;—that we made them dig their own graves and then kneel in them to be shot. . . . [and] that we were killing all the old ugly women and giving all the young and handsome women to our free negroes." On the road in front of one cluster of houses, an enormously fat woman in a panic, screaming about the murder of women and children, tried to waddle away from the soldiers but did not make much forward progress. Her whole body shook "like a mountain of jelly" and she started "to paddle the air with her hands like a seal fighting flies with its flippers." A crowd of young soldiers could not help roaring with laughter at the sight, but Kelso got some other women to calm her down. Many of the houses they passed were abandoned by similarly terrified residents. Some of them sent a letter to General Curtis: "We, as citizens, have left our homes and firesides" because of "a brutal soldiery that would lay waste our humble homes and outrage the chastity of our wives and daughters and place our own lives in jeopardy." In a public address, Curtis answered that the "falsehoods circulated concerning us have driven thousands from their homes . . . [and] have involved the whole community in the troubles" that they need not have experienced. Yes, his troops needed supplies, he explained, but if people stayed home, the army would pay for them instead of just taking them. Military prisoners were not mistreated, peaceable private citizens would be left alone, and there had been no complaints about his soldiers harassing women.[10]

When did the necessary foraging cross the line into pillaging and plundering? A newspaper correspondent praised the behavior of Curtis's army: the quartermaster paid for supplies as they traveled and the men displayed "far better discipline and less of that reckless disposition to destroy and lay waste the country" than on Frémont's march. An address to the soldiers from Curtis's headquarters lauded their diligence and encouraged further restraint. One evening, as the soldiers collapsed, hungry and exhausted after another day's forced march but without the benefit of the rebels' camp food, Kelso went out to conduct some necessary spoliation, enlisting an eighty-pound civilian pig into the Federal service. The next day, over half the infantrymen straggled from the ranks, looking for food. He saw some of them swarm an apple cellar, crowding in so tightly that he worried some might get trampled or suffocate. Backing away from the cellar and rejoining the stragglers on the road, he saw the results of their visits to the nearby houses. One soldier had run his bayonet "through two large middlings of bacon." Another had "two geese tied together by their necks, slung across his gun." Others carried turkeys and chickens, or sacks of flour, cornmeal, and dried fruit.[11]

Some came away with more unusual kinds of plunder: "Of these, one carried a large earthen jar filled with some kind of preserves. From the mouth of this jar, which he carried under his left arm, he constantly kept taking handfuls of preserves and cramming them into his [mouth], daubing a liberal portion of them upon his face. . . . Another carried a large wooden churn full of buttermilk . . . by locking his arms around it and hugging it to his bosom." Most bizarre was the plunderer "who cared more for the beautiful than for the useful." Kelso in his autobiography claimed to have seen this soldier, who "wore, upon the lower part of his body, the immense hoop skirt of some gigantic female; upon his shoulders, a large striped shawl; and, upon his head, a huge, funnel-shaped, straw bonnet, of the style of fifty years ago. Thus attired, this remarkable aesthete marched proudly onward, contemplating his various charms in a large looking-glass which he carried." As unlikely as this may sound, there are other references to soldiers donning bonnets or dresses to mock and insult the women they plundered. The previous summer, a squad of soldiers marching with Lyon emptied a small store, and afterward, according to a soldier's account published in 1861, could be "seen circulating around the camp—one with a parasol daintily held over his swarthy countenance, another tripping elegantly along with a coquettish 'flat' surmounting his unkempt locks, a third lugged a looking glass under his arm, a fourth minced in Broadway style, enveloped in a rotundant hoop skirt, and so on, each of the squad carrying a trophy." Another memoir of the march to Arkansas corroborates part of the scene Kelso described. Robert Pinckney Matthews, a private with the Phelps Regiment, wrote years later that he "saw some cavalry, who had confiscated a lot of ladies bonnets from a small store by the road side, riding along with the feminine head gear on their own heads, the ribbons fluttering like streamers in the air. I also saw another carrying a large looking glass and he amused himself, while the thunder of the artillery was shaking the hills, by holding it before the faces of his comrades to let them see how pale they were."[12]

Kelso may have embellished his account for comic effect, a narrative turn signaled by his description of the "remarkable aesthete" as "nearly seven feet in height" and by nodding to a "Sut Lovingood" story by the humorist George Washington Harris. Kelso certainly accented the ridiculous as he put his characters in motion at the sound of artillery fire. When "the thunders of heavy cannonading began to reverberate among the hills in our front . . . the whole vast mass of stragglers started forward on a run, all being eager to participate in the opening battle." Bacon swung on bayonets, geese and chickens flopped back and forth, and the sacks on men's shoulders bobbed up and down as they ran. "The man with the jar of preserves ran as fast as he could, taking out a handful of preserves, every few jumps, cramming vigorously into his mouth and daubing more liberally upon his face." The man with the churn of butter-milk ran well, but the "butter-milk splashed up through the dasher hole and around the edge of the lid, and came down in quite a shower upon the face and bosom of our hero, leaving many little lumps of butter entangled in his beard." The soldier in the hoop skirt ran "so fast against the wind [which] made the front part of the skirt come down against his legs, while the stiffness of the hoops and their great size made the back part rise high up and stick far out behind." This hero held tight to his looking glass and gazed at his reflection as he ran. "He evidently wanted to thoroughly regale his vision upon his own beauty before it was spoiled forever."[13]

More revealing than Kelso seeing comedy in a scene of plunderers rushing into battle is his choosing, as he wrote in the early 1880s, to describe the cross-dressing soldier as "a kind of Oscar Wilde." As Kelso wrote this passage, the national press was avidly covering the Irish writer's American tour, remarking on his flamboyant appearance and "effeminacy." For Kelso, the soldier's cross-dressing was not necessarily a sign of homosexuality, but his narcissistic self-regard was still a queer declension from the standard of true manhood. Perhaps the soldier was not all that different from that parlor lothario with the waxed moustache and silken tongue, Dr. Hovey, who was sitting out the war with Kelso's "dear Susie."[14]

The battle the plunderers ran to was not just another late afternoon skirmish. It was February 17, and they were at Sugar Creek Crossing. A hundred miles from Springfield, they were 6 miles across the Arkansas border when the cavalry battalions out front spotted what they thought were fleeing Missouri rebels—the tail of Price's army, as usual. Instead it was part of General Ben McCulloch's Arkansas Confederates, who had joined Price. The Confederates had deployed in a line crossing Telegraph Road—with three regiments on the eastern side, one on the west, and a battery of artillery in the middle. The artillery opened fire on the Federal cavalry. One Federal battalion immediately moved off the road to engage the enemy in the woods on the right, while the other did the same on the left. But the lead battalion, led by Major James Hubbard, perhaps not hearing the order to leave the road, charged straight ahead into the rebels' "hornet nest." Hit by a hail of bullets, they quickly pulled back. Curtis, hearing the guns, rushed reinforcements from behind. Kelso and the other stragglers ran forward, the calls of the regimental adjutants directing them to their positions: "Twenty-fourth Missouri, extreme right!" Kelso suggested to some other stragglers from the 24th that they go even farther to the right of the rest of the regiment so they could take positions behind the little trees and bushes growing there. But when they reached the spot, they found that every tree and bush already had a soldier behind it. "As the storm of bullets whistled about our ears, it was amusing to see some of the men and the officers, who were behind saplings not larger than a man's wrist trying to draw themselves in from both sides and to make themselves as slim, respectively, as were their protecting saplings." Kelso and the other stragglers, however, had to face the storm of bullets on the open ground.[15]

After at least an hour of intense fighting, the enemy retreated. Thirteen Federals had been killed and about twenty wounded. The Confederates lost twice as many, at least according to the Union soldiers who walked the frozen battlefield. George A. Cummins of the 36th Illinois wrote in his diary: "For the first time [I] saw men [who] were killed in battle and it was a nasty sight. I hope to see but few of such." Kelso saw pale, dead bodies in puddles of blood. One corpse, however, still had color in its cheeks. "I felt its wrist. Its pulse was strong and good. I put my ear to its nostrils. It held it[s] breath for nearly a minute and then let up with quite a puff. It was a strange corpse. We rubbed some prickly pear leaves under its nose. Its eyes flew open, a kind of sheepish smile lit up its countenance, and it explained: 'Hold on, boys, I'm not dead!'" The Confederate soldier had fallen and then hoped to play possum until darkness would allow him to escape. On another part of the battlefield, they found the body of an older man. "He lay upon his back. He had been shot through the brain, and his silvered locks were dabbled with blood.

The fierce look of battle was still on his ghastly countenance, and his stiffened hands still clutched his musket. While we were gazing upon him in silence, we were startled by a strange cry from one of our comrades: 'By God! Boys, he's my daddy!' And so he was." The son wiped blood from his father's face, calling his name and weeping. Kelso and the other soldiers wept, too, as they helped with the burial.[16]

As the men made camp for the night, the plunderers who had purloined the turkeys, chickens, bacon, and buttermilk a few hours before were cursing up a storm. They had thrown their stolen goods aside to fight, but after the battle the plunderers had been plundered, other soldiers making off with the booty. "One half of the army, who had just been engaged in stealing, seemed to be charging the other half with being damned thieves." Those like Kelso who had no plundered provisions got nothing for supper that night. He managed to steal an ear of corn from a poor half-starved mule. "When this mule saw me robbing him of his own scant fare, he seemed to reproach me with his sad eyes."[17]

In the newspapers of February 21–23, Susie Kelso would have seen the reports of the battle at Sugar Creek on the 17th, and of the next day's rout of a small Confederate force as the Federals took control of Bentonville, Arkansas. On February 28 and March 1, the press reported that on the morning of February 23, the Federals had taken Fayetteville, pushing out the Confederate picket guard who set fire to the main public buildings before they left. Readers now knew that Price and McCulloch had joined forces under General Van Dorn, and that the enemy, by any estimate, substantially outnumbered Curtis's Army of the Southwest. A big battle again seemed imminent, but the news went quiet for a week, aside from a brief dispatch on March 7 saying that the Federals had pulled back a few miles to set up camp and forage.[18]

Then, on March 11, the headlines: "Great Battle at Sugar Creek. Three Days Hard Fighting. General Curtis Victorious." The report itself contained more worrisome details: The Army of the Southwest had suffered a thousand casualties—a number that would rise with the official tally. The Battle of Pea Ridge, as it came to be known, would be the largest Civil War battle fought west of the Mississippi River. Van Dorn had led an army of over 16,000 men—Price's and McCulloch's divisions and three Cherokee regiments. On the morning of March 6, they attacked Curtis's 10,250. The Confederates had a four-to-three artillery advantage to add to their superiority in manpower. Curtis, however, knew they were coming, thanks to a local man who rode through a snow storm with the news and a spy who confirmed it.

Curtis deployed a division atop the steep bluffs to the north of Little Sugar Creek and had two artillery redoubts constructed on either side of Telegraph Road. On the first day, General McCulloch was shot dead from his horse, his second-in-command was killed, and his division fell apart. Kelso's regiment experienced heavy fighting a mile northeast, at Elkhorn Tavern. On the second day, General Sigel made up for some of his earlier blunders by leading an infantry charge, breaking a rebel line that was running low on ammunition. Van Dorn's forces scattered. The victorious Federals "lost 1,384 men at Pea Ridge: 203 killed, 980 wounded (of whom perhaps 150 later died), and 201 missing and presumed captured." Confederate losses are harder to ascertain. Of the 16,500 that started the march, "fewer than 14,000 reached Pea Ridge, and fewer than 13,000 were engaged," and they suffered at least 2,000 casualties. Although these details were not in the newspapers, Kelso's 24th Missouri had 3 killed, 16 wounded, and 7 missing.[19]

Susie would have read, and wondered, and worried. But John had not fought at Pea Ridge. He had left his regiment a week and a half earlier, as the Army of the Southwest stopped its pursuit, pulled back, and assumed a defensive posture while Curtis pondered what to do next. The general thought he was facing an enemy of 20,000 to 40,000 men, camped about 30 miles south in the Boston Mountains. His supply line, stretching over 200 miles back to the railhead at Rolla, was nearing its breaking point. On February 22 Curtis had written to Halleck asking for reinforcements (7,000 infantry and 3,000 cavalry), as well as 800 horses, and 10,000 pairs of pants. He did not mention shoes, but hundreds of his soldiers, including Kelso, had their shoes give out and were walking through the snow with their feet wrapped in rags. "Pants will be sent," Halleck responded, "but cannot now send more troops or horses." Curtis felt he could neither move forward to attack the larger Confederate force nor retreat to Missouri and risk letting Price back into the state. As the days passed in camp, Kelso had begun to grow restless. He and two friends, John McConnell and James Garrison, went to General Curtis with a plan to sneak into the Confederate camp and kidnap General Price. Curtis, unsurprisingly, rejected this scheme. For a moment he considered letting Kelso go alone on a spy mission, but then dropped that idea, too, since Kelso was too well known to the Confederates. Disappointed, Kelso asked permission to leave camp and return to southwest Missouri to recruit a company and earn a commission as a captain. Apparently, Kelso's kidnapping scheme had not convinced Curtis that Kelso lacked the judgment for field command; the general granted this request, and Kelso, alone, left the Army of the Southwest and headed north in a pair of new shoes he had somehow obtained.[20]

So, in the days before Pea Ridge, as Curtis was consolidating his troops at Little Sugar Creek, Kelso, trying to sleep in a corncrib outside of Bentonville, Arkansas, lost a battle with a skunk. As Van Dorn in the Boston Mountains made his plans to crush Curtis and march all the way to St. Louis, Kelso was vomiting the canned oysters and butter crackers he had gorged from an abandoned supply wagon. Forty-eight hours before the big battle, as the snow fell and the armies moved into their positions, Kelso sat by a warm fire in Springfield, writing a letter to Susie, describing the gallant "boys" of the Army of the Southwest chasing the rebels into Arkansas. He heard about the "terrible battle of Pea Ridge" a few days later and regretted missing his chance.[21]

His recruiting did not go exactly as planned. He gathered over a hundred recruits in Christian and Barry counties, more than enough to form a company. While on a scout with them, though, they were arrested, disarmed, and forced to ride under guard to Keetsville by a treacherous lieutenant in the 4th Iowa Infantry who refused to examine Kelso's authorizing paperwork. Then Kelso learned that Colonel Boyd had misled him again, telling him that he could recruit for the cavalry when the new men would have to be foot soldiers. Half of his recruits refused and joined the 14th Missouri State Militia (MSM) cavalry regiment instead, merging with recruits raised by Kelso's Buffalo friend, Milton Burch. Kelso got a transfer from the 24th Missouri Infantry and joined them. He lost a close election to Burch for captain, but was chosen to be a first lieutenant. If he had to serve under anyone in the company, he was glad it was Burch, "an excellent man in every way." Kelso was happy to receive his lieutenant's commission, having come to regret his impetuous decision the previous fall to enlist as a private to prove a point about patriotism. "I had now learned that a pair of officer's straps alone," he wrote, "outweighed the highest degree of valor, patriotism, intelligence, and moral worth without them." Besides, his "family sorely needed the fair pay that I would now receive" and his "social position in the army would be greatly elevated." Susie would appreciate the extra money and, perhaps, the new prestige.[22]

"MY DEAR SUSIE," Kelso began a letter to his wife from Springfield on June 6, 1862, narrating the disastrous Battle of Neosho, which had occurred on May 31. Kelso had just given testimony for an inquiry into the conduct of his commander, Colonel John M. Richardson of the 14th MSM Cavalry. The officer conducting the inquiry, Lieutenant Colonel James K. Mills, commander of the post at Springfield, noted that "there is scarcely a point upon which the testimony is not contradictory." The soldiers who fought told very different stories about the battle. The officers investigating the defeat came to different conclusions about who deserved blame. Richardson said that after he had been shot off his horse, the men panicked without his leadership. Mills gave Richardson the benefit of the doubt and seemed to shift responsibility to the junior officers, including Kelso, and to the undisciplined men. Brigadier General Egbert B. Brown, who headed the Southwestern Division of the MSM at Springfield, concluded that the blame rested almost solely on Richardson. So did Kelso, who, still fuming as he wrote to Susie, declared that Richardson was utterly incompetent and possibly treasonous.[23]

Before the war, John M. Richardson had been a lawyer, a newspaper editor, and a prominent politician in the Missouri Democratic Party. He served as a state representative and was Missouri's secretary of state under Governor Sterling Price (1853–1856), but he was a strong Unionist and voted for Lincoln in 1860. When the Missouri State Militia was formed, he helped organize a cavalry regiment of men from the counties surrounding Springfield. Commissioned as a colonel, he donned a uniform with eagles on his straps and called the green troops under his command his "Mountain Rangers," boasting that the mere name of his mighty men would scare all the rebels out of southwest Missouri. Kelso described the doughty colonel as a Don Quixote "burning with a desire to win for his own brows the laurels of the conqueror."[24]

The inquiry at Springfield must have begun, as the reports did, with the situation at Neosho, in the state's southwest corner, when the Mountain Rangers arrived on May 29. Five companies of the 14th MSM cavalry, including Kelso's Company H, along with a company from the 10th Illinois Cavalry, had marched the 40 miles from Mt. Vernon and set up camp on the edge of town. With Curtis's Army of the Southwest far away in central Arkansas and the Confederates just beginning to scrape together another army for the Trans-Mississippi in Little Rock, warfare in Missouri would be conducted by smaller forces. The Federals got word that about 400 men—or perhaps 500, or 600—under the joint command of Colonel Stand Watie and Colonel John T. Coffee were prowling the region. Stand Watie was a leader of the Cherokee Nation and had become a colonel of the Confederacy's 1st Regiment, Cherokee Mounted Volunteers. Coffee had commanded the 6th Missouri Cavalry of the State Guard, but he operated independently of Gen. Price's forces and from the Confederate army. Richardson claimed that the latest intelligence had the enemy at least 40 miles away. The Mountain Rangers were at that time, Kelso wrote, "Raw recruits" sitting on old saddles they brought from home and "armed with old style muzzle-loading muskets." Kelso, who had been out leading a ten-man scouting party, arrived after Richardson had established the camp and was alarmed at what he saw.[25]

How did you pitch your camp, Colonel Richardson? Lieutenant Colonel Mills would have asked the commander of the Mountain Rangers this central question as the wounded warrior—his arm in a sling, his stiff leg sticking straight out from the chair, his head, no doubt, held high—sat in Mills's Springfield office. "I was careful in selecting the camp," Richardson insisted. It was the same ground, he said, that the great General Sigel had chosen when he had been in Neosho before joining Curtis for the plunge into Arkansas a few months earlier. Kelso, however—and, he said, the other experienced junior officers—thought that the problems with the campsite were obvious and dangerous. On the side of the camp toward the enemy was a steep hill covered in brush. Attacking from that hill, the enemy would have a great advantage and, Kelso thought, "would be sure to defeat us." At first, he thought the colonel had only temporarily halted the troops on the vulnerable spot. "To my surprise and dismay, however, the men were soon commanded to [put] up their tents upon this ground—the very ground that the enemy would have selected for us, had the selection been left to them." Kelso suspected that Richardson had chosen to camp at Neosho because he wanted to set up his headquarters in a house in his former hometown, where he would drink wine, dine on oysters, and enjoy "the smiles and the wit of a bevy of rebel women, beautiful and bright, old friends of the Colonel."[26]

And how, Colonel Richardson, did you establish the picket guards? "I saw to placing the pickets in person," Richardson answered. Kelso testified, and then explained to Susie in his letter, that the camp was "very badly guarded," especially with the lack of pickets on the southwest hill, "the very place above all others that should have been guarded—, and no one was permitted to ascend it to see what might be there." On the night of May 30, Kelso was in command of Company H. He lay in his tent with Lieutenant Amos Norton, and they were "restless and uneasy." Richardson and some of the convivial officers were making merry in town, and men in the other companies were fiddling, dancing, singing, and playing cards. Kelso had ordered his men to keep their tents dark and sleep in their clothes with their guns at their sides and their cartridge boxes under their heads.[27]

So, Colonel Richardson, on the night before the battle, did you convene a council of war with your officers? Yes, Richardson said. "They were all of opinion there was no danger and no necessity of moving camp." That was not what happened, according to Kelso's account. He and Norton were worrying in their tent. Prisoners that Kelso's squad had taken had said that Stand

Watie's men were only a few miles away. A Black man from town had come to the camp, warning of an attack. "A Union woman, also, had sent us word that the college grounds, near her house, and *within rifle range of our camps*, were full of men and horses." Dogs barked on the hill, and someone thought he heard three gunshots from that direction, too. Kelso, placing his ear to the ground, thought he heard "a low rumbling as of the distant trampling of many horses."[28]

Kelso and Norton decided that they had to go see Richardson. On their way they were joined by Captain Stephen Julian and a few other "prudent officers." At Richardson's headquarters, the colonel and his officers gathered around Kelso's group as Kelso voiced their concerns and asked permission to go scout the hill. The colonel refused, and "the festive officers, who had never yet smelt gun-powder" made "some insinuations of cowardice" about Kelso, Norton, Julian, and the others from the camp. "Even the Colonel, with a very brave look, said: 'It is very natural for some men to be chicken-hearted.' He then proceeded to assure us that all the reports that had reached us were rebel lies fabricated for the purpose of scaring us away." Richardson was certain that the enemy was far off, and, in any case, would not dare to attack him. Kelso returned to his tent, "smarting under the covert insults," and pondered reconnoitering the hill without permission, but decided against it.[29]

Kelso expected the attack at dawn, but the sun rose and nothing happened. The men ate breakfast and by an order the colonel had issued the previous evening began to lead their horses, without bridles or saddles, to the creek to drink. A group of officers told Kelso they had orders to go to the town jail to search for ammunition supposedly hidden there. At the urging of some Neosho ladies, the colonel also ordered another group of officers to go to the courthouse to raise an American flag. Strange coincidence, Kelso said later: at the very time when the men were away from their weapons watering their un-saddled horses, and the officers were away from their men, the enemy attacked.

Colonel Richardson, what happened at 8:00 a.m. when the enemy opened fire from the brush from the southwest? "You may suppose that the camp was surprised," Richardson answered. "Such was not the case." I first noticed the enemy when a small detachment of rebels tried to capture the camp sentinels, and the alarm was raised, Richardson said. His troops immediately mounted and formed lines. The rebels began firing when still 300 yards away, too far for the bullets to reach the Mountain Rangers, and then the enemy advanced very slowly. There was plenty of time to prepare. "A careful inspection of the enemy satisfied me their main strength and best arms was in the center," and if we broke them there victory would be ours. Company A was positioned to make a charge, but it was in a state of confusion when Richardson reached it until its commander, Lieutenant Wilson, under heavy fire, reformed the men "into as perfect a line as I ever saw on dress parade. My heart bounded with joy at such noble and gallant conduct of the young officer and the steady firmness of the men." Richardson ordered a saber charge, and the rebels broke and ran back to the brush line. Meanwhile, Lieutenant Norton and Company H were exchanging fire with the enemy on the left. Confident that "the day would be ours," Richardson turned "to give orders for my troops to take position on ground selected by myself for the action." Then a bullet hit him in the arm, and his horse was shot out from under him. In his fall, he dislocated his shoulder and sprained his wrist; his horse fell on him, pinning his left leg to the ground. "My troops, supposing their commander killed, and no other field officer being present to take command, became discouraged, confused, and began to leave. . . . I attribute the loss of the day to my misfortune in being crippled and the want of another field officer to take command."[30]

But why wasn't another field officer there to take command? "Four of my best officers—Captains Julian and Burch and Lieutenants Worley and Kelso—were unfortunately absent, the three former on duty," Richardson explained. "They made a desperate effort to get into the action. These gallant officers in their effort to get by my side subjected themselves to the fire of one whole company of rebels. It was a terrible gauntlet to run, but they came through it unharmed; too late, however, to aid in saving the day. They proved themselves entirely worthy of my confidence and are entitled to that of the Government."[31]

Kelso's account was quite different. He had been told that he, too, had been ordered to go with the other officers to the jail to look for ammunition. While there, they heard some boys at the door shout, "They're shoot'n! They're run'n!" They then heard Indian war whoops and heavy fire. Dashing out to see "citizens scampering in all directions" and the soldiers "scattered about the town running toward our camps," they began to race back to their tents and their weapons—about 400 yards. As they were "streaking it down an open street, the bullets began to whistle uncomfortably thick and close about our ears. . . . As we drew nearer, the bullets flew thicker about us. One of our men cried out that he was shot. At this, several other men ducked their heads and dived in behind houses or any other objects that could shelter them. The rest of us kept right on." As they got closer to the bush-covered hill, they heard a rebel officer shout, "Fire on that squad coming in!" At the command, "a hundred guns thundered out at once, and the bullets pattered like hail around us in the dust, or screamed through the air around our heads. How so many of us escaped, I cannot understand."[32]

The men in the camp had bridled, saddled, and mounted their horses; they were in a ragged line under some trees in an open grove. As they struggled to control their frightened horses and manage their long infantry guns, they had not yet been able to return any fire. The running officers darted behind the line and the rebels fired another volley. "The terrific crash of bullets among the foliage around us seemed sufficient to wither every-thing before it. The roar of the guns, the fearful yelling of the Indians, the rearing and the plunging of our frightened horses, the cries of our wounded as they fell to the ground, made a scene dreadful almost beyond description." Kelso wanted to reach his own men at the end of the line; he planned to have the whole command dismount and move to the shelter of a steep creek bank from which they could safely fire into the field. "Just then I heard our Colonel command: 'Mountain Rangers, charge that hill!' I knew that this was the command of an idiot, a madman, or a traitor, and I felt that the day was certainly lost."[33]

At the command to charge, Kelso told Susie, only one man moved forward—a young soldier named Wesley Rice, a former student of Kelso's. Rice sprang ahead twenty yards or so, but when he saw he was alone, he turned his horse and returned to the confused line. Hit by gunfire, Colonel Richardson and his horse then crumpled to the ground. The line broke, and the men turned to flee, galloping back toward Kelso, crowding toward a corral gate behind him. In an instant, he was caught amidst horses rushing for the gate. "In a compact mass they ran over me, knocked me down, knocked my hat off; bruised my right knee and skimmed my right hand. I tried to rise, but could not succeed in doing so. There was no room for me between the closely packed bodies of the horses. My head was jarred and bruised by the knees and the hooves of the terrified animals, and I was again knocked down and rolled forward in the dust among their frantically trampling feet." He tried to stand up, but was knocked back down. "To keep my hands and arms from being broken, I now drew them under my body, and lay still with my face to the ground till the whole command had passed over me. By a strange kind of instinct, the horses, though they could not see me, avoided stepping directly upon me. Some of them, however, not lifting their feet quite high enough as they stepped over me, bruised the back of my head with the corks of their shoes."[34]

When they had all passed over him, Kelso arose, covered in dust—coughing, spitting, wiping his eyes. Instead of joining his retreating men, he sprinted closer to the enemy—he needed to get his gun and his horse. "Several bullets screamed past me as I entered my tent. Several more passed through it while I was inside of it. Snatching up my revolvers, but leaving my saber, I ran with my saddle and my bridle to my horse a few yards away." His horse, Hawk Eye, tied to a nearby apple tree, was rearing and trying to break away. Kelso tried to calm him, and then quickly bridle, saddle, and untie him. "During this process, my coolness was severely tested." He was the only Federal soldier left for the enemy to shoot at, so the firing grew brisker. Seeing a body of cavalry to the north crossing a cornfield, and thinking they were a Federal scouting party just returned, he galloped to join them.[35]

Because of the clouds of dust, and because his terrified horse was racing nearly out of control, Kelso had almost joined this group before realizing his mistake. When he drew close he saw that the horsemen were mostly Indians, "dressed in fantastic hunting shirts," standing in their stirrups with their guns ready to shoot. Apparently, they took the hatless, bedraggled, dust-covered soldier racing toward them to be one of Colonel Coffee's men, for they paid little attention to him. He turned and galloped back toward the camp. "Again the bullets began to scream through the air around me, and my horse was slightly wounded in his right shoulder." He saw loose horses and mules, and some that were dead or dying, but, surprisingly, only two dead men. Confederate infantry had come down the hill and into the camp to the west, the Indians were in the cornfield to the north, and another body of cavalry blocked his escape route to the south. The fourth side of the box he found himself in was a high fence by a house, and then another fence beyond it. "My scalp began to feel loose upon my head. I turned my horse to the first fence. Would he leap it? He did leap it, bounding over like a deer. Turning quickly around the house so as to have it between myself and the enemy who were still firing upon me, I charged the other fence. My horse, my brave old Hawk Eye, leaped that also in fine style." But then he almost crashed into the rear of another body of rebel cavalry. He turned to avoid them, and headed for the brush.[36]

As he approached the brush line, he started to see some Federals escaping on foot. "The first one of our own men that I saw was Col. Richardson himself, alone, on foot, and quite lame from the fall of the horse upon his leg. Badly as he had managed, I wished to save him. I tried to reach him to let him have my horse. Before I could overtake him, however, he reached the brush and disappeared." (According to a later county history, when Richardson, hobbling alone through the woods north of town after the battle, met a civilian who was also fleeing, the colonel, mistaking the man for one of the enemy, "offered to surrender to him.")

Kelso saw "the brave old Captain Julian," too, who was "making remarkably good time for a man of his age"—forty—"and his weight." Once Kelso made it to the shelter of the brush, he found James Brewer, a private in his company, lying partly in the water of a shallow creek with both his femurs broken. He then found a dozen or so other men in the woods, two badly wounded with buckshot, as well as a sick boy and an old man who had also fled the battle. Those who could travel walked all night. They suffered quite a bit from thirst along the way: "but, having found a mining shaft that contained water, we made rope of hickory bark and, tying these to our boots, managed to draw up enough water to quench our thirst. The water was pretty strongly flavored with the sweat in our boots and with the rotten flesh of rabbits that had fallen into the shaft and then drowned. It was drink this or die, however, and we drank it." They made it back to Mt. Vernon by noon the next day.[37]

On the first of June, Colonel Stand Watie happily described the rout to his brigade commander: "The enemy were taken completely by surprise. At the first fire of our troops, they attempted to form, returned a volley at random, then broke and fled in the utmost confusion, our troops advancing rapidly upon them all the time." It was a good haul for 10 minutes' work: "Fourteen tents, five wagons and teams, arms, horses, some commissary stores and ammunition, and, in fact, all the enemy's baggage, fell into the hands of the Confederates." The Federals lost everything they had kept in their tents; Kelso mourned the loss of his books. The American flag, Watie noted, had only been "allowed to wave about a quarter of an hour on the steeple of the court-house at Neosho."[38]

Lieutenant Colonel Mills, conducting the inquiry and sifting through the contradictory accounts, ended up deflecting blame from Colonel Richardson and casting suspicion upon the junior officers. Mills recommended against filing charges against the colonel. It may not have been wise to pitch the camp so close to the brush-covered hill, Mills acknowledged, but a final judgment on that matter could not be made without walking the actual ground at Neosho. Richardson had taken all the usual precautions in posting the picket guards, Mills wrote, "save the unaccountable neglect to post a picket upon the hill," but he had, Mills believed, sent someone to scout the hill the evening before the battle. Richardson had that evening also sent scouts to the college yard, rumored to be full of men and horses, but they did not find anything. That the colonel had ordered or permitted all his main officers to be away from camp at the same time "deserves reprehension," but on this point, too, Mills argued, "the colonel commanding had the right to exercise his own judgment and discretion" and "should be held accountable only in case the lack of prudence on his part was extreme."[39]

For Mills, the central questions about the affair were not about Richardson's actions at Neosho at all. First, why were "certain officers" absent from camp at the time of the attack? Since the colonel had testified to ordering the others, this must refer to Kelso, who in the colonel's account accompanied them to the jail of his own accord. Second, why, when Richardson fell, did the next ranking officer not assume command, and why did not all the officers try "to rally the men after they first broke?" The performance of the junior officers urgently required "further investigation." Third, why did the men flee within 10 minutes of the first shot? The "screaming and whooping of the Indians" may have made their "untrained horses unmanageable," and the panicked flight of the civilian residents and refugees may have confused and alarmed them, but neither of these were adequate excuses. About the behavior of the men, Mills could only conclude "that the regiment is deficient in both drill and discipline, having little confidence in the arms with which they are supplied."[40]

Kelso was stunned when he heard that Richardson was not going to be charged. He could only conclude that Mills had been bought off, and the only question, really, was how much Richardson had to pay. Kelso wrote in his autobiography that he learned later that the enemy had attacked at 8:00 a.m. because they had found out that the men would be away from their weapons, leading their horses to the creek. He learned, too, that getting the officers away to raise the flag and inspect the jail was a scheme executed by the colonel's lady friends: "Whether our Colonel weakly permitted his fair rebel charmers to make all these plans for him, including the time of their execution . . . [or] he deliberately contracted with the enemy to place us in their power, I do not know." Was Richardson an idiot, a madman, or a traitor? One more piece of information tipped Kelso toward the third choice. The officer who led the Confederates down that brush-covered hill, Kelso came to believe, was none other than "our Colonel's old friend and law partner, Rick Johnson."[41]

General Brown followed Mills' recommendation not to prosecute Richardson, though he did not fully agree with the lieutenant colonel's conclusions. Brown's final report was brief and blunt. He read the reports by Richardson and Mills, but also mentioned "other sources" of information. He faulted Richardson for placing the camp where he did. He concluded that a lack "of proper precaution against surprise and foolhardiness in not taking a defensive position when it was known by the commander that a force of about 600 men was near him, the want of discipline, and doubt of the men in their arms were the causes of Colonel Richardson's defeat." Richardson was

banished to a desk job in Rolla, "a safe distance," as Kelso put it, "both from
the enemy and from his own men." At least the higher-ups recognized, Kelso
thought, that it would be "madness" to let the colonel again command a regiment in the field. Unbeknownst to Kelso, apparently, this madness did come
to pass: Richardson was commanding the post at Cassville by November 1862
and leading troops in battle within a month.[42]

"MY DEAR SUSIE," Kelso began his letters to his wife throughout the
war—or he began with similar forms of possessive endearment: "My
Dearest Susie," "My Own Dear Sweet Susie," "My Own Loved Susie." And
he often concluded urging her to remain true to him—"Be my own dear
Susie yet"—or with exhortations about what they should both strive to be
for each other: "Be my happy gentle Susie, and I will try to be your brave and
noble Johnny." In these letters, most of which have not survived, he spoke of
how he loved and missed her and hoped she felt the same. He talked about
the children, and about mundane domestic concerns—his pay, her teaching
school, selling a wagon. He reported on friends he had seen during brief
stops at Buffalo: army wives fighting loneliness, old folks in health and sickness, and children growing up fast. He told her how her brother Tillman
and other soldiers she knew were faring in the army. But he also tried to give
her "almost a full account of all my military achievements" and his other
dangerous and thrilling "adventures." He composed these narratives, as he
had written his accounts of skirmishing with Price's army on the chase into
Arkansas or having bullets scream by his head at Neosho, seemingly oblivious that she might respond differently than he did. "Imagine your Johnny"
infiltrating a band of "thieves and murderers," he wrote in the spring of
1863: the "very great danger" that "menaced" his life as he did so held an
"indescribable fascination," he told her. When he wrote of gunfights with
bushwhackers or cavalry assaults on rebel soldiers, he expected her to share
the thrill and admire his courage rather than be consumed with worry or
knotted with anger that he so clearly seemed to seek out the most dangerous
assignments.[43]

In some letters, he looked toward the end of the war, and the happy life
they would be able to rebuild; in others he doubted whether he would survive
to see peace restored. In August of 1864, he chided her for not taking an opportunity to come visit him: "We may not be able to pass many more happy
times together. The storms of war are growing darker. Three days ago . . . I was
again in battle where the bullets flew thick as hail. I saw several of my brave
boys fall mangled and bleeding around me. As I stopped over one of them, he

looked up, his glazing eyes brightening, and said: '*Captain, I am killed; but, thank God! I die in a good cause!*'" Kelso expected Susie's love to reinforce his devotion to his "boys" and to their noble effort: "I have mourned deeply over three fallen heroes, and oh! how I have longed to see you and to hear your words of love," he wrote. "The boys seem to think that they can not fight without me, and I mean to go with them hereafter on every scout. . . . I shall strive to be foremost in every conflict, and, in so many scenes of carnage, I am likely soon to meet the death that I have always wished to die,—the death of a hero fighting for his country, for the cause of universal liberty, for the general good of mankind." He did not fear death, he told her, and at times he almost welcomed it. "All that I wish is that I might be permitted to breathe my last sigh on your bosom, Susie, and go from earth gazing in your love-lit eye. My love for you, Susie, grows stronger as the storms grow darker around us."[44]

His pleas for her emotional sustenance can seem pathetic. "I mean to be such a man as you will be proud of, if you *can* be proud of one who seems born for misfortune only, and who has, unintentionally, been the cause of so much sorrow and suffering to yourself. O Susie! how much I wish to be *worthy* of your admiration! Then you would *love* me with that devotion with which I have *so long clung to you*." When he learned that his mother had died, he mourned her, remembering how she had called him her "own dear boy" and had loved him all the more when others had forsaken him. "Whose '*own dear boy*' am I now," he asked Susie, "and who will love '*Johnny*' as she did? . . . In all the wide world there are now none to love me but my sweet Susie and my dear little ones. But you will love me more, Susie, now that I need your affection so much. . . . You have the key to my heart, and can make me happy and good, or wretched and reckless."[45]

Like a chivalrous knight crusading with a handkerchief of his fair maiden, Kelso needed to adore a woman as an angelic "idol," and he needed her to reciprocate not only to validate what he did but also who he was, or tried to be. With Susie, however, there was also something else gnawing at his insecurities. In 1862, when she was away at Collinsville, he worried she would be seduced by the charming Dr. Hovey. The doctor frankly professed his "free love" principles, not believing that the human heart—or perhaps one's "whole person"—needed to be constrained by social customs or marriage vows. Kelso sensed from the glances of this "fascinating but unscrupulous" man that the doctor was interested in Susie. She was obviously pleased with Hovey's kind attentions, but Kelso portrayed her in his mind as an innocent and unsuspecting victim of the doctor's charms. Dr. Hovey's wife, Caroline, an otherwise admirable woman, looked away from her husband's flirtations and philandering, though Kelso was sure that had she been in Collinsville, she would have protected Susie. Mrs. Hovey and her children, however, had returned to Missouri, leaving Dr. Hovey to linger indefinitely, attending to business, in Collinsville. Kelso wanted Susie to return, too, but in the summer of 1862 he thought southwest Missouri still too dangerous: "it seems almost useless for you any way to come back to a country in which men are almost daily shot down at their plows or in their own door-yards." Kelso was a man who could sometimes see secret intrigues and conspiracies where there were none, and in this case his jealousies could have been kindled by a soldier's loneliness and a husband's neediness. Separated from them by hundreds of miles, though, Kelso could not determine if his suspicions about Dr. Hovey and Susie had any merit.[46]

8

Thieves, Cut-Throats,
and Confederates

KELSO AND TEN of his men chased three rebel horsemen into the village of Dubuque, Arkansas, not far from the Missouri border. Sergeants John Smith and John Baxter, mounted on the company's fastest horses, were in the lead, with Kelso on Hawk Eye galloping not far behind. Smith, Baxter, and two of the rebels entered the village in a cloud of dust. Gunshots rang out, and the two enemies fell from their horses to the ground. The Confederates stationed at Dubuque, members of the 14th regiment, Arkansas Infantry, "were nearly all scattered about among the houses eating their dinners. Many of them did not even have their guns with them. Their surprise was complete, their panic uncontrollable." They didn't even try to resist and "fled like frightened sheep in all directions. Dashing up the streets after them, we cut them down like green mullein stalks in an old meadow," Kelso wrote. "I got two for my share. Smith and Baxter did better. All of my men did well. How many of the enemy were killed in all, I do not know. Not one of my party received any injury." After the fight—or, rather, "the slaughter"—was over, Kelso and his men "burned their barracks, plundered their sutler store and the village post-office, and then departed as we had come in a cloud of dust. Burch and the rest of our comrades were highly pleased with our report."[1]

On their way back toward Missouri, they "met a party of half a dozen or more rebel militiamen who had not yet heard of our approach. They fired upon us, and then fled, through an open wood, scattering as they fled. Several of them were overtaken and slain. I got one more here, making three for me that day." The next day they "captured a small party, mostly officers." One man refused to surrender and tried to escape through a cornfield. As the man's brother watched, the Union soldiers aimed and fired. The runner fell amidst

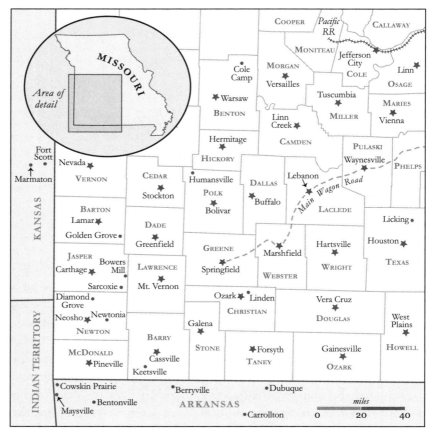

Southwest Missouri during the Civil War. Drawn by Rebecca Wrenn. Map source: "Southwestern Missouri in 1864," parts 1 and 2, in Bruce Nichols, *Guerrilla Warfare in Civil War Missouri*, vol. 4, *September 1864–June 1865* (Jefferson, N.C.: McFarland, 2014), 12–13.

the ripening corn. "Two of the captured officers were brothers of the name of Herd," Kelso recounted. "They were thorough gentlemen, and I feel sure that, by our courteous treatment of them while they were our prisoners, Burch and I made them our warm personal friends." In Civil War Missouri, occasionally combatants would invoke law or honor or even friendship to mitigate the cruelties of combat. More often, they cut each other down.[2]

IN THE SPRING of 1862, the Union command in Missouri faced several problems, the most prominent being a lack of manpower, nearly constant guerrilla warfare, and depredations by Kansas Jayhawkers on the western border. After Sterling Price's troops were defeated at Pea Ridge, the Union could redeploy forces to help the broader war effort. In early April, the Battle of Shiloh on the Tennessee River cost the Union 13,000 casualties. Farther east, General McClellan's Army of the Potomac had finally begun its Peninsular Campaign by moving from Washington down the Potomac River and Chesapeake Bay and up toward the Confederate capitol at Richmond, Virginia. McClellan's army would be defeated by Robert E. Lee's Army of Northern Virginia at the Seven Days' Battles in late June, costing the Union 15,800 men killed, wounded, missing, or captured. So the Federals needed more troops elsewhere. But the redeployment of Missouri infantry regiments left troop levels in the state dangerously low. Brigadier General John M. Schofield, who replaced General Halleck, reported that in June there were only 17,360 soldiers for the entire state. The recently organized MSM Cavalry, posted at small bases, would ride out on patrols to battle the numerous small bands of guerrillas that were sabotaging railroads, cutting telegraph lines, stealing or destroying property, ambushing soldiers, and murdering loyal civilians. The cavalry also engaged the larger bodies of irregulars—often numbering in the hundreds—operating quasi-independently from the Confederate command, or the companies organized by Confederate recruiters that moved through the state. After the debacle at Neosho, Kelso's 14th Cavalry MSM, particularly the companies of Greene County men (E, G, and H) commanded by captains Julian, Breedan, and Burch, became in the summer and fall of 1862 a potent counter-insurgency force in southwest Missouri. It was in these months, too, that Kelso emerged as a noted guerrilla hunter.[3]

The small, scattered cavalry regiments, however, still left the state exposed to larger forces that could strike quickly up from Arkansas. The state's military and civilian authorities created the Enrolled Missouri Militia (EMM), conscripting all able-bodied loyal men into local units that could quickly be called into active duty in an emergency. This call to arms, because it forced men who had tried to stay out of the fight to choose sides, had the unintended effect of driving more Missourians into the local guerrilla bands. So did the announcement of the Emancipation Proclamation.[4]

Union commanders despaired that guerrillas, often called bushwhackers, were infesting the countryside and spreading terror through the loyal populace. How to fight them and beat them proved to be an enormous challenge. Supported by their kin and by secret networks of Southern sympathizers, the bushwhackers seemed to be ordinary farmers until they donned elaborate shirts or the blue uniforms they stripped from the bodies of their military victims when they rode and attacked. Hiding in wooded hills and creek bottoms, striking from the bush on fast horses, shooting at close range with the multiple revolvers pulled from holsters strapped to their bodies and saddles, and then dispersing and vanishing back into the countryside, bushwhackers were an elusive and dangerous enemy. Because they violated the laws of civilized warfare, military commanders revised the rules of engagement. When Kelso explained to Susie, more than once, that "*We* do not trouble head-quarters much with prisoners. *We* prefer patronizing the *brimstone* head-quarters," he was not just expressing his own hardened attitude toward the enemy, or the harsh practices of his company or of the 14th Cavalry MSM. He was describing Union policy throughout the state and beyond.[5]

That policy took shape in the winter and spring of 1862. After saboteurs killed civilians in train derailments, General Halleck ordered on March 13 that guerrillas caught in the act of damaging railroads would be shot on sight, and that those accused and found guilty would be executed. Angered that General Price was encouraging the guerrilla bands and promoting war crimes, Halleck issued General Orders No. 18 on May 29: "The utmost vigilance and energy are enjoined upon all the troops of the state in hunting down and destroying these robbers and assassins. When caught in arms, engaged in their unlawful warfare, they will be shot down on the spot."[6]

The Missouri bushwhackers that cavalrymen like Kelso hunted were a mixed bunch. Some were former Confederate soldiers who wanted to serve the cause closer to home. Clifton Holzclaw, a Confederate commander at the Battle of Pea Ridge, became a guerrilla captain noted for his brutality toward Unionists who supported the enlistment of Blacks. Frank James (Jesse's brother) served in the regular Confederate army before becoming a bushwhacker and then a postwar outlaw. Other Missouri guerrillas were connected to the Confederate command through kinship. Bill Jackson, for example, was the son of Claiborne Fox Jackson, the secessionist governor. Jo Shelby, after serving as an officer in the State Guard, led guerrillas near his home in Lafayette County before becoming a Confederate officer and commanding some of the forces Kelso would face at the Battle of Springfield. Many of the men fighting with Sterling Price would spend part of the war as guerrillas and part as regulars.[7]

Other bushwhackers grabbed their guns and saddled up less in devotion to the Confederacy than because they imagined themselves protecting their own "Southern rights" in Missouri and their own families from Northern "tyranny." By Southern rights they meant a right to property, including the ownership of people of African descent, and the right to erect local, state, and national governments protecting that "property." They defended their families against any who threatened an economic well-being connected to the slave economy (even if they did not personally own slaves), against the depredations of Federal soldiers, and against the free Black marauders who, they imagined, would take their women if abolition ever came to pass. Some had few ideological motivations of any sort. Young men sought the thrill of battle without having to endure the discipline and deprivations of regular military life. The criminally inclined exploited the breakdown of civil order to rob for their own profit and kill people they did not like. Militant White supremacists were mythologized as freedom fighters and sociopathic criminals as folk heroes.[8]

Some Missouri bushwhackers fought, or claimed to fight, for personal revenge. After seeing relatives killed and his mother's house burnt down, and then being wounded himself by Federals, Sam Hildebrand in the spring of 1862 began his career as a prolific murderer of unarmed Unionists. A similar story has been connected to Bill Wilson, later fictionalized in a novel and a Clint Eastwood film as "the Outlaw Josey Wales," but Wilson was already "a well known Bushwhacker and Marauder" before Federal authorities burned down his house and harassed his family. "Bloody Bill" Anderson was already a guerrilla when the collapse of a prison roof injured one sister, crippled another, and killed a third, but his cruelty intensified after this accident, which he blamed on the Federals. Notorious guerrilla leader William Quantrill claimed he was avenging the death of his brother at the hands of Union soldiers, but he was lying: he had no such brother.[9]

Quantrill was an opportunist and petty criminal from Ohio who had courted anti-slavery men before switching sides. He usually found targets in west-central Missouri, as in Cass County in November 1862, when he and 300 of his men battled a Union detachment led by Kelso's comrade from the Neosho fight and the Medlock raid, Captain Mastin Breedan. Quantrill's gang was unusually large and especially brutal. Capturing a steamboat transporting escaped slaves to freedom, Quantrill's men lined up ten Black men in front of the other passengers and shot them in the head. After Quantrill's attack on Ft. Blair in Baxter Springs, Kansas in the fall of 1863, most of the 80 dead men, including General Samuel Curtis's son Henry, had suffered head wounds at close range, indicating that they had been executed while surrendering. Quantrill's most famous raid occurred two months earlier. He led 450 guerrillas into Lawrence, Kansas, where they plundered, burned, and slaughtered over 200 unarmed men and boys.[10]

"Bloody Bill" Anderson was a Quantrill sub-chief who helped depose the chief in the spring of 1864. Although in a newspaper manifesto Anderson, the former horse thief, claimed to disdain men who robbed and fought for self-interest rather than higher principles (by which he meant revenge), he stole from Northerners and Southerners alike, collecting a "tax" like a local warlord running a protection racket. He shot a man in the head for his watch, choked a woman for her valuables, shot another woman in the back when she tried to run away, and raped a twelve-year-old Black girl. To get information from an unarmed civilian about where loot was stashed, his men pulled out the man's toenails with pliers, cut off his fingers, and then hanged him almost to death, all in front of his wife and ten-month-old baby. Finally, they shot him and burned down his widow's house. In a "bacchanalia of drinking, theft, vandalism, and bloodlust" in Centralia, Missouri, in the fall of 1864, Anderson had his men pull 23 unarmed soldiers off a train and force them to strip off their uniforms. After taking one prisoner, they gunned down the other twenty-two. Anderson's guerrilla band became known for scalping, skinning, castrating, and decapitating their victims. One of his lieutenants, "Little Archie" Clements, was especially fond of slitting throats and mutilating corpses, but he was hardly the only one. Band member Hamp Watts admitted in his memoir that such men with "predatory instincts and natures" were useful and that "the time, opportunities and conditions" of Civil War Missouri "gave them power."[11]

Soldiers defending the Union were supposed to treat the uniformed Confederate combatants that they captured decently as prisoners of war; guerrillas, however, could be shot, their bodies left where they dropped. But when General Halleck issued his orders in the spring of 1862, he knew that not all the war crimes were being committed by the enemy. Union troops and ir-regular paramilitary bands from Kansas—collectively called Jayhawkers, with the irregulars sometimes identified as "Red Legs"—plundered, burned, and occasionally killed Missourians on the western border. The conflict there ex-tended and amplified the border war between anti- and proslavery forces that had raged in the 1850s; many of the Jayhawkers had been previously terrorized by proslavery "border ruffians" and were getting their revenge. Some attacked to liberate slaves, weaken slaveholders, and punish traitors who had risen up in arms against the United States. Others stole for their own profit and killed to settle old scores. In January 1862, the 7th Kansas Cavalry crossed the border and burned about 230 buildings in Cass and Johnson counties, killing at least nine men and cropping the ear of another, marking him like a hog. Within days of condemning Price's railroad saboteurs, Halleck proposed a similar fate for the Unionist Jayhawkers: "I will now keep them out of Missouri," he wrote to Secretary of War Stanton, "or have them shot."[12]

Not all Union soldiers committing crimes were from Kansas. Sometimes Missouri Union troopers, frustrated that conservative Unionists were coddling the very Southern sympathizers who were surreptitiously supporting the rebel bushwhackers, took matters into their own hands, freelancing as "Midnight Riders" to rob and murder suspected rebels. Others used the war and their uniforms to pursue their own agendas. As District of Central Missouri commander Brigadier General James Totten wrote in mid-April 1862, "Private quarrels of long standing, originating out of matters concerned with property, county politics, and neighborhood disagreement" were "made to appear as connected with the rebellion."[13]

Some crime rings, too, operated through or in collusion with local military units. Whether connected to politics and principle or not, cycles of local violence began and continued with the eye-for-an-eye logic of retribution. Unionists also used the tool of terror and committed atrocities: a soldier shot a rebel farmer as the man's small children clung to his legs; infantrymen took a fourteen-year-old boy who had aided bushwhackers and stuffed him through a hole in the river ice; troopers left a man pinned to a tree with bayonets; militiamen left a body missing its ears. By 1863, Unionist hit squads were operating near Springfield and in other locales across the state, answering attacks by guerrillas. Some of the violence meted out to civilians was administered by the part-time soldiers in poorly disciplined units of the EMM, but regular units had their problems, too. Kelso's own regiment, the 14th (later the 8th) MSM, was already known for abuses by the spring of 1862.[14]

The Union command tried—sometimes—to prosecute lawbreakers within their own ranks. After a punitive raid by 25 soldiers burned 23 homes and killed 10 men in southeastern Missouri, headquarters in St. Louis began a war crimes inquiry. In the northwestern part of the state, Union commanders arrested and jailed members of a Unionist vigilante group that called itself "Company Q" or the "Clear Fork Rangers," which was manned by EMM soldiers. In the northeast, after four local militiamen beat an accused guerrilla in front of a crowd and then shot him, they were arrested and tried for war crimes (though no record of the trial's outcome survives). After U.S. detective J. W. Terman went on a killing spree in Chariton County, claiming perhaps two dozen lives, he was arrested, tried, convicted, and imprisoned. In other cases, however, the Union brass simply tried to break the local cycle of violence by transferring troops committing depredations to a different part of the state. At other times, the authorities claimed to not be able to find the accused parties, often lacking the time, manpower, or inclination to look very hard.[15]

Confederates had a different view of irregular warfare and violence committed in the name of their cause. On April 21, 1862, Confederate President

Jefferson Davis legitimized guerrilla warfare and offered commissions to officers leading bands of what he called "partisan rangers." On June 17, General Thomas C. Hindman, the Confederate commander of the Trans-Mississippi Department at Little Rock after the Battle of Pea Ridge, called on men not in the regular military to organize themselves into independent companies, electing a captain when they had at least ten members, and "at once commence operations against the enemy without waiting for special instructions." The duty of these independent bands—many of which, as Hindman well knew, were already active—"will be to cut off Federal pickets, scouts, foraging parties, and trains, and to kill pilots and others on transports, attacking them day and night, and using the greatest vigor in their movement." Acting under Hindman's authority, Colonel Gideon W. Thompson mustered Quantrill's bushwhackers into the Confederate service in mid-August 1862. Both President Davis and General Hindman said that these independent guerrilla bands would be "governed in all respects by the same regulations as other troops." But it was not clear who would govern them. General Price cooperated with—but certainly did not control—rebel guerrilla chiefs in Missouri. Late in the war, on his October 1864 raid into the state, over a year after Quantrill led the massacre at Lawrence and a month after "Bloody Bill" Anderson commanded the slaughter at Centralia, Price welcomed the help of Quantrill and Anderson. Quantrill was still hiding out, but Anderson and his men, wearing plumed hats and "guerrilla shirts" embroidered by their wives and sweethearts, proudly rode into Price's camp and presented the general with silver mounted revolvers. Price objected to the scalps tied to the guerrillas' bridles but lauded Anderson, saying he wished he had 50,000 more Missouri men just like him. The regulars and the irregulars joined forces. "Little Archie" Clements, the cut-throat and corpse mutilator, helped guard Price's troops on their retreat to Arkansas, committing some side murders along the way.[16]

General Halleck in the spring of 1862 had tried to distinguish regular Confederate soldiers in uniform and on recognized battlefields from the outlaws without uniforms (or in disguise) behind the lines and in arms against the government. In August, 1862, as commander of the entire Union army, he asked Columbia professor Francis Lieber to refine the laws of war in what would become the famous "Lieber Code," issued as General Orders 100 on April 24, 1863. Lieber distinguished between "partisans" and other irregular fighters. "Partisans" were men in arms and uniforms but belonging to a corps detached from the main body of their army and operating in enemy territory. If captured, they were entitled "to all the privileges of prisoners of war." Other irregular fighters were not. Men who lacked commissions and uniforms, "armed prowlers," and rebels who rose up in arms against the occupying army, "whether called upon to do so by their own, but expelled, government or not," would be treated "as highway robbers or pirates" and given no quarter.[17]

These distinctions were much harder to make on the ground and in the moment. Few of the larger irregular military units battling the Federals in Missouri had been formally commissioned as partisan rangers. Confederate recruiting commands of several hundred men each—such as those led by Colonel John T. Coffee and Colonel Robert Lawther, who both fought Kelso's regiment—roamed through the state and the southwest prairie corridor to Arkansas. Many of the men recruited to the Confederate service were, when still in Missouri, not yet in uniform or officially mustered. The recruiting commands often joined with detachments of regular Confederate cavalry that moved up briefly from Arkansas and with local bushwhacker bands. Units led by recruiters were often indistinguishable from larger bands of raiding guerrillas, such as those commanded by Thomas R. Livingston of Newton County (the "Cherokee Spikes") or by William O. Coleman, who repeatedly attacked the Federal supply line between Rolla and Springfield. Kelso noted the mixed character of these forces when he mentioned encountering Colonel Thomas Roe Freeman's "regiment of semi-robber cavalry" on one of his spy missions. Union soldiers like Kelso sometimes captured irregulars and treated them as prisoners of war, and they sometimes shot regular Confederate soldiers who should have been taken captive. The shifting rules of engagement and quick ethical code switching depended less on the guidelines developed by General Halleck or Professor Lieber and more on the discretion of the men under fire and the exigencies of the moment.[18]

When Kelso, Breedan, and four dozen MSM cavalrymen attacked the Medlock brothers' hideout in the Ozark Mountains in the fall of 1862, they thought of their enemy as "a large band of rebel thieves and cut-throats." When he chased Captain Medlock into his cabin and shot him in the back at point-blank range, Kelso surely believed that the captain deserved what he got: the rebel outlaw was reaching for his gun when Kelso killed him. The wounded Lieutenant Medlock, however, lying on a cooling board in another cabin, also "deserved to die." Kelso would not have been blamed for finishing him off with another bullet because the man "had been guilty of committing several murders upon unarmed Union men." Kelso's commanding officers might have preferred that such an execution in the field occur after a quick "drum-head" court martial, for protocol's sake, time permitting. Kelso spared him, though, making a point about the difference between honorable and dishonorable warfare, telling Lieutenant Medlock to "quit this base robbing business, and go south and fight like a man for your cause." The younger Medlock brother lived rather than died that day because Kelso enjoyed playing the gallant in front of the man's pretty wife and glorying in his own power over life and death, saying: "Remember that it was *Kelso* who saved you."[19]

After defeating the Medlocks, Kelso and a few of his men went after a separate group of a half-dozen men at a house about 3 miles distant. He did not call them "thieves and murderers" the way he characterized yet another band in the neighborhood led by the notorious bushwhacker Alf Bolin, but merely as "armed rebels who constituted a little independent band of their own." The cavalrymen surrounded the cabin. A woman, hearing her dog bark, came to the door. Seeing Kelso taking aim from behind a fence, she grabbed two guns from the side of the house and ran at Kelso, shouting, "You cannot hurt them now, they are disarmed, they surrender." So Kelso and his men captured the rebels without incident. One of them even switched sides and joined Kelso's company. "He became a good soldier and a firm friend of mine," Kelso wrote. "How glad I have long been that I was prevented from killing him." A guerrilla could be a vicious cut-throat or an honorable man. It was hard to tell.[20]

Thomas R. Livingston was a former lead miner and saloon brawler who led his sizable band of guerrillas from 1862 through the spring of 1863 in Missouri's southwest corner. Regular Confederate commands moving through the region often teamed up with his veteran fighters. In a raid on Neosho, he seized twenty horses and twenty Black people; he kept the horses, but a few days later Black bodies were seen floating down the river. It is possible that Livingston was not responsible for these deaths, or that, if he were, Kelso had not heard of them, for he described Livingston as a daring and skillful "rebel guerrilla leader" who "carried on war in a somewhat respectable manner." Nevertheless, Livingston "protected, when they sought refuge in his camp, all the thieves and cut-throats that infected that portion of the country." Livingston's group of about 100 (though Kelso thought 300) "well-armed, well-mounted and desperate men" was too large for Kelso's MSM company to attack in an open field. The cavalrymen "had to operate secretly against smaller parties at some distance from his stronger force."[21]

The Federals learned that four officers of one of those smaller parties— a "band of murderers" led by Captain Wallace Finney—took their meals with some "women of doubtful reputation" at a house about a mile from Livingston's camp in Jasper County. Finney was "a notorious bushwhacker" who "had been guilty of murder before the war and was now an escaped convict,—a proper leader of such a band of brutal cut-throats as he had gathered about him. He boasted, and truthfully, no doubt, that he had with his own hands killed over *thirty* Union men." Most of his victims, Kelso noted, "had been unarmed citizens shot down at their own doors or while at work, and wounded men, sick men, and nurses left behind by our army. He spared none that he could reach." Burch, Kelso, and 25 of their men rode at night and approached the house at dawn.[22]

Creeping up to the house through a cornfield to scout the situation while Burch and the others waited at the edge of the forest, Kelso was spotted by some women in the yard, who started screaming. Fearing that the four rebels, inside eating breakfast, would be able to dash out to their horses and escape before Burch and his men could come up, Kelso charged the house on his own. Sprinting forward with revolvers in each hand, he started shooting when the four emerged from the doorway. One rebel, wounded, staggered into the nearby brush thicket. As Burch's men arrived and shot at two who had mounted and were escaping, Kelso pulled the fourth rebel from his horse, grappled with him, and shot him in the stomach while the man punched him in the head. The man did not drop until Kelso cracked him over the head with an empty revolver. Then Kelso finished him: "I clapped my foot on the back of his neck and pressed his head down. I drew my last revolver and put a shot through his brain." The troops soon learned that Kelso's "formidable foe was the notorious Finney himself. His dark dirt-covered face, even in death, looked like the face of a fiend. The man I had wounded was a Captain Wakeman, a brave man and so far as I know an honorable enemy. Wounded as he was he reached the brush and escaped after killing one of our own men, and severely wounding another." It is unclear why Kelso gave Wakeman, a member of the fiendish Finney's "band of brutal cut-throats," the benefit of the doubt as an "honorable man."[23]

In early December, 1862, Burch and Kelso decided to make an expedition across the border into Arkansas that would include an assault on another honorable guerrilla. The rebel captain Joseph Hale Mooney was the uncle of a friend in Kelso's own battalion, Second Lieutenant Reuben Mooney. The older Mooney had served as a private in the Confederate infantry from February to August; he was promoted to captain and by the fall was leading a band of about 75 irregulars in northern Arkansas at Tolbert's Ferry on the White River. Captain Mooney had captured some EMM soldiers, but despite the fact that the "no quarter" policy was now being regularly applied on both sides of the conflict, he treated his prisoners "remarkably well." He gave them back their blankets, filled their haversacks with provisions, and personally escorted them beyond his lines to release them, saying, "Go home, boys, and tell your friends that this is the way we treat our prisoners." Kelso wanted to return the favor: "Boys, we must go and capture that old Captain, and, by our kind treatment of him, repay him for the magnanimity which he displayed in his treatment of our prisoners."[24]

Burch commanded a detachment of forty men from the 14th, reinforced by 60 EMM militiamen, with Kelso leading the advance guard. They learned that most of Mooney's men lived at their homes, scattered through the surrounding hills, and the captain probably had only a dozen with him in camp near his large home. But first the MSM had to get past the picket station, several miles from Mooney's camp, without any alarms being sounded. Kelso's squad of 8 men captured the guards at a small two-room log cabin, and then at dawn, Burch's men surrounded Mooney's unguarded house. With Kelso in the lead, they burst through all the doors at once. One unarmed man was captured in his night clothes. Kelso rushed up the stairs, shouting that if anyone fired a shot, they would burn down the house with all of them in it. Captain Mooney met Kelso at the top of the stairs. "I'm here," he said. What did this mean? Was he surrendering? Did he propose to stand and fight? From his tone and look, Keslo thought the latter. He aimed his big shotgun at the captain, but did not pull the trigger. Mooney grabbed the gun and tried to rip it out of Kelso's hands. "He was a powerful man, above my size, and I do not know how the struggle would have terminated, had not one of my men, Sergeant Anderson, come to my assistance." When Anderson grabbed him, Mooney shouted: "I surrender! I surrender!" "Why did you not say that a good while ago?" Kelso asked, calling the Captain "several ugly names," for which he later apologized.[25]

Mooney, ever the gentleman, rewarded Kelso with a fine revolver, telling his captor that "no one but a brave man had ever carried it, and that he did not wish any man, but a brave man, ever to carry it." He asked Kelso not to part with it until the war ended or until Mooney could retake it by capturing Kelso. Kelso promised to keep it and said that if on some future occasion Mooney captured him, he would give him the pistol and another to match it. The captain then gave Burch a rifle, repeated his little speech, and invited them all to breakfast. The Federals afterward sent Mooney and the other prisoners back to Missouri under guard. When Kelso returned to camp, he made Captain Mooney, "one of nature's true noblemen," a guest in his home until the captain was exchanged for a captured Union officer and released. The two had become "warm personal friends." Mooney continued to fight "bravely and honorably" for the Confederacy until he was captured again in early 1863. "His hopes for the success of the Confederacy were now broken." After Kelso was elected to Congress in 1864, he worked to have Mooney "exempted from exchange and permitted to remain among us as a citizen." Mooney was not a Medlock or a Finney but a good man who had fought for a bad cause. When fighting the enemy, however, circumstances rarely allowed Kelso time to make that distinction.[26]

DURING THE SECOND half of 1862, Kelso was part of expeditions of as many as 200 men against enemy bases in northern Arkansas and against large bodies of horsemen riding through Missouri's southwest corner. He commanded detachments of 75 to 125 men on patrols taking rebel prisoners and killing bushwhackers, including one, Rude Arnold, who had helped burn down his house in Buffalo. He helped lead strike forces of 60 to 80 riders against outlaw nests and guerrilla hideouts. With squads of 8 to 10 men, he attacked small enemy camps. Sometimes he wound up charging a bush-whacker cabin by himself. As he fought cut-throats and Confederates, he also learned that not all the thieves were on the opposing side.[27]

In mid-July, Kelso's company moved from Springfield to Ozark, a small town of six hundred inhabitants about 15 miles south, where it would be stationed through the end of the year. He was assigned to be the provost marshal, a military officer enforcing martial law: conducting searches and seizures, making arrests, investigating citizen complaints. In his courtroom, Kelso "presided as judge, jury, attorney, and every thing else that chanced to be necessary." He made up laws and had them strictly enforced: "I was just, but I was severe." Men tried to bribe him with money, and women offered some-thing "far more powerful," but he withstood these temptations. He worked earnestly, but hated the job. He wrote to Major James H. Steger at Springfield, asking to be relieved of this duty and sent back to the field. After eight days he could tell that the sedentary desk job was bad for his health, he wrote. He was eager to serve his country in combat and make a reputation for himself as a soldier. What he did not say was that he was sure his regimental commander, Major John C. Wilber, had stuck him behind a desk out of jealousy. Kelso was successful in battle and popular with the men; Wilber was neither.[28]

In late July, Wilber marched out of Ozark with 80 men for a scout, leaving Burch in command of the remaining 75, mostly "sick men, nurses, teamsters, cooks, etc., who constituted a very poor fighting force." Burch, Kelso, and the other officers worried that they were vulnerable to attack by Confederate Colonel Robert R. Lawther's Missouri Partisan Rangers, said to be only a day's march away. (Kelso thought Lawther had "400 fine cavalry men"; Burch would report 120; Lawther himself would claim he only had 55 suitably armed for battle.) Burch and his officers decided to draw him in and fight on their own terms. They set a trap, similar to the one Kelso had tried to set for Mabary's men when he commanded the Dallas County Home Guard in the early weeks of the war. On the night of July 30, the Ozark Federals were camped in a large, open wheat field at the edge of town. At about midnight, they watched Lawther's men trot their horses out of the forest on the opposite side of the field and form a line, preparing to charge the camp. "We had expected this, hoped for it, and prepared for it. We had placed lights in our tents and had hung up coats and hats so that they would cast shadows, against the insides of the tents, resembling the shadows of men. We meant for the enemy to charge through our camps and empty their guns upon the shadows of our empty hats and our empty coats." They also stretched ropes across the camp to throw the attackers from their horses as they charged through. Kelso, commanding Company H, and Lieutenant Cleon Etter, the quartermaster, commanding Company G, hid their men near the ropes, guns ready; Captain Robertson and Lieutenant Mooney, commanding F and D on the right, would reinforce if needed or defend the opposite side if necessary.[29]

They waited. Then the silence of the still, clear summer air was broken by rebel yells and hooves that pounded like thunder as the dark mass of men and horses swept down upon the camp, firing into the empty tents. When the horses hit the ropes, they tumbled down, throwing their riders from their saddles. As Burch wrote in his report and as Kelso echoed years later in his memoir, "Then was our time." The Federals on the left opened fire. "Like young devils let loose, our boys raised their battle cry and lit up the darkness of night with the lurid flashings of their fire-arms." All was confusion. Horses reared and plunged, men scrambled on the ground, shouting, cursing, fleeing in all directions. Many ran—or, remounted, rode—for their lives through a dense grove of black-jacks, battered by low-hanging branches in their escape.[30]

Everything had worked according to plan, except that in their excitement the Ozark men had shot too high, as they saw the next morning from bullet marks high up on tree trunks and nearby houses. The MSM had only two men wounded. Burch thought the enemy probably had a dozen wounded, three perhaps mortally, and Kelso recorded a similar count in his memoir; Lawther reported only two men slightly wounded. In his report, Burch gave "the highest credit" to his men. "They seemed to regard the battle as a grand species of sport. Too much praise cannot be given to Captain Robertson and Lieutenants Mooney, Etter, and Kelso. . . . Lieutenants Kelso and Etter really seemed to enjoy the scene, and their men partook of their spirit." Kelso was a little more critical. Etter had ordered his men to fire too early. Worse, there had been "a few cowards" in the 14th Cavalry: two or three had hidden behind some large sycamore trees nearby, and one ran away entirely, going all the way to Springfield. But in general, Kelso wrote, the men "behaved remarkably well." The victory put them "into fine spirits and made them eager for another fight. It also raised Burch and myself still higher in the favor of the men and the loyal people generally."[31]

Colonel Lawther's report to the Confederate command described an utterly different battle. The Federals, he admitted, had been warned of their approach and had their tents lit up, but were posted behind the camp, in front of the Ozark courthouse and in surrounding buildings. "We charged upon those in the street, tramping them down and scattering them in all directions." Then the Confederates charged men sheltering in the courthouse and drove them into the nearby brush. Others refused to come out of their houses and give Lawther's Rangers a fair fight, and, the colonel wrote, since he was outnumbered eight to one, he thought it prudent to withdraw. He estimated Union losses at 10 killed and 20 wounded.[32]

A few days later, after the return of Major Wilber and his troops, Captain Burch took command of a hundred men and rode 30 miles south to Forsyth, a strategically important town on the White River. Burch and the cavalrymen were hoping for another shot at Lawther's Rangers. A bitterly frustrated Kelso was ordered to stay behind at Ozark to attend to his provost marshal duties. His comrades returned victorious. They had launched a surprise dawn attack on Lawther's camp. The enemy fled, most running off, like the colonel himself, "bare-foot and in his shirt and drawers." Among the documents in a captured trunk were Lawther's commission as a Confederate colonel, his fanciful report on the Ozark battle a few days earlier, and two hundred printed handbills in which he bragged that he "would rid Missouri of all the Yankee Hessians, and would also invade both Iowa and Illinois." Three weeks later Lawther was captured and sent to military prison.[33]

Kelso's pleasure at the success of his comrades was dampened less by his frustration at not being able to fight alongside them than by devastating news from Susie at Collinsville. Ianthus, his year-old son, had caught malaria and died. Kelso received the letter just as he was finishing guard duty on a mid-September evening. He paced his room all night, mourning the loss of his sweet little boy. In his grief, he composed "Ianthus," a poem of eight quatrains, the last of which reads, "And thou art gone, Ianthus, long years may pass away,/ And yet I'll think of thee, my child, I'll think of thee every day;/ Thy little image will remain, engraven on my heart,/ Nor time, nor distance can efface, or cause it to depart."[34]

He had long been anxious about Susie in Collinsville falling prey to Dr. Hovey, but Kelso had kept his family there for their safety. Death had nevertheless come, and in their time of loss and despair the family was separated by 250 miles. He could not take it any longer and summoned Susie and the children to Ozark. He set them up in "a small and scantily furnished house" in late September. "My wife was more cheerful and affectionate than I expected her to be," Kelso remembered. "I was comparatively happy, and I came to love my wife more devotedly than ever. I was proud, too, of my three children."[35]

Kelso was relieved of his duties as provost marshal but then was quickly appointed to three offices: quartermaster, ordnance-master, and commissary. Given only one clerk, he was responsible for payrolls and muster rolls and had to keep two sets of books: one for the MSM and one for the EMM. "This, of course," Kelso believed, "was again the work of my enemy, Major Wilber, who seemed determined to break me down, in some way, by putting upon me more duties than I could successfully accomplish." Kelso was determined, however, to do his jobs impeccably and still volunteer for every scout in the field, even though he had to miss meals and stay up late doing his paperwork, splashing water on his face to stay awake. He joined every expedition he could, "won fresh laurels," and "grew in favor with the men." Wilber's efforts backfired. "So far from breaking me down, Wilber's ill-disguised malice toward me reacted upon himself, causing him to be as intensely hated by the men as I was loved by them." Wilber and his few pet officers became so obnoxious to the men that, according to Kelso, they rose in mutiny against one of them, forcing him to resign.[36]

In early October, Major Wilber prepared to take nearly the entire available forces at Ozark and the post at Lawrence's Mill—125 MSM and 100 EMM soldiers—on an expedition. Kelso, Burch, and the other officers excluded from Wilber's circle were to be left behind in camp. They became suspicious, believing the major was acting without orders and they worried that the expedition's purpose might be plunder for personal profit. Relenting to pressure, Wilber allowed Kelso and Mooney to join him, though without telling the two officers their destination or mission. Kelso, relieved of his desk duties, was to be third in command behind Wilber and his "creature," Captain Samuel A. Flagg.

The story of this expedition, as Kelso told it, began with the march. Protocol dictated that Flagg, the senior company commander, lead the march on the first day and Kelso on the second. But Flagg took the lead on the second day, too, ordering Kelso to the rear. When the captain repeated the insult on the third day, Kelso refused until Major Wilber gave him a direct order to move back. "I will obey you, Major," Kelso said, ". . . because of your rank and not because I have any respect for such officers as you and Captain Flagg. I respect my two horses, Hawk-eye and Sigel, far more than I do such miserable substitutes for officers." As they made their way through a comparatively wealthy and populated part of Marion County, Arkansas known as Tolbert's Barrens, Kelso watched as Wilber, Flagg, and their toadies stopped at every prosperous farmhouse and "drank the milk, ate the provisions, and seized upon such valuables as they could find." The rest of the command was forbidden to break ranks.[37]

At one house, according to Kelso, Wilber and Flagg threatened to rape an attractive young mother until her loud pleas to the other officers stopped the assault. At another, Flagg claimed all the provisions for himself, and when a half-witted soldier tried to drink from a pan of milk, Flagg, in a rage, snatched it out of his hands and threatened to cut the man's throat. Kelso snapped. He jumped forward, grabbed Flagg, and thrust his fist under the captain's nose. "You infernal cowardly *thief*," Kelso roared, "talk to one who is in a position to defend himself! Talk to *me*, you vile *thief*!" Flagg "trembled from abject fear, set the pan of milk down, and, without replying a word, slunk around the house to where Major Wilber was, and actually got behind him for protection."[38]

Kelso told the major what had happened, and then unloaded on him, too. "Major, I look upon you as but little better than he is." Wilber had encouraged Flagg's disgraceful conduct when he allowed him to lead the march each day, and it was from the front, while the rest of the line was halted, that the thieving officers did their plundering. "You have done this just to give him a chance to disgrace our flag by robbing and outraging unarmed citizens and women. I hold you responsible for his base conduct." Wilber, like Flagg, was a thief but unlike the captain, he was not also a coward. In a cold fury, the major drew his revolver and aimed it at Kelso's chest. Kelso drew his, and aimed it at Wilber. "All of the men of three companies, and over half of Flagg's own company, instantly sprang into line by my side, every man with a revolver in his hand. The balance of Flagg's men stood scattered about not taking either side. Wilber ordered the men to disperse. . . . Not a man moved except to cock his revolver. Again Wilber repeated his order. The men were motionless as statues."[39]

Wilber then addressed Kelso: all right, he said, tomorrow you can lead the march. He gave in on the smaller issue, the insulting deviation from military protocol, but the larger one, disgracing the flag by robbing and outraging citizens, was left hanging in the air. Kelso, though he did not admit as much, latched onto this concession to deescalate a dangerous situation; he returned his revolver to its holster, turned to its men, and said, "Boys, let's feed." They too holstered their weapons and dispersed to feed their horses. Kelso's confrontation with Wilber and Flagg was defused, but it was not over. In camp that night, Kelso found himself protecting the valuables of two young ladies—"a gold watch, a trunk, a fine mare, and a $500.00 bank bill"—from the officers' thieving hands.[40]

The next day, Wilber sent Kelso and a small squad on a side scout, looking for rebels, while the major stopped at "the splendid mansion of a very wealthy man who was running a private bank, and who was said to have on hand several thousand dollars in coin." Kelso returned to the house sooner than the major expected. Talking his way past a guard the major had posted at the front door, Kelso found one of Wilber's men in the hall, Lieutenant John Cross, propositioning "a handsome young colored woman." Wilber and Flagg were also on the hunt for Black mistresses, hired as "cooks." "Proceeding to an inner room," Kelso later wrote, "I found Wilber and Flagg in the presence of the aged banker, who was lying upon a bed, very ill, and who died a few days afterward. Flagg was searching the room. Wilber was holding a fine gold watch which he had just taken from a young daughter of the banker." The girl was pleading in vain for her watch. "When Wilber saw me," Kelso recounted, "he looked surprised, frightened, and angry. 'Why Lieutenant,' said he, 'how did *you* get in?' 'I *came* in,' said I."[41]

Wilber went quickly to the door and reprimanded the guard for letting Kelso in. Then he gave Kelso new orders: the lieutenant was to take 10 men 10 miles south to a particular rebel officer's house. To do what, Kelso asked? The major stammered. He had not yet made up a purpose for this mission. Take what military supplies you find and return, the major finally replied. We'll be waiting. Kelso knew that Wilber was sending him away so he could finish his robbery and that he was probably being sent into a nest of bushwhackers to be gotten out of the way permanently. But he felt that he could not disobey the order. With Kelso gone, Wilber finished relieving the old man of his money. Instead of waiting for Kelso to return, the major left a 30-man rear guard commanded by the virtuous (and therefore expendable) Lieutenant Mooney and started beating a fast retreat to Missouri. Riding north that evening, Mooney's rear guard came upon a large camp, thinking it was Wilber's. It was instead a party of rebels, who opened fire. Mooney was severely wounded, but he and his men escaped to the forest, though three who had been thrown from their horses went missing.

Traveling south as ordered, Kelso found the road so full of rebels that he, too, was forced into the forest. His squad reached the rebel officer's house at midnight. Finding only women there and nothing of military value, they returned north, attacking small groups of rebels when they found them and hiding from larger ones. At dawn, they reached the dying old banker's mansion at Tolbert's Barrens and learned of Wilber's "cowardly flight." Some miles ahead, they came upon the abandoned rebel camp, saw signs of the conflict, and found some of their friends' hats in the woods. One of Mooney's men came out of hiding and related the story. They shortly picked up the other two unhorsed stragglers from Mooney's party.[42]

Crossing into Missouri, Kelso and his men reached the Union military post at Beaver Station, where they found Wilber, Flagg, the wounded Mooney, and the rest of the expedition. The soldiers had refused to retreat any farther until they learned what happened to Kelso and his men. "They had also let Wilber know that they suspected that he had sent me out and then abandoned me on purpose to secure my destruction, and that his life and Flagg's must atone for mine, if, through their machinations, myself and my party were lost." The men said they would wait two days, and the time had nearly expired. "No wonder, then, that these treacherous villains were glad that they had failed in their attempt to have me destroyed. On the next day, we proceeded to Ozark, where I was received as a hero, Wilber and Flagg as cowards."[43]

Nothing like any of this, of course, appeared in Wilber's official report of the expedition, which he filed on October 20, 1862, from Ozark. The expedition, Wilber wrote, had been authorized by Brigadier General Francis J. Herron, commander of the 2nd and 3rd divisions of the Army of the Frontier in Missouri. Its purpose was to march on Yellville, Arkansas, and take or burn Confederate military supplies there. Their advance to Yellville was prevented by the sudden rise of the White River, Wilber explained, and the area was "swarming with secesh scouts." He then learned that a Confederate force of 3,000 men was a day's march away and headed toward him. The expedition, therefore, after collecting "property useful to the military" such as horses and wagons, began its retreat. Lieutenant Mooney's rear guard was attacked in the night by a detachment from the large Confederate force. Mooney then, according to Wilber, led a charge "with such impetuosity and gallantry" that his little band broke through the enemy line, killing not less than 10 and wounding 20, though some of his men were thrown from their mounts and Mooney himself was wounded. Wilber's report said nothing about Kelso.[44]

On the next major expedition out of the Ozark post, Burch commanded and Kelso was at his side. They left on November 8. Eighty men rode down to Arkansas and hid in the woods near a rebel neighborhood 3 miles from Dubuque. They had a plan. Burch, as he afterward reported, "sent Lieut. John R. Kelso, with 10 Enrolled Militia, to play the part of rebels. They were to take four men . . . and conduct them as Federal prisoners into the vicinity of Dubuque, and assemble a sufficient number of rebel provost guards to take charge of the prisoners." At the right moment, Burch and the rest of his men would surround and capture them.[45]

Kelso recounts that he dressed himself and men "like rebel bush-whackers" and he "was now playing the role of a rebel guerrilla leader, one Lieutenant Russell." They marched their four pretend Federal prisoners out onto the road and up to the nearest house, owned, it turned out, by a rebel named Yandle. Men who had seen them coming "appeared with their guns at the windows and the port-holes." At Kelso's call, a woman came out to the gate. He told her his story. They were Southern fighters with four obnoxious Federal captives, and they wanted to hang them at 2:00 that afternoon. But they had traveled all night and were hungry and tired (this part was true). Could they come in to eat and rest for a while? The woman returned to the house and repeated Kelso's story to the armed men. Intrigued by the promise of a hanging, they welcomed Lieutenant Russell and his bushwhackers inside.[46]

The armed men left to spread the word in the neighborhood about the hanging, letting Lieutenant Russell put his four prisoners with their four guards in one of the house's two large rooms, while he and the other six bushwhackers stayed in the other with the women cooking them breakfast. Russell planned to send one of his men out each hour to guard his trail. When he ordered the first out, his "new rebel friends" assured him the precaution was unnecessary because no Federals were likely to venture into the surrounding hills, but if they did none would get out alive. The lieutenant insisted, though, because actually the men would be reporting to Burch. The plan was that after a good crowd of rebels had assembled for the hanging, Kelso would send word for Burch to come up. So, while he waited, the lieutenant ate his breakfast and chatted with "a pleasant and intelligent woman who was so enthusiastic a little rebel that she was eager to do a little fighting herself for the holy cause." Once his belly was full, and despite being anxious that something would go wrong, his weariness got the better of him. He took to one of the beds in the room for a nap, asking the women to wake him in an hour.[47]

Soon an excited woman was shaking him awake. He sprang to the door, heard two or three shots fired, and looked out to see their horses breaking loose and galloping about the yard while the house was circled by what seemed to be 200 horsemen. Confederate cavalry—caught in my own trap— he thought. But the rebels in the yard looked more alarmed than triumphant and they were forming a defensive line. As the rebels called to Lieutenant Russell, asking him to lead them in the fight, Kelso recognized the surrounding horsemen as Burch and 50 of his men. (As Kelso later learned, the soldier he had sent out to report to Burch, either misunderstanding the plan or nervous, had urged Burch to attack as soon as possible.) Russell ordered his own men, except two guards for the prisoners, to join the rebel line. When Burch roared "Surrender! Down with your arms," Russell, to the astonishment of his new rebel friends, answered, "We surrender! We surrender!" He had his own men lay down their arms, and ordered the rebels to do the same. "They hesitated. 'Lay down your arms quickly,' I repeated earnestly, 'or we'll all be killed.' They obeyed but they did so in a surly and dissatisfied manner." Once the rebels had been disarmed, Kelso and his "bushwhackers" took off their disguises. The rebels were indignant at the trick. Better to trick you, boys, and capture you instead of having to kill you, Kelso said with a smile. He even invited them to switch sides and join the Union army. "Won by our kind treatment of them," Kelso later claimed, "several of them did afterwards join our service."[48]

As they left Yandle's with their prisoners, Kelso asked Burch for permission to take 10 or 12 volunteers for a quick raid on the village of Dubuque. There he and his men cut down men "like green mullein stalks in an old meadow."[49]

A month later, in early December, Kelso and his comrades were again in rebel disguise. He, Burch, and 34 of their soldiers had "donned a number of Confederate uniforms, bush-whacker suits, etc.," making themselves "sufficiently motley to resemble the rebels in that section." They sat in their saddles in front of a Confederate army barracks on a bluff above the White River near Yellville, Arkansas. Their target was a Confederate saltpeter mine. Saltpeter, or potassium nitrate, is a major component of gunpowder. Destroying this site would deliver a powerful blow to the enemy's gunpowder production in the region. If successful, it would be their most successful strike yet.[50]

With only 36 men, they could not take the barracks guarding the saltpeter caves by direct assault, but they might by trickery. They had learned that a Confederate force of 2,000 men was approaching from the south. If they could pretend to be an advance detachment from those regiments, they might be able to capture the men in the barracks, destroy the equipment in the caves, and quickly escape across the river. Burch, in his report, did not mention their rebel disguises, since that was not a sanctioned tactic they were supposed to employ. According to General Halleck's rules, disguises forfeited their right, if captured, to be treated as prisoners of war and they could be executed as outlaws or spies. Accordingly, Burch wrote that the enemy soldiers in the barracks "mistook us for a company of their own men which they were expecting."[51]

A single guard let Burch's men pass, saying he was "expecting" them. It was noon, and the men in the barracks were eating. When the soldiers inside saw the Confederates and bushwhackers on horseback they exited the barracks to greet them, leaving most of their guns behind. A friendly Burch called out, "How are you, boys?" He asked if his men could come in for a warm fire and some food. The rebels welcomed the newcomers. Half of Burch's men dismounted to enter. But they lingered by the doors, so as to block anyone wanting to retrieve guns. Burch then bellowed, "Now, God damn you, give up your arms and fall into line, and be damned quick about it!" The soldiers from the barracks "seemed paralyzed with astonishment." Kelso hollered: "We are Federals; if you surrender without firing, you will be treated kindly, as prisoners of war. If a single shot is fired, every man of you will die. Now fall into line quickly."[52]

The surly Confederates reluctantly followed these orders. Captain Patrick S. McNamara, the commander of the post, was especially bitter, cursing himself for letting this happen. But he warned his captors that he would soon be trading places with them: a large Confederate force was only two hours away and the White River at their backs was too deep to cross.

Leaving Burch and the men to deal with the prisoners, Kelso descended the long flight of steps leading from the barracks at the top of the high bluff to the cave entrance on the riverbank. He realized as he reached the bottom that he should have brought several men with him. Too late now, he thought, and entered the saltpeter cave by himself. Fortunately, there was only one man there. The soldier made a move toward his shotgun, which was leaning against the engine house. "Move and you die! Stand right still!" Kelso shouted, aiming his own shotgun. The man froze. Shortly, Burch and some others appeared. The captain set some of the prisoners to work with axes and sledgehammers, destroying the kettles, machinery, and other things that might not burn. Captain McNamara at first refused to help destroy the operation that he had worked night and day for six months to get up and running. Kelso told him that when he was a child refusing to perform an unpleasant task, he got a whipping, until he finally learned that sometimes there was no avoiding disagreeable things.

McNamara "went to work, but cursed bitterly all the time." Then the Federals set fire, and hastily climbed the steps up the bluff.[53]

They were running out of time. Burch took 23 prisoners, including McNamara, paroled the rest, and led the horses to a place where they could descend to the riverbank. (McNamara had been lying—the Federals' guide knew a fordable spot.) Kelso and one soldier stayed behind to set fire to the barracks and the blockhouse. Women who lived nearby came and asked if they could take provisions out of the blockhouse—flour, salt, sugar, bacon, and so on—before the building was engulfed in flames. Kelso said yes, and he and his comrade helped them roll out some barrels. But in the distance, he could see clouds of dust rising in the trees: the Confederate force was coming.

Kelso let the soldier take his horse down the steep slope first, and then followed. His comrade forded the river. Turning to watch Kelso as the lieutenant descended, the soldier started to signal anxiously that they needed to move as quickly as possible. By the time Kelso and his horse made it out of the river, spent bullets from the Confederates firing from the bluff "began to patter like hail" around him. At the edge of the forest, the two escaping Federals turned briefly to admire their destructive work. It was a scene "of weird and wonderful grandeur." The air was still and the river placid, but flames from the blockhouse shot up a hundred feet. Billowing smoke rose far higher, reaching up toward some dark storm clouds spreading out "like a vast umbrella in all directions," a "grand dark canopy." On the ridge of the bluff, seemingly oblivious to the "wonderful beauty and grandeur of the scene," a hundred rebels fired their rifles at the two Union soldiers across the river.[54]

Burch's men knew they were still in a "tight place," and they hurriedly marched their prisoners through the woods. With a particular eye on the bold Captain McNamara, Kelso ordered the guards to shoot dead any prisoner who tried to communicate with his fellows or did so much as look around. As they raced north, knowing that a detachment of Confederates would be hunting them, a thunderstorm began, soaking them to the skin. When night fell and the rain continued, it was hard to even see the trail or the trees before them. Around midnight they reached a rapidly rising creek. They forded it just in time, knowing that when their pursuers reached it, it would be too deep to cross.[55]

They camped that night in the rain beneath sodden blankets, their heads on their saddles. The rain turned to sleet, and then to snow. By morning their clothes were frozen stiff on their bodies. By the time they made it back to Ozark the next evening, they were "weary, hungry, and almost frozen," but they were warmed by the knowledge of their victory and the cheers of their friends.[56]

Burch could report that they had destroyed a "gigantic" saltpeter works that had cost the Confederate government $30,000, an operation that could have produced, McNamara told him, $6,000 worth of saltpeter in three days. Burch praised the efforts of his men, concluding with a special note about his second-in-command: "As to Lieutenant Kelso, his reputation as an intrepid soldier and skillful officer is too well known to require any further comment at this time." Brigadier General Egbert Brown at Springfield added his praise in a communication to Major General Samuel Curtis, now commander of the District of Missouri at St. Louis, noting that this was the fourth "equally important and successful scout" by Burch's men in the past few months, and that they had done just as well in numerous smaller affairs. General Curtis, Kelso heard, called the raid on the saltpeter works "brilliant." The men of the 14th, meanwhile, started to think they might be invincible when led by Burch or Kelso.[57]

The year 1862, therefore, ended for Kelso on an optimistic note. In late September, in the largest battle in the Trans-Mississippi since Pea Ridge, 7,000 Union troops had been defeated by 11,000 Confederates at Newtonia, 65 miles west of Ozark, though the victors withdrew to Arkansas shortly afterward. On December 7, however, 10,000 Federals commanded by Brigadier Generals James Blunt and Francis Herron defeated 11,000 Confederates under General Thomas C. Hindman at Prairie Grove, Arkansas, and by the end of the month pushed Hindman's demoralized army south of the Arkansas River. Back East, the huge Army of the Potomac suffered a costly defeat at the Battle of Fredericksburg, Virginia, on December 13, losing over 12,600 men. Yet President Lincoln had signaled in the fall that an Emancipation Proclamation would be issued in January, which promised to shift the moral foundations of the war. Conservative Unionists, who had long argued that the war was merely to restore the Union, were losing ground to men like Kelso, who insisted that the larger cause was "universal liberty."[58]

9

I Am Kelso

IF YOU'RE LYING, you're dead men, Captain Burch told the two captured rebels. It was the evening of January 6, 1863. Burch, Kelso, and a detachment of about a hundred men from their regiment were on a scout headed into Carroll County, Arkansas. Stopped at Widow Fisher's place on Big Creek, about 6 miles from Dubuque, they found the two Confederate soldiers claiming to be advance scouts of a large rebel army marching quickly northward and about to overtake them: 6,000 men led by General John S. Marmaduke. When the prisoners stuck to their story after Burch issued his threat, the captain was convinced. Kelso had been off on his own, hunting turkeys for dinner. When he rejoined his men and found them anxiously talking about the advancing Confederate army, he was skeptical. The captured rebels suggested that he ride down the road half a mile to see for himself. So as the sun was setting, Kelso mounted his horse and rode off alone to investigate, while Burch readied the men for a quick withdrawal.[1]

Kelso had not gone more than a few hundred yards before he caught sight of a large body of men coming down the road and heard the "peculiar rumbling" made by thousands of horses' hooves. He galloped back, and Burch ordered a rapid retreat. Marmaduke's troops saw them and opened fire, which only prompted the Federals to coax their tired horses to go faster.[2]

Sending a messenger ahead, they raced the 30 miles back to Beaver Station at Lawrence's Mill, the small fort they had left earlier that day. The station by the mill on Beaver Creek in northwestern Taney County, Missouri, had a two-story log blockhouse about 150 feet long and 40 feet wide and ten smaller buildings serving as barracks for a garrison of about 75 local militia men. Major William Turner commanded the station. Burch, Kelso, and their men arrived at about 4:00 in the morning, but to their dismay they learned that Turner had not evacuated as the advance messenger had warned. "Turner was an old man," a local historian later remembered, who "had been long in the service, and had heard a great deal more of the Confederates than he had ever seen of them, and was incredulous about there being any more of them in the country than a squad of bushwhackers." Kelso was not as generous: Turner was "either a traitor or an imbecile," he declared. Even as Kelso and Burch argued with the fort commander, they heard the enemy firing on the picket guard southeast of the station.[3]

The 14th Cavalry quickly remounted. Before they could get to the blockhouse, 270 Confederate cavalry had taken it and from there began shooting at the Federals. The regiment was led by "Long-Haired" Colonel Emmett MacDonald, who, like Kelso, had vowed not to cut his hair until victory. With a rebel detachment in pursuit, Burch's men forded Beaver Creek and galloped to the far side of the frozen mill pond. Kelso heard bullets skip and rattle across the pond ice behind his back. As the men of the 14th rode hard toward Ozark, Beaver Station was overwhelmed. The Confederates killed 4 or 5 militia men, wounded several others, including Major Turner, captured about 14, slaughtered many of the hundred aging horses and mules not worth taking, helped themselves to about $15,000 worth of commissary and quartermaster supplies, and burned down the blockhouse, fort, and mill.[4]

When Burch's men reached Ozark late the next evening, they received an order for the battalion stationed there to fall back to Springfield, 15 miles farther north. Kelso rode to the house where Susie and his children were staying. Little could be said and nothing done. The army had to abandon tiny Ozark to the approaching Confederates and help defend the arsenal at Springfield, clearly the main target of Marmaduke's expedition. As the 14th Cavalry poured across the Finley River bridge, the rebels swept into the town behind them. On their way through Ozark, the Confederates torched the blockhouse and fort Kelso had helped build on Sugar Loaf Hill the previous fall. "[G]reat bursts of flame rose vividly upon the midnight air," Confederate Major John N. Edwards wrote, "as the fort, the barracks, tents, whiskey, bacon, flour, and everything belonging to the garrison caught fire and disappeared in the conflagration." The advancing army did not stay long. It took a few prisoners and grabbed needed supplies—including blankets from Susie Kelso's house—but mostly seemed intent upon chasing Burch's men into Springfield. As the two forces pressed northward on that January night, sometimes the Confederates got so close that Kelso could hear the rebels complain about the cold, taunting the 14th to stop and hand over their overcoats.[5]

Kelso and his men reached Springfield at midnight after two days of hard riding and no sleep the night before. But there was no time for rest.

Springfield's soldiers and civilians were scrambling to prepare for an attack they knew would come the next day. A crucial military depot for the Federal Army of the Frontier, the town was stocked with gunpowder, muskets, provisions, and hospital supplies. But it was weakly defended. Five forts and earthworks had been planned, but only two were finished and only Fort No. 1 had any artillery (two brass cannons that fired 6-pound shells). The biggest problem, as Springfield braced for an attack from an army said to be 6,000 strong, was a lack of manpower. General Egbert B. Brown, EMM commander of the Southwest District, was in charge, and Colonel Benjamin Crabb of the 19th Iowa Infantry commanded the post. Brown counted up the men stationed in the town from the 3rd, 4th, and Kelso's 14th MSM Cavalry and the 18th Iowa Infantry. The urgent call had gone out to militia men in the surrounding counties, and a few hundred arrived through the night. A few hundred convalescents, recently discharged from medical care, were in town or camp, and some of the sick or wounded men still in the buildings and tents serving as hospitals would have to be well enough to prop themselves up and fire a gun. Civilian men and older boys willing to fight were issued arms. Altogether General Brown estimated that he had a fighting force of about 2,000 men. The 250 men from the EMM would raise the total to over 2,300.[6]

General Brown was—understandably—worried. He thought it might be wise for the army to evacuate Springfield. He ordered that oil, turpentine, gunpowder, and wood shavings be readied at the Methodist church building on South Street, where the arsenal containing tons of ammunition and arms was stored, telling Captain Charles B. McAfee to be ready to set fire to it and blow it all to the sky if they had to retreat. Some of the other officers, though, including Colonel Crabb, urged Brown to stay and fight, suggesting that the defenders might withdraw to Fort No. 1 and hold out until reinforcements came. Kelso believed the men were eager to fight. He certainly was. Another observer summed up the general feeling: "We *may* hold the town, and we will not give it up without a fight; but we shall probably be whipped."[7]

Throughout the night, Springfield prepared as best it could. Civilians hid their money and valuables. Some packed up and left town to stay with friends or relatives in the countryside. Others threw their belongings into wagons and made their way through the dark streets to shelter at Fort No. 1, the largest fort (a pentagon enclosing 10 acres) and the furthest from the approaching army. Some citizens headed for their cellars, as if hiding from an approaching storm. The Confederate sympathizers in town looked forward to welcoming the liberators in gray, an army that included more than a few Springfield and Greene County men. "Long-Haired" MacDonald, the

"chivalrous and dashing" young colonel, had become something of a secessionist hero at the start of war for refusing Federal parole after capture and
for looking splendid in his Zouave-style uniform. He reportedly sent word
through a spy to a Confederate lady friend in town that he would be taking
tea with her the next afternoon. Dr. Samuel Melcher organized the sick men
from the hospitals into what would be called the "Quinine Brigade" after
their bitter malarial fever medicine. On General Brown's orders, soldiers
pierced walls of brick buildings for musket fire and hurriedly stocked the
forts with provisions. They hauled three old iron cannons that had been lying
on the ground near the Calvary Presbyterian Church to a blacksmith's shop.
There the guns were attached to axles and wheels from army wagons and then
rolled to the small but sturdy Fort No. 4 (about 160 feet long and wide) half a
mile south of the town square. At daylight on January 8, General Brown knew
that Marmaduke's forces were massing a few miles south of town. He ordered
about a dozen houses in front of Fort No. 4 burned to the ground, affording
the artillery there a clearer line of fire.[8]

Brown deployed his forces a few blocks south of the town square,
stretching from the unfinished Fort No. 2 in the west (on his right) to the
unfinished Fort No. 5 in the east (on his left). Everyone agreed that the town
was most vulnerable from the east, along St. Louis Street. Brown, Kelso, and
a newspaper reporter with the troops in the center at Fort No. 4 all expected
Marmaduke's main assault to come from the east, sheltered by the trees along
Wilson's Creek. Brown climbed the courthouse tower and through his field
glasses saw Marmaduke instead establishing his line of troops on the open
prairie directly to the south. But Brown believed that this would to be a feint.
The "real attack" would still come at "another point." That other point was
on his left, where General Brown posted the 14th MSM Cavalry, with an advance flanking party of 20 mounted men led by Lieutenant John R. Kelso.[9]

General Brown saw something else as he observed the enemy from the
courthouse tower. Marmaduke had far fewer than 6,000 men. In fact, the
Confederate force was about 2,300. Marmaduke had expected another 825—
a separate column under the command of Colonel Joseph C. Porter that had
also moved up from Arkansas and was supposed to rendezvous at Springfield.
But after having been detected by Burch's men near Dubuque, Marmaduke's
forces had had to accelerate their march on Springfield and were unable to get
word to Porter. Springfield's defenders, many of whom were green militiamen,
hospital patients, and civilians, might still not be a match for Marmaduke's
cavalry and artillery. But Brown now knew they had a chance.

As the sun rose higher, Springfield waited. Finally, at about 10:00, the
battle began as the advancing rebel army opened fire on some Federal scouts,

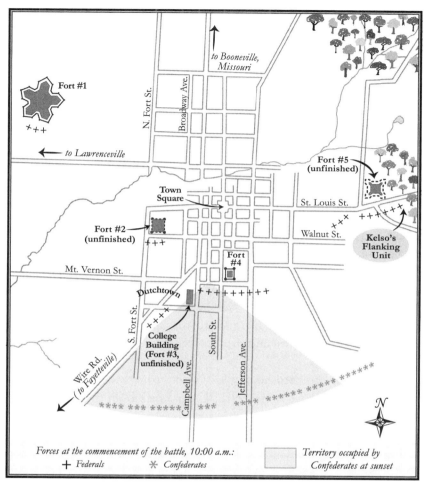

The Battle of Springfield, Missouri, January 8, 1863. Drawn by Rebecca Wrenn. Map sources: "Plan of Springfield, Mo., Showing the Location of the Forts," Record Group 77, National Archives and Record Administration, Washington, D.C., in Frederick W. Goman, *Up from Arkansas: Marmaduke's First Missouri Raid, Including the Battles of Springfield and Hartville* (Springfield, Mo.: Privately printed, 1999); Elmo Ingenthron, *Borderland Rebellion: A History of the Civil War on the Missouri-Arkansas Border* (Branson, Mo.: Ozarks Mountaineer, [1989]), 262; Larry Wood, *Civil War Springfield* (Charleston, S.C.: History Press, 2011), 106; Map: Battle of Springfield, Missouri, 1863, https://springfield1863.org.

who quickly pulled back. On the left and right of the Confederate line were cavalry regiments, and in the center about half the force had dismounted to fight as infantry. Behind Kelso on St. Louis Street were nearly 600 men—his own 14th Cavalry and the 3rd Missouri State Militia under Colonel Walter

King. King's group was ordered to charge forward to meet a Confederate cavalry force. The *New York Times* reporter at Fort No. 4 described the scene: "My blood quickened its flow, as I watched our brave boys gallop forward to the charge, then saw the enemy galloping in a long line to meet them, and heard the sharp, rapid firing of carbines, on both sides. After each charge and fire both sides would turn and gallop back, with small loss on either side." Colonel George H. Hall's 4th MSM made a similar charge at the Confederate center and then pulled back to Fort No. 4. Kelso and the 14th repulsed a Confederate assault on the left.[10]

The big guns then opened fire. General Brown, standing on the southwest bastion of Fort No. 4, was convinced the attackers had fired first, beginning a bombardment of the town without prior notification so women and children could be removed from harm's way, as protocol demanded. "Gentlemen," Brown shouted, the portly man standing erect and directing return fire as shells whistled over his head, "this is unprecedented; it is barbarous!" Kelso saw "several heavy shots sent crashing through our churches, our dwelling houses, our printing offices, etc.," and he was convinced that "several women and children were wounded by this barbarous fire." One shell did explode in a room where four women and two children were lying on the floor, covered by their feather beds.[11]

Marmaduke had been hoping for Porter's troops to arrive. If they had, the general might have launched the larger attack from the east that Kelso expected. The gaunt Confederate general—too near-sighted to detect the Federal troop movements well even through field glasses—consulted with his officers, including the dashing MacDonald and the talented Colonel Joseph O. "Jo" Shelby. At about 2:00 in the afternoon, Marmaduke decided to shift his forces to the southwest and to concentrate fire on Fort No. 4 in the center. The Confederates fighting as infantry advanced by crawling on the ground "like Indians," the newspaper reporter said, "from one stump to another, sheltering themselves as much as possible, but keeping up a deadly fire." It was later said that one of them, having strapped a large frying pan to his chest to serve as armor, bravely darted ahead of his comrades, but then lost his nerve. As he turned to run back, he was shot and killed, the bullet going through his back and lodging in the frying pan in front. General Brown rode out to the corner of South and State streets to rally his troops. Brown, who before the war had been a grain merchant and a railroad man, had been criticized for timidity, and Kelso, who had spoken privately with the general before the battle, was among those who doubted him. But here he was, riding high in the saddle, in full view of the enemy, not even flinching under heavy fire. Even a Confederate observer was impressed: Brown was "clad in bold regimentals, elegantly mounted and ahead of all so that the fire might be concentrated upon him." A shot knocked him from his horse—his adjutant suspected a sharpshooting rebel civilian from the town. The bullet shattered the bone in his upper left arm. He was helped to the rear and had to transfer command to Colonel Crabb. Later that night he dictated a dispatch to General Curtis in St. Louis, calling his men heroes, but had to stop because he was losing too much blood.[12]

Kelso was ordered to remain with his small group guarding the far left flank as Burch and the rest of the 14th, along with King's 3rd, were shifted to the south and southwest. Kelso and his men continued a frustrating game of cat-and-mouse with about 50 mounted Confederates. They chased each other back and forth, "neither party accomplishing much except some fine feats of horsemanship." Dashing in as close as they dared to Kelso's defensive position in rifle pits, the Confederates would stop and call out to the Federals to give up their overcoats and Lincoln coffee. "They would also make obscene gestures, turning up their buttocks toward us and patting them with their hands." Once, at about 3:00, when Kelso and his men were chasing the enemy back to their position, they stopped on a hill to get a better look at the battle raging a mile to the southwest. Kelso watched a desperate and deadly struggle over one of Springfield's cannons.[13]

The Confederates had pressed into the southern end of town, shooting from behind the cluster of houses and outbuildings known as "Dutchtown," and had advanced to capture a two-story brick building. Before the war the building, surrounded on three sides by a stockade, had been a college; until the previous evening it had served as a military prison housing 50 Confederates. Empty but accidentally left unguarded by Federal troops, it offered the attackers a strong position just 250 yards from Fort No. 4. A detachment from the 18th Iowa led by Captains John A. Landis, William R. Blue, and Joseph Van Meter came down from Fort No. 1 to help fend off the attack with a field piece—one of the brass 6-pounders—but they wound up beyond the Federal line and exposed to the enemy. A detachment of Confederates led by Major John Bowman sped forward to capture the gun. One of the Iowans, seeing the Confederates charge, suggested that they abandon the artillery piece and retreat to the fort. But Blue and Van Meter drew their pistols and threatened to shoot anyone who tried to leave. Galloping forward, Major Bowman demanded that the Federals surrender. When Captain Landis refused, Bowman shot at him, the bullet snapping the captain's shoulder strap. In the gunfire that followed, Bowman, shot right below his heart, fell from his

saddle. The Federals' horses were all shot down. Landis got hit and fell, severely wounded. Captains Blue and Van Meter went down in the gunfire;
each would die a few days later. In a few moments, 8 or 9 Confederates and 4
or 5 Union soldiers were dead or dying, and more than a dozen on each side
were badly wounded. As Kelso saw from his hilltop, the attackers captured
both the gun and the college building.[14]

The fighting at the southern end of town and into the cemetery to the
west intensified. Members of the Quinine Brigade moved to occupy a house
between Fort No. 4 and the stockaded college. Suddenly emerging from the
cellar of the house, Mrs. Jane Toney "refused to leave until the solders, in language more forcible than elegant," insisted. They chased her off, "with the
Confederate bullets singing about her ears quite lively." The soldiers at Fort
No. 4 kept up the artillery fire, with Dr. David V. Whitney on one bastion
shouting "Give them hell, boys! give them hell!" and the Post Chaplain Fred
H. Wines on the other urging the soldiers to "Put your trust in Jesus, boys,
and *aim low*!" A little to the west on Fayetteville Road the 72nd EMM, a
regiment of mostly local men led by Colonel Henry Shepard, a Springfield
merchant, fought desperately against Shelby's well-trained Missouri Cavalry
Brigade.[15]

Captain Burch and the rest of Kelso's 14th Cavalry had been moved nearby,
on Booneville Street, 50 yards from the town square, and had to try to stop
the advance of Marmaduke's troops toward the center of town. Lieutenant
Colonel Pound was in command of the battalion, but Captain Flagg was at
the head of the column and was again "dog drunk," according to Burch. The
men rode down the street, four abreast, to within 20 yards of the enemy, and
then both sides opened fire. Burch, from behind, "saw the peril that we were
in." He rode ahead to Pound. "Colonel, what are you going to do?" "What
had we better do?" Pound asked in response. "Dismount and charge," Burch
answered. With Pound's assent, Burch ordered the men to dismount, organized them into a line, and ordered them to charge and fire their pistols. At
this moment, Confederates turned their big guns, too, on the Federals in the
street. Still, "we made the charge notwithstanding the artillery fire and the
galling fire of small arms. Our boys raised the Indian war whoop and we drove
the rebels back into the stockade." The heavy fire continued. Though doing so
made him a better target, Burch had to stay on his horse because of his lame
foot. A bullet tore through his horse's head, and when the animal fell, its body
rolled onto Burch's leg and "mashed it severely." He limped to the rear, got his
other horse, and returned to the front, but his leg swelled up so much that
later he could not stand.[16]

As Burch and the rest of the 14th were in the thick of the fight a few blocks south of the town square, Kelso and his small group were still jousting with the Confederate cavalry on the open land past the eastern edge of town. As the sun began to set, Kelso and his men were drawn out farther from their rifle pits than ever before in one last attempt to catch or kill some of the enemy. Throughout the day a reserve group of several hundred Confederate cavalry had been standing by their horses some distance away, watching Kelso's unit and the small group of rebel horsemen charge back and forth. This reserve force had been so removed from the action that Kelso and his men had stopped paying much attention to it. But on this last charge, as Kelso came too close, the reserves quickly mounted and galloped to try to cut off his retreat. Suddenly Kelso's soldiers were racing back toward town, riding for their lives. Kelso was in the rear, behind Sergeant McElhaney. When they passed just in front of the rebel riders trying to intercept them, their pursuers yelled and opened fire, making such a terrific noise that they frightened Kelso's horse. Hawk Eye "shied from the road, sprang into a pile of stones, and fell, throwing me over his head and hurting me quite severely." McElhaney saw Kelso fall and reined up his horse. Kelso cried out "Leave me! Save yourself." As Hawk Eye arose, Kelso "sprang upon him without catching my stirrups, threw my arms around his neck, and thus, with my face to his mane, let him dart into the thick cluster of hawthorns that fortunately for me lined that side of the road." Kelso escaped—the enemy merely 20 yards behind him. When he made it back to the rifle pits, hatless, badly scratched, and thoroughly bruised, his men were glad to see him, surprised he was still alive.[17]

The 20 men of the 14th looked out at the long line of Confederate cavalry that was forming about 300 yards away, apparently readying an attack. Kelso sent a messenger back into town, calling for reinforcements. But the fight was still hot in the southern and southwestern parts of the town, and no more than 15 sick "skeletons" from the Quinine Brigade could be spared. So Kelso bluffed. From their sheltered position, his troops aimed some effective shots into the enemy line as Kelso called out and taunted the enemy, pretending his reinforcements had been substantial and daring them to attack. Night came, but the attack did not. The Confederate cavalry withdrew. Gunfire quieted in the town, too. "Dense darkness and an oppressive silence gathered around us." After a while, Kelso's men quietly and cautiously made their way to the town square, not knowing which army held it. There they encountered a small party of men who turned out to be Burch and other members of the 14th. The battalion's men stood around crunching on some hardtack, feeding their horses, and awaiting orders. Kelso learned the names of comrades who had fallen.[18]

Kelso went to see Colonel Crabb, who had taken command after General Brown had been shot. Crabb, a hotel manager before the war, had already earned a reputation for bravery, and Kelso trusted his judgment. Every few moments, as Kelso made his way through the dark streets to Crabb's office, "a flash of light would be seen, a heavy shot would crash through the houses or scream through the air over our heads, and the thunders of a cannon would burst forth on the silence of night." What was the enemy doing? Would there be another attack that night? A telegram had been received from General Curtis in St. Louis at 9:00 p.m., promising reinforcements. "You and your troops are heroes," Curtis wrote to Brown. "I hope God will spare you strength for to-morrow. I expect a desperate effort early in the morning. All the troops, especially the cavalry, should be ready. . . . Don't weary in doing well. The eyes of the country are on you. Your general feels for you deeply. God grant you success."[19]

When Kelso found Crabb, the commander was frustrated that he could not get better intelligence about Marmaduke's movements and intentions. Kelso offered to go out spying. Crabb said that he would have called upon Kelso for the job, but he knew the lieutenant had not slept or rested for days and must be exhausted. But Kelso insisted. He did not explain to Crabb, and perhaps did not admit to himself, that because he had been away from the main action all day, he was desperate to do something heroic.

Kelso may also have been eager to do something for the honor of the 14th Cavalry. Colonel Crabb's report to General Curtis was full of praise for the bravery of Sheppard's Greene County militia, for the Iowans, and for the Quinine Brigade, all of whom "fought like heroes, Spartans, and veterans." His one criticism concerned the 14th. Crabb would tell Curtis that at a critical moment late in the day as the battle raged near the college building, an officer commanding a company in the 14th ordered his men to remount "and the whole battalion came running to the rear." Crabb tried to rally them, but "they seemed panic-stricken." This caused other troops to falter but Crabb was able to reorganize them, he reported, and get them to return to the fight. It took longer for Lieutenant Colonel Pound to reestablish order among the "panic-stricken" 14th. But the order for the men to take to their horses came, Burch told Kelso, from the battalion commander, not from a mere company officer. It was a strategic repositioning, not a panicked retreat: "[B]y the order of Colonel Pound, we mounted and moved to the left to feel of the enemy. They threw a shell very near us. Then Colonel Pound had us fall back two hundred yards and dismount." Moreover, according to Burch, the 14th's move, rather than weakening the Federal line to the point of collapse, had no negative effect at all: "As if with solid walls, we now held the rebels on every side. . . . We held the rebels there till dark." Still, Burch had said that Captain Flagg was "dog drunk" and had mentioned Pound's earlier indecisiveness. Burch also made a cryptic remark about Kelso knowing "how the other field officers acted." Kelso may have sensed that not everything had been glorious for the fighting 14th.[20]

But the battle was not yet over. The enemy still occupied Dutchtown and the college. Confederate batteries were still firing shells into the town, and the guns at Fort No. 4 were answering. Springfield's defenders all expected another attack to come by daylight if not sooner. Kelso left Crabb's office carrying his big shotgun and walked southwest toward the enemy on Fayetteville Road. A hundred yards in front of Fort No. 4, he got down on his hands and knees and began to crawl. Close by, he heard men coughing. The sound seemed to be coming from rebel guards in a blacksmith shop at the edge of Dutchtown. Creeping closer, he began to move over ground where the battle had raged a few hours before. Dark forms, dead bodies lying in the cold dirt, were scattered around in an empty lot near the shop. Suddenly a light flashed and a cannon thundered some distance in front of him. Another Confederate artillery shell crashed into the town. Then behind him, closer, another flash of light and another roar as Fort No. 4 returned fire. Then again from the Confederate lines, and again from the fort. Kelso flattened himself on the ground. The shells seemed to be screaming through the air right over his back. "I felt the wind that they made, and saw the burning fuse pass like a faint streak of lightning." He crawled to get out of the direct line of fire. And then the shelling stopped. The rebel batteries were moving, he thought. But moving where?[21]

Still on his hands and knees, crawling over the frozen ground in the dark, Kelso made his way toward what appeared to be the smoldering ruins of houses destroyed in the battle. Some soldiers were asleep on the ground, huddled for warmth next to the embers. He crept silently past them and farther out into the open battlefield. More bodies—not sleeping men but dead ones. But also the wounded and the dying. Some of them could have been men from his own regiment, he thought, friends and comrades who had been fighting earlier that day with Burch and the rest of the 14th. Friends or enemies, the men around him on the ground were dying in the dark and the cold: "Some of these were calling for help and for water. After calling a while in vain, some of these men would curse; others would pray. Some were evidently delirious.

They seemed to be talking to their mothers and other dear ones in their far away homes." After a while, some of these stopped speaking and were still. "And there they lay alone in the darkness stiffening upon the frozen ground." They would be found the next morning, Confederate and Union dead, including, as Kelso had guessed, some from the 14th, "their upturned faces covered with frost."[22]

He did not dare help any of the wounded as he lay still among them on the ground. Rebel troops were close by. He strained to hear and make sense of a commotion among them a little way off. It was about one o'clock in the morning. "The enemy seemed to be organizing some movement which they wished to execute as secretly as possible. There were no bugle calls, no loud commands. The officers were rousing the sleeping men as quietly as possible and getting them into line. Those nearest our lines were not yet being disturbed." Kelso, lying still among the wounded, the dying, and the dead, could not quite figure out what they were up to. But then he heard. The enemy was withdrawing about a mile and a half to the southeast to a farm owned by Congressman John S. Phelps.[23]

Kelso needed to get this information back to Colonel Crabb as quickly as possible. Just then, though, a Confederate ambulance wagon approached with a small group of soldiers carrying lanterns. Some of the wounded men near Kelso called out to them. Kelso lay flat on the ground, face down in the dirt, tucking his shotgun beneath him. The ambulance detail approached, lanterns bobbing. They lifted a moaning man nearby into the wagon. One soldier approached a body on Kelso's right. "Here's a dead man," he said. Kelso, eyes closed, trying to be as still as death himself, felt his heart flop violently in his chest. The soldier hovered over him. "And here's another," he said, lowering the lantern to the side of Kelso's head and pushing his boot gently against his side. Kelso did not breathe. "Well," said another soldier farther off, "damn it, don't fool away your time with the *dead* men! Find the *wounded*!" The soldier took his lantern and moved on.[24]

Soon Kelso was alone again with the dead men in the darkness. Fighting the almost irresistible urge to get up and run from the cold battlefield as fast as he could, he turned around and began creeping back by the same route he had taken to get there. But soon he could not bear crawling any longer. He stood and started walking. He was about 30 yards from the blacksmith shop. He had taken only a few steps when someone called "Halt!" from the shop's doorway. Kelso froze. There was enough moonlight for him to see three guards stepping outside, and for them to see him. "Who goes there?"

"A *friend*, I reckon, who are you?" Kelso answered.

"You come up!" one of them demanded, and the three cocked their guns and aimed at him.

"Well, I will come up," Kelso replied. "But I wish to know whether you are Federals or Southern soldiers."

"We are Southern soldiers," a guard answered.

"Oh!" Kelso said, feigning relief. He told them he was a Southern soldier who had gotten separated from his regiment in the battle before it got dark.

"Well," said the guard, "You are all right now. Come up!"

"Boys, if I was sure you were Southern soldiers I would not care, but—" At the word "but" he took off, sprinting past the corner of a building, then alongside a hedge and away into the night toward Fort No. 4. The guards were too surprised to even fire a shot after him.[25]

Kelso ran through the Springfield streets to Colonel Crabb's office and made his report. On the way he concocted his next plan. Crabb was so pleased to have the information about Marmaduke's movements that he gave Kelso permission to do his "devilment." Had Crabb forgotten that Kelso had not slept in three days? Perhaps the colonel did not wait for the lieutenant to share details of his scheme and just sent him off to do what he wanted.[26]

First, Kelso thought, I'll dress myself and a half-dozen of my men in civilian clothing and go back down to those guards in the blacksmith shop. They'll challenge us—"Halt, who goes there?"—and we'll say we're Southern men eager to join Marmaduke's army. They'll call us in—"Come up!"—but when we do we'll grab their guns and place cocked revolvers to their heads, threatening to blow their brains out if they make a squeak. Then we'll make our way into the enemy's camp and capture the soldiers still sleeping by the smoldering houses, too. Easy!

But by the time he had recruited his men, got them dressed, and made it back to the blacksmith shop, the Confederates had gone. On orders from Marmaduke, Colonel Shelby had quietly roused his men sleeping by the smoldering houses and withdrew from the town. So Kelso and his men got their horses and went to reconnoiter Phelps' homestead. There the rebel army had set up camp, using fence rails for firewood, the men feasting happily on the apples, bacon, beef, and bottled beverages Mrs. Phelps had left behind in her larder. Kelso dismounted about 200 yards away from the nearest rebels, and then left his men behind and moved closer alone. Again he was crawling through the dark on his hands and knees, this time through thickets and bushes. The sun would rise soon, and before it did he hoped he could at least capture some men—especially officers—and some horses. He would have to devise a plan quickly.[27]

But as he was thinking this, hunched behind a small bush in a relatively open field, he heard a soldier about 30 yards to his right shout "Halt!"

Had they seen him? He did not move.

"Who goes there?"

Another man replied: "Officer of the Day."

"Advance, Officer of the Day, and give the countersign," said the first.[28]

As the Officer of the Day relieved the guard, Kelso imagined creeping over and giving him the compliments of his big shotgun. But then the officer was joined by 30 mounted men who fanned out and started moving slowly across the field. Some were headed right toward Kelso, and there was no good place to hide. Others would soon cut off his escape route back to his men. So he jumped to his feet and sprinted away as fast as he could. The officer's shouts of "Halt! Halt!" behind him only made him run faster. "Again," he thought, "I had failed to distinguish myself, as I had hoped, by any remarkable feat of personal prowess."[29]

He sent two men back to report to Colonel Crabb, and with the remaining four watched the Confederates from a safer hiding place. The rebels all seemed to be in a foul mood. "Some damned thief has stolen my overcoat," Kelso could hear one yell. "God damn you! You never had an over-coat," another yelled back. A mule brayed. An officer cursed his troops: "Fall in! God damn you, fall in!" One man swore at another soldier for not taking care of his horse. Another officer roared at his troops to march. Marmaduke's men were breaking camp again, getting ready to make another move. Kelso sent more men off to update Crabb. The sun rose above the hills in the east, and it was clear that the Confederate army was headed in that direction, toward the St. Louis Road and the timberland in the Wilson Creek valley. It looked like they were planning the assault that the town's defenders had expected the day before—an attack from the east on Springfield's weakest point.[30]

Kelso sent his last man off to Crabb with that warning and watched the army by himself. "I never saw a finer body of cavalry," Kelso later wrote. "The light of the morning sun, gleaming from the polished weapons, added to the brilliance of their appearance. Presently they halted, just where I feared and expected that they would, due east of town. Here they formed in order of battle. Expecting them soon to come in a charge . . . I now hastened back to town." What Kelso had not been able to see from a distance was that Marmaduke's gleaming army was in fact a ragged bunch—cold, exhausted, and sick. They had raced up from Arkansas, covering the last 50 miles in only twenty-four hours. They had marched with only the supplies each man could carry, hoping to live off the land and feast on the provisions waiting for them in Springfield.

A good number of the cavalry lacked horses. They had called out for overcoats because many did not have any—Major Edwards described overcoats as "an article more desirable than purple and fine linen." Some Confederate soldiers, trudging through the snow and the mud, even lacked boots.[31]

Springfield had prepared for the next attack. With daylight, Crabb could confirm Kelso's reports as he watched Marmaduke's troops through field glasses from the top of the courthouse. Springfield's soldiers punched through more brick walls facing east and placed a sick or wounded man with a gun behind each new porthole, propping up the feeble with flour sacks. But then the Confederate army seemed to move away from the town, farther east down St. Louis Road. A message came in from Marmaduke under a flag of truce. Kelso thought it was an order to surrender, which Crabb refused. Instead it seems to have been merely a customary request for the town to take care of the Confederate wounded left behind and for proper burials for the dead. Union reinforcements were reaching the town and Marmaduke's reinforcements from Porter were still nowhere to be seen. So the Confederate general declared victory and retreated. The Battle of Springfield was over. In the grim bookkeeping that followed, the Union commanders reported 14 killed, 146 wounded, and 5 missing, though another dozen would suffer and die from their wounds in the days that followed; Marmaduke reported 19 killed, 105 wounded, and 26 missing, though Dr. Melcher knew of 80 Confederate burials and there were probably more like 200 wounded.[32]

Later that day, a long wagon train came into town from the south. About a hundred wagons of every description arrived, driven by men, women, and boys. They were Confederate sympathizers. Marmaduke had sent word a few days before that he was certain to take Springfield. Since the town was stocked with far more coffee, sugar, flour, and other provisions than his army would be able to haul back to Arkansas, the general had suggested that rebel civilians might come and share the plunder. The news of Marmaduke's retreat, however, had not reached the wagon train. Even after they had gotten into town, some of the wagon drivers did not understand that the Federal army still controlled Springfield. One old man approached Kelso and asked to see Marmaduke. He wanted to sell the Confederates four of his horses, he said, before the Federals took them. Yes, he snorted, he had taken the loyalty oath to the United States, but that oath "was only from the teeth out." Kelso pleasantly told the man that General Marmaduke was busy at the moment but that he could attend to his business.[33]

That's exactly the number of horses I needed, Kelso said with a smile, and he had a sergeant lead the animals away.

The old man waited uneasily. "Of course you will give me a receipt for them," he said.

"Oh! No," Kelso responded, "You will not need any receipt."

"But how will I get my *pay*?" the man asked, becoming flustered.

"You will not get it at all," Kelso said cheerily, "Can you not give that much for the good of the cause? . . . You will get no pay, and besides this, you will have to help us fight."

The old man look frightened, his zeal for the rebel cause fading. "I do not *want* to *fight*," he said.

"Of course you *do* want to *fight*," Kelso responded. Then one imagines Kelso dropping the bantering tone, his voice lowering, flattening, his gaze piercing the old rebel. "I will also place a man behind you to shoot you dead instantly if you do not perform your full duty in battle. In violation of your oath, you came here to help our enemies. Now you shall help us or die. You do not deserve to be treated as a prisoner of war, and you shall not be so treated. We are *Federals*; I am *Kelso*; now you know what to *expect*."[34]

KELSO WAS NEARLY delirious. His eyes burned and hot tears streamed down his cheeks. His tired horse trotted along the road. He was leading 25 other exhausted mounted men out to meet and guard a wagon train coming from Cassville. Marmaduke's troops were out there somewhere. What day was it? He tried to think. The morning of January 10. The Battle of Springfield had been on the 8th. With Burch and the others, he had been on the scout to Arkansas two days before that, and he had not slept since. He did not even remember how he had come to be on this wagon train guard duty. Had he been ordered? More likely, he realized, he had compulsively volunteered. The events of the past hundred sleepless hours jumbled together in his mind.[35]

The memories tangled, and he could not unravel them. His mind, like the sight from his tearing eyes, was failing. Men slumped and sleeping rode next to him on listless horses. Maybe this was just some sort of distressful dream. He pinched himself, but the flesh on his arm just felt numb. Where were they and what were they supposed to be doing? The enemy was still out there.

He had not stayed long at Springfield the day before. The courage of the town's defenders had risen higher the farther away Marmaduke's army marched. "We felt that we could whip the devil himself, if he would only venture to appear in our presence." Relenting to this exuberance in the flush of victory, Colonel Crabb sent out 300 men to pursue the Confederates. Not a pursuit to engage the enemy, or even to pursue them so closely that Marmaduke might notice. "But we were chasing him all the same." Lieutenant

Colonel Pound was in command of the expedition, Captain Flagg was second in command, and Kelso was third.[36]

After marching for two or three hours, Pound and Flagg got too drunk to even stay in their saddles. "They were rolled into an ambulance and hauled along like a couple of dead hogs." Kelso, in charge of the lookouts and the advance guard, looked behind and saw that the troops had halted. An officer rode up and told him that the men were "in a state of mutiny, refusing to advance nearer the enemy under the command of a couple of officers, gibbering, slobbering, and idiotic from beastly drunkenness." Kelso said that he was in charge up front, and if any real danger threatened he would put Pound and Flagg under arrest and take command himself. The officer rode back with this message, and Kelso heard the men cheer when they were told. They kept marching until midnight, when Pound ordered them to halt at a farmhouse. Then the colonel and the captain with a few of their toadies climbed from their wagons, went into the house, and flopped onto beds to sleep, without giving any orders to the men. Kelso and the rest of the soldiers could see the lights of Marmaduke's campfires in the distance. The men tried to get some sleep while holding their bridle reins in their arms. Kelso stayed awake all that night on the lookout. At daybreak the 300 men returned to Springfield, tired and disgusted.[37]

Somehow, not long after he had returned to town, Kelso managed to get himself assigned to ride back out to find and then guard the wagon train coming in from Cassville. So now he was nearly falling off his horse, his whole body, his whole being, weary beyond description. He had gone nights without sleep before on scouts and patrols, staying alert for hours on end and ignoring cold and hunger. But never had he suffered like this. The desire for sleep seemed to thicken the air and amplify gravity, weighing him down, clouding his mind, draining the life out of him. He gave up trying to think about what had happened yesterday with drunken Pound and Flagg, or about the Battle of Springfield, or the race from Beaver Station and Ozark in the days before. "At last I concluded to give up all thoughts but two: 'Look out for the *enemy*! Look out for the train!'" He clung to those two floating thoughts like a drowning man trying to fight the current pulling him down. He tried to fight sleep, too, by shifting from side to side in his saddle. Still he would feel himself being pulled down to sleep, so he would slide to the ground and try to walk, leading his horse, moving his legs one after the other as if he were hauling bags of sand. But he would even fall asleep while walking. He would start to fall, and then in a dream he would hear guns firing and the sound would startle him awake. So he would climb in his saddle and go through the same routine all over again.[38]

Kelso and his men were briefly roused from their "death-like lethargy" when, near sunset, they met up with a small party of Federal soldiers going in the opposite direction. The wagon train had already returned to Cassville, the soldiers told them, and they went on their way. Now what? the men thought. They were about 20 miles from town. Neither the horses nor the men would be able to return without rest. It would not be safe to set up camp without posting lookouts—even if the main body of Marmaduke's men was not close, the Confederates could have sent detachments out, and they could be anywhere. Kelso and his men would be asleep—none would be able to stay awake as lookouts—and the rebels could be upon them as fast as Emmett MacDonald's cavalry had swept into Beaver Station or Jo Shelby's troops had pushed into Dutchtown. So Kelso led his men about a mile from the road into a dense hazel thicket. He had them tuck down into the bushes, each hidden 50 yards apart from the next. Going another 50 yards past the last man, Kelso hitched his horse, tumbled to the frozen ground, and finally let sleep take him.[39]

General Marmaduke and his men had moved northeast toward Rolla after leaving Springfield. "On the morning of the 9th, I deemed it best not to renew the attack," the general reported. He mistakenly thought that Springfield had already been reinforced, and he added that his "troops, from forced marches, sleepless nights, and the hard-fought battle of the 8th, were not in condition for another desperate struggle." Colonel Jo Shelby reported—in the flowery prose of his adjutant, former journalist John N. Edwards—that his brigade "suffered seriously in the attack upon Springfield, but it covered itself all over with glory, and won imperishable laurels." His men had been "lion-hearted," bravely hurling them themselves against the "Gibraltar of the Southeast," and the fallen were "Southern martyrs." "The mission had been accomplished," Shelby (through Edwards) declared, noting that they had destroyed the forts at Lawrence's Mill and Ozark and had captured an artillery piece from the Federals. The Confederates, "after making almost a circuit of the town with floating banners and waving pennons, left it alone in its glory, because all had been done that could be done."[40]

On January 10, as Kelso fought death-like lethargy on the road to Cassville, Marmaduke's troops marched through Marshfield, 40 miles to the northeast, and burned the small Federal fort there. They finally met up with Colonel Porter's troops. On Sunday morning, January 11, the combined command galloped toward Hartville to engage a force of 880 Union men under the command of Colonel Samuel Merrill. Porter, who had successfully recruited hundreds of Missouri men for the Confederate service the previous year, led the charge.[41]

As Marmaduke's men—"in splendid spirits," according to Shelby's report—advanced on Hartville, Kelso awoke in the hazel thicket 70 miles to the southwest, feeling remarkably refreshed. Everything around him was white with frost. He located his men, who were still asleep, by following the sound of their horses breaking and eating brush. "Some of my men were beardless youths and, as they lay there still before me in the frost upon the frozen ground, their faces looked so blue" that he almost feared they were dead. They looked like the soldiers lying on the cold streets of Springfield on the morning after the battle. But these men stirred, rubbed sleep from their eyes, and told Kelso as they got to their feet that they had never slept better.[42]

Kelso's party got back to Springfield at two in the afternoon, just as the funeral procession was leaving Fort No. 4. The band, with two companies of infantry marching as an escort, the bodies of the Union soldiers in wagons, their horses with their empty saddles, then the rest of the infantry, cavalry, officers, and citizens processed from the fort back to the town square and then out North Street. Colonel King was the day's field marshal, but General Brown was back in command of the army. By the next morning, Springfield heard the good news from Hartville. Merrill's troops, with their sharp-shooting artillery, had inflicted heavy damage on Marmaduke's much larger force, until the Federals ran out of ammunition and had to retreat. Among the Confederate dead was Colonel Porter. "Long-Haired" Emmett MacDonald, shot in the thigh, bled to death, his dying wish supposedly being that General Marmaduke remember his last "gallant charge." The Confederate army, trudging back to Arkansas through the Ozark mountains, would get caught in a bad snowstorm and some of the men, still wanting those overcoats, would lose fingers and toes to frostbite. The Confederates congratulated themselves: Marmaduke's expedition had destroyed some forts, exposed some of the enemy's vulnerabilities, and caused Federal troops to shift and scramble. But there were still no Confederate flags flying in Missouri. "The enemy got nothing but a good thrashing and one gun," General Curtis concluded.[43]

Springfield's residents patched the holes that Confederate shot had left in their houses and outbuildings, replaced the broken glass in their windows, and repaired fences that had been knocked down. Several buildings, such as the Lyon Hotel, the Methodist Church, the college, and the newspaper printing shop, had been hit especially hard. Shells had exploded inside more than a few homes. Refugees from the south filed into the town, and there were not enough beds for them. The post chaplain, the fighting parson Fred

Wines, tried to keep the refugees fed and warm, and the Western Sanitary Commission established a hospital for them. Kelso, though, was able to buy "a pretty little house" and move his family up from Ozark. He dreamed of staying in Springfield after the war and opening an academy.[44]

Over the next few weeks, Kelso and the men of the 14th Cavalry went on several scouts of three or four days each, probing into the counties to the south and east of Springfield, looking for bushwhackers and thieves that Marmaduke's army might have stirred up on its way. They captured a few rebel prisoners, horses, and guns, but there was no fighting. These expeditions followed the pattern set by the pursuit of Marmaduke the day after the Battle of Springfield. Kelso was third in command. The troops would stop at night at a farmhouse, and while the other officers went inside to warm themselves by the fire, eat at the farmer's table, and sleep in soft beds, Kelso stayed outside with the men as officer of the guard. One night, in the midst of a heavy snowstorm, they stopped at the farm of "a wealthy old rebel." Kelso's commanding officers went into the warm house as usual, and, as usual, sent out the order putting Kelso in charge of the guard. In deference to their host, the scout's commander also ordered Kelso to prevent the men from taking any of the farmer's corn, oats, or hay for their starving horses; to forbid them from killing and eating any of his pigs, sheep, chickens and turkeys; and to stop them from burning any of his fence rails, the only source of firewood in the storm. Kelso was indignant. In the biting winter storm, soldiers and horses alike would suffer severely.[45]

Kelso called the men together and read them the orders. He watched their faces darken and heard them begin to mutter curses. Then he gave them his interpretation of the orders. They could not make their fires from fence rails, but if they happened to find what they could designate merely as "*split timber*," they could use that. They could feed their horses with any "*dried vegetables*" they found in the barn. And they could eat any pigs, turkeys, or chickens that just "happened to fall and break their damned necks or happened to be kicked and killed by the horses." Kelso's men took the hint, and soon the horses were feeding, great fires were blazing, and the air was filled with the sweet savory smell of roasting meat. Kelso found some of the rebel farmer's apples and honey, too, which he distributed to the troops. His men "were in fine good humor, and I had a little to eat a little with every mess in the entire encampment."[46]

Kelso had had about all he could take of Captain Flagg, and the captain felt the same way about Kelso. In late January, they were back on the charred campground at Ozark. Flagg ordered Kelso to march his company to Forsyth,

30 miles to the south. The subsequent exchange between the two men prompted Flagg to file charges against the lieutenant, and seven weeks later, on March 11, 1863, Kelso found himself facing a court martial at Springfield. The court was made up of three captains and three lieutenants from Kansas regiments and Captain Alvah R. Conklin of 4th MSM Cavalry acting as judge advocate. Kelso was charged with "conduct to the prejudice of good order and military discipline." Flagg's complaint held that Kelso, in front of the men, absolutely refused to obey the captain's order to march the troops to Forsyth. The lieutenant then said, according to Flagg, that he would not "move his company on any wild goose chase" and would not march until he saw the written orders that Flagg had received.[47]

None of the three witnesses called by the prosecution could testify that he had heard any conversation between Flagg and Kelso that day at Ozark, and only one, Captain Madison Day of Company F, seemed to be under the impression that Kelso had disobeyed orders. Kelso then introduced the first witness for the defense, Sergeant William Crumpley, who said that he had indeed heard the conversation. Both officers had walked toward Crumpley's wagon. Kelso asked Flagg about the orders to move. "Flagg said that he would show them when he got ready." Then the captain asked if Kelso were refusing to obey orders. The lieutenant, Crumply testified, said nothing when Flagg asked this the first time. "Flagg then said if you refuse to obey my orders, I will report it as such." I'm not refusing, Kelso replied. The lieutenant "formed his men and was soon on the march." Crumpley then added that "Kelso addressed Flagg in a gentlemanly manner."

The judge advocate, Captain Conklin, perhaps raising an eyebrow, pressed the witness on this last point: "What was Lieutenant Kelso's manner towards his commanding officer that day?"

"His manner," Sergeant Crumpley answered, backpedaling, "was positive and plain but not insulting." Then the sergeant further revised his testimony: "Part of his language might have been insulting but it was deserved."

"What was the language of Lieutenant Kelso that was insulting?" the judge advocate continued.

"When Kelso started off to form his company," Crumpley answered, "he (Kelso) said he had been obeying drunken officers as long as he was willing."

"During the conversation," the judge advocate went on, "did you hear Kelso say anything in regard to marching his men on a wild goose chase?"

Yes, Crumpley admitted, Kelso had said that too.

"Did not Lieutenant Kelso's whole manner and conversation seem to doubt and question Flagg's having received orders to march the command?"

Yes, Kelso seemed to doubt at first, the sergeant answered, but when Captain Flagg said he had the order Kelso seemed convinced.

The final witness was William C. Day, an assistant surgeon. Day testified that he had gone with Kelso to ask Flagg if the captain actually had orders to march to Forsyth. Flagg had answered: it should be enough for Kelso that I gave him an order. Kelso said, in a "gentlemanly and courteous" manner, that of course he would obey the order. Captain Conklin, seemingly suspicious, then asked Day if he and Kelso had had any subsequent conversations about this exchange with Flagg. Day answered that he did not think so.

The judge advocate's final question to Day seemed to hint which way he might be leaning: was not this a simple case of insubordination to a commanding officer?

"Was Captain Flagg the ranking officer in the camp at this time?" he asked.

"He was," Day responded.

The accused then made a closing statement to the court. "When I enquired of Captain Flagg if he had orders to move," Kelso began, "I did so for the purpose of silencing any doubts about our being ordered off improperly. In regard to the remark that I was weary following drunken officers. I did so from the fact that many grievances have grown out of my superior officers being intoxicated. I made this remark also from the fact that I was suffering under abusive language made to me when I asked to see Captain Flagg's order."

The prosecution's witnesses could not persuasively establish the three central points: that Kelso had challenged Flagg's order, refused at first to obey it, and spoke to his commanding officer in an insulting manner. Strangely, the defense conceded all three charges. The courtroom was cleared, and the seven officers deliberated. Apparently, in this instance at least, facts (Flagg was a drunk and he did issue improper orders) trumped the demand for respectful obedience by subordinates required by "good order and military discipline." The court found Kelso not guilty and recommended that he "resume his sword" and return to duty.

At the time of Kelso's trial, the Missouri State Militia was being reorganized and reduced from 13,000 to 10,000 men to bring it into accord with the federal law that authorized and funded it. The 14th was disbanded and two of its companies were incorporated with the 8th Regiment MSM Cavalry, commanded at first by Colonel J. W. McClurg, but soon afterward by Colonel J. J. Gravelly. Kelso's Company H became Company M in this new regiment. Captain Flagg had already been transferred, with Lieutenant

John R. Kelso's sword. Photo courtesy of Rhiannon Kelso.

Colonel Pound, to the 4th Regiment on February 4, two weeks after the incident at Ozark. The court martial was Flagg's parting gift to Kelso. In having the charges dismissed by establishing in court that Flagg was an irresponsible drunk, Kelso more than returned the favor. In July Flagg resigned from the army.[48]

10

Hero of the South West

"THE HERO OF the South West." That's what they called him. It was early May in 1864, and Kelso was briefly on leave from his company at Neosho and staying overnight at a hotel in Sedalia, 180 miles north, before taking the train to St. Louis. Sedalia, in west central Missouri, was a small town of about a thousand people that had sprouted up at the end of the Missouri Pacific Railroad only three years earlier. Like Rolla to the south, it was a town where the trains stopped and the stagecoaches and wagon trains to the West began. So throughout the war various regiments were stationed there—Missouri Cavalry and Enrolled Militia units manning the fort on East Main Street, but also troops from Indiana, Iowa, and Kansas camping just outside the town center. A huge government warehouse on the north side of Main Street supplied the soldiers, and the cattle in a 5-acre corral extending south from the block between Osage and Ohio streets fed them. The town's business district was a string of false-front wooden buildings extending two and a half blocks along a treeless street that was either dust or mud: shops, stores, stables, and saloons but not yet a brick school, church, or courthouse. The town fathers, though, were proud of the place, and imagined a great future. They had staged an elaborate July Fourth celebration the previous summer and just three months before Kelso's visit had secured a charter for the city and its designation as the new Pettis County seat. A delegation of these leading citizens, including the alderman and dry goods merchant Elias Laupheimer, called on Kelso at his hotel. They asked if they could take him for a ride through town in an open carriage because "there was a general desire on the part of the people to see 'The Hero of the South West.'"[1]

Kelso took his ride through the streets of Sedalia. "The sidewalks, the balconies, the windows,—every place, from which a view could be obtained, all were crowded with men, women, and children," he later recalled fondly.

John R. Kelso, ca. 1863-4. John R. Kelso, carte de visite, folder 25, Charles Lanham Collection, State Historical Society of Missouri, Columbia. State Historical Society of Missouri.

"Wherever we appeared, we were greeted with enthusiastic cheers and the waving of flags, hats, and handkerchiefs. The impromptu ovation, so full of heartiness, was a complete surprise to me and rendered the occasion one of the proudest in my life." That evening he was invited to an exclusive party at Laupheimer's home. Several officers of higher rank attended, but Kelso "was the observed of all observers,—the lion of the party." Stories about him, it was clear, had spread from the state's southwest corner to its center. When he reached St. Louis, he saw that word of his exploits had made an impression there, too, and he "received many marks of honor." By the spring of 1864, he had made a name for himself: "No other officer of my rank had ever excited so much public attention. No other Union officer in the South West was ever so loved, so praised, so idolized by the Union people, or so hated, so feared, so bitterly cursed by the rebels. No one regarded me with indifference."[2]

Stories about Kelso spread by word of mouth during the war and afterward. Wiley Britton heard many of them. A native of Newton County,

Missouri, Britton served the Union in the 6th Kansas Cavalry on the Missouri-Kansas border. He heard more after the war as he conducted several thousand interviews while investigating pension and property compensation claims for the War Department. Stories of Kelso's "fearless operations against Southern bandits," Britton wrote in one of his postwar histories, "were familiar to nearly every family in Southwest Missouri." Britton heard from "the many witnesses examined who had reminiscences to relate of [Kelso's] daring acts in the war." But Britton also had a brother and a brother-in-law who had served with Kelso, and the historian had corresponded with the man himself. While those who sympathized with the Confederacy hated Kelso and even called him a monster, Britton thought of him as a hero who "was without fear and a genius in many respects and like a tiger in his warlike activities." Kelso's daring deeds made Britton think of Ulysses and Diomede in the Tenth Book of the *Iliad*, Greek warriors who entered a Trojan camp at night, slaughtered enemy soldiers, and triumphantly returned with trophies. "But this grandest of scenes in the description of individual heroism in war scarcely surpasses some of the daring acts of Kelso, the student, teacher, and soldier."[3]

Kelso was remembered as a polite and scholarly man, always pacing about camp with a book in his hands, but especially as a fighter with remarkable courage. Britton commented repeatedly about Kelso's reputation for fearlessness. Describing one skirmish, Britton wrote that Kelso "displayed his usual tact, daring, and coolness. In fact, it was asserted by those who had served with him from the beginning of the war that he never became disconcerted under the most trying situations." Kelso "frequently exposed himself in the most perilous situations without any outward signs of fear or excitement. He was always equal to an emergency. When in a fight or dangerous situation, no interposing obstacle disconcerted him at the critical moment." Britton recorded several stories to illustrate the point that "[a]s far as outward signs were concerned, [Kelso] seems to have been absolutely without fear."[4]

Britton wrote that on one occasion, Kelso went out alone into the Ozark Mountains, disguised as a bushwhacker. He joined a rebel camp, but most of the bandits left him behind with two who did not trust him—they "never took their hands off their guns for a moment." Kelso acted as if he did not notice their distrust, and chatted with them affably. One afternoon, he pretended to have gotten a splinter stuck in his finger and complained that he could not get it out. He went to the two bushwhackers for help, holding out his hand for them to inspect the injury. As they leaned forward to look, they slightly relaxed their vigilance, "so that each let the butt of his gun drop to the ground while holding it with one hand near the muzzle." In a flash,

Kelso "with his left hand seized the gun of the nearest bandit and in another moment with his right hand drew his revolver and shot him, and the other bandit also." Kelso took their horses and guns and rejoined his command.[5]

On another occasion, Britton wrote, Kelso was scouting in southern Taney County with a small detachment of his men when he learned that several Southern families were sheltering some pro-Confederate bandits. Early one morning, Kelso and his men surrounded a house. He "saw three bandits within, and keeping his eyes on them and his hands on his shotgun in the position of 'ready,' crossed the fence and started for the door." As he did so, "a big dog came snarling and growling at him and seized him by the calf of the leg. Not in the least disconcerted by this unexpected attack of the dog, he stopped, and keeping his eyes on the bandits took with his right hand his revolver from the scabbard, and feeling for the dog's neck shot the beast dead. He proceeded as if nothing had happened, and entering the door, found that the bandits had escaped through the opposite door." His daring had so amazed them that they fled without firing a shot.[6]

Kelso's "name was connected with so many acts of daring adventure in Southern and Southwest Missouri during the war" and he "was so much talked about by the Unionists and secessionists" in that region, Britton wrote, "on account of the numerous victims upon whom his avenging hands had fallen." Of course, "he was popular with and liked by the Unionists and sincerely hated by the Southern people." R. I. Holcombe, a less sympathetic local historian writing in the early 1880s, called Kelso "a desperate man" who was "fanatical in his Unionism" and who believed that all Confederates were traitors deserving death. "It is said of him that he killed many a man without a cause. Stories are told of him that make him appear . . . fit only to be denominated a monster, and entitled only to execration. Doubtless some of these stories are exaggerations, but the fact remains that Kelso was a 'bad man,' and held human life in very cheap estimation."[7]

After Kelso's death, in 1893 the *St. Louis Republic* published an article of over 5,300 words that conveyed something of both sides. "The Scout of the Ozarks: John R. Kelso's Mysterious and Bloody Career in Southwest Missouri" was based on interviews with people who had known him or known of him, including three men who had fought at his side. Kelso's name, the reporter wrote, was still "spoken with a shudder by many people along the Missouri and Arkansas border, though nearly thirty years of peace have helped to sustain or palliate the deeds of this fanatical partisan of the Union cause." Some of the stories about the man might "sound like the nursery tales of mythical desperadoes," but, the journalist assured his readers, they were "well authenticated by witnesses still living." The article described Kelso as "brave to the point of recklessness" and marveled at his preternatural composure under fire: "Kelso was a man of phenomenal self-control. He never lost his cool, methodical judgment in the most perilous situations.... He loved to fight, but the intoxication of hand-to-hand encounter only steadied the man's nerves and sharpened his perceptions." The reporter also described him as a remorseless, ferocious, inhuman "rebel-killer" who "butchered his victims" with an "unforgiving heart."[8]

Even in Britton's appreciative account Kelso's darker side can be seen. In the episode with the dog, for example, after Kelso entered through the front door "he shot the man of the house and severely wounded his son, holding that those who gave aid and comfort to the bandits were as deserving of punishment as the bandits themselves." The author of "The Scout of the Ozarks," who heard the same story from an eyewitness, added details that painted an even more brutal picture: "An old man was found in the cabin, whose wife and son, a young man hardly grown, completed the family. Kelso shot down the aged husband and father as soon as the fleeing soldiers dodged his aim." The boy ran from the house and "was climbing over the fence around a little 'truck patch' when the Captain fired the other barrel of his shot-gun at him. The lad fell down among some pea vines and Kelso thought he was killed. The wounded youth crawled under the matted vines and escaped to tell in after years his sad story. Kelso went back into the house and searched for more soldiers and left the helpless old woman alone with her dead husband and, as she thought, murdered boy."[9]

The author of "The Scout of the Ozarks" in the *Republic* presented another account of Kelso's cold-bloodedness, claiming he heard it, thirty years after the fact, from a lieutenant in Kelso's company. Kelso and the lieutenant, heading a scouting party southeast of Springfield, came across a party of rebels. They charged them and routed them, killing several. The lieutenant found a young Confederate shot in the chest. "The boy was suffering great pain and asked the officer to kill him. He said his wound was mortal and he wanted to escape the pain of a lingering death." The lieutenant tried to convince the soldier that the wound might not be fatal. But then Kelso rode up, "radiant with the flush of victory." The "wounded boy" made his "desperate wish" known to "the stern rebel hater." Kelso immediately drew his gun and fired. " 'Somebody's darling' had added another score to the bloody record of the remorseless scout who killed with such inhuman delight."[10]

Kelso did not tell this story in his memoir (nor the ones about the splinter in his finger or the dog biting his leg, either). But he did present a parallel one, with a different ending. He and Burch, leading 60 men, were chasing a large but retreating and exhausted body of rebels near Dug Springs, about 20 miles southeast of Springfield, in the fall of 1864. They charged and routed the enemy, killing several. "At Dug Springs, I found a well-dressed and intelligent wounded rebel lying upon the ground. He asked me to dismount and come to him. I did so, asking him where he was hurt." He had been hit in the spine and was paralyzed below the neck. "Then I am bound to die, am I not?" he inquired. "Yes," Kelso answered, "you will die very soon, but you will die without pain." The wounded man requested a favor. Would Kelso write to the soldier's mother and sister in Cole County? "Tell them that I died a true soldier fighting for what I believed to be a righteous cause." Kelso took down the address and said he would. "The sun was now down," Kelso later wrote. "The shades of night were gathering in the forest. A solemn silence reigned where the sounds of battle had so recently been heard." As Kelso turned to go, the wounded soldier asked one more favor: "Please shoot me," he said. "I would much rather die quickly than to linger on here alone and to be torn, perhaps, by wolves before I am dead." But Kelso could only mount his horse, silently and sadly, and ride away. "I sent back for this poor fellow as soon as I could, but when the party sent for him arrived, he was cold and stiff; and there, in that forest, where he fell, he was laid to rest."[11]

Friend and foe alike marveled at "the fearless and energetic manner in which Kelso had hunted down the bandits, frequently penetrating their most secret hiding places and engaging them in hand-to-hand conflicts." Both his admirers and detractors remembered a story about a trophy quilt. The reporter for the *St. Louis Republic* heard it from Mart Hancock, who had served in Kelso's cavalry regiment. Britton told the tale by describing Kelso making his way alone through the night woods toward a bandits' camp, "moving along cautiously over the dim path . . . carefully scanning every object in front, with revolver in hand and ears alert to the slightest sound in any direction. After he gets up near to the marauders' camp, who can follow him through his careful reconnoitering of it on up to the commencement of his terrible slaughter, without his heart beating audibly?" Kelso found three bandits sleeping under their crude shelter, and six horses saddled nearby. "He ascertains that the sleeping bandits are covered with a beautiful quilt, which he desires to take unstained with blood as a trophy, and carefully draws it off them, and in another moment like a tiger springs on his victims and shoots them to death before they are conscious of danger." Kelso then mounted one of the horses and led the others back to his own camp "as trophies of his bloody adventure." Ulysses and Diomede, too, had slain sleeping Trojan soldiers before making off with their horses and chariot. Britton was quick to explain that, despite Kelso's interest in trophies, "he was never charged with committing acts of plunder, or of turning captured property into channels of private gain." But the writer admitted that Kelso's "acts were of course characterized as cruel by those who sympathized with the South."[12]

Britton admired Kelso's intellect as well as his courage: "He was a great student of languages, philosophy, and mathematics," Britton wrote; "He had an insatiable thirst for knowledge—knowledge, too, of the profoundest depths." Holcombe, the Missouri historian writing in the early 1880s, called Kelso a "transcendentalist" who was "well versed in all the dogmas of the schools of modern thought. It is said that he always carried a book of some sort in his saddle pockets, and frequently engaged in the study of mental philosophy and the subtleties of metaphysics while lying in the brush by the roadside waiting to 'get the drop' on a rebel!'" The *Republic's* reporter wondered how "this strange man could return from a bloody scout and take up his studies with as much earnestness as though he had been at college preparing for commencement." Britton commended Kelso's "characteristic earnestness." Holcombe concluded that "[m]uch learning made him mad." Britton noted Kelso's self-discipline: "He was strictly temperate in his habits of life, and he prided himself in asserting that he had never taken a chew of tobacco, nor used the weed in any form; nor touched a drop of intoxicants of any kind. No language ever escaped his lips that was not fit for the most refined and cultured ears." Holcombe recorded that Kelso "believed in diet and plenty of exercise as brain-producing elements" and dismissed him as a "crank."[13]

Britton did not dismiss Kelso, but he struggled to explain what drove the man to pursue his foes with such relentless determination. Britton speculated that as a spy who had entered the enemy's camps, Kelso had seen firsthand how Confederates mistreated Union prisoners and heard how rebels, conspicuous before the war "for their domineering conduct towards political opponents," boasted of killing Union men for trifling causes. According to Britton, Kelso refused to be promoted any higher than a captain of a company because he did not want to miss "the opportunity of participating in the personal conflicts with the enemy, which appears to have been almost a burning desire with him."[14]

Scenes of "individual heroism" in "personal conflicts," especially featuring the "intoxication of hand-to-hand encounter": Kelso himself told some of these stories. Sometimes he went out of his way to confront enemies by himself. Once, in the summer of 1863, he went on "a sly hunt for bushwhackers" 3 miles southeast of Newtonia with only one other man. Then he sent that soldier back to camp for reinforcements while planning to fight two bushwhackers on his own because he "greatly wished to add to my fame for personal prowess." He hid in the bushes next to their camp. In the brush beyond them, there was a sound—branches snapping, as if someone were approaching. The bushwhackers listened, grew alarmed, and then ran to untie their horses. That's when Kelso bounded out into the open, shouting, "Halt, you sons of bitches, you have *Kelso* to deal with now!"[15]

The bushwhackers, at the mention of his name seemingly "frightened almost out of their wits," left their horses and fled on foot. Kelso chased them. The smaller bushwhacker turned and fired one barrel of his shotgun; the shot tore through Kelso's shirt at the left shoulder but left him unharmed. Kelso answered by blasting his shotgun at the other man, hitting him in the right thigh. As Kelso approached, the wounded man dove into a thick cluster of bushes and vines and thrust his Mississippi rifle out through the foliage at his pursuer. Kelso grabbed the gun; the bushwhacker, with a "tremendous pull," yanked Kelso into the bushes. They both dropped the rifle, Kelso seizing the bushwhacker's collar and the wounded man wrapping his arms around Kelso, and they began to wrestle. "He was a powerful young man, weighing at least 200 pounds. For once, I had my match. His strength was prodigious."[16]

Kelso was wearing his spurs, which became tangled in the vines and made him fall to the ground, flat on his back, bringing his opponent right down on top of him. Kelso realized that he was suddenly very vulnerable—the man could have freed himself from Kelso's grasp, pulled a revolver, and shot the Hero of the South West dead as he lay there, tangled in the vines. But instead the man grabbed Kelso's throat and tried to choke him to death. A fatal mistake. Kelso pushed upward on the man with his left hand, freed his right, drew his revolver, quickly held the barrel to the man's head, and pulled the trigger. "He dropped upon me like a log, his hot blood gushing out upon my face and neck."[17]

Just then, his reinforcements, a 10-man squad led by Sergeant John Baxter, appeared from the brush. "Seeing me dripping with blood, panting violently, and scarcely able to speak, they turned pale as corpses, thinking that I was dripping with my own gore and that I was about to give up the ghost." Gasping, he sent them off after the other bushwhacker. No sooner had they gone than that man ran from the woods back into the open space of the small camp, nearly crashing right into Kelso. With no time to draw his gun, still panting from the fight with the first man, Kelso tackled the second one. "I was in no condition for another such struggle. This bushwhacker, however, was also out of breath from running, and was, moreover, a mere pigmy as compared with his herculean fallen companion." This second wrestling match ended like the first. Baxter and his men returned, having found and killed a third bushwhacker at his cabin, and they all returned to their camp. "This really desperate and thrilling adventure of mine lost nothing in the telling among my friends, and it tended to still heighten my fame for wonderful personal prowess."[18]

Kelso knew that sometimes, however, he would not have survived these hand-to-hand encounters with the enemy without help from his men. Britton described Kelso's conquest of the notorious bushwhacker Wallace Finney as a simple thing: Kelso merely "ran up and pulled the bandit [Finney] off his horse before he could loose it, shot him, and took his horse and brace of revolvers from him." Kelso's version depicts a more desperate struggle. Kelso, spotted spying from the cornfield while Burch and the men waited at the edge of the woods, ran at the house firing his revolvers as the four bushwhackers raced to their horses, which were hitched under some small trees twenty steps from the doorway. He hit one—Captain Wakeman—who stumbled toward a brush thicket. Two others mounted, started toward the thicket, but "then stopped a moment to see on which side the danger lay." The fourth— Finney—was slower unhitching his horse. Kelso was almost upon him. The bushwhacker mounted and began drawing his revolver. The revolvers in Kelso's hands were empty. He had two more on him, but could not draw in time. He lunged for Finney's arm, preventing the rebel from grabbing his gun, and pulled him off his horse.[19]

"As his face met mine in his fall," Kelso recounted, "I read the look of despair on his dark features." Kelso landed on top of Finney and at first tried to pin him to the ground. But the two mounted rebels—Bellsmire and Stoker— were close by, and they leveled their revolvers at Kelso. So he quickly pulled Finney to his feet and tried to use the bushwhacker's body as a shield. "Hope and a terrible resolution took the place of despair in [Finney's] look. He saw what his comrades were trying to do. Throwing his arms about me, he whirled me around so that his comrades could shoot me with less danger to himself. With all my power, I whirled him so that, if they fired, they would hit him. And thus in this violent waltz of death we whirled till all things around seemed to be bands of different colors all whirling." Bellsmire and Stoker aimed to shoot, but hesitated. But where, Keslo wondered, were Burch and his men?[20]

Gunshots, close by. Joel Hood, a young scout in Kelso's company, had raced across the cornfield to help Kelso, and his shots, just in time, made the two mounted bushwhackers turn away from the death waltz and spur their horses. It was only then that Kelso was able to "try to fix my waltzing partner." Kelso's left hand held Finney's right; Finney's left delivered "several staggering blows" to Kelso's head. Kelso drew, fired into Finney's stomach, hit him over the head with the empty gun, and then, after Finney finally fell, took out his last revolver and finished him. But Kelso knew that he owed his life to Hood, and he gave the scout Finney's brace of revolvers as a sign of his gratitude.[21]

If not fighting alone, Kelso at least liked to be outnumbered. In April of 1863 he described in a letter to Susie a scout of what he said were 50 men into Indian Territory—land owned by the Seneca Nation—led by Captain Ozias Ruark. Their goal was "to destroy a band of thieves and bushwhackers who were infesting that part of the country." Kelso went forward with a detachment of four men "dressed like bushwhackers in butternut-colored clothing," pretending to be dispatch bearers from General Marmaduke's Confederate brigade. They even carried forged dispatches and orders to back up their story. They were hoping to infiltrate the cattle rustlers' camp and then report back to Ruark and the larger force. Finding a camp of only 10 men, though (40 others being scattered through the countryside in houses), Kelso changed the plan. He wanted to try "to accomplish with my four men that which had been looked upon as a hazardous undertaking for fifty men. It would be quite a feather in our caps, if we five could break up this band ourselves."[22]

Kelso and his "dispatch bearers" met five of the rebels and fooled them. They agreed to join the thieves and help them collect two hundred head of cattle, herd them into a hundred-acre pasture at Cowskin Prairie, and then help drive them over 200 miles south to Boggy Depot, a major Confederate supply station in Indian Territory, for sale to the Southern army. So the disguised Federals rode with their new friends deeper into Seneca country. The land was fertile, the farmhouses richly appointed, and the "prairies were alive with cattle," but they saw few people because the bushwhackers had driven most of the Seneca away. The thieves themselves were "half-breeds and white men, fantastically dressed and loaded with formidable looking weapons, rifles, shotguns, revolvers, and bowie knives."[23]

Kelso rode most of the time with a man named Swan, "a dark, sullen, cruel, villainous looking man who would undoubtedly be an ugly customer in a conflict for life." Swan spoke at length, peppering most of his sentences with profanity, bitterly cursing the Federals in general and the cavalrymen posted at Neosho in particular who, he knew, were devoted to exterminating bushwhackers like himself. "He was specially venomous in his remarks about *Kelso*. He said that that damned son of a bitch had played off on many Southern men and had thus managed to either kill or capture them." Let that

Kelso just try, he said, to play *him*. Yes, Kelso nodded, just let that damn Kelso try to play *us*. Swan said that he had never set a man on fire, "but that, if he could take Kelso alive, he would burn him. He said that he would really enjoy seeing Kelso dance to the tune of a slow fire." Swan said that he had a plan to catch Kelso, and asked his new confidante, Marmaduke's messenger, if he would help once they were done driving the cattle. Kelso "readily agreed."[24]

Kelso's men, in their slouched hats and butternut clothes, rode with the rustlers that day, rounding up cattle suitable for Confederate beef and herding them into the pasture. At night, all ten men ate their suppers around a campfire, talking and laughing. "Our genuine thief comrades boasted of the number of Union men they had murdered, the number of Union families they had driven off, and the amount of Union property they had stolen." Several bragged about having taken the oath of loyalty to the United States and showed the certificates they had attesting to that fact, papers that offered protection against harassment by Federal troops. Kelso knew that he and his men could have killed or captured "these five villains," but he wanted the other five as well, including the band's captain, who were due to arrive that evening. He knew that his men, too, "wanted the glory of finishing up twice our number of these well-armed desperadoes." So he waited. As darkness came, he spread out his blankets, listened to the owls hoot, and thought about Swan's eagerness to capture and burn that son of a bitch Kelso. He found the whole situation fascinating, a thrill heightened by the danger he faced.[25]

After the darkness deepened on the prairie, they heard someone call from a hazel thicket beyond the rail fence at the edge of their camp. It was the captain and the other four men. One of Kelso's soldiers was at a distance, tending to his horse, but the other three knew to casually position themselves around the five cattle rustlers at the campfire. Each would take a man, leaving Kelso with two: Swan and a thief named King. Swan answered the captain and told him to come inside the rail fence. No, the captain called, *you* come out *here*.

"No, Cap, I have my boots off, come in!" Swan replied.

"Come out here!" the captain repeated.

"Oh, damn it, what's the matter with you?" Swan asked.

"Do you know who the men are that are with you in camp?" the captain called.

"Yes," Swan said, "they are Southern men."

"I don't know that, come out here!" the captain hollered.

The captain's suspicion finally sparked a response in the five cattle rustlers by the fire. They went for their guns, but the Federals already had their revolvers in their hands. "Swan sprang up with his gun," Kelso wrote. "I sprang toward him. He brought the muzzle of his gun to my breast. I caught it quickly with my left hand and turned it aside while I put two shots into King, who was just rising with his gun. . . . Then turning upon Swan, I emptied the other four chambers into him as well as I could while clinging, with my left hand to the gun which he was jerking with all his might." But Swan did not fall. "Throwing down my empty revolver and seizing the gun with both hands, I wrenched it from him, and, quickly turning it upon him, I literally blew his head off with it, scattering his brains around for some paces upon the grass."[26]

Kelso's men killed the other three. The "cowardly Captain," after the sound of gunfire, did not lead his men out of the hazel thicket. Kelso and his squad did not wait for them: as soon as they caught hold of their frightened horses, they quickly galloped off into the night, 6 miles back to Captain Ruark and the rest of the men, killing two more rebels along the way. At daylight, the whole party rode back to the pasture. "Then we beheld a sickening sight. Five mangled bodies lying in their blood, their ghastly features distorted and covered with blood and dirt. One of them had crawled several yards from where he had fallen. He was now growing stiff, however, like the others."[27]

The day after returning to camp, on April 22, 1863, Kelso wrote his letter to Susie, describing all the details of the scout into Seneca country. Right after describing the dead, stiffening bodies, Kelso mentioned that he was studying Spanish in his leisure hours and had composed a play, called "The Gambler," to be performed in camp that night.

Captain Ruark's report said that his detachment had numbered 30, not 50 men, and that Kelso took 5, not 4, soldiers ahead. Ruark reported a total of 4 enemies killed, not 7. Official reports frequently miscounted the dead and wounded, so Kelso was not necessarily exaggerating the body count. Ruark gave no details of how the killings occurred, saying only that two Kelso had found at "a kennel of bushwhackers" had "fought till they died," and that two more found later did the same. Wiley Britton, though, heard the story and recorded it as another hand-to-hand struggle of a lone hero. "On leaving the detachment that afternoon Lieutenant Kelso had little trouble in passing himself off . . . as a Southern officer in that section on important business," Britton wrote. Earning the confidence of two cattle rustlers, Kelso "agreed to assist them in collecting the cattle to sell into the Southern army, and actually helped them drive in a few head." The friendly conversation turned from one subject to another, "until it came to their arms, and then in such a manner that he was permitted to seize hold of one of their guns and in the struggle wrenched it from his hands. The moment he disarmed the bandits, he opened fire and shot them down, and then mounting his horse with his trophies, joined his comrades, who had been stationed a short distance off, and rode into camp with them." Ruark's report, however, had other details from Kelso's account—the disguise as Marmaduke's dispatch bearers, the bushwhackers' boasts and loyalty oaths, the specific plans for the cattle rustling. And more than Kelso himself, Ruark presented the whole scheme as Kelso's idea. "Too much praise cannot be bestowed upon Lieutenant Kelso," Ruark concluded, "for the daring and cunning he displayed."[28]

The conversation with Swan about catching Kelso was not the only time the Hero of the South West heard enemies speak about him while not knowing he was listening. On four other occasions, he claimed, he overheard rebels discussing Old Kelso the preeminent guerrilla hunter, the opponent they most hated and feared. Spying alone in the woods one night and eavesdropping on two bushwhackers chatting by a fire, Kelso heard his name mentioned. One asked if there had "been any Feds" at a place about 8 miles away. "None but old Kelso," his companion answered. "He seems to be everywhere." The first then wished that "some plan could be devised to cut off the old son of a bitch's head." The second bushwhacker revealed that he did have a plan to get Kelso: a rebel woman at a house Kelso visited had agreed to throw a party and drug his food or drink so he could easily be captured. Kelso later found out that the bushwhackers had in fact approached the woman but that she had refused to cooperate.[29]

Another time, he overheard a rebel woman bragging about how her father had outfoxed "Old Kelso." Kelso was part of a large expedition hunting guerrillas in the summer of 1863. Scouting ahead at night with a squad of 10 men, he came across a man moving through the brush. Kelso's men went after him, but he signaled surrender, and Kelso ordered them to spare him. The grateful captive admitted that he was a local man serving as a guide for the rebels, but he promised to serve Kelso—the man who had just prevented his death—in any way he could. He guided them toward the rebel camp, but as they got close he asked to stay behind at a large tree, promising he would wait there to guide them back, declaring "in the most solemn manner that he would rather die than prove false to the man who had so recently saved his life." Kelso went forward and spied on the camp, but when he returned to the tree the man was gone—and the noise at the camp suggested that he had left and alerted the guerrillas. Making his way back toward his own camp, Kelso stopped by what he knew was the guide's house and heard the man's daughter talking to two or three rebel soldiers in the yard.[30]

Her father had just been at the house, she gleefully told the soldiers, and had just left with a party that would ambush "Old Kelso" up the road. They were nearly sure to get him, she said, and her father would get a "big reward for his head." But, one of the soldiers warned, if they miss him, Kelso might someday get your father's head. Oh, she laughed, they would have to catch him before they could hang him. In the darkness, Old Kelso slipped away from the side of the house, determined to punish the guide for his treachery.[31]

A few days later, Kelso heard that the treacherous guide had pitched a tent in a brush thicket not far from his house. He found the man gathering wood a dozen yards from his tent and his gun. When the guide realized that he could neither escape nor defend himself, he turned to Kelso, "looking like a corpse. 'Why did you betray me that night when I left you by the tree?' I asked. 'I--- - I----- I----,' stammered he, and stopped. Without waiting to hear more, I put three bullets through his heart and left him dead upon the ground."[32]

Crouched under a window outside a rebel house on another occasion and listening at a door that was slightly ajar, Kelso eavesdropped on a conversation between several women and two teenaged boys. The boys insisted that they were going off to be bushwhackers as soon as they could get their hands on some guns. "But what if you should meet old Kelso," one of the women asked. "Old K-e-l-s-o," sneered one of the boys, "we'd like to get one good look at him." Kelso then kicked in the door in the door and sprang into the room, with his shotgun at the ready. The boy who had just spoken "bounded upward, threw his heels into the air and shot under a bed at a single leap, just as a frightened frog dives into the water." The other, younger teenager jumped behind one of the women, and, "winding himself so in her skirts as to almost trip her upon the floor, began to cry, "Oh! sister, don't let him kill me!" Seeing Kelso laugh, the women laughed, too—nervously. They begged his pardon, politely calling him "Lieutenant" rather than "Old" Kelso. He left the women and the quivering teenagers, but outside on the road, in the distance but within range, he saw a man riding a horse that had been stolen from Kelso's comrade Sergeant Banks, who had recently been killed by bushwhackers near Newtonia. Kelso fired one barrel of his shotgun into the rider's side and then, as the man wobbled in his saddle and turned the horse to gallop in the opposite direction, fired the second into his back. The bushwhacker managed to keep his mount and escape, but learning that he later died of his wounds, Old Kelso "added one more, therefore, to my rather long personal list of slain enemies."[33]

In the fall of 1864, during General Sterling Price's final raid on Missouri with a large army marching up from Arkansas, Kelso tried to collect intelligence by eavesdropping at night outside rebel homes in Neosho. "At every house," Kelso claimed, beggaring belief, "I heard my own character discussed in an unfavorable manner." From a conversation overheard from two women who arrived very late in a creaky old wagon from near the enemy's camp in Granby, 10 miles away, he learned that General Price had considered sending troops to defeat the Federals at Neosho, "but that he had finally abandoned this thought, fearing that the detachment would be ambuscaded by that terrible '*Kelso*.'"[34]

The terrible Kelso sometimes played up his developing legend to his advantage. Scouting with a partner on the prairie near Newtonia, he met a fourteen-year-old local boy who declared that there were no bushwhackers in his neighborhood. A few hours later, as he spied on two bushwhackers at their camp in the woods, Kelso saw that same boy appear through the bushes and talk to the rebels. "Boys, you'd better look out," he said, "I saw two Federals a little while ago out on the prairie!" The lad then gave them details about the size of Kelso's unit, the guns they carried, and the direction they headed. When the boy left the camp, Kelso decided to follow him home. He found him at his house with several younger brothers. When the younger children howled as Kelso dragged the fourteen-year-old outside, Kelso warned them to stay in the house: if they stepped out the door they would be instantly shot dead by the soldiers he pretended were hiding in the surrounding woods.[35]

He then brought the eldest brother to a secluded part of the forest. "'Bud, I will have to hang you!' 'What for?' said he, beginning to blubber quite lustily. 'For lying,' replied I. 'Do you not know that it is a dreadful thing to lie? Why all along the routes by which I have marched, the trees at the side of the road are white with the bleached skeletons of boys that I have hung for lying.'" Kelso reminded him that, when they first met, Bud said there were no bushwhackers in the neighborhood. Then Kelso repeated exactly what the boy had told the bushwhackers in the woods. Bud looked astonished. How on earth could this Federal solider know what he said to the two men? You need not be surprised, Kelso said. "Of course you've heard of Kelso? Yes? Well, do you not know that he is not like other people—that he knows all things? I am Kelso." I can read your thoughts—but I'll give you one more chance to tell the truth, he said. Bud spilled everything he knew, and Kelso, before heading back to kill the bushwhackers, sent the boy home and warned him to stay inside with his brothers.[36]

Kelso's growing reputation did not go unnoticed by women. "On every hand I was lionized, and especially by the women, many of whom always" (and here, writing his autobiography, he added in pencil the phrase "I regret to say") "are inclined to go wild over any man who has distinguished himself by deeds of desperate daring." He insisted that he never took advantage of these attentions. The recollections of him in later years, on this topic as on others, were divided. The journalist writing about the "Scout of the Ozarks" nearly three decades after the war reported that there were "contradictory stories told about Kelso's treatment of women. Some of his men say that he never offered an insult to a woman. Other citizens of Southwest Missouri who knew the Captain well during the war have brought serious charges against the character of Kelso on this ground." During the war itself, however, his wife, Susie, heard things. Perhaps it was no more than some young belles sighing for the Hero of the South West, or perhaps she heard slanders circulated by enemies keen to destroy his reputation if they could not get his scalp. In any case, she grew infuriated.[37]

"My wife was constantly hearing of my gallant deeds, my popularity among the soldiers, my admiration by the women, etc., and although she had her lover, she could not bear that I should be praised and admired so much by other women," he later wrote. "The result was that she treated me with real cruelty when we met, refusing, both at meeting and at parting, my proffered kiss, pushing me from her, and, with a face dark with jealous rage, calling me foul names and telling me to go to my 'mistresses for such favors!'" Kelso was deeply hurt by these accusations. He had been ever-faithful, he protested—he had never even thought of enjoying another woman's affections. He claimed that he "had never, except to my wife, spoken a word to any woman that I could not with propriety have spoken to my mother, my sister, or my daughter." He protested his innocence "in the sight of heaven and on the honor of a gentleman and a soldier." But Susie would not listen. "Go, old polygamist," she said, "go to your mistresses!" Kelso was crushed.[38]

Shortly after this blow up, John and Susie seemed to have come an understanding. It is not clear if they had a frank conversation about Dr. Hovey yet. But Susie, in a very different mood than when she erupted in what John described as a jealous rage, told John that she planned to "go into company" at Springfield and "enjoy herself," and said that he should do the same 70 miles away at Neosho. She meant to "catch beaus." In a tender letter he wrote to her on Christmas Eve, 1864, which looked forward to their happy life together after the war, he told her to "[a]ttend parties, if you wish, and if you '*catch a beau*' once in a while, no matter, *so* [long as] *he is a true gentleman and you do not fall in love with him*." John did start socializing with respectable women. In another letter to Susie, he mentioned being eager to see his "pretty squaw," a "half-breed Cherokee" widow named Boynton, who was "well educated" and "very intelligent." In his memoir, he admitted that, "with the usual audacity of a soldier," he once kissed a handsome rebel lady, and he gave a few hints of other flirtations. In the copy of his Christmas Eve letter to Susie, though in a crossed-out passage, he wrote that "I have sparked the girls some, it is true, but they are Union girls and are about the best to be found. The more I see and know of other women, however, the more I feel that I am blessed in the possession of my dear good Susie." He insisted in his memoir that he "always acted toward these girls just as I would wish any other gentleman, whom I might trust, to act toward my own daughters." At the end of the war, however, Susie discovered on his desk a letter John had written to a widow named Augusta Miller and flew into a rage. John said the letter was about buying some cows; Susie was convinced it was in code, arranging a tryst.[39]

Confederate women, of course, did not lionize Kelso as the Hero of the South West. The handsome rebel lady he wound up kissing had expected him, from the terrible things she had heard about "Old Kelso" the "rebel killer," to be "a monster rather than a man." But after he behaved like a perfect gentlemen in her house and even offered to share the food from his haversack when he discovered that her cupboard was bare, she came to see him as "a kind and generous friend." Her changed opinion, and even Kelso's kiss, somehow became known. At the next Neosho quilting bee, when other rebel ladies, as they often did, denounced Old Kelso as a monster who ought to be shot, hanged, or poisoned, she defended him. The other rebels brought up the scandalous kiss, questioned her virtue, and, even worse, called her no better than "a black abolitionist." Kelso's champion and her friends fought back, leading, Kelso heard, to quite a row at the bee.[40]

Kelso sympathized with other rebel women, many of whom suffered serious deprivations during Missouri's Civil War. Some in the southwest, with their men gone and their farms destroyed, were so destitute that they would have starved without provisions from the U.S. government. Once on a night scout a few miles from Neosho, Kelso spotted a campfire and crept closer to investigate. "I beheld three women sleeping on the cold, bare ground with their feet to the fire and little sacks of shelled corn for their pillows," he wrote. "I looked down close upon their weary sleeping faces, I saw their tattered shoes. My heart ached. I knew them all. They were rebel women uncomplainingly suffering thus for their cause that they loved." Those women, he thought, "never knew that the dreaded Kelso had knelt by their sides, as they slept by that lonely camp fire, and had wept over them tears of real sympathy."[41]

His attitude hardened, however, when he found rebel women more actively supporting the "cause that they loved." Once, entering a "palatial residence of a wealthy planter," he found a dozen women busily making Confederate uniforms from gray cloth. He ordered one of the house slaves to fetch some kindling so he could burn the cloth in the fireplace. When the boy looked to his mistress and did not move, Kelso stamped his foot and thundered, "When I speak I must be obeyed!"

"By what authority,"' the mistress asked him haughtily, "do you enter my house and give orders to my servants?"

"By the authority of the present master," Kelso replied, "myself being that important personage."

When he offered to transport her seventeen slaves away from her plantation, encouraging them to take whatever provisions they needed from her house, she again challenged his authority. By what authority, he shot back, did she obtain all those provisions in the first place from the "unrequited labor" of the enslaved? Another time, he found two women in a cabin who were also in the uniform business—in this case, washing the blue uniforms that had been stripped from the dead bodies of Federal soldiers and then giving the clothing to bushwhackers. Kelso burned these uniforms, too, and when one of the women tried to sneak ahead and warn the bushwhackers of the Federal presence, he burned down her cabin.[42]

Sometimes encounters with rebel women provoked neither tears nor anger but laughter. At a house in Arkansas, when Kelso tried to take a rebel prisoner at gunpoint, he was attacked by seven women—the man's mother, three sisters, and three sisters-in-law—who screamed and tugged and tore at Kelso's clothes. While the seven swarmed Kelso, an eighth, "a fine buxom girl of sweet sixteen," skipped over to the bashful young Sergeant John Anderson, embraced him, pleaded with him, and made him blush beet red. The other soldiers present found this all very entertaining. On another occasion, it was Kelso who got hugged. An enormous and powerful woman practically pulled Kelso from his horse in an amorous embrace, professing her love and begging him not to harm her tiny, stuttering father (Kelso had drawn his weapon only to scare information out of the man). Off balance and worried his gun would go off, Kelso surrendered to her, and fell to the ground when she released him. His men got another good laugh. When they got back to Neosho, Kelso was surprised to see them line up on all four sides of the town square. As he crossed the square, the men on the right called out, "Who got hugged?" Those on the left answered "Lieutenant Kelso." Then the line in front asked, "Who hugged him?" and those behind called out the woman's name. The Hero of the South West could take a joke. He spent ten dollars and rolled out a barrel of hard cider for the men, which "was duly disposed of."[43]

REGULAR CONFEDERATE FORCES moved up from Arkansas three times to strike Missouri in 1863. After the Battle of Springfield in January, General Marmaduke tried again in April, though this time the Confederates targeted Cape Girardeau on the Mississippi River, far from Kelso and his regiment. Marmaduke knew that Union defenses had been weakened because Missouri troops had been moved south to support General Grant's siege of Vicksburg, Mississippi, but Marmaduke's 5,000 men were unable to take the fortified city and again had to retreat to Arkansas. General Jo Shelby's "Iron Brigade" raided in October right up through Missouri's southwest corner, and Kelso would help chase him back south. Between the Springfield battle and the Shelby raid, Kelso and his men fought nearly constantly against groups of guerrillas, battling local bushwhackers and chasing Colonel Thomas R. Livingston's larger band of seasoned partisans.

One of the most notorious of the local bushwhackers was Alf Bolin. The Union sources described him as a horse thief, highway robber, and murderer who liked to pick off travelers from a place near the Arkansas line that came to be called Murder Rocks. His victims were said to include a twelve-year-old boy and an eighty-year-old man. The government put a high price on his head, but when Kelso and his men paid a call during the Medlock raid the previous fall, Bolin was not at home. In early February, however, while Kelso's unit was stationed briefly at Forsyth with an Iowa cavalry regiment, an Iowa private, Zack Thomas, in league with a Confederate prisoner on parole, arranged to meet Bolin with a promise to sell him some stolen goods. As they chatted by a fireplace and Bolin stooped to blow his nose, Thomas hit him over the head with a heavy fireplace iron and killed him. Bolin's head, as Kelso heard, was severed from his body, shipped to Ozark, and subsequently stuck on a pole, where children threw rocks at it.[44]

Kelso would have been dismayed to read later historians mention him as "the Union counterpart to Alfred Bolin." He would have expected the slander from Confederate zealots, but not from dispassionate scholars. The lazy false equivalence seems to have emerged when the sour assessment of Kelso by Greene County historian R. I. Holcombe in the early 1880s was distilled by the next generation's Greene County historian in the early twentieth century, who compared Kelso to "Bloody Bill" Anderson. Kelso's doppelganger was then downgraded to Bolin, a bush-league Bloody Bill, by the mid-twentieth century, a linkage then carried into the twenty-first. During the war, Kelso was the Union's admired protector and the Confederacy's feared enemy; his placement in a fraternity of "fanatics" was the product of a later ideological moment. By the time Holcombe wrote, Radical Republicans had lost the postbellum culture war. The Lost Cause propaganda of former Confederate Major John N. Edwards, who had gushed at the gallantry of the attack on Springfield, had romanticized the rebel guerrillas after the war, and led the campaign in the 1870s to make the bushwhacker-turned-murderous outlaw Jesse James into a folk hero. In the conservative backlash of the later nineteenth century, it was difficult for many White Missourians to admire a Federal Radical who had hunted local rebels. Holcombe classed Kelso as a "fanatic" as much for his politics as for his war record, which the few later writers who mentioned Kelso at all simplified further, reducing him to the equivalent of a senseless killer like Bolin.[45]

In the summer of 1863, though, the Hero of the South West, or Old Kelso the Rebel Killer, was spending most of his time in a large force hunting Colonel Livingston's hundred or so crafty and battle-hardened Cherokee Spikes. Known for executing their prisoners, in March Livingston's men had captured two men in Kelso's regiment who were outside the stockade at Granby, tending to a sick family. The guerrillas shot the soldiers as they begged for mercy. Kansas troops tried to track the Spikes into Indian Territory, but Livingston and his men disappeared. In April, Major Edward B. Eno of the 8th MSM Cavalry had led a command that broke up two of Livingston's camps, killing eight of the guerrillas, but the rest dispersed. In mid-May, Eno marched out with a hundred men, hoping to destroy the Cherokee Spikes once and for all, but after fighting them twice in two days, leaving more than a dozen men dead on each side, Livingston's men escaped again.[46]

On May 18, Livingston launched a surprise attack on 60 soldiers from two Kansas regiments, one being the 1st Kansas Colored Infantry. The Cherokee Spikes chased and cut down fleeing soldiers for 8 miles, killing 30 and wounding 28. Nine days later Livingston was writing to General Sterling Price at Little Rock, complaining about Black regiments "who have all the hellish passions belonging to their race" and pleading for reinforcements.[47]

In June, Kelso and Burch were part of another large expedition, commanded by Major Thomas W. Houts of the 7th MSM Cavalry, going after Livingston's men, but they found it impossible to flush them out in the open. They tracked the Cherokee Spikes, but Livingston cleverly dispersed his men so the trail would dwindle and then disappear. Then Livingston's men regrouped, as if toying with their pursuers, 4 miles behind them, and were now traveling in the opposite direction. Houts turned to follow. Kelso, scouting ahead, saved his men from riding into an ambush, but the next day they lost the trail again. After finding Livingston's camp, Kelso sent two men, privates Joshua Black and William H. Anderson, back to Major Houts to urge him to bring the command forward. But Houts never got the message and never came up. Black and Anderson had been captured by the guerrillas. Livingston's men led them into the woods to kill them. Anderson was shot dead but Black, "springing from his captors, bounded away in the darkness amid a shower of bullets, and made his escape. He reached Newtonia on foot the next day looking wild from fright. He took to having fits from which he never recovered. He might as well have perished. His life was ruined forever."[48]

Having ridden back to Houts's camp the next day, Kelso and 20 men were sent ahead again to scout the rebels' movements. Reaching the top of a ridge on the edge of a prairie, Kelso suddenly saw all the Cherokee Spikes emerging from the forest 400 yards away—and they spotted Kelso's small squad. The Federal scouting party, in a desperate situation, could turn and run for their lives, but across the open prairie only the few on fast horses would escape: guerrillas were usually better mounted than Federal soldiers, most of whom had to ride the government's "regular issue nags" worn out from constant patrolling. Or they could retreat to a small log house they had just passed and try to make a stand. Kelso ordered the men to the house. Some objected, not wanting to reenact the Alamo, and one, wide-eyed with fear, spurred his horse and deserted them.[49]

As the rest moved back to the house, Kelso tried to send the soldier on the fastest horse, Levi Scott, on a dash across the prairie to get help from Major Houts. But as Scott galloped off, Kelso and the others watched 6 rebels, also on fast horses, peel away from the rest of Livingston's force and race to cut him off. Scott, riding for his life, had to change direction and head for Newtonia. Kelso watched him disappear on the horizon, and knew that he and his remaining 18 men would have to "fight it out alone."[50]

While the men occupied the two-room house and made portholes in the log walls for their rifles, a young woman on horseback trotted up the road out front and stopped to ask directions. Some of the men, however, recognized her as a Livingston spy, sent to discern their numbers. Kelso ordered her, too, into the house. "You surely would not keep a *woman* here in time of battle," she said. But Kelso answered: You came to help get us killed, so why should we care about *your* life? He told her she could shield herself from the bullets by hiding beneath a strong wooden box that had stored salt pork. Then he organized the men. There was no door between the two rooms. He put 8 men in the smaller room and placed Sergeant John Grantham in charge, dubbing the room "Fort No. Two" while promoting Grantham to major general and all his men to brigadier generals and colonels. He and the remaining men, with similar promotions, would fight from the larger room, "Fort No. One."[51]

The men, pale but determined, laid out their cartridges and caps and looked out the portholes. They saw Livingston's men about 300 yards away on the top of the prairie ridge, the sunlight gleaming from their weapons. One of Kelso's soldiers, a young lad, started to panic. "They're dismounting! We'll all be murdered! We'll all be murdered! Let's get out and leave while we can!" Joel Hood sprang toward the boy and put a cocked revolver to his ear. "Another scream and you die," Hood said. "Yes," Kelso added, "kill him instantly if he opens his mouth again." As the boy sank down to the floor with a whimper, Kelso thought that he and Hood had stamped out the panic before it could spread to the others. But then a brave old veteran jumped up from his porthole. "There *are* too *many* for us!" he blurted. "Let us get away!" "No, they're not," Kelso said calmly, "We'll whip them easily! Get down to your place." The old soldier returned to his porthole. The only sound they heard was their own breathing.[52]

Then, with a great yell from the enemy, a storm of bullets slammed into the house, a few penetrating the portholes and whistling past their heads to strike the opposite wall. Wait to shoot until you can see the whites of their eyes, Kelso told the men. Have a good rest for your gun. Aim carefully. Each of us can take out four men before they reach the house. Livingston wasn't stupid—he won't want to lose so many. He'll decide to leave us alone.

But Livingston's men stopped firing. Why? Kelso and the defenders of Forts One and Two peered out to see another, larger body of horsemen thundering over the ridge. Rebel reinforcements?

"They're our own men!" Grantham called out from the next room, and he was right: it was Major Houts and the Federal cavalry to the rescue. The Cherokee Spikes galloped away, escaping again. "Well, Lieutenant," Houts said when he met Kelso in front of the house, "we came up in time to get you out of a very tight place." "On the contrary," Kelso replied with a straight face, "you came up just in time to rob me of a glorious victory." The expedition returned to Newtonia without having inflicted any damage on Livingston's guerrillas. As Kelso later wrote, he and his men were "covered with dust but not with glory."[53]

Still, Kelso's reputation grew. If he had not done anything to stop Livingston (who would be killed a few weeks later charging a small group of Union militiamen holed up in a courthouse), he had in the same couple months outfoxed the cattle rustlers in Indian country, outwrestled the two bushwhackers in the woods, and won the waltz with Wallace Finney. Later chroniclers of the legend of John R. Kelso wrote that he became known for riding his claybank horse, Hawk Eye, and for carrying an extra-large shotgun rather than a rifle. "Hawkeye seemed to possess, like Kelso, a charmed life," according to later recollections. "The horse was never touched in battle, though often the most conspicuous target for Confederate bullets." As for Kelso's favorite weapon, a reporter later wrote that "Kelso killed his first Confederate with a shotgun and he would never exchange the weapon for any of the improved army rifles." Yet when his luck finally evaporated in the late summer and early fall of 1863, it was a shotgun blast and an accident with Hawk Eye that gave him injuries that would trouble him the rest of his life.[54]

It was August 7, 1863. Three rebel bushwhackers had visited the home of Sergeant Banks, a member of Kelso's and Burch's company. They had stripped the dresses off of Mrs. Banks and her mother, killed a harmless old man, murdered an eleven-year-old boy in his sick bed, and then, after plundering everything they could, burned the house down. "Take as many men as you want and get those devils," Burch told Kelso, "if you have to follow them to hell."[55]

Kelso and his 10 men found the bushwhacker camp at night. He recognized the last of the 3 to flee the camp as someone he had shot and left for dead before; this time he fired several shots into the man's back and, after he fell, gave him two more at close range to make sure. Riding into a small open space in the woods, he saw the other two bushwhackers. One fired one barrel of his shotgun at Corporal Francis Henderson, who was coming at him from the left. "Henderson reeled in his saddle, but did not fall." Then the man turned and, as Kelso rushed him, fired the second barrel. At the last second, Kelso slid to the right on his saddle, an instinctive move that he thought saved his life because he was hit "slantingly" instead of straight on. He "felt the shots, like heavy hot irons, tearing through my flesh on my left breast and in my left hand."[56]

His horse kept charging forward. Kelso shot the bushwhacker once in the chest, but then his revolver's chambers were empty. The bushwhacker had dropped his shotgun and aimed at Kelso with a handgun. "Just as he pulled the trigger, I threw my revolver with all my force across his eyes. The blow staggered him, and his shot, instead of entering my right side, went tearing though my already wounded left hand, cutting the first finger about half off near the hand." To dodge the man's next shot, Kelso leapt off his horse, but his boot caught for a moment in his stirrup. The enemy rounded the horse and, 6 feet from Kelso, aimed to fire. As he pulled the trigger, one of Kelso's men, Ab Smithson, who had always kept his comrades laughing, dove in front of Kelso and took the bullet for him. Smithson's nephew Andrew came up, and the wounded, furious bushwhacker, gnashing his teeth like a wild animal, shot him in the thigh before Kelso could grab another revolver and shoot several times, finally dropping him. Kelso's men killed the third bushwhacker farther out in the woods, but sending the three devils to hell had come at a price. Henderson, Kelso, and Andrew Smithson were wounded, and Ab lay dying. "Lieutenant, I am gone," Ab said, "but thank God! I got up in time to save you." He asked Kelso to tell his sons that he had tried to live and die like a man, and was proud to sacrifice his life for his country. Kelso knelt by his side and wept.[57]

The lieutenant could not fully assess his injuries until he made it to a nearby house. He had fifteen wounds. The shots in his chest from the shotgun gun blast "had passed slantingly through the thick padded breast of my military coat, through my vest and through two shirts. They had then entered the flesh slantingly ranging to the left. They now remained, looking like a cluster of ugly blue bumps, just under the skin. Their presence there was producing inflammation and causing pain. I therefore took my pocket-knife, which was quite sharp, and cut them all out." His chest wounds did not hurt too badly, but his left hand did, "a shot having imbedded itself between the second and third metacarpal bones. Without danger of severing the tendons of my hand, this shot could never be extracted." It would remain there, and his left hand would be forever slightly disabled.[58]

When, by the evening of the next day, he arrived home at Springfield wearing a sling, his children treated him tenderly, but Susie was far more vexed than sympathetic, blaming him for exposing himself to danger. The camp surgeon examined him and said that he should rest and heal for a month, and probably extend his sick leave another month after that. Kelso reported back for duty twelve days later. His unit was stationed at Carthage, 60 miles west of Springfield and 30 miles north of Neosho. A couple weeks after he arrived there, in early September, the camp heard that a large bushwhacker band had attacked a wagon train. Burch and 75 men mounted and galloped off in pursuit. Kelso, staying at a private house on the other side of town, leapt on his horse and rode off at full speed to catch up. His picket rope, coiled upon the saddle, fell to the ground and got tangled in Hawk Eye's legs or got caught on a stump. Horse and rider did a somersault. "The great weight of the horse with so great a fall crushed me to the earth, rupturing me badly in the right groin, partially dislocating my hips, and seriously injuring them in the joints. My left shoulder was also severely injured, my head and left ankle severely bruised." He was stunned and bewildered. He could not remember afterward how he got out from beneath his horse. Hawk Eye was on his back, not moving, his neck badly bent. Kelso assumed the horse had broken his neck and was dead.

But when he took hold of Hawk Eye's hooves and tried to roll him over, the charmed horse sprang to his feet and "proved to be but little hurt except in his pride and a few skinned places on his face." Kelso himself was not so lucky.[59]

He rode forward and eventually found one of his comrades, James Briggs, dying in the grass. When he caught up to Burch, he took 6 men to pursue some straggling bushwhackers who had captives while the captain and the main force pressed ahead after the larger body of guerrillas. The stragglers had already executed one cavalryman, Samuel Hutchinson, and were about to shoot two others when Kelso and his 6 arrived to scare off the bushwhackers and rescue the captives. It was not until he returned to Carthage, after midnight, and the excitement of the chase had faded, that he felt the full force of his new injuries. He had to be lifted from his saddle and carried to his tent. The pain became so excruciating that he was partially delirious that night.[60]

But he refused to be kept from the field. "The men wanted me on every scout, and I could not bear to be left behind." He had to be carried to his horse and placed on his saddle each morning, and then carried from his horse and placed on his blanket each evening. He did not, however, mention to anyone that having to spread his thighs to ride caused such intense pain that several times he almost fainted and fell from his saddle. Gradually, he could mount and dismount without help, but these injuries, too, would never completely heal.[61]

A few weeks later he was suffering from typhoid fever as well, staying behind and trying to see through tearing eyes to make out the payroll while Burch led a successful scout into Indian Territory. Kelso was envious that Hood and Baxter were the heroes this time—Baxter by himself killing 6 rebels in one day, doubling Kelso's best single-day body count, as the sick and injured lieutenant noted ruefully. But as Kelso later wrote, "I was not left long to grieve over my absence from this action." Early in the morning on October 4, General Jo Shelby and his "Iron Brigade," 1,200 men with two artillery pieces, began their fall raid into Missouri by advancing on Neosho.[62]

Burch and 40 men, out hunting bushwhackers, came within a mile and a half of Neosho and found a burning farmhouse. Scouts sent ahead saw the town full of rebels and gathered that the large force was headed north, right at their own post at Carthage. Burch hurried the 30 miles back to camp and prepared to make a stand. Shelby's raiders ended up bypassing Carthage by a few miles that night. The Confederates did send 15 men dressed in blue toward the town, and the disguised rebels killed John Wells, one of the company's scouts. Burch received orders from Major Austin A. King of the 6th MSM Cavalry to take a detachment and follow Shelby, so the captain called for 30 volunteers to chase the Iron Brigade's tail and to attack when they caught up to it. But only a dozen men stepped forward. Kelso was watching this from his ambulance wagon. Still suffering from typhoid, but insisting on being with his men, he was on doctor's orders to ride on a feather bed next to his bottles of medicine. He saw the men, when Burch made the call, look toward his wagon. So he staggered out with his medicine bottles in his hand, threw them high into the air, and called for his horse. This dramatic gesture prodded enough of the others to join Burch. But once in his saddle, Kelso almost lacked the strength to stay upright. Sweating, weak, exhausted, and not thinking clearly, he tried to break his fever by sheer force of will. [63]

In a couple days, as Kelso began to feel better, they joined a larger force commanded by Major Edward B. Eno of the 8th MSM Cavalry. But where was Shelby going, and how could he be stopped? In St. Louis, General Scofield, commander of the Department of Missouri, was busy at the telegraph office, trying to gather information and consolidate troops scattered over the 120 square miles and thirty-seven posts of the Central District to confront Shelby's brigade. But some telegraph lines were cut, and some messengers were intercepted in the field. Federal commanders, unclear about the enemy's movements, struggled to coordinate their efforts. Major Eno was first ordered to chase Shelby, and then to stay south of him to catch him on his retreat. They needed better information. Burch and a couple of his men were ordered to stop and question some of the locals as they rode. On the front porch of one house, Joel Hood, the man who had run to Kelso's rescue in the Wallace Finney fight, was blasted in the belly with buckshot fired from a window by a jittery Unionist who thought he was a bushwhacker. Hood died two days later.[64]

The Iron Brigade continued to march north, growing larger with new recruits. It brushed aside small Federal forces and swept through Missouri towns—Greenfield, Humansville, Warsaw, Cole Camp, Tipton, Boonville—filling wagons with supplies, torching railway bridges, tearing up track. Kelso blamed what seemed to be an inept Federal response on Brigadier General Egbert Brown, the officer left with only one functioning arm after being shot from his horse at the Battle of Springfield. Kelso had already been suspicious of Brown, a political conservative who, he thought, was too soft on local rebels; Kelso would agree with the 120 citizens of Lexington, Missouri, the following year who signed a petition calling Brown "the personification of timid inefficiency." But Brown, the commander of Missouri's Central District, did manage to consolidate his forces and, with 1,600 men, on October 13, sandwiched Shelby's brigade at Marshall, Missouri, and beat the rebels badly.

Shelby, suffering 125 casualties by his own count, was forced to divide his brigade and retreat. Trying to put the best spin on the defeat, his report later claimed that his men "retreated in splendid order"; a Union officer reported that "the enemy is running like wild hogs." To move faster, the rebels ended up sinking their wagons of proud plunder in the Missouri River.[65]

The retreating enemy ran south, toward the Osage River at the fording spots like Warsaw, where Kelso and his men waited. A flurry of telegrams and dispatches tried to ready the troops. A message from a brigadier general at the state capital to a colonel in the field urged that capturing or exterminating the rebels, in their flight, was "the all-important thing"; General Scofield in St. Louis wired General-in-Chief Halleck in Washington, D.C., that Shelby's escape seemed "hardly possible." Then to his astonishment Kelso heard that Major Austin A. King, his commanding officer at Warsaw, received orders to disperse all his companies in different directions just as they learned that a division of Shelby's army was indeed crossing the Osage only 4 miles away. Schofield, too, seems to have been startled to hear that units had broken off the pursuit and were "apparently leaving the enemy to go off at his leisure." Kelso the conspiracy theorist would later wonder whether General Brown was intentionally helping Shelby escape. Although the records are not clear, Brown seems to have had two reasons for the order. First, he and other commanders thought that the enemy would be breaking up into several small bodies that would spread out and raid through the countryside, and he wanted Federal detachments to fan out and protect abandoned property. Second, he thought that Brigadier General John McNeil, below the Osage, with fresher troops and horses, would be better able to pursue Shelby back down into Arkansas.[66]

Kelso and the other officers at Warsaw, however, went and pleaded with King to let them chase and attack the fleeing rebels. Why not, they asked? "The orders," the major answered. "Oh! damn the orders," Kelso said. Circumstances had changed—the enemy was only 4 miles away. "But I may be court-martialed," the major said. If it comes to that, Kelso responded, I'll take the blame. "I will do the same," Captain Ruark said emphatically, and the other officers agreed. "That decides it," said the major, and he ordered the bugler to sound "*Boots and Saddles.*"[67]

At 11:00 in the morning, the 375 cavalrymen splashed across the Osage and began the chase. The day was clear and the roads very dry, and soon they were galloping through clouds of dust with their heads down, trying not to choke. It was so hard to see that riders ahead called back so those behind could swerve around a dead horse or dead man in the road. They raced hard for more than 50 miles and finally caught the enemy's tail in Humansville.

Kelso came upon Federals and Confederates fighting over a rebel cannon. All the artillery horses had been shot dead and the opposing teams of men were pulling at the weapon in opposite directions until the rebels gave up and the Union soldiers cheered. The Federals continued their pursuit until, as Major King reported the next day, "it was too dark to do anything; besides, my cavalry [had] given completely out."[68]

Kelso, Burch, and 14 men from the 8th MSM Cavalry continued the chase with Major King. They and another force soon joined General McNeil, who therefore, by October 19, led a command of 600 cavalry and 300 infantry and pulled four artillery pieces. Kelso served as a scout, following Shelby's trail into Arkansas. The enemy finally stopped to camp in War Eagle Valley, over 260 miles south from where they had started running after the defeat at Marshall. Shelby consolidated his forces there, and soon had, General McNeil estimated, 2,500 men. Kelso proposed a plan to McNeil: the general would take 600 men and the big guns around and ahead of the valley, while 300 cavalry would attack Shelby's rear. Although several officers in the command outranked him, Kelso volunteered himself to lead the cavalry charge. According to Kelso, the general seemed to like the plan, but he did not act upon it. The Federals moved ahead into War Eagle Valley, but by the time they did so Shelby was gone. On October 24, McNeil led his men over the Boston Mountains. Finding Shelby's men leaving another valley two days later, the Federals attacked the rear of the Confederates' departing column—what Shelby in his report dismissed as "a weak charge, easily repulsed."[69]

The blues chased the grays another 70 miles south to the Arkansas River. Burch, Kelso, Baxter, and the other 13 men of the 8th MSM Cavalry went on side scouts to find rebel stragglers. Pretending to be bushwhackers from Livingston's band looking to join Shelby, they took captives and horses, and when they had about as many of these as they could manage comfortably, Kelso proposed a change of tactics. "I told Burch that I thought we had enough prisoners for that day, and that I thought it would be better to vary our exercise a little from that time on by doing a little killing. Burch liked my plan very well, and Baxter, always eager for fighting, delighted with it." Baxter shot a fleeing rebel off his horse that afternoon, and Kelso did the same the next day. When McNeil's command neared the Arkansas River and learned that Shelby had already crossed it, the general, his horses exhausted, gave up the pursuit. The soldiers of the 8th MSM rode slowly back north in cold rain and snow, arriving in Springfield in mid-November, having spent thirty-five days without changing their clothes or pulling off their boots.[70]

The men finished the year reposted to Neosho. Most of the larger guerrilla bands had left with Shelby to winter in Arkansas, but there were still local bushwhackers to hunt. On a bitterly cold Christmas night (as Kelso remembered it), two bushwhackers had pitched a tent on the snowy ground in the woods and sat talking beside a blazing fire. Burch's report would identify them as Martin Levacy and a man named Woods. It was not a night that they expected the Federal patrols to be out, but Kelso watched them from the bushes. He, Burch, and 20 men had been out patrolling when they had spotted the campfire, and Burch sent Kelso forward to investigate. He heard them talking about the plan to poison Old Kelso, and then about their amorous conquests of particular women in Neosho. Finally, one of them went to the tent to sleep while the other spit tobacco juice into the fire for a while and then joined him. Kelso did not know how many bushwhackers might be in the tent, so he went back to get Burch and a few other men. They crept back to the campsite, threw the tent flaps open, and Burch roared, "You damned sons of bitches, what are you doing here!" There were only the two men in the tent, and as they reached for their guns, the Federals opened fire.[71]

The cavalrymen then rode to a house about 5 miles away where they had heard that bushwhackers would be dancing at a grand "Officer's Ball." The Federals surrounded the house and were able to disarm and capture the dancing bushwhackers without firing a shot. To describe the scene that closed the year 1863, Kelso in his memoir turned to verse, parodying lines from Lord Byron's *Childe Harold's Pilgrimage*. Byron's stanzas describe a ball tragically interrupted by the Battle of Waterloo; Kelso's lines laugh at a bushwhackers' dance comically cancelled by the heroes of the 8th MSM Cavalry:

> *There was a sound of revelry by night,*
> *And the neighborhood's capital had gathered then*
> *His beauty and her chivalry and bright*
> *The tallow candles shone over fair women and brave men;*
> *A dozen hearts beat happily; and when*
> *Music arose with its voluptuous swell,*
> *Soft eyes looked love to eyes which spake again,*
> *And all went merry as a marriage bell,*
> *But hush! hark! A deep sound strikes like a rising knell.*
> *Did ye not hear it? Yes, you bet we did. It was*
> *Burch's voice bellowing out: "Surrender in there, you*

infernal scoundrels, surrender!"
Ah! then and there were hurrying to and fro,
Many there who'd tripped the light fantastic toe,
And gathering tears, and tremblings of distress,
And cheeks all pale, which but an hour ago,
Blushed at the praise of their own loveliness;
With mouths chock full of chewing gum,
The girls cried "Good Goddle mighty, boys, the Feds. have come."[72]

Electioneering with a Big Shotgun

THE "GENTLEMANLY" SEMPRONIUS Hamilton "Pony" Boyd—a skilled lawyer, former Springfield mayor, colonel who had commanded the 24th Missouri Infantry, and the sitting member of Congress for Missouri's Fourth District—hardly knew what to make of his main challenger in the 1864 election. It was not the candidate for the district's anemic Democratic Party, circuit court clerk Martin J. Hubble. Nor was it the eccentric Dr. P. B. Larimore, a perennial independent who ran on his love for children and sympathy for women. Although Boyd was a leading Radical Republican in the state and served as a member of the Republican National Committee in 1864, his main challenge came from within the same wing of his own party.

Boyd must have been shaking his head when he told a sympathetic journalist about his opponent. Kelso was a half-breed Indian, it was said—a school teacher before the war, embittered and radicalized when rebels burned down his library. Canvassing for the vote, he made a "ludicrous" sight, according to what the newspaper writer heard from Boyd. "Bearing upon his shoulder a loaded shot-gun, with an antique powder-horn upon his breast, riding upon a braying ass whose altitude did not quite enable the rider's feet to clear the ground, his long black hair streaming in the wind, his pantaloons eternally working their way up over the top of his boots and leaving a broad belt of genuine Aboriginal calf exposed, he traveled over the district." Most of the voters were soldiers who flocked to him and cheered when he "declared so earnestly and energetically his intention of shooting every rebel, thrashing every Copperhead, and voting against every Democrat in Congress."[1]

From the spring of 1861, when Kelso denounced secessionists from the Buffalo courthouse steps, to the spring of 1864, when, between scouts, he delivered his first political speech, the transformation of political sentiment in the state had been extraordinary. Charles D. Drake, who emerged as a

Sempronius H. Boyd, ca. 1850s. Library of Congress, Washington, D.C.

leader of the state's Radical Republicans, noted in May, 1864, "the progressive development of opinion in regard to slavery" over the previous thirty-six months—progress resulting from "an education by current events." The provisional government that had replaced Governor Claiborne Fox Jackson and the fleeing secessionists in July 1861 had been dominated by conservative Unionists who considered both secession and abolition to be madness. Many were as ardently proslavery as Jackson but they thought that their "Southern" way of life would be better preserved in the Union than outside of it. Governor Hamilton Gamble's inaugural address in July promised that slavery would continue to be protected. Charles Drake, then still a Democrat,

defended the Union in a July Fourth address that year but said he detested antislavery agitation. In the fall, President Lincoln nullified General Frémont's
offer of freedom to the escaped slaves of disloyal citizens. But the enslaved
themselves helped force the issue. As slave patrols collapsed with the onset
of regular and irregular warfare, enslaved men and women left the farms and
plantations where they had been held and presented themselves to Federal
troops. General Halleck, who took command in Missouri at the end of 1861,
did not want any of his soldiers to act as either "negro-catcher or negro-
stealer," but his effort to keep escaped slaves away from his lines failed.[2]

By the spring of 1862, more and more White Unionists in Missouri,
shocked by the damage wrought by the slaveholders' Confederacy outside the
state and angered by the depredations by the proslavery guerrillas within it,
began to see that slavery was the key to the rebellion. The press color-coded the
factions that emerged within Missouri Unionism: "Snowflakes" still wanted
slavery preserved; "Claybanks" were willing to consider some plan of gradual
emancipation with compensation to slaveholders; and "Charcoals" called for
immediate emancipation. The emancipation question dominated the fall 1862
election. In Missouri's Fourth Congressional District, the Emancipationist
Boyd defeated the sitting congressman, Anti-emancipationist John S. Phelps.
In the state at large, too, the tide had turned in favor of ending slavery, but
with the vote nearly equally divided between gradualist Claybanks and
immediatist Charcoals, no emancipation plan emerged from the new state
legislature.[3]

By the spring of 1863, with slaves continuing to flee their bondage,
slave prices falling, and the enlistment of Blacks in the army a reality, even
conservatives like Governor Gamble started to come out in favor of some
form of emancipation. In June, he called the 1861 Constitutional Convention
back into session, and that body, after much debate, approved a gradual plan
proposed to take effect on July 4, 1870. Slavery in Missouri would end on
that date, the ordinance declared. However, slaves younger than twelve would
continue in bondage until age twenty-three, and those older than forty would
remain in bondage for the rest of their lives. With yet another sweetener for
slaveholders, the act waived all taxes on slave property. Charcoals considered
this plan a sham, a tactic allowing conservative Snowflakes to masquerade as
Claybanks, pretending to solve the slavery problem while in fact hoping to
stall until a more favorable political climate allowed them to repeal the law.
Rather than take slavery off the table, the emancipation act galvanized the
Radical Republican opposition.[4]

On September 1, 1863, the Missouri State Radical Emancipation and Union Convention convened at the state capital, Jefferson City, bringing together over seven hundred delegates from three-quarters of the state's counties. As Charles Drake said in his keynote address, they were not afraid to be known as "Radicals" because they recognized the root of treason and rebellion was slavery. The speeches and resolutions framed much of the political argument that Kelso would carry forward the following spring. The opening address by Judge Robert W. Wells set out three of the main planks of the Radical Republican platform. First was a demand for immediate emancipation. Second was a call for new elections and the opportunity both to replace Gamble and the conservative state officers appointed by the emergency constitutional convention in 1861 and to choose delegates to a new constitutional convention. Third was to secure "a *constitutional* provision, by which those engaged in the rebellion shall be prevented from voting in our elections." Congressman Boyd was one of the ten men who had signed the call for the Radical Convention, served as a delegate to it, and then worked on the committee that drafted its resolutions.[5]

The Radicals lost a close state judicial election later in the fall of 1863, but their stock was rising both in Missouri and nationally. With U.S. victories at Chattanooga and Knoxville in late November ending the year's major military campaigns on an optimistic note, attention throughout the Union turned to reconstruction policy and political maneuvering for the coming presidential election year. After President Lincoln issued his "Proclamation of Amnesty and Reconstruction" on December 8, which welcomed rebels back to full citizenship upon taking a loyalty oath and proposed to rehabilitate the governments of seceding states once a mere 10 percent of a state's voters took that oath, Radicals sent up trial balloons for candidates who might challenge Lincoln for the nomination: Treasury Secretary Salmon P. Chase and generals Frémont and Grant. Most Radicals on the national stage, though, like Congressman Boyd, played their cards close to the vest. In a speech on the House floor, Boyd denied that he and his Radical colleagues had made a "covert assault" upon the president and voiced his continued support for the administration, even if he differed from it "widely and materially" on some questions, such as easy amnesty for traitors. Back in Missouri, Radicals consolidated their power in the state assembly and managed to get one of their own—Benjamin Gratz Brown—elected to the U.S. Senate. By February 1864, they had corralled enough votes in the state legislature to put a referendum for a new state constitutional convention on the fall ballot.[6]

The Missouri Congressional delegation was a fitting emblem of the state's politics. Its nine representatives split into three groups: four Radical Republicans, including Boyd; two conservative Republicans, led by Lincoln's "hatchet man," Frank Blair; and three Democrats. As an editorial in Missouri's leading radical paper argued, the major fault line was less between Republicans and Democrats than between Radicals and Conservatives (now capitalized as party labels): "Old parties were unequal to the new crisis." (Adding to the confusion for outsiders, Missouri's leading Republican paper was the *St. Louis Daily Democrat* and its leading Democratic paper was the *St. Louis Daily Republican*.) In Congress, on key legislation the nine representatives voted as two opposing blocs. The Radicals voted in support of the draft, to repeal the Fugitive Slave Law, and for the constitutional amendment abolishing slavery, while the Conservative Republicans and the Democrats voted against these bills. In the spring, the Radicals were frustrated with Lincoln: the German-Americans were vocal for Frémont for president and the *Democrat* seemed to move in that direction, too. Frank Blair and the Conservative Republicans, meanwhile, hoped to form a cross-party coalition with the Democrats that could rally behind Lincoln and ride to victory in the fall.[7]

Kelso delivered his first political speech on April 23, 1864, at Mt. Vernon, 45 miles northeast of where he was stationed at Neosho. Since he was, like Boyd, a Union officer with Radical Republican positions (vigorous prosecution of the war, rebel disfranchisement, and immediate emancipation), his challenge would be to distinguish himself from Boyd, the polished politician. In these desperate times, he said, when they found themselves called to act within a revolution that would have world historical consequences, it was better to "select plain, honest farmers and mechanics, with only good common sense, to fill our high places, than trust wire-working politicians, tricky lawyers, or dram-drinking gamesters, however great may be their talents." He reminded the voters that he was just such a man: "For my own part, I have always been a laboring man, and my interests and sympathies are with that class."[8]

Like Boyd's House speech six weeks earlier, Kelso's address portrayed the suffering of southwest Missouri as the essential context for political decision making. Both men contrasted the peaceful, prosperous, happy antebellum Missouri to the terrible "desolation" that war had created. Boyd had mentioned exile, but Kelso had experienced it: "You and I, my fellow countrymen, have had to flee . . . . Our wives and our little ones, robbed and abused, have had to flee, without money, without food, and without clothing sufficient to protect them from the pelting storms, through which they have had to travel."

Boyd described a countryside filled with graves; Kelso pictured a land where "wolves and vultures feast upon the unburied bodies of our slain."[9]

Boyd blamed it all on the traitors who "without cause raised up their might and power to destroy the Government" and "invaded the happy circles of every family . . . rich and poor" alike. Kelso blamed "all this wretchedness" on "*Treason,*" and rooted treason in slavery. But he also turned back to the Free Soilers' language of the corrupt Slave Power and linked his indictment to class exploitation. Corrupted by slavery, "the wealthy classes of the South came to regard *honest labor as disgraceful, wealth as the only necessary virtue, and their own selfish interests as the principal object for which a government should exist,*" he argued. Long dominating politics, when they saw their power threatened they "resolved to *ruin* what they could no longer *rule.*" They conspired against the government, "appealed to the low passions of bad men," duped "the great masses of the poor and the ignorant," and then launched the rebellion that brought the terrible storm of war upon the country.[10]

Slavery seemed even closer to extinction when Kelso spoke at the end of April than when Boyd had spoken in early March. Lincoln's Emancipation Proclamation of the previous January, though politically important, went no further than previous congressional action and applied only to the slaves in the Confederacy—areas over which the federal government had no control. But on April 8, 1864, the U.S. Senate passed a joint resolution abolishing slavery and approving the Thirteenth Amendment. Although the House would not endorse the amendment with the required two-thirds vote until January 31, 1865, the national wave seemed to be carrying Missouri to freedom's shore, despite misgivings by the state's Conservatives. Still, it was important for Kelso to make the point that slavery, even when it was legal, was immoral, and that he had never been a proslavery man, despite being raised in a proslavery family. He had in fact, he said, been "banished from the great family circle" because of his antislavery principles. Many in the audience would surely have known that Boyd, the son of a wealthy farmer in Greene County, had a different history in this regard. Before the war Boyd's father held thirteen slaves, and Pony himself had three—a young Black woman and two "mulatto" boys.[11]

Boyd was vulnerable to the charge that he was an unprincipled political opportunist. A satirical piece in the Conservative *Missouri Republican* savaged him a few weeks after his House speech. "Great and marvelous are thy works, Oh Pony!" The writer recalled that before the war Boyd had been a Whig, then a Know-Nothing, and then a Democrat, before becoming a Radical Republican. Previous to this last incarnation, the article claimed, Pony had declared that German Americans were "unfit to vote," that "slavery was the natural and proper condition of the nigger," and that abolitionist "negro thieves" from Kansas needed to be resisted by violence. But then Pony had realized that the semi-secretive Union League clubs were "the only successful avenue to power and profit," and suddenly the "Dutchmen" were true patriots, the Kansans were allies, and the Blacks were not only equal but the superior race. Kelso more obliquely linked Boyd's self-interested pursuit of power to his conversion to Radical Republicanism. In 1862, Kelso said, he (Kelso) was talked about as the best man in the district to challenge (and almost certainly defeat) Democratic Congressman John Phelps. But then "Mr. Boyd, suddenly leaving the Democratic party, announced himself as a candidate for the Republican ticket." Not wanting to split the Republican vote and give the seat to Phelps, Kelso withdrew his name. In 1864, they were back in the same situation. Boyd, however, lacking Kelso's magnanimity, was not willing to step aside. Here Kelso again echoed the "rule or ruin" language that he had borrowed from a famous 1860 speech by Senator Benjamin Wade of Ohio, and he aligned Boyd with the aristocratic, self-interested slaveholders who had brought on the war: Boyd was, Kelso said, "determined to rule the party, in this district, or ruin it."[12]

When Kelso advised voters not to choose "wire-working politicians, tricky lawyers, or dram-drinking gamesters," his reference was quite clear. The last of the three insults probably referred to a story about Boyd that many of the soldiers in his audience would have known. During the campaign of 1862, Boyd, stumping in the district, was riding one night from Springfield to Mt. Vernon with a newspaper editor named Charles E. Moss and a military escort to defend against bushwhackers. The men had all been drinking. As a later county historian told the tale, Moss, "with more than half a pint of Dutch courage . . . was soon declaring his contempt for any kinds and all sorts of danger." So Boyd decided to play a practical joke on him. He got some of the soldiers to sneak off, ride ahead, and stage a "sham ambush." When Boyd and Moss rode up, the pretend bushwhackers fired their revolvers in the air. A terrified Moss spurred his fine white stallion and streaked the 18 miles back to Springfield, sure that he had "barely escaped with his life." Rather than a liquor-fueled practical joker, Kelso said, Republicans should "nominate our most thoroughly tried men;—men who have, from the beginning, stood by our cause;—men, too, of untiring energy, and who are always sober and always at their post."[13]

Kelso's speech raised an issue that Boyd's had not mentioned, but which had flared up in in the state legislature in February: "negro equality" and the threat of "miscegenation." With the end of slavery, what would be the place of

Blacks in American society? Democrats and Conservative Republicans also asked the question of their Radical opponents, race-baiting being the most effective card they had to play in the long campaign leading up to the fall elections. The Radicals had turned the war to save the Union into a war for abolition, their opponents charged. They had pushed for gradual, compensated emancipation, then for Black troops, then for immediate emancipation, and now began whispering about Black suffrage, panting over the prospect of Black votes that could help keep them in power. The obvious endpoint, the Conservatives charged, was the horrible prospect of full political and social equality for people of African descent—and, with that, the amalgamation of the races.[14]

In the Missouri House on February 11, Representative Thomas H. Allin of Lafayette County demanded a vote on his resolution: "That the loyal people of Missouri are opposed to negro equality or extending to the negro the right of suffrage or other political or social privileges." The Radicals tried to dismiss the resolution as a joke or a political stunt, and then tried to prevent a vote by parliamentary maneuvering. No Missouri Radicals, they said, were proposing Black equality or suffrage. Allin, though, wanted to get them on the record. One of the Radicals who answered him seemed to speak for nearly all the rest: "I am now, sir, and have always been opposed to negro equality and amalgamation." The resolution passed, 86 to 3.[15]

A week later, one of the more outspoken racists in the U.S. House of Representatives—Samuel Sullivan "Sunset" Cox, a Democrat from Ohio—rose from his chair with what he described as proof of the goal of Republican policy. A pamphlet, anonymously published two months earlier, called *Miscegenation: The Theory of the Blending of the Races, Applied to the American White Man and Negro*, argued that racial mixing would lead to a higher type of mankind. Endorsed by some leading abolitionists, the pamphlet revealed, Cox charged, the true colors of Republicanism. The term "miscegenate"—from the Latin for "to mingle and generate"—was new; racial theorists had previously spoken of "amalgamation." The neologism, though, seemed to fit the pseudo-science and fevered philosophizing of the text. The pamphlet was a hoax. Concocted by two Democratic newspapermen in New York, it was sent to abolitionists for comment, and some of them took the bait. It was an effective propaganda weapon, and politicians and the press—including those in Missouri—took up the argument.[16]

A few days after Cox's "Miscegenation" speech in Washington, Thomas Allin delivered a similar address, "Negro Equality," to the Missouri legislature. Arguing for the Conservatives—the "law and order party"—against the Radical "Jacobins," he charged that his opponents were still agitating on the slavery question "to cloak their real purpose of elevating the negro to the standard of the white man." "Sambo," he predicted, would first be allowed to attend political conventions, then to vote, and then to hold office and make laws for White men. Black children would go to school with Whites. Young Black men and White women would socialize. "*Amalgamation* just as naturally succeeds admission to the social circle." When that happens, "*our Anglo-American status is lost and lost forever*. We are no longer a distinct race, no longer a nation of white people." Like Congressman Cox, Allin proceeded to quote several paragraphs from the pamphlet *Miscegenation* as proof of real Radical Republican attitudes.[17]

As he gave his April speech, Kelso knew that people in his audience would "like to ask whether or not I am a believer in '*negro equality*.'" Like Lincoln, he still clung to the old and increasingly unpopular idea of colonization. Kelso proposed colonizing freed slaves in Mexico; Lincoln had supported an 1863 experiment that funded the resettlement of over 450 freed slaves on an island near Haiti, but the survivors of this mismanaged disaster had already returned to United States the month before Kelso spoke. On colonization Kelso was out of step with other Radicals in the state, who painted it as a failed Conservative policy and pinned it on Frank Blair in particular. In any case, in the short term Kelso was happy to have Blacks help win the war. To him, the "great out-cry against using negroes as soldiers" made no sense. "They are good enough to fight rebels, and their lives are no more precious, in my estimation, than are the lives of loyal white men."[18]

But what about the status of Blacks in society? Was Kelso in favor of "negro equality," or not? "Far from it," he said. "I no more believe that the negro is, in all respects, equal to the white man, than I believe that the least boy on the ground, is equal to me in stature. Individuals are unequal in most respects, and so are nations and races. There is but *one respect* in which all men are born equal, and that is in respect to their *rights*." He then quoted "the sublime language" of the Declaration of Independence: "All men have certain unalienable rights, among which are life, liberty, and the pursuit of happiness." As far as these rights were concerned, he said, he endorsed "negro equality"—but no farther. "In most other respects, the races are unequal and unlike."[19]

He also addressed fears about "miscegenation," and like many Radicals, he threw the charge back in the faces of Conservatives. It was the White slave masters, after all, taking their Black slaves to bed, who had been "miscegenating" for generations. "There are also many persons who greatly fear lest their daughters marry free negroes, and lest, in a few years, certain devilish little mulattoes may be calling them '*grand pap.*' . . . They know from *experience* how dreadful a thing miscegenation is, and knowing their *own* proneness to mix with the kinky heads, they may well tremble for their *posterity.*" He was confident, however, that "[n]o truly loyal man has any fears that either himself or his children will ever miscegenate with negroes under any circumstances." Kelso thought that racial mixing was a violation of "a natural law of repulsion between the two races, which makes them inclined to separate, when both are left free to act. Miscegenation, then, or the mixing of the two races, must always involve a violation of this natural law of repulsion." Slavery had unnaturally brought together these two distinctive peoples—coming from very different parts of the world, shaped by dissimilar climates, and suited to incongruous modes of life. "When both races are free to act, they as naturally tend to separation as do oil and water when at rest," Kelso reasoned. He opposed slavery because it violated "the eternal laws of justice" and he supported colonization because it harmonized with this apparent natural law of repulsion. But he placed much more weight on the former: "To detain them among us, will be to continue the violation of the same great laws, lest we grant to them all the rights enjoyed by other freemen." So he committed himself to "labor earnestly" both for the emancipation of slaves and for "the entire removal of the African race from among us." Should colonization prove impractical or unpopular, however, he would "contend for the removal of all legal distinctions on account of color."[20]

Calling for a color-blind legal code propelled him toward a related issue that was gaining more attention: Black voting. When the war began, every Northern state except five in New England barred Blacks from voting in one way or another. Antislavery Republicans held a range of opinions on the issue, and most through late 1863 considered it too controversial to discuss. Black abolitionists such as Frederick Douglass, however, began arguing for the necessary linkage of freedom, full citizenship rights, and the franchise. Freedmen in Leavenworth, Kansas, in December 1863 met with White reformers and called for the Black vote as a natural right. White abolitionist Wendell Phillips, too, in a speech before the American Anti-Slavery Society in Boston in January 1864, endorsed the idea. Leading Missouri Radical Charles Drake in a February speech was still waffling, speaking vaguely about the Black man's "new status" and of "negroes" as an "enfranchised race": "I say not that he is to be lifted into equality with the white man; but that he is to be assigned a position above that of his former days."[21]

But "negro suffrage" was gaining political saliency, both as a policy position for the most progressive Radicals developing plans for reconstruction and, for their opponents, as a propaganda cudgel. In Congress at the end of February, Missouri Conservative Frank Blair denounced his state's congressional Radicals in a floor address, mentioning Black suffrage as part of the "Jacobin" plot. When, in mid-March, two free men of color from New Orleans met with President Lincoln, Senator Charles Sumner, and Representative William D. Kelley, they presented a petition with over a thousand signatures asking that all men born free, regardless of color, be added to the voter rolls in Union-controlled Louisiana. Lincoln, after the meeting, expressed the hope that at least some Black men—literate ones, and soldiers—be allowed to vote in that state. Sumner pushed the idea in the Senate a few days later. Between February and the end of April, Black suffrage surfaced in other congressional discussions, too. Opponents slapped down the idea as a new heresy "to inflame and embitter the great controversy to come off in the ensuing presidential election."[22]

Thomas Allin in the Missouri State House tried to pin his opponents to the wall with a direct question: were they "in favor of negro suffrage?" One of them, B. R. Bonner of St. Louis, responded: "It depends on the circumstances. A loyal negro who shoulders a gun and fights for the Union is more entitled to a vote than a returned rebel." Allin, looking for a yes-or-no answer, considered this a dodge: "The gentleman don't answer my question! 'Ah! how they squirm.'" Kelso's response was similar: "I am aware that the bare idea of negro suffrage is terrifying to all persons in the least tinctured with rebel sympathies, and it is regarded with suspicion, even by many whose loyalty can not be questioned. For my own part, however, I would rather the loyal negroes be allowed the right of suffrage, than that the same right be allowed to rebels and their sympathizers. I think it safer to trust ignorant friends than intelligent enemies." This was no evasion. The question of the Black vote was entangled with that of re-enfranchising "returning rebels." For Kelso and many of the voters he addressed, the prospect of welcoming former rebels quickly back into the polity was far more politically dangerous, morally objectionable, and emotionally fraught that the possibility of voting next to a former slave on some future election day.[23]

Kelso understood the electoral arithmetic, but principled resentment rather than political calculation determined his position. The men with the loudest cries against Blacks voting were also those most eager to grant amnesty to the rebels who had left the state and to the remaining Southern sympathizers who had been disfranchised by the loyalty oath of 1861. These former rebels, who would far outnumber enfranchised freedmen in Missouri, would quickly become "flaming *conservatives*," he said, joining the loyal men who still pined for "the Union as it was." The Conservatives would once again become the dominant political power in the state. These champions of "Southern rights," Kelso argued, would try to return as much as possible to the social and political principles that had led to all the destruction and carnage in the first place. He acknowledged that there were "loyal and brave men who still clung to the *name* of *conservatism*." They needed to shun rather than embrace these traitorous thieves, these murderers with blood on their hands. "I tremble for the fate of our cause, when I see many of the bravest and best men of our nation still bearing the same name with these returned thieves and cut throats, endorsing the same principles, and voting the same ticket. The crisis is too terrible. The loyal should unite with the loyal." The disloyal should have some of their property confiscated to pay for the damage they caused; they should be made to wait at least as long as a loyal German immigrant—five years—before again enjoying all the rights of citizenship.[24]

Kelso closed his April speech at Mt. Vernon by reminding the voters that he was not yet officially a candidate. He still worried about splitting the Republican vote. The Republicans needed to have a district convention. If they chose him over Boyd, he said, he would gratefully accept their nomination. Three days after Kelso's speech, Boyd published a letter to his constituents. He stressed his commitment to the Radical cause, explained why he was running, and promised that as soon as he finished doing the people's business in Washington he would visit every county in the district. He said that the fate of the state and the nation depended on the success of the Radical agenda, and that a vote for Boyd was a vote for Radicalism. "I am anxious that the people—who are sovereign, and to whom I only look for delegated power and honor—shall have a fair chance to indorse radicalism, and pass judgment upon me as their representative. I am not to be laid aside except by the honest voice of the citizens and soldiers of my district."[25]

In the spring of 1864 Kelso's nomination looked unlikely, to say the least. The Springfield correspondent to the *St. Louis Democrat* wrote that citizens in the Fourth District were very happy with the job Boyd had done in Washington. Looking at the whole state, the influential *Democrat* urged in an editorial that all the current Radical Congressmen, including Boyd, deserved to keep their seats. In the summer the paper was dismayed to learn that in some districts personal disagreements among Radicals threatened to divide the Radical Republican tickets. This must not happen, an editorial warned: the stakes were too high.[26]

The *Democrat's* correspondent from Kelso's adopted hometown of Springfield, who had praised Boyd and predicted that the colonel would almost surely win reelection, also wrote in high praise of Kelso as a guerrilla fighter. A month before Kelso had indicated his interest in the congressional seat, the writer had suggested that Kelso would make a good secretary of state for Missouri: "He is *the* man who will suit the Radical voters of this country . . . [and] he should not be overlooked." After the Mount Vernon speech, however, a Springfield correspondent predicted that Kelso "will be elected by a larger majority than any man ever got here"—but the writer mistakenly reported that Kelso was trying to run for the state senate.[27]

Meanwhile, as the Radicals consolidated power, Boyd was emerging as one of the state party's rising stars. Both the third party movement behind Frémont and the Conservative effort to dominate the Republican Party failed. Congressman Boyd gave what was described as a well-received impromptu speech to a rally of five thousand people in St. Louis. He candidly admitted that Lincoln had not been his first choice, and that the president had made some poor decisions that hurt Missouri (in part from being misled by bad advice from the Blairs). But Lincoln, Boyd said, was an honest man, and all Unionists needed to unite behind him to prevent the disaster of a Democratic victory. Nodding to the strong contingent of German-American Radicals in St. Louis, Boyd said that he admired General Frémont, but stressed that he and his staunchly Radical Fourth District in the southwest corner knew that a vote for Frémont was a vote thrown away. Fourth District women, Boyd joked, with broomsticks in their hands, would drive out anyone not willing to vote for Lincoln. His speech, according the newspaper report, was punctuated by laughter and applause. The next day the *Democrat* praised the address on its first page and reiterated that voters in the Fourth District "could not do a better thing" than to reelect Boyd.[28]

Republican voters in the Fourth District did gather to choose their candidate. But—according to Kelso—only hand-picked Boyd men from five of the district's twenty-one counties attended the meeting. When they voted for Pony, he claimed the nomination, but this "fraudulent concern," Kelso later wrote, "was so evidently a farce and an outrage that the loyal people, and especially the soldiers, called for an independent Republican candidate, and I responded to that call." Boyd was canvassing the district, giving speeches. Kelso, unable to get leave from his post, was still going on scouts, hunting guerrillas. In the summer, though, Kelso was appointed to gather information on fortifications in southwest Missouri for Major Albert J. Myer, the chief signal officer for the Division of West Mississippi. This meant, as luck would have it, that Kelso was ordered "to visit and report the condition of all fortified places in my Congressional District," taking the opportunity to give stump speeches as he did so. Someone up the chain of command—Kelso professed not to know who—was doing him a favor.[29]

Congressman Boyd toured with a squad of soldiers serving as his bodyguard; Captain Kelso, armed and in uniform, traveled only with his "colored servant." His speeches were apparently a big success. "In great alarm, Boyd hurried himself to the General commanding our district"—Brigadier General John B. Sanborn, stationed at Springfield—"and urged him, for '*God's sake*,' to order me back to my command and not let me make any more speeches." So Kelso returned to his post at Neosho. "My electioneering, therefore," he wrote, "had to be principally done in the brush, with my big shot-gun, shooting bush-whackers."[30]

THE UNION OPTIMISM of 1863 had been nearly blotted out by the lengthening shadows of death in the spring and summer of 1864. General U. S. Grant, who had become the commander of all Union Armies in March, launched a coordinated multipronged operation in early April: George Gordon Meade would chase Robert E. Lee, Benjamin F. Butler would move against Richmond, Franz Sigel would march through the Shenandoah Valley, and William T. Sherman would campaign through Georgia. Across the Mississippi, Nathaniel P. Banks would march up the Red River in Louisiana to seize cotton and then, joined by Frederick Steele coming south from Little Rock, would drive east to take Mobile, Alabama. But the hard fighting of the aggressive Union offensive in Virginia piled up unprecedented casualties without breaking Lee's lines: by mid-June, Grant had lost 65,000 men killed, wounded, or missing. Closer to Missouri, the number of men involved was smaller but a soldier's chance of being killed or maimed was just as high. Banks's force of 12,000 suffered 3,600 casualties in two days and withdrew. An 800-man foraging party under Steele's command in Arkansas suffered 300 casualties in a Confederate attack that helped stall Steele's movement south. In Missouri itself, the bloody guerrilla war ground on.[31]

Kelso had written a short note to Susie in late February 1864, "worn out from a long and toilsome scout," his hand "so unsteady" that he could barely write. There were many more long and toilsome scouts through the first half of 1864. He had been promoted to captain and had launched his political career, but it was not a particularly glorious campaign in the bush for the Hero of the South West running for Congress. The war dragged on. Good officers, well-intentioned and able, could make mistakes, and men died. Brave soldiers, doing their duty, could be just a step wrong or a second slow, and men died. By August he was writing to Susie that "the storms of war are growing darker." A year to the day after he had been seriously wounded, he was again fighting in battles "where the bullets flew thick as hail" and seeing "several of my brave boys fall mangled and bleeding around me." He mourned the dead and was weary of mourning. He thought that he, too, might be nearing his own end. He did not fear death, and at times, he told his wife, he "could almost welcome" its approach—as long as sacrificing his life could mean something.[32]

On May 29, 1864, Kelso led a scout of 30 men down into northern Arkansas. He filed his official report of the expedition after he returned to his post at Neosho on June 2. To set that report alongside his recollection written two decades later for his autobiography marks the distance between a chronicle of military activities and the emotional resonance of lived experience.

Following form, the report is written as a letter to the reporter's commanding officer, in this case, Captain Henry D. Moore. It describes where the troops went, what they did, and what resulted from their encounter with the enemy— supplies and horses captured, men wounded or killed. It closes with commendations for the men generally and of particular soldiers for specific accomplishments. These reports, though, are not just bare recitations of facts, or alleged facts; they are narratives, not infrequently containing rhetorical flourishes that convey hints about the author's character. In his reports, for example, Milton Burch tended to employ a conventional trope by inflating the personal pronoun to contain the entire military unit, as if the actions of all the soldiers individually or collectively were the unmediated expression of the commander's will: "I marched down on Turkey Creek. . . . I received information that 40 armed rebels had passed . . . I started on the trail and followed them . . . . I reached Carthage . . . preparing to give them a warm reception." Burch did, however, occasionally drop in a colloquialism, a wink in an otherwise formal document: charging an enemy camp in mid-May, 1864, he reported, prompted a "general skedaddle." Kelso winks, too, but there is less of the imperial "I": "We found a hidden tanyard, which we destroyed. . . . [W]e proceeded in a south westerly direction . . . where we learned a dancing party was going on, attended by the notorious thief, Lieutenant McGhee, and 7 of his men. . . . We arrived too late to dance any ourselves, but we made Lieutenant McGhee and his men dance in the following manner . . ."[33]

It is clear who made the decisions and gave the orders, but Kelso nevertheless recorded the expedition as a collective effort, and he celebrated the accomplishments of his men, rather than himself, with paternal pride: "I sent Lieutenant [Malcolm] Hunter with the main body of my command with instructions to move slowly up the valley. . . . The keen cracks of rifles and revolvers soon rang out on both sides of me, accompanied by the hearty yells of my brave boys. The fight soon over, I found my boys all unhurt, and 2 bushwhackers dead on the ground." Later, Lieutenant Hunter and three others caught up with McGhee and seven of his men, "charged them like madmen, killed 2 on the spot, wounded another, and chased the balance more than a mile." Kelso concluded with praise for his men: "I am proud to command such men as formed my detachment on this occasion. Lieutenant Hunter, of Company H, is an officer after my own heart. Every man also did his duty well. Hunger, fatigue, loss of sleep, every privation was borne without one word of complaint. With such officers and men under my command, I feel sure of success in almost any enterprise."[34]

Twenty years later, some of the specifics had faded. May 29 became "about the close of May" and a scouting party of 30 men became "some 25 or more." His men kill two of the enemy and then another two, but the names of the dancing McGhee and the brave Lieutenant Hunter disappear into the generic crowd of soldiers and bushwhackers. Yet other details come into view in the memoir's richer narrative, which is alternately more humorous and more somber. The report merely mentions coming upon "a bushwhacker rendezvous" at a house owned by a man named Waitman, where the soldiers discover "a considerable quantity of provisions and some Federal clothing." The memoir describes a whole scene there, not with the house's male owner but with its two female occupants. The dramatis personae are a shifty middle-aged farmwife who tries to hide the washed uniforms in her cellar and an old woman who tries to distract Kelso by feigning a fit, lying stiffly on the floor and "rolling her eyes about in a very theatrical manner." Kelso, though, while throwing the uniforms into the fireplace, is able to "cure" her by tossing a pair of home-made non-military pants onto the fire with the rest. Seeing this, the old woman quickly bounded "from the floor like and acrobat, and snatching the badly scorched pantaloons from the flames," exclaimed, "Good goddlemity, mister, them's my husband's pants. I made them myself."[35]

Missing entirely from the report is the soldiers' discovery of where the bushwhackers' women had gotten those uniforms. Exploring the hills near Butler Creek in northern Arkansas, Kelso and his men came across the trail taken by "a considerable party of Federals" that had been ambushed and "cut to pieces" a few months before—probably Sergeant Isaac T. Jones and two dozen men of the 11th Cavalry, Missouri Volunteers, who were attacked on January 21. Kelso and his men found, scattered along the trail for 2 miles or more, the bodies of the slain soldiers, stripped of their clothing, skeletons with only a little dried, blackened flesh still on the bones.[36]

Some distance from the trail and the other bodies, Kelso found a dead soldier the bushwhackers seem to have overlooked after the slaughter. "He sat with his back against a tree, his right elbow resting upon his right knee, and his right cheek resting upon his right hand. He had evidently crept to this place mortally wounded, and had died sitting in this position." He still wore his uniform, "but his garments hung very loosely upon him, for his flesh was now all gone except the cartilage that held the bones together. In the bones of his left hand which rested by his side he clutched a faded photograph. It was that of a beautiful woman, with [a] happy smiling face." Kelso wondered: a wife, or a sweetheart? A sister, or a daughter? He imagined the man carrying the photograph on many long marches. He imagined the ambush: green troops, caught by surprise—the sudden explosion of gunfire— the rearing horses and falling men—the soldier, wounded, bleeding, crawling from the trail to the tree. The dying man takes the photograph out of his pocket and looks at her beloved face as the last thing he will ever see. Then he places his weary head in his other hand and closes his eyes. Kelso imagined the woman, too, somewhere, hearing only that the soldier was missing and presumed dead, not knowing that the man had died this way. Had she seen what Kelso saw, he thought, she would not be able to bear it. He slipped the photograph back into the soldier's hand "and left him as I found him." None of these meditations on death and pain and loss, of course, were part of Kelso's official record of his detachment's late May scout into northern Arkansas.[37]

The day after Kelso and his men returned to Neosho, a woman named Madeline Goode rushed into headquarters to tell the officers that her rebel ex-husband and a group of his men had just attacked a couple of soldiers who had been swimming in Shoal Creek a mile north of town. They shot and killed Private Robert Poag as he tried to escape by swimming to the creek's opposite bank. They captured Sergeant Joshua Ruark, "one of the bravest men" in the party that had just returned with Kelso, and the brother of Kelso's friend and fellow officer, Captain Ozias Ruark. They then grabbed a Black man named Simpson, who worked for Major Burch, and one of Burch's horses.[38]

Captain Moore, commander of the post, immediately ordered Captain Ruark and 30 men, including Kelso and Lieutenants Hunter and John T. Smith, in pursuit. Major Burch went too. While Ruark and the others ran to get their horses saddled, Kelso took the company's best trackers and ran to pick up the trail at Shoal Creek. They followed, bending twigs and stripping leaves to mark the way for the horsemen behind them. They were after John R. Goode, formerly First Lieutenant in the 11th Missouri Infantry, C.S.A., now called "Captain" Goode, who was on furlough recruiting for the Confederates and had turned to bushwhacking. He had gathered about 20 men so far. Captain Ruark and the others caught up to Kelso and the trackers after about 3 miles. They knew that time was working against them: they were sure that the bushwhackers, as soon as they could, would stop to question Sergeant Ruark and Simpson and then murder them. Yet the trail led up into the flinty hills, where the horses' hooves barely made impressions. Furthermore, the bushwhackers had split up to confuse their pursuers. But the trackers were skilled woodsmen who "could run and trail like fox-hounds." An occasional bent grass blade or displaced piece of flint was all they needed. The hunters kept on; the hunted, thinking they surely must have lost the men who chased them, regrouped and turned down into a small, bush-covered valley.[39]

Kelso, in the lead, knew they were close, and they moved slowly, wary of an ambush. "Parting the bushes in front of me with my gun barrel, I perceived about 30 yards in advance, a large party of men, most of them seated in a circle upon the ground. One of them, upon seeing me, cried out: 'There's Kelso now!'" They sprang up and bolted for their horses. Sergeant Ruark rushed toward his rescuers with his hands up; so did old Simpson, after first grabbing the reins of Captain Burch's stolen horse.[40]

The bushwhackers galloped away across a dry creek bed and made a brief stand, firing from behind bushes. The MSM charged. Lieutenant Smith was in front, following closely behind a fleeing bushwhacker, but when Smith entered the creek bed, the enemy turned in his saddle and fired. The bullet tore through Smith's head and he fell dead from his horse. In a moment, Kelso was charging through the creek bed, too. A bushwhacker in front of him whirled around to shoot. Kelso shifted to the right in his saddle as the man fired. If he hadn't, he would have fallen dead from his saddle like Smith, for the bullet grazed the left side of his neck. Kelso answered his assailant with his shotgun. Blasted at close range, the man "uttered an unearthly scream and fell dead." The bushwhackers rode hard through the brush, scattering from the creek bed in different directions. Kelso chased two of them for a couple miles, giving them the second barrel of his shotgun and emptying his revolvers in their direction, but they got away.[41]

The cavalrymen returned to Neosho, glad that their quick response had rescued Sergeant Ruark and Simpson. Ruark had thought that his fate was sealed when the bushwhackers went through those flinty hills to hide their trail, but then he knew he was saved when he saw Kelso's "big eyes peering through the bushes." The laconic Captain Ruark noted the day's events—the deaths to two Union soldiers and four bushwhackers, and the capture and rescue of his brother and Simpson—in a twenty-seven-word diary entry and a six-sentence official report, the latter of which concluded by noting that "[l]ike a brave soldier" Lieutenant Smith had "died at the post of duty and honor." Smith's wife, who had just arrived in Neosho to spend time with her husband, had to watch a wagon bring his body back into town for burial.[42]

Billy Cloe would have a different memory of that June day's events. In the summer of 1864, Cloe was a thirteen-year-old Jasper County boy living about 18 miles north of Neosho. His friends and kin were all Southern sympathizers. As an old man, sometime before his death in 1935, Cloe dictated his recollections. Through the first years of the war, he said, his people "just tried to exist. It would have been easier without the Union thieves, robbers, and killers." He described local Federal officers as leaders of "gangs" who had murdered local men Cloe knew. "Old John Kelso, murderer," Cloe recalled, "always talked to my step-brother, Mike Hickey, 15 years old, about joining the army. Kelso often threatened to press him in." When Captain Goode returned to the area in the spring of 1864, he encouraged Hickey to enlist in the Confederate army, and Hickey's mother gave her consent. "In some way, word reached Kelso. When a few of the Southern boys came to enlist . . . they were surrounded by Lieutenant Smith, Kelso and others. Kelso knew Mike, and killed him, saying 'The hogs should eat him.'" There was nothing in Cloe's account about Goode's raid, the murder of Private Poag, the capture of Sergeant Ruark and Simpson, or the battle at the dry creek bed. Just vicious Federals murdering young boys in cold blood. Cloe, his mother, who was "almost insane with grief," and her young niece took a cart to retrieve the bodies. In moving the corpses, Cloe got "as bloody as if I had butchered a hog." He claimed that later, "old Kelso, came with his bunch, [and] bragged to Mother of killing her son, saying, 'I'll say he was as brave a boy as I ever met. Look at this powder burn on my face . . . he put it there.'"[43]

Cloe also heard about how Captain Goode met his end two months later. He said that "[t]he Neosho 'bunch' came along and located where Captain Goode watered his horse, waylaid him and shot him in the back of the head." Kelso thought that Captain Ruark had been able to get personal revenge by killing Goode "in single combat." Major Burch's report on August 5, 1864, however, described how Ruark's men (not just the captain himself) concealed themselves in bushes around the watering hole. When the bushwhacker captain and two others arrived, they heard a noise in the thicket but it was too late to escape: "the sharp report of a revolver was heard and Goode rolled from his horse dead. The ball penetrated the left side of his upper lip and ranged upward." Captain Ruark added to a brief note in his diary about the killing of Goode, the man responsible for the deaths of Private Poag and Lieutenant Smith: "He who so sheddeth man's blood by man shall his blood be shed. Bible."[44]

In the June 3 fight at the dry creek bed, Lieutenant Hunter and the other cavalrymen saw Lieutenant Smith up ahead get shot from his horse. Then, in an eerie repetition, they saw another bushwhacker turn and shoot, and Kelso, apparently hit, reel in his saddle as he fired his shotgun. His comrades dashed past him. When the chase was over and Kelso had not yet returned, they listed him among the dead. Hunter and most of the men rode ahead to Neosho, and then Burch sent Hunter immediately to Springfield with an account of the battle, including the news that Kelso, too, had died—though, Hunter said, "in the act of falling, he killed the bushwhacker that had killed him." Worried about the effect such news would have upon his family, the next day Kelso, after helping to bury Poag and Smith, headed for Springfield, 80 miles northeast.[45]

When he arrived at the town square he saw that a speaker's stand had been erected and a crowd was assembling for a public meeting. He made his way to the stand, spotted a friend—Lieutenant Lycurgus Lindsay—and asked what was going on. Lindsay stared at him, shocked. "Can I believe my eyes?" he gasped. "Is it *you* . . . . And are you *alive*?" Lindsay explained that they were gathering to hear funeral orations for Captain Kelso. Other people now started to come up to Kelso, surprised and smiling. "Every body seemed rejoiced to see me alive except those who had come as the orators of the occasion. . . . I had spoiled their opportunity to deliver themselves each of a spread-eagle speech in eulogy of the *'Fallen Hero of the South West.'* "[46]

Kelso made other scouting expeditions in the summer of 1864. On one, separated from his command with four of his men and lost in the rugged hills of northern Arkansas, he got out of a scrape with a cut-throat named Tall Thomas and his 25 bushwhackers by bluffing that he had dozens of men waiting in the woods and opening fire at close range. On another, larger expedition of 100 men led by Colonel Joseph Gravely, Kelso crept alone into a rebel house and killed the "noted bushwhacker" Lieutenant Baxter, who was, Gravely noted in his report, carrying dispatches for Confederate General Stand Watie. Toward the end of June, Kelso and his company were transferred to Granby, 9 miles northeast of Neosho, to help guard the lead mines. But when his men were sent out with someone other than Kelso or Burch in command, bad things started to happen. A small foraging party that went to Diamond Grove was routed by bushwhackers and two of his men—Privates Andrew J. Campbell and Joseph H. McGhee—were killed. Kelso was especially worried when a large scouting party left for McDonald County without him.[47]

Kelso remembered it as a detachment of 150 men, but the records show 60. It was commanded by Lieutenant Malcolm Hunter, with Lieutenant Robert M. McReynolds as his second and William Haycock—who would become famous after the war as "Wild Bill" Hickok—as the scout. Kelso was at first comforted that, if he was not allowed to go (being kept back in case Granby itself was attacked), at least McReynolds and Haycock would be there—they were both "heroic and skillful leaders." But his opinion of Hunter had dimmed since he had extolled the lieutenant as an officer after his own heart in his early June report. He still believed that no man was braver than Hunter and that no man was better to execute someone else's orders. "But, in a dire emergency, he was totally incompetent to act judiciously for himself. And, like most other incompetent men, he utterly refused to listen to other men more competent than himself." Hunter was likely to engage a large band of rebels, too, led by the crafty Confederate Major Andrew J. Piercey. Kelso feared disaster.[48]

From a friend's front yard, he watched the light-hearted and merry troops leave town. They smiled and waved, kissed the girls goodbye, and bid their friends a fond farewell. Kelso's foreboding turned into a premonition. "All my life," he later wrote, "I have been subject to strange impressions, which, account for them as we may, have always correctly fore-shadowed important coming events. . . . Call this superstition or any thing else you choose. . . . On this occasion, I had a very powerful impression of this kind. I *felt* that, if I did not get off with this party, the expedition would be a *very unfortunate one.*" As they passed, the men all had friendly words for him and said they were sorry he could not come along. He broke out in a cold sweat. "Many lives of dear brave comrades that I might have saved were now passing beyond my reach,— I would never see those comrades again." He calculated the time it would take them to ride out, be beaten by Piercey, and come limping back, with their hats gone, their horses covered in dust and foam, and their list of the dead. They did come back, just when he predicted and in the way he expected. "The *doomed* were now *dead.*" It was terrible, but also something of a relief: "Their lives were no longer *depending* on *me.*"[49]

Hunter and his men had first encountered the enemy's pickets near the McDonald County town of Rutledge. The Federals drove the guards toward their camp, but found it evacuated. Despite warnings from McReynolds and

Haycock, Hunter ordered the troops slowly forward. It was not long before gunfire erupted in their rear and on their flanks. They had marched right into an ambush and faced what seemed like 250 to 300 men nearly surrounding them. As Kelso understood the battle from what he was told and what he imagined, "when defeat was inevitable, when the slaughter had begun, when [Hunter] became utterly helpless, when the men ceased to look to him, when they were crying: '*Oh! that Captain Kelso were only here,*'" McReynolds and Haycock "virtually took control of the party and saved most of its members." They staged an orderly retreat, a running fight for over 4 miles, until the rebels gave up the chase. Kelso thought that about 10 men were lost; the records say 6.[50]

Three days later the Federals sent 175 men back out into the field, this time commanded by Major Burch and including Captains Kelso and Ruark. They tracked the enemy 30 miles until they found them occupying a strong position in a forest beyond the banks of Buffalo Creek. In reconnoitering the rebels' position, Burch had his horse shot out from under him, and Kelso and Lieutenant Baxter received "terrific fire" from the enemy that, miraculously, left them without a scratch. Uncharacteristically, "Burch seemed at a loss what to do." He did not, for a time, consult Kelso, and then when he finally asked Kelso's advice, he dithered a long while before taking it. When he sent an advance party to the left, as Kelso had recommended, he (in Kelso's view) sent the wrong man to lead it, and Sergeant Grantham led his 6 men into an ambush at a horseshoe bend in the creek. Grantham's party stopped at the creek to let their horses drink. "Instantly the whole semicircle flashed into a blaze, and every man and every horse of Grantham's heroic little band was riddled with bullets. . . . The wounded men all clung to their horses and the wounded horses all turned about and reach[ed] the near shelter of the woods, several of them hobbling away with some of their legs broken."[51]

Kelso rushed forward to help the wounded. The worst off was Corporal Jonathan C. "Caz" Thomas, who had several bullet wounds. He pointed to a wound and asked Kelso if it would kill him. No, Kelso said. Then Caz moved his finger and pointed to another with the same question, and got the same answer. And then to a third. Yes, Kelso answered, that one will kill you. In a few minutes. Well, Caz said, then don't spend any more time with me and go help those who can be saved. "I am killed, but, thank God! I die in a good cause!" A few minutes later, Kelso, weeping, helped carry his dead body away in a blanket.[52]

As the sun set, the MSM abandoned the pursuit of the still-unseen enemy and began their retreat through what Burch described in his report as "an everlasting jungle of brush and weeds." Kelso stayed behind on foot to see if the rebels sent any pursuit. "The ground was covered with blood from the wounded men and wounded horses," he remembered. "Bloody boots that had been cut from broken legs lay scattered around." With twilight, the silent forest began to darken. "Several horses were standing there slowly bleeding to death. They stood in great puddles of blood. I went to them, and patted their necks. They looked pleased and grateful. They looked around at their bleeding wounds, and then pleadingly in my face, begging in their poor dumb way for the help which they expected at my hands but which I was not able to give them." Kelso turned away and started to follow his men. "The poor creatures, seeing that I, their last friend, was deserting them, began to neigh piteously, and to hobble along after me, giving me looks of reproach almost human in their expressiveness. One of them dragged, tumbling along in the dirt, a hind foot that had been entirely shot from the leg except a small strip of skin." Kelso went back to pat their necks and try to soothe them. "They exhibited signs of great joy and again, in their way plead for help. Again I hurried away, thinking that I would not look back at them anymore." When about 100 yards away, however, he did look back. "And there they were, hobbling along after me, their necks stretched out pleadingly toward me, while, by their neighing, they were trying to call me back to them. I quickened my footsteps and was soon out of sight of them, but, for some time, I could still hear the piteous neighings which they kept up after they felt that their last friend had deserted them in their time of greatest need."[53]

ON ONE SCOUT in the fall, 20 miles south of Neosho, Kelso and a small squad flushed 3 rebel soldiers out of a farm house. He had to make sure his men did not kill the farm's owner, Joshua Miller, though he could not tell them why: Miller's wife, though known as one of Kelso's bitterest critics, was actually an important Union spy. The other two Confederates who ran across the cornfield, however, were fair game. Kelso took aim and brought one of them down. From the body, a man Kelso identified as a Lieutenant Gunter, Kelso found some interesting papers pertaining to a secret society known as the "Knights of the Golden Circle."[54]

Founded in the later 1850s by George W. L. Bickley, a Virginian living in Ohio, the Knights of the Golden Circle (KGC) was initially a secret society promoting the annexation of Mexico and the spread of the American slaveholding empire there and into Central America and the Caribbean. After John Brown's raid on Harper's Ferry in 1859, Bickley and his small "castles" of Knights turned to supporting Southern vigilante groups and then, in late 1860, to promoting secession. The KGC's strength in the spring of 1861 was in Texas and Arkansas, and Confederate General Ben McCulloch, the former Texas Ranger who fought at Wilson's Creek and died at Pea Ridge, was said to have been a prominent member. With the war, castles in the South mostly became dormant, though the group became a vehicle for men of Southern sentiments in Border States and in the North. A Louisville newspaper exposed the KGC's subversive activities in Kentucky in the summer of 1861; a federal grand journey in Indiana was convinced it had spread through the Midwest in the summer of 1862; and Bickley's arrest brought still more exposure in the summer of 1863. The extent of the group's membership and influence was a topic of intense debate, during the war and subsequently. Republican leader Thaddeus Stevens declared on the House floor in 1863 his belief "that the Democratic party through the North are holding secret meetings under the name of the Knights of the Golden Circle, and are plotting to seize the government and depose the President." Democratic Representative Samuel Sullivan Cox of Ohio declared a year later that he "had no knowledge of such an order." It is clear, however, that by the time Kelso took the KGC papers off of Lieutenant Gunter in 1864, pro-Confederate secret societies were still operating in the Border States and the North. That summer, a Michigan man arrested in Louisville had a KGC oath in his pocket—a document similar to what Kelso had found.[55]

Kelso's KGC papers described a ceremony used to induct new members. The candidate would first respond to a series of questions:

Question: "Do you believe in the existence of an Almighty God?"
Answer. "Yes." . . .

Q. "Do you believe that the white race is superior to the black race?"
A. "Yes."

Q. "Do you believe that it is right for the white race to enslave the black race?"
A. "Yes."

Q. "Do you believe that it is right to attempt the overthrow of the U. S. Government for the extension of slavery?"
A. "Yes."

Q. "Are you willing to take a solemn oath, in the presence of God and these witnesses, to use all the means which God hath placed in your power for the overthrow of the U. S. Government and the extension of slavery, and will you consider as null and void all other oaths that you ever have taken or that you may hereafter take if these oaths are in conflict with this oath?"

A. "Yes, God being my helper."

Accounts of the KGC's initiation ceremonies and oaths published during the war differed, acknowledging that forms and practices changed over time and varied from place to place. An 1861 exposé had a candidate swear to defend "Southern rights" and place his duty to his state and to his "home and domestic interests" above any obligation to the U.S. Constitution. An 1864 oath used in Indiana required that an initiate vow to defend the Democratic Party and do all in his power, through honorable means or not, "to subvert, or overthrow, the present damnable, Yankee Abolition Administration, so help me God."[56]

When he was next in Springfield, Kelso handed the Golden Circle papers over to C. C. Dawson, the office foreman at the Springfield *Patriot*, who promised to publish them in the town's Republican newspaper. Had Kelso known the background of Christopher Columbus "Lum" Dawson, however, he would never have handed over the documents. Dawson had been a proslavery journalist in Jasper County in 1857, a secessionist in 1861, and a printer for the pro-Confederate Missouri government in 1862. He took the Union loyalty oath (which, as Kelso knew, did not necessarily mean much) and registered for the draft in November 1863. Dawson never published the papers Kelso gave him in the fall of 1864, claiming they had been stolen off his desk. Kelso later learned—or came to suspect—that Dawson himself was "*a member of the treasonable order which these papers would have exposed.*"[57]

Kelso thought that secret societies of plotting traitors were nearly as much a threat as Confederate armies marching up from Arkansas and guerrillas terrorizing the countryside—and he was not alone. On July 28, 1864, the first page of the *Missouri Daily Democrat* featured a long exposé by Missouri's provost marshal general, Colonel John P. Sanderson, summarizing the report he had submitted in mid-June to General William S. Rosecrans, commander of the Department of Missouri since January. The report described secret societies operating in the state to conspire against the U.S. government. Together, Rosecrans and Sanderson had seen the problem early, so they greatly expanded the surveillance of suspected individuals and groups and began begging Washington for more troops to guard against civilian saboteurs and more money to fund their detectives. Citing discovered documents, affidavits, reports from undercover agents, and confessions, the report argued that a secret society in Missouri and several other states—Iowa, Indiana, Kentucky, New York, New Jersey, and Pennsylvania—linked the Copperhead Democrats led by exiled Ohio politician Clement L. Vallandigham in the North to the Confederacy through General Sterling Price in the South.[58]

According to Federal investigators, the society—originally the KGC, but then reformulated as the "Order of American Knights" (OAK) and then as the "Sons of Liberty"—hoped either to restore the "Union as it was" or to create a northwestern confederacy to ally with the southern one. Through an interstate communication network, the Knights (or Sons) smuggled letters, rebel propaganda, and guns. Members schemed to resist the Union draft, demoralize Federal troops, and liberate Confederate prisoners. They plotted assassinations and, in direct contact with Confederate generals such as Price and Marmaduke, planned a civilian uprising to coincide with the next Confederate attack from Arkansas. Some Democrats—like Vallandigham himself—admitted that there were Democratic clubs but insisted that these were merely to defend constitutional rights. Sanderson, however, and other dogged investigators such as Brigadier General Henry B. Carrington in Indiana made arrests and published detailed reports that convinced many—including, eventually, Secretary of War Edwin Stanton—that the threat was real. Sanderson believed there were twenty to thirty thousand members in Missouri and one hundred forty thousand in Illinois. If too ready to accept inflated numbers and too quick to draw direct conspiratorial connections among Peace Democrats, local fraternal societies, and the Confederate high command, Union investigators and commanders were not conjuring conspiracies out of thin air. The KGC and its offspring were more than figments of Republican propaganda.[59]

For Kelso, the KGC merely confirmed his already acute sense that there were no clear lines between battlefield and home front, between warfare and politics. Both sides of the Civil War, he argued, were engaged in a revolutionary struggle—one to confirm, once and for all, that the cornerstone of White republicanism was Black slavery and the other to establish, at long last, the commitment to universal liberty at the heart of the republic's constitution. If the contrast of principles were clearly drawn, though, the legions on either side were not. Secret traitors publicly pledged allegiance to one flag while conspiring to support the other. Other people—both the manipulators and the manipulated—moved back and forth, depending on how the wind blew. Powerbrokers could find their pawns among the fearful, the ignorant, and the confused. It was hard to tell who was who. If in the bush enemies only sometimes wore uniforms to identify themselves, in politics they never did.

ON SEPTEMBER 20, 1864, Confederate General Sterling Price and his Army of Missouri moved across the Arkansas line into the southeast. Price had been eager to return to Missouri since he had been chased out and beaten at Pea Ridge in early 1862. John Marmaduke and Jo Shelby had led cavalry raids into the state in 1863—including the attack on Springfield—but had been repulsed each time. The Confederate movement up from Arkansas in the fall of 1864, however, was no mere raid of a few thousand men. Price, with Marmaduke and Shelby commanding two of his three divisions, was leading more than 12,000 soldiers. The invasion intended to conquer St. Louis and Jefferson City and place the entire state under Confederate rule. The governor of Missouri's Confederate government in exile, Thomas Caute Reynolds, who had replaced Claib Jackson when the latter died in late 1862, accompanied the invasion force, ready to assume what he considered to be his rightful place on Missouri soil.[60]

Price had looked forward to this day for two and a half years. He had lobbied, complained, even pounded Jefferson Davis's desk. The military and political situation in the late summer of 1864, however, rather than "Old Pap's" pressure or petulance, set the invasion in motion. The Union's Red River campaign in western Louisiana had collapsed in the spring and the Federals had also been beaten in Arkansas, leaving a large number of rebel troops there to threaten Missouri's southern border. Meanwhile, Federal forces in Missouri were depleted and scattered through the countryside to fight guerrillas. Although the state had recently recruited an additional 69,000 men, most of them had been sent east, leaving only 11,000 garrisoned soldiers in the entire state. Price thought that he could march in with his army, rally tens of thousands more true Missourians to the Confederate flag, take the two cities, and, with infantry reinforcements from the South, pry the state free from Federal control. The Confederate leadership, growing more desperate as Grant and Sherman pressed hard in Virginia and Georgia, hoped that Price's strike might force the United States to shift men away from the eastern theater. Ultimately, though, the deciding factor may have been more political than military. An embarrassing and demoralizing Union loss of Missouri right before the fall election might encourage voters to choose McClellan over Lincoln, opening the way for a negotiated peace.

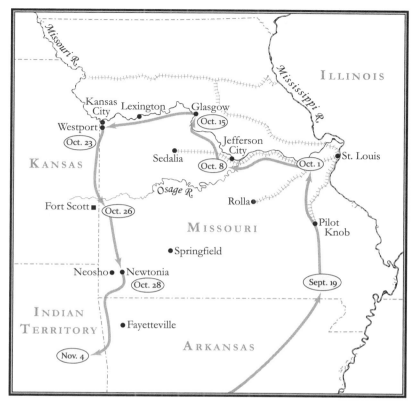

Sterling Price's Missouri Expedition of 1864. Drawn by Rebecca Wrenn. Map source: Charles D. Collins, Jr., *Battlefield Atlas of Price's Missouri Expedition of 1864* (Fort Leavenworth, Kans.: Combat Studies Institute Press, 2016).

Price's Army of Missouri marched north in three columns 10 to 30 miles apart. The divisions united at Fredericktown on September 24. Price had sent word ahead to guerrillas, including "Bloody Bill" Anderson and William Quantrill, asking them to attack railroad lines and harass Federal scouting parties. But the guerrillas were more interested in following in the army's wake to plunder and spread terror. On September 27, Anderson and his men pulled the 23 soldiers off the train in Centralia and executed them. Two weeks later, they rode into Glasgow and tortured the town's richest man until he gave them $5,000. Price, who had little sway over the guerrillas, also had trouble maintaining discipline among his own men. The Confederates were more intent on revenge than on winning hearts and minds. They harassed and pillaged; they shot down captured soldiers and murdered random civilians, especially Blacks.[61]

The first major battle was on September 27, the attack on Fort Davidson at Pilot Knob, near the terminus of the Iron Mountain Railroad that Kelso and the 24th Infantry had rushed to defend back in 1861. The 1,300 men defending the fort, commanded by Brigadier General Thomas Ewing, held off an assault by a much larger force, inflicting heavy casualties (perhaps 200 killed and 600 to 800 wounded). As the Confederates withdrew into camp for the night and planned the next morning's attack, Ewing and the Federals knew they would have to evacuate. In the middle of the night, they opened the gate and silently exited the fort, their horses' hooves wrapped in hay bags and their wagon wheels in blankets to muffle the sound as they crossed the drawbridge. They crept through the darkness, passing within 80 yards of the enemy's camp. The last ones out trailed a line of gunpowder that led back into the fort's powder and ammunition magazine. As the last of the Federals disappeared into the night mist, a match was struck, and a few moments later a tremendous explosion blasted flames hundreds of feet into the air, blew in windows in the surrounding town, showered debris and dirt over the nearest campers, and shook the earth for 20 miles.[62]

As a cavalry detachment went after Ewing's escaping Federals, the bulk of Price's lumbering army moved north toward St. Louis. The Union commander of the Department of Missouri stationed at the city, Major General William S. Rosecrans, had been in the job for eight months. Before coming to Missouri, some early battlefield successes were followed by a bad loss at Chickamauga and a bewilderment at Chattanooga that prompted Lincoln to describe Rosecrans as "confused and stunned like a duck hit on the head." The president, though, hoped the general had the political savvy and bureaucratic skills to manage Missouri. Rosecrans did reorganize the militia, help expose the KGC and its progeny, and navigate fairly well amidst the state's rancorous political factions. But his response to his greatest Missouri challenge—Price's invasion—was criticized as feckless both by press accounts and later by General Grant. Rosecrans was slow to comprehend the size of Price's force, had difficulty locating where the enemy was on any given day within a hundred miles, and misread his opponent's intentions. Once he understood the threat, Missouri's Federal commander was afraid to concentrate his forces and face Price in the field: pulling men from their outposts would expose much of the countryside to guerrilla attacks, and in going on the march, his forces might be outflanked, leaving St. Louis vulnerable. So he did little at first besides bluff that he had twice the 6,000 experienced troops actually defending the city, and he allowed small militia units to be swept aside as Price's army marauded through the state at will.[63]

Fortunately for Rosecrans, though, in Price he faced an opponent who, as a critical Confederate officer put it, "had a voice like a lion and a spring like a guinea pig." Weighing over 300 pounds, Price was obliged to ride to battle in a buggy, and was frequently ill (or, it was rumored, drunk). He began to lose confidence as they approached St. Louis. A circular issued by the leader of the KGC-like Order of American Knights in the city urged its members to rise up, attack the Federal occupiers, and await further orders from Price. But the general had no orders. Deciding that St. Louis was too well defended, he turned west toward Jefferson City.[64]

The defenders of the state capital had, after reinforcements, about 6,000 to 8,000 men. A Federal force from St. Louis was supposed to be pursuing Price but, slow off the mark, it had given the Confederates a five-day head start and would be no help. On October 5–7, the rebels and the Jeff City men battled on the outskirts of the city. But again Price believed the reports that doubled the number of enemy troops. So he broke off the attack and moved northwest. In leaving Jefferson City behind, Price and his army also abandoned their larger goals for the campaign. It became merely a raid, aimed at destroying military resources, inflicting pain on Federal troops and their supporters where possible, stealing supplies, and then quickly retreating back to Arkansas. They could stop hoping to reclaim Missouri for the Confederacy and could pretend, as a later commentator put it, that every stolen Unionist farm wagon was a victory. Price's soldiers won many such victories as they marched across the state: by the time they reached Lexington, according to some accounts, they had six hundred wagons, many of them loaded with plunder, and three thousand head of rustled cattle—though these numbers, like most of the assessments of troops and casualties associated with this campaign, remain in dispute.[65]

Major General Samuel Curtis, who had beaten Price at Pea Ridge and was now the commander of the Department of Kansas, saw the Confederates plow across Missouri toward the Kansas line and was ready to meet Price there and beat him again. Pulling together what he called the "Army of the Border" from Kansas volunteers and militia and troops from Wisconsin and Colorado, Curtis had fortifications built, creating three lines of defense for Kansas City. He sent out 2,000 cavalry led by Major General James G. Blunt to engage Price's army and slow it down, giving the forces sent in pursuit by Rosecrans—4,500 cavalry and 9,000 infantry—time to catch up. On October 23 at Westport, a little south of Kansas City, the Federals routed the Confederates, but left an escape path to the south, which Price's beaten and bedraggled army took. With two Federal divisions in pursuit, the rebels swept down along the Kansas border and toward Missouri's southwest corner, shedding baggage and booty and deserters as they went.[66]

The soldiers of the Confederate Army of Missouri bore down upon Kelso and Burch and the few hundred militiamen stationed at Neosho and Newtonia. Though perhaps half the size of the force that had entered the state a month earlier, Price's army was still many thousands strong and his men were desperate and dangerous. The Confederate invasion had roused local bushwhackers to action like angry hornets, and Kelso and his men had been scouting constantly. On the morning of October 27, Kelso returned to Neosho from a scout and found Burch readying an evacuation of the post's 300 men to Newtonia, 11 miles east. Reports had Price's army only a day's march away. After doing some reconnaissance, Kelso and his 40 men rode to join Burch at Newtonia, having to swing wide to the right to make it around one of Price's advance units.[67]

Burch and Kelso had a few hundred men; Price had several thousand. The only thing for the Federals to do was to retreat farther northeast toward Springfield. Strangely, though, Burch was in no hurry. He had waited until the morning after his arrival to evacuate Newtonia and even then moved only a few miles east over the prairie to the edge of the forest. Federal divisions led by generals Curtis and Blunt were close behind Price, Burch reasoned, and if the two armies collided at Newtonia, the men of the 8th MSM might be able to move around Price's left flank and join the attackers. So they waited and watched. When the sun rose higher and nothing happened, Burch ordered Kelso to take 10 men back into town for a closer look.[68]

For perhaps the first time in his military career, Kelso regretted the honor of being chosen for hazardous duty. Because of the long scouts he had just completed, his horse was nearly exhausted. And he was riding into a situation where he would almost certainly need a fast horse. Kelso was always the one to argue for staying and fighting rather than retreating, but in this instance he felt that he and his small squad were "running into the very jaws of death."[69]

One of the men who volunteered to go back into town with Kelso was 1st Lieutenant Robert H. Christian, known as "Old Grisly," of the 15th Missouri Cavalry. Kelso respected Christian as a "successful hunter of Bush-whackers," but Old Grisly's reputation for ruthlessness exceeded even Kelso's. Christian supposedly shot four old Southern men in cold blood—one in his sick bed— and had tried to poison some others. There was a story that he once brought home a severed head from one of his scouts. He lived in Newtonia near the fort. His wife was confined to her bed—dying, it was thought—and he wanted to visit her one more time. So Old Grisly, "splendidly mounted and formidably armed," his long gray beard waving in the breeze, rode with Kelso back into Newtonia.[70]

Kelso had sent two lookouts to a high point on the prairie a mile and a half outside of town. They signaled "immediate danger" and came galloping back. They had seen Price's entire army—in a line that stretched for miles—heading for town, with an advance party of several hundred cavalry in the lead. Kelso knew he and his men had to leave quickly. Then Burch rode up. Informed of the approaching cavalry, the major decided that Kelso's small squad could hold them off from the blockhouse until the rest of the 8th MSM came up from the tree line. Burch then galloped off without waiting for Kelso's reply.[71]

Kelso saw another body of cavalry coming from the north, with two horsemen riding straight toward him at full speed. They handed him orders from General Sanborn, the commander at Springfield, to evacuate immediately. Kelso did not know whether to believe the messengers or not: their blue uniforms could have been stolen, the orders forged. As they galloped away, Burch returned. "[W]e must get away at once," Kelso told the major. "But a hundred more men will soon be here," Burch said. "Then just a hundred more will be lost," Kelso replied, pointing to a summit to the west, 3 miles long, the whole length of which was growing dark with approaching enemies. Corporal Barnes, Kelso's brother-in-law, on a horse next to Burch, looked, and his eyes grew wide. "Je-e-e-s-us Chri-i-i-st! That is too much for me," he cried. Though "a brave man, generally," Barnes, without waiting for orders, put spurs to his racing mare and streaked away toward the timberline. "Yes, we must be off," Burch agreed, and galloped off after Barnes. Kelso ordered the rest of his men to follow, but waited for Old Grisly, who had lingered, visiting with his wife.[72]

Christian was on his horse, coming around the side of his barn, about 80 yards behind Kelso and 40 yards in front of the approaching Confederate horsemen. The rebels spurred their horses and charged. Realizing that he had lost the opportunity to escape on his exhausted horse, Kelso planned to leap onto Christian's when the lieutenant rode by. But Old Grisly, instead of dashing toward Kelso, stopped his horse, turned toward the rebels, and began firing. "The rebels rushed right on, closing upon him as they came. The bullets that missed him, whistled past me. I sat upon my horse facing him watching the fight that could have but one termination. He was throwing away his own life and mine also. I saw him fall. I turned around and put spurs to my excuse for a horse." As he learned later, the men who killed Lieutenant Christian then "*scalped* Christian's *head* and also his *chin*, which was covered with [a] long grisly beard; and they *showed these bloody trophies to his sick wife as she lay almost dying in bed*." Kelso believed the men had to be bushwhackers

rather than regular soldiers in Price's army because "they did what no honorable Confederate soldiers would have done." He assumed that they were
connected to a local group that had tortured a Newtonia man for money, first
burning his feet and then, when that did not work, shoving hot coals into
his mouth, "which so cooked his tongue that it came off." But the distinction between regulars and irregulars no longer made a difference. The man
who killed and scalped Christian was Lieutenant Samuel Moore, who rode
in Price's army in Jo Shelby's division. Moore, who said his father had been
killed by Christian, had asked to lead the advance party into Newtonia. He
showed the bloody trophies to other women in town, too. One of Christian's
neighbors, Jane Sanderson, a Southern sympathizer and a bushwhacker's
widow, saw Old Grisly's body and came to town in tears. "I am called a rebel,
but I cannot stand such sights as this."[73]

Kelso, on his tired horse, had looked back to see Christian's killers dismount to do their bloody work. But plenty of other rebel horsemen galloped
from Newtonia's streets and headed right toward him. Ahead, Burch and his
hundred men were nowhere to be seen. Kelso could not expect to be rescued.
Perhaps, though, the enemy would not recognize him as a Federal officer. He
was, after all, dressed more like a bushwhacker than a soldier—except for his
hat, which he quickly took off and tossed away. The first rider who caught up
to him "was a large, dark, fierce looking man with long hair," a bushwhacker
wearing an elaborate hunting shirt and a belt loaded with revolvers. The rebel
eyed the man on the broken down horse suspiciously and asked a question
Kelso pretended not to hear above the clattering of horses' hooves. "Our boys
got one of them back yonder," Kelso called back. The bushwhacker repeated
his question. Still pretending not to hear, Kelso answered, "My horse is nearly
given out running so far." Flashing another dark look, the man "waved his
revolver in the air, gave a keen war whoop," spurred his horse and left Kelso
behind in the dust. Other riders galloped past Kelso too. If any of them suddenly suspected that Kelso was their enemy, he had a plan: he would open fire
with both barrels of his big shotgun and then jump to the ground and empty
his revolvers at the enemy swarming around him. He figured he could take
out a dozen before being killed. He also thought, "What a strange place this is
for a candidate for Congress to be in so near the day of election!"[74]

He wondered if he was approaching the moment of his death. But a distinct feeling rose up within him—more than resolve, more than intuition, it
was a certain premonition not only that he would survive but that he would
"live to perform a great work after the close of the war." He was riding at the
rear of the group of rebels heading toward the timberline, where the 8th

MSM waited and then opened fire. But his comrades in the woods saw him, and Kelso was able to leave the rebels, maneuver around a small knoll between the battle lines, and rejoin his men without getting caught in the fusillade from his friends in front or his enemies behind.[75]

With the main body of Price's army moving through Newtonia, the Federals in the woods risked being surrounded. A narrow passage through a rocky gorge was only way out. Kelso and ten men were to wait at the entrance of the defile, mostly visible to the enemy but masking the retreat of the rest of the troops. Kelso's squad had to wait as thousands of rebels poured across the prairie and through the town, wait until a single gunshot signaled "all clear." As Kelso and his small rear guard sat on their horses with thousands of enemy soldiers nearly surrounding them, with the chances of their survival dwindling with every passing minute, he proposed to tell his men a humorous story to pass the time. Recounting his storytelling years later in his autobiography, he set the scene. The men got comfortable as they listened to their captain describe his first courtship—the tale of Adelia's suitor, the haughty young man pacing about in his orchard, trying to memorize a prayer, and his embarrassing performance at the prayer meeting. "Picture to yourself if you can that little party of ten men in the edge of that forest, looking out on a great prairie covered with 30,000 enemies," he wrote. "[P]icture them, all young men, scarcely more than boys—sitting there side-wise on their saddles with death before their eyes, quietly puffing their smoke and smiling at the laughable story which their tall, dark, long-haired, bare-headed leader—who has just reached them through the jaws of death—is telling them in so jocular a manner,—picture all this to yourself and you will have a picture of heroism unsurpassed in the annals of the world." At the end of the story, they heard the single rifle shot—the signal—and bolted through the defile to safety.[76]

Behind them, artillery started to boom. An advance party of Curtis's Union troops, commanded by Major General Blunt, clashed with Price's rear guard, commanded by Brigadier General Jo Shelby. The two forces blasted away at each other for two hours across a field on Thomas McClain's farm, a thousand Federals facing considerably more Confederates. Blunt's men were running out of ammunition and stretched to the breaking point when reinforcements appeared atop the prairie ridge: Brigadier General John Sanborn's 3rd Brigade, with four wagonloads of ammunition. General Curtis was close behind. Burch and Kelso had wanted to make their way around the enemy's flank to join Sanborn, but not knowing how to reach him, they continued their retreat. At Newtonia, with the appearance of more Union troops, the Confederates withdrew. Both sides claimed victory: the Federals took the battlefield, but the Confederates bought precious time for Price's retreating army. About 200 men were killed or wounded.[77]

Kelso and his "boys" did not miss any "adventures" by not being able to join the Federal troops chasing Price's disintegrating army into Arkansas. General Curtis's pursuit sputtered to an anticlimactic conclusion. Plagued by political infighting among his commanders and initially thwarted by an order from Rosecrans to stop at Missouri's southern border (Curtis had to appeal over Rosecrans's head to Washington), the chase ended with the Federals firing thirty-four artillery rounds across the Arkansas River at the fleeing ragged rebels. The day after the battle at Newtonia, Burch, Kelso, and a detachment of 60 men were sent after a force of over 300 irregulars who had broken off from Price's army. Burch's orders were to harass their rear as they retreated south, delaying them so that Lieutenant Colonel John Brutsche, commanding a much larger force, could get in front of them and cut them off.

The 8th MSM tracked the rebels through a rough, hilly region covered in bushes. The trail was easily marked by the foam from the enemy's exhausted horses. To make sure they would not be ambushed, Kelso dismounted and walked ahead of the troops alone to draw the enemy's fire. When he saw a puff of smoke flashing 100 yards ahead, he hit the ground. "Quite a storm of bullets tore through the bushes over my back, and a sliver from a wounded bush near my face stuck into my left cheek." Burch and the rest of the men came up and they skirmished briefly with the enemy until the rebels fled. This process was repeated five more times. "How I escaped, as I did, un-hurt, I do not myself understand." The Federals pressed ahead, continuing to harass the enemy's rear. On the trail they started to encounter abandoned horses, some lying upon the ground panting, others standing, feet splayed, trembling from exhaustion. When the soldiers came upon dismounted stragglers stumbling along the trail up ahead, they shot them. Three more times, the rebels "made a feeble attempt to fight; but they were so demor-alized now that we did not dismount any more to fight them, nor did I go forward any more to draw their fire. We charged at once on horseback." The battle turned "into a rout and a slaughter," Kelso wrote. "Haver-sacks, blankets, guns, packages of stolen goods, fallen horses, and dead rebels, now strewed the ground for many miles. Utterly panic stricken, the rebels were dispersing in all directions."[78]

The cavalrymen fanned out, pursuing the fleeing rebels, picking them off one by one. By the time they reached Lieutenant Colonel Brutsche's com-mand at the end of the trail, there was no enemy force left for Brutsche to fight. Many had been shot down, and the rest had scattered like autumn leaves in the wind. "We turned back upon our own trail to gather our own stragglers, to pick up plunder, to form an estimate of the rebel slain, etc. For fifteen miles back . . . the trail was literally strewn with dead men, dead or exhausted horses, guns, revolvers, blankets, etc., etc. We had made a fearful slaughter, and had ourselves suffered no loss except that of the two men wounded in the first engagement."[79]

On this expedition, Kelso's horse was so broken down that his front legs would sometimes collapse beneath him, pitching Kelso into the grass. He asked Burch for a better mount, and the major had him switch with Sergeant McElhany, but this exchange cost Kelso. Kelso's horse soon collapsed again and pitched the sergeant through the air. "[T]he Sergt. arising from the ground, in the broad light of day, and without the fear of god before his eyes, blasphemed my name aloud, declaring that by the Great-jumping jingo, he'd vote against me; and when he said a thing, he meant it. He did vote against me."[80]

By the time they made it to Springfield the next day, Kelso had given McElhany his horse back and instead rode "a very small pony" he had captured. "When mounted upon this pony, my feet were within a few inches of the ground. My hat was gone, and my long dark hair hung upon my shoulders. The legs of my pantaloons had been torn off at the knees. Exposure had made me dark almost as an Indian," he wrote. "I wore a bush-whacker's coat and carried my big shot-gun. My belt was full of large revolvers and an enormous hunting knife. Besides all these things, I carried a cartridge box, a shot pouch, and a powder horn. . . . Entering the city thus, I probably looked more picturesque than beautiful." In his memoir, he made a joke about Jesus riding into Jerusalem on a little jackass, but crossed it out. "In the midst of the public square, I was stopped by the crowds of eager people who gathered about me. The windows and balconies were soon filled with women waving handkerchiefs and cheering for the '*Hero of the South West*.'" A week later, men in the Fourth District cast their votes, and Kelso was elected to Congress.[81]

ON FRIDAY, MARCH 3, 1865, Representative S. H. Boyd and the other members of the 38th Congress completed their long final day of the session. William T. Sherman marched through the Carolinas, Philip Sheridan through the Shenandoah Valley, and Ulysses Grant planned the final push to break Robert E. Lee's defense of Richmond and Petersburg, Virginia. Jefferson Davis still hoped for divine deliverance. Abraham Lincoln, preparing for his second inauguration the next day, also wrote to Grant, telling him how to handle the enemy's surrender.[82]

In northwest Arkansas on March 3, a woman was angry. She had supported the Southern cause, and she was pretty sure that cause was lost, but that was not what infuriated her. A small party of armed Southern men had ridden up to her farm and taken nearly everything she had. They grabbed all the bacon she had put up after slaughtering her hogs and made off with all her seed corn for the coming spring planting. So when some Federal cavalrymen rode by not long afterward, she went out to them, told them what had happened, and pointed the direction the guerrillas had taken.

Up a long winding trail, through a ravine, and into some wooded hills, a man sat against a tree, cutting slices of the woman's bacon. His horse, hitched in front of him, chomped on the seed corn. Suddenly a shotgun blast sprayed the dirt by his boots. Springing to his feet and believing that there was not a Federal soldier within 50 miles, he thought it must have been one of his friends—thought the shot was some dangerous mistake.

"What the devil are you shooting at *me* for?" he cried. But then the answer came from the woods, about 50 yards away: "I want your scalp." The man lunged to his horse for his gun. As his hand pulled the weapon from its holster the shotgun fired again. One shot went through his head, and he died as he hit the ground.[83]

As Kelso walked from the woods, he tore a piece of paper from his notebook, wrote a note and pinned it to the corpse's coat. This was a practice the bushwhackers themselves had started. "Bloody Bill" Anderson had pinned a note to one of his victims the previous summer, proudly attributing the scalping and corpse mutilation to his right-hand man Archie Clements. Jim Jackson's guerrilla band in northeast Missouri made this a common practice, leaving notes pinned to the Black men they murdered in the spring of 1865. Kelso's note read: "I hereby send my kindest compliments to the friends of this bush-whacker and inform them that he makes *twenty-six* rebels in all that have fallen by my hand. I had vowed to kill *twenty-five*. I have more than fulfilled my vow. I am content. I will now cut my hair. John R. Kelso." On his last scout, it was the last shot fired and the last kill by Congressman-elect Kelso in the Civil War.[84]

12

Captain Kelso Goes to Congress

AS HIS TRAIN neared Washington, D.C., in late November 1865, Kelso would have seen dilapidated farms, dingy houses, and small tobacco plantations in among the pine thickets, scrub forests, and swamps. Near the district line were the grim earthworks built to defend the city. But he was too excited to notice. "I had always thought of Washington as something almost fabulous. . . . Yet here I was approaching it in reality. Here I was about to realize one of the fondest dreams of my life. I approached it with a strange feeling of awe. I was entering a kind of fairy land." Then, as the train began to slow, out the window, looming on the left, was "the great snow-white dome of our magnificent National Capitol." The new dome had been completed just two years before, in the midst of war, as a new powerful nation rose on the foundations of the old Union. "It is formed almost entirely of cast iron," a Washington correspondent wrote, "resting upon the old Capitol edifice, which, to support so vast additional weight, has been trussed up, buttressed, and strengthened, so that it seems to cower beneath the threatening mass of its superimposed burden." A 19-foot-6-inch statue called "Freedom Triumphant in War and Peace" and weighing nearly 20,000 pounds had been hoisted to its perch on the top in December 1863, to the salute of artillery guns. "The outer dome," the correspondent wrote, "is government as the vast mass of citizens behold it, white and monumental and crowned with liberty." Inside the dome, however, in "its hungry hollow belly, is government as you find it, familiar with its gluttonies and processes, its dyspepsias and cramps." But Kelso, arriving on the train, had not been inside the belly yet. He sat, staring out the window, feeling "entranced."[1]

As soon as he stepped off the train, though, he "was rudely disenchanted." Two dozen hackmen surrounded him yelling "Want a carriage?" Another observer described the usual scene at the train station. The visitor "is greeted by a series of shouts and yells which startle and bewilder him unless he be a man of uncommon nerve. A dense line of omnibuses and hacks is drawn up before the station entrance, each and all yelling at the top of their lungs the names and merits of their respective hotels. 'Metropolitan 'otel, Sir, best 'ouse in the City, Sir.' 'National, Sir, National. This way, Sir.'" Trying to make his way through the crowd, Kelso "was beset by a small army of boys, each of whom insisted upon carrying my valise, and several of whom seized it and began to pull for its possessions." Next were the newsboys, "each of whom thrust a newspaper up toward my head yelling the name of his paper with all his might." Then "a small army of boot-blacks, most of them little negroes. For some distance, they all marched along with me in fine style, some before me, some behind, and some at each side, all pointing to my boots, and yelling: 'Bla-a-a-ck yer boots! Shi-i-i-ne um up! Only ten cents!'" Last were the panhandlers: "I fell into an army of little dirty beggars, each of whom held out its little paw, 'Pl-e-e-ase give me a penn-e-e-ey to buy a loaf of bre-ea-ea-ead!'"[2]

As Horace Greeley quipped, in Washington, D.C., "the rents are high, the food is bad, the dust is disgusting, the mud is deep, and the morals are deplorable." It had always been an odd little city, a grand plan plotted onto isolated, swampy acres along the Potomac, its stately public buildings surrounded by all the amenities of a shabby Southern town. Visitors found its boarding houses dirty and poorly furnished; in the hotels the air was hazy from cigar smoke and the floors slick with tobacco juice. In 1865 it was also suffering from having had its 1860 population of 75,000 nearly double and then recede to 120,000. The troops in tens of thousands of tents were mostly gone now, but so were the city's trees, which the soldiers had hacked down for firewood. Carcasses of the mules that had pulled army wagons still rotted behind makeshift stables on the mall. Pennsylvania Avenue was impressively wide, and lined with handsome three-story red brick homes down toward the White House, but it was filled with ruts and potholes, and goats and pigs wandered its side streets. Kelso's boarding house was at 393 First Street—convenient to the Capitol but not a fashionable address (no other congressmen stayed there). In the few days before the session opened, he visited the usual tourist attractions, including the White House, the Smithsonian, and the War Department. He mentioned the Washington Monument, but not the fact that in 1865, seventeen years after its cornerstone had been laid, the obelisk was still an unfinished stump. He got lost inside the Capitol on his first visit, but described the view of the city from the dome as "magnificent."[3]

The 39th Congress would begin on December 4 with great expectations. Much had happened since the adjournment of the 38th Congress in early

March 1865. A month later, Lee had surrendered to Grant at Appomattox Court House. A week after that, Lincoln was dead and Andrew Johnson, a former slaveholding Democrat from Tennessee brought on to balance the ticket in 1864, became president. Although initially promising to take a hard line against the beaten Southerners, Johnson quickly offered amnesty to most common rebels and granted presidential pardons to thousands of former Confederate leaders. Without any congressional input, he moved swiftly to patch up state governments and courts and encouraged constitutional conventions to put the former Confederate states on a fast track to be fully restored to the Union. Soon the state legislatures, organized according to his plan and filled with former rebels, passed "Black Codes" to trap freed people in a peonage status that was as close to slavery as possible. When the Congress convened in early December, it faced momentous challenges in a continuing national crisis. By the end of the term, it would have historic achievements, notably the Civil Rights Bill of 1866, the first Reconstruction Act of 1867, and the 14th Amendment to the U.S. Constitution. It would also begin, for the first time in American history, the process of impeaching a president of the United States.

Freshman congressman John R. Kelso, known for haunting the "dark and bloody vistas" of the border war, as the *New-York Daily Tribune* put it, would try not to seem out of place beneath the Capitol dome. He worked diligently for his constituents and with his colleagues. He cast mundane votes to turn the gears of government and important ones to forward the great work of Reconstruction. He submitted petitions, proposed bills, drafted constitutional amendments, and was among the first to call from the floor of the House for the impeachment of Andrew Johnson. But a challenge to his election victory, to his right to the seat, threw him off balance right from the beginning of the term. His intemperate response led him to blunders that would spark rumors of a drift toward conservatism, wounding his political reputation back home in Missouri's Fourth Congressional District.[4]

Kelso had seven months to transition from soldier to legislator. He and his men of the 8th Missouri State Militia Cavalry had been discharged on April 18 in a ceremony at Springfield. Kelso made a short speech, his men gave him three cheers, and "tears, manly tears, flowed down all their cheeks." He felt a deep sadness, sensing that "the best of my life was gone forever." He returned home to Susie and the children. John and Susie sat down, had a frank conversation, and tried to rebuild their life together. "My wife had declared her intention to overcome her unfortunate love for Doctor Hovey . . . and to become a good and true wife to me." Kelso worked in his garden and on his

John R. Kelso, ca. 1864-7. Portrait of U.S. Representative John R. Kelso, Springfield, Missouri, Charles Lanham Collection, State Historical Society of Missouri, Columbia.

grounds, taught his children, and prepared to be a congressman. He read and reread the congressional manual—the parliamentary rules of order. As one congressional reporter observed, few representatives seemed to have studied the manual and others seemed never to have opened the volume at all. But those who learned all the complex rules of House procedure could use them to their advantage. Kelso, as ever, wanted to be one of the clever ones. He also studied the newspapers, "informing myself in regard to the political condition of our country." Susie gave birth to another son, "our little Freddie, who became the most lovely child, without any exception, that I ever knew."[5]

Kelso looked back on this period "as one of the pleasantest" in his life. Still, for many months he "felt lost." He "pined for the tented field and the excitement of war. I often roused from a reverie, with a start, under the impression that the faint sound of a distant bugle had reached my ear, and that I must rush to my post to command my men." The thought that he would never again lead "brave men to victory and to glory" left him with "a feeling of unutterable loneliness." For the rest of his life he would have dreams that he was still in battle, waking himself by crying aloud, "Charge! boys, charge! we'll get every one of them!"[6]

On September 19, 1865, Kelso had given a speech at Walnut Grove, in Greene County, Missouri, twenty-some miles northwest of Springfield, in which he outlined his political agenda for Congress. He began by asking his audience to remind themselves about the origins and nature of the war they had just endured, "the mightiest struggle ever recorded in the annals of the world," the "bloodiest, the most stupendous tragedy ever enacted on the stage of time." Unlike most wars, which sprang from trivial causes, political accidents, or the caprice of ambitious rulers, the American Civil War had been a violent opposition "of antagonistic principles which, from the beginning, have underlain the whole fabric of government." Liberty and slavery had both been woven into the Constitution, and the result, he said, using a line from a famous 1858 speech by William H. Seward, was an "irrepressible conflict." Kelso compared the titanic struggle between the "minions of Slavery" and the defenders of Liberty to the battle of God's legions and Satan's fallen angels in Milton's *Paradise Lost.*[7]

The war was over, but the struggle of antagonistic principles continued in political form, Kelso argued. The rebels changed their tactics. Like the serpent in Eden, "so do they now glide among us, *professing* an interest in our welfare." With blood still on their hands, they proudly posed as honorable men. "Even our great and good Executive," President Johnson, who in the spring had promised to "hang traitors and make treason odious," had been duped. The Southerners professed to have relinquished slavery, but they were forging a new set of shackles for Blacks; they professed loyalty to the United States, but only to get federal troops removed from the South as soon as possible. Their vows of allegiance meant nothing, Kelso charged. Hadn't the Knights of the Golden Circle taught them to make and break such oaths as expediency demanded?[8]

Since there could be no secure peace "until the rebels are rendered totally powerless to do harm," the first pressing question for the new Congress was obvious: "What, then, shall be done with the rebels?" The question would be easily answered, Kelso said, if, like God in *Paradise Lost*, we had a Hell to put them in. Traitors deserved death and the confiscation of their property; loyal citizens deserved protection and reparations. Depriving the rebels of their rights as citizens for at least five years and the forfeit of some of their property seemed a modest request of justice.[9]

Kelso did not pretend, however, that this stance toward rebels was only the abstract dictate of justice. The suffering experienced by loyal people should not be casually set aside. "We can *forgive*, but can we *forget*?" He, for one, could not forget the winter of 1861, he said, when their wives and children were driven from their homes into a snowstorm, all to suffer and some to die. "I can not forget the fearful *vow* I made to *avenge* these wrongs." He remembered when he led his men in battle and when he crept alone "upon the traitor foe." He remembered "while taking aim and pulling trigger, and have felt a strange, wild pleasure while beholding my foes fall, before my own fatal shots. Yes! I have thought of these things; and so help me God! I expect to think of them, whenever I see rebels intermeddling in the affairs of our government."[10]

Another issue that was being debated in the press and would be argued in Congress was the status of the rebellious states. Politicians and political writers had wrestled with the question of "whether the Rebel States are *in* the Union or *out*." Lincoln had thrown up his hands at what seemed to devolve into a "merely metaphysical" conundrum. Kelso, like Radical Republican House leader Thaddeus Stevens in a speech earlier that month, argued that by illegally seceding, treasonously rebelling, and making war against the United States, the rebel states "ceased to be states at all, and the country they occupied has relapsed to its original *territorial* condition." As such, their governance would be supervised by Congress until they were judged to be rehabilitated and ready to return to the Union as states on an equal footing with the others.[11]

The third main question for the upcoming Congress was about who should rule in the formerly rebellious states. Here again Kelso confronted the status of people of color in American society. He tried to push further past the racial bias that had blighted his stump speeches a year earlier. "We have prejudices to overcome, old almost as our lives, and strong as our innate passions," he said. We need to lay aside these prejudices in favor of the sublime principle of equal rights in the Declaration of Independence. "[I]f we incorporate this principle into our Constitution and thus make it equally applicable to all parts of the nation, we shall humble the haughty power of the aristocratic traitors of the South, lift to liberty and joy the millions of down-trodden and oppressed, and make our country glorious among the nations as indeed, 'the land of the free and the home of the brave.'" If instead, "we yield to our old prejudices" and insist that the United States is a "*white* man's country," then the victory will be lost. Who should rule the rebel states—or any states? The loyal people, regardless of color.[12]

Kelso disavowed any plans to remove people of African descent and colonize them outside the United States. He had become convinced, he said, that colonization "would be *unwise, unjust,* and *impracticable.* I therefore relinquish this doctrine, and join issue upon the grand practical question, now before the American people, of *universal suffrage.*" He now boldly declared "for the equal rights of all men." He hoped that his "colonization friends" did not blame him for abandoning that position since he did so "from *honest convictions,* and since this is the only political change I have made."[13]

The goal, then, included voting rights and not just equality before the law in civil matters. Men who fought bravely in the war certainly deserved the ballot. To those who decried the Blacks' lack of intelligence, Kelso said that the same was true for most Southern Whites, and he would support a colorblind literacy standard or intelligence test as a qualification for voting. However, he noted, during the war "the negroes had intelligence enough to be loyal, while their masters were rebels." Freedmen could acquire skill in voting by practicing the art. The 13th Amendment had set the slaves free; the next task was to secure freedom not just in name but in fact—to give people of color political power so they could protect themselves from abuse and better their condition.[14]

Kelso's "great day" finally arrived on December 4, 1866. In the Hall of the U.S. House of Representatives, the great clock on the wall above the main door and opposite the Speaker's desk ticked toward the noon hour. The hall was unusually crowded. The galleries ringing the floor were divided by iron railings into sections for ladies, gentlemen unaccompanied by ladies, the diplomatic corps, and the press; together they accommodated twelve hundred people, but on this day there seemed to be more than that. The floor was thronged, as an observer described it, not only by the members but also by "a great crowd of pages, office-seekers, office-holders, and unambitious citizens" milling about on the new carpet and among the desks. Light from the skylight 30 feet over their heads flooded the large room. The sound of a hundred conversations, as members greeted and congratulated one another, bounced off the walls. Spectators new to the scene looked around and took it all in. There in front were the three tiers of white marble desks for the Speaker of the House, the Clerk and his assistants, and the congressional reporters. Portraits of George Washington and the Marquis de Lafayette were on either side of the desks, and on another wall a fresco depicted the Revolutionary battle of Yorktown. The floor rose as an amphitheater and the desks were arranged in semicircles. Kelso would be assigned a desk in the last row, just off the center aisle, beneath the great clock.[15]

He looked around at his colleagues. He was glad that they were not as extravagantly attired as the Missouri legislators he had seen in Jefferson City on the trip out, whose "stylish, dandified" appearance had made him wonder if U.S. congressmen would dress like kings. But here the men were greater, but the style simpler: most wore plain dark suits. Kelso was the third-youngest man in the House. The men around him were experienced, perhaps wiser, some of them with "world-wide" reputations. None was more prominent than "Thaddeus Stevens whose every word moved the nation." In their presence, Kelso wrote, "I felt small."[16]

At noon the clerk, Edward McPherson, gaveled the House to order. The members took their seats and everyone else withdrew behind the last row of desks. Then the clerk began to call the roll, but in the 39th Congress, even the opening roll call would be fraught with political drama. Representatives from the formerly rebellious states were seated at some of the desks on the floor, believing they ought to be recognized. When the clerk skipped over the first Southern state, Tennessee, Horace Maynard, elected by that state, rose with his election certificate in hand and tried to interrupt, but he was silenced by the gavel. The point, everyone knew, was clear: readmission to Congress would not occur by votes in a former Confederate state or by presidential decree but by an act of Congress itself. After some parliamentary maneuvering, the House proceeded to the main business of the day: electing a speaker (Schuyler Colfax of Indiana) and voting to create a Joint Committee on Reconstruction.[17]

Some of the men sitting on the floor of the House with Kelso were called "radicals" and some "conservatives"; in the political discourse of the day, a moderate center did not hold. In Missouri, "radical" and "conservative" had become the shorthand for the political parties. In Washington, D.C., and the nation at large they were political orientations that translated into more fluid political factions depending upon the particular argument being waged or the specific piece of legislation being voted upon. An angry President Johnson would come to denounce all who opposed him as "radicals," led, as he thought, by the grim tyrant Thaddeus Stevens in the House and the self-righteous windbag Charles Sumner in the Senate, while the president's supporters would be called "conservatives." But even within the congressional

Republican caucus battling Johnson there were radical and conservative wings. Conservative Republicans were to the left of the ultraconservative Democrats. (Although acknowledging—sometimes begrudgingly—the death of slavery, Democrats openly opposed reconstructing the South and wanted to restore the Union as close as possible to its prewar status). At the other end of the spectrum were the radical reformers fueled by abolitionist fervor who believed that Southern political, social, and economic life had to be remade for there to be a new birth of American freedom and justice. Charles D. Drake, elected to the Senate from Missouri, further discovered that there was such a thing as "conservative radicalism" in Congress, and it differed from "profound radicalism" not over general principles but about the strategies, policies, legislation, and constitutional provisions those principles ought to entail.[18]

The range of opinion within the Republican Party was marked out by two speeches early in the session, one by the radical Thaddeus Stevens and another by the conservative Henry J. Raymond. Though ailing, the septuagenarian Stevens remained a commanding figure in the House. Kelso watched him limp down the aisle toward his desk, his dark brown wig sometimes sitting crookedly on his head, but his mind was razor sharp and his tongue sharper still. With the chiseled features that observers likened to a Roman senator or Indian chief and deeply set eyes that flashed like coals, Stevens, intensely committed to the cause of equal justice, was famous for dispatching opponents with masterful parliamentary tactics and dry, cold sarcasm. He opened debate on Reconstruction with a speech on December 18.[19]

Stevens began, as he had in his published campaign speech, with the current status of the formerly rebellious states, since the warrant for Reconstruction rested upon that premise. "It matters little," he said, "whether you call them states out of the Union" or "only dead as to all national and political action." Even the president's acts assumed they had "lost their constitutional relations to the Union, and are incapable of representation in Congress except by permission of the Government." According to international law as well as Supreme Court cases, Stevens contended, the former Confederate states ought to be treated as a conquered belligerent power. According to the fourth article of the Constitution, the federal government had the duty to ensure a republican government in each state. But since evidence suggested that White Southerners would not be prepared to accept such governments for another several years, the federal government should treat the former Confederate states in the interim as territories. The Constitution already had provisions for territorial governments, giving Congress exclusive and universal power over them.[20]

During this period of territorial probation—Reconstruction properly conceived, in Stevens's view—at least five things ought to happen before the prodigal states could be restored. First, powers and procedures needed to be clarified. Congress needed to reassert that the former rebel states had no say in the approval of any new constitutional amendments until they were fully restored, and also reassert that Congress itself—not the president or the courts—had the power to restore them. Second, the Constitution would need to be amended, bringing the power the South had in the House and the Electoral College in line with the number of people actually being represented (previously, with the Three-Fifths Compromise, White Southerners had additional seats by partially counting unrepresented Blacks). Third, the states had to have stable republican governments, which would include giving their large Black populations the vote. Fourth, the federal government needed to provide freed slaves with homesteads and also "hedge them with protective laws." Fifth, the South ought to help pay down the national debt. Stevens did not here talk, as he had in his earlier speech, about confiscating rebel property, but proposed instead an export tax on cotton.[21]

Henry J. Raymond, congressman from New York, editor of the conservative *New York Times*, and a close ally of Secretary of State William H. Seward, was considered the Johnson administration's spokesman in the House. A few days after Stevens's speech, Raymond rose to counter it. The New Yorker denied that the Southern states were either "dead" or "out" of the Union. How could either condition have been achieved? Not by secession, since that was illegal and therefore null and void. Not by armed rebellion, because the rebels had lost on the battlefield and had failed to achieve their independence. Moreover, the states themselves had not rebelled—only individuals within them. How, then, should the federal government deal with these Southern states? Not, Raymond answered, with the sovereign will of conquerors over conquered territory, but according to the constitutional restrictions on the federal government in regard to any state.[22]

Raymond favored a quick and complete restoration of the Union. That did not mean, however, that he or the Johnson administration agreed with the ultraconservative Democrats that the Southern states should simply send their representatives back to Congress to be seated with no further questions or conditions. There were conditions, Raymond argued, which the president had already asked for and the Southern states had prepared to meet: They had to ratify the 13th Amendment abolishing slavery, repeal their state ordinances declaring a right of secession, and repudiate the Confederate debt. Once those were met, the states should be restored to their full constitutional functions, and "we should cultivate friendly relations with them."[23]

Kelso's comments during the campaign and in the September speech at Walnut Grove made it clear that he was a radical on the Stevens end of the spectrum. In Congress itself, though, he was mostly quiet, listening and learning, for the first two months.[24]

On the second day of Kelso's congressional career, December 5, the Speaker of the House received a petition from Sempronious Boyd challenging the result of the election in Missouri's Fourth District. By unanimous consent the case was sent to the Committee on Elections. Boyd's lawyers had started gathering evidence nine months earlier, and the first set of documents was delivered to the House on December 12. He would compile an evidence file—including depositions, poll books, military muster rolls, and county clerk certificates—that would fill 130 printed pages. The file would contain an abstract of election returns certified by Missouri's Secretary of State that put Kelso only 84 votes ahead. Boyd claimed and intended to prove that Kelso had received at least 400 illegal votes and that Boyd was the rightful winner of the 1864 congressional election.[25]

Kelso, on December 19, rose in the House on a "question of personal privilege." When Boyd had delivered legal notice to Kelso's home on March 25 that depositions from witnesses would be taken nine days later, Kelso was stationed at Neosho. The war was still going on; the mail was delivered irregularly, if at all; Susie was confined to a sick bed and could not attend to the business. Because of these extenuating circumstances, Kelso did not even hear about the depositions and was not able to arrange to have an attorney present to cross-examine the witnesses. Nor was he able to have his lawyers conduct investigations of their own before the legal deadline had passed. Kelso asked for an extension of sixty days to have his attorneys gather evidence and testimony. The issue was sent to the Election Committee, which gave him fifty days and allotted Boyd another thirty beyond that. On January 12, Boyd sent Kelso notice of two more hearings; the next day, Kelso sent Boyd a notice of the first of another two.[26]

As his legitimacy as a representative was being challenged, Kelso had to carry on with his work. Although Reconstruction was the burning issue of the day and dealt with profound questions that would define the character of the nation going forward, the regular work of governance had to proceed as well. Every morning, when not in committee meetings, Kelso did paperwork, responding to petitions and requests from constituents. He claimed

that he wrote about thirty letters and dealt with five hundred documents
a day. Other members hired clerks to deal with this avalanche of paper; to
save money, Kelso did not. He did not have much income beyond his annual $5,000 congressional salary and needed to spend up to $2,000 of that on
attorneys' fees for his election challenge. Those legal expenses would eventually be reimbursed, but until then he had to economize. He regularly worked
late into the night and was chronically short on sleep. His health began to
break down.[27]

The House met every day at noon until at least four or five in the afternoon, and sometimes on evenings and Saturdays. An English observer
described the scene: "Except when some remarkably good speaker has possession of the floor, the members, instead of attending to what is spoken, are
busy in conversation, in writing letters, rapping sand off the wet ink with their
knuckles, rustling countless newspapers which deluge the House, locking or
unlocking their drawers, or moving up and down the avenues which divide
the ranges of seats, and kicking before them, at every step, printed reports,
letter covers, and other documents strewed on the floor." A couple of boys ran
to and fro carrying papers and delivering notes. "Representatives talked and
laughed in the aisles, sat reading with their feet on their desks, and sometimes
napped." Yet when House business turned from the banal and the trivial to the
pressing and profound, or at least when debate and discussion finally yielded
an opportunity to vote, they were expected to snap to attention. Innumerable
hours were spent on the House floor devoted not to Reconstruction and the
fate of the nation but to matters of concern only to particular districts and
the interminable details of tax and appropriation bills. In the army, Kelso
had complained to his commanding officer after two weeks that he was unsuited to desk work and begged to return to the field. In Congress, the Man of
Action was forced to do nothing but listen to talk and deal with paperwork.[28]

Like Boyd before him, Kelso was assigned to a seat on the Post Office
Committee. It was not a top-tier assignment like Ways and Means or the
Judiciary Committee, but it did important work. In the nineteenth century,
the U.S. Postal Service, linked to the telegraph lines, was the nation's communications infrastructure. As the federal government's largest bureaucracy, it
had an outsized impact upon citizens' lives. Before the war it employed more
than three-quarters of all federal officials. By 1865 there were nearly 29,000
post offices in the country, with an operating revenue of $14.5 million. As
part of a nine-member House committee, Kelso worked with the postmaster
general's office to write bills to bring to the floor. Some of these addressed
weighty issues, like the government's relationship to the telegraph monopoly.

Others, like a long bill to amend postal laws, dealt with mundane matters such as the sale of stamped envelopes, the return of prepaid letters, or the fees for money orders. Some members grew frustrated with this minutiae, but sometimes such small things were linked to larger political struggles. The question of who could sell stamps, for example, was tied up with the requirement in the South for postmasters to take a loyalty oath. A bid to give the postmaster general more administrative flexibility, as Thaddeus Steven reminded the House, diminished Congress's power of the purse and strengthened the hand of the administration. Working to improve the national system, Kelso also tried to serve his constituents. During the first session, for instance, he tried to get a daily mail line through his district and also lobbied to get Post Office advertisements placed in Fourth District newspapers.[29]

Constituent service was not the only way that a congressman could use the Post Office to link federal power to local influence. For decades the postal service had been a patronage machine. The president claimed the power to appoint or dismiss the postmasters of larger offices, and the postmaster general, a cabinet position named by the president, appointed and dismissed the rest. In practice, members of the House in the president's party got to nominate men to be postmasters in their districts. Even if they had few other ways to reward their supporters back home, one observer wrote, congressmen had the post offices, which were "as plentiful as blackberries, and their pickers equally so." During Lincoln's first term, nearly all the postmasters in the country had been removed and replaced with Republicans. President Johnson began by accepting Republican nominations, but after his relationship with Congress soured, he installed a loyalist, Alexander Randall, as postmaster general and purged 10 percent of the country's postmasters in four months for purely political reasons, sending a clear message to the rest. Republicans in Rolla, Missouri, complained that Johnson replaced a Republican veteran wounded at Pea Ridge with a notorious rebel; in Springfield, Johnson ignored Kelso's radical nomination for a position at the new Land Office and gave it to the current conservative postmaster, Pony Boyd's father Marcus.[30]

As Kelso settled into the rhythms of his work after the holidays, the first bill to be extensively debated was not, strictly speaking, about rebuilding the rebel South, but it had profound implications for Reconstruction. With H. R. No. 1, the House directly confronted the issue of race in America. The bill proposed to remove the word "white" from the qualification for voters in Washington, D.C. Supporters of Black suffrage recognized the broader symbolic power of changing racial politics in the nation's capital and knew that the peculiar status of the District (where Congress had direct authority over local affairs) would avoid conflicts between state and federal jurisdiction. Giving Blacks the vote in D.C., then, could lay the groundwork for the larger campaign. Conservative White supremacists knew the stakes and showed in their response that abolition did not have to smooth the jagged edges of American racism.

Kelso listened to seven days of debate in mid-January. The conservative Democratic case was made by Andrew J. Rogers of New Jersey, John Winthrop Chanler of New York, and Benjamin M. Boyer and Philip Johnson, both of Pennsylvania. Rogers opened by declaring that there never had been "a bill which involved so momentous consequences." If passed it would end up "disturbing and embittering the whole social system" and "fill our history with a record of degradation and shame." The wisdom of the ages had "handed down to us that grand principle that all Governments of a civilized character have been and were intended especially for white men and women, and not for those who belong to the negro, Indian, or mulatto race." In 1776 every state had slaves and at the ratification of the Constitution "no persons . . . were considered citizens but the white race." Boyer explained that people of African descent were not prohibited from participating in American government just because of the color of their skin: skin color was an outward badge "of a race by nature inferior in mental caliber, and lacking that vim, pluck, and poise of character which give force and direction to human enterprise, and which is essential to the safety of popular institutions." The "white democracy" the forefathers built and we have inherited, Chanler summed up, "is a white man's government, founded by white men to preserve and perpetuate the laws and customs of their race." Blacks had no literature or art of their own and even with the extinction of slavery they would be forever dependent upon Whites for the blessings of civilization. We all "agree that the negro race is inferior to the white or European race," Johnson concluded, and he proposed that American politics ought to reflect that truth.[31]

The Republicans leading the charge for the D.C. suffrage bill denied that the United States was a "white man's government." John F. Farnsworth of Illinois imagined that phrase being spoken to a wounded Black veteran hobbling home from the war. "Shame! I say, eternal shame! upon such a doctrine and upon the man who advocates it." For the right of the elective franchise, he argued, the "test should be that of manhood, not that of color or races or class. Is he endowed with conscience and reason? Is he an immortal being?" When our forefathers declared that all men are created equal, Farnsworth argued, they did not mean equally rich, strong, intelligent, or handsome. They meant that all were equally endowed with the rights to life, liberty, and the pursuit of happiness; they said that government was instituted to protect these rights, and that it rested on the consent of the governed. William D. Kelley of Pennsylvania pointed out that most states at the nation's founding did allow free men of color to vote; that right was then stripped from them by a later generation whose moral vision had dimmed. Iowans James F. Wilson and Josiah B. Grinnell reminded the House that the District's Blacks—like Blacks in America generally—had been intensely loyal during the war; they owned property, paid taxes, and built schools and churches, and they deserved the political right to vote as much as any other citizen. Indiana's George W. Julian contended that suffrage was not a privilege or a social convention but an absolute political right. There was no security or freedom without the ballot, he said—it is "the vital principle of all democracy."[32]

Others waffled between the stark bigotry of White supremacy and the radical aspiration for racial political equality. "I do not doubt that the negro race is inferior to our own," said Martin Russell Thayer, a moderate Republican from Pennsylvania. But the question was, he continued, whether Blacks were "so ignorant and degraded that they cannot be safely intrusted with the smallest conceivable part of political power." Some mediators proposed a "limited" Black suffrage similar to what Lincoln had suggested—giving the vote to veterans and Black men who could read the Constitution. "Impartial" suffrage was another option: it would impose colorblind literacy or property-owning restrictions on the franchise (though these, critics pointed out, would disproportionately bar freedmen). When the vote was held, it was a 116–54 majority (including Kelso) for "universal" adult male suffrage in Washington, D.C. Hearing, however, that President Johnson planned to veto the bill, Republicans, still hoping to avoid a break with him, let it linger in the Senate for another year.[33]

Meanwhile, Kelso was feeling the strain of Boyd's challenge to his seat. In late January, he wrote a long letter that he had sent home to have published in Missouri newspapers. Kelso's remarkable "Circular," addressed to the "People of Southwest Missouri," announced his candidacy for reelection. He did so by combining a truculent attack on Boyd with a pathetic plea for the voters' support—more than that, for their sympathy and love. He described Boyd's election challenge as an "unjust persecution" and recounted his tortured political history with Pony. You remember, he wrote, that I was an antislavery candidate in 1862. But then Boyd, who not long before had been "a fire-eating *pro-slavery Democrat*" wanting "to aid in driving Free State men out of Kansas," switched parties—so I withdrew to avoid splitting the antislavery vote. Then in 1864, we were both candidates, and while I was battling guerrillas he was making speeches and preventing any newspapers from supporting me or printing my letters. On Election Day, he spread lies that I had withdrawn. "Yet after all these, and many other mean advantages had been taken by my enemies, I was elected fairly and legally, as you all believe. Still my competitor was not satisfied." Boyd started his suit when I was still away in the army; he served papers on my sick wife, making sure I would be unprepared to answer his challenge when Congress convened. Now the "great expense" involved in having lawyers take testimony and gather documents "is inflicting a deep injury on my family."[34]

Boyd was simply being vindictive, Kelso wrote. Though Missouri's governor had named him to the lucrative post of circuit court judge, "he seems bent at all hazards, upon crushing the old soldier, whose long and faithful services, whose many battles, whose wounds (all in front) so completely eclipse [Boyd's] career." Boyd ought to feel ashamed, Kelso wrote, but he was incapable of it. "He has wealth on his side, and is skilled in all the tricks which unscrupulous politicians practice, while I have nothing upon which to rely but the justness of my cause and the integrity of my heart." Kelso reminded readers of his own virtues: "You know that I am always sober and always at my post; you know, also, that neither fear, favor, nor partiality can cause me to swerve one particle from what I believe to be just and right. You know that I have always depended upon merit alone."[35]

As he wrote, he stopped addressing all the "People of Southwest Missouri" and focused only on the soldiers. You know I never ate while you were hungry or took shelter while you were exposed, he reminded them. "You remember our long marches, our night scouts, and our fierce conflicts." You remember how we rested on rocks for pillows, ate our hardtack, and talked of home as the rain froze on our uniforms. Where was Boyd through all this? By the end, Kelso's letter became a heartfelt plea to the "boys" of his own cavalry company: "You remember Ozark, and Forsyth, and the Tolbert Barrens, and the Saltpeter Cave, and Marmaduke's long chase after us, the desperate battle of [Springfield on] the 8th of January. . . . You remember the time when we joined those rebels in the Seneca Nation, and after helping them steal cattle all day 'wiped them out' at night." You remember a hundred other such places, he wrote. "You remember the time when I was wounded, and you sheltered me with your own bodies—when poor, brave Ab. Smithson, in saving my life, lost his own. You remember the times we mourned together over the cold forms of our fallen comrades." He reminded them that "your Kelso" had led them in battle sixty-six times "and you know he never turned his back upon the foe. In the hottest of the battle, you could always hear the roar of his 'old shot gun.' That was his way of electioneering, and now you wish him to rest from war in the field, and fight rebels in the halls of Congress. . . . He will do the best he can, if you do not let Boyd deprive him of the seat he has tried so hard to earn." Kelso concluded by blending the political contest with nostalgia for the tented field and the sound of the bugle: "Give him, then, such an overwhelming majority as will show how much you love him, and then, with your consent, he will retire from public life until a new war may render his services necessary in the field. Then he will again lead you in battle."[36]

The blowback was immediate. The *St. Louis Democrat* published the circular, but made clear that it was in no way endorsing Kelso, noting that the Fourth District Radical Unionists would choose their candidate in the summer. The *St. Louis Republican* commented that Kelso seemed to be "in a hurry to announce" his candidacy and was neither "diffident in setting forth his claims, nor is he remarkably complimentary" to Boyd, whom in the past he had called a "wire-working, dram-drinking, political demagogue." But the *Springfield Patriot* angrily disapproved of the circular. Much of it seemed to be motivated by a personal feud between Kelso and Boyd. More troubling was that Kelso was apparently declaring himself a candidate in the general election whether or not he became the duly elected choice of the party at its district nominating convention, which is what he had done in 1864. "We don't approve of him as an independent candidate and won't support him unless he is the nominee of the [Radical] Union party," the *Patriot* declared. Another concern about Kelso was "the company he keeps." Why did he use his franking privilege to send more free government publications to Conservatives than to Radicals? Why did he send the circular itself to Conservatives to read and edit at their pleasure before they passed it along to the press? These were disturbing signs. The *Patriot* warned that Kelso was "permitting the wily and experienced Conservatives to make a tool of him. They are deluding him with the idea that they will support him at the next election, whereas it is palpable that their object is to divide the Radical party."[37]

Kelso, the *Patriot* charged, was politically naïve at best, possibly disloyal to the party, and perhaps even drifting toward conservatism himself. The paper added that he was also wrong on some of the facts of the 1864 election, and ungrateful. The congressman's charge that Boyd had bought or bought off the only newspaper that had been open to Kelso in the last campaign besmirched the *Patriot* itself, which in fact had supported Kelso. Finally, the paper questioned "the general character of the Circular—the taste displayed by the vigorous blowing of his own horn."[38]

In a response printed on February 1, Kelso beat his chest in regret and apology and tried to make amends—another performance that did not speak well for his political savvy. "I now regret having written the circular at all," Kelso confessed. "It was untimely and written when I was angry and excited by the real injuries" inflicted by Boyd. He had no intention of running as an independent and would abide by the party's decision at the nominating convention. As for his ties to Conservatives—that was all a misunderstanding. He had sent his circular to two trusted friends for circulation, one whose judgment he trusted despite his conservatism and the other whose conservatism Kelso had not suspected at all. But he denied that any Conservatives had ever promised to support his candidacy.[39]

He was particularly sorry that his comments had insulted the *Patriot*. When he said that Boyd had bought off the only paper open to him, he had meant the defunct *Missourian*; the *Patriot* had only begun publication fairly late in the campaign. As he apologized to the Springfield paper and its editor, Archibald F. Ingram, though, Kelso was perhaps too frank about the mutual back-scratching involved in the politics of patronage. "I felt really grateful for [the *Patriot's*] support," he wrote, "and hope yet to show that I am so. I recommended it for the Post Office advertising." In addition, he had "recommended the senior Editor of the *Patriot* to the best position in the district—that of Receiver of the Land Office, which is to be established soon at Springfield." Kelso was especially "anxious," he wrote, that Ingram accept this position, "for I am very sorry to be thought ungrateful, and my high esteem for the talent and integrity of the man is not at all diminished by having lost his confidence and friendship, which I have unintentionally done." Another paper mocked the congressman's very public courtship of the *Patriot's* editor: it was doubtful that the relationship, if consummated, would be productive, the Springfield *Journal* jabbed, because Kelso was a "warhorse," Ingram a "jack-ass," and the result would be a "mule."[40]

Despite Kelso's apologies and clumsy attempts to court favor, the damage was done. "Since Capt. Kelso published that most remarkable electioneering circular," a correspondent from Cedar County wrote in the *Patriot*, "his warmest friends are rather doubtful about the propriety of again supporting him. The Thirty-Ninth Congress must think the inhabitants of the 4th Congressional District of Missouri need schoolmasters, if their Representative addresses them in such a style."[41]

Kelso tried to redeem himself with statesmanlike performances in Washington. On February 5 he submitted a resolution for a constitutional amendment and two days later he gave a speech on Reconstruction to the House. That a freshman congressman with only two months' experience was drafting a constitutional amendment was less unusual in the 39th Congress than at most other points in American history. By the time Kelso submitted his, more than seventy others had been proposed. President Johnson complained that proposed amendments had become as numerous as resolutions at a town meeting, and he groused that this was diminishing the dignity of the document and the confidence people had in it. But the need to bind the nation's wounds and make good on the promise of a new birth of freedom convinced many reform-minded Americans both inside and outside Congress that the country's constitutional foundations needed to be repaired and improved. Kelso's proposed constitutional amendment simply stated that a rebellious state "forfeited all its rights and privileges as a state" and "reverted to the condition of a Territory." It would make constitutionally explicit, in other words, what Stevens had argued was already implicitly the case. The conservative St. Louis *Republican* denied that any such thing could be inferred from the Constitution, but admitted that Kelso's and Stevens's position reflected the current sentiments of many as well as how in fact the rebellion had been subdued.[42]

Kelso delivered his speech to Congress on Wednesday evening, February 7, 1866. The House tried to give every member at least one opportunity to give an hour-long speech on the floor each term: printed and circulated back home in the congressmen's districts, the speeches were important as campaign documents. The House held evening and sometimes Saturday sessions just for speeches rather than regular business. The performances offered a range of oratorical styles: one would seem like a legal brief, bristling with legal citations, and the next a casual conversation encouraging questions from other members on the floor. Kelso was lucky that his turn came up relatively early in the session. Even by early February, though, speakers on Reconstruction began to apologize that because "so many great minds, at both ends of this Capitol, have exhausted so thoroughly all views and phases of this question," listeners ought not to expect "anything new." Moreover, Kelso was the third speaker that Wednesday evening, at the end of a long day. But he had shown his carefully prepared text to some of his Missouri colleagues and a few other old hands, and they had pronounced it, Kelso later wrote, "better than any that had yet been delivered in that Congress." This was encouraging. "Knowing the excellence of my voice at that time and my powers as an elocutionist, I had no fear of failing in the delivery," and he began his speech with confidence.[43]

Kelso again addressed three main questions: What was "the present *status* of the rebel States?" "What shall be done with the rebels?" and "What shall be done with the negroes?" The first section seemed to be a direct response to the exchange of speeches by Stevens and Raymond that had opened the congressional debate on Reconstruction six weeks earlier. To establish the status of the rebel states, Stevens had cited authorities in international law, specific Supreme Court cases, and legal rules of evidence. Kelso argued from the dictionary definition of a "state" and reasoned by analogy. A state was a body of people in a particular area organized for government. Each element—the people, the land, and the governmental organization—was essential for its existence as a state, just as water without hydrogen was no longer water. If a state's governmental organization is destroyed, even if the same people continue to inhabit the same patch of land, it is no longer a state, just as a ruined house was just a pile of debris and could no longer function as a house until reconstructed.[44]

Were the states, then, "dead" or "out" of the Union? Raymond and other conservatives had said that secession did not take the states out of the Union because secession was illegal and therefore "null and void." Stevens had answered that this argument was like saying that because murder was illegal no murder could occur. Kelso echoed Stevens: "By [this beautiful theory] we could prove that Lincoln was not murdered." Stevens had called the states either out of the Union or "dead as to all national and political action." Kelso described them as either dead or in a coma, a "protracted catalepsy, in which their functions are suspended while their vitality remains." President Johnson and advocates like Raymond held the "cataleptic doctrine," which seemed premised on a belief in "state immortality," but Kelso argued that they were dead. They had reverted to territories under the authority of Congress. New states needed to be made, he argued—but not necessarily by just breathing life back into the old ones, as Stevens had said. Congress could draw new state borders and make up new state names.[45]

In his House speech, Kelso went no easier on the rebels than he had at Walnut Grove. Strict justice, he said, required that the traitors be put to death. Since the president's amnesty proclamation had spared their lives and given them the liberty of their persons, what should now be done? With a series of rhetorical questions, Kelso made the point that the rebels could never fully make amends: "Can the rebels ever restore" all the property they damaged? "Can they restore" the innocence and happiness lost? Health to the hundreds of thousands wounded? Life to the hundreds of thousands dead? But they must pay *something*.[46]

Stevens had argued for confiscating property from wealthier rebels in his September campaign speech but not in his December address to the House.

Kelso did: "Let us, then, confiscate the property of the rebels, or at least so much of it as will pay our entire war debt. This could be done without reducing any of the wealthy rebels to less than $10,000 worth of property." He also repeated his call that they lose their right to vote for at least five years because they could not yet be trusted. He refused Raymond's plea to set aside animosity and welcome them back as friends. "Has treason made them more loyal?" Kelso asked. "Has war made them more friendly? Has murder rendered them more humane? Has perjury rendered them more honest?" Kelso confronted the "high-toned" Southern gentlemen who asked to be seen as men of "instinctive frankness and honor" with his own experience: "I cannot so see them. I see them now as I saw them when they were burning our homes, when they were driving our wives and our little ones out in the winter storms, when they were butchering our gray-haired sires, tearing off their bloody scalps, roasting their feet, or burning out their tongues." This was the political rhetoric of the "bloody shirt"—but perhaps those who would come to smirk at the rhetoric had not had to wear an actual bloody shirt themselves.[47]

When he turned to his final question, about the place of Blacks in postbellum American society, he offered an eloquent defense of African American citizenship. "Though I never was a pro-slavery man," he admitted again, "yet reared up in a slave State, and by ultra-proslavery parents, I unconsciously imbibed many of their prejudices." The war, however, had taught him some profound lessons. "In the darkest hour of our country's need [the loyal Blacks] never faltered, though their fidelity to us subjected them to unheard-of outrages and to death in a thousand terrible forms." They gave succor to Federal prisoners of war escaping from Confederate pens. By the tens of thousands they rushed into battle and fought heroically. They fought for freedom—for theirs and for ours. Yet now we tell them, "We are done with you niggers; now lay down your arms and either leave the country or go to work for your old rebel masters. This is a white man's country, and you have no rights here which a white man is bound to respect." Slavery is abolished in name but not in reality. "Does not every southern breeze bring to the ear the sound of the lash, the baying of the bloodhound, the cries of the slave, and the screams of murder?"[48]

However, these loyal citizens, Kelso argued, deserve legal and political equality not just out of our gratitude for what they did in the war but as a matter of natural right and eternal justice. No government was truly republican if it discriminated on account of race or color. Their equal rights had to include the vote.[49]

As he had at Walnut Grove, Kelso concluded with the hope "that we may all live to see our redeemed country glorious among the nations, as indeed—'The land of the free and the home of the brave.'" The House stenographer noted "Applause in the galleries" when Kelso finished. He later wrote that his Republican colleagues, and then even the Democrats, the chief clerk, and the sergeant at arms, formed a line to shake his hand in congratulations. This may have been a ritual for a representative's maiden speech, but Kelso claimed that "no other member had received such an ovation. So great a victory made me very proud and happy." Thirty-five hundred copies of the speech were printed and distributed. Three months later, it appeared on the front page of the *Springfield Patriot*.[50]

As Kelso tried to push Reconstruction forward, the challenge to his seat continued to hang over him. His lawyers had taken depositions, but one of the witnesses remembered seeing seventeen nonresident soldiers in Kelso's regiment cast illegal votes for him. He sat at his desk on the floor and watched as seven times between December and April more evidence in the case was submitted to the House and sent to the Election Committee. And he watched as other contested elections spilled from the Election Committee to the House floor. The *New York Herald* had warned that *Boyd vs. Kelso* might provoke broader controversy because it raised questions about soldier voting. Most states, Missouri among them, had passed laws in 1862 and 1863 allowing soldiers to vote from their military posts and camps. This became a campaign issue in 1864, and after the election, voter fraud scandals in New York and Pennsylvania gave some support to the *New York Tribune*'s panicked speculation about the Union (Republican) party's being cheated out of 30,000 votes nationwide. The contest between Boyd and Kelso did not have partisan complications—they were both Radical Republicans—but it could conceivably become entangled with questions about the soldier vote, which was heavy in Missouri's Fourth District (two-thirds of them had voted for Kelso). But he could only worry, and wait, and pay his lawyers.[51]

Kelso's votes in the first session, like his speech and proposed amendment, did not support the *Springfield Patriot*'s insinuation that the congressman might be drifting toward conservatism. He supported two crucial pieces of legislation in the Republican agenda: the Freedmen's Bureau Bill and the landmark Civil Rights Bill. The first was intended to extend the authorization and expand the role of the agency created a year earlier to help freed people make the transition from slavery to freedom. The Civil Rights Bill defined U.S. citizenship and committed the national government to protecting the rights of individual citizens (the Constitution had done neither). Countering

the Supreme Court's infamous *Dred Scott* case (1857), which had denied
that people of African descent could be citizens, it declared that all persons
born in the United States (except "Indians not taxed"), "without regard to
any previous condition of slavery or involuntary servitude," were citizens.
Countering the notorious Black Codes enacted by the defeated Southern
states, the bill declared that citizens "of every race and color" had the same
legal rights. Crafted by moderates so the bills could get the president's signature, the Freedmen's Bureau Bill tried not to run roughshod over states' rights
and the Civil Rights Bill avoided any mention of Black suffrage.[52]

But Johnson vetoed both. He explained his actions by condemning the
principles animating both pieces of legislation. Having already worked to
undermine the efforts of the Freedmen's Bureau, Johnson now repudiated
the agency, decrying what he characterized as an immense and costly federal bureaucracy that only encouraged Blacks' indolence. In his veto of the
Civil Rights Bill, he expressed open hostility to any legislation that acknowledged people of color as full citizens. Trying to snub congressional radicals,
he alienated moderate and conservative Republicans too. Republicans in the
House had the votes to override Johnson's veto of the Freedmen's Bureau
Bill, but they fell two votes short in the Senate. Both houses overcame the
president's veto of the Civil Rights Bill, the House passing it 122–41 on April
9, the same day it received the veto message (with Kelso, of course, voting
with the majority), to great applause in the galleries.[53]

A month later on May 8, Kelso watched and listened as Thaddeus Stevens
finally brought the Joint Committee's Reconstruction plan to the House.
The committee proposed a constitutional amendment accompanied by two
bills. The bills prevented former Confederate officers and high officials from
holding office in the United States and would admit to Congress any former
rebel state that ratified the new amendment and conformed its laws to it.
The amendment itself was a conglomeration of existing proposals, smoothed
and blunted by the grinding necessities of compromise and practicality. It
was "not all that the committee desired," Stevens admitted. "It falls short of
my wishes, but it fulfills my hopes. I believe it is all that can be obtained in
the present state of public opinion. . . . I will take all I can get in the cause
of humanity, and leave it to be perfected by better men in better times." The
first section, with language pushed by John A. Bingham of Ohio since the
beginning of the term, constitutionalized the Civil Rights Act by defining
citizenship and guaranteeing equal protection under the law. This part of
what would become the 14th Amendment would have vast consequences in
America's future.[54]

The second part of the proposed amendment was a clever—too clever, it turned out—solution to the problem of how to count the residents of the former slave states when apportioning their representation in Congress and the Electoral College. According to the original constitutional compromise, each slave counted as three-fifths of a person in the calculation. This peculiar math was abolished along with the "peculiar institution," and freed people would thereafter count as whole persons. But if Blacks were not allowed to vote, this change would give White Southerners even more national political power than they had before. That, for Republicans of all stripes, was unacceptable. Republicans could not figure out a way to give African Americans the vote solely in the South, and they feared that voters would reject a constitutional amendment that ended voting discrimination everywhere. So the second section of the proposed 14th Amendment would apportion representatives according to "the whole number of persons in each State"—with the catch that if any state deprived any male citizens (excluding criminals and former rebels) from voting, its basis of representation would be reduced proportionately. Therefore, while the amendment did not prevent states from imposing discriminatory voting laws (a feature Stevens disliked and other radicals condemned as a violation of moral principle), its new math did impose a stiff political penalty on states choosing that path.[55]

The amendment's third section would prove to be contentious, pitting Stevens against Bingham and other centrists and conservatives in the floor debate. It prohibited former rebels from voting for Congress or the president until 1870. Bingham argued that it was unenforceable and useless, and others contended that it was too vindictive. Stevens countered that the third section was "vital." Without it, the House would "be filled with yelling secessionists and copperheads. Give us the third section or give us nothing." He pushed back at those who found it too restrictive. "It is too lenient for my hard heart. Not only to 1870, but to 18070, every rebel who shed the blood of loyal men should be prevented from exercising any power in this Government. That, even, would be too mild a punishment for them." He had little patience for those urging brotherly reconciliation with no period of probation. "Gentlemen have said you must not humble these people. Why not? Do not they deserve humiliation? Do not they deserve degradation? . . . Let not these friends of secession sing to me their siren songs of peace and good will until they can stop my ears to the screams and groans of the dying victims" of the continuing violence being committed against Blacks in the South. Kelso, who had been sorry he could not confine rebels to a special place in hell, voted with Stevens and the slim 84–79 majority to move the amendment forward. On the final vote, Republicans united and passed it, 128–37.[56]

The amendment, however, returned in mid-June from the Senate with its third section enfeebled. Instead of disfranchising rebels, it merely prevented former Confederates who had previously sworn oaths to the United States from again holding office. "In my youth, in my manhood, in my old age," Stevens sighed in a speech before the final vote on the Senate's version in the House, he said he had dreamed of freeing American institutions from the degradation of inequality. That dream was gone. "I find that we shall be obliged to be content with patching up the worst portions of the ancient edifice." Why accept such an imperfect amendment? "I answer, because I live among men and not among angels; among men as intelligent, as determined, and as independent as myself, who, not agreeing with me, do not choose to yield their opinion to mine." Flawed as it was, the old political warrior argued, it was essential that it become part of the constitutional fabric. Every House Republican agreed, approving it with a vote of 120–32.

Adopted two years later after being ratified by the required three-quarters of the states, the 14th Amendment was a constitutional landmark. It recognized national citizenship and committed the federal government to protecting the equal rights of citizens. Although limited for decades by narrow court rulings, in the twentieth century it was recognized as doing what most of its framers—Bingham, Stevens, and the rank-in-file Republicans like Kelso who endorsed it—understood it to do: it demanded that the states and not just Congress respect the Bill of Rights.[57]

As the House turned from historic votes on constitutional amendments to the grind of tariff and internal tax bills, the Committee on Elections finally submitted its report on Boyd's challenge to Kelso's seat. Boyd had challenged the votes in six of the Fourth District's twenty-one counties. Some voters (usually soldiers) in counties that had gone strongly for Kelso, he charged, were minors or nonresidents, and their votes should be excluded. In two of the counties, officials had so mishandled the election that the entire return should be discarded. In two others, votes for Boyd, he claimed, had been undercounted by a total of 380. Kelso denied all these claims and added some of his own. There had been gross irregularities in four counties polling strongly for Boyd, he argued. In other precincts, including the hometown of both men, Springfield, hundreds of illegal votes had been cast for Boyd. In addition, Kelso directly charged Boyd's campaign with dirty tricks: soldiers in two regiments were told that Kelso had withdrawn and Boyd was the only remaining Republican candidate. The evidence that Kelso's lawyers collected did a poor job of sustaining his charges. But the burden of proof was on Boyd.[58]

The Election Committee found Boyd's charges "very general, vague, and indefinite" and his evidence "defective." The testimony was contradictory. Many of the documents Boyd had submitted were irrelevant to the six named counties. The relevant ones were not much better: "the evidence certified from the office of the secretary of state, as well as from the offices of several county clerks, is very defective, both in substance and in arithmetication, and is very unsatisfactory and inconclusive." Missouri Secretary of State Francis Rodman's "true and complete abstract"—which put Kelso up by only 84 votes—was not a certified tally of the final vote. The committee surmised that Rodman, "either with or without the consent of the contestant [Boyd]," had excluded some returns and some votes he presumed to be illegal, "thus to relieve the committee and the House from the labor of investigating and passing [judgment] upon them." Whether or not Rodman had colluded with Boyd, the secretary had put his finger on the scale. The committee did not even need to attend to Kelso's claims or evidence, because Boyd's case collapsed. The committee reported its unanimous decision to the House on June 25. That evening, Kelso sent a dispatch to Springfield to have the news published in the *Patriot*: "John R. Kelso is entitled to his seat in Congress."[59]

At about this time, Susie Kelso arrived in Washington to find her husband exhausted and ill. She tried to nurse him back to health, and he did begin to show some improvement. But in mid-July, as the heat and humidity in the city grew oppressive and the first session of the 39th Congress neared its end, Kelso asked for and received permission from the House to leave two weeks early. Congressman Kelso and his wife headed home to Missouri.[60]

The Great Mistake

KELSO HAD LONG intuited that he was destined for greatness. He would make a mark in the world, and not just through his exploits in the war. Facing death on the battlefield, the Hero of the South West had been emboldened by deep "impressions" he could not explain, convictions that he would survive the moment and go on to accomplish grand things after the guns had gone quiet. His election to Congress had seemed to be the next step for this "child of destiny." But then he made a choice—a single decision during his congressional career—and the course of his life, he reflected later, seemed to swerve. A "great mistake," he called it, a mistake that began a new era where he seemed to stumble at every major decision, "a period of my life, continuing several years, that was so crowded with mistakes, misfortunes and sorrows that I would fain blot every vestige of the memory of it from my mind if I could." He had made a political decision—one of many, and he had made it, he thought, like all of them, from "good motives" and using his "best judgment." Only later did he see it as a major fork in his life's road.[1]

Kelso had made plenty of political decisions during the first session of the 39th Congress, and the things he had said and done—his votes, resolutions, speeches, and circular—were before the Fourth District's voters as they began to choose candidates for the fall 1866 election. Missouri's Conservative Unionist party had rallied around Andrew Johnson, forming "Johnson Clubs" in the state, including one in Springfield. The Conservatives cheered when the president opposed the 14th Amendment. When they read the June 25 call for a National Union Convention of Johnson's Democratic and conservative Republican supporters, they planned to send delegates. Missouri's Radical (Republican) Unionists, meanwhile, worked to strengthen their local organizations and state party apparatus, the Executive Committee urging the formation of "Radical Union Clubs." They held local mass meetings, like those in Greene and Dallas counties in March, which condemned Johnson and supported Congress. In the Fourth Congressional District, Conservatives knew that their only chance would be to have more than one Radical running in the general election and split the vote. Radicals knew that too, and party organizers were determined to come out of the district convention in late July unified behind one candidate. Whatever damage Kelso had done with his circular, he was still in the running.[2]

The leading Radical candidates were Kelso, Boyd, and Col. Joseph J. Gravely. A former state senator, Gravely was described was a "self-made man" who, like Kelso, had begun the war as a private and had then risen up through the ranks. He had commanded posts at Lebanon and Springfield and fought in the field against Shelby and Price. He was a lawyer and a good stump speaker, and he had solid Radical credentials. County caucuses, choosing delegates for the district convention, showed support for all three candidates.[3]

When Governor Fletcher had been in town to give a July Fourth speech, he gave a wink and a nod to his friend Boyd as the Fourth District's once and future congressman. But Kelso had political allies, too. Back in May, his congressional colleague Henry T. Blow of Missouri's Second District had traveled through Springfield and endorsed Kelso. Some puff pieces for Kelso appeared in the local press by the summer. The *Warrensburg Standard* praised Kelso's morality, industry, and lack of political self-interest. "Only give him half a chance," the paper said, "and the political record of John R. Kelso will be as honorable as his military record was brave and glorious." A letter in the Springfield *Patriot* lauded Kelso for standing up to Democrats, Conservatives, Copperheads, and presidential obstruction. Another reminded readers that Kelso was "emphatically the soldier's candidate in the last election," and that in Congress he was "always at his post, and cast his vote for the Freedmen's Bureau Bill, the Civil Rights Bill, and all the great Radical measures."[4]

On July 21, Kelso got to speak for himself at a political meeting held at the Springfield courthouse. The account in a conservative paper has Kelso spending more time attacking Boyd than defending his record or looking to the future. Boyd was "an unprincipled, dishonest, corrupt, scheming trickster," Kelso reportedly said, "and a disgrace to the great Radical party." The sitting congressman charged that Boyd had "applied to the President for a foreign appointment and promised to support the administration if he received it." Like John M. Richardson, the bumbling colonel who had led his Mountain Rangers to defeat at the Battle of Neosho and had just jumped from the Radicals to the Conservatives to secure a job in Johnson's Treasury

Department, Boyd was willing to be reborn as a Johnsonian conservative if he could secure a lucrative position from the president. However, Kelso said, according to the report, "the President having no faith in [Boyd's] moral or political integrity refused to appoint him," so Boyd "returns to the people . . . and becomes a candidate for Congress on the Radical ticket."[5]

"The contest waxes hot and hotter between the candidates," a correspondent to the *St. Louis Republican* reported a few days before the Fourth District's Radical nominating convention. "The indications are that Boyd will be nominated, unless the friends of Kelso and Gravely unite and defeat him." Kelso was confident that either he or his friend Gravely could defeat Pony Boyd in a two-way race, though the result of a three-way race was harder to predict. Kelso considered dropping out, and he had other motives besides wanting to ensure Boyd's defeat. He had been worn down by his labors in Washington. In addition, he later recalled, "I was very weary of being so long absent from my family, and my wife complained so much because she was left to bear the burden of caring for the family alone." He went to talk to Gravely, and the colonel proposed a gentleman's agreement: "He said that if I would withdraw, and let him have the nomination, he would work faithfully for me the next time and see that I received the nomination if I wished it." That settled the matter. When the delegates assembled at 11:00 in the morning on Thursday, July 26, Kelso had a friend from Jasper County withdraw his name. By the next afternoon, Boyd, having seen the delegate count, also withdrew. The Radical press praised Kelso and Boyd for their selfless patriotism. Gravely, the nominee, went on to win easily in November, part of another decisive Radical victory in Missouri and Republican electoral triumph nationwide.[6]

But Gravely's 40th Congress would not convene until later in 1867. Kelso's 39th would hold its second session from December 3, 1866, to March 3, 1867. A few days after Radicals held a late November torchlight procession and political rally in Springfield, Kelso headed for Washington.

Missouri's radical press urged the Republican-dominated Congress to act on the mandate they had received at the ballot box. The Republicans had been timid in the last session, the *Democrat* wrote, but now they had the thunder of local majorities behind them. Moreover, events through the second half of 1866 had shown the folly of trying to cooperate and compromise with obstructionists. The Southern states (except Tennessee), with President Johnson's blessing, had rejected the 14th Amendment. Former Confederates also showed their utter opposition to building a new South by striking out violently against Blacks. Whites rioted for three days in May in Memphis, killing nearly fifty Blacks and burning their houses, churches, and schools to the ground. In New Orleans in July, the violence was as bad and the political implications even worse. After President Johnson had telegraphed local authorities, urging them to break up a political meeting of Black and White loyalists, a police force manned mostly by ex-Confederates complied, leading a White mob that killed nearly 40 and wounded nearly 150. In August, Johnson then undertook an unprecedented speaking tour aimed at the election, a "Swing around the Circle" from Washington to Chicago and back. At political rallies, he lashed out at Congress and demonized his political opponents. At one stop, when a heckler urged him to "hang Jeff Davis," Johnson shot back, "Why not hang Thad Stevens?" Radicals, he charged, promoted tyranny, treason, and disunion, while he, the Union's much-maligned leader, was doing God's work preserving liberty. His belligerent, undignified harangues alienated moderates and contributed to the shellacking of his supporters in the midterms. Radicals had begun talking about more aggressive Reconstruction policies and even openly considering impeachment even before all the votes were counted.[7]

Most Republicans, however, had run on the comparatively moderate principles of the 14th Amendment and had avoided divisive issues like Black suffrage on the stump. One group that had tried to push Black voting was the Southern Loyalist Convention, held in Philadelphia in September to counter the Johnsonian National Union Convention a month earlier, but it too had divided over the issue. (Kelso had signed the call for the Southern Loyalist meeting, but did not attend.) When Congress reconvened in December, the House Republicans were so divided that Stevens wondered if the radicals should just caucus separately.[8]

Economic problems also put a strain on the Republican agenda. When Kelso had entered Congress in 1865, economic concerns were muted, though inflation was a concern. Like nearly everyone else, he supported a limited, cautious reduction in the money supply. A slowing economy and market instability in the fall of 1866, however, sharpened economic policy differences: contractionists wanted to further tighten the money supply, suspensionists wanted to halt the current contraction, and expansionists wanted to increase the supply of greenbacks. These differences did not map onto Reconstruction's radical-to-conservative spectrum: radicals and non-radicals alike had contractionists, suspensionists, and expansionists in their ranks. As the economy dipped toward recession in early 1867, Kelso, like Stevens, swung toward expansionism. But early in the session economic policy debates were still being crowded out by conflicts over Reconstruction.[9]

Had Andrew Johnson been a better politician, he might have exploited economic policy differences among the Republicans. Instead, his belligerent obstructionism repeatedly united them. Some radicals, like Thaddeus Stevens, had been long convinced that Reconstruction would never succeed with Johnson in the White House. The president of the United States was supposed to execute the laws passed by Congress. Johnson, they complained, had done the opposite. In actively thwarting the expressed will of the legislature, whose mandate was strengthened by the election of 1866, he had abused his power as commander-in-chief of the military, perverted the authority of his office, and even questioned the legitimacy of Congress itself. There had been whispers about impeachment as early as the fall of 1865. In the spring of 1866, radicals outside of Congress, in meeting halls and in the press, began to push the case for Johnson's removal. As the election campaign heated up in the summer and fall, some congressional candidates—particularly Benjamin Butler in Massachusetts and James A. Ashley in Ohio—began calling for Johnson's impeachment in their stump speeches. Ashley was widely reported to have vowed to "give neither sleep to his eyes nor slumber to his eyelids" (a reference to Psalms 132:4) until articles of impeachment were brought against Johnson.[10]

Other Republicans, however, even other radicals, saw impeachment as legally dubious, politically reckless, and ultimately dangerous for the country. Even the *New York Tribune*, which agreed that Johnson "has been a bad president, but also a foolish one," thought his removal highly unlikely and the attempt unwise. Had he really committed "high crimes and misdemeanors," the constitutional warrant for removal, or rather had he merely opposed Congress by exploiting the same patronage and discretionary powers that all presidents, at least since Andrew Jackson, had used to exert their executive will? Would the impeachers really be able to get enough conservative Republican votes to pass an impeachment resolution and begin a trial in the Senate? Would two-thirds of the Senate vote to convict? Both Houses had veto-proof majorities—wasn't Johnson's ability to do damage already limited? The public might see an impeachment attempt as Republican overreach and rally to the president. The process, too, would drain time and energy away from the work of Reconstruction and regular legislation. Moreover, with the economy so fragile, and currency speculators on Wall Street betting on or against every move in Washington, a constitutional crisis might produce economic chaos.[11]

The fifty or so radical House members, probably including Kelso, who caucused on December 3 at the opening of the second session, thought

Congress needed to battle against Johnson's obstructionism more aggressively. To this group, Stevens presented a draft of what would become the Tenure of Office Act, which limited the president's appointment and removal powers. Representative George S. Boutwell of Massachusetts introduced the topic of impeachment and proposed the creation of a special House committee to consider it, an idea endorsed by every man at the meeting. Ashley attempted to create this committee with a resolution in the House on December 17. Appealing to moderates and conservatives, he did not mention the president specifically but framed it to authorize a committee to inquire whether *any* civil officers had committed "high crimes and misdemeanors." Kelso voted with him, but the vote fell far short of the two-thirds necessary for the required rule change.[12]

Ashley let it be known that he intended to introduce an impeachment resolution anyway, and when private counsel would not dissuade him, House Republicans held a caucus on Saturday evening, January 5, 1867. About fifty or sixty attended, including conservatives and moderates. For two hours they argued about impeachment. Rufus P. Spalding of Ohio proposed a resolution that no representative would present articles of impeachment without the measure first being approved by the Republican caucus. Stevens was opposed. Caucus votes were screens for cowards to hide behind, he grumbled. He agreed with Ashley that impeachment should be proposed to the House immediately, and he argued that each man should then "take his stand openly and fairly before the country." Ashley, slightly more open to compromise, proposed to amend the language of Spalding's resolution so that it would be against a member ordering articles of impeachment but not opposed to a resolution for a committee to inquire into impeachment. This passed, 31–20. The caucus majority then resolved that any impeachment inquiry needed to be vetted by the Judiciary Committee. Stevens was reported to be "in a towering passion" over the decisions of the caucus. But even with the caucus's constraints, Ashley had a path for bringing the topic of impeachment to the floor of the House.[13]

Word went out, and the press reported the Ohioan's intentions. On Monday, January 7, the galleries were full, and reporters noted a sense of anticipation and excitement in the air. But then something happened that no one expected. Missouri Congressman Benjamin Loan, with Kelso's help, became the first representative to call for the impeachment of Andrew Johnson.[14]

Every Monday, what was called the "morning hour"—actually noon to 1:00 p.m.—was reserved for a call from the states for bills and resolutions to be disposed of without debate. On this day, when Missouri's turn came,

Loan, from the state's Seventh District, read a resolution with a preamble and four parts. In order to secure "the fruits of the victories" gained in the war and to effect the will of the people expressed at the last election, Loan declared, it was the "imperative duty" of Congress, without delay, to accomplish four objectives. First, impeach the president, convict him "of the crimes and high misdemeanors of which he is manifestly and notoriously guilty," and remove him from office. Second, ensure that the presidency operates "within the limits prescribed by law." Third, reorganize the former Confederate states "upon a basis of loyalty and justice" and restore their practical relations to the Union. Finally, to achieve this last end, secure "by the direct intervention of Federal authority" the voting rights of all "loyal citizens" in those states, "without regard to color."[15]

What was going on? The correspondents in the press gallery, darting from their seats to the telegraph operator, were confused; the stenographic congressional record of parliamentary moves and motions veils motives and consequences; later historical accounts hurry past these initial steps to the impeachment process itself. Loan had clearly not coordinated with Ashley: the latter immediately sprang to his feet to try to offer an amendment. Loan wanted to hear Ashley's offer, but he learned from the Chair that if he agreed to do so he would lose his chance for an immediate vote without debate (having to withdraw his call for the "previous question") and postpone further discussion for another week ("go over under the rule"). So Loan pressed forward.[16]

Was Loan trying to steal Ashley's thunder and push a hyper-partisan agenda? That is what some hostile commentators in the press would charge. The *New York Tribune* called Loan's "manifesto" an "incoherent and amusing resolution" by a man who was "evidently a morbid person, with the weakness of getting into print, or in some way of attracting attention." The *New York Herald* would come to see him as "a radical politician, with more ambition than brains" trying to create "a sensation." The *Baltimore Sun* looked beyond Loan himself to the cabal of extremist Republicans trying to drive the entire party—and thus the entire Congress, and the entire country—toward radical Reconstruction. Loan's resolution, the *Sun* editorialized, "set forth the considerations of partisan expediency which require the impeachment of the president." The resolution "precisely" expressed the position of House leader Thaddeus Stevens: "that the impeachment of Mr. Johnson is essential to the consummation of the congressional scheme of reconstruction, which otherwise is a failure." The paper was wrong to dismiss the resolution as mere partisanship, but right to see that Loan—and Stevens, and, apparently,

Kelso—were trying to make the case that reconstructing the presidency had to be part of rebuilding the republic.[17]

Loan's resolution did not order specific articles of impeachment against Johnson, but it broadly declared the president to be "manifestly and notoriously guilty" of "crimes and high misdemeanors." It did not merely call for an investigation; it demanded bold and immediate action: Congress's final solution to a law-breaking president and the direct intervention of federal power in the conquered but still-rebellious Southern states. In effect, it proclaimed a philosophy of Reconstruction that had as its main pillars impeachment, congressional supremacy, Black suffrage, and a thorough reorganization of Southern political life. Loan was thumbing his nose at the conservative roadblocks propped up by the Republican caucus. He wanted to force the impeachment issue to the floor, not have it limited by the caucus or stuck in a committee.[18]

Then Ralph Hill, a moderate Republican from Indiana, raised a point of order. Since the resolution's third and fourth clauses were about representation in the former Confederate states, they were specifically about Reconstruction. And Congress had the year before made a rule that all Reconstruction bills and resolutions would be sent immediately to the Joint Committee on Reconstruction. When the chair agreed, Loan knew that his impeachment resolution was in trouble. If his radical resolution was sent to that committee, it would never again see the light of day. So Loan quickly asked the Chair if he could drop the third and fourth clauses (about Reconstruction) and just keep the first two (about the presidency). No, the Chair answered, it was too late—the resolution could not be altered after a point of order had been raised. Upon the Chair's ruling, the resolution was sent to the Joint Committee, "amid a murmur of approval on the Democratic side of the House."[19]

Just after the impeachment resolution died, Kelso resurrected it. Seated behind Loan at the back of the hall, Kelso had obviously been aware of what his Missouri colleague was doing, if not collaborating with him from the start. The Missouri delegation still had the floor for the Monday "morning hour" call for resolutions from the states. "On the instant," according to a reporter who watched the scene, Kelso took a copy of Loan's resolution, crossed out the third and fourth clauses, and rose to be recognized. He then reintroduced the resolution to impeach Andrew Johnson.[20]

Kelso, like Loan, Stevens, and some other aggressive radicals, wanted a vote on the floor so congressmen would have to take a stand on impeachment before the country. But time was running out—the morning hour had almost expired, and once it did, by rule, the issue would be postponed until the following Monday but remain alive as a topic of discussion on the floor. Observers watched members gathering around Ashley's desk. What was he planning to do? The motion to table (and thus kill) the resolution came to a vote and was defeated, 40–104—a test vote that one report described as "ominous." Loan's—and now Kelso's—impeachment resolution would carry over into the next week.[21]

Reporters in the gallery thought the excitement was over for the day. Yet as soon as the morning hour expired, Ashley arose and interrupted the resumption of regular business with a "high question of personal privilege," which, by rule, took precedence over everything else. Ashley charged Andrew Johnson with "high crimes and misdemeanors," specifying that the president had illegally usurped power and corruptly pardoned rebels, appointed officials, vetoed legislation, and disposed of public property. The resolution would authorize the Judiciary Committee to investigate with subpoena power, and then, if appropriate, report articles of impeachment back to the House. As Ashley spoke, according to a correspondent, "members came from the lobbies down the aisle to their seats; the galleries became more compact than ever; the gold speculators vibrated rapidly between the reporters' gallery and the telegraph in its rear; all present were full of excitement and anxiety."[22]

Ashley called the question. Opponents moved to table but were defeated in a vote almost identical to the tabling motion on Kelso's: 39–105. Then they tried to get Ashley's resolution referred to the Judiciary Committee before a vote could be taken to authorize the investigation, but they failed again. Finally, the House voted on the impeachment investigation resolution itself, and it passed, 107–39.[23]

Ashley would become known as the "Great Impeacher." In the radical Missouri press, Loan got some credit, too, for being the first to bring the issue to the House floor. A headline in an Ohio paper summarized the day's events: "Impeachment. Exciting Scene in the House. Two Impeachment Resolutions. Messrs. Loan and Ashley the Movers. The Latter's Measure Passed." Kelso, who kept the impeachment issue alive on the floor and forced the first test vote, was barely mentioned in some accounts and completely absent in others. One newspaper report misidentified him as "Mr. Kelley," a Republican from Pennsylvania. Another called him "Retzer."[24]

A week later in the House, Benjamin Loan hurled an even more explosive accusation against the president: he charged Johnson with having been complicit in the assassination of Abraham Lincoln. As the Judiciary Committee's investigation began and was quickly shrouded in secrecy, discussion of impeachment continued on the House floor, thanks to Kelso's efforts on January 7.

On Monday, January 14, Kelso opened debate by withdrawing his demand for the previous question and yielded ten minutes of his allotted hour to his colleague. Loan had not gotten far into his speech before he made the charge. We have learned, Loan began, that Lincoln's death was not the desperate act of a lone gunman but the result of a rebel conspiracy. Defeated on the battle-field, rebel leaders had realized that the best way to further their cause was to replace Lincoln with the "life-long pro-slavery Democrat" who had, in a ges-ture of reconciliation, unfortunately become vice president. "The crime was committed. The way was made clear for the succession; an assassin's bullet, wielded and directed by rebel hand and paid for by rebel gold, made Andrew Johnson President of the United States of America. The price that he was to pay for his promotion was treachery to the Republic and fidelity to the party of treason and rebellion."[25]

Robert S. Hale, a Republican Johnson supporter from New York, rose to interrupt Loan with a point of order. Had he just heard what he thought he heard? Hale asked the Chair if such an outrageous charge could possibly be in order in a speech made from the floor. The Chair, Speaker Colfax, ruled that it was, since it was specifying one of the crimes and misdemeanors mentioned in Kelso's resolution, so the Chair could not restrain Loan's remarks. Considering the gravity of the issue, however, the Chair asked for and re-ceived a vote upholding his ruling. Then Loan continued. "Has [Johnson] performed his part of the agreement as faithfully as the rebels did theirs?" Loan then explained Johnson's obstruction as collusion intended to bring former Confederates back to power both in their own states and in the fed-eral government. When Loan's ten minutes expired, Kelso yielded as much more time as Loan needed to finish his speech. When Loan concluded, Hale rose again to challenge the Missourian to "specify any particle of proof" to support his sensational charge. Loan answered that he would do so "in my own way and in my own good time," before the proper tribunal.[26]

Conspiracy theorists had floated rumors about Johnson and the assassina-tion before, but it was still a shock to hear such allegations made by a U.S. con-gressman on the floor of the House. On the night that John Wilkes Booth shot Lincoln at Ford's Theater and another plotter stabbed and severely wounded Secretary of State William H. Seward at his home, Johnson, too, had been a target—but the man assigned to kill the vice president lost his nerve and no attack was made. Still, subsequent political events suggested to some—Mary Todd Lincoln, for one—that Johnson must have been involved. James Ashley was convinced that Johnson had blood on his hands, and the congressman had worked to prove it even before the Judiciary Committee had begun its investigation. He mentioned to House colleagues that he had obtained evidence. But he later admitted under oath that this "evidence," while enough to convince Ashley himself of his theory, was not really "legal" evidence. All he had, in fact, were vague statements he heard in jailhouse interviews with a convicted perjurer, statements so useless as proof that he had not even voluntarily mentioned the assassination question to the committee. His initial boast to his House colleagues about having "evidence," however, may have been what emboldened Loan.[27]

The conservative press denounced Loan's "disgraceful" speech as "border ruffianism in Congress" and hammered the Missourian as a "restless" man in an "obscure" position who was trying to outdo the extremism of Thaddeus Stevens by "glibly" linking Johnson to the assassination. Even the radical *St. Louis Democrat* backed away from Loan, cautioning that such charges, "so grave as to be hardly credible," ought not to be made without proof. Kelso, who had a predilection for conspiracy theories, left no record of what he thought about this one.[28]

When it returned to the issue, the House sent Kelso's resolution to the Judiciary Committee, in effect folding it into the process that Ashley had launched. The Committee's investigation lasted for many months after Kelso left Congress. It finally reported in late November 1867 and by a 5–4 majority endorsed articles of impeachment. The House voted on December 6, and impeachment failed, 57–108. Too many representatives, even many furious with Johnson, were persuaded that impeachment could not be used to address merely general malfeasance and mendacity, and they were not convinced that the president had broken any laws. But in late February 1868, Johnson fired Secretary of War Edwin M. Stanton in violation of the Tenure of Office Act. The House quickly passed an impeachment resolution in a party-line vote, 128–47. After a five-week trial, the Senate vote in mid-May fell one short of the two-thirds necessary for conviction and removal.[29]

Kelso's 39th Congress had begun the impeachment process at the beginning of 1867, but there was much else for the House of Representatives to do before the session ended in early March. Amidst the battles over impeachment and Reconstruction and the daily tug-of-war over regular legislation, Kelso, either looking toward his election campaign in 1868 or eager to put a broad statement of principle in the record in case he never returned to Congress, offered another constitutional amendment on January 28.[30]

Kelso's proposed amendment looked toward a future when the egalitarian idealism of the Declaration of Independence would be finally concretized in fundamental law. His resolution had four sections. The first ensured that "no citizen" twenty-one years and older could be deprived of the right to vote. This was not just another insistence that Black suffrage was essential to a reconstructed South. It also secured race-blind citizenship in those Northern states that continued to deny it. Kelso's proposal presupposed the notion of citizenship defined in the 14th Amendment and anticipated the actual 15th Amendment (1870), holding that political equality could not be abridged according to race, color, or previous condition of servitude.[31]

Moreover, Kelso's amendment treated suffrage as the right of adult citizens and not adult *male* citizens. This surely was not because he simply assumed the voter's maleness and thought it unnecessary to be gender specific. That might have been true some years earlier, but the issue of women's suffrage had come to the fore during the Reconstruction debates. Some conservatives tried to use it as a debater's tactic against the claim that the rights of adult citizenship necessarily included equal political rights, appealing to gender bias by analogy to justify racial bias: if White women were citizens but could still be held unsuited for voting, so could Blacks. Other politicians and political writers deployed women's suffrage cynically to oppose reform: if, as some bills proposed, representation in the House and the Electoral College were changed to reflect the number of voters in a state rather than the number of inhabitants, states would take the otherwise unimaginable step of enfranchising women just to increase their share of federal power.

Feminists had been campaigning vigorously for women's suffrage. Elizabeth Cady Stanton and Susan B. Anthony condemned the provision of the 14th Amendment that, for the first time, specified "male" inhabitants as it linked voting rights and representation. Some Republican lawmakers acknowledged that gender discrimination in the political sphere was as unjust as racial discrimination. But few endorsed a constitutional amendment to remedy that injustice in the midst of the bitter fight over Reconstruction. Those like Kelso, who did, were a minority within a minority. Ohio Republican Senator Benjamin F. Wade got in trouble with his own party for endorsing women's suffrage on the campaign trail in 1866. Missouri Senator B. Gratz Brown voiced his support for women's suffrage in a floor debate in December, but Brown was retiring. Back in Missouri, the Woman Suffrage Association formed in the spring of 1867.[32]

The second section of Kelso's proposed amendment endorsed equality of opportunity in the economic and social spheres. "All men being equal before the law, and endowed with an inalienable right to the pursuit of happiness," it read, "no law shall be passed by Congress or by any State depriving any citizen of sound mind and unconvicted of any crime from following any lawful business in life, but shall leave all honor, all avocations, and all positions open alike to each and every citizen of lawful age." Again, Kelso proposed protecting the rights of all citizens, not just men. This constitutional provision would open all professions and forms of labor—and the social status that came with them—to everyone. The third section declared that any laws or previous constitutional provisions inconsistent with the first two provisions would be null and void.[33]

Kelso's fourth section established the duty of every state to establish free public schools for all its inhabitants between the ages of five and twenty-one. Others in Congress—Senator Charles Sumner most forcefully—had been long trying to incorporate an education plank in the Reconstruction platform, both to answer opponents claiming that former slaves were too ignorant to vote and for the greater good of the country. Kelso, ever the schoolteacher, wanted to affirm the broader civic value of education in the Constitution. Such schools, his resolution read, needed to be sufficiently advanced "to enable each and every scholar to thoroughly fit himself for an efficient and intelligent discharge of all the duties of a citizen of an enlightened commonwealth and to fill creditably any office or position in the state or nation." (Kelso's school in Springfield, a private academy, would not have benefited from the public funding.) The proposed amendment's fifth and final section, mirroring the apparatus of the 14th Amendment, directed states to carry out all the provisions but empowered Congress and the federal government to step in if the states failed.[34]

Kelso's resolution was immediately sent to the Judiciary Committee, where it disappeared from sight—except in Missouri's Fourth Congressional District, where the Springfield *Patriot* printed the full text on its front page on February 14, 1867.[35]

As Kelso helped to impeach the president and dreamed of enshrining racial, gender, and social equality in the Constitution, Congress, in January, 1867, finally passed, over Johnson's veto, the bill enfranchising Black men in the District of Columbia. It also extended manhood suffrage to the territories. But it bogged down in debates over Reconstruction policy. Three bills emerged to open a path forward. The first, coming out of the Joint Committee on Reconstruction and reported to the House on February 6, was a centrist proposal to place the Southern states under temporary military authority. The move was required because of the continuing unrest there and it was justified by Congress's war powers, still in effect according to the "grasp of war" theory (which held that a vanquished foe, though having surrendered on the battlefield, could still be treated as an enemy until it submitted to the victor's reasonable peace terms). Still, it its original form, it was just a police bill—a method for maintaining law and order—not a plan to reconstruct and restore the former Confederate states.[36]

The second—and much more radical—bill came before the House on February 11 from the special committee formed to respond to the New Orleans riot the previous summer. The Louisiana bill framed a new provisional government for the state, one that would be controlled by loyal Unionists, require universal manhood suffrage, exclude all former rebels from holding office (and most of them from voting), and exist under the supervision of the military and Congress. Southern Unionists lobbied to make this the template for reconstructing the entire South.[37]

A third, conservative, option emerged out of opposition to the military government bill in the House. Conservatives feared that the bill delegitimized the existing state governments, prolonged military occupation, and raised the specter of military despotism. Bingham and James G. Blaine from Maine wanted to turn the military government bill from a police bill into a Reconstruction act. Blaine's amendment to the military government bill assured the Johnsonian state governments that if they only ratified the 14th Amendment and passed impartial (not universal) suffrage laws, Congress would recognize their legitimacy. Nothing dislodged former rebels from controlling the state machinery and the process fulfilling these requirements.[38]

On February 12, Blaine used a sharp parliamentary maneuver to attach his amendment to the military government bill, in effect trying to hijack it and turn it into Congress's Reconstruction Act. He moved to refer the bill to the Judiciary Committee with instructions to add his amendment and immediately return it to the floor. When the House agreed 85–78 to vote on his motion (Kelso voting with the majority), Stevens saw a conservative victory looming. The frail but fiery and determined old man rose to address his colleagues, his voice so weak that members had to crowd around his desk to hear him.

I see a great party "about to destroy itself," Stevens began. "For the last few months Congress has been sitting here, and while the South has been bleeding at every pore, Congress has done nothing to protect the loyal people there." We had a Reconstruction bill last month, he complained, but the gentleman from Ohio (Bingham) doggedly worked against it and finally killed it. The military government bill was meeting the same obstructions. The amendment by the gentleman from Maine (Blaine), Stevens declared, was a "step toward universal amnesty [for rebels] and universal Andy Johnsonism" in its approval of the existing state governments. The old House leader derided the "small criticisms" that other "young gentlemen" with a slew of proposed amendments and substitutions brought against the bill. But the Blaine amendment was the worst of all: the House needed to "understand that the adoption of it would be an entire surrender of those States into the hands of rebels." Stevens took his seat, the House voted, and Blaine's motion failed, 69–94. Seventeen Republicans had swung back to Stevens's side. But not Kelso. After the vote was announced, the old political warrior inquired of the Speaker "if it is in order for me to say . . . that heaven rules as yet and there are gods above." The Speaker, to laughter, ruled that it was in order for Stevens to say so.[39]

Kelso had voted for the radicals' Louisiana bill the day before. But the votes he cast on that single day, February 13, 1867, for the Blaine amendment and against the Stevens military bill, would cause later historians to categorize him as a "conservative" among the Republicans in the Second Session of the 39th Congress. Three votes on a single day should not erase the rest of Kelso's record during his term in Congress. Kelso being listed as a conservative in two different analyses of congressional voting has more to do with statistical quirks and the vagaries of sorting than with his actual ideological position or political strategy. Still, what explains Kelso's vote for Blaine and against Stevens—his apparent swing in a more conservative direction—on this important day? Absent commentary by Kelso or anyone else, we can only speculate.[40]

In one scenario, Kelso was persuaded to vote for Blaine's more conservative option in order to break the legislative logjam, reach a compromise with Johnson and his supporters, and finally move forward on Reconstruction. On the evening of February 12, President Johnson had sent two of his supporters to meet with a group of Republicans—mostly conservatives—at the Metropolitan Hotel. The president was signaling that he was open to seeking a compromise on Reconstruction (and privately hoping to split the Republican Party in doing so). Surely Kelso, a man who had called for Johnson's impeachment a month earlier, was not at the meeting. But his centrist-conservative colleague and friend Henry T. Blow, the representative from Missouri's Second District who had vouched for Kelso during the 1866 campaign, was. At the meeting, Johnson's representatives and the congressmen could not reach an agreement, but compromise was in the air. The next day, Blaine made his parliamentary maneuvers to amend Stevens's bill. It is not inconceivable that Kelso spoke with Blow and, with the close of the session only three weeks away, was persuaded to vote with Blaine as a necessary compromise, a last best chance to pass a Reconstruction Act.[41]

But there is another, more likely scenario. James F. Wilson, chair of the Judiciary Committee, lobbied radicals to vote to commit the bill to his committee with Blaine's instructions to add his amendment and send it immediately back to the House. But Wilson promised that the committee would add a stricter provision disfranchising former rebels. In other words, as William Lawrence from Ohio explained on the floor a few days later, some radicals voted for the Blaine amendment not to endorse its conservatism (its relative lenience toward rebels) but as a tactic to move the bill in the opposite direction. Kelso may have voted to refer the bill to the committee on this understanding.[42]

Such procedural maneuvering, however, does not explain why, after Stevens's dramatic speech rallied radicals back to his standard and the Blaine gambit failed, Kelso did not join most of the other radicals and vote for Stevens's version of the military government bill. Kelso's vote here may have arisen from a (not unusual) combination of principled conviction, inflated self-confidence, and personal pique.

The day before the votes, Kelso's friend William D. Kelley, a radical from Pennsylvania speaking on the floor in favor of Stevens's original military government bill, mentioned that he had recently reviewed all the amendments that had been filed at the clerk's desk. He mentioned two complete substitutions for Stevens's bill that he liked, one from Kelso, "which I regret has not found its way into print, for if any were to be adopted, it would command my preference." No record remains of Kelso's substitute bill. But evidently he thought he could do better than the venerable Stevens and the Reconstruction committee.[43]

When Stevens had taken the floor on February 13, he had not hidden his impatience with all the proposed amendments and substitutions. In warning that the party was about to destroy itself, he had aimed most of his venom at Bingham and Blaine. But he had also lectured the "young gentlemen" around him to rise above their petty quibbling over adverbs and adjectives and realize their historic responsibilities. Then he had started going through the amendments and substitutions one by one, dismissing each in a sentence and noting that even the decent ones would wind up killing the bill entirely. He mentioned three and had planned to notice "two or three more" from the clerk's file, perhaps including Kelso's substitute, but after being interrupted instead returned to his criticism of Blaine's amendment. After the Blaine amendment failed, it was time to vote on Stevens's bill. Kelso clearly thought that Congress could do better—that he himself had done better. And he may have been miffed that Stevens had brushed him aside without a word. In any case, Kelso voted no.[44]

In the subsequent twists and turns in the road toward the passage of the first Reconstruction Act, Kelso voted with the radicals. When the military government bill came back from the Senate with the Blaine amendment restored, Kelso voted with Stevens against concurrence, even as more moderate and conservative Republicans denounced them as impractical idealists. When amendments were finally attached that pushed the bill in a more radical direction—giving the vote to Blacks and taking it away from more rebels—Kelso voted with Stevens and the Republican majority, 126–46, to pass what became the first Reconstruction Act on February 20, 1867. When President Johnson's veto arrived on the Hill on March 2, both Houses immediately mustered the required two-thirds vote to override it.[45]

The act was a far cry from how radicals like Stevens and Kelso had envisioned Reconstruction at the beginning of the term. It did not dismantle the Johnsonian state governments dominated by former Confederates and replace them with provisional territorial governments supervised by Congress. It did not confiscate land from traitors and distribute 40-acre homesteads to loyal Blacks, or create a system of public education to shape an enlightened, interracial democratic society. But it did temporarily divide the former Confederate states (excluding Tennessee) into five military districts with commanders empowered to protect freed people and loyal Whites from abuse. And it held that Southern states could deny Black male suffrage only if they paid a steep political price.[46]

Back in Missouri, the radical press celebrated a surprising victory. The *St. Louis Democrat* said that the Act that had become law at the very end of the session was the best Reconstruction bill that had been considered in either House. The 39th Congress, an editorial proclaimed two days after that body had adjourned, "will be memorable in history as the best and bravest this country has yet seen. Never before have the people been so worthily represented." A week and a half later, the *Springfield Patriot* welcomed Kelso home. Its congratulations, however, had a valedictory tone, as if acknowledging that his political career was over. "It is fitting to say to him on behalf of the Radical party of the Southwest, which clothed him with official honors, 'well done good and faithful servant,'" the *Patriot* concluded. "He has made a record for himself in the National Legislature, of which he and his friends may be proud. So far as we know, he has always voted for the right, and has never been made to falter in the least, in the discharge of the grave and solemn trials and duties of the most important Congress that ever convened in the capitol of the nation."[47]

AS KELSO CAME to his congressional career when writing his autobiography, he left a note to himself on the inside cover of one of his composition notebooks: "The political part of this book to be most briefly given." After narrating his Civil War experiences with extraordinary detail, seemingly re-experiencing each scout and skirmish as he wrote, he backed away from the political fights of the 1860s with little comment about the issues that had so engaged him and the nation. Writing this chapter of his life, he gave more attention to the sights he saw traveling to and from Washington than to the news he had helped make in the capital. He says he worked hard, but not what he worked on. He describes his speech on Reconstruction as well received, but not what points he argued. He skips over Boyd's challenge to the election and the circular he sent to the folks back home. He mentions no votes, no policy debates, no resolutions for constitutional amendments. He passes by the success or failure of the Reconstruction program and his role in the impeachment drama without a word.[48]

By the time he wrote, Reconstruction had collapsed; it was remembered by some as a political blunder and by others as a tragic failure. To secure the presidency, Rutherford B. Hayes had agreed in 1877 to return troops in the South to their barracks and give up on the idea that the federal government would try to protect voting rights and fair elections there. But two years before that, the Democrats had taken the House, ensuring that there would be few federal dollars to sustain Reconstruction anyway. And years before that, as early as the election of 1868, other issues moved forward to displace those that had animated the 39th Congress: taxes and tariffs, gold and greenbacks, monopolies, lobbyists, and corruption. The radical Republican coalition in Congress did not die with Thaddeus Stevens in August 1868, but it did not long outlast him.[49]

Political corruption and the undue influence of corporate power did not suddenly appear in the scandal-prone Grant administration. Observers claimed that corruption had metastasized with the massive growth of government spending during the war. During the 39th Congress, Kelso would have seen lobbyists sitting at members' desks on the House floor, influencing legislation as it was being debated. A "Whiskey Ring"—a systematic evasion of taxes by distillers and shopkeepers, with revenue officials and congressional committees induced to look the other way—became notorious during the Johnson administration. There were other such rings, some involving speculators in tobacco or cotton, others bilking the customs houses or manipulating government contracts supplying Indians on the frontier. By the end of 1868, a corruption scandal flared up in the Post Office Department, implicating Johnson's loyal postmaster general Alexander Randall. A guide to Washington, D.C., written before the close of the Johnson era, described a city filled with log-rolling lobbyists, parasitic office-seekers, and government officials easily manipulated or simply on the take. As Kelso looked back upon his congressional term, he may have remembered Washington less for the stately white dome of the capitol adorned with the statue of Freedom than for the horde of hack drivers, paperboys, bootblacks, and panhandlers who accosted him when he first stepped off the train, calling out, crowding around, tugging at his luggage, doing anything they could to extract coins from pockets.[50]

In the years following his term in Congress, Kelso had come to think about politics differently. The corrupt politician arm-in-arm with the plutocrat had become central characters of the Gilded Age, bloated gents with top hats in a Thomas Nast cartoon, feeding at the public trough. Behind the speeches and the votes and the resolutions, the real movers of the government machine, Kelso had come to believe, were corrupt conspiracies driven by corporate power. And in the 39th Congress, no influence-buying interest group had been more powerful than the railroad lobby. He had seen its work firsthand—had even been tempted by some of the favors it offered. During the Christmas recess in 1866, he remembered, "the various rail-road companies of the South combined and invited the entire Congress to take a free ride throughout the entire South on board a train of palace cars furnished with every known luxury, wine, wom[en]—everything that could be thought of or desired. I greatly wished to take this princely ride, but, looking upon the whole thing as a kind of bribe for which the various companies involved in it would ask subsidies for their various roads, I declined the tempting invitation. My suspicion soon proved to be well founded."[51]

Kelso also declined the offer of Credit Mobilier stock, though he saw many of his friends—including House Speaker Schuyler Colfax and Congressmen William D. Kelley and James A. Garfield—get caught up in the scandal. Credit Mobilier was a shell company run by Union Pacific Railroad directors that evaded laws for selling government bonds and grossly overcharged for road construction. Shares, which earned huge dividends, were offered to congressmen at considerably below their market value. When the scheme was exposed, the congressional investors denied that they knew what they were buying or that they subsequently did any special favors for the railroad men. Kelso did not believe them. They "did vote the [railroad] subsidies notwithstanding the cowardly denials of these damaging facts which many of them subsequently made."[52]

Kelso's "great mistake," the political miscalculation that he believed, in retrospect, changed the course of his life, was not in declining the lobbyists' tempting offers. It was not his commitment to radical Reconstruction or involvement with the impeachment of the president. It was not any vote, or speech, or resolution. Looking back, Kelso remembered when he first entered Congress. He met and got to know both President Johnson and Secretary of State Seward before the relations between the administration and the Republican Congress had broken beyond repair. The Andrew Johnson who briefly appears in the autobiography is not the stubborn racist who opposed meaningful reform at every turn but a "truly great and good" man who flattered Kelso by inviting him to the White House for some fine dinners and "pleasant conversations." In one of those pleasant conversations, Kelso later wrote, Johnson or Seward floated a tempting offer: might Kelso be interested in becoming the minister resident to the Court of Sweden? Such an offer was not entirely implausible—Kelso's friend Henry T. Blow had jumped from the Missouri Senate to become Minister to Venezuela in 1861. There is no evidence that the post in Sweden was actually open: James Hepburn Campbell had been appointed to the position by Lincoln in the spring of 1864 and would serve until the end of March 1867. But Johnson and Seward may have had motives for raising such a possibility anyway. "I was greatly pleased with this offer and meant to accept it," Kelso recalled. "I now think that I made a great mistake in declining to accept that honorable office."[53]

Kelso had to have known in 1866 that the Johnson administration was using the president's patronage power to shore up his political capital. Kelso had to have understood that such an offer was a gesture of "friendship" that the administration hoped would be reciprocated by the congressman's committee work and votes on the floor. An actual appointment would have removed a radical from the Republican caucus and would have been seen as Kelso's endorsement of Johnson's policies. Perhaps Kelso told himself that he would not actually disavow any of his professed political principles, would not explicitly do what he had accused Boyd of offering to do: switch positions and jump parties in exchange for a lucrative foreign post. But if the administration's proposition was not the same as a railroad lobbyist's offer of a princely junket or a lucrative investment opportunity, it was close. Kelso ended up declining not because of moral qualms, but through self-interested political calculation: "When I consulted my friends, however, in regard to the matter, they dissuaded me. They said that for me to accept this appointment from Johnson at that time, when he was so unpopular, would ruin me forever with the Republican Party; and that, since Johnson was likely to be impeached and removed soon, I would not be likely to retain this office long even if I should accept it."[54]

Nearly two decades after his "great mistake," he was thinking not at all of Reconstruction politics and only of the course his life had taken. What if he had left Congress and had moved his family to Sweden. How different everything, from that moment forward, would have been. Instead, that great mistake was followed by another—his withdrawing from the race in 1866—and then came a cascade of "mistakes, misfortunes and sorrows" that he wished he could forget. But as he wrote, he did not linger long to berate himself for making the wrong decision: "And yet, who can tell whether I did or did not err? I acted from good motives, and used the best judgment I had; and it may be that, by taking the course I did take on each occasion, I will have done more good for the world, at the close of my life, than I would have done had I taken any other."[55]

In the years following his term in Congress, Kelso had also come to think about life differently. In the 1870s he had come to embrace a philosophy of hard determinism. In a lecture called "Influences" he argued that a person's every action, like every other event in the universe, was determined by a chain of causes and effects operating by fixed laws. A single cause in a person's life is a concatenation of influences—from historical conditions and social institutions to inherited traits and prenatal neurological development—that determine what can delusively appear to the actor himself as a free choice. Applying that philosophy to his own life and pondering the "great mistake" of his political career, he was determined to see himself as "a child of destiny, and my course through life, like the course of a planet through the heavens, was fixed for me by an inexorable law entirely beyond my control.... I will not now repine at what *'might have been.'* "[56]

14

The Cold, Dark River

ONE BEAUTIFUL LATE summer evening at dusk, Kelso, walking in his yard, stopped to look back at his house, at a window glowing from the light within. His ten-year-old daughter Iantha, the sprightly girl he called his "little weasel," sat in the window reading, her face aglow with pleasure at what she read. "How happy she looks, and how beautiful," Kelso thought. He could hear peals of laughter from his other children in the room. Several moths, resembling humming birds, had gotten in and fluttered near the ceiling, and the children named them and made a game of it. Steadfast and loving Florella, his eldest at fifteen, was there talking and laughing with the younger children: his delightful Freddie, five-and-a-half, and rambunctious little Johnny, three. Only Kelso's eldest son, Florellus, fourteen, was absent. The father stood watching and listening, his heart full. This "scene of joy" would long dwell in his memory "like a beautiful picture." It was one of those ordinary yet precious moments in life. Kelso was both fully in it, bathed by the light from within, and yet a step outside of it, watching from the lengthening shadows, experiencing the joy and reflecting upon it at the same time.[1]

After the war, Kelso had worked hard to build his new life in Springfield. The future looked bright. The population of Greene County surged 65 percent between 1865 and 1870, and Campbell Township (Springfield and its environs), spurred in particular by the coming of the railroad, grew from 3,500 to 8,600. The military camps disappeared and industry returned. Enterprising men rebuilt the foundry on Campbell Street and opened a steam mill, a plow factory, and a large brickyard. After fires destroyed several town buildings in 1867 and 1868, Springfielders rebuilt in brick. Plenty of rough characters still brawled in the saloons and cavorted in the whorehouses—Wild Bill Hickok had gunned down fellow gambler Dave Tutt on a Springfield street in the summer of 1865. But the town fathers, aiming for respectability, regulated the dram shops, cleaned up the town square, and put up lamps on downtown streets. In the spring of 1867, Kelso's was the lone house on a 5-acre town lot on North Campbell Street; he bought the rest of the lot and "built several beautiful cottages upon it." He also bought some property just across an alley to the south of his home and built Kelso Academy on the corner of North Campbell and Pine streets, a "fine-furnished" school building that could hold one hundred students and cost him $5,000.[2]

The 1870 census, recorded six weeks before Kelso stood outside his home admiring the "beautiful picture" of his children, offers one measure of his material prosperity. Kelso by that time had $1,400 in real estate and $500 in personal property. This placed him among the town's middling farmers, small shopkeepers, skilled craftsmen and advanced clerks but well below its leading professional men. Over three hundred households (16 percent in Campbell Township) lacked any assessed property, and many propertyless adult laborers lived in Springfield's boarding houses. Of the property-holders, about a third owned less than $500 worth and nearly two-thirds owned less than Kelso's $1,900. One hundred and twenty-nine (9 percent) had property worth $10,000 or more, sixty (4 percent) were assessed at $20,000 or more, and the ten highest—three merchants, two lawyers, a broker, a real estate speculator, a druggist, and a farmer—were assessed at $56,000 to $125,000. The town's laborers and wealthier families were both supposed to be the keys to Kelso's success. The laborers would rent his cottages. His wealthier neighbors would lend him money and send their children to his private school—or so they had initially promised.[3]

After serving in Congress, Kelso became a simple school teacher and family man in Springfield. But his deeds during the war had not been forgotten. Grudges and vendettas had not been set aside with the Confederate surrender. A group of outlaws, former rebels known as the Texas Avengers, targeted some southwest Missouri men for assassination, and Kelso was one of them. On a warm August evening in 1866, Spencer Pettis Wright of Marshfield, a town about 25 miles northeast of Springfield, was at home reading a newspaper by candlelight and quietly rocking his baby to sleep. Wright had fought for the Union as a first lieutenant in the 24th Missouri Infantry. His pregnant wife was in an adjoining room when she heard the gunshot. She "came into the room," the account in the Springfield *Patriot* said, and "beheld her husband sitting with the paper and candle in his hand, motionless in death." Someone had crept up to the house in the darkness and from the front doorway shot Wright in the head. The following spring, Judge Hiram C. Christian received a letter warning that the Texas men were looking for him. Christian had been a Texas Unionist who served the U.S. govern-ment as a provost marshal in Bell County, Texas, during the war. Two weeks after receiving the letter, on a Friday evening in May 1867, he was working late in his market house on the corner of Mill and Boonville streets in Springfield. Two men entered, and one of them shot Christian in the head with a revolver. The judge was found "lying dead behind his counter, his pocketbook lying on the floor beside him, and a one dollar greenback on his knee."[4]

On a sultry summer night, John R. Kelso sat in his house with his back against an open window. He was reading a large book with one red cover, and one cover missing. Two men crept to the window and "one of them," he later wrote, "placed a cocked revolver within a few inches of the back of my head." Just before the man fired, several of the boarders in Kelso's cottages arrived at the gate. The would-be assassin's accomplice "placed his hand on his comrade's arm and kept him from firing." Kelso got up to speak to the boarders and did not return to the window, so the men hiding outside in the dark left, with Kelso none the wiser. He learned of the attempt from a letter he received from a U.S. detective who had infiltrated the band. The detective said that the Texans took credit for the Wright and Christian murders and described the scene at Kelso's house, with all the details, including the book with one red cover. Kelso, who had already been threatened by the relatives of the local bushwhackers he had killed in the war, knew that he must be con-stantly on guard, with his revolver close at hand. But other than spotting a sus-picious man hiding behind his woodpile one morning, he knew of no other attempts.[5]

In 1867 the former guerrilla hunter and former congressman returned to the schoolhouse. "Many of the wealthy men in the city had encouraged me to build this Academy and had promised me their full patronage," he wrote. He had an impressive Board of Trustees. Colly B. Holland, a brigadier ge-neral during the war, was a retired merchant and the richest man in town. Henry Sheppard, formerly a colonel, was a retail dry goods merchant who was wealthy enough to retire in his mid-forties. William E. Gilmore was a lawyer soon to be elected mayor. James Vaughan was a hotel keeper and prosperous businessman. Archibald F. Ingram, a real estate agent, had been the founding editor of the *Patriot*. Kelso wrote in his late summer advertisement that he was grateful for the encouragement he had already received and urged the general public to also patronize the noble enterprise. He was confident that the Academy would soon be incorporated and, alluding to recent interest in bringing a college to Springfield, expected his school to soon develop in that direction.[6]

He made a great push for the September opening of the eight-month 1867–68 school term with an elaborate newspaper advertisement. "This Academy," he wrote, "is situated in a beautiful and healthful part of the city, at a distance from the noise and confusion of the business portion, and its grounds being ornamented with shade trees and shrubbery, render it a truly delightful place." He was not shy in drawing attention to the sacrifices he had already made and to his ambitions for success: "The Principal has invested all his means in the erection of the building and the ornamenting of the grounds, and is determined to render it the model school of the Southwest."[7]

The content of instruction was unexceptional: the textbooks were the standard ones in the "National Series" published by A. S. Barnes of New York and available at a local shop. What would set the school apart was its rigor: "The discipline of this Academy is far more rigid than is customary in most other schools of the Southwest," the ad claimed. "No student is admitted who is known to be addicted to any immoral habits, and all are required both in school and out, to deport themselves with strict propriety. During study hours all will be required to observe *strict silence*. . . . [and] all are expected to *study with all the powers of their minds*, and no disorder is permitted which would disturb them." This was not to suggest that Kelso Academy was all work and no play. There would be frequent recesses devoted to "healthful amusements," and the tone throughout the day would be pleasant and encouraging: "While the Principal is firm in enforcing discipline, he is, at the same time, cheerful and kind. He strives to win the confidence and affection of his students, and to render them happier at his school than anywhere else."[8]

The main selling point was Kelso himself. He would devote two to three hours more each day to teaching than was customary, and the advertisement for the school promised that "by his indomitable energy, [Kelso] inspires his students with much of his own zeal and arouses them to such exertions as enable them to accomplish nearly twice the amount of learning than is usually accomplished in the same time. By thus saving time he makes this the *cheapest* school in the Southwest for those who are *willing to strive*." Kelso also advertised that he was prepared to board up to two dozen high school students and would also offer a night school, principally for his own children and the boarders but $2 per month for others who wanted to attend.[9]

With a hundred students paying $5 a month in tuition, he expected to earn an income equal to what his congressional salary had been and begin paying off the considerable debts he had incurred. But when he opened his doors, fifteen students showed up—and a third of these were orphans and poor children he had agreed to teach for free. "My disappointment was overwhelming." The economy had soured—people everywhere were tightening their belts. Those wealthy families who once thought Kelso Academy was a great idea now saw a cheaper option in the rapidly expanding public school system, which by 1867–68 was teaching over five hundred students at a cost to taxpayers of $3.15 per pupil per term. Kelso felt personally betrayed: "My faith in humanity was shaken, and the future promised nothing better." With interest payments on his debts, taxes, and monthly expenses far exceeding his income, Kelso was desperate to economize at home. He fired his gardener and did the work on the grounds himself before and after school, getting up before the sun and working until dark. He was a success in the classroom, though, and as news of his talents spread, enrollment into early 1868 gradually improved.[10]

Perhaps the continuing financial pressures helped rekindle his political ambitions. The schoolteacher decided he wanted to return to Congress. In early June 1868, he sent out another circular letter to the Republican newspapers in his congressional district, announcing his candidacy. He was confident that most of the voters already knew where he stood: "You know my course during the war, and you know my course during the 39th Congress, and you know that I am not one of those political weathercocks that change with every wind that seems likely to blow them toward office or gain. You know that I was one of the first Radicals of Southwest Missouri, and that I have so steadily adhered to my principles that even my political enemies give me credit for honesty and consistency." As far as "the political issues now before the country," he reiterated his support for congressional Reconstruction, tried to clarify his position on Black equality, supported the Republican national ticket, and vowed to fight for lower taxes and the completion of the railroad through the district. His central appeal, however, was to character and the politics of political virtue. Beware of demagogues, he warned, the cliques and the tricksters who try to use the party machine for their own self-interest. "Ask yourselves who of the aspirants for Congressional honors was *first a Radical? Who suffered most for his loyalty? Who fought the most battles in defense of your homes? Who has always been the most strictly sober man? In whom, under any and all circumstances, would the people place the fullest confidence?*" He offered himself as "their plain old soldier friend . . . a true and faithful servant of the people."[11]

The story of what happened next in the 1868 election is at least three-sided, and none of the accounts is entirely trustworthy. Kelso's recollections were written a decade and a half later when he had long since grown disenchanted with electoral politics. In his autobiography it was a tale, quickly told, of betrayal, corruption, and the degradation of democracy. Not so much inaccurate as incomplete, his narrative may elide moments of his own complicity. Newspaper accounts from a highly partisan press are useful less for fact checking than for juxtaposing alternate political narratives. The Republican press attacked him as precisely the sort of politician he condemned: a selfish, disloyal, demagogic weathercock. The Democrats cast him as a bully whose incoherent policy positions showed him to be a dupe or a dissembler. Kelso's course through the 1868 campaign can be plotted only through a kind of triangulation among these three points of view.

Political alignments in 1868 were beginning to shift, both in Missouri and nationally. In the state, two issues were expected to dominate the fall campaign: the Black suffrage amendment to the state constitution, and the tighter voter registration law that Radicals had pushed through the legislature. Nationally, however, monetary policy was beginning to divide both parties. Although Republicans would eventually ally with the hard-money financiers in the East, and Democrats would warm to greenbacks and currency inflation, these had not yet formed as clear partisan divisions. Missouri, too, saw the beginnings of a "Liberal Republican" national movement that would end up destroying the Radicals' power within the Republican Party. Retiring Senator B. Gratz Brown, rising star Carl Schurz, and the new editor of the *Missouri Democrat* had begun championing amnesty for former Confederates (along with free trade and civil service reform). Change was in the wind, though few—and certainly not Kelso—could chart the course.[12]

When he sent out his letter in early June, Kelso was not sure that he would face opposition for the Republican nomination. He had been told that Pony Boyd would not run. Yet he had heard disturbing rumors that Joseph J. Gravely, the sitting congressman, might want to seek another term: "I hope this is not so, for he cannot honorably be a candidate while I am one, for in 1866 *he personally and through his friends, fairly promised that if I drew off from the Convention and threw my support to him, he would not be a candidate in 1868, if I wished to be one....* Will he now forget that magnanimity and violate his promise, or will he keep it sacred?" A letter from Gravely in the *Patriot* confirmed the congressman's intentions. Gravely wrote that he had received many flattering letters from all over the district asking him to serve again, and he would be honored to do so, pointing to his impeccably Radical voting record. A neighbor of Gravely's who claimed "personal knowledge of the facts" testified in the *Patriot* that the colonel had never made any promise to Kelso in 1866. According to one account, Kelso in his stump speeches began reading from a private letter from Gravely to prove that the Fourth District's current congressman was just another faithless politician; in the letter, Gravely pitied

Kelso for being such a fool for taking their 1866 conversation as a binding promise that Gravely would step aside for the next election.[13]

Springfield's conservative Democratic newspaper, the *Leader*, chortled that one of the two Republican candidates had to be lying. If Kelso was the honest one, though, it hardly showed him as being very "shrewd and discerning" if in 1866 he had been "gulled by such a simpleton." The *Leader* nodded in approval, however, about what Kelso's June circular had to say about race. Kelso had written that in a short letter he could not give his views on Black suffrage "at length." But he paused to explain that he believed legal and political equality did not entail equality of any other sort. The congressman who two and a half years earlier in the House of Representatives had spoken of laying aside old prejudices and who praised people of color as "sober, honest, industrious, loyal and brave," now, to a local audience, back-pedaled: "As to '*negro equality*,' . . . I regard it as something which cannot exist. The God of nature has made the African and the European races unlike and unequal and no human legislation can make them equal or alike. . . . I do not believe that the same laws, modes and customs, that are adapted to the whites, in their advanced stage of civilization, would be equally well adapted to the less advanced, less energetic and less talented negroes." Congressman Kelso had abandoned colonization as not just impractical but also as unwise and unjust; candidate Kelso now only lamented its impracticality: "[T]ime will prove that neither race can ever attain its highest degree of prosperity and happiness when a large element of the other race is present. I have long entertained these views, and so long as there appeared to be any hope of successfully colonizing the negroes, I was in favor of doing so." Still, if colonizationists could devise a workable plan, he wrote, "I will give *ten percent of my income for the rest of my life to aid them in their enterprise.*"[14]

The *Leader* pronounced all of Kelso's remarks on Black inequality as "sound Democratic doctrine." Moreover, Kelso's vagueness on Black suffrage in the June circular allowed the paper to infer that he might only support a limited Black franchise (that is, with a literacy test), and only in the South (and not in Missouri or the North). Kelso's announcement also avoided mention of President Johnson or impeachment and contained not a single harsh word about the "defeated rebels." Opponents who had suspected Kelso of trying to cozy up to the conservatives now had some evidence.[15]

The *Patriot* was neutral about Kelso's candidacy, but, like other Republican newspapers in the district, it was enthusiastic about Gravely's. By the late July district convention the sitting congressman had built a commanding lead among pledged delegates, with 52 of 71. The convention opened in the

Springfield courthouse at 10:00 on Monday morning, July 27, with an address by Boyd. The judge and former congressman told the assembled delegates, dignitaries, and crowd of spectators that the central issues in the fall campaign would and should be Reconstruction and Missouri's suffrage amendment; other issues were merely distractions that the Democrats were trying to drag in. Then, before the convention could begin voting on the nominees, L. M. Andrews of Lawrence County rose and moved that they should first approve the resolutions of the national and state Republican Party platforms. After a long debate, the delegates agreed to Andrews's motion, a procedural tussle that to many must have seemed pointless—until it wasn't. After the resolutions were unanimously adopted, the convention turned to nominating and voting for their congressional candidates. One delegate rose to formally nominate Gravely; another did the same for Kelso. But before voting could begin, delegate Andrews rose again and objected to Gravely's nomination. In June, Andrews said, Gravely had voted for an unsuccessful bill in Congress that would have taxed the interest payments on government bonds. But such a vote contradicted the Republican platform that the convention had just endorsed. Gravely's position, Andrews argued, was disqualifying. Gravely's friends leapt to their feet and argued for their candidate "with much earnestness" until the meeting recessed for lunch at 1:30.[16]

During the lunch break, the county politicians must have been huddling and scheming. A trap had been set for Gravely, and he had been caught. Clearly, a cabal was at work—but what was its next move? Surely not to clear a path for John R. Kelso, whatever Kelso himself might have been thinking over the lunch recess. Then, when the convention reconvened, came what the *Leader* described as "the sensation of the day." A delegate from Webster took the floor and said that his county delegation (with its five votes) could no longer support Gravely, and therefore nominated a new candidate: Pony Boyd. Laclede County, whose delegates had been instructed to vote for Gravely, seconded the Boyd nomination. The Gravely men howled at the betrayal. One of Gravely's defenders said that the Lawrence County delegates who had first challenged the congressman's nomination "were mean enough to destroy their marriage certificates and brand their children bastards if they could make anything by it."[17]

But another Gravely supporter, J. L. Tracey, knew who was really behind the whole scheme. It was clear, Tracey charged, that "the opposition to Mr. Gravely's nomination was a concocted and well understood plan on the part of the Greene county delegation." Congressman Joseph W. McClurg, Tracey reminded the assembly, had voted exactly the same way on the tax bill, and he was Missouri's Republican candidate for governor! If McClurg was not disqualified, why was Gravely? The Greene County delegation (11 votes) professed innocence and claimed that they had supported Gravely until they had heard about his bond vote that morning. But, the Greene spokesman said, it was important that the Fourth District's candidate support the party platform in all its particulars. The argument, according to the account published in the *Patriot*, "continued at great length and became quite stormy."[18]

Finally the delegates took an informal ballot. Dallas County, where Kelso lived before the war, and which had a delegation that included his old friend Milton Burch, gave its five votes to Kelso. So did Christian County. But the other nineteen counties split between Gravely (29 votes) and Boyd (32 votes, four short of the necessary majority). On the next ballot, four counties swung to Boyd, giving Pony 48, Gravely 18, and Kelso 5. Missouri's Fourth District had its Republican congressional nominee for the fall 1868 election.[19]

In the aftermath, Gravely, Kelso, and the Democratic press all agreed: the coup was engineered by a courthouse cabal of wealthy investors at Springfield. Boyd arguing that financial questions were mere distractions, along with the fact that Gravely was initially challenged and Boyd nominated by delegates not from Greene County, were but feints disguising the real purpose. That purpose was not to use the bond issue to elect Boyd; it was to elect Boyd to secure the right vote on the bond issue. "Everybody knows," the Springfield *Leader* wrote, that Boyd "is owned by a clique of bondholders in this city"; they will have a "mortgage" on him and he will champion their interests. Gravely denounced the new "Bondholders' Party" christened at Springfield and refused to endorse its candidate. Kelso later described a bondholder "conspiracy" behind the election of his old nemesis, "the '*Great Steal and Let Steal*' candidate," Pony Boyd.[20]

The bonds had become a topic of national debate. The federal government had issued bonds paying 6 percent annual interest to finance the war. Of the $2.5 billion the government owed in 1868, $1.6 billion was in (or convertible to) bonds called "5/20's" because they were callable by the government in not less than five years and payable in twenty. Half a billion dollars' worth were issued in 1862 and had become redeemable in 1867. Two main questions concerning these bonds agitated the campaign of 1868. First, did they have to be paid in gold, or could they be paid in paper currency (greenbacks)? Custom said gold, but the authorizing legislation did not specify. Because in 1868 a dollar in gold equaled $1.40 in greenbacks, this decision could make a difference worth many millions of dollars. The second question was, could the interest payments be taxed? Gravely and McClurg had voted for a bill that would tax them at 10 percent. Bondholders argued that paying in greenbacks or taxing interest amounted to outright theft. Those who supported greenbacks and/or taxes pointed out that creditors, who had bought the bonds at far below face value in the first place, were already making huge profits; that all other sorts of property (that is, the kind owned by poorer folks) was taxed; and that all sorts of other loans (that is, those paid to ordinary creditors rather than wealthy investors) were paid in greenbacks. The bondholders' demand for tax-free payments in gold, when neither condition was specified in the legislation, amounted to, as Kelso argued, robbery of the public coffers on a grand scale.[21]

The division over the bonds, however, did not break down along neat partisan lines. The greenback plan had made its way into the Democratic Party platform, along with support for taxing interest payments. But Eastern capitalists in the party opposed it, as did the Democratic nominees for president and vice president, New York's Horatio Seymour and Missouri's Frank Blair. Republicans were divided over the issue, with many party leaders such as Thaddeus Stevens and Benjamin Butler supporting greenbacks and/ or taxation. The national Republican Party platform had vague language supporting the letter and spirit of the law, which could accommodate both positions. Missouri's Republican platform did not mention greenbacks or taxation but it condemned "the evasion of our national obligations, as proposed by the Democratic convention, as ruinous to the credit and material interests of the country." Missouri's Fourth District Convention's resolution was more specific. After endorsing the national and state platforms (right before the convention dumped Gravely), it had "further affirm[ed] as the cardinal and common sentiment of this convention, that the payment of the national bonds, both principal and interest, should, and must be, made according to the understanding of the parties at the time of purchase . . . and that the interest on the same should . . . be paid without reduction or taxation."[22]

Gravely did not go away quietly. He did not declare himself an independent candidate, but through August and into early September, he continued touring the district and making speeches defending himself. He argued that his position on the bonds was in line with the national and state platforms as well as the views of many eminent Republicans, if not "the clique that runs [the party] in Southwest Missouri." He said that he "could not see the justice of taxing the poor man for the support of the Government and let the rich man go free from all taxation." He declared that he would never vote for a man like Boyd who would "rob the poor man to increase the wealth of the bondholder."[23]

The Republican newspapers in the Fourth District turned on Gravely with a vengeance—Kelso later charged that the bondholders had bought off all but the one in Gravely's home county. The *Neosho Tribune* had expected Gravely to do what he had promised to do: cordially acquiesce to the judgment of the nominating convention and cheerfully support the party nominee, whoever it was. What he had done instead was "strange and mystifying to his best friends." The *Bolivar Free Press* said Gravely's actions were making people doubt his character. A letter from Ozark in the *Patriot* accused him of colluding with district Democrats. Calling him a "disorganizer," the writer asked, "Why don't he go home and respect the will of the people?" Newton County Radicals were "astonished and mortified" at Gravely's conduct: "But let him go, and good riddance. He must be taught, as many other inordinately ambitious political aspirants have been and must be—that MAN is nothing to the Radical party, but principle is the all." The *Patriot* at once denounced Gravely and, as it backed away from Black suffrage, elevated the bond issue to preeminence. Gravely's selfishness, the editor wrote, betrayed a heart "full of dissention and opposition to one of the greatest and most clearly defined principles of the party."[24]

In mid-September, the campaign shifted again: Gravely went quiet, and Kelso announced himself as an independent candidate for Congress. Although Gravely reportedly endorsed Kelso, there is no evidence of another agreement between the two. Gravely apparently decided to stand down to preserve what was left of his tattered reputation (and he did recover, becoming lieutenant governor in 1870). Kelso thought he could repeat the campaign of 1864 and again beat Boyd in a three-way race with a Democrat.[25]

The Republican newspapers quickly turned their artillery on Kelso. The *Neosho Tribune* wrote that if "Kelso possessed the discernment of ordinary men, he would know that he is not wanted by the people of this District as a Congressman." The *Patriot* explained why he was running: "Heart-broken because the Radical party failed to appreciate his wonderful abilities, he means to be revenged on the party by defeating the nominee." Or perhaps he was only driven by "a bitter personal hostility" toward Boyd. Or maybe it was just blind ambition: Kelso "don't like school teaching no how," the paper wrote; "*Kelso* means to go to Congress—he does—platform or no platform—principles or no principles—any way to get there." The Springfield paper also reported that Kelso was consorting with Copperheads. The Mt. Vernon *Fountain* condemned his lust for "place and power," the Lebanon *Chronicle* denounced him as "a sore head bolter," and the *Bolivar Free Press* dismissed him as "a political demagogue of the lowest and most degrading character."[26]

The conservative Democratic *Leader*, at first, held its fire. At the announcement of Kelso's revived candidacy in mid-September, the editor wrote that Kelso's position seemed "more favorable to the interests of the people than Col. Boyd's," but reserved judgment until he got more details. With the bonds and Black suffrage, the Democrats had their two main issues of the campaign: class and race. The Republicans, the *Leader* argued, wanted to widen the gap between wealthy aristocrats and everyone else; they "have not one sentiment of sympathy for the poor laboring man." The lyrics to "The Bondholder" made the point:

> *Oh, the Bondholder rests in a cushioned chair*
> *   As he sits at his table to dine.*
> *While before him is spread out the daintiest fare,*
> *   And the choicest of foreign wine.*
> *Then he thinks of the wealth he has made by the war*
> *   For his heart has grown selfish and cold;*
> *And he laughs, and he quaffs, and smokes a cigar,*
> *   As he counts up his interest in gold.*
> *Chorus—Oh, a rollicking fellow is he, is he,*
> *   And his life passes smoothly away,*
> *And what careth he for you, or me,*
> *   When he has no taxes to pay?*

At the same time, Republicans, Democrats charged, wanted to erase the distinction between Black and White. They would "force nigger children into the free schools with your children," would "have you consort with niggers and . . . think you no better than a nigger," and thought "a respectable young negro boy as good a husband as a poor white girl in the country is entitled to." A "New Radical Campaign Song" that the *Leader* printed in mid-October used the word "nigger" thirty-one times in sixteen lines. Would Kelso, who stumped as a laboring man against the bondholders and spoke about Black inequality in his June circular, appeal to Democratic voters?[27]

Kelso later said that Republicans who had been angered by the bondholders' coup at the district convention had urged him to run as an independent. Democratic leaders in his district, too, he claimed, who were "opposed to the monstrous conspiracy" of bondholders nationwide, "also urged me to run, promising to support me as they had supported me before." The leading Democrat in southwest Missouri was John S. Phelps, a nine-term antebellum congressman who was running for governor. Phelps's law partner,

Charles B. McAfee, was the Democrats' candidate for Congress in the Fourth District. Kelso knew both men well, having hired the firm of Phelps and McAfee for his election case in 1865. It is hard to fathom why Kelso thought Democrats would favor him over their own candidate, McAfee, who showed he was taking the campaign seriously by stumping the district and challenging Boyd to a debate. Kelso must have still been entranced by his victory in 1864. "I knew that their support would elect me, and, since they had kept their promise with me before, I concluded again to trust them although I had now become very suspicious of the promises of professional politicians."[28]

Kelso sent around another circular, but the newspapers did not print it: The *Patriot* extracted only a few quotations to criticize, and the *Leader* excerpted only his diatribe against Boyd. He found himself shut out of the press. He offered to pay advertising rates to publish his articles, but the district's newspapers refused—they had been paid more to refuse, he charged. He began a speaking tour of the district in his old hometown of Buffalo and planned to conclude it in Springfield on October 31, a few days before the election. In the campaign's last eighteen days, he traveled to thirteen towns, spending $300 and wearing out a good horse. But few heard his speeches. The press mocked the poor attendance he drew, but Kelso knew the cause: "the conspirators had my posters pulled down as soon as they were put up; and in many instances had a man precede me to my appointments and disperse the meetings, just before my arrival, stating that he did so by my order,—that I was sick and would not be there."[29]

If the Democratic *Leader* had reserved judgment about Kelso in September, in October it flatly denied that it supported him in any way. Kelso, the paper determined, despite some wobbling on policy was still "a Radical of the darkest dye." The choice of "Pony Boyd or Shot Gun Kelso" was "a dreadful alternative." Boyd had no "political integrity," and Kelso had a soul "stained with the blood of his victims." During the war, Boyd had wanted to murder prisoners, and Kelso had "assassinat[ed] the innocent and the guilty alike!" Boyd despite his bluster was actually a coward, and Kelso was still a brute. At a Springfield political rally and bonfire that turned into a brawl, the paper reported, Kelso was heard to say that he "regretted he hadn't his shot-gun with him." How could any honest, patriotic Christian vote for either man? And no matter what Kelso said about bonds and Blacks, he endorsed Grant and the Republican platform and therefore supported aristocracy and miscegenation.[30]

The version of candidate Kelso that appeared in the Republican press was neither the selfless crusader against the bondholder conspiracy nor the

Republican unsuccessfully pandering to the conservative Democrats by filing down some of his rough Radical edges. Weeks before the district convention in July, the papers argued, Kelso, enraged at Gravely for allegedly breaking the 1866 agreement, had tried to destroy the sitting congressman's reputation. First he spread the scurrilous rumor that in 1861, before siding with the Union, Gravely had attempted to raise a rebel militia. Then Kelso came across an article in the Mt. Vernon *Fountain* that criticized Gravely's vote on the bond tax. At the Christian County nominating convention in Ozark, Kelso used this vote to argue that Gravely was in effect repudiating the national debt and ought to be disqualified from being re-nominated. Kelso, therefore, the ringleader of the anti-Gravely faction, was one of the first to push the very issue that blew up at the district convention. Before that July 27 convention, Kelso, the papers said, favored payment to bondholders in gold and was against taxing the interest. At the convention, he fully supported the district platform and the move against Gravely in the morning session. Only after the delegates ignored him in the afternoon and elected Boyd did he denounce the convention as a fraud. Only after that vote, and perhaps not until Gravely himself declined to run as an independent candidate, did Kelso switch sides on the bond questions. Thus the Fourth District's "old soldier friend" revealed himself to be "a political demagogue, of the lowest and most degrading character."[31]

How much of this is true? Or, if accurate in broad strokes, what portion emerged from Kelso's Machiavellian calculation and what was the result of him plunging ahead with the current of events, in the dark about much of what was going on? The newspaper's details of his attack on Gravely's bond tax vote have a ring of authenticity. Furthermore, when Kelso wrote a response to the *Patriot*, he did not deny—or at least the papers did not print his denial—of his criticism of Gravely. Considering, though, the vehemence of his later denunciations of the bondholders' greed for gold, it seems hard to imagine that before the end of July Kelso himself was a "gold man," as the Republican press alleged. Perhaps he separated the issues of greenback payment and interest taxes. He might have supported greenbacks in early summer but opposed taxation, and, trying to promote himself as a low-tax candidate generally, saw an opportunity to score points against Gravely. It is hard to know—he did not mention the bond issue at all in his June circular. Or he might have been confused about the financial legislation and how the platform language was being interpreted—the *Patriot* claims that he offered this ("laughable") explanation for his flip-flop. It is possible that he had not paid much attention to the bond issue in June, tried to use it as a partisan weapon before fully understanding it in July, and then settled—for principled as well as self-serving reasons—on his full-throated anti-bondholder position in August. However Kelso got to Election Day, his horse was not the only thing that had broken down by the end of the campaign.[32]

Boyd won easily in early November with 58 percent of the vote—not as commanding a win in the district as the top of the Republican ticket, Grant for president (72 percent) or McClurg for governor (69 percent), but Boyd only lost one county. That one county went to Kelso: Cedar, Gravely's county, which had had the only district newspaper not pitched against Kelso. Still, Kelso ran a distant third overall, with only about 9 percent of the vote. In his former home county of Dallas, he received only 37 votes, or under 4 percent. In Greene, his new home county, he did just as badly, with only 74 of the 1,959 votes cast.[33]

Kelso blamed his enemies. The Democrats betrayed him, the bondholders bought off the newspapers, and Boyd's men sabotaged his speaking tour. The final stroke, as the election neared, was the forged letter his opponents circulated to the voting precincts. Purportedly from Kelso himself, it announced that he had withdrawn and was endorsing Boyd. But the voters, too, Kelso later wrote, shared some of the responsibility. They had been too easily duped, too easily nudged from the path of political virtue: "the people had given the preference to a well-known drunkard and notoriously corrupt man. . . . The people deserved to be robbed and effectively they have been robbed." His own "standing in the Republican party" had been crushed by "the bondholders and other great monopolies" that had taken over that party. "I was thoroughly disgusted as well I might have been."[34]

By the next congressional election cycle, Kelso was a figure on the fringes. He was mentioned in the press a few times in 1870 along with Gravely and a couple others who had bucked party discipline and "bolted" in 1868. In 1870, however, Missouri Republicans had bigger problems. With the ratification of the Fifteenth Amendment giving Black men the vote, discussion in the state turned to the re-enfranchisement of former rebels. "Liberal" Republicans, a group led by Senator Carl Schurz, argued for quick re-enfranchisement and caused a schism at the state convention. Nationally, Liberal Republicanism (initially focusing on free trade and civil service reform) would emerge as a powerful movement reshaping Republican (and therefore American) politics. In Missouri, the Liberals briefly prevailed due to a short-lived coalition with a resurgent Democratic Party, and most Radical leaders fell, as Kelso already had, into political obscurity. With former rebels voting, the Liberal movement collapsed after 1872 and Democrats would rule Missouri for the next three decades. By 1875, a former Confederate general was representing Missouri in the U.S. Senate and former Confederate President Jefferson Davis toured the state to appreciative crowds. By November 1877, Springfield's conservative Democratic newspaper, the *Leader*, was remembering Kelso, a half-dozen years after he had left town, not as a congressman but as a fanatical killer. Recalling the year 1865–66, the paper pitied the "[p]oor, broken down, disheartened and impoverished Rebels returning to their homes" only to be "shot down like dogs by such men as Kelso and his murderous band of Loyal Leaguers." The political climate that helped mythologize rebel bushwhackers as Lost Cause heroes recast Kelso as a fanatical villain.[35]

ON JANUARY 5, 1870, the following notice appeared in Springfield's newspapers: "All who are in favor of equal rights, religiously and politically; equal wages for the same labor performed without regard to sex, will meet at Mr. Kelso's school house," next Saturday afternoon at 2:00. Springfield's churches and temperance societies, the notice went on to lament, had failed to close the town's saloons and gambling houses, and therefore its "fathers, husbands, and sons are on the 'broad road to ruin.' " Give women the ballot, the anonymous writer agued, and the saloons would become houses of prayer and virtue. "Men and women come out! If you have no personal interest in the reformative work which is spreading so rapidly in Europe and America, come from curiosity on next Saturday to Kelso's school house."[36]

The "high cockalorum," as a critic called her, behind this fusion of women's suffrage, temperance, and moral reform was Mary Whitney Phelps, wife of prominent Democratic politician John S. Phelps. Kelso was one of her most vocal supporters. She had become well known for her humanitarian efforts during and after the war. In 1861, Mary Phelps had safeguarded the body of the fallen martyr of the Battle of Wilson's Creek, General Nathaniel Lyon. She nursed the wounded at the Battle of Pea Ridge in 1862 and then turned her home into a hospital. In the fall of 1864, her home became an orphanage. When the number of indigent children outgrew the large house, she appealed for funds, first in St. Louis newspapers and then with a petition to Congress. (She also held an "Orphan's Fair" in town, and Susie Kelso lent a hand.) Receiving a grant of $20,000, she built a Gothic-style twenty-two room building and cared for an estimated two to three hundred children by the end of the decade. The size of the grant caused some resentment in town. In defending herself against detractors in 1868, she noted that "Mr. Kelso could speak from his own knowledge [about the orphanage], for he saw me struggling day and night to feed and clothe hundreds who were starving and without shelter." She had labored nearly alone, with "the assistance of a few generous souls (Mr. Kelso one of them)." When the population of orphans declined, she created Phelps Institute, a school for girls and young women, which in 1870 had thirteen students and was being advertised in the Springfield newspapers alongside the notice for the women's rights meeting.[37]

Reconstruction politics focused what had been a more variegated antebellum women's rights movement upon the question of women's suffrage. Debate over Black suffrage and the 14th and 15th amendments spurred discussion about the vote for women. In Missouri, Senator John B. Henderson took a petition for women voting to the U.S. Senate in 1866 (though he would vote against it), and in 1867 Senator B. Gratz Brown gave a speech on the Senate floor in favor of the idea (though he later reversed himself). Shortly after Brown's speech, a group of St. Louis women organized the Missouri Women's Suffrage Association. In early February, 1869, a delegation of women including Mary Phelps went to Jefferson City to petition state legislators. Phelps was one of two women to deliver formal addresses in the Hall of Delegates. At a National Woman Suffrage Convention the following October in St. Louis, Phelps was named, along with Susan B. Anthony (the dominant figure at the convention), as one of seven vice presidents of the new National Woman Suffrage Association. The gathering at Kelso's schoolhouse in January was an attempt to bring the movement to Springfield.[38]

The coverage in the local press was skeptical and either condescending or sarcastic. Someone writing as "Wife" in the *Leader* reported that only nineteen people—twelve women and seven men, including Kelso—attended the first meeting on January 8. There was a lot of informal talk, the *Patriot* reported, "that woman was very badly treated under the laws of the country, and that no power less than the ballot in their own hands will secure them justice." When one woman wondered how many women would actually run for office if allowed to do so, Kelso answered quickly, according to the account: "He said he believed that very few would ever hold office, as he knew by experience that after one good beating they would never care to run again." The main business was to appoint Mary Phelps to write up a constitution for the new organization.[39]

The second meeting the following Saturday afternoon, held at the courthouse, drew a much larger crowd, most being curious spectators rather than participants. Kelso called the meeting to order, made a short speech explaining its purpose, and called on Mrs. Phelps to present the constitution she had drafted. She handed the pages to Kelso, who began to read the proposed articles aloud, but a gentleman—J. W. D. L. F. ("Alphabet") Mack—rose and moved that Phelps read it herself, and, after borrowing a pair of spectacles from Mack, she did so. It was then decided that anyone who signed the constitution would be considered a member of the society. Kelso, perhaps imagining himself as John Hancock signing the Declaration of Independence, told Phelps "to head the list with his name, and 'write it in just as large letters as you please.'" Most who were present hesitated to sign. A man identified as "R. C." stood up and complained, "with a very long lackadaisical face," that his wife was forcing him to help with the housework, including making mince pies all that morning. He got no sympathy from Mrs. Phelps: "Just right—just what you ought to do," she retorted, and the "hen-pecked" R. C. suddenly looked as though he wanted to slink home.[40]

The next—and last reported—meeting of the Springfield women's suffrage society opened with Mrs. Phelps reading from a prepared text, although the *Leader*'s reporter could not hear her distinctly. Then Kelso rose and gave "a somewhat disconnected speech, but very good for an impromptu one." He suggested that a man should take his whole family with him to the polls, and they should all vote together. After Kelso sat down, a Mrs. Stephens took the floor. The reporter smirked: "What a splendid picture of woman in search of her rights she made, with her shawl slipped from her shoulders and lying at her feet, her sunbonnet pushed back, and her arms akimbo, she stood eying the enemy (man)." She argued that there should be no taxation without representation. Then Mrs. Eversoll stood up. She charged that half the men in town did believe that women should have equal rights, including the vote, "but had not the moral courage to say so in public; and the other half were so ignorant they knew nothing about it whatever." Animated discussion continued, but the reporter left and dismissed it all: such talk trampled on laws human and divine that cast woman as man's companion, not his competitor, and recognized that the fairer sex was suited to the home and not to "public life."[41]

Women's suffrage did not seem to take hold in Springfield. Nationally, the movement continued, though it was hurt by a schism that produced two organizations: the National Woman's Suffrage Association, led by Susan B. Anthony and Elizabeth Cady Stanton, which objected to Black men getting the vote ahead of White women and used racist language to appeal to conservatives, and the American Woman Suffrage Association, led by Lucy Stone, which supported the Reconstruction Amendments and tried to keep advocates of racial and gender equality working together. This split affected Missouri's state suffrage association, too, in 1871. A suffrage lecturer, Lydia

Fuller, visited Springfield in 1874 and reported "little general interest" in the cause there. She found no formal organization, but met with "a small circle of earnest men and women" around Mary Phelps and Mrs. Dr. Augusta Smith, a physician, "who believe in the gospel of emancipated womanhood." Phelps lived "almost alone" with a Black servant and a single grown orphan in the large building that had been the orphanage. Phelps, Smith, and Fuller tried again to formally organize a society, and Phelps promised to again "take the field" and continue "this last and crowning crusade against slavery."[42]

Kelso never wavered in his commitment to women's suffrage. In a speech delivered in the mid-1880s, he said that he had long taken the Declaration's proclamation that "all men are created equal" in "a generic sense": "[the] *female man* as well as the male man is entitled to all the rights of *man* in general. And this includes voting, holding office, and all other political rights and privileges. Indeed, I hold that, outside of the marriage relation, sex should be practically unknown." For years he had seen debauched men, reeking of whiskey and tobacco, being dragged up to the polls "by some petty hot-house politician, in the interest of the pope or of some other foreign potentate unfriendly to our best interests; or . . . of some monstrous monopolistic despotism of our own country." Yet, outrageously, intelligent and virtuous women, like his own mother, sister, wife, or daughters, could not cast a ballot. As a "true man," he considered "every woman . . . my mother, my wife, my sister, my daughter. If she stumbles and falls I will do nothing to keep her down."[43]

So Kelso thought that "outside of the marriage relation" the rights of men and women were identical and distinctions based on gender ought to be "practically unknown." What about inside the marriage relation? According to Return I. Holcombe, the county historian writing a dozen years after Kelso left Springfield, Kelso had "forced his wife and daughter to adopt the Bloomer costume"—pants under a short skirt. The claim prompts two questions: Did Susie and Florella actually wear Bloomers in Springfield? If so, did John R. "force" them to adopt this radical attire? Women's rights advocates promoted Bloomers beginning in 1851, but the dress reform had caused such an uproar, distracting from more substantive issues, that Anthony, Stanton, and Amelia Bloomer herself abandoned it by the late 1850s. Health advocates continued to push for more sensible women's clothing, and there was some revival of interest in Bloomers by the early 1870s. But the sight of a woman wearing the Bloomer costume during the St. Louis suffrage convention in 1869 provoked the woman's arrest for indecency (she was showing some ankle). The convention condemned the arrest but refused to let another female pants advocate make her case. In Southwest Missouri, the Bloomer outfit seems to have been an even rarer sight. When two young "belles" donned pants for a hunting excursion in Marshfield in 1869, it made the local newspaper, and the item was reprinted by both papers in Springfield.[44]

Though unlikely, perhaps Susie and Florella Kelso did start wearing the Bloomer costume. But did the man of the house "force" them? Holcombe, the county historian (who never knew Kelso personally), thought so: it fit the writer's portrait of a man made "mad" from much learning, a "crank" with a head filled with "modern dogmas," a "desperate" and "fanatical" fellow with many "whims and failings." Maybe Susie had chosen to wear the pants herself. Through the long years of war and when John was away at Congress, after all, she had run the household. She may have come on her own to a version of women's rights that he found less congenial. Looking back at this period in his autobiography, he bitterly complained that Susie "had fallen in with a little bevy of grass-widows who gave her to understand that all men were brutes and that I was no exception to the general rule."[45]

"Grass-widows" were women who had informally separated from their husbands. Mary Phelps could have been considered a grass-widow: she and her husband John spent a lot of time living apart and independently before the war, and were estranged after it; when he was elected governor in 1877, she stayed in Springfield. Perhaps Kelso's relationship with Mary Phelps deteriorated dramatically over the course of 1870–71, and he came to imagine her as one of the man-haters whispering into Susie's ear. Of the women in Susie's "little bevy," Kelso mentioned only one by name: "a Mrs. Chandler"— Sarah Chandler, who was thirty-seven in the summer of 1870 and the mother of five children between the ages of sixteen years and eleven months. According to the census taker in 1870, at least, she still shared a home with her second husband, Daniel, sixty-one, a tenement landlord. Kelso thought that she "possessed all the truly mischievous elements that can enter into the composition of a she-devil."[46]

Men behaved like brutes, according to Susie and her bevy, in part through the sexual demands they made upon their wives. But for John, sex was the foundation of the marital relation. "I hold that marriage consists essentially in a sex union founded upon pure sex love," he argued in a lecture on "Marriage," written and delivered later in the 1870s. True marriage was "that silent union, harmonious and even happy, into which, by a law of nature, a man and a woman of congenial natures are irresistibly drawn … and in which they mutually supply to each other all the demands of sex." He agreed with the women's rights advocates that the modern institution of marriage still betrayed its ancient origin in a kind of slavery. It was perpetuated as "a purely commercial institution founded upon the false, the unjust, the degrading idea that women were mere property, and that, consequently, they had no right at all to say when their own bodies should be used, how they should be used, or by whom they should be used." Free people—men and women alike—owned their own bodies and ought to have a legal right to give and receive sexual pleasure as they so choose. Seeking to gratify a natural "sexual appetite" and responding to a natural "magnetic" attraction to a particular person, a man and a woman formed a unique bond through the sexual act: "In this union,—this only marriage, every sexual element in the one of the parties finds and by a natural law of affinity, combines with its corresponding sexual element in the other party. All the sexual demands of the one, therefore, are fully satisfied in the satisfying of the corresponding sexual demands of the other."[47]

He denied, however, that his criticism of the false, ceremonial marriage authorized by the state made him a promoter of "free-love," as that term was so frequently misunderstood and misused. He was neither severing sex from love nor licensing promiscuity. In having sex merely to satisfy your sexual appetite, he argued, you turn your partner from a person into a thing, and her body becomes little more than a masturbation aid: "Are not the bodies of women" in many (false) marriages, he asked, "mere passive *machines* upon which their so-called husbands, in a very unsatisfying manner, manage to commit a species of self-abuse?" Are women who consent to sex without love by marrying for money any better than prostitutes? The "higher demands of sex" were met only in love, a union of hearts and minds as well as bodies. Such an intimate reciprocity could only occur with one's magnetic match, one's true love: "Some of you will doubtless charge me . . . with favoring the general prevalence of sexual promiscuity. And yet no charge was ever more false," he insisted. "I hold marriage to be the highest and holiest of all human relationships, and, so far from favoring sexual promiscuity, I earnestly advocate the strictest fidelity—the most absolute exclusiveness, in act and in thought, in time and in eternity, to the one true conjugal companion to whom we have been united by the God of nature, with the law of love."[48]

John and Susie's marriage, however, fell considerably short of this ideal. And one of their problems was sex. It was a "fruitful source of unhappiness" between them, he wrote in a passage of his autobiography that he—or someone else?—subsequently tried to blacken out with a pencil. He described a "vast difference of our views, or rather, of our feelings, in regard to those nameless caresses which are usually expected to take place between a husband and his wife. Like any other well-sexed man of good health and loving disposition,

I desired these caresses quite often, and loving her as I did,—loving the very dust she trod upon, I could not sleep by her side and be denied of these caresses." What did she expect? "I was not a *eunuch*, an *anchorite*, or an *angel*. I was a *man*, and I held then, as I hold now, that, as in the case of food and drink, nature through an unperverted appetite guides us correctly in regard to this matter." His sexual desire, he thought, was an essential dimension of his manhood. It was natural (a basic appetite), moral (grounded in love), and healthy: "To me, while living thus, three times a week were not intemperate. Indeed, that many were physiologically needful. The unalloyed excitement on my part attendant upon a greater degree of abstemiousness than this deprived me of sleep and did my health real harm." Susie, though, felt otherwise. "My wife, on the contrary, seeming to feel a sexual antipathy, in regard to myself at least, instead of sexual desire, rarely ever received my embraces lovingly or even cheerfully." Kelso continued writing on this topic, but the next page was torn out of the notebook.[49]

John, who thought a woman's natural desire to procreate was at least as powerful as her sexual appetite, could not fully grasp the extent to which pregnancy and childbirth had taken a physical and emotional toll upon Susie—who, after all, had been only fifteen when he married her. The birth of their daughter Iantha in 1860 had been followed by Ianthus in 1861, who died the next year. Freddie came in 1865 and Johnny, a very difficult birth, in 1867. Susie lost one baby prematurely in 1868 and another in 1870. She had continuous ailments: she traveled to New York in the late 1860s to stay at a "water cure establishment" and in Springfield kept a local physician on retainer. After Johnny's birth in 1867, she "finally became so averse to bearing children," John later wrote, "that when she found herself pregnant, she would become furious and would abuse me as the vilest of monsters for having so 'outraged' her as to put her in that condition." John finally "proposed that we live entirely apart sexually, occupying separate rooms and separate beds. To this she objected on account of the gossip that it would create. She wanted me to lie by her side like a *stick* of *wood*, and I, not being a *stick* of *wood*, could not do this."[50]

As the trust between them evaporated, John became suspicious of Susie's miscarriages. In both cases, she had "tried to get her physician to give her relief; and, this being refused, she finally gave an untimely birth to her child anyway; when, in my opinion, she could have borne it to the full time and let it live. In her unreasonable tantrums of rage against me, she would do whatever would hurt me most deeply, and each of these abortions followed one of these tantrums."[51]

Sex was a problem—but so was money. In the fall of 1867, when Kelso's Academy was not even bringing in $50 per month, let alone the $500 he had hoped for, Susie refused to economize. "Not only must we keep up our expensive style of living, but she must have a physician employed by the year at a regular salary, equal to the entire profits of my school for her especial benefit." She still insisted on going to her water-cure resort in New York. "She would never permit me to explain the condition of our affairs. . . . that we must retrench or come to poverty," he complained. "To speak of economy was simply to put her into a passion and to get myself abused for a miser, an unfeeling wretch, etc. Caring little for her home, she spent most of her time with these enemies to domestic happiness," the grass widows and she-devils.[52]

By the fall of 1868, after his failed political campaign, Kelso realized that he could not risk opening another session of his private school, so he made an arrangement with the local school board to teach a public school in his Academy building. Each month he would get $100 for rent, $40 to teach, and another $40 for his assistant, Florella. That seemed a good deal compared to the paltry income he had made the previous year. He spent $100 on firewood and school supplies. But after the term was over, every time he approached the board for his reimbursement, rent, and pay, the trustees assured him that all his money, in a lump sum, would be forthcoming. Yet he never received it. "When I tried to collect my money by law," he later wrote, "these good Christians laughed at me, they knowing very well that there was a flaw in the matter through which they could escape and never pay me at all. Four other teachers, in the same district, lost a year each. *And of such is the kingdom of heaven.*"[53]

In early January, 1869, Kelso opened a small "Select School" in one of his cottages. Students, his advertisement read, needed to "be willing to perform nearly twice as much hard study as is usually required. Thoroughness will be required in every thing taught, and at the same time, the teacher, devoting his entire attention to a few, will crowd them forward in their studies. . . . Those who can excel shall have a chance to do so.—*Idlers are not wanted.*" The star pupil in the Select School was his own eldest son. "Florellus was the best educated boy of his age, I suppose, in America," the proud father later wrote. "He rarely ever misspelled a word. He was not only a good reader but a fine elocutionist. In penmanship, he was so skillful that, when only twelve years of age, he was offered a place in the city public schools as a teacher of penmanship. He was the best geographer I ever knew. He was thorough in English Grammar, and was reading and speaking German very well. He was also a fair Latin reader and was thorough in Natural Philosophy. He was well posted, too, in ancient and modern history. . . . He was also good in Geometry." His talents were physical as well as intellectual: "He was the best gymnast in the city and could take his playmates through the manual of arms and many forms of military drill." In that classroom, Florellus seemed to be stepping from childhood to manhood right before John's eyes. "I shall never forget with what pride I looked upon Florellus' splendid form and magnificent forehead as he sat among my pupils. Superiority was marked in his every lineament. He seemed a picture of perfection." The father was proud of Iantha and Florella, too: "I was truly blessed in my children," he wrote; they were all "indomitable workers." All the twenty or so "select" students during that term did well: "Though the school was not a profitable one, it was a very pleasant one."[54]

Times were hard all around by the summer of 1869. Several of his renters and boarders fell months behind in their payments and then skipped town. Kelso himself was drowning in debt and realized that he would have to sell some of his property. "My beautiful academy upon which I had built such high hopes must go." The town's Catholics bought the building for $3,900 (a loss to Kelso of $1,100), and turned it into Springfield's first Catholic church, the Church of the Immaculate Conception. He also sold some of his books, including his volumes of the *Congressional Globe*, which contained the record of all the speeches and votes of his term in Congress. A lawyer took the collection off his hands, promising $170, but never paying. Then his creditors sued him and took possession of much of the rest of his city property. He wound up selling his house to the Catholics, who turned it into a convent for a half-dozen Sisters of Mercy. He then put his last thousand dollars down on "a beautiful little farm about three and a half miles southeast of the city" and took out a mortgage for the remaining $4,500. Soon he was struggling to make the interest payments.[55]

Financial strain led to the further deterioration of the Kelsos' marriage. "When my wife could no longer hide from herself the fact that I was a poor man and hard pressed," John later wrote, "so far from trying to cheer me, she spoke of my poverty as a crime,—as an outrage against her. She harped almost daily upon what she had done and suffered for me and my children, and oft lamented her folly in marrying a poor man. She often declared that, if she was ever free from this union, she would never get into another such scrape;— that, if she ever married again, she would marry none but a rich man."[56]

Jealousy also clawed at their relationship—an irrational jealousy on Susie's part, John believed, but a perfectly understandable response on his. Whenever teenage girls in his school or young mothers of his pupils sang John's praises,

Susie would fly into a rage and accuse him of flirting with them or worse. He was constantly on edge that she would one day make a public scene with these groundless accusations and ruin his reputation as a schoolteacher. John, for his part, again had to be concerned about the suave dentist, Dr. Eleazer Hovey. Hovey was back living in Buffalo but he visited Springfield frequently. If Kelso's stock was falling, Hovey's was rising: he owned $20,000 in real estate and had designed the handsome new Dallas County courthouse. By the fall of 1871, Susie was no longer even trying to conceal her rekindled affections for Dr. Hovey. When the doctor came to Springfield for some lectures, Susie arranged to go into town and stay at the same boarding house. That night, John walked the three-and-a-half miles from his farmhouse into town in a state of high agitation. "In the darkness of the night I went to the town and wandered back and forth before her window, hoping to get a glimpse of her face. I was not gratified. In my fevered imagination, I pictured her smiling sweetly into the Doctor's face, or nestling in his arms as she had admitted nestling on former occasions." John was, he admitted, "*madly jealous*"—but, he argued, didn't he have a right to be? "My wife was here with her acknowledged illicit lover, in the house of a woman who would put no obstacles in their way." Would they—this night—go further than they had acknowledged going before and sleep together? "For what but the illicit *fruition* of their illicit *love* do illicit lovers wish to *meet* and to be *alone* with each other?"[57]

He never found out what happened that night. He said he did not want to know. He never mentioned any anger toward Hovey, who had a different philosophy of "free love" and a wife willing to overlook the dalliances that philosophy justified. Kelso did not record the rage of a cuckold, did not confess to wanting to wring Hovey's neck or put a bullet through his brain. He focused only on his relationship with Susie—on his jealousy, on his painfully broken heart, on why "she would thus deliberately cause him the most exquisite torture known to humanity."[58]

Long before this "finishing stroke"; long before the confrontation that followed the night at the boarding house, when, "with a look so fiendish in its vengeance" it made him shudder, she told him she wanted to kill him; long before she then cried and begged him not to make the separation permanent with a divorce; long before he walked out the door on the last day of November 1871 and left Springfield forever, he had wanted to leave her. But he dreaded "the disgrace of a second separation." Even more, he worried about his children. He could take Florella and Florellus with him, but he was sure he would have to leave his "little weasel" Iantha, sweet Freddie, and little Johnny behind with Susie. He felt hollow at the thought of living without his younger children and worried about the possible effects of depriving them of the care of both parents.[59]

He knew they were not growing up in the happiest of households and that he and Susie were not the best of parents. Susie had never treated her two stepchildren, Florella and Florellus, in a loving, maternal way and was especially hard on Florella. His wife had not wanted to become pregnant with Iantha, and John, who was convinced that the mood of an expectant mother shaped the personality of her child, felt that Iantha had been "in her very constitution . . . impressed with a *feeling* of *unwelcomeness.*" Susie had suffered with Johnny's difficult birth and seemed to resent him for it, and he was "so impressed with a want of love" that he could hardly express love himself. "Of all the children my present wife had borne me, Freddie alone had been entirely welcome to her, and his superior sweetness of disposition was doubtless greatly due to this feeling of welcome, on her part, while bearing him."[60]

Upon reflection, John felt that he, too, had made some bad impressions upon his children. He was too much the disciplinarian. Despite his many fine qualities, Florellus was moody and rebellious. John punished him for his disobedience, just as his parents had punished him. The balance was tilted too much toward discipline and away from displayed affection. He loved his children deeply, profoundly, but did not know how to express that love. "I never knew how to be demonstrative in my love and especially in my love for my children. This love has been too deep for any demonstration. They will understand this only when, for themselves, they know how deeply a *parent can love.*" Would his children be worse off in a broken family? He worried, and he delayed leaving. In retrospect, he wondered if this was another great mistake. Perhaps if he had left Susie sooner and broken up the family, the greatest tragedy of his life would not have occurred.[61]

A BEAUTIFUL LATE summer evening at dusk, on Saturday, August 30, 1870. Kelso had been quite ill, confined to his bed for a few days, but was recovering. Freddie was in a sickbed, too. Romping merrily with his little brother Johnny a few days before, Freddie had jumped off a swing and dashed across the yard, but stepping on an upturned garden rake in the grass he pierced the bottom of his foot on the rake's iron teeth. "The wound did not seem to be a very severe one. It was poulticed and yet it pained him a good deal for four days. Then the wound was running quite freely, and seemed much better." Kelso went in to see him. "I talked with him for some time. I told him how proud I was of him, and that because he had borne his sufferings like a brave little soldier, I would get him a little drum the next day. This pleased him very much." A bit later,

Kelso stepped outside to get some air. Walking in his yard, he stopped to look back at his house, at the window to Freddie's room, glowing from the light within. Iantha sat in the window, happily reading. He could hear his other children laughing about the moths that fluttered near the ceiling. The father stood watching and listening, his heart full. This image would long dwell in his memory "like a beautiful picture." He would remember it as "the last scene of joy that I ever beheld in my own house-hold. The sun of happiness in my home was setting forever and this was its departing glory."[62]

Later that evening, as Susie and John drifted off to sleep, their hired girl came to the bedroom door. "The girl spoke calmly, and yet there was something in the tone of her voice that made me fear the worst." The parents rushed to the boy's bedside. A doctor was summoned. Tetanus—lockjaw—nothing could be done. "Alone he had entered the cold river of death and was struggling in its dark waters." By Saturday, September 3, Freddie was dead.[63]

Still weak from his own illness, Kelso was nearly overwhelmed by grief. His eldest, Florellus, was a great comfort. "He had never before seemed so grand, so noble, and so strong. Upon him, more than upon any other, I leaned in this time of my great affliction. With a solicitude in his tone and manner that deeply touched my heart, he would every day ask: '*Për, you feel some better today, do you not?*'" A week or so after they buried Freddie, John and Florellus had a conversation. Or perhaps it was a conversation that Kelso wished he had had, that he so needed to remember having, just to be able to go on:

[Florellus] told me that he would make me proud of him yet.

I SAID: "I believe you will make me proud of you. Indeed, I am proud of you now; and, whatever may be your faults hereafter, I do not mean ever again to give you an unkind word. In all cases I shall trust to your own honor and your own manhood."

HE REPLIED: "Për, you have never been unkind to me."

I ANSWERED: "I have not meant to be unkind, it is true, but I have often used harsh measures when mild ones would have been better."

"But, Për," said he, "I have not done right and have always deserved the punishments you have ever inflicted upon me."[64]

At the end of the following week, on Friday, September 16, Kelso went to town for a political rally. His old friend from the 39th Congress, Governor Joseph W. McClurg, was giving a speech. Kelso returned home near dusk the next day with small presents for his family. The best present of all was good news for Florellus: he had been accepted to the Naval Academy at Annapolis.

But where was he? Probably still out doing his chores. After half an hour passed, Kelso sent one of the children to call him in. But they heard no reply. Who had last seen him? Iantha remembered seeing him sitting on the swing. "She said that his face wore an expression of extreme sadness, and that, in low sad tones, he had asked her about a certain rope that had been lying about the yard." Hearing this, Kelso felt a cold, fearful chill. Then Florella told him that, earlier in the day, while mending her brother's clothes, she found some tobacco in his pocket and reproached him for it. Kelso taught that chewing or smoking tobacco were disgusting and unhealthful habits and had been angry and disappointed with his son for going near the stuff. Just a few days before, Florellus had sworn, on his honor and manhood, never to use tobacco again.[65]

Kelso saw it all—felt it all—in a flash. Stricken with fear, he ran to look for his gun. The belt was there, but the revolver was gone. "Filled with horror, I took a lantern and searched all about the premises. I called his name. My own voice was so hollow that it frightened me. It did not seem to penetrate the surrounding darkness. It seemed to fall back scared upon my own ears." No, no, others said. Some of Florellus's friends had just run off in search of an adventure, and he probably went with them. Kelso grasped at this straw.[66]

On Sunday, the father had nearly convinced himself that his son running off with friends had to be the explanation. On Monday, Kelso went to teach at the local schoolhouse. At the end of the day, just before he dismissed his students, a neighbor appeared in the doorway. The man's face said it all.

Kelso ran to the spot, a ravine four hundred yards from his house. There was Florellus. "He lay upon his back with his hat folded under his head. His right hand, still grasping the revolver, lay across his breast. His thumb was still upon the trigger. In the center of his forehead was a bullet hole." The following day, they buried him next to Freddie.[67]

At first there was a strange numbness. The indescribable anguish that followed was far worse than anything he had faced in battle. Florellus! His beautiful, remarkable son. If he had a "rebellious disposition," Kelso thought, it was because he had been made so by a stepmother who hated him and a father who beat him when he disobeyed. The father would be forever haunted by "the memory of his pleadings: 'Oh! Për, please do not whip me and I will not do so again!' " Kelso clung to the memory of that last meaningful conversation, of hearing his son say, "Për, you have never been unkind to me."[68]

With the loss of Freddie and Florellus, Kelso felt years of his own life drain away. Sometimes it seemed as though he would forget to breathe. "For some time after the death of these boys, I would wander about our grounds in a dazed kind of way, visiting their neglected gardens and play grounds, listening for their voices, the faint sounds of which seemed often to reach my ears," he wrote. "I felt impelled to search for my boys, each evening on my return from school, among their former haunts, although I knew that I should not find them. At every step my search, however, I met some object that reminded me of them and opened my wounds afresh. In a few weeks, my hair began to turn gray, and the few friends who understood me best advised me to go far away and try among new scenes to rally from my great and crushing sorrows. I finally took their advice."[69]

15

Great Infidel

WHEN HE WAS in Congress, Kelso would have seen a vast mural on the north end of the Capitol's west corridor, facing the marble staircase leading to the third floor. Lit from the skylight above, *Westward the Course of Empire Makes Its Way* (1862) by Emanuel Leutze depicts a wagon train crossing the Rocky Mountains. The emigrants pause, catching their first view of the great Far West stretching to the Pacific. As two men clear a fallen tree from their path, another two in the center background have scrambled to the craggy summit to plant an American flag. Others point to the glowing sunset, San Francisco's distant harbor, and the world of possibilities opening before them. This is an empire making its way west through the effort of rough-looking White men holding guns (and a single Black man leading a mule); their wives hold children in their arms and clasp their hands in prayer.[1]

Kelso had never been farther west than eastern Kansas, but he had absorbed the mythology as a young boy reading by firelight. After leaving Springfield with Florella at the end of November 1871, and then leaving his daughter with relatives in Colorado, Kelso had made his way farther west to find employment for both of them. By the spring, he was writing letters back to Florella describing the wonders he beheld. He crossed the Sierra Nevada Mountains not by wagon but by train. He began in cold, hard winter. "In a few hours, however, we passed from the bleak scenes of winter, down the western slope of the mountains, into what seemed to me to be a fairy land. I fell asleep among the scenes of winter. I awoke among the scenes of summer." When he opened his eyes, he was "whirling among forests of beautiful trees, all clothed in green, and among meadows of waving grass and flowers . . . past gardens in which the vegetables were ripe for market, and past groups of barefoot children at play. The change was so sudden and so great that it seemed like one of the transitions of a happy dream." A month later he was writing "in the shade of a vast spreading live oak on the summit of one of the low mountains that enclose the Valley of Suisun." He was thrilled. "The lands of the gods! I have *heard* of them, I have *read* of them, I have *dreamed* of them, and now I *behold* them.... the beauties of Paradise or the Land of the Fairies." When he reached the summit, he "felt a glow of returning health pervading my whole system. I threw off my hat, and, invoking the spirits of the hills, I made them an enthusiastic speech. Oh! how much I wish that you and all my other dear ones were here if only for one hour. My whole bosom swells, and I feel that I can almost burst forth into a real gladness which I have not known for more than twenty years."[2]

But the abundance of the "Great West" did not immediately come within Kelso's grasp. Before coming to California he had spent the winter in Virginia City, Nevada, "the richest and wickedest mining camp in the world." Ill with a bad cold when he arrived, he quickly contracted erysipelas, an acute skin infection; his eyes swelled shut and his face "soon lost the appearance of humanity." He had to coat his face twice a day with a lotion containing mercury and iron, which turned the top layer of skin black and caused it to peel off. Alone, sleepless, and delirious with fever, he thought that he "was very near the brink of the cold dark river." Out of money and in debt, as soon as he was well enough he began teaching school to pay for his meager meals and room at the boarding house. The students were horrible, and without having the strength to restore order to the "bedlam," he quit after a month. Getting his pay, he celebrated alone in his room: after living for weeks on dried meat, bread, and vinegar water, he splurged on a can of peaches, a can of oysters, and a melon.[3]

Still recovering from his ailments, Kelso was determined to hike up Mount Davidson, which rose above Virginia City, before he left Nevada. He had to go up alone, since all the locals thought mountain climbing in the winter was more than a little daft. He ascended the south side, which had little snow, took in the grand view from the summit, and then tried to go down on the north side, which was covered in snow and ice. "[T]he declivity became so steep that I could not keep my feet in the snow which was hard and smooth almost as ice. I then got down and crept backward on my hands and knees, holding myself as well as I could by sticking the blade of my pocket knife into the ice." This did not work for long. "My knife blade was not strong enough to bear my weight. It broke and I was helpless." His heart began to thump in his chest in a way he had not felt since the war. He could not go back up, but if he slipped down he was not sure what might happen. Seeing no alternative, he flipped onto his back, lifted his head and feet off the ice, and launched himself like a sled down the steep slope. "I closed my eyes and shot down with a velocity that caused the friction to make my back burn as if it was in contact with a red hot frying pan. Presently I shot out upon a nearly level position of ice, and I lay there awhile not sure that I was *all* there. Finding but little gone except a portion of the back of my coat, I arose and went on my way rejoicing."[4]

Virginia City—when he lay in bed delirious with peeling, blackening skin and his eyes swollen shut—was not the low point of Kelso's westward journey. That occurred in San Francisco, between his March descent into fairy land on his way to Oakland and his April paean to the celestial beauties of Suisun Valley. After reaching Oakland, he crossed San Francisco Bay on a ferry and found cheap lodging on Pacific Street. But he was sick again—this time with diarrhea and hemorrhoids. His spent his first night in San Francisco unable to sleep, staggering back and forth to the water closet and then sitting in a wash bowl of cool water to try to relieve his discomfort. On one of his trips out of the room, someone snuck in and stole his watch, the last of his money, and his only pair of pants.

He discovered the theft the next morning. He told the landlord, who called in a couple policemen and described a suspicious lodger across the hall who had left the boarding house in the night. The policemen dutifully scribbled down the information, shrugged, and departed. Kelso was left alone in his room, sick, friendless, penniless, and pants-less. "I put on my coat, my vest and my boots, and then walked back and forth across my room in my drawers, viewing my image in a large looking-glass," Kelso wrote later. "I was at the '*end of my rope.*'" Eight years earlier he was being hailed as the Hero of the South West. Five years earlier he was standing up in Congress, calling for the impeachment of the president. Looking at himself in the mirror now, he did not know whether to laugh or cry.[5]

He would come to see the moment as yet another test of his resiliency, his "indomitable will" spurred to action by mysterious external forces. "I began to feel amused at the ridiculousness of my situation. My dauntless spirit began to rise to the necessities of the occasion. That strange impression, that '*still small voice*'—if I may use such a term—which has always come to me in times of great need and of great danger, assured me that all would be well." He sat down with a city newspaper and spotted a notice for a meeting of religious Liberals to be held later that Sunday afternoon at Dashaway Hall on Post Street. "I felt impressed to attend that meeting; and, by these impressions, I was assured that, in some way, I would soon surmount all my present difficulties." From the landlord he borrowed a small pair of old brown pants (they were ten inches too short) and fifty cents for breakfast. In the afternoon, he headed to Dashaway Hall.[6]

The room was crowded with about 1,200 people listening to a debate on a religious topic. Kelso learned that anyone who desired could have his say for ten minutes, so he put his name in the queue. When he was called up to the dais, he saw the crowd ogling his long legs and short pants. He used his outlandish appearance to his advantage. Having gotten their attention, he made a forceful argument that won the debate. He then proposed to lecture as soon as possible in that same hall to raise money to buy a new pair of pants. "Several men offered to secure the hall for me on the following evening, and to pay for it themselves." Someone called out that he should be paid for the speech he just delivered, and the crowd applauded. "[O]ver forty dollars, all in silver, were soon jingling in the capacious pockets of my little pantaloons. On my lecture next evening, I made $22.00 after paying all expenses." It seemed an auspicious start to his career as a public lecturer.

FROM THE EDUCATIONAL lyceum movement in the 1820s through the rage for entertaining public speaking in the 1850s, lecturing by the 1870s was becoming increasingly dominated by commercial bureaus scheduling celebrity speakers on national circuits. Still, the local lecture hall remained a venue that could be rented by anyone trying to reach an audience, spread a message, build a public reputation and, perhaps, earn a little money. Kelso had written some of the lectures he delivered in California during his final year in Springfield. In them he publicly wrestled with the big philosophical questions and profound experiences that had shaped his life: God and faith, free will and determinism, sex and love, the excitement and trauma of war. Early on, he delivered lectures on his "War Adventures," advertising himself as "the great guerrilla fighter of Missouri." He did so at Suisun and Vacaville in April, 1872, and tried to speak in Sacramento in May, but the fellow in charge of turning on the lights in Hamilton Hall never showed up.[7]

Kelso's impulse to make sense of his wartime experience, though, quickly turned into a desire to write a serious history. In early 1874, he wrote back to Missouri, placing a notice in the newspapers calling on his old comrades to send him accounts and records so he could write "a history of the Guerrilla warfare in Southwest Missouri." He asked for sketches of "thrilling personal adventures" but even more wanted military records so he could specify "places, dates, and circumstances as correctly as possible." Milton Burch sent him descriptions of two skirmishes Kelso had missed, but the historian was never able to get hold of muster rolls and official battlefield reports, even after a trip several years later to the War Department in Washington, D.C. So in the early 1880s, instead of writing a broader history, Kelso composed his autobiographical account.[8]

His lecture on "Influences," too, seems to be an early effort. That lecture's emphasis on how parents' moods and motivations during conception and pregnancy shaped the character of offspring echoed the standard understanding of heredity in the nineteenth century. Kelso joined nearly everyone else commenting on the topic in assuming that offspring inherited the acquired characteristics of their parents—that is, that the psycho-biological being of the parents, the cumulative product of their own inheritance and the predominant habits, mental states, and illnesses that had shaped their lives, imprinted their children (as embryos, fetuses, and nursing babies) with tendencies or predispositions to different characters, temperaments, and susceptibilities to chronic diseases. Fathers and mothers transmitted these tendencies in different ways, and Kelso used the analogy of photography to explain it. Fathers did so in the flash of conception, like the burst of light and opening of the camera's shutter allowing the image to imprint upon the film. Mothers did so more gradually, through gestation, birth, and breast feeding, like the photo's image emerging gradually in the dark room's chemical bath. Like other commentators, too, he linked hereditarian arguments either to determinism or to agency depending on the needs of his discussion. How much can we influence the conditions under which the photograph is taken and developed to affect the quality of the image produced? To parents, reformers could urge virtuous habits and cautious propagation; to children, they could say, "It's not your fault."[9]

His larger deterministic point—that we are all products of chains of causes and effects, and our free will is an illusion—led to his argument about the cruelty of punishing people for their mistakes. The memory of his hand raised against Florellus silently haunted his text, but his personal torment was transmuted into a plea for prison reform. Criminal dispositions proceeded from disordered minds, and these minds from brains deformed by the fetus's prenatal environment and the child's subsequent development. We should no more punish the criminal for his deformed brain than the consumptive for his bad lungs, Kelso argued. Dangerous criminals, of course, needed to be confined, just as people infected with smallpox had to be quarantined to protect others. But such criminals belonged in compassionate asylums, not punitive prisons. Criminal dispositions, Kelso thought, might be cured or at least prevented from producing criminal acts through therapeutic interventions, though he did not specify what these might be. Punishment, though, was worse than useless as a corrective or as a deterrent. It was just cruel. And the desire for vengeance that powered so much of the criminal justice system was itself a morbid inclination.[10]

By the time Kelso in 1881 visited the Tombs in New York City, the nation's largest prison, what he saw there was refracted by his theories of "influences" and criminality. It was a massive, gloomy, damp, three-story stone building built in Egyptian Revival style four decades earlier, with shut windows covered in moss and vines. Inside, its 8-by-6 foot cells, each built for a single inmate but sometimes holding two or three, stank of sewer gas. On the first floor he found "genteel-looking young men with intelligent countenances and gentlemanly manners" in clean and well-furnished cells. Many were reading and none were smoking. He judged that "as a rule, these young men belonged to comparatively good families and that it was their fast habits rather than their depraved natures that led them into criminality." A "harder set" was incarcerated on the second floor. Less comfort and cleanliness, more tobacco smoking and spitting. Some had "hard-looking countenances," though others "looked sorrowful rather than wicked." The worst were on the third floor, wretched men sitting on hard, dirty beds, glaring at him as if they wanted to tear his eyes out or staring into space with despair. Nearly all of them had "bad heads and bad countenances"—criminality etched into their physiognomies, misshapen skulls phrenologically marking their destiny from the womb. Kelso saw only what he expected to see. The floors were roughly divided by type of crime (from misdemeanors to burglary to Murderers' Row) but also varied by class. Many of the prisoners had been charged but not convicted and simply could not afford bail; wealthier inmates could pay fees to obtain single cells and nicer accommodations. Socio-economic class rather than parentage was the most pronounced "influence" shaping experience at the Tombs.[11]

Kelso's lecture on marriage was probably written in 1874–75 after his marriage to Susie dissolved. After the lecture contrasted an ideal, loving, sexual union to the false loveless marriages endorsed by society, he looked back to Mima as his one true love, his magnetic match, lost to him forever. He presented himself as a lonely wanderer, wounded by that lost love (rather than by two failed marriages) and throwing himself into battle and politics to try to fill that hole in his life.[12]

John and Susie had not broken completely when he left Springfield in late 1871. She had begged him not to file for divorce immediately, and they had agreed to hold out the possibility of a reconciliation. In the spring of 1872, she sent him loving letters suggesting they might reunite in California: "Last night I woke up at two o'clock, and lay awake two hours thinking of you; and the fear of losing you was so terrible, and my impatience to see you once more, and to hear you speak kind loving words was so great that it seemed that I could not endure life till we should meet again. You seem now to be the only one in the wide world whom I could love." She told him that she would send him a photograph of herself as soon as she could have one taken. "I will think of you at the twilight hour and will try to send love and endearing words to you. I am saving all the kisses, love, and—and—for My Dear Johnny." The letter that followed, however, was cold and bitter, insulting him with old accusations that he had cheated on her during the war.[13]

Kelso had left her with all his remaining property and sent her back small sums from what little he earned in California. After selling most of his last books to send her $40 more, he received a letter that seemed like a final demand for divorce: "On no account would I inaugurate another hell and be one of the principal actors therein. I loathe the very thought of the sexual embrace," she wrote. Then she mirrored back the same deterministic philosophy he had described in "Influences" and closed with language he might have applauded at a women's suffrage meeting: "I do not say this to reproach you, for you have been true to your organization. I only wish you to understand that you are what your parents made you, and that you have made me what I am," she wrote. "Oh! I can not tell the terrors of the suffering I have endured on account of the cruelties and the injustice you have heaped upon me. But it is all over now! I am free! I possess my own person! It is owned by no one else!"[14]

A few weeks later, in late April, John received a very different letter: "Now I want to go to you," Susie wrote. "Let us bury the past, and try if we can not yet live in peace and harmony together. . . . Now please consider the matter; don't give me a hasty reply. I must have the sympathy and love of someone, and as I never have met any one who so nearly filled the bill as you do, I think it is not worth while to try to find one now." In a letter dated May 12, 1872, she wrote: "I so yearn for your love and society. I have always admired your talents and your noble qualities of heart and mind; but the fact that I have not felt myself your equal in these things has rendered me discontented and unhappy. I shall try to live a good life, . . . and it may be that, in sometime in the future, I may be worthy of you and your love." John thought she was probably sincere both in her bitterness and her affection, but he had had enough. He wrote to his lawyers in Missouri to start divorce proceedings; the final decree was issued on January 30, 1874.[15]

KELSO ALSO ATTEMPTED to write about his deepest trauma, the twin tragedy of his sons' deaths. Since his teenage years he had tried to make sense of his emotional life by writing poetry. The poems he copied into his "Works of John R. Kelso" volume in 1873 and his "Miscellaneous Writings" manuscript in 1887 turned deeply felt experiences or soaring flights of imagination into the rhyming quatrains of conventional Victorian sentimentality. They lamented lost love and pondered whether death meant the finality of absence or the possibility of reunion. Sometimes he invented speakers or characters, rubbing out the specificity of experience to create poetic types—the absent lover, the blind girl, the returning soldier, the old schoolmaster. Other poems were more clearly autobiographical. Two wistfully recalled his lost love: "The Lock of Hair" and "Dost Thou Remember, Mima?" Another, "To Adelia," marked the dissolution of his first marriage. The poem opens with tender recollection:

> I loved thee too fondly, I think of thee yet,
> Though far, far asunder we be;
> Though years have departed, I can not forget
> The joys that I tasted with thee.

It closes with a resolution to move on:

> Farewell! Then, Adelia, let no thought of me
> To thy heart bring a moment's regret;
> For since I forever am now lost to thee,
> It is better that thou should'st forget.

"To the False Wife," a bitter wail written after his separation from Susie, fantasizes about the cheating spouse being tormented by guilt for the rest of her life. Kelso also preserved somber poems commemorating the deaths of his mother Anna and young son Ianthus. But the loss of Freddie and Florellus seemed too terrible for words.[16]

He tried to convert his pain into poetry, but even years later found it impossible. "Several times, I have thought to write a poem, entitled The 'Unfinished Lives' concerning these two dear boys so cruelly torn from me," he wrote in the mid-1880s. "On each occasion, however, I have abandoned the attempt. I have felt that, in order to pour out in poetry the full soul of my sorrow, I must again suffer the full weight of that sorrow to come upon me." The closest he came was when sometime between 1873 and 1875 he added

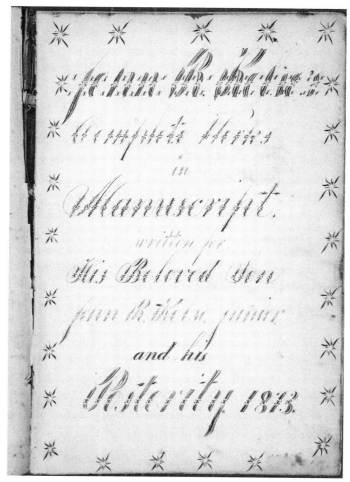

"John R. Kelso's Complete Works in Manuscript," 1873, title page. Huntington Library, San Marino, California.

a final stanza to a poem he had written as a teenager. "The Better Land," written when he was a believing Christian struggling to feel the assurance of a born-again faith, wondered whether he would know his friends and family in heaven. By the time he added the stanza about his children, he had lost his belief in God but still clung to the hope that there was some sort of afterlife in which he could see them again, "in robes of white," coming to him "on their wings of light."[17]

Kelso never wrote "The Unfinished Lives." At every attempt the sorrow caused what he described as a pressure on his brain so intense he feared it would kill him. Even more than a dozen years later, as he wrote the bare description of the tragedy in his autobiography, he felt his brain "threatened with paralysis. I could not now bear any great sorrow or any intense excitement. Even the writing of this account has caused a pressure upon my brain extremely distressful and by no means free from danger to my life. I could not omit the account, however, without breaking the integrity of my story. And now that it is written, I hope that it is not without benefit to those who may see fit to read it." Perhaps, he thought, it was just as well that he was unable to fully express his grief in writing—not just for him, but for his reader, too. "What I suffered then . . . what I suffered afterwards, I will never try to tell. If ever you watch the idols of your own hearts expire, you will understand it. Even if I *could* make you understand it before that time, I *would* not do so cruel an act."[18]

After the deaths of Freddie and Florellus, he did turn to writing verse as a kind of "mental refuge," but with a project that had a vastly different topic and tone. "The Devil's Defense" was a satiric poem of over 2,500 rhyming couplets. In the spirit of Voltaire or Thomas Paine, it mocked Bible stories and Christian doctrines. In a preface to the poem, Kelso recounted his own passage from evangelical enthusiasm to enlightened skepticism—from "the darkness of ignorance and superstition" and his trembling fear of damnation to "the light and gladness of truth," a transformation made possible because he found the "moral courage" to "read and reason" for himself. The poem itself purports to be a long speech by the Devil, who has been brought before a human court. Here Satan is not the being who had terrified the young Kelso, or the rhetorical emblem of treason he had invoked to damn secessionists in his Buffalo broadside before the war, but a playful voice demolishing the "fairy tale" of Christianity with "*reason, science*, and *common sense*." He recounts Bible stories, lingering over Creation, the Fall, the Flood, and Exodus, exposing absurdities, impossibilities, and ridiculous details in the scriptural accounts. How did God create night and day three days before creating the sun? How did Noah muck out the tons of dung that would have accumulated in the ark each day? In the Cain and Abel story, where did the people in the Land of Nod come from? Did Moses really glimpse God's hind parts? Turning to the New Testament, the Devil also noted discrepancies in the Gospel accounts and described the Book of Revelation as resembling a drunken man's hallucination.[19]

Like many deistic critics in the Age of Reason, the Devil indicts Jehovah's moral character—the God who forbids lying, adultery, and killing yet tells untruths, gives his patriarchs concubines, and commands his people to slaughter their neighbors. But unlike Kelso's hero Thomas Paine, Kelso's

Devil—and Kelso himself—went beyond replacing the Judeo-Christian God with a moral Creator inferred from Nature. With Epicurus, he contended that if God were willing to prevent evil but was not able, he was not omnipotent; if he were able, but not willing, he was not benevolent; and if neither omnipotent nor benevolent, why call him God? He then argued against positing a Creator of any sort from a position of naturalistic atheism:

> *No valid reason I can see,*
> *Why matter may not also be*
> *Like them [time and space] from all eternity.*
> *And if these things were never made,*
> *They had of course no Maker's aid;*
> *And, though the statement may seem odd,*
> *There never was such thing as God.*
>   *These three vast elements sublime,*
> *Of all that is—space, matter, time*
> *With their inherent mighty powers,*
> *Can fashion dew drops, worlds, and flowers;*
> *Form living beings everywhere,*
> *That walk the earth and cleave the air;--*
> *In fact can do, as may be shown,*
> *Just what tis thought God does alone.*[20]

The point of it all was to use humor to demystify and demythologize. Kelso admitted that sometimes his humor was "open to criticism on the ground that it verges on the obscene." But he protested that his style was bold and his satire severe because the topic demanded it. God was a powerful and dangerous fiction. So was the Devil, who admitted as much in his closing lines:

> *I am not what your Priests try to make me appear,*
> *Nor should wise men regard me with hatred or fear;*
> *For I was invented to scare only fools*
> *And make them more pliable Priest-serving tools.*[21]

IN A LETTER to Florella in early May 1872, Kelso mentioned having delivered "several lectures" but he was beginning to doubt he could make a living as a public speaker. Back in San Francisco, he gave a lecture at Charter Oak Hall but cleared only about two dollars after expenses. He took a steamer to Sacramento, rented a theater, and delivered two more lectures, with disappointing financial results. "I had now learned that, as a mere lecturer, I was a real success; while as a business manager, I was a total failure." Returning to San Francisco at the end of the month, he had to resort to "dirty work at low wages in the company of the lowest class of Irishmen." With six dollars left in his pocket, he took deck passage on a steamer to Stockton, crowded next to "Chinamen and other disagreeable persons," hiding beneath a slouched hat to avoid being recognized by anyone who might have known him as a lecturer. In Stockton, after breakfasting on five cents worth of dry crackers, he took the train to Modesto, where he had heard there was work.[22]

Five minutes after he had stepped off the train he was hired to help with the harvest on a farm 5 miles back on the Stanislaus River: 700 acres of wheat, 60 acres of barley, and some considerable alfalfa fields, operated by two Missourians and a Texan, all former Confederates. Kelso spent the next weeks having to swim through a large slough of ice-cold mountain water to reach the fields and then work the day stooped, under the blazing sun, pulling weeds. The former schoolmaster's hands quickly blistered and bled. "The juice of the weeds, getting into the raw fresh sores in my hands, caused pain so acute that it sometimes made me feel faint." His muscles became so sore that for a week or so it was hard to stand up in the morning. The heat in the fields, on the days when the breeze from the ocean failed, was incredible. "The mercury then rises occasionally to 115° or more in the shade," he reported to Florella. "At such times, the sand becomes so hot that it can not be touched with the naked foot. If driven into it while it is so hot, hogs lose their hoofs. To keep my feet from blistering, I am wont to pour cold water upon my boots," he wrote. "Chains and all other such things, when left in the sun, had to be handled with gloves or with rags. The backs of our hands blistered as did our noses and our lips. At such times, the whole surface of the ground would seem to glow with heat. The air would become visible and would quiver as you have seen it quiver over a hot fire out of doors. Objects at a distance would look wavy and indistinct. Every thing would cease to look real." Working in such conditions was not easy. "To stand or to sit still in heat so terrific was out of the question, and yet to keep constantly going throughout the long days was a severe trial of the strength of the men and of the horses."[23]

Nights were cool, though, and he slept well under the stars on a haystack covered with an old wagon sheet. "Sometimes, however," he wrote to Florella, "I can not sleep. I think of the past, of my life so full of strange vicissitudes. My heart aches and I grieve for my children,—for the living and for the dead." Yet he found that hard work was a good remedy for despair. "While it gives us but little time to think and to grieve, it gives us a good appetite and sound sleep. Hard as my labor has been here, my physical powers have improved under it, and I again stand among the strongest of men. Instead of the almost constant mental suffering that had so nearly worn me out, I now suffer in mind only occasionally."[24]

Kelso wrote again to Florella at the end of the harvest in late July. He tried to explain where he was. Stanislaus County, in the center of the state, stretched across the San Joaquin Valley. The plains extending for miles on either side of the San Joaquin River, from the Diablo mountains in the west to the Sierra Nevada range on the east, were almost perfectly flat, and "except narrow strips along the banks of the rivers," nearly treeless. "The soil is composed of coarse sand and small gravel, mixed with enough dirt to render it quite productive when irrigated." But he had seen enough of Stanislaus and the San Joaquin Valley, he thought. "This would never suit me. It is too monotonous, and, for me, it has no society at all. I am eager to be off." He would live there, however, for the next thirteen years.[25]

After working the harvest that first summer in 1872, he spent three months as a bookkeeper and general manager for John Murphy, a grain merchant in Salida. From November through April he taught a school there and slept in Murphy's barn. Murphy offered him $2.75 per cord for all the stove wood he could chop in his leisure hours. Rising before the sun and, wearing only his boots and his drawers, Kelso chopped until he had to walk the 4 miles to open the schoolhouse at 9:00, then chopped by lantern light each evening after school until 10:00, and then chopped all day Saturday and Sunday. He was able to earn $80 a month teaching, $30 a month chopping, and $12.75 a month from his army pension, sending nearly all of it to his children. He felt good being a provider, but also came to believe, as he later wrote, that the "overwork of that period did me real harm," the effects of which lingered for the rest of his life.[26]

Florella came out to California from Colorado in the fall of 1872. "When we met," Kelso remembered, "she hardly recognized her genteel father in the bronzed hired man before her dressed in canvas." He had left her with his father and married sisters in Colorado, where he hoped she would be better off than in Susie's household. He could not have been certain of this, however. His family had broken off communication with him at the start of the war; it is not clear when they resumed a correspondence, but he had not seen any of them in a dozen years. Yet they welcomed him and his daughter warmly and took to Florella right away. She was then "a splendid young woman in her eighteenth year. The cowed look that she always wore in the presence of

her step-mother was gone. She became brilliant and happy; and, by her unselfish and loving disposition, soon endeared herself to all my people and to all
others who knew her." Florella herself recalled going West as the fulfillment
of a dream, entering the sunlight of a new world and leaving the dark clouds
of her past far behind. She finished high school in Oakland and came to visit
her father again in the summer of 1873 as he worked another harvest for the
farmers who had hired him the previous year. One of those farmers was Lynn
Atchinson Finney, a twenty-nine-year-old from Missouri. Finney and Florella
made "a good impression on each other," as Kelso put it, and were married a
few months later.[27]

Through the end of the 1870s Kelso would continue to be what he had
been in the 1850s, an itinerant schoolteacher. But he had not set aside his intellectual ambitions. Even during that first exhausting harvest in the summer of
1872 he had tried to engage his fellow farmhands in philosophical discussion
and religious debate. The men sleeping with him each night on the haystack
under the stars were "a good specimen of the mixed society of California,"
he had written to Florella: "two Americans, one Irishman, one German,
one Chinaman, and a Javaman." The other American was a Protestant, who
hoped to escape hell on Jesus's "ticket." The Irishman was a Catholic named
Patrick. He expected to "bamboozle" his "praste" with a one-dollar confession. His praste would then somehow bamboozle the "Howly Vargin," the
Vargin would bamboozle her son, and the son would bamboozle his father.
By "this chain system of bamboozling," Patrick expected to secure the safety
of his soul. The German was some sort of Spiritualist who spoke little but
liked to hear Kelso talk. "The Chinaman worships a celebrated Asiatic God
by the name of Juss" who could be bamboozled by the offerings of roast pork.
"The Javaman worships a celebrated god by the name of Allah" and prayed
five times a day for his heavenly reward—a reward (a harem) that Kelso
thought was far better than the "penny trumpet" the Christian God handed
out to the members of his heavenly host. Kelso spent his time "extolling the
superior merits of the Devil"—presumably the spokesman of reason, science,
and common sense in "The Devil's Defense." The farmhands, Kelso claimed,
seemed half convinced by his arguments.[28]

Kelso took two months off from teaching during the winter of 1873–74
and spent the time in Modesto, writing. He also delivered two lectures to
Modesto's "Scientific Association," which led to an "exciting debate" with
two local clergymen. Kelso claimed that he had so thoroughly thrashed his
opponents that by the end of the debate he had demoralized one, converted
the other, and made a name for himself in the county as an intellectual force

to be reckoned with. But this victory also prompted the Christian contingent, led by County Superintendent of Schools James Burney, to conspire against him. According to a friend who was at the "secret meeting" where the plan was hatched, and to a letter Kelso later obtained written by the "slimy hypocrite" Burney, they would write and visit clergymen and other pious school board members in the county and try to blackball Kelso from teaching to protect the youth of Stanislaus from his infidel philosophy. They also persuaded a college in San José to renege on its offer to make him an instructor of Greek, Latin, and Higher Mathematics. The opposition only fueled Kelso's determination to become a freethinking crusader.[29]

WHEN THE CENSUS-TAKER came knocking in the summer of 1880, he recorded Kelso's occupation not as "schoolteacher" but as "scholar." Kelso had begun writing the six lectures of "Deity Analyzed" in the spring of 1876 and then incorporated them into a twenty-lecture series called "The Bible Analyzed," completed sometime before 1881. Whatever his aspirations, however, Kelso had neither the training, the resources, nor the time for advanced scholarship. Rather than cloistered in a library, surrounded by books and manuscripts, he wrote in "an old deserted warehouse; my seat has been an empty goods-box; my table has been an old board propped up at both ends . . . and my company has been the bats that have kept up their monotonous circlings over my head." The writer's textual poverty, though, was part of the point. Ethan Allen claimed to have written *Oracles of Reason* in 1783 with only a Bible, a dictionary, and quotations from a handful of books beside him; Thomas Paine wrote the first part of *The Age of Reason* in 1793 without even a Bible, quoting verses from memory. Like these freethinking forebears, Kelso's only "guides" were "reason, science, and common sense." He did not claim to be a scientist, but simply to draw upon the natural facts science had established. Reason and common sense were the mental powers he applied to the concept of deity and the texts of the Old and New Testaments.[30]

Rather than a "scholar," Kelso aimed to be more like what would come to be called a "public intellectual," a figure like the nineteenth-century freethinkers' hero, Thomas Paine. Freethinkers had celebrated Paine's birthday since 1825. In a lecture and a poem about Paine at one such commemoration in the later 1880s, Kelso described the eighteenth-century deist as a man of unparalleled greatness. He had struck "mighty blows . . . for the overthrow of kingly and of priestly despotism, and for the establishment of civil, of religious, and of mental freedom." He imagined Paine composing *Common Sense* (1776), the great call for American independence: there was Paine, a poor man wearing a faded brown coat, walking in front of the Philadelphia State House. Kelso envisioned Paine as he had once described himself composing poetry: walking back and forth, hands behind his back, head bowed, lost in thought until the words emerged from the "deep womb" of his mind. Paine's *Age of Reason* (1794, 1795) was an even greater accomplishment, Kelso believed, but it was a century ahead of its time. The world was not ready for the truth it proclaimed: that many if not all the dogmas of the Christian religion were false. So the "bats of ignorance" screamed in fearful rage at Paine, the "skunks of slander" sprayed him, and the "serpents of bigotry and ignorance" hissed and harassed him until he died. But if Paine could return to America in the late nineteenth century, Kelso wrote, he would be hailed as a hero by "the rapidly increasing ranks of the mighty armies of free-thought." Kelso wanted to lead one of those armies and continue Paine's work.[31]

Kelso also had a model closer at hand: Robert G. Ingersoll, the popular Gilded Age orator known as "The Great Agnostic," one of whose signature lectures, "The Great Infidels," attacked the doctrine of hell. Ingersoll, a prosperous lawyer from Peoria, had been a colonel in the war, the attorney general of Illinois, and a prominent Republican speaker. With lectures extolling Paine and Voltaire in the early 1870s, Ingersoll emerged as a popular champion of freethinking and secular progress. He had a resonant voice, a sparkling wit, graceful and emphatic gestures, and a knack for turning Bible stories upside down. The orthodox were shocked by his blasphemy; the folks in the seats were delighted by his delivery. In 1877 he had set out on his first transcontinental lecture tour, earning hundreds and then thousands of dollars per lecture. Kelso considered Ingersoll one of the greatest orators since Demosthenes. After hearing one of Kelso's lectures on the deity in the summer of 1881, a writer signing as "Nancy Prattler" in the *Sonoma Democrat* called him one of Bob Ingersoll's "imps."[32]

Ingersoll was the most prominent figure in what has been called "The Golden Age of Freethought" in the last third of the nineteenth century. Skeptics, secularists, agnostics, and atheists—radicals who had been marginalized, shouted down, and silenced by Christian crusaders and pious patriots earlier in the century—were now more vocal and visible as traditional religious beliefs seemed ever more out of sync in a scientific, industrializing, materialistic modern age. Freethought organizations such as the Free Religious Association and the National Liberal League that were formed to promote the cause through publications, lectures, and clubs were puny and weak compared to the churches, religious reform associations, Bible and tract societies, and Christian missions that continued to dominate Gilded Age

America. Nonetheless, the freethinkers, who believed they were speaking modern truth to illegitimate religious power, articulated pervasive doubts about traditional forms of faith.[33]

The ideas sustaining these radical critics of religion could be found in the pages of free-thought periodicals, particularly *The Boston Investigator* and the *Truth Seeker*, published in New York City. Kelso began contributing to both publications in the early 1880s; whenever in the 1870s that he first started reading them, he must have felt immediately at home. The *Investigator*, the nation's oldest and most read free-thought paper, had been founded in 1831 and continued to champion the philosophy of materialism and an atheistic, reformist secularism. D. M. Bennett began *The Truth Seeker* in Paris, Illinois in 1873 and relaunched it in New York City in 1874.[34]

Behind the nineteenth-century freethinkers stood the eighteenth-century deists like Paine, Voltaire, and Matthew Tindal, who much preferred the God of Nature found through universal Reason to the Bible's defective deity. Behind the deists stood a renegade Jew in the Netherlands, Baruch de Spinoza, who in the wake of bloody wars of religion gave impetus to a radical strain of what would come to be called the Enlightenment. Spinoza took the historical-critical and philological techniques earlier humanists had developed for the study of classical texts and applied them to the scriptures. He argued that the Bible was merely a collection of human compositions, written in different historical contexts, mangled as they were transcribed, translated, and handed down from century to century, and filled with contradictions, discrepancies, and incomprehensible passages. Moreover, his philosophy countered the Augustinian tradition, which described human beings as depraved sinners needing to be disciplined by church authority and redeemed by God's grace, with a vision of a society where individuals could freely use their reason in a pluralist democracy. Kelso was joining a long tradition that linked criticism of the gods to ideological critique, exposing a false faith as a mask of social and political power. He wanted his readers to understand that orthodox religious ideas made no sense, that the sacred texts were flawed forgeries, and that the modern priesthood and its enablers were duping them to pursue their own profit and prestige.[35]

Anti-Christian radicalism was not the only or even the dominant form of the Enlightenment: most of the devotees of reason, science, and common sense in the eighteenth century found ways to reconcile their philosophy and their religious faith. Most who carried on the historical and philological analysis of the scriptures, too, did not come to Spinoza's radical conclusions, even as they confronted interpretive problems and admitted that it was no longer possible to see the Bible as a unified, inerrant Word of God. In the late seventeenth century, nearly all biblical scholars followed tradition and believed what Spinoza denied: that the first five books of the Old Testament (the Pentateuch) had been written by Moses and the first four books of the New Testament (the Gospels) were reliable eyewitness accounts of the events they described. Sophisticated and painstaking scholarship in Germany in the next century and beyond, however, deflated both of these assumptions. The Pentateuch, the German scholars demonstrated, had been stitched together out of different sources that had been written centuries apart, had arisen in vastly different social and political contexts, and had pursued different theological agendas. The Gospels depended either on oral traditions or on earlier written sources now lost. Unlike Spinoza and the Deists, though, instead of tossing out the testaments they tried to explain how these texts came to be and argued that religious meaning could still be extracted from them. Rather than dismiss the miracle stories as lies or delusions, they began to describe them not as factual historical reports but as myths—accounts not necessarily false but whose relation to historical fact was unclear; powerful stories that expressed an "oriental" and "primitive" consciousness far different from that of modern Western man but that nonetheless communicated profound religious truths.[36]

Few articles in free-thought periodicals like the *Boston Investigator* and the *Truth Seeker*, aiming at a popular audience, showed much awareness of the German scholarship. A liberal critic complained that the *Investigator* was a century behind the times, chiefly reflecting "the spirit of the eighteenth century" with its "negatively dogmatic" dismissal of "God and immortality as not only unproved but unprovable." Paineite common sense critiques of the Bible's inconsistencies and absurdities continued to appear in the publication's pages through the 1870s. Readers complained that articles doing more sophisticated forms of source criticism or historical investigation were boring. The *Truth Seeker* steered even further away from anything that seemed like dry erudition.[37]

America's Christian theologians and Bible experts, however, were not much better. Aside from some outliers like the Transcendentalist Theodore Parker, few before the 1870s knew the German biblical scholarship beyond a superficial abhorrence to what they perceived to be a new form of infidelity, and most of those who dug deeper still kept it at arm's length. Divinity school professors and the pastors they trained tended to hold tightly to an accommodating form of Enlightenment rationality fused with traditional Protestant ways to read the Bible. Scottish Common Sense Realism, very popular among

Americans with philosophical inclinations from the 1790s through the 1860s, was confident that normal human faculties could grasp the real world. People could make rational judgments without a lot of fancy philosophizing. They could trust their instincts and make reasonable inferences, and in most cases rely on the testimony of other people. Similarly, common people armed with literacy alone (the Reformation's priesthood of all believers) could depend upon the Bible's basic message through a literal reading of the text. They could rely on their intuitions or inferences of divine authorship just as, when they beheld the wonders of Creation, they were led to ponder the Creator. They could trust the testimonies of the scriptural writers, yet also have confidence in the marvels and miracles described there, even if they seemed at first glance to defy common sense, because the fulfillment of prophecies showed a divine power at work.[38]

The clergymen that Kelso challenged to debate at the end of his lectures, therefore, could say they shared his faith in reason, science, and common sense. The truth of the basic Bible message could be apprehended by any reasonable, sensible person, they contended. Moreover, that truth could be elaborated through the scientific method, as they understood it: collect facts and then draw broader conclusions. Kelso and the writers in the *Boston Investigator* and the *Truth Seeker* may have been rehashing old arguments from the Deists and Spinoza. But their main opponents were literalist Bible believers in the age of trains and telegraphs who still thought, Kelso sighed, that the first humans were duped by a talking snake and Jesus exorcised demons by casting them into a herd of pigs.

Kelso's *Deity Analyzed* lectures overdrew dichotomies, pitting naturalism against supernaturalism, reason against faith. He described "an irreconcilable conflict . . . between science and religion," perhaps alluding to John William Draper's *History of the Conflict between Religion and Science* (1874) and Andrew Dickson White's *History of the Warfare of Science with Theology in Christendom* (1876), which together had caused a stir by positing a sharp antagonism between the two realms—a break that Common Sense Realism and so much of the Anglo-American intellectual establishment had worked so hard to avoid. Following well-blazed trails in the natural history of religion, Kelso described the invention of the gods as "personifications of man's ignorance," explanations for natural phenomena primitives could not otherwise fathom. As in "The Devil's Defense," he ridiculed the flawed and finite personal God and flat-earth-and-firmament cosmology of the Bible, and dismissed the impossibly infinite and eternal God of the philosophers. Like an eighteenth-century deist in full lather, he hauled the biblical God before the court of justice and convicted him of gross immoralities. To the theologians scrambling for cover under the notion that some scriptural verses had to be taken figuratively rather than literally, he asked how that interpretive rule could be reasonably drawn. If the six-day creation were to be taken figuratively, why not the resurrection? How could the scripture's "larger truths" about the origin, nature, and destiny of man be trusted if the facts were wrong?[39]

The Fall was a myth, and so was the Redemption. Jesus, the historical figure upon whom the salvation story was pinned, had been a "tramp and a vagrant" strolling about the countryside, preaching good if unoriginal doctrines like the Golden Rule together with bad ones, telling people they needn't work for the morrow since the end was near. Jesus made fairly modest claims for himself as the "Son of Man" and was only promoted to the godhead by Constantine in the fourth century, who bullied the Council of Nicaea and turned the Nazarene into a demigod like Prometheus. Kelso concluded that all forms of deity in Christianity—God as Creator, Supreme Ruler, and Savior—were remnants of pagan mythology "founded entirely upon ignorance and superstition."[40]

The longer lecture series, *The Bible Analyzed*, appears similar at the outset. Also seemingly written to be delivered from a podium rather than studied at a reader's desk, the lectures generally cite few books that might have informed Kelso's thinking, aside from occasional nods to Bible dictionaries. "Except when making direct quotations," he explained, "I have not thought best to burden this, or any other of my lectures, by giving my authority in every instance. Those who are well posted in regard to the matters under consideration do not need any references to authority; and those who are not thus well posted would not be likely to make any use of those references." In the second lecture on the Old Testament, however, the text becomes flecked with citations. By the third, on the New Testament, he has apparently plunged into a variety of histories and bible commentaries. His argument about the composition of the Pentateuch illustrates how Kelso engaged the broader world of biblical scholarship while writing in his spare Modesto warehouse with the bats circling overhead.[41]

Kelso set out to demonstrate that the Old Testament was "a book full of obscurity, absurdity, triviality, falsity, immorality, gross ignorance, bad grammar, and many other faults and imperfections." His first step was to establish that the Pentateuch—Genesis, Exodus, Leviticus, Numbers, and Deuteronomy—had not been written by Moses and did not appear until several centuries after his death. Internal evidence (mention of people and places) dates the texts.

But who wrote them? Kelso fingered two forgers. The first was the high priest Hilkiah in 625 BCE, eight centuries after Moses, who claimed to have discovered the long lost book of Mosaic law to prop up his own authority and persecute religious enemies (2 Chronicles 34: 14, 15, 18, 30). Then, after eighty years of captivity in Babylon caused the sacred texts to be lost again, the scribe Ezra rewrote them (2 Esdras 14: 20–22). This process, Kelso asked incredulously, preserved the inerrant Word of God?[42]

At the end of his third lecture, Kelso acknowledged that "for many of the historical facts . . . I am indebted to the researches of other parties, and especially to those of that able writer, Robert Cooper." Cooper's *Infidel's Text-Book* (1846) did not just supply Kelso with his historical facts but also gave him his scholarly citations and several of his rhetorical flourishes. More importantly, Cooper gave Kelso his central argument about Hilkiah and Ezra. By the looser early modern standards of textual borrowing in the republic of letters, or in the stew of the nineteenth-century popular press, where writers freely summarized for non-expert audiences, Kelso was merely highly dependent upon Cooper, though more than he admitted; by the stricter definitions of intellectual property in modern scholarship, he crossed the line into plagiarism. Cooper's *Infidel's Text-Book* itself, though, was simply a compendium of "the best arguments of the Infidel world against the divinity of the Jewish and Christian Scriptures."[43]

In any case, Kelso was less concerned with being original than with being right and being persuasive. He persuaded himself, at least, of the value of his lectures. He was persuaded enough in the early 1880s to take a trip back East, take a financial risk to get his work published, and try to launch a new career as a free-thought orator and author, another Great Infidel like Robert G. Ingersoll to do battle against superstition.

L. C. BRANCH'S *HISTORY of Stanislaus County, California*, published in 1881, was an elaborate folio volume illustrated by over two hundred "lithographic views." In it, Branch celebrated the "elastic energy, unconquerable enterprise, and unsurpassable progress" of the county's people and cheered their county seat, Modesto, as "one of the best business and progressive towns on the Pacific coast." In the drawings of farms, ranches, town residences, and places of business, everything is laid out with a geometrical orderliness, every aspect of the built landscape is tidy and neat. Beside handsome Victorian homes, fountains burble and windmills stand silent watch. Ladies play croquet on immaculate lawns as gentlemen arrive driving buggies to be greeted by capering dogs. In the background, a few workers bring in the harvest, using machines that puff a little black smoke into the clear air. More modest houses still have pruned shade trees, well-trimmed shrubbery, and perfect picket fences. Downtown stores, empty and waiting for customers, sparkle inside and out.[44]

The county's prosperity had sprung from wheat, the railroad, and the work of only the past decade or so. In the blink of an eye, Stanislaus had become "the banner wheat county in the state." Kelso, too, marveled at the wheat. "I suppose that it is the greatest wheat country of its size in the world," he wrote. "Very little of anything else is cultivated." Farmers planted vast farms, sometimes over 10,000 acres. They plowed with gang plows, sowed with machines, and harvested with headers pulled by eight horses and cutting 16-foot swaths through the grain. "Wheat here is everything. Nothing else of a profitable nature can ripen before the dry weather sets in. The people sow wheat, and harvest wheat, and thrash wheat, and haul wheat, and sell wheat, and buy wheat, and ship wheat, and eat wheat, and feed wheat, and make hay of wheat, and talk of nothing but wheat. Entire counties are in a single wheat field. . . . You may ride for days and never get out of wheat."[45]

Modesto quickly sprouted on land purchased by the Union Pacific Railroad in 1870, became the county seat in 1872, and by 1880 had more than 1,800 people. Though he lived all over the county depending on where he was teaching, Kelso participated in Modesto's civic life. Passing a series of difficult tests, he earned a lifetime teaching certificate from the state, became involved in the Teachers' Association, and participated in teacher training conferences in the town. He was the poet laureate for the Modesto July Fourth celebrations in 1876 and 1884. Despite the bruises that had not quite healed from his last Missouri election campaign, he again also dabbled in politics. In the 1870s, Kelso wrote for and helped edit the *Modesto Herald*, a Republican newspaper in a strongly Democratic town and county. He spent his summer vacation in 1877 "in Modesto doing most of the political writing on the Republican side in a very exciting campaign." Nearly all of the editorials in the *Herald* that summer merely jousted with the Democratic *Stanislaus County News* and complained about the corrupt local party machine. Kelso's hand is probably evident in the pieces that likened the Modesto "Court House Ring" to Boss Tweed's infamous Tammany Hall ring in New York City. In one editorial, the writer lifted his head from local squabbles to address larger principles. Encouraging honest Democrats to vote for the best men rather than from party loyalty, he praised Republicans for having crossed party lines in the 1876 presidential election. Putting patriotism above partisanship, they voted Democratic because they thought their own party had become too mired in corruption. Kelso offered himself as one of those best men, running for County Recorder.[46]

The *News* smeared Kelso by printing a long rambling letter from Missouri's Democratic secretary of state (and former Confederate private) Michael K. McGrath. McGrath, after making a great show of citing official records, lied about Kelso's political and military career. Kelso went to the *News* office in Modesto with his commission and discharge papers signed by the U.S. Secretary of War, his signed pension certificate, and a "living witness" who had served under him. The newspaper printed a retraction the following week—after the election. All the Republicans running for county offices lost in September. Kelso got fewer votes than all but one.[47]

Kelso's political career would not be reborn in Modesto. In 1879, he was a delegate to the New Constitution Party State Convention, delivering a speech, he reported, that was wildly applauded. In his autobiography he does not mention that his speech, summarized in the *Sacramento Daily Union*, was a humorous one. A friend from Sonoma nominated him to be the party's candidate for state superintendent for public instruction, calling Kelso a "self-made man" who had graduated college in four months and "was

Teachers' Institute, Modesto, California, ca. 1880. Kelso: far right, second row. McHenry Museum, Modesto, California.

in some respects the most remarkable man in history." Kelso took the stand and said he had come to California with nothing—no money, no pocket to put money in, and indeed no breeches to hold a pocket. He explained how he lost his pants his first night in San Francisco, eliciting "roars of laughter." But he lost a close vote to be the nominee. His only political victory would be, a few years later, defeating his nemesis, former school superintendent James Burney, to become a justice of the peace. By that time, his relationship to the *Herald* must have ended, since during the presidential campaign of 1880 he gave several speeches in the county supporting the Democrat Winfield Scott Hancock rather than Kelso's Republican colleague from the 39th Congress, James A. Garfield.[48]

Kelso's Modesto, however, was not the clean, prosperous, and peaceful town depicted in the 1881 county history. As the *Herald* reported in August, 1879, the Stanislaus County seat was notorious as "the rendezvous of gamblers, thieves, rollers and gentlemen of that ilk. . . . Dance houses and opium dens loomed up in the distance and these places were thronged nightly by these human hyenas, their orgies being kept up until a late hour. Drunken men were rolled and robbed on the streets, ladies were insulted, young lads were enticed into their dens of iniquity and numerous offenses committed." Solomon Elias, who grew up in Modesto and later returned to be the city's mayor, recalled that the "liveliest mining camp possessed no edge upon Modesto in the years from 1879 to 1884. . . . Money was spent with a recklessness and prodigality that baffled understanding." The saloons on Front Street, the dance halls on Eighth and Tenth Streets, the grog shops in the alleys, and the opium dens in the Chinese section ran "wide open" and "at full blast." Young and old from the farms came to town to slum with the "painted ladies" and "the most daring sports, gamblers and saloon hangers-on that could be gathered together in the state." The saloons controlled politics in Modesto and in the county. Their leader was the Front Street boss, Democratic Party power broker, and owner of the Marble Palace Saloon, Barney Garner, who had shot and killed gambler and brothel owner Jerry Lockwood in 1871. When the *Stockton Herald* called Modesto "a God-forsaken and devil-ruled town," it was repeating a commonplace, not reporting news.[49]

On two occasions, local citizens, tired of the carousers, the brawlers, and the drunks, the pimps, the whores, and the opium smokers, tried to take matters into their own hands. The vigilantes—about 150 men—"were the most substantial and prominent farmers and businessmen in Modesto and vicinity." They were called to night meetings by messengers or by coded messages posted in downtown shop windows. They came armed, singly or in pairs, and met in darkness. "They were led by a 'Captain'—a man of family, of property, a farmer in whose veins flowed Revolutionary blood." On Thursday evening, August 14, 1879, they assembled wearing black masks and carrying shotguns and revolvers. Marching down Tenth Street, they deployed in front of Sullivan's dance hall. The Captain called out Sullivan, and when the owner appeared, he was ordered to close his place and leave town the next morning. Then "pandemonium reigned in the house," with the barflies scattering and frightened "scantily dressed" women running off down the street. The vigilantes then marched to Johnson's dance hall on the corner of H and Eighth streets, and repeated the performance. After that they hit the other saloons and grog shops. The Captain and his crew finished their night's work in Chinatown. "Ropes were placed around some of the opium shanties, and with the combined tugging of the Vigilantes they were razed to the ground." From the ruins, the masked men gathered up "pipes and other smoking paraphernalia, fan tan layouts and faro tables," and made a bonfire on the public square.[50]

Modesto's two main newspapers, the *Herald* and the *Stanislaus News*, applauded the vigilantes' efforts. But the effects of the 1879 raid lasted for only a few months. The saloon faction kept its tight grip on politics and law enforcement, and things soon returned to normal: "There were the brutal pistol duels, the customary bruising, drunken brawls and fights, the wide open gambling, the highway robbery, pocket picking, petty thievery, and thuggery, and all the other accompaniments of saloon and tenderloin control."[51]

In 1884, a more controversial exercise of vigilante justice threw Modesto and Stanislaus County into turmoil. The catalyst was the arrest of two men accused of raping two young girls. John J. Robbins, sixty years old and with a flowing white beard, came to town in 1882 and hung out a sign as an attorney. "His clientele did not keep him very busy, and soon it was observed by persons in the vicinity of his office that he was fond of little girls, 'and often asked them into his office, petted them and giving them candies told them stories.'" John H. Doane, fifty-seven, who had spent some time in prison for shooting a man in Tuolumne, had a small saloon about 6 miles from town. Robbins and Doane were charged with having taken criminal liberties with sisters Lulu and Dora MacCrellish, whose ages are given as eleven and fifteen in one account or nine and "over ten" in another. The MacCrellish family, however, were considered "shiftless in the extreme"; the parents had been chased out of another town for suspected blackmail, a scheme involving their daughters, and had let Dora sleep at Doane's place for three nights.

10th Street, Modesto, California, ca. 1875. McHenry Museum, Modesto, California.

Doane was released on lack of evidence (and it was claimed that Dora had given her consent). Lulu at Robbins's trial claimed that the old man had a distinctive tattoo on his body, but he was acquitted when, after stripping for the jury, no tattoo was found. "There was subdued whispering among small knots of men gathered at the street corners." At one point, a mob formed and some men brought a rope intending to have "a necktie party," but nothing came of it.[52]

Not long after Robbins was released, on March 1, 1884, three notices were sent by unknown persons signing as the "San Joaquin Valley Regulators" to Doane, Robbins, and John MacCrellish: "Leave this county within ten days, fail not on pain of death." The MacCrellish family, after begging for (and receiving) funds to pay for their travel, did leave. Robbins scoffed at first, but then he left too. Doane defied the Regulators. He brought the letter to a Modesto saloon, vowed to fight, and then, after getting suitably liquored up, staggered up and down Front Street, yelling challenges into the dark. He drew two pistols on a passing farmer, but bystanders intervened.[53]

On Wednesday night, March 19, 1884, the San Joaquin Valley Regulators assembled and put on their masks. Twenty-five men went to the nearest bridge and waited. Another twenty-five, on horseback, made their way up Waterford

Road to Doane's saloon. Others were stationed along the roads between the two points. The plan was to capture Doane, put a noose around his neck, and hang him from the bridge. Seven or eight Regulators, masks pulled up and weapons drawn, entered the front door. Doane was there, playing cards with three other men. The Regulators shouted to the men to put their hands up. Three of them did, but Doane tried to bolt to his bedroom to grab his gun, and a shotgun blast dropped him to the floor, where he died.[54]

Two days later a notice was posted and published, signed by the San Joaquin Valley Regulators, listing twenty-five names and warning them all, along with "all gamblers and persons without any visible means of support," to leave Modesto and never return, "under peril of your lives." The notice concluded: "Remember Doane's fate." The train leaving town was crowded the next morning. On Saturday evening, April 7, the Regulators paid another visit to Chinatown, and again destroyed the opium dens. Ten days after that they issued another edict, this one directed to the disreputable people who had been driven out but were still said to be "lurking in the vicinity of Modesto," waiting for things to cool down so they could return. The Regulators demanded that they leave the county.[55]

This time, however, the opponents of the Regulators pushed back. Some of the names listed in the March 21 notice belonged to the wild young sons of prominent families. Saloon boss Barney Garner publicly denounced the vigilantes. When the Regulators then threatened Garner directly, he had the letter published and decried in the *Stanislaus News*. Other newspapers in the region, too, criticized the vigilantes. The San Francisco *Daily Alta California* deplored the "mob government" ruling Modesto. The *Stockton Herald* and the *Morning Union* condemned the Regulators' "reign of terror" and called for a rival "vigilance committee" to rise up and oppose them. Or perhaps California's governor should call out the National Guard. "Stanislaus County ought to be disorganized and its territory divided up and attached to neighboring counties," the papers concluded. The Regulators, in a final notice issued on April 25, apologized for nothing, saying that they had made the town and the county safer and better.[56]

Political tensions were directed back into more conventional channels that summer with the move to incorporate Modesto and create a more robust local government, which included a city marshal. After a raucous mass meeting at the beginning of August, both sides ended up in the same place. As Sol Elias, the later mayor and chronicler, wrote: "To the anti-Vigilante electorate the plea was made that incorporation would save them from the Regulators. To those who favored the Regulators, the argument was made that incorporation would obviate the further neces-sity for the activities of this extra-legal body." The vote for incorporation passed by a large majority. With the new government, the saloons and the brothels did not immediately disappear, but Modesto gradually started to become a more orderly and law-abiding place—especially after Front Street boss Barney Garner, reaching for his pistol, was shot dead by the marshal.[57]

Where was Kelso in all of this? It is hard to imagine he was not involved, or at least keenly interested. The Regulators spoke to the same inclinations that called him to be a freethinker and reformer. Conscience discerned a moral outrage, but traditional structures of authority had failed. Virtuous manhood demanded action—even violent action—to make things right. The 1884 incidents occurred as he was writing the later chapters of his autobiog-raphy, but he does not say a word about them. Of course, considering the strict secrecy of the Regulators, and the legal jeopardy he might have risked had he been among those donning masks to clean up the town, he was wise to remain silent. He was probably not the "Captain" leading the group, however well that role seems to fit him, if the Captain was in fact a farmer and a man of property (Kelso was neither). Did he enter Doane's saloon that night, car-rying his shotgun? Or did he, like most everyone else, just read about it all in the newspapers?

IN THE SUMMER of 1881, Kelso traveled to Colorado to visit relatives and deliver his "Deity Analyzed" lectures. In late July he took some time to explore the region around Mt. Evans, one of the highest peaks in the state, 35 miles west of Denver. There were three people in his party ascending Deer Creek Canyon, which, he claimed, "had never before been ascended by tourists, and rarely by even the most brave hunters and prospectors." Out front was their guide, a man named Freeman, who was clearing the trail with an axe. "Next came two little donkeys all invisible under their enormous packs except their immense ears." Driving the donkeys, "hidden under a mammoth slouched hat, *a la mode* Mexican highwayman," was Kelso. "Last of all, bringing up the rear in grand style, ... ensconced in a prodigious sun-bonnet, and mounted upon a beautiful, intelligent, and sure-footed mountain pony," was Kelso's daughter Iantha, a smart and lovely woman of twenty-one. Susie had moved to California too, and Kelso had first reunited with his younger children in 1874, three years after he had left them in Springfield, and thereafter could see them occasionally. (Susie married a Fresno farmer named Ransom McCapes in 1883.) Iantha had enrolled in the same Oakland high school that Florella had attended, and then entered the Normal School at San Jose, graduating with highest honors in the summer of 1878. Kelso was delighted to be able to share this Colorado adventure with her.[58]

They groped their way through dark, damp forests and twisted through bright, tree-less valleys. They clambered over fallen trees and broken rocks, "and along the ragged edges of frightful chasms and the almost perpendicular faces of gigantic walls of solid rock." Pitching camp in the afternoon "in a lovely little valley, covered with fine tender grass," they had a delicious supper of trout and grouse and told stories by the evening's campfire. Night brought a sweet and refreshing sleep. "When we awoke, the waters were sparkling, the birds were singing, and the squirrels were chirping around us in the glorious light of the morning sun."[59]

The next day's journey took them over rougher and more dangerous ground. They left the donkeys behind and went on, but Iantha's pony would tremble when the footing became treacherous. "On such occasions," Kelso wrote in a letter, "my daughter's eyes—although she is an almost recklessly daring young woman—looked at least 50 percent larger than was absolutely necessary." Iantha would dismount, and "with almost the agility of a gazelle," would lead the pony to safer ground. At last they made it through the gnarled and twisted spruces and firs crowding the tree line and they burst out into the open to behold "scenes of grandeur and beauty almost too glorious to be of earth." They marched upward, reached the summit by 5:00, and took in still grander views. To the north and west they spotted two even higher peaks, which, according to Freeman, had not yet been named or measured. "One of these, the highest and the nearest—only about 4 miles from Mt. Evans—was, at once by the unanimous vote of our entire party, named the '*Great Infidel*,' in honor of myself, the first Liberal lecturer that has ever visited this part of the state. The other, standing a little to the left of this one, by a similarly unanimous vote, was named '*Mt. Iantha*,' in honor of my daughter, the first woman that ever ascended the Deer Creek Canyon."[60]

A week later, after giving his lecture demolishing deity to a small audience of astonished Coloradans at the Salvert House in the town of Bailey, Kelso returned to climb Great Infidel alone. On the afternoon of August 16, he reached the base of Mt. Evans and began fishing for his dinner. But before he could catch more than one trout the skies opened up and soaked him. Searching for shelter in the heavy rain as night fell, he finally found a small dry spot at the trunk of a large fir tree. After managing to kindle a fire and eat his trout, he sat with his back against the tree and his chin upon his knees, and tried to sleep. "I had learned this method of retiring to slumber long ago, during [the] strangely eventful life which I spent fighting bush-whackers in Missouri, Arkansas and Indian Territory." When he woke himself to re-plenish the fire, "it seemed that I ought to hear the voices of my dear war-worn old comrades or at least to see their forms reposing in slumber around me. A strange sad loneliness crept over me when, instead of these slumbering forms, I saw nothing but the dripping boughs sparkling in the fitful light of my solitary camp-fire . . . in the dark and dreary forest." He thought of those who had fallen in battle and wondered how many of those who had survived the war were still living.[61]

The next day, he made his way along the northern side of Mt. Evans and then up the north side of what a week earlier they had named "Mt. Shepherd" because they had spotted some bighorn sheep. Mt. Shepard still had ice and snow in its rocky crevices. He watched a small storm cloud below him crash into the mountain, deliver a load of hail like buckshot, and then go skidding down the valley as the sunlight around it produced a series of concentric rainbows. Finally he reached Great Infidel and headed up its eastern slope. The terrain was extremely rugged. Though "[n]ever a timid man," there were times when he "dared not look down." From the summit, he looked down upon a blanket of dense, dark clouds. The view was at once "grand" and "beautiful," but also "desolate" and "terrible." Then suddenly the cloud blanket lifted and enveloped him. The wind howled, thunder rumbled, and a cold rain began to fall. He took shelter under a large rock shelf, watched the rain turn to snow, and became chilled by the piercing wind. "While lying there, benumbed and shivering with cold, waiting for the storm to abate a little, I could not help thinking that this desolate and storm-beaten mountain had been well named for me, so fit an emblem it was of my now desolate and storm-beaten life."[62]

16

Mirages

IN LATE APRIL 1881, the Modesto Liberal League said goodbye to their president, who was stepping down to get ready for a lecture tour to the East Coast. The National Liberal League had been founded in 1876 to seek the total separation of church and state and combat religious groups lobbying to get a constitutional amendment endorsing Christianity. Kelso had been quick to help organize a local chapter in Modesto. The Secretary, S. S. Hanscom, made a fine speech, the members presented Kelso with a lovely engraved cane, and Samuel Gates, "one of the oldest Liberals in the county of Stanislaus," gave him a twenty-dollar gold piece for good luck. Turning fifty and looking back at the past decade, Kelso was surprised at the thousands of pages of writing he had produced despite all his hours in the classroom. It was time, he had decided, to enlist his life "in the invincible little army of Liberalism" by lecturing across the country and publishing his books. He announced his intentions in the *Boston Investigator* and the *Truth Seeker* and set out at the end of May.[1]

He planned to file reports from the road. One of the first was an "independent scientific article" on mirages for the *Investigator*. He had been fascinated by mirages since coming to California, and here did his best to analyze the "wonderful natural phenomenon" that was "so little understood." He tried to explain the different forms of the optical illusion—a phantom lake shimmering in the distance, for example, or the way a low cottage could appear to loom upward like a castle, or how an inverted image of a church steeple could float in the air above the actual steeple. It was light reflecting or refracting or some combination of the two on different layers of atmosphere, all relative to the location of the observer's eye, he explained. To the *Truth Seeker* he began sending letters that would function as a kind of travelogue, commenting on the sights he saw, the "adventures" he had, and the state of

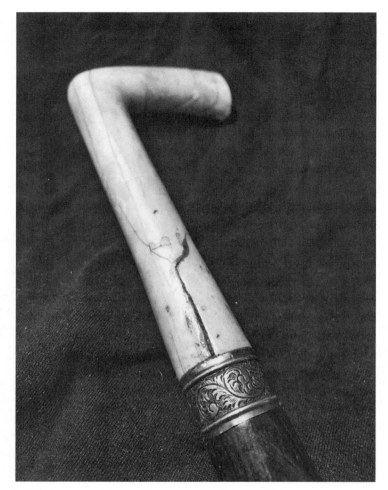

John R. Kelso's ceremonial cane. Photo courtesy Rhiannon Kelso.

liberalism in the towns and villages he visited. He wrote too much, so he decided to save the accounts instead for a book.[2]

He lectured in Petaluma and Galt in California, and then traveled through Reno and lectured in Virginia City, Nevada. After that, he headed to the Colorado mountains, visiting family and lecturing for three months. Near Georgetown, he climbed Kelso Mountain, named for his cousin, William Fletcher Kelso, who owned several mines there. The cousins hiked to the top like "two happy, old gray-haired boys," reminiscing about their childhoods and talking about the different paths their lives had taken in the years since. From the six lectures he delivered (four on "Deity Analyzed," plus "Influences" and "The Sunday Question") to good audiences in town, however, he cleared only seventeen dollars. By early September, he was in Kansas City, meeting up with his brother Robert, whom he had not seen in eleven years. Then the brothers took a train to Robert's hometown, Trading Post, Kansas, where John would lecture on the topic of "The Creation and the Creator." To John, the attractiveness of Trading Post seemed confined to the landscape surrounding the town, not the town itself. "It is an ill-built village of about 300 inhabitants. . . . The water is abominable and the health bad. . . . The inhabitants, almost universally, have a sallow, sickly look, and, as I pass along the street, my ears are saluted . . . by the sound of energetic vomiting, which shows that the tri-weekly emetic is successfully operating." Trading Post, at least, had been a good place for Robert, a physician.[3]

On September 14, the two went to a state fair at Kansas City, crowded with over twenty thousand people. While they sat packed in an amphitheater waiting to watch a horse race, a fire broke out. Black smoke filled the air. Flames shot upward from the roof of the main exhibition building and raced toward the amphitheater. Alarms sounded and a few women screamed. But the crowd did not panic (they must have been Missourians, John thought). Men tore down a fence to create an avenue of escape. John and Robert helped women and children jump down from the bleachers. The next morning, the tents were back up on the charred ground and the fair went on as if nothing had happened.[4]

From Kansas City, his train passed through the entire state of Missouri at night while he slept, rolling past thirty years of memories. In Chicago he attended the National Liberal League Congress (September 30 to October 2), and then lectured twice, but made only enough money to cover his expenses. He was impressed by the city's size and vitality but not its appearance. The women, too, seemingly influenced by their surroundings, struck him as being less attractive than the norm. "The men are generally not great beauties either; but men, you know, do not so much need beauty. They need money." Kelso had $1.85 in his pocket.[5]

By mid-October, Kelso was at last in New York City and immediately visited the Secretary of the National Liberal League, T. C. Leland, on 71st Street and then George E. Macdonald, acting editor of the *Truth Seeker*, at the printing office on 8th Street. Decades later, Macdonald would remember Kelso as "the author of some excellent Freethought books" whose "arguments were as clear as mathematical demonstrations." At the *Truth Seeker* office, Kelso arranged to have two of his five manuscripts—"The Devil's Defense" and "Deity Analyzed"—published in a single volume. By the publishing agreement, he would "lose quite heavily" on the first edition of five hundred copies but "make a fair profit" on subsequent editions. When he was wired $700 from California, nearly his "entire fortune," he handed most of it to his publisher, $200 of which went toward funding the paperback publication of a third manuscript, "The Real Blasphemers," a four-lecture critique of Christianity. For the next six weeks, Kelso saw the sights of the city.[6]

He visited many of the city's parks, including the grandest, Central Park, some of them strangely lit at night by electric lights on tall masts—an

John R. Kelso, c. 1884. In John R. Kelso, *The Bible Analyzed in Twenty Lectures* (New York: Truth Seeker Office, 1884), frontispiece. Photo courtesy of Homer Babbidge Library, University of Connecticut, Storrs, Connecticut.

artificial glow, he thought, resembling a three-quarters eclipse of the sun and producing a "phantasmagoria" where every object cast six shadows. He saw the Brooklyn Bridge being built, and marveled; he visited Wall Street and was disappointed—it was narrow and crooked, with dull buildings and broken sidewalks. He watched the belles parade on 5th Avenue and stopped in at a revival meeting at Chickering Hall to smirk. He toured four museums on the Bowery, each advertising that it had the fattest woman alive on display. One day he got lost and wound up "bewildered in a labyrinth of curved and crooked streets, lined with old, dingy, tumbled-down buildings, the sidewalks almost hidden with goods of all kinds, and the streets packed with market wagons of all sorts and of all sizes. Many of the people here were foreigners, and nearly all of them were very dirty." The people yelled out the names of the goods they were trying to sell, promising high quality and low prices. Others marched around with advertisements on signboards, front and back. "Cocks were crowing in the market wagons, ducks were quacking, geese were gabbling, and pigs were squealing. Among these vehicles, and on the sidewalks, cats were mewing, dogs were barking, children were squealing, women were scolding." A variety of unsavory odors hung in the air. "Bold young women beckoned to me from their windows and shrieked, '*Come in, Darling!*' Blear-eyed, heavy-jawed cut-throats, at the doors of whiskey dens, told me by their furtive and peculiar glances that they would try to 'fix' me if the hour was only a little later." But there were worse places in this Christian city, where millionaires lived atop "thousands of miserable creatures that are supposed to be men," and people survived in filthy dens and at the service of their masters.[7]

He also participated in the progressive intellectual life of the city. On Friday evenings he attended the Manhattan Liberal Club meetings at Science Hall and heard the "rising stars" of liberalism speak on topics ranging from "The Irish Land Question" to "Problems of Life and Mind." He gave a lecture there himself, and at the Newark Liberal club, as well as delivering a speech at a meeting of the National Greenback Labor Party. He became acquainted with some men he considered to be advanced thinkers. Kelso thought that the attorney Thaddeus B. Wakeman, president of the Manhattan Liberal Club, was one of the most "profound logicians" of his day. "Like myself, he is writing and otherwise laboring for the good of humanity. He is, however, teaching only the world's teachers. He is too far in advance of the masses of this age to be fully understood and appreciated by them." The old banker Charles Moran, too, had a "great mind," but he could only teach other "great thinkers." The notoriously abstruse Stephen Pearl Andrews and his "purely scientific body of real thinkers" at the Alwato Club were "wrestling with the problem of '*Universology*,'—that is . . . trying to reduce all knowledge, including the knowledge of language, to one simple science." Andrews had proclaimed some years before that his new system of thought was "more abstractly and metaphysically profound than Kant and Hegel, more analytically and specifically positive than Comte," more powerfully synthetic than Fourier, more scientific than Spencer, and so on. Kelso, after paying the club a visit, thought they were "really accomplishing a good deal in their great undertaking," but believed that "the world is not yet prepared for anything of the kind."[8]

These Olympian thinkers, though, may have inspired Kelso to write his *Universe Analyzed* a half-dozen years later. Here he plumbed more deeply the eternal, self-sustaining universe that remained after his logic had discarded deity; it was also his effort to tackle the topic of evolution. Like the geniuses at the Alwato Club, he was not afraid to be boldly original, "leaving the beaten track usually pursued by writers of science." If space, matter, and motion could be posited as basic features of the universe, he argued, why not duration? He imagined matter moving through time at a constant rate as a fixed natural law, like the speed of light through space.[9]

On evolution, he mainly reasoned from college textbooks and was inspired by Robert Chambers's anonymous bestseller *Vestiges of the Natural History of Creation* (1844), a pre-Darwinian treatise that left God out of the story but also lacked a mechanism—which Darwin supplied with the theory of natural selection. Kelso's chapter on the origin, evolution, and destiny of man, though, waved off Darwinian logic in a few sentences. After contending that life could be spontaneously generated (the right chemistry plus heat equals biology), he conceded it plausible that species could evolve by random mutations making individuals fitter—more likely to procreate—in their particular environments. But he preferred the teleological notion of natural laws tending toward producing the "ultimate form" of an organism, marching the entire species forward, just as an individual fetus deterministically develops into its mature form. Kelso did not posit a godlike conscious intention operating behind or through these laws pushing species toward their "ideal" forms, but neither did he offer an explanation for why or how the process worked. An illustration of "Arbor Hominis" (humans on the tree of life) that Kelso included in the book indicated both that all men were brothers and that the Caucasian "division" of humanity was higher than the Mongolian, Ethiopian, Malaysian, or Indian. (The Caucasian head on the top of the tree, the pinnacle of evolution, was a portrait of Kelso himself.) So despite Kelso's boast in his preface about his radical, independent thinking,

The Universe Analyzed—which he said had been written "at irregular times, while resting from manual labor on the farm, my pen alternating with my hoe"— voiced the same racial doublespeak that he had learned from his schoolbooks a half century earlier.[10]

Kelso left New York City on November 30, and after a visit to Washington, D.C. (during which he sighed while gazing down from the gallery at his old seat on the floor of the House), he traveled to Rochester, New York, and delivered lectures on spiritualism. He gave his first talk at the home of Mrs. Amy Post, a prominent reformer now eighty years old. He had befriended

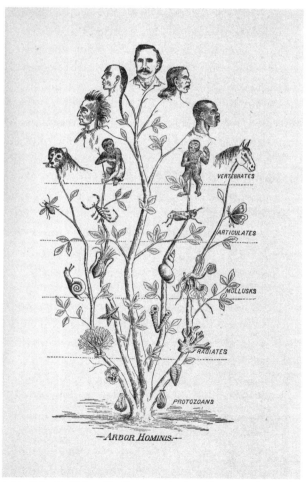

"Arbor Hominis," in John R. Kelso, *The Universe Analyzed* (New York: Truth Seeker Co., 1887), facing p. 156. Library of Congress, Washington, D.C.

Mrs. Post at the National Liberal League Congress in Chicago a couple months earlier. Rochester, an Erie Canal boomtown, had long sprouted varieties of revivalists, reformers, and spiritual adventurers, and the Posts, Amy and her husband Isaac, had been leaders in the temperance, abolitionist, and women's rights movements. Their home was called "the hottest place" in a town reputed to be a "hot-house for isms." In 1848 the Posts' parlor had been a site for the séances that would make the Fox sisters, Kate and Margaret, from nearby Hydesville, famous. The sisters claimed that they could communicate with departed spirits who made mysterious sounds—the "Rochester Rappings." Other seers, mystics, and spiritual visionaries had claimed to visit heaven or chat with the dead, but the Fox sisters became a public phenomenon and launched a popular movement. Not easily explained away, the rapping had soon led to hundreds of séance circles, and thousands, and then tens of thousands, of people witnessed or read about amazing communications with the dead—first with the rapping "spiritual telegraph," then through entranced mediums who would write or speak, and finally with materialized apparitions. Some of the curious came to investigate or scoff, and others to be entertained, but many, restless with the constraints of conventional faiths, shaped spiritualism into a new religion. Some spiritualists would call Rochester "the Bethlehem of the new dispensation."[11]

Freethinkers in the 1880s divided over spiritualism. Some who rejected religion and supernaturalism as superstition, like the materialists at the *Boston Investigator*, delighted in debunking fraudulent clairvoyants and sham séances, thinking the movement merely another form of credulous foolishness. Others, like the editors of the *Truth Seeker*, supported spiritualism or were at least open to continued investigation and discussion. The Liberal League movement tried to erect a big tent for skeptics and seekers of various stripes to unite against the churches' intolerant social and political power and the Christian majority's infringement upon the rights of conscience.

To the small group in Mrs. Post's parlor, and to two larger audiences at the Odd Fellows' hall the following week, Kelso delivered versions of lectures on spiritualism he had first written in the 1870s. In them he defended modern spiritualism on the authority of the Bible, the history of the Christian Church, and the logic of God's government of the universe. This was an odd approach, to say the least, from a professed atheist who had publicly argued that the Bible was a pack of forgeries and fables and the history of the Christian Church a chronicle of dishonesty and delusion. He was acting as a defense attorney for spiritualism, he explained, making his case according to the orthodox Christian's best witnesses. Conceding for the sake of argument the veracity and authority of God, the Bible, and the Church, Kelso would show Christians that the "angels" in the Bible were best understood as human spirits communicating with embodied humans. If Christians acknowledged that, they endorsed the two main principles of modern spiritualism: that consciousness continues after the death of the body, and that disembodied spirits can and sometimes do communicate with people in the flesh. Admitting these, Christians would realize that they were spiritualists themselves. If instead they denied the Bible's authority, Kelso would welcome them into the camp of infidels. "In either of these cases my object will have been accomplished. They will have been freed from the slavish mental chains in which priestcraft has so long held them bound, and will take their places in the ranks of the grand army of liberalism." He acknowledged that, by the end of the three lectures, his audience might wonder whether the whole performance was merely a rhetorical exercise to place Christians on the horns of a dilemma. Did Kelso himself believe in spiritualism, or not? The answer was complicated.[12]

Kelso had heard and read about spiritualism since the early 1850s, but he had not thought "the subject as worthy a serious investigation." In Springfield during the spring of 1871, however, nine months after the death of his sons, and "seeing great numbers of honest and intelligent persons becoming victims of the '*strange delusion*' as I regarded it, I determined to analyze it to the very bottom, and then, in the interest of truth and humanity, expose it to the world." So in June he attended the spiritualist lectures of Alexis J. Fishback and then participated in a debate with Fishback and three other men at the courthouse. The next month, the "Seer" Ebenezer V. Wilson came to town and gave a series of lectures and demonstrations. It is not clear exactly what went on at these meetings. Five years later Wilson culled anecdotes from his diary and published *The Truths of Spiritualism: Immortality Proved beyond a Doubt*, giving a sense of how he operated. He would lecture on the theory of magnetism or on spiritualism in the Bible and then perform tests or demonstrations of his powers. Selecting members of the audience, he would give accurate assessments of their characters or their ailments by sensing their magnetic fields. Then he would convey messages from the attending spirits of departed loved ones or townspeople, messages containing information that, the audience was to believe, Wilson himself could not possibly have known.[13]

Kelso conducted empirical tests of some kind and, to his surprise, became convinced—at least initially—that the spirit phenomena were real. Wilson, or some other medium, apparently conveyed messages from the afterlife that Kelso thought really could be from the dearly departed. In late

1871, when he left Springfield and visited his father in Colorado for the last time, Robert, who had always laughed at spiritualism, too, confessed that he had been conversing with the spirit of his late wife. In Virginia City, Nevada, a couple of months later, a medium named Mrs. Maynard, a banker's wife, conveyed communications from the spirits, she said, of Florellus, Freddie, Ianthus, Kelso's mother, and his grandfather. The spirit of Florellus said: "I and Freddie often come to your lonely bed, where you are sleeping, care-worn and weary, and smooth your hair and wish to comfort you. We hope soon to be able to make you feel our hands touch your head and your face." His grandfather's spirit told him that he was "one of those specially chosen to work in the cause of humanity. For this work, your life has been preserved by spirit influence amid untold dangers. Your property has been taken from you to prevent you from devoting to the pursuit of wealth the time, the talent and the energy that ought to be devoted to your great work. Nothing will prosper with you till you engage earnestly in this work." Although he wrote to Flora that "these professed communications did tend to give me comfort and hope," he admitted that he was "not very strong in the Spiritualistic faith." When he wrote about his sons' deaths in his autobiography in the early 1880s, the question was still open: at his death, would he go to meet his "loved ones on the blissful shores of a beautiful '*Summer Land*,'" or "simply sink into the mystic silence of an autumnal and dreamless sleep"? In the spring of 1885, he would still be describing his position on spiritualism as "extreme skepticism."[14]

In Amy Post's parlor in 1881, Kelso's lectures defending spiritualism must have seemed like weak tea to the hard-core Rochester believers: they had been floating tables, transcribing messages from luminaries like Franklin, Washington, and Jefferson, and materializing spirits for thirty years. But they treated him warmly, inviting him out to rides in the country and to a Christmas party where he danced a quadrille with old Mrs. Post. They asked him to read some of his poems and old speeches aloud and seemed to enjoy them. When "two of the most prominent Spiritualistic Liberals of the city," Dr. Augustine E. Tilden and Mrs. Martha Van Auken, shared a prophetic spiritual communication with him, he wanted to believe. It was easier in this case to do so, however, because the spirits confirmed one of his own predictions: "that a mighty revolution is about to come upon us;—a revolution in which an attempt will be made to change our government into an empire, to unite the church and the state, and to make the laborer the virtual slave of the capitalist." Kelso differed with the spirits only in the role he thought former president Ulysses S. Grant would play. The spirits said Grant would be "a defender of liberty" in the crisis; Kelso predicted Grant would "be the leader of the imperialists and of the church,—the candidate for the office of Emperor of the United States."[15]

Whatever Kelso may have learned about the spirit world when he visited Rochester on his East Coast trip in 1881, he learned more about his dream of becoming a liberal lecturer. He had been sick in Chicago, and sick again in New York City. In Rochester, he was ill most of the time. He had a cough he could not shake, despite lots of hot tea and cough medicine, and his lungs felt very sore. He felt he had no choice but to give up his plans and, at the end of December, began the trip home to California. By New Year's Day 1882, he was on a train crossing the cheerless plains of Kansas. A few days later, traveling through New Mexico, he watched four "three card monte men" cheat some passengers out of their money. After Tucson and then Yuma, his train crossed the line into California, and he stared out at a bleak desert and grim black mountains on the horizon. Reading a romantic novel, Augusta J. Evans's *Infelice* (1875), only added to his melancholy mood. "The reading of this book had brought upon me a feeling of sadness," he later wrote. "Indeed, the reading of romances nearly always does bring upon me this feeling of sadness. I enter too fully into sympathy with heroes of the same in all their misfortunes and in all their brave and noble deeds. The living of a romance, however, often brings upon me a feeling of still more sadness. For many years, the romance of my life has made me feel very sad nearly all the time. When will the denouement of this romance come, and what will that denouement be?"[16]

For some fresh air and sunshine, he went out and stood for two hours on the flat car. In the distance, he saw a mirage—a beautiful phantom lake, receding before the train as it advanced. "So real did this mirage appear that most of the passengers believed it to be a genuine lake, and some of them were as ready to stake money upon its being so as they had been a few days before on the game of the three card monte sharps." Even Kelso began to wonder if the lake might be real. But then it suddenly disappeared, "and left in its stead only a vast waste of burning sand. How many a weary traveler has left the only safe trail to follow these phantom waters and to perish of thirst in the hot sands! So in life; how many leave the road that leads to the real good to follow that which proves to be only a phantom. This is particularly true of those who have left the paths of reason, science, and common-sense to follow the phantoms which priest-craft, in the name of religion, holds before their eyes."[17]

One of the tantalizing phantoms in front of Kelso had been his new life on the lecture circuit, receding just beyond his grasp and then disappearing completely. "And thus closed, in disappointment, my short career as a Liberal lecturer," he wrote after reaching Modesto. "I was now satisfied that my health, especially my fading voice, would never permit me to follow lecturing as a profession. I had hoped to win fame on the rostrum and to greatly advance the cause of liberalism. My lectures, too, had been so well received that my hopes seemed about to be realized." But the dream had evaporated. "To have to abandon the field, therefore, thus early, and to be compelled to return, with shattered health, to the drudgery and the monotony of the school room, was one of the greatest disappointments of my life. The prospect made me feel sick at heart." Through the spring of 1882, he taught school but stopped writing and did no physical labor. "I was suffering from an oppression of the brain that produced indescribable mental suffering. At times, my brain became so nearly paralyzed that a numbness pervaded my whole body." His depression spawned a crippling paranoia. As he put it, he "suffered an abnormal dread of the malice of enemies, although, with the exception of my divorced wife, Susie, I had no enemy living. I dreaded a malice that would seek, by false charges, to destroy, before the world, the fair name which I valued so highly, and to which a long life of the strictest uprightness so justly entitled me." Susie, who, he thought, continued to hate him with a passion and whisper poison into the ear of his fifteen-year-old son Johnny, loomed large as a threat. "So much was I afflicted by this strange, abnormal dread that I often felt glad that I had death to fall back upon, should this dread be realized;—that I had it in my own power to snap the taut thread of life and to thus, with my own hand end all my dread, and all my earthly sorrows. This condition of my brain continued many months." Even years later, he felt traces of those dark moods lingering.[18]

FAILING TO REINVENT himself as a lecturer, Kelso looked backward, trying to make sense of his "eventful career" by writing his autobiography. He began on June 6, 1882. Or perhaps that was just the day he began copying it from another draft into his "Works of John R. Kelso," the eight-hundred-page folio he began nine years earlier with the elaborate calligraphy on the title page dedicating the work to his son, John R. Kelso Jr. After filling 667 pages with his speeches, lectures, and poems, he began the autobiography's preface by dedicating the narrative to all three of his surviving children. He told them he was not sure he would publish his life story in his lifetime. If not, they could do so, making "any changes, comments, and additions" they thought proper. If one of them (and perhaps he was thinking of Johnny here) did not want anything to do with the project, the other two could publish and share in any profits. The point of writing it, though, was not to make money but to explain himself—to them, to the world, and to himself. "While I wish you to be indulgent critics, I do not wish you to be blind to my many errors," he wrote. "I wish you to see, to forgive and to avoid those errors. If you do all these things, even my errors will not have been utterly in vain. The world will be at least a little better off for my having lived in it, and the great desire of my heart will be realized." By the volume's last page, though—page 800—the narrative had only gotten a few weeks past the Battle of Springfield in January 1863. He was turning again to his suspicions about that "smooth-tongued serpent," Dr. Hovey, and the seduction of Susie. "Will those who have loved, who have trusted, and who have been betrayed," he wrote in his last line at the bottom of the page, "blame me for writing about these things?"[19]

On May 9, 1884, staying at Florella's house while she delivered another grandchild, he began copying (and expanding) the autobiography in a series of school composition books. The earlier version contained about 95,000 words; the new one, about 116,000 up to the same point in the narrative in 1863. Then Kelso wrote another 136,000 words, eventually carrying the story through the early fall of 1885. The new preface was this time addressed just to Florella, but it had the same instructions for all three children about publication and the same declaration of purpose.

If the narrative of his childhood suffers from excessive nostalgia and the account of his teenage years is weighed down by pathos, the poignancy is deepened by the shadow Florellus cast backward in time. After Kelso's extraordinary account of his wartime experiences, his later chapters sometimes lapse into a dull chronicle of teaching appointments and a travelogue. He is too often struck speechless by sublime scenes of natural beauty, a travel guidebook trope: "How gladly would I describe all that I beheld here. To do so, however, would require a volume. I will simply say, therefore . . . '*Had I missed this view, my life would never had been complete.*'" More often, though, he is a keen observer and a skillful writer, seriously engaging ideas and conveying deep feeling with unwavering earnestness and flashes of wit. His account of the death of his sons is all the more harrowing by being a raw description of what happened rather than an extended meditation upon his pain. "I am not composing what I am now writing," he paused to say while recounting that tragedy. "I am giving my thoughts without reflection just as they well up in my mind. If I am saving you from suffering such as I have endured, I am not writing in vain."[20]

John R. Kelso's Civil War took up twenty of thirty-eight chapters in his life story. He wrote at a time when many other veterans were committing their reminiscences to paper. For the first fifteen years or so after the war, as one study of Civil War memory put it, "ex-soldiers groped for ways to express the trauma of their personal experiences as well as its larger legacies." After this period of "incubation," though, former soldiers in the early 1880s began writing their accounts—leaving narratives for their children, delivering papers on particular battles to local veteran's organizations, flooding the marketplace with memoirs and stories. Vernacular autobiographies emerged that usually focused on martial manhood—"individual honor" and the "culture of character"—rather than the causes of the war and its larger moral meanings; the writers pursued accuracy almost as a measure of "moral rectitude" but mostly avoided frank depictions of battlefield horrors. Like other memoirists, Kelso sometimes got drawn into the "petty realism" of daily detail and his prose sometimes purples when his reflections turn sentimental. But like the best memoirists, he seems to try to reckon honestly with the many dimensions of his wartime experience.[21]

The Civil War was the central defining event of Kelso's life, and as he wrote about it in the mid-1880s, he endowed the chronicle with the emotional texture of his experience, breathing life into the narrative by blowing on the embers of memory and rekindling the moods and passions of the past. As he describes hiding from the enemy, heart thumping, cold sweat trickling down his back, one imagines his heart thumping and the sweat trickling again as he writes. But punctuating passages that seem to relive the war on the page are moments where he pauses to reflect and try to make sense of it all. One perceptive twenty-first-century reader wrote that "Kelso's coldblooded depictions of the day-to-day grind of soldier life foreshadow the imaginative work of Stephen Crane and others, but they are also interspersed with treacly homilies and a residual Romanticism that is jarring in its quaintness." The jarring juxtaposition, however, may be less between "coldblooded" depictions and quaint sentimentality than between Kelso re-inhabiting the experiences in the 1860s and his halting attempts to render a moral judgment in the 1880s. The shifts in register to stilted apostrophes—"Oh! war! war! why shouldst thou ever exist?"—mark a profound ambivalence: war is brutalizing, but war is ennobling; war is heroic, but war is hell; he was good at it, but should he be ashamed?[22]

When he sat remembering, writing, feeling again the bitter snowstorm in November of 1861, thinking about his home left in ashes, hearing the secessionists refuse shelter to the weeping women and children, forgetting that many of the rebels had their own reasons to seek revenge, sensing his gentleness die and his blood grow hot, and vowing to kill twenty-five rebels with his own hands—when he sat remembering and writing all of this, he described his vengeance as a kind of insanity: "for surely it was madness," he wrote; "I vowed to slay with my own hand *twenty-five* rebels before I cut my hair. If it was madness to *make* such a vow, what was it to *fulfill* that vow, as I *did*?" A few pages later, though, he defended it: "Why should we not avenge ourselves upon those who have done us very great wrongs? I know that, when we are calm, when no war excitement is upon us, when no wrong has been done us, it is easy to moralize. I can now do this myself." He knew it was especially easy for those who had never experienced war "to say that a soldier should feel no animosity against those whom he may be killing, or who may be killing him." And clergymen preached about loving thy enemy even as they sent young men off to shed blood. "At the time of which I am speaking, however, I did not have grace enough to proceed in this godly manner. . . . I did not pretend to *love* those that I killed, and I did not try to kill them in a *loving manner*. I did not ask a blessing before killing a man or eating a dinner. I did both as a man, not as a Christian." The deluded Christian soldier marching off to war tries to mask two opposed truths—what the moralist in his armchair accurately sees as madness, and what the soldier on the battlefield honestly understands as a call to virtuous manhood. Without the evasions of religion, Kelso in the mid-1880s was still caught between these two positions.[23]

Kelso wrote and then rewrote the first half of his autobiography during vacations while he was still teaching. In the fall of 1883, he taught a school at Turlock, 15 miles southeast of Modesto, and boarded at the Turlock Hotel. Unruly students at the school caused him "a great deal of trouble." The hotel had "[d]runken and boisterous men coming and going at all hours," and this "bedlam of noises," along with "the overwhelming odor from a pig pen near my window," kept him up at night. His physical and mental health were already fragile. He had not been able to do hard physical labor since the harvest of 1876, having accumulated a variety of ailments including something he described as a partial paralysis of the stomach brought on, he thought, by drinking too much cold water in the summer heat. And he was still burdened by his dark anxieties. Growing more alarmed as his health continued to decline, he bartered copies of his books for a forty-dollar "suit of magnetic clothing" devised by Dr. L. Tenney of Cincinnati. With a similar arrangement, he tried a more expensive though (temporarily) more successful treatment prescribed by Dr. Liebig and Company of San Francisco: Liebig's "Wonderful German Invigorator," medicine sent in an amber bottle, promised to cure "Nervous and Physical Debility, Vital Exhaustion, [and] Loss of Manhood," all connected to prostate problems and a malady known as "spermatorrhea." Still, after an academic year in Modesto, 1884–85, he felt that his "health was so broken" and his "nervous system so shattered," that he had to retire from teaching.[24]

In mid-May 1885, he went to San Francisco to apply for a job at the U.S. Customs House, which he did not get. While in the city, he attended a materialization séance conducted by Mrs. Elsie Reynolds. Reynolds was known for materializing various spirits, including an Indian named "Star Eye." Kelso saw and felt the apparitions, but knew that they "were undoubtedly *real women* in the *flesh* and *not materialized spirits*." If he had read the local papers, he could have saved himself fifty cents. Reynolds had been exposed ten days earlier by a reporter who grabbed Star Eye and re-lit a lantern, revealing Reynolds herself in his clutches. She used low lighting, a cabinet with a false back, a dark curtain, a chemise covered in phosphorescent chemicals, masks, and an inner circle of true believers who usually kept the skeptics at bay during performances. Repeated exposures, however, did not halt Reynolds' career—she went on materializing for years and was still advertising séances in 1913. The Fox sisters themselves would confess three years after Kelso saw Reynolds that the whole thing was a hoax, demonstrating before a large audience in New York that they had made the "Rochester Rappings" forty years earlier by cracking their toe joints. Spiritualists acknowledged that there were some charlatans bilking the gullible, but argued that the existence of counterfeits did not invalidate the authentic.[25]

At the end of the month, Kelso attended a spiritualist camp meeting which was being held for more than two weeks at the fairgrounds in San Jose. Although he was "not known as a Spiritualist," he had been elected by the state association and asked to lecture there. He found the campsite beautiful, the speakers engaging, and the crowds large and enthusiastic. The mediums were "excellent," he wrote, some of them possessing "wonderful powers," and, unlike Mrs. Reynolds, they were persuasive. "They gave me many tests of such a nature that, in spite of my extreme skepticism, I was compelled to believe that we do have a conscious existence after the dissolution of the body." The experience marked more than his intellectual acceptance of spiritualism; it was a profound, emotional conversion: "I was compelled, too, to believe that my departed loved ones, in spirit forms, were then hovering about me. When these facts, in the full force of their magnitude, forced themselves upon my mind, I shed tears of joy,—the first in over forty years." He made many friends and his lectures were well received; "It was the happiest fortnight that I had known since my boyhood."[26]

When he finally published *Spiritualism Sustained* two years later, he could state that he was "now a believer in this beautiful philosophy," though "only a recent convert." His conversion, he admitted, had nothing to do with the arguments from the Bible and Christian history that he gave in his lectures. He had been persuaded by empirical evidence—"direct tests" to his own senses. He argued, as many spiritualists did, that his embrace of spiritualism did not indicate a turn toward the "supernatural." Spiritual manifestations appeared to him "to be just as strictly in accordance with the laws of nature as are any of the other phenomena with which we are acquainted. Indeed, I do not know any such thing as the supernatural. Supply the necessary conditions, and communications between man and a spirit become just as easy and just as natural as are those between one man and another." Other proponents also contended that spiritualists could still be materialists. Following the eighteenth-century mystic Emanuel Swedenborg, as one commentator has explained, "they replaced a spirit/matter dichotomy with a hierarchical spectrum in which the ordinary matter detectable by the senses shaded off into higher and more elusive forms and higher spirits were composed of finer matter than lower ones." Kelso, however, wrote about his "materialistic prejudices" being overcome, of being freed from what he had once called "the cold barren rock of absolute materialism," and he now inclined toward an ill-defined dualism.[27]

Accordingly, humans must be dual beings, he thought, with physical organs for the material world and another set for the spiritual one. He believed it a mistake, though, for spiritualists—or mystics, or Methodists, or believers in spiritual experiences of any sort—to focus on cultivating those spiritual faculties while still living as embodied beings in the material world. There would be time enough for that in the afterlife. Ministers, he argued, should encourage their flocks to focus on the health of the body, on the consequences of the first birth into the material world and not the second birth into the spiritual one. He wavered on whether a spiritual afterlife meant immortality: in *Spiritualism Sustained* he endorsed the idea; in *The Universe Analyzed*, published in the same year, he argued that eternal life for an individualized entity was impossible, and that consciousness would eventually cease. Believing in an afterlife for finite spirits beyond the death of the body, however, did not at all persuade him of the existence of an Infinite Spirit. "I am a thorough atheist myself," he continued to say."[28]

17

Heaven on Earth

HOW WOULD IT all end? By the time he was fifty, Kelso, in the mournful conclusion to an early 1880s lecture, observing the furrows on his face, the gray at his temples, and the weariness in his bones, was thinking that his "journey is almost ended" and his "work is almost done." Most of the people he had loved in his life, he said, were dead and gone, and he was ready to join them. His interest in spiritualism kept alive a hope that he might be reunited with them in some sort of godless heaven on the "farther shore" of death's cold, dark river. Several years later, however, after copying that lecture into his "Miscellaneous Writings" manuscript, he was able to tack on a cheerier note. Describing himself as "now one of the happiest of men," he concluded that "the stormy day of his life's eventful career promises to close with a remarkably serene and beautiful eventide."[1]

But even as he wrote those words, he was in the midst of another storm. In the spring of 1886, he opened his newspaper to read news that both shocked him and confirmed his worst fears. Angry, impassioned, and rethinking some of his core beliefs, he decided that events had exposed, once and for all, the hopeless rot of the American political and economic system. In his last years, he turned from his own story to the story of the nation he had fought and bled for, looking for a better way forward.

BETWEEN 1882 AND 1885 Kelso had another project besides writing his autobiography. Tired of being alone, he was looking for a new wife. He knew "many charming marriageable women" between the ages of "fifteen and fifty years or more." After the spiritualist camp meeting at San Jose in May 1885, he traveled to Monterey with a "Mrs. F. B. Clark of Connecticut, a charming widow, and her niece, Mrs. S. M. Kingsley, a still more charming widow. By the latter, I was so charmed and cheered that I constantly called her Little Sunbeam, a pet name with which she seemed well pleased." He also conducted an extensive correspondence with women. From his male friends to whom he wrote about "purely business" or "purely literary" matters, he obtained introductions to eligible women. Eventually, he claimed, he secured "over thirty" female correspondents "in various parts of the United States and Canada." He enjoyed the epistolary flirtation, and "several of the most desirable of these women" seemed interested in him, but, apparently, charm was not enough. "I did not find any one that I thought would make me an entirely harmonious conjugal mate and an earnest helper in the great work to which my life had been consecrated," he wrote. "I finally almost despaired of ever finding one that I could love, as I had once loved, and as I felt that I was still capable of loving. I had almost come to the conclusion, that I would have to continue, to the close of my earthly career, the desolate and unnatural life of celibacy that I was then living."[2]

However, through the courtesy of a correspondent in Colorado, Morse Coffin, Kelso was introduced to Coffin's sister-in-law, Etta S. Dunbar. Born in 1837, Etta had grown up in Otsego, New York. Her parents were transplanted New England Congregationalists, and her father at various times worked as a butcher, a farmer, and a merchant. In 1868 she had graduated from Illinois State Normal University, and then taught and served as principal for schools in Blackburn and DeKalb, Illinois, until stepping down for health reasons in 1874. After taking care of her invalid mother for three years she moved to Colorado to be near her younger sister Julia and Julia's husband Morse. Etta bought a 160-acre farm 6 miles east of Longmont. She loved art, literature, and music, and, in the spring of 1885 as Kelso wrote to her, she bought a piano on installments. Like her sister, she was a "dynamic and progressive" woman; a visiting freethinker described Dunbar as having "passed altogether beyond the bounds of Orthodoxy," enjoying "the broad and breezy commons of the universe."[3]

From her first letter, Kelso felt a connection. Subsequent letters only strengthened the feeling that Miss Dunbar might be the one. From the photograph she sent, Kelso saw "a very plain woman. Her features possessed very little of what the world calls beauty. In her form, however, she was perfect, and beneath the plain surface, I could read in her a rarely beautiful nature,—a wonderfully perfect womanhood. She was forty-seven years of age, though she looked ten years younger." (Perhaps her youthful appearance was already being aided by hair dye—a bottle of which was hidden beneath a floorboard in her room.) She was "highly educated," had been a popular teacher, and she possessed, Kelso thought, "a brilliant intellect." She had socialized, as he

Etta Dunbar [Kelso], Self Portrait. Photo courtesy of Sandstone Ranch, Longmont, Colorado.

understood it, with the leading families of Illinois and Colorado. "Her hand had often been sought by men of wealth, education, and high social standing." But no one ever measured up to her ideal. On her farm she spent her time painting, tending to her flowers and shrubbery, and enjoying a quiet life with a small circle of friends. "Her only want was congenial companionship,— some one to love her and be loved by her."[4]

Still struggling with illness, Kelso had planned a restorative July trip to the Sierra Nevada Mountains, but Miss Dunbar invited him to Colorado. So after a six-day journey, during which he got progressively sicker, he got off the train at Longmont, stayed the night at a hotel, and the next morning walked the 4 miles east to Morse and Julia Coffin's Sandstone Ranch. Morse, an early White settler in the region, was considered a "pioneer." In 1859, then in his early twenties, he left Illinois during the Colorado gold rush, made some money sawing timber, and established a prosperous 360-acre farm on the banks of the St. Vrain River. After returning to Illinois to marry Julia in 1865, the couple returned to become civic and social leaders in a community that developed rapidly with the arrival of the Denver Pacific Railroad in 1870. Longmont was founded in 1871 by the Chicago-Colorado Colony, a cooperative venture that laid out a 60,000 acre grid and developed an irrigation system. The Coffins' handsome home, built of stone quarried from bluffs right behind it, had a two-story back porch and an adobe-brick summer kitchen. Kelso, after going back to Longmont in a wagon to fetch his luggage, stayed with the Coffins that night.[5]

On the following day Mrs. Coffin took him to Miss Dunbar's residence. "Her cordial and yet dignified welcome," Kelso wrote not long afterward, "made me at once feel entirely at home." But Kelso's illness intensified. "The remainder of the day, we spent very pleasantly in conversation, I, by a strong effort of the will, repressing the feeling of illness that was upon me. On the next morning, Miss Dunbar perceived that I was ill and I had to admit that I really was so. It was, indeed, the beginning of a long attack of malarial fever." Kelso collapsed into bed and Etta took care of him. She immediately saw that he had been brought down by more than malaria. She thought, as she recalled three years later, that his years of teaching had "so prostrated the nervous system that at the time of our meeting he was as incapable of mental as of

Coffin Home at Sandstone Ranch, Longmont, Colorado, ca. 1900–1910. Photo courtesy Longmont Museum, Longmont, Colorado.

manual labor." For the next couple weeks, John was the patient and Etta the nurse. "Through this long illness," he wrote, "Miss Dunbar nursed me with a skill, a carefulness, and a solicitude that fully won my admiration, my gratitude and my love. And in her patient, she found something to win her love." As he convalesced, they read to each other from the composition books containing his handwritten autobiography, and through this she learned all the details of his "checkered career," and in the way he wanted them to be known. "When she thus learned of the many dangers I had known and of the many sorrows I had suffered, she was, in sympathy, drawn closer to me than ever; and I loved her more because of her sympathy in all these dangers and sorrows."[6]

By August he was able to putter in her gardens. A few weeks later he felt well enough for the couple to go on a camping trip up Long's Peak with Morse, Coffin's daughter Neva, and two other friends. They set out in a two-horse wagon and camped on a rainy second night with another camper and his wife in their large tent. A photograph preserved in Coffin's photo album shows the camp, the long-bearded Morse recognizable in front of the tent. The trip would not go well. They left their wagon behind to hike up the mountain, but a horse ran off with their provisions and many of their blankets. A cold rain soaked them. Kelso, weak from his recent illness, could not keep up. Etta stayed back with him. He was thoroughly exhausted by the summit on the second day, and still struggled after lunch and an hour's rest when they made their descent. A marker on the way served as a warning to tourists who were too casual about the dangers of mountain hiking: "Here Carrie J. Wilton lay down to rest and died alone Sept. 23rd 1884," read the inscription on a plain board.[7]

When they reached a plateau called Boulder Field and cold rain again drenched them, Kelso and Coffin disagreed about the direction they ought to take next. Coffin was worn out, too, and apparently bewildered, but as the self-appointed leader of the expedition, he insisted on going in the wrong direction. They spent the night in a canyon with immense snowbanks, sheltering from the rain as best they could next to a boulder, trying to dry their clothes by a fire and rub the chill from their limbs. The next morning Coffin, averring he could find the trail back to their base camp, marched off alone. The others followed Kelso, who walked gingerly, worried that one wrong step could dislocate his bad hip. After tiptoeing past a large black bear, they finally reached a hunter's cabin. The hunter told them that he had already seen Morse Coffin three times that day: the pioneer was walking in circles.

Not until they had rested a few days at Coffin's ranch did Morse announce that he was opposed to John and Etta marrying and "would prevent it if he

Coffin Family Camping Trip, August, 1885. Morse Coffin, bearded, stands in front of the tent. Kelso may be the figure on the far left. Photo courtesy Longmont Museum, Longmont, Colorado.

could." As Etta's brother-in-law, he seemed to think that he was also her "proprietor," and that she could not marry without his consent. Etta resented Morse's presumption. Kelso resented it even more. "His language on that occasion, and his conduct on various other occasions, revealed the fact that he was a treacherous and unprincipled man totally unworthy of my friendship," he wrote not long after. "I therefore cast him off forever." The next Friday, on September 5, 1885, Etta and John went to Denver and were married at the home of a Superior Court judge.[8]

Kelso had long criticized the "false marriage" propped up by ceremony and law. He had lectured against it since the 1870s. From 1883 to the summer of 1885 he participated in an extended exchange with the editors of the *Boston Investigator* about polygamy. He despised both Mormonism and polygamy as much as they did, he said. But he thought antipolygamy laws unconstitutional. He argued not for the religion or the marriage practice but for the citizens of Utah to establish their own forms of marriage without outside interference. When the assistant editor of the free-thought journal *Lucifer the Light-Bearer* was arrested for marrying the editor's daughter by private contract rather than state license, Kelso published letters in *Lucifer* and a pamphlet in support, and Etta, he said, "heartily" agreed. So why did John and Etta marry conventionally in 1885? The same reason, he explained in 1886, why he had put down his gun when twenty rebels aiming muskets at his chest demanded he surrender: not because they were in the right, but because they had more power. "So, a year ago when I married knowing that the enemy was too strong for me . . . I marched up, like a big fine coward," and bowed to the demands of law and ceremony to protect himself and his wife from "fines, imprisonments, social ostracism, etc., if not mob violence."[9]

In arguing about marriage, Kelso was again thinking through the relationships between individuals, local communities, and the state. It was wrong for majorities to turn personal opinions and prejudices into legislation, he argued. He possessed "equally strong prejudices against the intermarriage of whites and negroes" as he did against polygamy, he admitted. When the editor of the *Boston Investigator* asked if he would want his own mother, sister, or daughter in a polygamous relationship, his answer was no—just as it had been when his White Southern neighbors had asked him before the war if he wanted to see his mother, sister, or daughter marry a Black man. He would rather see them dead first, he said. Raised in the South, where Blacks were treated "like cattle," he could not deny those feelings. "I am duly ashamed of these prejudices, so unreasonable and so unjust, but I am not able to cast them off. I *am*, however, able to rise above them in my treatment of the negroes, just as I am able to rise above my prejudices against the Mormons in my treatment of them." Blacks and Whites who loved each other should be allowed to marry, and Mormons should be allowed to enter into polygamous relationships, no matter how distasteful to the rest of us, without the interference of the state.[10]

The antipolygamy laws were wicked, and like all wicked laws they ought to be resisted, he advised a (monogamously) married Mormon woman who wrote to him. However, open opposition to the national government, which continued to consolidate power and increasingly encroached upon citizens' rights, would be madness. He encouraged the Mormons instead to organize forms of passive resistance and peaceful civil disobedience. The *Boston Investigator*, aghast, decried this notion of ignoring or opposing laws one did not like as dangerous anarchism. In another three and a half years, Kelso would embrace the label.[11]

KELSO CONCLUDED HIS autobiography with his marriage to Etta in the fall of 1885: after the wedding, he wrote in his last lines, "we devoted our time to labor and to literary amusements, growing more and more happy in the pure and unspeakable love that existed between us. We found that, after marriage, the sweetest part of our courtship had just begun. More than ever, we were true and devoted lovers." The free-thought lecturer and writer Samuel P. Putnam reported visits to the Kelsos in 1886 and 1887, describing a "pleasant home" with a "genial gentleman" and a talented wife who shared his philosophy and his commitments. Kelso was indeed happy with Etta and his new life in Colorado, and he may have been able to put a brave face on for visitors like Putnam, but physically he was a wreck.[12]

So in the spring of 1886, with Etta's help and encouragement, he again applied for a full disability pension. For the shotgun blast in August 1863 that had maimed his left hand and the fall beneath his horse a month later that had left him with a hernia, he had received a two-thirds disability right after the war, with payments of $11.33 per month. In 1869, he had applied for an increase, and although he was kept at two-thirds disabled, his monthly rate was raised to $12.75. In 1874, he had tried again. His hernia was worse, he had testified: he could not even leave his room without wearing a truss, and the constant pressure of the truss, in turn, seemed to have injured his kidneys. Rejected, he had applied again in 1877, arguing that he was totally disabled for manual labor (the pension law's measure of disability). His payment went up to $17 per month, but this was still short of the $24 he could receive with full disability.[13]

In 1880, he had tried to get an increase based upon a different injury: the dislocation of his right hip, caused by the fall of his horse, which had left lingering and worsening problems besides the hernia. The dislocation had been mentioned in his 1865 medical exam, but he had not pressed the point fifteen years earlier, thinking the injury would eventually heal. By 1880, however, it would be difficult to obtain witness affidavits attesting to the details of the accident and verifying that it had occurred in the line of duty. He had been riding hard a few hundred yards behind his men when his horse had fallen on top of him. All of the four soldiers who had seen him right afterward, he thought, were now dead. His company had been on detached service, away from the regimental hospital and surgeon, so there was no medical record of treatment immediately after the injury. Failing on these technicalities, Kelso tried to appeal to his record of service overall: "He finally states," he testified, writing in the third person and concluding his 1880 affidavit, "that he was never absent from his post of duty, that he took part in over fifty engagements, that he was victorious in many hand to hand conflicts, that he tried to be a good, faithful, and brave officer, that he was three times brevetted for *'gallant and meritorious services.'*" But his appeal was rejected. "Cannot prove new disability of right hip," the notation in his file reads. "No increase. Inability to furnish the testimony of officers or enlisted men who have personal knowledge of circumstances under which the injury to hip was received. Reject."[14]

He would go all out for a total disability military pension in 1886. He hired the Washington, D.C., law firm of Charles and William B. King to serve as his claim agent. He based his claim on his wounds, his injuries, and a chronic disease, all stemming from the gunshot and horse accident in 1863. The injury to his hand had been permanent, the severity of his hernia had "greatly increased" over the years, and now he also described a bad left shoulder, detailed serious problems with both hips, and complained of a chronic kidney ailment. He gave the fullest account of his condition in an affidavit sworn at the end of July. "Instead of getting well, as I hoped they would, these injuries have grown worse," he testified. "The hernia is now about twice as large as a goose egg and is down all the time, except when held up by a strong truss. My hips are sore in the joints, the balls sometimes slipping in the sockets, rendering me unable to walk without great pain. The flesh upon my hips is greatly shrunken and is too soft. My left shoulder is a little elevated and is stiff and sore in the joint, so much that I can hardly put on a coat without help." There was more: "My kidneys pain me nearly all the time. A brick-dust deposit of a slimy nature appears in the urine. The long pressure of a truss has aggravated the trouble in my kidneys, injured my organs of generation, and produced varicose veins on the right leg. The hard manual labor which I have had, and still have to perform, has greatly aggravated all these injuries. I can scarce perform labor at all now."[15]

Etta testified with clinical details about her husband's body. She first met him on July 10, 1885, she wrote, and became acquainted with his intimate physical details "soon after." The hernia "has greatly increased in size during these three years, and which renders the wearing of a truss imperative." As several other witnesses also remarked she noted a "distortion of the left scapula causing the shoulder to be much protruded and elevated, rendering action of the left arm, at times, very painful and the putting on or off of a coat (especially an overcoat) always very difficult." She mentioned the bullet buried in his left palm and the limited use of the second and third fingers on that hand. His kidney problem, she noted, "causes him to rise often in the night." She did not discuss his hips, but testified that his "glutei muscles are in a constant state of wasting, so that in their stead, on each side, is a marked depression." Unlike any other witness, she also commented upon his mental state: his prostrated nervous system rendered him "as incapable of mental as of manual labor."[16]

Kelso knew he had to gather new testimonies about the origins of his wounds and injuries. Andrew Smithson, who had been a private in the 14th MSM Cavalry, and had been shot in the thigh by the same bushwhacker who had unloaded his shotgun at Kelso, had not witnessed the fall of the horse but saw Kelso badly hurt in camp later that day. Other soldiers testified seeing Kelso unable to walk "a few minutes" after he had been crushed by his horse and having to be lifted in and out of his saddle for many days afterward. Sergeant Peter Humphrey remembered Kelso's injuries, and though he "never saw the ingered parts," he "saw the captain a limpin a round the camps for quite a while." Sergeant Ozias Ruark could not remember details, but like the other soldiers testified to Kelso's bravery, integrity, and veracity. Major Milton Burch, who had seen Kelso's buckshot wounds and listed Kelso's injuries from the horse accident, added that Kelso had "done as much to help put down the rebellion as any man in the Government service. Those last words may be superfluous, but they are facts."[17]

Kelso knew he also had to establish the continuity of his injuries from his medical exam in 1865 through his time in Missouri, California, and Colorado. This would be difficult, too, because he had done his best to hide his ailments from anyone outside his family. Tilman Barnes, his brother-in-law, and June Doherty, a housekeeper, had lived in his household for several years in Missouri and could have spoken about his disabilities, but Barnes was dead and Doherty could not be located. Kelso managed to secure Missouri testimony from Jared Smith, who remembered Kelso as being perfectly healthy before the war and having a limp and a crippled shoulder after it. Another Missouri neighbor, E. D. Ott, remembered the shoulder and heard Kelso complain about his hips and back. For the California period (1872–1885) he had affidavits from Samuel Gibson and J. D. Harp. Gibson testified that Kelso "could scarcely put on a coat without help," and a "mis-step or stumble would make him quite lame for several days." After 1879 Kelso lived for two years with J. D. Harp, who remembered the truss and recalled that Kelso "often went to his room to lay down for he said he was easier in a reclining position."[18]

The fullest account of the Missouri and California years came from his daughter Florella. She testified to the weakened hand, the hernia and truss, the stiff shoulder, the kidney medicine, the pain in both hips, and the femur occasionally slipping out of its socket. "All these injuries have grown worse with time, except that of his left hand." However, Kelso mistakenly thought that pension law and Pension Bureau procedures excluded testimony from family members. He resented the rule and submitted Florella's affidavit anyway. Because of the private nature of most of his ailments and the difficulty of getting other testimony, he felt he had to submit a sworn affidavit from Etta, too, in which she had to promise that she would not personally benefit from the pension because the money would be put toward publishing Kelso's books rather than be added to the family's general fund. Besides Etta's, Kelso had sworn depositions from two Longmont neighbors, John and Georgiana Rice, who described him having to weed or hoe in the garden while on his knees, since he could neither stand long nor stoop.[19]

All of the affidavits made their way to the Pension Office in Washington, D.C., a government bureaucracy housed in a new, enormous building occupying an entire city block—the largest brick building in the world, with many of the Bureau's 1,500 employees. The documents came to the Mail Division, where they were date-stamped and sent to the Record Division. The claim was then evaluated to see if it met all the formal requirements (such as being sworn before a notary public) and then filed with the claimant's prior claim(s), if any. A request for a report on the claimant's military service made its way to the War Department. Medical evaluations were ordered, and requests for additional information were made. In Kelso's case the Bureau asked three witnesses for more detail, sought to secure affidavits verifying the reliable character of three others, and required proof from the War Department showing the military witnesses were in fact present for the occasions of Kelso's wounds and injuries. Kelso was summoned to a medical examination before a three-person board of surgeons in Denver at the end of October 1888.[20]

When the evidence was complete—and its collection could take many months or even years—an examiner indexed the file and prepared a brief for the chief of division who, if all was well, referred the file to the Board of Review. The Board ruled according to the law (the increasingly complex pension statutes) and the facts as presented in the evidence. Then the case was sent to the Medical Referee's Office for medical review.[21]

The medical reviewer focused on a single question: did the claimant deserve a higher rate? Claims for an increase on account of new disabilities (any not mentioned in an earlier claim) raised "strong legal presumption that such disabilities did not exist at the filing of the original declaration." The pathological sequence of diseases, too, had to be established by competent evidence. Did a disease suffered by a claimant during the war really lead to a permanent or eventual impairment? The medical reviewer had to follow the general rule "that lay testimony, when unsupported by the record or by medical evidence, and dated years after the discharge of the soldier, cannot be accepted as proof of service origin of obscure diseases"—that is, diseases not obvious to the lay observer. Approved claims were then rated according to an eighteen-point scale, a formula where full disability—18/18—was equivalent to the loss of a hand or foot. Some disabilities (blindness, deafness, loss of limbs) were rated in the statutes; many others were listed in a Pension Office table. The loss of one eye, for example, was worth 18/18; a thumb and index finger, 16/18; a big toe, 6/18. An inguinal hernia that had passed through the external ring got 10/18; one that had not so passed, 6/18. Medical examiners and reviewers rated injuries that were not specified in the statutes or the table according to their best guesses.[22]

The evaluation of Kelso's last pension claims in the 1880s occurred at a time when military pensions had become an important political issue. When applications began to dip in the late 1870s, claims agents who saw their fees start to dry up launched a lobbying effort and propaganda campaign, led by leading pension attorney George E. Lemon's newspaper, the *National Tribune*, to broaden pension requirements and liberalize benefits. When the Arrears Act passed in 1879, backdating pension payments to the date of discharge and thus offering large lump sums as well as monthly stipends to pensioners, applications and payouts soared: In 1875 the government paid 213,000 invalids and their widows or dependents nearly $27 million; in 1885 there were nearly 325,000 pensioners getting over $63 million. The Grand Army of the Republic, the leading Civil War veterans' organization, made pension liberalization a rallying cry in the early 1880s. Pensions became a cornerstone of patronage politics for both Democratic and Republican politicians courting the soldier vote. As pension statutes became more complex, congressmen began receiving fifty letters per week from constituents seeking help with their applications. The volume of correspondence between Congress and the Pension Bureau ballooned from nearly 40,000 inquires in 1880 to 94,000 in 1888. During the 1884 presidential election season, the Pension Commissioner was accused of speeding up applications in electorally significant states and slowing them down elsewhere. Pensions were again a hot topic in the campaign of 1888.[23]

That election came and went and Kelso still waited. The process dragged on. After twenty-one months and still no decision, Kelso submitted a final, frustrated affidavit in December 1888. He told the story of his wounds and injuries one more time and summarized the evidence he had submitted to sustain his claim. In an affidavit two months earlier he was indignant: "He is certainly entitled to the increase claimed, and feels that a *great* injustice is being done him by long delays." Now he was plaintive: "Three years ago, I had to give up teaching on account of my nervous afflictions. Will my country let me suffer want and perish for having so faithfully served her? I can not last long. Will she make me comfortable so far as she can while I do live? The testimony is now all in. Please let the case be adjudicated at once." In his desperation, he revealed a final injury, one only hinted at previously, concealed from everyone but his wife. This was "the most serious injury of all." Now he felt he had to stand naked before the Government, exposing not just the goose egg-sized hernia in his scrotum but the most intimate wound to his manhood. "One injury received at the same time as the others and by the same accident I have concealed so well that even my daughter does not know if its existence," he wrote. "This is injury to my generation organs, producing spermatorrhea, from which I have never been free since the reception of the injury. This is the most serious injury of all, affecting my whole nervous system and producing a depression of spirit that has often lead [*sic*] me to seriously meditate suicide. And yet knowing that I could not furnish the required proof of the origin and the continuity of this injury, I have not included it in this claim."[24]

Spermatorrhea was a mysterious—and imaginary—malady at the center of anxieties about men's health and male sexuality in the second half of the nineteenth-century. It first came to attention with a three-volume treatise by French physician Claude Francois Lallemand, which was translated into English in 1847 and published in America the following year. The subject was quickly taken up by medical writers and then popular healers. Quacks pushing tonics and treatments exploited men's anxieties about sex and their bodies. (The ads for "Dr. Liebig's German Invigorator," which Kelso was taking by the mid-1880s, had much to say about spermatorrhea.) Much of the concern was rooted in hysteria over masturbation, but Lallemand and those who followed him also warned about an involuntary emission of semen and described a man's vital fluid unconsciously draining away through the urine or feces. Proceeding from a variety of conditions, diseases, or injuries, involuntary spermatorrhea was said to produce the same host of dire effects as excessive masturbation. These included a variety of afflictions from hemorrhoids to stuttering, but commonly involved chronic muscular weakness and general lassitude, along with serious mental conditions: melancholy, anxiety, mania, even delusions. This trickling away of seminal fluid, even when it did not cause impotence, could drain away masculine vitality and produce "effeminacy, and sometimes extreme pusillanimity." By later in the century some physicians began arguing that such involuntary seminal leakage was in fact very rare; they lamented that Lallemand's mistaken views, fueled by quack advertisements, had so taken hold of the popular imagination. "Imaginary" spermattorrhea and spermatorrhea as a "neurosis" became the focus of some of the medical literature even as popular health publications and advertisements continued to obsess about actual spermatorrhea as a dire threat to American manhood. Kelso apparently became convinced that his wartime injuries had produced a physiological cause to his depression. He seems to have feared that his manhood was literally dribbling away.[25]

On April 7, 1890, the Pension Bureau's Medical Referee at last reviewed Kelso's file. The referee turned to Form 3-111, the medical examination that had been conducted in October 1888, in order to fill out Form 3-146, recording the final decision. The report described the buckshot lodged in Kelso's hand and the scarring around his fingers. It recorded that his left shoulder was 1½ inches above his right and caused pain when he moved his arm upward and backward, but found "no objective evidence of injury." It noted a hernia the size of a "goose egg," but said that it "can easily be reduced & retained by truss." The examining physicians also noted the "apparent atrophy of his gluteus maximus muscles," which, they said, may have been caused by the truss and which in turn could have caused the tenderness in his joints and pain in his back. "There is no evidence of disease of Kidneys elicited by chemical examination of Urine," the report stated. The physicians then rated his injuries: 0/18 for kidneys, 2/18 for back pain, 3/18 for hips, 4/18 for his hand, and 8/18 for the hernia. The Medical Referee in 1890 simply did the arithmetic: "Combined disabilities not to exceed 17/18 at any time," he concluded. Kelso remained 1/18 shy of total disability, and his pension would stay at $17 per month, less $25 for his attorneys' fee.[26]

IN EARLY MAY 1886, at Haymarket Square in Chicago, workers rallied for an eight-hour workday and to protest a police shooting that had killed a reported six strikers the day before. As policemen tried to disperse the crowd, someone threw a bomb, killing one officer and wounding others. The police opened fire, the workers fired back, and before it was over four more people in the crowd and six more policemen were mortally wounded and 130 people were injured. Eight anarchists who had organized the labor protest were arrested and put on trial in the summer of 1886. All were convicted, seven of them condemned to death. Two had their sentences commuted to life in prison, one committed suicide, and the remaining four were hanged on November 11, 1887. Kelso was among those in an international chorus who condemned the result as an outrageous miscarriage of justice. Lacking a bomb thrower and any real evidence of a conspiracy, the critics charged, a biased judge and jury condemned men for their radical ideas for labor reform.[27]

"Bombs and Blood," the first front page headline in the *Rocky Mountain News* of May 5, 1886, had read, the sub-headlines outlining a slanted account of Chicago's Haymarket "riot" the day before: "Terrible Slaughter of Police by Anarchists in Chicago"; "The Matter Evidently Preconcerted, the Socialist

Paper Having Advised Just Such a Work"; "The Police Forced onto the Scene by Inflammatory Speeches of the Socialist Leaders"; "Three Bombs Thrown by the Socialists Among One Hundred Twenty-Five Policemen"; "Terrible Scenes of Suffering Among the Wounded Policemen." The police fired into the crowd because they were defending themselves, according to the report. The "mob" fired back because it "appeared crazed with frantic desire for blood." If Kelso sought a different view of the Haymarket affair in the free-thought journals he read, he would have been disappointed. *The Boston Investigator* condemned anarchism as an "unmitigated evil" and the Chicago anarchists and socialists as "foreign ruffians" and "murderous wretches" who ought to be hanged or imprisoned for life. *The Truth Seeker* was only a little less vehement against the foreign "fanatics" and lamented that the bloodshed would set back the labor movement for years.[28]

Even Moses Harman's *Lucifer the Light-Bearer* assumed the guilt of the anarchist leaders and denounced them. *Lucifer*, the radical journal focusing on marriage reform and women's rights, had probably introduced Kelso to anarchist ideas in the first place. The principles of free-thought, Harman had consistently argued, logically led to anarchism. Statecraft and priestcraft were both based on fear of the supernatural, and freethinkers should oppose the state's despotic claim to sovereignty over the citizen's body and material interests just as they opposed the church's despotism over individual conscience. But the Chicago rioters, Harman believed, were false anarchists and socialists whose mob violence needed to be opposed as well.[29]

Kelso got an entirely different view of Chicago's anarchist leaders in Denver's *Labor Enquirer*, which denounced the biased coverage in the capitalist press. It argued that the police provoked the violence, the anarchists had nothing to do with it, the bomb-thrower was a lone "idiot," and the farcical, corrupt trial, violating law and fundamental principles, produced no evidence to convict. Kelso's first Haymarket essay was published in Chicago, and then in the Denver paper. After the essay was printed separately as a pamphlet, John and Etta visited the *Labor Enquirer's* office and "impressed all who met them with their deep earnestness in the cause of reform."[30]

Other than on church and state issues, Kelso had not publicly spoken or written about politics since he gave some speeches during the presidential campaign of 1880. In conversation with the Rochester spiritualists a year later he had predicted that the United States was nearing a great political crisis, a revolutionary effort to unify church and state, enslave workers to their capitalist imperialist overlords, and crown former president Grant as emperor. Grant died in the summer of 1885, but in March, 1886, Kelso used him as a figure of the continuing exploitation of downtrodden laborers by capitalist plutocrats. He published "Our Great Non-needy and Non-Deserving U.S. Paupers" in the *Truth Seeker* protesting the exorbitant pension that Congress had awarded Grant's widow. The political puppets of the bondholders, bankers, and monopolists who had benefitted so lavishly from the notoriously corrupt Grant administration further bled the poor toilers of the nation to pay Mrs. Grant more than $5,000 a year, he complained, while a fully disabled Civil War soldier got less than $100. The essay, though, could do little more than sputter in indignation. Its maudlin scenes—the crippled soldier unable to buy a coat; the seamstress sewing late into the night for 3 cents an hour to buy a coffin for her dead child; the fifteen-year-old girl turning to prostitution to survive—sought to shame Mrs. Grant into repudiating her pension. When anarchism suddenly flashed into focus a few weeks later with the Haymarket bomb, it gave Kelso an ideological framework for his disillusionment with the American experiment, his outrage at the injustices of Gilded Age society, and his hopes for a better future.[31]

Kelso had been primed for anarchism by *Lucifer* and by an obscure book he read in 1884, *The New Republic, Founded on the Natural and Inalienable Rights of Man* (1883) by Edwin J. Schellhous, a California physician. Schellhous, apparently inspired by Henry George's bestselling *Progress and Poverty* (1879), tried to combine ideas from anarchism, socialism, and republican liberalism to rejuvenate the republic. Like the anarchists, he proposed replacing corporations and banks with worker cooperatives and voluntary associations. Like the socialists, he recommended nationalizing transportation and communication (railroads and the telegraph). And like liberal activists, he wanted electoral reform (direct balloting, proportional voting, and women's suffrage). Kelso shared—or would come to share—many of Schellhous's views. Both lauded the Declaration of Independence and far preferred the U.S. government that had been created by the Articles of Confederation in the 1780s to the one established by the Constitution that followed. Both detested tariffs, advocated paper currency rather than the gold standard, and called for the judicial system to be replaced by arbitration. Schellhous, though, never used the words "socialism" or "anarchism" and framed his book as advocating a return to the Founding Fathers' first principles. Kelso, too, in his first public response to the Haymarket affair, written in mid-October, 1886, began by invoking the spirit of 1776.[32]

He followed the Haymarket trial closely and felt it his "duty as a man" to speak out in defense of the accused anarchists. The trial, he argued in the essay published in Chicago and Denver, tested the principles of the Declaration of Independence: a government was formed by the consent of the people, and citizens had the right to speak out against it. Citizens could even call for their government's dissolution if they believed it had become destructive to its primary purpose, which was to secure their inalienable rights. He believed the Chicago anarchists had correctly diagnosed the fatal flaws of the United States government. The murder charge against them, he argued, had little to do with the evidence presented at the trial. "We all know that these men were really tried and condemned for being bold and able leaders of the labor movement in Chicago,—leaders whose arguments could not be answered by their monopolistic enemies, and whose voices so dangerous to monopolistic despotism could be hushed only in death. They are doomed to die simply for teaching *abolitionism* to *slaves*."[33]

Condemned to die, the Chicago anarchists would be martyrs in the coming revolution, and Kelso was ready to join them. He felt his "whole soul burning with indignation." As the prisoners waited while their lawyers prepared an appeal to the Supreme Court of Illinois, Kelso's allegiance to the United States hung by a thread. "I have never been an Anarchist. Hitherto, how fondly I hoped that the government which I once so dearly loved, for the salvation of which I suffered so much and fought so long and so well, might yet be redeemed from her monstrous corruptions and suffered to live for the protection of the inalienable rights of her citizens," he wrote. "If, however, she permits this most horrible of all murders to be committed, this fond hope in my bosom will die out forever. I shall regard her redemption as impossible, her deserved doom as desirable and inevitable. And, taking my position in the foremost rank of socialistic Anarchism, I shall try to fill the place of at least one of these heroic spirits who will then have gone to the martyr's doom, the martyr's rest, the martyr's glory."[34]

As the condemned men waited in the spring of 1887, Kelso read *A Concise History of the Great Trial of the Chicago Anarchists* by Dyer D. Lum. Like Kelso, Lum had been a conventional Protestant who rejected traditional religion and then investigated spiritualism and supported women's rights. He had also served with distinction in the Union army, rising to brevet captain. In the 1870s Lum turned to labor reform and then, in the next decade, to anarchism. He was close friends with the convicted Chicago Eight. But he presented the *Concise History* merely as a compilation from the trial record, and many readers, at the time and subsequently, read it that way. Author William Dean Howells, for example, thinking he was just reading trial excerpts, found Lum's conclusion utterly persuasive: "The defendants," Lum wrote, "were condemned less for the murder . . . than because they were Anarchists, because they held theoretical views at variance with those in general acceptance—in short because they were *social heretics*." Lum's *Concise History*, however, was in fact propaganda, masterfully paraphrasing and quoting selectively from the abstract of the trial record prepared by the defendants' lawyers. Lum's work would help shape the narrative of the Haymarket affair for the next 125 years. A twenty-first-century analysis of the eight thousand pages in the actual trial record persuasively showed that Lum distorted the evidence to present his portrait of innocent martyrdom. The Chicago anarchists, committed to revolutionary violence on the principle of "propaganda of the deed," had manufactured bombs matching the one that had exploded, and had conspired to attack the police in the days leading up to the May 4 rally. Kelso, however, embraced them not as bomb-throwing terrorists but as persecuted social heretics like himself.[35]

On November 11, 1887, four of the Chicago anarchists—George Engel, Adolph Fischer, Albert Parsons, and August Spies—were hanged, and Kelso made good on his pledge to become an anarchist himself. In a speech before the Rocky Mountain Social League commemorating the second anniversary of the execution, Kelso's anger was still white hot. He addressed the assembly as "Fellow Slaves." He denounced "this absurdly so-called free country" for cruelly murdering the Chicago anarchists. "Our Martyrs" went to the gallows for "having dared to exercise their inalienable right to free speech; for having dared to expose the monstrous villainies of the mighty corporations and monopolies which, like huge anacondas, are crushing the life out of the people;—for having dared to expose the hideous corruptions that prevail in all the departments of our government, municipal, county, state, and national." He reviewed the scene on the street near Haymarket Square, where Pinkerton detectives and police, both tools of the capitalists, marched on a peaceful rally with a plot to destroy or at least damage leaders of the eight-hour strike. A bomb was thrown. Who threw it? Kelso the amateur detective had discovered "indubitable indications of a monstrous conspiracy" and was continuing to investigate. Surely there had been a plan among the moneyed men to set off a bomb, blame the anarchists, and discredit the entire labor movement. The only mistake was that the hireling bomb-thrower had bad aim or a weak arm, and the explosive landed too close to the police—unless sacrificing some policemen was part of the scheme from the beginning, in order to better stoke public outrage.[36]

Kelso the conspiracy theorist took easily to this interpretation of the Haymarket affair, but he was not alone: Dyler Lum had planted the idea of a capitalist conspiracy in the first paragraph of the *Concise History*, repeating a charge familiar in the radical press. In his speech, Kelso also denounced the trial, with its bought witnesses, biased judge, and paid-off jurors, as "the foulest blot in the history of American jurisprudence." He described the dignified stoicism of the men on the scaffold as the assembled audience of capitalists gaped in ghoulish satisfaction. "And this, fellow slaves, is the fate held in reserve for *us* if we do not hurrah for our masters, and, like humble curs, lick their feet when they kick us."[37]

In the red-scare crackdown that followed Haymarket, it was dangerous to fly the flag of anarchism, though as always Kelso was a defiant moth drawn to the flame of public outrage. But what was anarchism? Kelso would explain by turning to etymology in his last book, *Government Analyzed*, arguing like the French theorist Pierre-Joseph Proudhon that "an-archism" meant not the absence of order but the absence of coercive rule. American anarchism in the 1880s had two major branches, each with separate ideological roots, radical liberalism and libertarian socialism. Benjamin Tucker, leader of the individualist Boston branch, wrote that "Anarchists are simply unterrified Jeffersonian Democrats. They believe that 'the best government is that which governs least,' and that which governs least is no government at all." These individualist anarchists proclaimed two principles above all else: individual sovereignty and equal liberty. After the destruction of the coercive state, workers would be able to reclaim what was theirs (the value of their labor) in a free society rebuilt on producer cooperatives and voluntary associations. They called themselves individualist socialists, too, and opposed the state socialist response to capitalist exploitation (such as Marxism) as inevitably authoritarian. The collectivist anarchists in Chicago, dominated by immigrants from Russia, Germany, and Bohemia, wanted to organize proletarians as a revolutionary class and abolish private property. Kelso, like Dyer Lum, would try to bridge these individualist and collectivist impulses.[38]

Kelso began *Government Analyzed* as he had begun the *Devil's Defense*, *Deity Analyzed*, and *The Bible Analyzed*—with a preface sketching the religious despair he suffered as a young man and his subsequent deliverance from superstition by reason, science, and common sense. *Government Analyzed* added, though, that while he lost his religious faith, his faith in government— his "political religion"—had lingered. Without really knowing it, he had replaced God and the Bible with the United States and the Constitution. Government was the new "Supreme Ruler," a "sacred personality" endowed with powers and rights of its own, demanding and deserving allegiance and obedience, worth fighting and killing and dying for. Only late in life did he come "to regard all governments, like all gods, as the mere personifications of mythical monsters invented by selfish and crafty men, as instruments with which to rob and enslave the ignorant toiling masses."[39]

In the thirteen chapters that followed, Kelso explained his new philosophy and politics. His first chapter made the case that no form of (coercive) government had legitimate authority. His second reviewed the various forms of government—patriarchy, monarchy, aristocracy, oligarchy, and so on. Democracy in its pure form would not be a "government" at all (an institution ruling over people), but the United States was far from being a democracy or a republic (a representative democracy): "Our government is usually called a republic. Like most other so-called republics, however, it is simply a wretched conglomeration of the worst elements of monarchy, hierarchy, plutocracy, oligarchy, and all other forms of government." An anarchy—in which people would not have rulers to be obeyed but would elect committees to serve the public needs of the commonwealth—would be democracy actually realized. The third and fourth chapters reviewed the principles and functions of government, concluding that "all the real governments of the world. . . . are all essentially criminal organizations," trampling on the rights of the many to benefit the ruling few. Another chapter imagined the origins and evolution of government from stronger primates dominating the herd through the various forms of civilized oligarchy. Others examined the Declaration of Independence (almost anarchistic!), the Articles of Confederation (its so-called weaknesses were admirable), and the U.S. Constitution (a clever mechanism to protect property holders). He then spent eighty pages decrying tariffs as larceny and taxation as slavery.[40]

Many reformers who recognized the exploitative character of government made the mistake, he argued, of thinking that government itself could be the solution. Liberals thought they could tinker with it, checking and balancing its powers, keeping it on a short leash. But Kelso went beyond his hero Paine, who thought government was a necessary evil. Kelso no longer thought it necessary. It was society's "tumor" or "cancer," a "vampire" or "parasite" sucking the life out of the body politic. State socialists thought all would be well if they could just hand the government over to a new ruling class—the toiling many—and then use the state apparatus to reshape society according to the wisdom of that class. But Kelso recoiled at this authoritarianism. These state socialists "seem to believe that a government ought to be simply a vast molding machine, of prodigious power, into which, as raw materials, all the people of a country—except themselves, who are already good enough—should be shoveled, no matter how widely they may differ from one another in every conceivable respect and (op)pressed into the form of human bricks, all of a uniform shape, size, weight, color, density, value, etc."[41]

After warning that all signs pointed to a coming bloody revolution, as the people finally rose up against their oppressors, Kelso turned to his final chapter, "War." He now believed that a state had no right to wage war except for purely defensive purposes. Murder was murder, whether done by an assassin in the night or a uniformed army flying flags and beating drums. This made him reevaluate the Civil War. The great conflict had not been a just war, he decided. The North had in fact done an injustice to the South. What right did Northerners have to compel Southerners to give up their slaves without remuneration—Northerners who themselves had profited from the slave trade in the seventeenth and eighteenth centuries, and who had continued to profit from the slave economy in the nineteenth? Kelso here ignored that plans to reimburse slaveholders had in fact been discussed—as late as 1862, with Lincoln's offer of compensated emancipation to the border states—and had been rejected by the slaveholders.[42]

"But," Kelso imagined his reader protesting, "did we not . . . preserve unbroken our great Union of States?" Yes, he answered, the carnage had saved the Union, the North's great war aim at the outset. However, in "preserving the Union, we did ourselves an incalculable injury." The Leviathan, the powerful nation state that emerged from the war, had all the more ability to oppress its own people. "But did we not," Kelso had his imagined reader ask, "by means of this war, give freedom to the slaves of the south?" Kelso answered by denying that the slaves had actually been freed. "We simply *changed* the *form* of their *slavery* from a *bad* to a *worse.*" Antebellum slaveholders, he argued, "from motives of a pecuniary interest if not from any higher motives," at least protected their slaves and "amply supplied all their physical wants just as they did those of their very valuable horses and cattle. In place of these protecting masters, we gave them, as masters, soulless corporations and monopolists of all kinds, who work them harder, and, in return from their labor, afford them a much poorer living than did their old individual masters, and who yield them no protection at all." Here Kelso echoed the proslavery apologists in the antebellum South, who insisted that Southern chattel slaves were better off than the Northern wage slaves of industrial capitalism. He did not go quite so far as the postbellum Southern mythologists of the Lost Cause, who imagined happy slaves fiddling and dancing for kind Massa in Ole Dixie. Kelso did not argue that chattel slavery was good and antebellum bondspeople happy, but he did claim that the lives of Blacks were even worse in the late nineteenth century, as they were "cruelly mocked" while suffering in "the utter empty shadow of liberty."[43]

In any case, the Civil War was not really about slavery, or the Union, or constitutional rights, Kelso argued. "The war is known to have been a result of a vast conspiracy of the capitalists of Europe and of America. The object of this conspiracy was through the war, to create an immense national debt, through this debt, to obtain full control of our government, and, through this control, to reduce our *entire laboring population* to the *most helpless forms of slavery*," he wrote. "These capitalists were the *full managers* of the entire arena upon which the battle between *capital* and *liberty* was to be fought. It was *they* who *planned* and *carried out*, to *full success*, the whole *bloody*, the whole *hellish programme*. By them, the question of slavery was used simply as a *red flag* to excite the *powerful* but *silly bulls*, *North* and *South*, to *gore* and *lacerate each other* until they were *both so weakened* that they could be *easily brought under the yoke*. Here you have it all."[44]

Where did this leave the Hero of the South West? Like most people, even among the enlightened, he reflected, he had not carried his emancipation from superstition far enough. "When, however, men discovered the utterly mythical nature of all the gods—the assumed source of all governmental authority—and the consequently fraudulent nature of all the governments claiming to derive their powers from these mythical monsters, they unfortunately failed to discover, at the same time, the equally mythical nature of all governments, per se, and the consequently equally fraudulent nature of all the claims to rulership founded upon the authority of these mythical monsters." They unfortunately still believed that governments "possessed the *power*, by their simple commands, to make it right for their subjects to slaughter their fellowmen, to burn their villages, towns, and cities, to carry away or destroy their goods, to make slaves of their women and children and to do any and all other acts which it would be horribly cruel and criminal to do without this authority."[45]

Kelso himself had been enchanted by the myth. "I once believed this very way myself; and when our own government called upon its ignorant and superstitious devotees to go out and butcher our brothers of the South, I promptly responded to the call," he wrote. "I did not for a moment, think of questioning the righteousness of the required butchery. It was sanctified by the commandment of my *government*; and, to me, this was the commandment of my *god*. Believing that I was thereby fulfilling a sacred duty, and proving myself a good, brave and patriotic man, I cheerfully bore, for more than three years, every conceivable hardship and privation; took part in nearly a hundred bloody engagements; [and] with my own hands, slew a goodly number of brave men." After the war, "I looked back with exultation upon the part I had enacted in their achievement; and viewed with pride my own once well-formed and iron-like frame riddled and broken with many wounds. How blind I was, and yet how honest. How blindly, how piously, how patriotically inhuman even the best of us are capable of being made by superstition, whether with regard to those mythical monsters, called gods, or those equally mythical monsters called governments."[46]

After finishing his discussion of the Civil War in *Government Analyzed*, Kelso turned back to the topic of war in general. "When we consider that the principles upon which all, but purely defensive wars are waged, are those of pure and unmitigated robbery and murder,—" But here, as Etta marked the spot in the published text, was where Kelso "laid down his pen in early January 1891." He died a few weeks later. Etta finished the chapter. She then composed the next six chapters—"Punishments," "Marriage," "Religion," "Prohibition," "Money," and the concluding chapter, which was also published separately, "What a Government Should Be." For these, amounting to 216 pages of the 519-page book, she drew from Kelso's lectures, stitched together his fragmentary notes, and added some of her own material. Etta, a friend believed, "was in such close sympathy with [Kelso] as to reflect his very thought." A confirmed spiritualist, she felt his presence guiding her as she wrote. She even consulted a clairvoyant, who communicated a vision of John in the spirit world, "surrounded by a group of fine looking men he seemed to be teaching." In 1892, Etta published *Government Analyzed* to the world.[47]

A sympathetic reviewer in the *Freethinkers' Magazine* called *Government Analyzed* a "*great* book," though "more a book for the future than the present." Another reader saluted Kelso as a "true friend of humanity," though found his positions too "extreme." The most substantive review appeared in *Liberty (Not the Daughter But the Mother of Order)*, a journal of ideas conducted with intellectual rigor by the individualist anarchist Benjamin Tucker, who led a stable of sharp writers including his protégé Victor Yarros. The five-column review of *Government Analyzed* by Yarros was scorched-earth criticism.[48]

Yarros began sarcastically: surely this master of analysis who had dissected the Bible, the Deity, and the Universe would find analyzing government to be "a trifling matter." Then he pulled out the dagger. The pathetic announcement on the book's title page that the author had died while writing it, he pronounced, would not soften the verdict: "I condemn the book in question as utterly worthless. To say of it that it is unscientific and unphilosophical would not meet the requirements of justice; no, the truth simply is that the book, instead of being in the least degree enlightening, is confusing and confused, the pitch of absurdity attained being unparalleled." Elsewhere in the issue,

YOURS FOR PROGRESS,

JOHN R. KELSO.

John R. Kelso, ca. 1890. John R. Kelso, *Government Analyzed* (Longmont, Colo.: Privately printed, 1892), frontispiece. Photo courtesy of the Huntington Rare Book and Manuscript Library, San Marino, California.

Tucker the editor seconded the opinion of Yarros the reviewer: "Mr. Yarros is not a whit too severe in his condemnation . . . of the late John R. Kelso's book, 'Government Analyzed.' Impudence attains its climax when such a work is offered to the public as an exposition of Anarchism."[49]

"Tucker the Terrible's" *Liberty* was known for its savage takedowns of writers who disagreed with the journal's positions. Convinced that anarchism was misunderstood even by self-described anarchists, Tucker was especially eager to distance "true" anarchism from the foreign collectivists in Chicago after the Haymarket bomb. The abused objected to the dogmatic browbeating and said that issues of *Liberty* were published as so many papal bulls. In 1890, the anarchist writer and Chicago labor organizer Lizzie M. Holmes complained that the *Liberty* writers assumed they had "a right to call a man a fool who shows that he does not reach the conclusions they have reached." Later that year, Yarros denied that he and his colleagues, "like religious enthusiasts, ask people to seek salvation in perfect obedience to the truth as we see it and pay no heed to the surroundings. We do not demand from anybody the carrying out of 'the perfect law,' and we do not profess to be holier and purer than others." But *Liberty*'s tone did not change. Three years later, Holmes, along with an associate editor of another journal, complained specifically about Yarros' "cruel and harsh" review of Kelso's book. Yarros responded just as Kelso himself would have: "If I have been in the slightest degree unjust to the authors of 'Government Analyzed,' I am ready to retract and humble myself." But not until you make a persuasive argument, based on the evidence of the text, proving I was wrong.[50]

Kelso wrote that governments were merely human institutions that had become personified, exalted into sacred beings with rights and powers compelling obedience, like the gods of religion. Yarros dismissed this idea as "silly and manifestly untrue," but did not explain why. Perhaps he would say that states are not mythical (existing, like gods, only in the imagination); they have real physical power, as anyone coerced by the police could attest. But Kelso was suggesting that much of a government's power does rest on strategies that cultivate a social-psychological buttress of authority, ideological mystifications (as Marx recognized) not dissimilar from those used in religion. Yarros also faulted Kelso for imagining that an anarchistic society would have no prisons. Yarros countered that anarchism meant the absence of physical compulsion for people who do not infringe upon others. For those who did aggressively invade others' rights, there would still be prisons, though prisons run by voluntary defensive associations rather than the state and funded by voluntary contributions rather than compulsory taxes. Kelso would have agreed with the practical point—any society has to protect itself from dangerous criminals, incarcerating them by force if necessary. His rehabilitative reformatories, though, would not be "prisons" in any conventional sense. Yarros charged that Kelso fundamentally misunderstood the place of coercion in anarchism and misconstrued the practical outcomes of anarchistic principles. But in a passage such as the one Yarros selected, where Kelso turned to project an anarchistic future and imagined no prisons, no prostitution, and no poverty, he was not spelling out policies and programs, but dreaming of an ideal world. Anarchism for Kelso was less a blueprint than a vessel of hope.[51]

Yarros was driven nearly to apoplexy by the inconsistencies in the book. Indeed, a later, friendly notice of *Government Analyzed* in another journal allowed that there was some "discrepancy" between the chapters, a lack of "coherence" to the whole, "probably due to the fact that the book is the product of two different minds, each an independent thinker." But Yarros would have none of this. The first part of the book was "Worthless," the second part worse than worthless, and inconsistencies ran through the whole—every chapter, nearly every page. The book seems to endorse voluntary communism in one paragraph, and then the "tyrannical" state socialism of Edward Bellamy's bestselling utopian novel *Looking Backward* in another. The Kelsos supported greenbacks (government issued paper currency) but also "free banking" (financial mutual associations premised on the rejection of government currency). The book applauded the anarchists' withdrawal from conventional politics and then reprinted the platform of the People's Party. Yarros could only throw up his hands.[52]

Government Analyzed is not always clear about the relation between means and ends, between the short-term and the long-term, between pragmatic compromise and principled idealism. But neither is it the hopeless muddle that Yarros described. Kelso did admire the utopian society described in "Bellamy's wildest dream, the glorious ideal of national Socialism." A paragraph later, he qualified his praise of *Looking Backward* by objecting to the "*modus operandi* of attaining to this desirable condition," the "despotic principle" of compulsory taxation at the heart of Bellamy's state socialism. So he liked the idealistic goal but not the authoritarian strategy Bellamy proposed to reach it. In another chapter, Kelso described communism as man's primitive social condition and the natural mode of sharing resources within families. Could it be extended to modern society as a whole? Anarchists agreed that individuals should not be forced into communes, and disagreed over the likelihood of them voluntarily choosing communism in the modern age. Kelso thought people would become communists, but only "when all men come to regard one another as brothers, as members of one great family"—a crucial (and challenging) precondition.[53]

As for other inconsistencies, doctrinaire anarchists themselves distinguished between their preferred, principled strategies (such as noncooperation with the coercive state) and opportunistic tactics that were not in themselves anarchistic but which might help move toward the larger goal. If Yarros and Tucker could flirt with unions and dabble in voting for tactical purposes, why could not Kelso support greenbacks or the Popular Party in the short term while hoping for free banking and the end of conventional politics someday?[54]

Although his criticism was overblown, Yarros was right that *Government Analyzed* lacked the sophistication to join the conversation at *Liberty*, where writers were fluent in Proudhon and Marx, Smith and Mill. Yet if the book should not be read as a masterwork by "a keenly analytical mind," as another journal put it, it might be appreciated as a meditation in a prophetic voice—prophetic not merely in the sense of predicting the future, but in a biblical register. It offered what Kelso took to be revelatory insights of a radical new order that, as Jesus had said, was both "within you" and "at hand"—speaking to your deepest needs for freedom, equality, and justice, and just over the horizon of the present, determined and certain yet nonetheless requiring your active participation to be realized.[55]

That prophetic voice was best heard in Kelso's last speech, "The Kingdom of Heaven," delivered before the Rocky Mountain Social League in Denver on November 16, 1890. Red circulars distributed for several days had drawn a large crowd to Coliseum Hall for the annual ceremony commemorating the Haymarket martyrs. Kelso was the featured orator, and, according to a reporter from the *Rocky Mountain News*, he mingled with his "many admirers" in the crowd before the proceedings began. The stage was "lavishly" bedecked with red and black banners. Flowers surrounded an imposing monument with a portrait of the martyred Spies beneath a gallows and, to symbolize hope, an anchor. The assembly sang two songs, "The Flag of Scarlet" and "La Marseillaise," and heard remarks from two other speakers. Then Kelso took the stage. When he spoke, he again invoked the Declaration's statement of human equality and inalienable rights, almost as an incantation. He preached the catechism of anarchism as he understood it. And then he turned to the passages in the Bible about the Kingdom of Heaven. He once more explained that the scriptures recorded an archaic idea of the sky as a firmament, an inverted bowl, and the superstitious belief of another, better realm—a heaven—on the other side. In response to very real suffering in this world, though, the Jews of the Roman Empire, "feeling the heel of oppression on their necks," yearned for "the happy social conditions" that they imagined heaven signified. "We must, of course, reject, as purely mythical, the local heaven just described. We must not, however, thus reject the soul yearnings of the people which led to the invention of this myth. These yearnings are a *reality*;—a *genuine demand* of *nature*. They have their meaning and use."[56]

The yearning for liberty, harmony, love, and justice is natural and universal, he said. It was the desire for "a system in which all men are brothers, all equals, all free to do whatever they severally will, provided that, in the doing thereof, they infringe not the equal liberty of one another." It was the demand for "a system in which every man receives the proceeds of his own labor . . . [and] in which the words, monopoly, trust, syndicate, tax, tariff, rent, interest, debt, mortgage, want, wretchedness, vice, and crime are never heard; . . . a system, in short, which is the *realization* of all that of which the heaven of the pagan and the Christian is the *idealization*." A social system not in some supernatural realm but in this world, here and soon.[57]

Kelso then turned to the New Testament and to Jesus. In *The Bible Analyzed*, Kelso had spent two chapters demonstrating that the New Testament texts were a collection of fables and forgeries. The theology of the Christ, the sacrificed god-man who redeemed the sins of humanity, was an absurd holdover from ignorant paganism. Reason, science, and common sense left the Christian edifice a useless pile of ancient rubble. The historical Jesus, too, from what could be known, was hardly an admirable figure. Kelso had described him as a "tramp," with unwashed hands and dirty clothes, who strolled about the countryside teaching his followers not to work and to abolish normal family and sexual relations. But now Kelso returned to the New Testament, finding a myth that reflected something real, a myth that still had some use. Jesus, he argued, preached the doctrines of anarchism, and, like the Haymarket martyrs, was executed for it. His Kingdom of Heaven was to be established here (in the Roman Empire and beyond) and soon (before his current generation passed away). That is, the ideal values of an imagined heaven were to be actually realized on earth: "Thy kingdom come, thy will be done, on earth as it is in heaven." In the new heavenly system, coercive government would end (Matthew 23:13), and public officials would serve and not rule over the people (Matthew 20: 25–28). Property would be held in common (Acts 4:32–35), and all would be equal (Matthew 23: 8-10). The glad tidings of this new way of organizing society was Jesus' good news, his "gospel."[58]

Jesus was neither God nor the Son of God, Kelso said, but a great reformer. However, he failed to bring about this new Kingdom of Heaven on earth. He failed because he was still captive to ancient superstitions, because he believed that his kingdom would be realized by supernatural power, by the hand of his imagined god, rather than by the hard work of the people themselves. "Why the 'kingdom of heaven,' the anarchistic commune established by Jesus finally failed, I can now scarcely notice," Kelso said. "The principal cause of its failure seems to have been that Jesus unwisely discouraged all labor among his followers, condemning the accumulation of property among them, and fanatically taught them to depend for their subsistence, not upon their own exertions, but upon the miraculous interposition of God, who, whatever he may have done for the rich, has never been known to assist the poor."[59]

The creation of heaven on earth would come about only by a great struggle. Kelso wished the transformation could be achieved peacefully, but he expected it to be "the bloodiest revolution the world has ever known." Unlike the Chicago anarchists, he did not endorse revolutionary violence as a strategy. But neither had he become a pacifist. The people could—and would have to—defend themselves against Pinkerton thugs and the police state shock troops that the monopolists and the corrupt politicians would set upon them. He imagined himself in Haymarket Square or some similar place. Attacked, he would reach for his gun. If someone handed him a bomb, he would throw it. In an earlier speech, he had paraphrased Jefferson, acknowledging that "the wheels of every revolution must be lubricated with the warm life-blood of its earliest and ablest promoters." He asserted his manhood and predicted his own destiny: "A little further on in this great revolution, I shall probably die any way;—die, as I have always wished that I might, on the field of battle fighting for the rights of man; or, like these men, 'die it may be ignominiously and on the scaffold.' Let our enemies, then, demand my life." He was growing old, he said. He probably had only a few more years anyway. "In nearly a hundred engagements, I fought for the preservation of the Union and the overthrow of chattel slavery in the South. And now, as the result of nearly a score of wounds, my life is slowly ebbing away. The balance of it I give to liberty. Let the enemies of liberty, then, take it as soon as they please. I am ready. And, as I have lived so will I die—a *man*." In mid-November of 1890, nine weeks before his actual death, he was still ready: "I am prepared to do my whole duty in affecting that revolution. After that, feeling that I have not lived in vain, I shall be able to lay me down in peace."[60]

Conclusion

REPRESENTATIVE MAN

But, at last, we shall cease to look in men for completeness,
and shall content ourselves with their social and delegated
quality.
—RALPH WALDO EMERSON, *Representative Men* (1850)

JOHN R. KELSO DID not die in the streets, fighting for a new revolution, or on a scaffold as a martyr for liberty and human rights. He died from a wound inflicted during the Civil War—at least, that is what he and Etta thought as he neared the end. On her application for a widow's pension in 1891, Etta listed John's cause of death as "chronic gastric inflammation of the stomach[;] cause supposed to be an incisted [encysted] rebel bullet, [Kelso] having been shot 14 times and one of which was not extracted[,] causing the above trouble." In her 1888 affidavit listing his injuries and ailments she had mentioned a "depression . . . just at the base of the sternum. Just below this hollow is a protuberance in which an imbedded bullet may be felt, but upon which pressure cannot be borne." When he started feeling an intense burning pain in his belly and had trouble eating in the spring of 1890, Kelso told the doctor about the "minni ball" lodged over the pit of his stomach. There was not much the physician could do, and Kelso's health continued to deteriorate through the year. When the doctor visited on Christmas Eve, he found his patient's condition "very poor." Kelso had a "chronic intolerance of food, fetid breath, acute pain in stomach, general emaciation, muscles flabby, features pinched." Toward the end, "his suffering was intense except what relief he got from morphine. A constant burning pain in the stomach. The last five days was spent re[t]ching and vomiting Bloody mucous." Unable to take nourishment, he finally died, on January 26, 1891, of "Starvation"—all of it caused, they thought, by that last rebel bullet beneath his heart, festering for a quarter century until the Civil War finally killed him.[1]

However, when Kelso in the early 1880s had written his account of getting hit by the shotgun blast in 1863, he described thirteen shots under the skin, which he cut out with his pocket knife. "After that," he had written, "although my breast was quite discolored, ragged and sore, it did not pain me very much." There was no mention then of a fourteenth bullet left behind. In all the discussions of his injuries over the years in his pension file, that festering fourteenth bullet did not appear until Etta's affidavit of November 1888. Milton Burch's last affidavit a month later also mentioned Kelso's thirteen buckshot, all of which caused merely superficial wounds except "one shot [that] was supposed to go deeper than the rest," but this detail may have been prompted by a letter from Kelso rather than Burch's memory, which the major confessed was "not good." The attending physician thought it was possible that an old gunshot wound caused the trouble, but that the problem more likely was stomach cancer. The story of the last rebel bullet may have been more of a useful myth than a medical fact, but it was what Kelso believed as he lay dying.[2]

He left behind little besides a few personal items and his manuscripts: the unfinished *Government Analyzed*, which Etta would complete; "The Works of John R. Kelso in Manuscript," the eight-hundred-page folio volume dedicated to John R. Kelso Jr.; the 519-page "Miscellaneous Poems, Speeches, Lectures, Etc.," which he copyrighted in 1887 and prepared for publication; and his autobiography, written in fourteen school composition books, which he gave to Florella. His children chose not to publish any of it. Perhaps the decision was financial. Etta, who published *Government Analyzed* at her own expense, ended up donating many of the volumes to Moses Harman, editor of *Lucifer the Light-Bearer*, and Harman was still trying to sell them as late as 1908. Still, there would have been interest in Kelso's life story. Historian Wiley Britton, author of *The Civil War on the Border* (1899) and other works, for one, had heard about the existence of the manuscript autobiography and would have been eager to shepherd it through the press. Florella thought the autobiography might correct some of the extravagant stories about her father that still echoed through the Ozarks. But perhaps he had written with too much frankness. Even within his own family he seems to have remained a controversial figure. The break with Susie had left a rift between John and John Jr. Lynn Finney, Florella's husband, had been a staunch Confederate. An oil portrait of Kelso, probably painted by Etta, was said to have been consigned to an attic. By the early twentieth century, outside the family, Kelso was largely forgotten.[3]

After John was gone and *Government Analyzed* finished, Etta resumed the life she had led before he had appeared at her door in the summer of 1885. She read, painted, visited with friends, and tended her gardens. After filing and then abandoning a claim for a widow's pension in 1891, she tried again in 1897. At the time she was leasing 200 acres to a tenant farmer, owned three horses and four cows, was paying 10 percent interest on a $3,000 loan, and had to take in boarders to make ends meet. But the Pension Office ruled that she had too much property to merit a pension (she was rejected again in 1904). In 1899, her nephew and his wife came to live with her and took over the farm. By 1910 she was seventy-three, ill, and living with her sister and brother-in-law at the Sandstone Ranch. A photograph shows her at a gathering there at about that time. But in that year she was nearly defrauded out of every cent she owned. George B. Fisher was a Denver purveyor of mail-order elixirs, the president of a family business he named the Fisheropathic College Association, and the author of a promotional book called *Murdering God Is the Science of Obtaining Health* (1905–1906), a title that would have intrigued Kelso. Fisher finagled Etta into signing a note for over $15,000 for Fisheropathic stock. He said his business was worth $60,000; the assessor at the August 1910 trial said $750. Fisher was convicted, but Etta was declared mentally incompetent to handle her own affairs, and her property was put in a trust. She died in 1923.[4]

Susie tried to get a widow's pension too, in 1916, thinking she was eligible since she had been the soldier's wife during the war. Writing from Porterville, California, she was in her seventies, had been divorced from her second husband for twenty-seven years, and was going blind from cataracts. But the Pension Office rejected her: she was one of Kelso's divorced wives, not his widow. She died in 1924. His first wife, Adelia, went on to have nine children with her second husband, Thomas Lynch. In California, Kelso happened to meet one of them, her eldest son Willis, whom he described as "a most excellent young man of rare intelligence." Adelia died in Missouri in 1921.[5]

Kelso's three surviving children lived out their days in California. He had seen his son Johnny only occasionally, even after Susie had brought the younger children to California in the mid-1870s. Kelso, traveling through Fresno in 1882, remarked on having the pleasure of grabbing a few minutes' conversation with his son, who was in school there, "a bright manly lad in his fifteenth year." Two summers later, John Jr. came to stay with his father for a few weeks. He "was now a handsome and cheerful young man," but the father had "grieved, however, to learn that he had acquired the habit of chewing tobacco and of squandering his money very foolishly." When he looked back on his relationship with his only surviving son, Kelso had had only regrets. In the mid-1880s, he wrote about "poor, wandering Johnny, my baby boy, whom I have known only long enough to make me love him in spite of his faults, he does not know how bitterly I have wept to-day to know that his young heart has been poisoned against me and that he has thus been cruelly rendered virtually fatherless." In 1900, John Jr., thirty-three, was an unmarried Fresno farmer living with his mother. Ten years later he was living alone and earning wages as a "pumper" on a Santa Barbara oil field. He later worked on the railroad, drove a twenty-mule team hauling borax and a water truck spraying dusty roads, and spent time as a prospector, a lumberjack, a ranch hand, and a woodchopper. Sometime in the early twentieth century, he changed his name to John Howard Kelso. He married Leura Mae Dehart in 1911, had three children, and died in 1935.[6]

In the autobiography, Kelso last described seeing Iantha in 1884, three years after he had gone mountain climbing in Colorado with her. She had taught school for a few years, but, being a woman with "a delicate and nervous constitution," the long hours in the classroom had injured her health. She had married William Rutledge Cooke, an engineer and superintendent at a mill. Having taken up landscape painting, she gave her father his favorite of her works, a scene among the "Big Trees." Kelso was proud of the generous, gentle woman Iantha had become, but still liked to think back to when she was ten, "a ray of sunlight," skipping ahead as they walked to school, collecting berries and delighting in saving the very best ones for her father. She would have two sons, and live until 1948.[7]

Kelso had been closest to his first born, Florella, who, he wrote, "has accompanied me and cheered me through more years of my life's journey than any other." Her mother, Adelia, had given her up when she was a toddler, and then she had to endure her stepmother Susie's severity and mood swings. As a child during the war, she might have saved her father's life when she ran to woods where he was hiding to warn him of the suspicious neighbors, and she suffered when the family was driven into exile, shivering in the snow and getting her foot run over by a wagon wheel. As a teenager, she surely felt anguish about the role she had played in the circumstances leading to her brother's suicide. But then she had blossomed into a "glorious" young woman—strong, patient, and unselfish. "She does not know," Kelso wrote, "how fondly I have treasured every word and every token of her love so deep and so pure." She would have six children and live into her eighty-seventh year. Sometime before her death in 1940, she handed a treasured heirloom to

John Howard Kelso (formerly John R. Kelso Jr.), ca. 1900–1910. Photo courtesy Rhiannon Kelso.

her eldest son: the fourteen school composition books containing her father's remarkable autobiography.[8]

KELSO HAD BEEN a teacher, a preacher, a soldier, and a spy; a congressman, a lecturer, and an author; a Whig, a Radical Republican, a Democrat, and an anarchist; a Methodist, a spiritualist, and an atheist. His nineteenth-century American life was both ordinary and extraordinary.

Ralph Waldo Emerson's "Representative Men," in the famous collection of essays by that name published in 1850, achieved greatness by embodying

Florella Kelso Finney, Oct. 26, 1885. Photo courtesy Trudie Sheffield.

Ideals: Plato the Philosopher, Shakespeare the Poet, Napoleon the Man of the World. Kelso, too, wrote about Great Men who represented areas of thought or behavior because their genius forever changed the course of human progress. They were giants towering above others in their age—Plato, Shakespeare, and Napoleon are in his list, too—who came to be regarded as the "representatives" of "the principles they have taught, the modes of character they have illustrated, the arts and sciences in which they have excelled, [and] the systems they have founded." Whatever Kelso had aspired to be when, as a young boy, he read biographies by firelight, he was not a Great Man in this sense—he never achieved greatness by his exemplary accomplishments or his historical influence. But Kelso was a representative man of nineteenth century America in a different way—embodying, with his own peculiar vitality, "modes of character" enmeshed in larger systems and principles not of his own making.[9]

Or perhaps he was (at least) four such characters: the Evangelical Christian, the Enlightened Critic, the Sentimental Hero, and the Radical Reformer.

The Evangelical Christian finds himself born into a world of suffering and sin, hungering for salvation. He is thrown onto a difficult, uncertain path through a fleeting life, seeking a peaceful eternity. The brute fact of mortality, if nothing else, teaches him that the familiar sources of love and comfort are ultimately unreliable, so he turns toward the promise of a Perfect Parent. He does not just assent to Christian doctrine. He is flooded first with the awareness and experience of his own incompleteness and inadequacy. Honestly confronting all his faults and failings, he passes through the fire of humiliation, fear, and regret. He realizes that he deserves horrific punishment for the contempt he has shown, with his every breath, to Infinite Goodness. But what he learns to seek, he finds. He knocks, and the door is opened. Then, with the unmerited gift of grace, he feels the exhilarating joy of God's forgiveness and love. He feels this new connection, this saving faith, in his body and soul. He senses it reorienting his life. But the door that opens can also close; the joyful presence can be replaced by a desolate absence, the assurance of love and comfort by doubt and despair.

Vast numbers of Americans in the nineteenth-century lived and died as such characters, in the chrysalis of evangelical Christianity. Kelso experienced it and then left it behind for a strain of modern rationalism that was less pervasive than heartfelt religion but that still permeated American culture. He left John Wesley for Thomas Paine. Again and again Kelso recounted how the turn to reason, science, and common sense rescued him from the emotional turbulence of evangelical Christian religious experience. It was a massive shift to a new way of seeing, of being in the world. The tortured soul was reborn as an enlightened self. The Enlightened Critic detaches himself from the sway of passions and affections to see them for what they are: subjective moods rather than disclosures of cosmic truth. He believes that natural human faculties, flawed as they are, are the best guide to life. He pauses to doubt and reason about what before had been taken for granted. He has the courage to ponder, to weigh, to analyze, and to criticize what Authority has told him he must believe and do. What if, he has the temerity to ask, the Bible stories we have taken as truth from our cradles are just fables inherited from the past? He has the confidence to rest on facts as he finds them, but also to revise beliefs in light of new evidence. He puts his trust not in the divine and supernatural light of grace but in the everyday enlightenments of common sense. He looks not to faith to guide him to bliss in a future world but to reason to muddle through, as best he can, in this one.

Yet for all his efforts in his lectures and books to demystify religion through hard-headed analysis, cool rationality was hardly Kelso's defining characteristic on the page, the orator's stage, or in daily life. He may have thought that reasoned analysis of empirical evidence was the best way to determine what was true and right. Once determined, though, the true and the right had to be voiced and defended. Speaking truth to power became a compulsion, a repeated test of "manhood"—which itself was a fraught fusion of maturity, virility, and self-possession. Moreover, the act of standing up to speak and fight like a man for what he thought was true and right became more important than the position being defended. Earnest sincerity and the courage to act on his convictions overshadowed what those convictions were, or the reasoning that led to them in the first place. When Kelso tried to sum up his life in the preface to his "Miscellaneous Writings" in 1887, he could not help but notice how his written work over forty years recorded profound transformations in his religious and political beliefs, "from the strictest Methodism to the rankest Atheism, and from the semi-monarchical doctrines of the old Whig Party to the most radical doctrines of Autonomy or Anarchism." Readers would recognize that the position expressed on one page might be "irreconcilably antagonistic" to a stance taken on another, he acknowledged. If those different views were bridged by an overarching ideal of true manhood they were also, he thought, harmonized by his honest sentiments: Kelso advised readers to use their own judgment, accepting the good and rejecting the bad, "simply giving me credit for sincerity in each shade of opinion at the time I expressed it."[10]

Credit for his honest sentiments and sincerity was in fact crucial to Kelso's image of himself as a Sentimental Hero. Kelso said that he sympathized with the heroes in the popular romantic novels of his day, "in all their misfortunes and in all their brave and noble deeds," because he felt he was living a "romance" himself. Compelled to speak and fight for difficult truths and unpopular but righteous causes, the Sentimental Hero needs to get sympathetic credit from others to sustain his heroism. Kelso could march off to war and do his daring deeds on the battlefield, but he needed an ideal woman at home to love him for it, a lady fair to inspire the noble knight on his crusade. When Susie failed to fulfill those emotional needs, he raced back to camp: first, as a mere foot soldier, to the fatherly approval of General Samuel Curtis and later, as a cavalry officer, to the "boys" he led in battle, who admired his courage, respected his leadership, and wept with him when they lost one of their own. The civilian men who cheered and the ladies who waved their handkerchiefs at the Hero of the South West validated him, told him that all the hardships he endured and the dangers he bravely faced were worth it because he was accomplishing something great in the larger scheme of things.[11]

In his political campaigns, Kelso expected the same sympathetic dynamic, addressing voters as if they were all soldiers from his old regiment and asking for their votes as further validation of the heroic character he had earned on the battlefield and the honest sentiments they had shared as comrades in arms. As a free-thought lecturer, he seemed to expect sympathetic credit for sincerely saying unpopular things. "One of the saddest words in our language is the word 'alone,'" he paused to tell an audience at a lecture in 1885, though he could have said the same when he addressed the Methodist conference in 1856, the Dallas County secession rally in 1861, or at any of his other political speeches or free-thought lectures. "I cannot tell you how much I crave your sympathy," he continued. "I have tried to deserve it by being true to my own manhood and my own conscience. I would grieve to know that any expression of mine would drive your sympathies from me. I would speak what I believe to be the truth, however, even though my bleeding heart should find me standing all alone. I would rather stand thus all alone, in my honest convictions, than gain the applause of the whole world at the cost of my conscience, my manhood, my self-respect." He wanted sympathetic credit for having the manly courage to stand and speak for his honest convictions, even if he failed to win anyone over by reasoned argument.[12]

These "modes of character" that Kelso personified in the "romance" of his life—the Evangelical Christian, the Enlightened Critic, and the Sentimental Hero—did not form a tidy sequence, one replacing the previous. Even as he cast ideas and beliefs aside, old habits endured within larger, persisting patterns of experience. As he himself eventually recognized, ways of being that he thought he had left behind when he walked out of the church—faith in a higher power, reverence for sacred doctrines, obedience to authority's commands—were instead transferred to his "political religion." Something like religious enchantment, too, lingered in his reliance on his intuitions about his destiny. Later, when empirical evidence convinced him that the spirits of his dead children hovered about consoling him, he joined scientific rationalism to Victorian sentimentality.

The Radical Reformer combined aspects of the other three. As a Radical Republican, he was willing to overturn nineteenth-century America's racial, gender, and political order: he wanted to disfranchise rebel Whites and enfranchise Black freedmen, give the vote and equal rights to women, and dissolve the defeated Southern states for an extended period of democratic tutelage under Reconstruction. As an anarchist, he would have gone much further, destroying corporate power and dismantling the state to reorganize social life on the basis of liberty, equality, and voluntary association. Here again he foregrounded an enlightened critical analysis that claimed to demystify political superstitions, unmask powerful forces of economic oppression, and use reason and common sense to topple tyranny. Here again he voiced a passionate faith in a higher cause. And as he publicly proclaimed his unpopular opinions, he again appealed to his audience's sympathy for his brave sincerity and invoked the language of heroic martyrdom. If as a Christian he had modeled himself after Jesus, as a soldier he enjoyed being compared to the crafty Revolutionary War hero Francis Marion, and as a freethinker he idolized Thomas Paine, as an anarchist he turned back to Jesus—Haymarket Jesus, at least, preaching the gospel of radical, anarchistic reform and willing to die for the truth that would set others free.

If in nothing else, Kelso can be seen as a representative man of nineteenth-century America in this complex intermingling of sentimentality and rationalism, sympathy and self-assertion, aspiration and despair, violence and tears. But more importantly, in the end, he was himself. Biography and autobiography are not efficient conveyances of some neat historical thesis: if they do not portray the irreducible singularity of a particular life, they have failed. When Florella handed down the fourteen composition books containing her father's handwritten autobiography to the next generation, she included a note: "Do not be too severe in criticism of a life laid bare with few reservations. Be as charitable as you can. Not knowing and loving him as I did and do, I do not expect you to understand the mistakes he made." Perhaps, though, even without a daughter's love, readers of a life laid bare might come to understand.[13]

Acknowledgments

I HAD BEEN working on Kelso for several years when, out of the blue, the phone rang. Joe Dieu identified himself as "the great-great-grandson of John R. Kelso" and said he "had some manuscripts." I almost fell out of my chair.

I had long fantasized that the second half of Kelso's memoir might be out there somewhere, continuing the story from where it had broken off in January 1863, on the last page of the manuscript "Works of John R. Kelso" at the Huntington Library. But I had run out of places to look. Finished with the annotated version of his partial Civil War memoir (*Bloody Engagements: John R. Kelso's Civil War*), I had begun this biography, piecing together the story of his post-January 1863 life from other sources. And then Joe called. Not only was he happy to have me photograph and transcribe the full autobiography Kelso had written out in fourteen school composition books, he transported the manuscripts across the country so I could do so, and shared other materials and stories about Kelso with me. No historian or biographer could be in greater debt for a source, and none could feel more grateful. This book is for you, Joe.

Joe's son and daughter-in-law, Martin Dieu and Holly Elwood, welcomed me into their home to photograph the manuscripts. They were there when I first sat down with the composition books and verified that they did in fact contain the second half of Kelso's autobiography, written in his own hand. Martin and Holly were kind and understanding when, at that moment of realization, the stranger at their dining room table nearly wept. They also rephotographed some pages for me when my images were blurry, shared other materials, and supplied the photo of Kelso in 1861.

Another Kelso family descendant, Angela Goldin, then came forward with another Kelso manuscript, his "Miscellaneous Writings," completed in 1887.

Over five hundred pages long, it contained some of the poems and lectures I had already seen in the "Works" volume at the Huntington, but also some I had not—especially later lectures and essays that illuminated his thought in the last dozen years of his life. Angela sent me beautifully clear images of every manuscript page. Once again, the family generosity was extraordinary.

Kris Stoever, another descendant, helped me with Kelso family genealogy. Even more important, though, Kris, an author, professional copy editor, and discerning reader, read the entire first draft of the biography, providing extensive and crucial feedback at a time when the fate of the project was uncertain. Her comments helped me make this a better book.

Trudie Sheffield, from the Finney side of the family (JRK's daughter Florella's husband), helped with genealogy and shared family photographs and some typescripts of a couple of Florella's letters and a short reminiscence of her by one of her sons. John Kelso and his daughter Rhiannon helped solve a mystery: what happened to John R. Kelso Jr.? He disappeared from the records in the early twentieth century because, it turns out, he changed his middle name to Howard. John and Rhiannon contributed photos of JRK's sword and ceremonial cane, and passed on the story of JRK's famous shotgun, which stayed in the family until the middle of the twentieth century.

I am deeply indebted to these generous Kelso family descendants.

THIS BOOK WOULD not have been possible without research in archives in Washington, DC, Missouri, California, and Colorado. Special thanks to the following archivists: Jill D'Andrea, National Archives; Anne E. Cox, Laura R. Jole, and Dennis Northcut, all of the State Historical Society of Missouri; Charles E. Brown, Mercantile Library, University of Missouri at St. Louis; Steve Haberman, Greene County Missouri Records and Archives Center; Steve Weldon, Jasper County Missouri Records Center; Olga Tsapina, Huntington Library; Erik Mason, Longmont Colorado Museum; Laura Mesa and Janet Lancaster, McHenry Museum, Modesto, California; and especially John F. Bradbury Jr., formerly of the State Historical Society of Missouri (Rolla), for sharing his research file on Kelso. Thanks also to Samantha Calhoon and Robin Boden of the Sandstone Ranch in Longmont, Colorado.

I'm grateful to John Demos, Martha Hodes, and George Rable for supporting the project in its early stages and to Roy Ritchie, Karen Halttunen, and Deborah Harkness for enabling research time at the Huntington. Joseph Beilein, William Foley, Gary R. Kremer, Christopher Phillips, William Piston, and Bruce Nichols offered advice on Missouri research. Jon White helped connect me to other scholars in the field. Thanks to Josh Rivkin, P.P.P., and Adina Berk for reading early drafts of a few chapters. Michael Les Benedict provided expert feedback on Chapters 12 and 13. Dermot Trainor located some important articles in the radical press relevant to Kelso and anarchism. Stan Huzarewicz, Babbidge Library, University of Connecticut, helped with a Kelso image and Dan Nelson helped with some genealogy. Funds from the dean's office and the history department at William & Mary supported my research and writing.

Once again, it has been a delight to publish with OUP. My editor, Susan Ferber, has been so helpful and supportive throughout the process that my spouse insists she hears "soft hosannas" whenever Susan's name is mentioned around the house. Both reports from the anonymous referees were extremely helpful. Thanks also to Elizabeth Bortka for the expert copyediting, Eric Anderson for the index, Rebecca Wrenn for the maps, the wonderful Joellyn Ausanka (with help from Gwen Colvin) for shepherding the manuscript through the production process, and the OUP design team.

In a book about a devoted teacher, I would be remiss not to thank my own teachers, especially Kate Burgess, Jerry Berenty, Mark Heidmann, Charlotte Wing, Jon Butler, and Harry Stout.

Although this time the dedication page has been reserved for others, my deepest debts are still to my spouse, Karin Wulf, who has lived with my Kelso project for a long time. She thinks Kelso is "kind of a nut"—but she says this about her husband, too.

Notes

INTRODUCTION

1. "Radical Literature," *Lucifer the Light-Bearer* (June 15, 1901): 176. Long after I had titled this project, Ernest B. Furgurson published "Teacher, Preacher, Soldier, Spy: How the Methodist Headmaster of a Boy's School Became a Rebel Secret Agent—and Tried to Kidnap Lincoln," *MHQ: Quarterly Journal of Military History* (Autumn 2012): 82–86. We both nod to John le Carré's 1974 novel, *Tinker Tailor Soldier Spy*, which in turn borrowed its title from a nursery rhyme.

2. [Advertisement], *Sacramento [Calif.] Daily Union* (May 9, 1872): 2.

3. *[Harrisburg, Pa.] Weekly Patriot and Union* (Nov. 30, 1865).

4. *New York Herald-Tribune* (June 20, 1866).

5. "Captain Kelso," *[Springfield] Missouri Weekly Patriot* [hereafter, *Patriot*] (July 5, 1866): 2; "'Wild Bill,' Harpers' Monthly and 'Colonel' G. W. Nichols," *Patriot* (Jan. 31, 1867): 2.

6. "The Autobiography of John R. Kelso," Dieu manuscripts (privately held), Vol. 5, 422, hereafter cited as D mss, with volume and page number.

7. D mss 5: 427.

8. Ibid., 428–29.

9. Ibid., 429. Kelso first wrote "son of a _____," then later, in pencil, replaced the phrase with the word "cutthroat."

10. Ibid., 434.

11. Ibid., 434.

12. *Sacramento Daily Union* (May 11, 1872): 5.

13. "Suicide of a Boy," *Sacramento Daily Union* (October 4, 1870): 1. Newspaper accounts misnamed Kelso's son: it was Florellus, not JRK Jr.

14. John R. Kelso, "Auto-Biography," in "John R. Kelso's Complete Works in Manuscript," Huntington Library, San Marino, Calif., 668–800, esp. 688–89.

15. Wiley Britton, *The Union Indian Brigade in the Civil War* (Kansas City, Kans.: Franklin Hudson, 1922); Wiley Britton, *The Aftermath of the Civil War: Based on Investigations of War Claims* (Kansas City, Kans.: Smith-Grieves, 1924); Wiley Britton, *Memoirs of the Rebellion on the Border, 1863* (Chicago: Cushing, Thomas, 1882); Wiley Britton, *The Civil War on the Border,* 2 vols. (New York: G. P. Putnam's Sons, 1899, 1904). John R. Kelso, "Reconstruction," a speech delivered in the House of Representatives, Feb. 7, 1866 (*Congressional Globe* [hereafter *CG*], 39th Cong., 1st Sess., Feb. 7, 1866, 730–33).

16. Kelso's main published works are *The Real Blasphemers* (New York: Truth Seeker, 1883); *The Bible Analyzed in Twenty Lectures* (New York: Truth Seeker, 1884); *Spiritualism Sustained in Five Lectures* (New York: Truth Seeker, 1886); *The Universe Analyzed* (New York: Truth Seeker, 1887); *Deity Analyzed in Six Lectures* (New York: Truth Seeker, 1890); and *Government Analyzed* (Longmont, Colo.: privately printed, 1892).

17. John R. Kelso, *Bloody Engagements: John R. Kelso's Civil War*, ed. Christopher Grasso (New Haven, Conn.: Yale University Press, 2017).

18. D mss 2: 187.

19. R. H. Dana, "True Manhood," *Young American's Magazine of Self-Improvement* 1, no. 3 (May 1847): 172; Horace Greeley, "Manhood—Its Hindrances and Its Hopes," *Nineteenth Century* 3, no. 1 (Jan. 1, 1849): 161–74; W. W. Everts, *Manhood: Its Duties and Responsibilities* (Louisville, Ky., and New York, 1854); "American Manhood," *Genius of the West* 5, no. 6 (June 1856): 161–63; Wm. Clift, "Farm Life, a School of True Manhood," *American Journal of Education and College Review* 3, no. 1 (Jan. 1, 1857): 5–23; "Slavery Hostile to Manhood," *Oberlin Evangelist* 20, no. 2 (Jan. 20, 1858): 13; T. D. Tooker, "Our Manhood," *Moore's Rural New-Yorker* 9, no. 25 (June 19, 1858): 200; "True Manhood," *Page Monthly* 1, no. 4 (Oct. 1858): 98–100; William Landels, *True Manhood: Its Nature, Foundation, and Development* (London and New York, 1861).

20. D mss 2: 183. There is a large literature on nineteenth-century manhood. For synopses see Bryan C. Rindfleisch, "'What It Means to Be a Man': Contested Masculinity in the Early Republic and Antebellum America," *History Compass* 10/11 (2012): 852–65; Brian Craig Miller, "Manhood," in Aaron Sheehan-Dean, ed., *A Companion to the U.S. Civil War*, Vol. 2. (West Sussex, UK: Wiley Blackwell, 2014): 795–810. See esp. E. Anthony Rotundo, "Learning about Manhood: Gender Ideals and the Middle-Class Family in Nineteenth-Century America," in J. A. Mangan and James Walvin, eds., *Manliness and Morality: Middle-Class Masculinity in Britain and America* (New York: St. Martin's Press, 1987), 35–51; Judy Arlene Hilkey, *Character Is Capital: Success Manuals and Manhood in Gilded Age America* (Chapel Hill: University of North Carolina Press, 1997); Dana D. Nelson, *National Manhood: Capitalist Citizenship and the Imagined Fraternity of White Men* (Durham, N.C.: Duke University Press, 1998); Shawn Johansen, *Family Men: Middle-Class Fatherhood in Industrializing America*

(New York: Routledge, 2001); Amy S. Greenberg, *Manifest Manhood and the Antebellum American Empire* (New York: Cambridge University Press, 2005); Kevin Murphy, *Political Manhood: Red Bloods, Mollycoddles, and the Politics of Progressive Era Reform* (New York: Columbia University Press, 2008); Lorien Foote, *The Gentlemen and the Roughs: Manhood, Honor, and Violence in the Union Army* (New York: New York University Press, 2010); John A. Casey, *New Men: Reconstructing the Image of the Veteran in Late Nineteenth-Century American Literature and Culture* (New York: Fordham University Press, 2015); Joseph M. Beilein Jr., *Bushwhackers: Guerrilla Warfare, Manhood, and the Household in Civil War Missouri* (Kent, Ohio: Kent State University Press, 2016).

21. D mss 2: 122, 4: 298, 4: 296-7.

22. D mss 3: 215, 4: 297–98. Kelso's underlines, here and throughout, rendered in italics.

23. "Courage—Physical, Intellectual, and Moral," *Nassau Literary Magazine* 24, no. 5 (Feb. 1864): 229; "The Weak Side of Our Armies," *Boston Daily Advertiser* (June 30, 1863): 2; Augustus Woodbury, *Courage* (Providence, R.I., 1861), 4; Taylor Lewis, *The Heroic Periods in a Nation's History* (New York: Baker and Godwin, 1866), 33; Ernest F. M. Faehtz, *The National Memorial Day: A Record of Ceremonies* (Washington, D.C.: Grand Army of the Republic, 1870), 189; Joshua L. Chamberlain, *Dead on the Field of Honor* (Portland, Maine: B. Thurston & Co., 1866), 16; O. W. Holmes quoted in Casey, *New Men*, 81. See also George P. Putnam, *The Man and the Soldier* (Boston: American Unitarian Assoc., 1861); Charles E. Norton, *The Soldier of the Good Cause* (Boston: American Unitarian Assoc., 1861); Theodore Parker, *Speeches, Addresses, and Occasional Sermons*, Vol. 3 (Boston: R. Leighton Jr., 1861): 159, 231–32; "Purpose the Basis of Improvement," *[Brooklyn, N.Y.] Circular* 10, 52 (Jan. 30, 1862), 1; "The Contest of the Hour," *Circular* 11, no. 77 (June 5, 1862): 68; S. H. Winkley, *An Enemy within the Lines* (Boston: American Unitarian Assoc., 1863); "Voice of the Hour," *[New York] Christian Inquirer* 17, no. 44 (Aug. 1, 1863): 1; John F. W. Ware, *Manhood, The Want of the Day* (Boston: American Unitarian Assoc., 1863); Henry T. Johns, *Life with the Forty-Ninth Massachusetts Volunteers* (Pittsfield, Mass.: for the author, 1864), 152; John F. W. Ware, *A Few Words with the Convalescent* (Boston: American Unitarian Assoc., 1864); "The Manhood Developed by the War," *Monthly Religious Magazine* 32, no. 4 (Oct. 1864): 265; Soldiers and Sailors National Union League of Washington, D.C., *An Address to All Honorably Discharged Soldiers and Sailors* (Washington, D.C., 1865); Lydia Minturn Post, ed., *Soldiers Letters from Camp, Battlefield, and Prison* (New York: Bunce and Huntington, 1865), 103, 167; Frank More, ed., *Memorial Ceremonies at the Graves of Our Soldiers* (Washington, D.C., 1869), 240, 531.

24. D mss 4: 379, 376; Stephen W. Berry II, *All That Makes a Man: Love and Ambition in the Civil War South* (New York: Oxford University Press, 2003), 12. In a poem Kelso wrote called "The Soldier's Visit Home," he contemplated a visit home when

he could "fling aside the cares of life—forget my manhood's pride" (*Miscellaneous Writings*, 386).

25. Putnam, *The Man and the Soldier*, 8; Robert Collyer, *A Letter to a Sick Soldier* (Boston: American Unitarian Assoc., 1862), 5; [Anon.], *The Camp and the Field* (Boston: American Unitarian Assoc., 1861), 5; John F. Ware, *The Home to the Hospital* (Boston: American Unitarian Assoc., 1861), 14. See also John F. Ware, *The Home to the Camp* (Boston: American Unitarian Assoc., 1861).

26. Eugene Debs quoted in Hilkey, *Character Is Capital*, 143; Kelso, "The Kingdom of Heaven" (1890) in "Miscellaneous Writings," 498.

27. D mss 10: 48; 11: 22; 11: 47; Kelso, "Kingdom of Heaven," in "Miscellaneous Writings," 519.

CHAPTER I

1. D mss 1: 24.
2. William Henry Perrin, ed., *History of Delaware County, Ohio* (Chicago: O. L. Baskin & Co., 1880), 581, 437, 58; D mss 1: 22.
3. D mss 1: 27–28.
4. Ibid., 16.
5. Ibid., 3–4.
6. Ibid., 4–6; George Washington to Brig. Gen. William Maxwell, Feb. 24, 1779, www.founders.archives.gov; George Washington Papers, Series 7, Applications for Office, 1789–1796: Robert Kelso, Library of Congress, https://www.loc.gov/item/mgw758384/. Thanks to Kris Stoever for the latter two references. On the uniform: Florella Kelso Finney, "Notes and Explanations" [reminiscence—typescript], March 5, 1928, Trudy Sheffield Collection (privately held), 60–61.
7. D mss 1: 7, 11–14.
8. Ibid., 16–17.
9. Ibid., 17.
10. Robert S. Kelso, purchase of 80 acres, Sept. 18, 1834, document 2699, United States, Bureau of Land Management, *Ohio, Homestead and Cash Entry Patents, Pre-1908*, ancestry.com; [W. H. Perrin and J. H. Battle], *History of Morrow County and Ohio* (Chicago: O. L. Baskin & Co., 1880), 449–50, 492.
11. *History of Morrow County*, 175–94, 452; Martin Welker, *Farm Life in Central Ohio Sixty Years Ago* (Cleveland, Ohio: Western Reserve Historical Society, 1895).
12. *History of Morrow County*, 453, 496, 502; Perrin, *History of Delaware County*, 436, 577.
13. D mss 1: 50; *History of Morrow County*, 401.
14. D mss 1: 29.
15. Ibid., 30–31.
16. Ibid., 39.
17. Ibid., 36–37.

18. Ibid., 40–42.

19. *History of Morrow County*, 503.

20. *History of Morrow County*, 457; D mss 1: 45.

21. D mss 1: 42–45.

22. Ibid., 46–47.

23. Ibid., 47–48.

24. D mss 10: 33.

25. Ibid., 31–32.

26. Ibid., 32–33.

27. Ibid., 34.

CHAPTER 2

1. D mss 1: 74.

2. Ibid., 53.

3. On Indians in northwestern Missouri see William E. Foley, *The Genesis of Missouri: From Wilderness Outpost to Statehood* (Columbia: University of Missouri Press, 1989), 145–46, 155–56, 174–75, and Willard H. Rollins, *The Osage: An Ethnohistorical Study of Hegemony on the Prairie-Plains* (Columbia: University of Missouri Press, 1992) (the Osage were primarily south of the Missouri River). On the response to the Black Hawk War and trade, see I. A. Holcombe, *History of Daviess County, Missouri* (Kansas City, Mo.: Birdsall & Dean, 1882), 149, 154. On the Heatherly War (a murder initially blamed on Indians), see *History of Daviess County*, 156–59, but a fuller account is in Albert J. Roof, *Past and Present of Livingston County, Missouri*, Vol. I (Chicago: S. J. Clark Pub. Co., 1913): 214–18.

4. To determine land ownership I have used: Daviess Co., Mo., Recorder of Deeds, Deed Record Books A (1838–1843) and B (1844–1849), microfilm; Daviess Co., Mo., Recorder of Deeds, Deed Records (Daviess County, Missouri), 1838–1902, Indexes, microfilm: (Salt Lake City, Utah: Genealogical Society of Utah, 1974–2010), https://familysearch.org; Missouri Digital History, "Land Records, 1777–1969," https://s1.sos.mo.gov/records/archives/archivesdb/land/default.aspx; U.S. Department of the Interior, Bureau of Land Management, General Land Office Records, www.glorecords.blm.gov; Gregory A. Boyd, *Family Maps of Daviess County, Missouri* (Norman, Okla.: Arphax Pub. Co., 2006). On Bingham see also *History of Daviess County*, 189; LaMar C. Berrett, ed., *Sacred Places: A Comprehensive Guide to Early LDS Historical Sites, Vol. 4: Missouri* (Salt Lake City, Utah: Deseret Books, 2004), 366–70; "Those Three Bingham Kids," http://thosethreebinghamkids.weebly.com/james-and-the-mormons.html. On Wilhite see also Thomas D. Casper Affidavit, Quincy, Ill., 1840, in BYU Religious Studies Center, "Individual Affidavits from the LDS Historical Center," https://rsc.byu.edu/archived/mormon-redress-petitions-documents-1833-1838-missouri-conflict/part-ii-first-appeal-1.

5. On the Mormon War in Missouri see Missouri State Archives, Mormon War Papers, 1837–1841, https://www.sos.mo.gov/archives/resources/findingaids/rg005-01; *Document Containing the Correspondence and Orders, &c. in Relation to the Disturbances with the Mormons* (Fayette, Mo.: Published by the Order of the General Assembly, 1841); James H. Hunt, *A History of the Mormon War, with a Prefix, Embracing the Rise, Progress, and Peculiar Tenets of Mormon Doctrine* (St. Louis, Mo: Ustick and Davis, 1844). The best study is Stephen C. LeSueur, *The 1838 Mormon War in Missouri* (Columbia: University of Missouri Press, 1987). On Mormons in Missouri in the 1830s and the Mormon War, see also Leland H. Gentry, "The Land Question at Adam-ondi-Ahman," *BYU Studies Quarterly* 26, no. 2 (1986): 45–56; Stephen C. LeSueur, "Missouri's Failed Compromise: The Creation of Caldwell County for the Mormons," *Journal of Mormon History* 31, no. 2 (Fall 2005): 133–44; John Hamer, "Mapping Mormon Settlement in Caldwell County, Missouri," *Mormon Historical Studies* 9, no. 1 (Spring 2008): 15–38; Jeffrey N. Walker, "Mormon Land Rights in Caldwell and Daviess Counties and the Mormon Conflict of 1838: New Findings and New Understandings," *BYU Studies Quarterly* 47, no. 1 (2008): 1–55; Leland H. Gentry and Todd M. Compton, *Fire and Sword: A History of the Latter-Day Saints in Northern Missouri, 1836–39* (Salt Lake City, Utah: Greg Kofford Books, 2011); Steve LeSueur, "Mixing Politics with Religion: A Closer Look at Electioneering and Voting in Caldwell and Daviess Counties in 1838," *John Whitmer Historical Association Journal* [hereafter *JWHAJ*] 33, no. 1 (Spring/Summer 2013): 184–208; Matthew B. Lund, "A Society of Like-Minded Men: American Localism and the Mormon Expulsion from Jackson County," *Journal of Mormon History* 40, no. 3 (Summer 2014): 169–200; William Shepard, "Transformation of the Mormon Hierarchy at Far West, Missouri," *JWHAJ* 35, no. 1 (Spring/Summer 2015): 62–83; Diane Mutti Burke, "A Contested Promised Land": Mormons, Slaveholders, and the Disputed Vision for the Settlement of Western Missouri," *JWHAJ* 36, no. 1 (Spring/Summer 2016): 13–34; Bill Shepard and H. Michael Marquardt, "Mortal Enemies: Mormons and Missourians 1839–1844," *JWHAJ* 36, no. 1 (Spring/Summer 2016): 35–80.

6. Sydney Rigdon quoted in LeSueur, *Mormon War*, 50.

7. Letter from Citizens of Daviess and Caldwell Counties to Gov. Lilburn Boggs, Sept. 12, 1838, Missouri State Archives, Mormon War Papers; Gov. Boggs to Gen. John B. Clark, Oct. 27, 1838, in *Document Containing the Correspondence*, 61; William Reynolds quoted in Ora Merle Hawk Pease, *History of Caldwell and Livingston Counties, Missouri* (St. Louis, Mo.: National History Co., 1886), 149.

8. On the Bingham fine and land sale see Daviess Co., Mo., Recorder of Deeds, Deed Record Books A (1838–1843), p. 72 (microfilm).

9. On Edgar Kelso settling in the region in 1834, see Holcombe, *History of Daviess County*, 786.

10. D mss 1: 59–60.

11. Ibid., 56–57.

12. Holcombe, *History of Daviess County*, 688–92, 786–87. Analysis of 1850 U.S. Census, Daviess County, Missouri: Of the male household heads (730) whose occupations are known (708), 627 (almost 90%) were farmers.

13. D mss 1: 13, 92, 68, 90; James M. Hunt, *History of the Mormon War* (St. Louis, Mo., 1844), quoted in *History of Daviess County*, 189; Daviess Co., Mo., Deeds, Indexes. The discussion of Robert's and Edgar's comparative wealth is based on an analysis of the 1850 U. S. Census for Daviess County. Of 792 householders, 454 owned real estate (57%). Only 8 householders in the county owned more land than Edgar, whose holdings were valued at $2,500; 79 householders owned less than Robert's $500 and 320 owned more. Robert Kelso was 44 years old in 1850. Of the 164 middle-aged (age 39–49) male household heads identified as farmers, 35 (21%) had no real estate (they were farm laborers, tenants, or squatters); 18 (11%) equaled Robert's $500; and 86 (52%) had more than $500. Among landowning farmers in this age group, Robert was in the bottom third. The details about Kelso's farm are from U.S. Bureau of the Census, Manuscript Census, Missouri, Daviess County, Schedule II (Agriculture), 1850, microfilm. Edgar's 930 acres (100 improved) had more of everything, including livestock worth $1,375 (compared to Robert's $255).

14. D mss 1: 59, 68, 73, 89.

15. Ibid., 51, 52, 59; Holcombe, *History of Daviess County*, 691; Noah Webster, *The Elementary Spelling Book* (Concord, N.H.: Moses G. Atwood, 1832); Samuel Kirkham, *English Grammar in Familiar Lectures*, 53rd ed. (Rochester, N.Y.: Wm. Alling, 1841).

16. D mss. 1: 52; J. Olney, *A Practical System of Modern Geography*, 27th ed. (New York: Robinson, 1838), 277. An earlier edition (Hartford, Conn.: D. F. Robinson, 1833), had a different frontispiece illustrating the four varieties of mankind.

17. D mss 1: 57. Kelso would have read Charles Rollin's *Ancient History of the Egyptians, Carthaginians, Assyrians, Babylonians, Medes and Persians, Grecians, and Macedonians* (12 vols., 1730–1738) and Sir Walter Scott's *Life of Napoleon* (9 vols., 1827) in compressed American one- or two-volume editions with small-font text crammed into double-column pages. For example: Rollin, *Ancient History*, 2 vols. (New York: Harper & Bros., 1839, 1842); Scott, *Napoleon*, 1 vol. (Philadelphia: E. L. Carey and A. Hart, 1839).

18. D mss 1: 17, 65–66, 70, 60.

19. Ibid., 72. On the death of Sarah Lisle (Jeremiah Lenhart's granddaughter), see Holcombe, *History of Daviess County*, 786.

20. D mss 1: 73; Kelso, "*Works*," 46–47.

21. D mss 1: 74; *History of Daviess County*, 692, 787.

CHAPTER 3

1. D mss 2: 106

2. Ibid., 106. On Hell Town see *History of Clay and Platte Counties, Missouri* (St. Louis, Mo.: National Historical Co., 1885), 894. On barring-out rituals and schoolmaster-schoolboy conflicts see Barbara Finkelstein, *Governing the Young: Teacher Behavior in Popular Primary Schools in Nineteenth-Century United States* (New York: Falmer Press, 1989), 95–106 and primary documents on 163–65, 172–74, 183–85, 214–18. For another description of barring out, see Martin Welker, *Farm Life in Central Ohio Sixty Years Ago* (Wooster, Ohio: Clapper's Print, 1982), 9.

3. D mss 2: 108.

4. Ibid., 110–11.

5. Ibid., 111.

6. Ibid., 112.

7. Ibid., 113–14.

8. Ibid., 115.

9. D mss 2: 75; Holcombe, *History of Daviess County*, 691; Ralph Edward Glauert, "Education and Society in Antebellum Missouri" (PhD diss., University of Missouri, 1973).

10. D mss 1: 75. Jacob Abbott and the Boston Association of Masters of Public Schools quoted in Finkelstein, *Governing the Young*, 118. For a rich portrait of the teaching experience, see William A. Alcott, *Confessions of a School Master* (Andover, Mass. and New York: Gould, Newman and Saxton, 1839).

11. D mss 1: 88-9.

12. Ibid.; Finkelstein, *Governing the Young*, 44–45, 138.

13. On early Methodism see esp. Frank Baker, *From Wesley to Asbury: Studies in Early American Methodism* (Durham, N.C.: Duke University Press, 1976); David Hempton, *Methodism and Politics in British Society, 1750–1850* (Stanford, Calif.: Stanford University Press, 1984); Russell E. Richey, *Early American Methodism* (Bloomington: Indiana University Press, 1991); Russell E. Richey, et al., eds., *Perspectives on American Methodism: Interpretive Essays* (Nashville, Tenn.: Kingswood Books, 1993); A. Gregory Schneider, *The Way of the Cross Leads Home: The Domestication of American Methodism* (Bloomington: Indiana University Press, 1993); Christine Leigh Heyrman, *Southern Cross; The Beginnings of the Bible Belt* (Chapel Hill: University of North Carolina Press, 1997); Cynthia Lynn Lyerly, *Methodism and the Southern Mind, 1710–1810* (New York: Oxford University Press, 1998); John H. Wigger, *Taking Heaven by Storm: Methodism and the Rise of Popular Christianity in America* (New York: Oxford University Press, 1998); Ann Taves, *Fits, Trances, and Visions: Experiencing Religion and Explaining Experience from Wesley to James* (Princeton, N.J.: Princeton University Press, 1999); Dee E. Andrews, *The Methodists and Revolutionary America, 1760–1800: The Shaping of an Evangelical Culture* (Princeton, N.J. Princeton University

Press, 2000), Nathan O. Hatch and John H. Wigger, eds. *Methodism and the Shaping of American Culture* (Nashville, Tenn.: Kingswood Books, 2001); Lester Ruth, *A Little Heaven Below: Worship at Early Methodist Quarterly Meetings* (Nashville, Tenn.: Kingswood Books, 2000); Lester Ruth, *Early Methodist Life and Spirituality: A Reader* (Nashville, Tenn: Kingswood Books., 2005); David Hempton, *Methodism: Empire of the Spirit* (New Haven, Conn.: Yale University Press, 2005); Phyllis Mack, *Heart Religion in the British Enlightenment: Gender and Emotion in Early Methodism* (New York: Cambridge University Press, 2008); John Wigger, *American Saint: Francis Asbury and the Methodists* (New York: Oxford University Press, 2009); Jeffrey Williams, *Religion and Violence in Early American Methodism: Taking the Kingdom by Force* (Bloomington: Indiana University Press, 2010); Anna M. Lawrence, *One Family Under God: Love, Belonging, and Authority in Early Transatlantic Methodism* (Philadelphia: University of Pennsylvania Press, 2011); Christopher Cannon Jones, "Methodism, Slavery, and Freedom in the Revolutionary Atlantic World" (PhD diss., College of William and Mary, 2016).

14. D mss 1: 76, 74.

15. Ibid., 77, 82-3.

16. Ibid., 78, –81-2. The identification of Kelso's rival as John Cravens's son Robert is speculative. Kelso refers to him only as "Mr. C." But Kelso describes him as the son of a slaveholder, and the only slaveholder with a surname beginning with "C" and having a son the right age is Cravens. The census actually recorded the number of slaves residing in a household; some of those slaves could have been hired from other owners, not owned by Cravens. Returns from the few Missouri counties where the tabulators distinguished residence and ownership suggest that anywhere from 4% to 31% of slaves were hired out. See Diane Mutti Burke, *On Slavery's Border: Missouri's Small Slaveholding Households, 1815–1865* (Athens: University of Georgia Press, 2010), 108.

17. D mss 1: 89; John W. Kelso, 1850 U. S. Census, District 27, Daviess Co., Mo., family no. 156; "Letter from Berea, Ohio. How Grindstones Are Made," *Cincinnati Daily Gazette* (June 2, 1869): 1.

18. D mss 1: 89–90.

19. Ibid., 89–91; Carol Shammas, *A History of Household Government in America* (Charlottesville: University of Virginia Press, 2002), 11; James D. Schmidt, "'Restless Movements Characteristic of Childhood': The Legal Construction of Child Labor in Nineteenth-Century Massachusetts," *Law and History Review* 23, no. 2 (Summer 2005): 315–25), esp. 319.

20. D mss 1: 92.

21. Ibid., 92–96. On Lexington as a market town, see Jeff Bremer, *A Store Almost in Sight: The Economic Transformation of Missouri from the Louisiana Purchase to the Civil War* (Iowa City: University of Iowa Press, 2014), 151–52; on cholera in antebellum Missouri see ibid., 66–67.

22. D mss 2: 98. See also "The Flood," *[St. Louis, Mo.] Daily Missouri Republican* (June 5, 1851): 2.

23. D mss 1: 77–78, 2: 99–102 (including copy of letter to Ursula Kelso, Sept. 23, 1851).

24. D mss 2: 103.

25. Ibid., 116.

26. Ibid., 116–17, 119–20.

27. Ibid., 119.

28. *History of Clay and Platte Counties, Missouri*, 542–653; Perry McCandless, *A History of Missouri, Vol. II: 1820–1860* (Columbia: University of Missouri Press, 1972), 258–88; Christopher Phillips, "'The Crime against Missouri': Slavery, Kansas, and the Cant of Southernness in the Border West," *Civil War History* 48 (March 2002): 60–81 (Phillips develops and expands this argument in *The Rivers Ran Backward: The Civil War and the Remaking of the American Middle Border* [New York: Oxford University Press, 2016]); Jeremy Neely, *The Border between Them: Violence and Reconciliation on the Kansas-Missouri Line* (Columbia: University of Missouri Press, 2007), 25–58.

29. D mss 2: 121. Platte County census figures, Missouri state census, 1856, cited in Benjamin Merkel, "The Antislavery Movement in Missouri" (PhD diss., Washington University, 1939), 246 (Merkel also notes 63 free Blacks in the county, 178 n. 26). See also 1860 U.S. Census, Slave Schedules: Platte County, Missouri; *History of Clay and Platte Counties, Missouri*, 600 (census figures, but with a lower slave count than in actual returns); R. Douglas Hurt, *Agriculture and Slavery in Missouri's Little Dixie* (Columbia: University of Missouri Press, 1992); Burke, *On Slavery's Border*, esp. 309–10.

30. D mss 2: 121–22. On Campbellites in Missouri see Mary K. Dains, "Alexander Campbell and the Missouri Disciples of Christ, 1852," *Missouri Historical Review* 77, no. 1 (Oct. 1982): 13–46.

31. D mss 2: 122-3. On William Phillips see *History of Clay and Platte Counties, Missouri*, 644; Harrison Anthony Trexler, *Slavery in Missouri, 1804–1865* (Baltimore: Johns Hopkins University Press, 1914), 198–99, and David Grimsted, *American Mobbing, 1828–1861: Toward Civil War* (New York: Oxford University Press, 1998), 250.

32. D mss 2: 122.

33. John R. Kelso, "Mormonism," *Boston Investigator* (May 7, 1884): 3; "Dangers that Threaten the People," delivered at the Spiritualistic Camp-meeting at San José, CA, June 7, 1885, in Kelso, "Miscellaneous Writings," 374–75.

34. By 1863, Edgar held a whole family of Blacks in bondage; in December of that year, two White men from Iowa tried to free them. See [St. Joseph, Mo.] *Morning Herald and Daily Tribune* (Dec. 12, 1863), 2. On Free Soil see Eric Foner, *Free Soil, Free Labor, Free Men: The Ideology of the Republican Party before the Civil War* (New York: Oxford University Press, 1970). On fears of a slave power conspiracy see David Brion Davis, *The Slave Power Conspiracy and the Paranoid Style* (Baton Rouge: Louisiana State University Press, 1969); Leonard L. Richards,

The Slave Power: The Free North and Southern Domination, 1780–1860 (Baton Rouge: Louisiana State University Press, 2000); Michael William Pfau, *The Political Style of Conspiracy: Chase, Sumner, and Lincoln* (East Lansing: Michigan State University Press, 2005).

35. Neely, *Border between Them*, 48–49; Foner *Free Soil*, 270.
36. Burke, *On Slavery's Border*, 263; Neely, *Border between Them*, 45–59.

CHAPTER 4

1. D mss 2: 145.
2. Ibid., 120, 124; 1850 U.S. Census, Buchanan County, Missouri, family no. 942. Snyder was not listed as a slaveholder on the census slave schedule.
3. D mss 2: 125. On religious liberalism see for example W. H. Channing, "The Gospel of To-day," *Harbinger* 6, no. 4 (Nov. 27, 1847): 26–27, and "Orthodox and Liberal," *Monthly Religious Magazine* 10, no. 7 (July 1853), 293–94. See also Leigh Eric Schmidt, *Restless Souls: The Making of American Spirituality* (New York: Harper, 2005), 10–14; Schmidt, "Introduction: The Parameters and Problematics of American Religious Liberalism," in Schmidt and Sally M. Promey, eds. *American Religious Liberalism* (Bloomington: Indiana University Press, 2012), 1–14; Christopher G. White, *Unsettled Minds: Psychology and the American Search for Spiritual Assurance, 1830–1940* (Berkeley: University of California Press, 2009), 7–9.
4. John R. Kelso, Preface to "The Devil's Defense," in "Works," 64, 65. This work was published, but no copies seem to have survived.
5. Kelso, "Deity Analyzed," in "Works," 280, 346, 276, 284. I have used Kelso's manuscript copy, but this work was published: John R. Kelso, *Deity Analyzed. In Six Lectures* (New York: D. M. Bennet, 1883).
6. Kelso, "Deity Analyzed," in "Works," 273, 336, 310.
7. A version of the preceding five paragraphs also appeared in my *Skepticism and American Faith: From the Revolution to the Civil War* (New York: Oxford University Press, 2018), 460–62.
8. D mss 2: 141.
9. D mss 1, 66; 2: 143.
10. [Anon.], *The History and Philosophy of Animal Magnetism* (Boston: J. N. Bradley, [1843]); Charles P. Johnson, *A Treatise on Animal Magnetism* (New York: Burgess and Stringer, 1844); *Saint Louis Magnet*, esp. "Mesmerism in St. Louis," July 1, 1845, 54, and Aug. 1, 1845, 103; Joseph H. Bagg, *Bagg on Magnetism, or the Doctrine of Equilibrium* (Detroit, Mich.: Bagg and Harmon, 1845). On animal magnetism and mesmerism see esp. Robert Darnton, *Mesmerism and the End of the Enlightenment in France* (Cambridge, Mass.: Harvard University Press, 1968); Robert C. Fuller, *Mesmerism and the American Cure of Souls* (Philadelphia: University Press of Pennsylvania, 1982); Eric T. Carlson, "Charles Poyen Brings Mesmerism to America," *Journal of the History of Medicine and Allied Studies* 15, no. 2 (April,

1960): 121–32; Fred Kaplan, "'The Mesmeric Mania': The Early Victorians and Animal Magnetism," *Journal of the History of Ideas* 35, no. 4 (Oct.–Dec. 1974): 691–702; Terry M. Parssinen, "Mesmeric Performers," *Victorian Studies* 21, no. 1 (Autumn 1977): 87–104; Peter McCandless, "Mesmerism and Phrenology in Antebellum Charleston: 'Enough of the Marvelous,'" *Journal of Southern History* 58, no. 2 (May 1992): 199–230.

11. *The Magnet*, ed. by La Roy Sunderland; see esp. Sunderland, "Living Magnetism," 1, (June 1842): 7. On Sunderland see Taves, *Fits, Trances, and Visions*, esp. 128–9, 140–48, 201–6. On phrenology see Stephen Tomlinson, *Head Masters: Phrenology, Secular Education, and Nineteenth-Century Social Thought* (Tuscaloosa: University of Alabama Press, 2005); White, *Unsettled Minds*, chap. 1.

12. D mss 1: 77; 2: 124. W. Byrd Powell, *The Natural History of Human Temperaments; Their Laws in Relation to Marriage* (Cincinnati, Ohio: H. W. Derby and Co., 1856). For a later example combining magnetism, phrenology, and physiognomy, see Edward B. Foote, *Plain Home Talk about the Human System: The Habits of Men and Women . . . Our Sexual Relations and Social Natures* (New York: Murray Hill, 1880).

13. D mss 2: 125.

14. Ibid., 123.

15. Ibid., 125–26.

16. Ibid., 127.

17. Ibid., 127.

18. Ibid., 127.

19. Ibid., 129.

20. *The Revised Statutes of the State of Missouri* (St. Louis, Mo.: Chambers and Knapp, 1845), 224–25; *The Revised Statutes of the State of Missouri* (Jefferson City, Mo.: James Luck, 1856), 662–66. See Joel Prentiss Bishop, *Commentaries on the Law of Marriage and Divorce, and Evidence in Matrimonial Suits* (Boston: Little, Brown, and Co., 1852), 270–637, esp. 286–87, 389, 396–403, 454–501. See also Norma Basch, *Framing American Divorce: From the Revolutionary Generation to the Victorians* (Berkeley: University of California Press, 1999); Robin C. Sanger, *Marital Cruelty in Antebellum America* (Baton Rouge: Louisiana State University Press, 2016); Martin Schultz, "Divorce in Early America: Origins and Patterns in Three North Central States," *Sociological Quarterly* 25, no. 4 (autumn 1984): 511–25; Lyn Ellen Bennett, "Child Custody, Custodial Arrangements, and Financial Support in Late 19th c. Kansas," *Kansas History* 37, no. 1 (March 2014): 83–112.

21. D mss 2: 130.

22. Ibid., 138. The chapel had been named for the Rev. Middleton R. Jones, an early settler in the Platte Purchase and currently one of the traveling preachers on the Plattsburg Circuit who preached there regularly. On Jones and Jones's Chapel see *History of Clinton County, Missouri* (St. Joseph, Mo.: National Historical Company, 1881), 163; *A History of Buchanan County, Missouri* (St. Joseph, Mo.: National

Historical Company, 1881), 117; C. I. Van Deventer, *Sketches of Methodism in Northeast Missouri* (St. Joseph, Mo.: Combe Printing Co., 1894), 31, 44. On the relationship of local preachers and preachers traveling a circuit, see *The Doctrines and Discipline of the Methodist Episcopal Church South* (Nashville, Tenn.: Stevenson & Owen, 1854), 228.

23. D mss 2: 132, 134, 135, 139. Missouri Marriage Records, 1805–2002, Jemima R. Snyder and Evans W. Ray, Nov. 18, 1856; the 1860 U.S. Census, Tremont, Buchanan Co., Mo., family no. 1550, shows Mima's husband owning 10,800 acres. Mima ("Fannie J. [Snyder] Ray") died in 1878 (headstone, Mount Mora Cemetery, St. Joseph, Buchanan Co., Mo., Lot 1, Block 10, Section L, Find-a-Grave.com).

24. D mss 2: 139–41.

25. Ibid., 140.

26. Ibid., 142.

27. E. M. Marvin, *The Life of Rev. William Goss Caples of the Missouri Conference of the Methodist Episcopal Church South* (St. Louis, Mo.: Southwestern Book and Pub. Co., 1871), 166–67, 317. See Charles F. Deems, ed., *Annals of Southern Methodism for 1855* (New York: J. A. Gray's, 1856), 25–27, and Deems, ed., *Annals of Southern Methodism for 1856* (Nashville, Tenn., [1857]), 20–22; see also *A History of Clinton County, Missouri* (St. Joseph, Mo.: National Historical Company, 1881), 479; W. S. Woodward, *Annals of Methodism in Missouri* (Columbia, Mo.: E. W. Stephens, 1893), 162–66; C. I. Van Deventer, *Sketches of Methodism in Northwest Missouri* (St. Joseph, Mo.: Combe Printing Co., 1894), 31.

28. Marvin, *Life of Caples*, 148, 150; D mss 2: 142–43.

29. D mss 2: 143–44. See Marvin, *Life of Caples*, 322, and see 192–93 and 224.

30. Marvin, *Life of Caples*, 258; D mss 2: 142.

31. D mss 2: 145.

32. Ibid., 144. See Dick Steward, *Duels and the Roots of Violence in Missouri* (Columbia: University of Missouri Press, 2000), esp. 38–39, 58–74, 88, 114, 132, 181; see also Steward, *Beyond the Sabbath: Missouri and Her Violent Heritage* (Marceline, Mo.: Vintage Publications, 2005).

33. Steward, *Duels and the Roots of Violence in Missouri.*

34. D mss 2: 155.

35. Ibid., 132, 156.

36. Ibid., 145.

37. Ibid., 146. On Walker and antebellum filibustering, see esp. Robert E. May, *Manifest Destiny's Underworld: Filibustering in Antebellum America* (Chapel Hill: University of North Carolina Press, 2002), esp. 105. For propaganda, see William Wells, *Walker's Expedition to Nicaragua* (New York: Stringer and Townswend, 1856), esp. 13; George W. Peck, *Nicaragua and General Walker. Speech of the Hon. Geo. W. Peck of Michigan* (Washington, D.C.: Union Office, 1856); Anna Ella Carroll, *The Star of the West; or, National Men and National Measures* (Boston: J. French, 1856), 172–73. For criticism by a Missouri politician, see Francis Preston Blair, *A*

Voice from the Grave of Jackson! (Washington, D.C.: Buell and Blanchard, 1856), 3. For Walker in Missouri newspapers, see for ex. articles in the *Weekly St. Louis Pilot* from April 21, 1855, through Sept. 6, 1856. On Walker in the press, see Amy S. Greenberg, "A Gray-Eyed Man: Character, Appearance, and Filibustering," *Journal of the Early Republic* 20, no. 4 (Winter 2000): 673–99; on Walker and literature, see Brady Harrison, *Agent of Empire: William Walker and the Imperial Self in American Literature* (Athens: University of Georgia Press, 2004).

38. D mss 2: 145.

39. Ibid., 146. *Second Regular Annual Catalogue of the Officers and Members of Pleasant Ridge College* (St. Louis, Mo.: Republican Book and Job Office, 1855). Cf. "Course of Instruction," *Catalogue of the Officers and Students in Yale College, 1849–50* (New Haven, Conn.: B. T. Hamlen, 1849), 31, and "Course of Instruction," *Catalogue of the Trustees, Officers, and Students of the University of Pennsylvania, Session 1851–52* (Philadelphia: L. R. Bailey, 1852), 30–33. On Pleasant Ridge College see *Laws of Missouri, Eighteenth Gen. Assembly, First Session*, 1854–5, State Documents Collections, Missouri State Archives, Jefferson City (act of incorporation, approved March 5, 1855); Nathan H. Parker, *Missouri As It Is in 1867* (Philadelphia: J. B. Lippincott & Co., 1867), 358–59; *History of Clay and Platte Counties, Missouri*, 772, 777; Paxton, *Annals of Platte County*, 337, 437. Still advertised in *The Christian Advocate* (Sept. 25, 1867), the college seems to have burned down shortly thereafter.

40. D mss 2: 146, 152; "Text Books," *Second Catalogue, Pleasant Ridge College*, 8; John Abercrombie, *Inquiries Concerning the Intellectual Powers and the Investigation of Truth* (Boston: Otis, Broades, and Co., 1843, orig. pub. 1833); Samuel Whelpley, *A Compend of History, from the Earliest Times*, 6th ed., 2 vol. (Boston: Richardson and Lord, 1822); Francis Wayland, *Elements of Moral Science* (Boston: Gould, Kendall and Lincoln, 1849, orig. pub. 1835).

41. D mss 2: 148, 150.

42. Ibid., 154, 157.

43. Ibid., 157–58.

44. D mss 2: 158–59; 1: 58–59, cross writing.

CHAPTER 5

1. D mss 2: 184. William E. Parrish, *Turbulent Partnership: Missouri and the Union, 1861–1865* (Columbia: University of Missouri Press, 1963), 1–17; Louis S. Gerteis, *Civil War St. Louis* (Lawrence: University Press of Kansas, 2001), 67–96; Gov. C. F. Jackson to Sec. of War Simon Cameron, April 17, 1861, *The War of the Rebellion: A Compilation of the Official Records of the Union and Confederate Armies* (hereafter cited as *OR*), Ser. 3, Vol. 1 (Washington, D.C.: Government Printing Office, 1899), 82–83; and see Christopher Phillips, *Missouri's Confederate: Claiborne Fox Jackson and the Creation of Southern Identity in the Border West* (Columbia: University of Missouri Press, 2000), 247–48. Kelso remembered the day being a Friday (May

10?), but also wrote that "The news had just reached us of the seceding of several more states" (D mss 2: 184) not long after the attack on Fort Sumter (April 12). Virginia seceded on April 17; Arkansas and Tennessee on May 6 (the Tennessee referendum would be on June 8). Other pro-Southern towns celebrated May 7 as "Secession Day": see the *Rolla Express*, May 13, 1861, cited in John F. Bradbury Jr., *The Old Phelps County Courthouse and the Civil War* (Rolla, Mo.: Old Courthouse Preservation Committee and the Phelps County Historical Society, 1999), 4.

2. D mss 2: 181, 184.

3. Ibid., 163; Greene County, Missouri, Circuit Court Records, File 6689, Divorce of John R. and Mary [Adelia] Kelso, filed March term, 1858; marriage dissolved September term, 1858, Book D. JR p. 136, 225–26, Greene County Records and Archives Center, Springfield, Missouri (thanks to Steven Haberman for helping me obtain this document); Marriage Record, John R. Kelso and Martha S. Barnes, Sept. 23, 1858, Missouri Marriage Records, Greene County, Missouri State Archives, Jefferson City, Mo., microfilm reproduced in Missouri Marriage Records 1805–2002, ancestry.com.

4. D mss 2: 172, 174, 175.

5. D mss 2: 186. Gov. Jackson, on May 3, 1861, called out the Missouri Volunteer Militia. His later proclamation calling for all loyal Missourians to rise up and drive out the Federal invaders was published in the *Boonville Times* on June 12, 1861. On Jackson see Phillips, *Missouri's Confederate*. For his May 3 speech, see "Governor's Message," *[St. Louis] Daily Missouri Republican* (May 4, 1861): 2, and Jackson, "Special Session Message," May 3, 1861, in Buel Leopard and Floyd C. Shoemaker, eds., *The Messages and Proclamations of the Governors of the State of Missouri*, Vol. 3 (Columbia, Mo.: State Historical Society of Missouri, 1922), 343–48; for the text of his June proclamation, see Silvana R. Siddali, ed., *Missouri's War: The Civil War in Documents* (Athens: University of Ohio Press, 69–71.

6. D mss 2: 185–87.

7. Ibid., 188.

8. William E. Parrish, *A History of Missouri, Vol. III: 1860–1875* (Columbia: University of Missouri Press, 1973), 6–8; Mark W. Geiger, *Financial Fraud and Guerrilla Violence in Missouri's Civil War, 1861–1865* (New Haven, Conn.: Yale University Press, 2010), 12; R. Douglas Hurt, "Planters and Slavery in Little Dixie," *Missouri Historical Review* (hereafter *MHR*) 88, no. 4 (July, 1994): 397–415; and Robert W. Frizzell, "Southern Identity in Nineteenth-Century Missouri: Little Dixie's Slave-Majority Areas and the Transition to Midwestern Farming," *MHR* 99 (April 2005): 238–60. "On the dominance of conservative Unionism, see Aaron Astor, *Rebels on the Border: Civil War, Emancipation, and the Reconstruction of Kentucky and Missouri* (Baton Rouge: Louisiana State University Press, 2012) and Phillips, *The Rivers Ran Backward*.

9. James Denny and John Bradbury, *The Civil War's First Blood: Missouri, 1854–1861* (Boonville: Missouri Life, 2007), 68 ("Secesh"). An analysis of the 1860 census

reveals some socio-economic differences between "greater Buffalo" and the rest of Dallas Co., Missouri. Benton Township, which included Buffalo, was on average wealthier than the other five townships in the county ($2,076 in real and personal estate per household as compared to $1,582/household). Benton had the three richest households in the county and eight of the top 20. The ten wealthiest households in Benton were 10% richer than the ten wealthiest in the rest of the county. Over 18% of Benton households listed occupations other than farming, as opposed to fewer than 4% for the rest of the county. In Dallas Co., as in the state at large, about 70% of the electorate in the 1860 presidential election voted for either Douglas or Bell, the compromise candidates, though in Missouri as a whole Douglas barely edged Bell by a few hundred votes, while in Dallas Douglas received 31% and Bell 41% of the vote. In the county, Breckinridge, the Southern candidate, received somewhat more support than in the whole state (24% to 19%) and Lincoln significantly less (less than 3% to over 10%). The Southern tilt of Buffalo can be seen in the 1860 governor's race. Sample Orr, Constitutional Union Party, got 42% of the vote in Missouri, 55% in Dallas Co., and only 12% in Buffalo. Claiborne F. Jackson, a Democrat with what were thought to be moderate Southern sympathies, won in Missouri with 47%, received 43% in Dallas, and 70% in Buffalo. Hancock Lee Jackson, the Breckinridge Southern Democrat, got 7% in Missouri, 6% in Dallas, and 18% in Buffalo. Parrish, *History of Missouri*, 2; "Missouri Returns," *[St. Louis] Missouri Daily Republican* (Nov. 14, 1860): 2; "Election Results, 1860," Western Historical Manuscripts Collection–Columbia, University of Missouri, Columbia, Missouri Digital Heritage, www.sos.mo.gov/mdh/ (hereafter cited as MDH). On the state's smaller slaveholders see esp. Burke, *Missouri's Small Slaveholding Households, 1815–1865*; for the culture of poorer Whites in the region see also T. J. Stiles, *Jesse James: Last Rebel of the Civil War* (New York: A. A. Knopf, 2002), and Jeremy Neely, *The Border Between Them: Violence and Reconciliation on the Kansas-Missouri Line* (Columbia: University of Missouri Press, 2007). On the Ozark region generally in this period, see Brooks Blevins, *A History of the Ozarks, Volume 2: The Conflicted Ozarks* (Urbana: University of Illinois Press, 2019).

10. D mss 2: 183–84.
11. A similar rally was held in Newtonia, Newton Co., Mo., on April 24, 1861: "Peter S. Wilkes of Springfield Mo. made an Eloquent and stirring speech on behalf of Southern Rights." Judge M. H. Ritchey also spoke. Then a committee passed resolutions in support of Governor Jackson and the Southern cause. "Resolutions of a Public Meeting Pledging the Participants Support on the South and Gov. Jackson," April 24, 1861, Missouri Provost Marshall Papers, Reel F 1611, Frame 0481, File 9049, www.sos.mo.gov/archives/provost. Peter S. Wilkes (b. 1826 in TN) was an attorney, but one source also describes him as a minister. He served in the Missouri legislature and was one of the leaders of the pro-Southern party in Springfield, Mo., in 1861. He would be a member of Capt. Dick Campbell's

Company of the Missouri State Guard, organized near Springfield in May, 1861. He would serve in the Confederate Congress in the last year of the war. George S. Escott, *History and Directory of Springfield and North Springfield* (Springfield, Mo.: Patriot-Advertiser, 1878), 101; Holcombe, *History of Greene County*, 404; Obituary, *San Francisco Call* 87 (Jan. 1900): 3.

12. D mss 2: 189–91. John Newton McConnell (1837–1905) had come to Missouri from Tennessee after 1856. In 1860 he was a merchant living with his wife, Sarah, and his father-in-law in Benton Township, Dallas Co., Mo. (1860 U.S. Census, Benton Township, Dallas County, Missouri, family no. 230).

13. D mss 2: 189, 192. Rev. 1:20: seven stars, golden candlesticks, angels, and churches; Gen. 41:29: seven years of plenty.

14. D mss 2: 192.

15. D mss 3: 193–94. William B. Edwards (b. 1810 in Tenn.) was a prosperous farmer in Dallas Co. (1860 U.S. Census, Benton Township, Dallas County, family no. 154). Kelso thought Edwards had been wounded in the War of 1812, but Edwards' pension record, filed by his widow Sarah in 1890, lists his previous military experience as "Indian War" (*U.S. Civil War Pension Index: General Index to Pension Files, 1861–1934*, Washington, D.C., National Archives and Records Administration, T288, ancestry.com [hereafter, *Civil War Pension Index*]). Edwards, though a slaveholder, was a strong Unionist: in 1860, he owned 8 slaves, ages 2 to 55 (*1860 U.S. Federal Census—Slave Schedules*, ancestry.com).

16. D mss 3: 194–95.

17. Christopher Phillips, *Damned Yankee: The Life of General Nathaniel Lyon* (Columbia: University of Missouri Press, 1990), 185–99; Gerteis, *Civil War St. Louis*, 100–15.

18. On Hickory County: F. Marion Wilson, *Wilson's History of Hickory County* (Hermitage, Mo., 1909), 65–66, 78–79. On Newton County: "Resolutions of a Public Meeting Pledging the Participants Support on the South and Gov. Jackson," April 24, 1861, Missouri Provost Marshall Papers, Reel F 1611, Frame 0481, File 9049, www.sos.mo.gov/archives/provost. On Matthews in Springfield: Robert Pinckney Matthews, *Souvenir of the Holland Company Home Guards and "Phelps" Regiment, Missouri Volunteer Infantry*, ca. 1890, State Historical Society of Missouri, Columbia, C 1160, typescript, 7.

19. "Fight near Fairfax Court House," *Daily Missouri Republican* (June 3, 1861): 2; "Latest from Fortress Monroe: The Repulse at Great Bethel—The Killed and Wounded," *Daily Missouri Republican* (June 15, 1861): 2; Phillips, *Damned Yankee*, 211–22 (quotation on 214); Gerteis, *Civil War in Missouri*, 32–40. Lyon's remark, however, comes only from Thomas Snead, who attended the meeting as a member of Jackson's party and who was writing a quarter century later in *The Fight for Missouri: From the Election of Lincoln to the Death of Lyon* (New York, 1886), 200. On the skirmish at Boonville on June 17 see also Paul Rorvig, "The Significant Skirmish: The Battle of Boonville, June 17, 1861," *MHR* 86 (Jan. 1992): 127–48.

20. D mss 3: 196. Milton Burch was a 39-year-old Buffalo merchant with a wife (Mary) and two small children (U.S. Census); the family had moved to Missouri from Illinois in the mid-1850s. Burch's pension record, which he filed as an "invalid" in 1886, twelve years before his death, listed him as a captain in Co. H, 1st Illinois Volunteers (Mexican War) (*Civil War Pension Index*); he is listed as a private in that company in Isaac H. Elliott, *Record of the Services of Illinois Soldiers in the Black Hawk War, 1831–32, and in the Mexican War, 1846–8* (Springfield, Ill.: H. W. Rokker, 1882), 204. Many Unionist citizen militia units that had already been organized (in Springfield, for example) were officially recognized as Home Guards. The U.S. government quickly sent 10,000 stands of arms. Home Guard units existed for one to six months. The Dallas Co. companies were mustered in on June 24 and were intended to serve until Sept. 24, 1861, but were disbanded Aug. 10–11. See Holcombe, *History of Greene County*, 280–90; Britton, *Civil War on the Border*, 1: 1–31; U.S. Pension and Record Office (War Department), *Organization and Status of Missouri Troops (Union and Confederate) in Service during the Civil War* (Washington, D.C.: Government Printing Office, 1902), 146–64; Phillips, *Damned Yankee*, 129–217; Phillips, *Missouri's Confederate*, 233–61; Gerteis, *Civil War St. Louis*, 78–131; Gerteis, *Civil War in Missouri*, 8–40. The roster for the Dallas County Home Guards lists Col. William B. Edwards, Lt. Col. Eleazer Hovey, Maj. John R. Kelso, and Milton Burch as first lieutenant (before he was promoted to captain). See "Soldiers' Records: War of 1812–World War I," Missouri Digital Heritage, www.sos.mo.gov/archives/soldiers (hereafter, "Soldiers' Records," MDH); see also Gary Swift, Dallas County Home Guards, Reconstructed Roster, http://mogenweb.org/dallas/home_guard_roster.html.

21. F. Marion Wilson, *Wilson's History of Hickory County* (Hermitage, Mo.: Wilson Bros., 1909), 65–66, 78–79; Capt. John Mabary, Mabary's Missouri Company, C.S.A. ("Soldiers' Records," MDH). On Benton County see Britton, *Civil War on the Border*, chap. 5, "Action at Cole Camp, Missouri," 1: 40–50; James Henry Lay, *A Sketch of the History of Benton Country, Missouri* (Hannibal, Mo.: Winchell and Ebert, 1876), 71–72.

22. "Important from Missouri: Battle near Cole, Missouri," *New York Herald* (June 22, 1861): 1; Lay, *Sketch of the History of Benton County*, 71–72; Britton, *Civil War on the Border*, chap. 5, "Action at Cole Camp, Missouri," 1: 40–50; Gerteis, *Civil War in Missouri*, 40–41. Brig. Gen. Nathaniel Lyon described it as a "massacre" (Lyon to Col. Chester Harding Jr., June 21, 1861), *OR*, Ser. 1, Vol. 3, 385.

23. D mss 3: 197–98. I have changed Kelso's spelling of "Mabry" to "Mabary," the form used in other sources.

24. Ibid., 198–99.

25. Ibid., 200. Black Oak (Point) became Preston. See Arthur Paul Moser, "A Directory of Towns, Villages, and Hamlets Past and Present of Hickory County, Missouri," https://thelibrary.org/lochist/moser/hickorypl.html.

26. Ibid., 203–204.

27. Ibid., 204–205.

28. Ibid., 205.

29. Ibid., 207.

30. Ibid., 208.

31. *OR*, Ser. 1, Vol. 3, 9–52; Phillips, *Damned Yankee*, 215–47; William Garrett Piston, "'Springfield is a Vast Hospital': The Dead and Wounded at the Battle of Wilson's Creek," *MHR* 93 (July 1999): 345–66; Piston and Hatcher, *Wilson's Creek*, 45–145; Gerteis, *Civil War in Missouri*, 32–65.

32. D mss 3: 210–11; Phillips, *Damned Yankee*, 251 (Lyon quotation), and 245. See also Piston and Hatcher, *Wilson's Creek*, 132, 145.

33. D mss 3: 212; Letter from N[athaniel] Lyon, Springfield, Mo., to Col. William B. Edwards, Dallas Co. Home Guards, Aug. 9, 1861, Missouri History Museum, Civil War Collection, http://collections.mohistory.org/archive/ARC:A0286_6908.

34. *OR*, Ser. 1, Vol. 3, 53–130. For the fullest account of the battle, see Piston and Hatcher, *Wilson's Creek*; on Mrs. Phelps and Lyon's body, see Phillips, *Damned Yankee*, 258–61.

35. D mss 3: 215.

36. Ibid., 200–201.

37. Ibid., 209.

38. D mss 4: 379, 376.

39. D mss 2: 183; 2: 122; 4: 298; 4: 296; 3: 215, 4: 297–98.

CHAPTER 6

1. D mss 4: 317–18.

2. D mss 3: 264, 266; 4: 309.

3. D mss 3: 216; Brig. Gen. Ulysses S. Grant to Capt. Speed Butler, Jefferson City, Mo. August 22, 1861, *The Papers of Ulysses S. Grant, Vol. 2: April–September 1861* (Carbondale: Southern Illinois University Press, 1969), 128. On Jefferson City, Mo., see Gary R. Kremer, "'We Are Living in Very Stirring Times': The Civil War in Jefferson City, Missouri," *MHR* 106 (Jan. 2012): 61–74; see also Eldon Hattervig, "Jefferson Landing: A Commercial Center of the Steamboat Era," *MHR* 74 (April 1980): 277–99.

4. D mss 3: 217; Fred Albert Shannon, *The Organization and Administration of the Union Army, 1861–1865* (Cleveland, Ohio: Arthur H. Clark Co., 1928), 22–47; 261–62; *Organization and Status of Missouri Troops, Union and Confederate, In Service during the Civil War* (Washington, D.C.: Government Printing Office, 1902), 7–21; Gerteis, *Civil War in Missouri*, 79: Col. James A. Mulligan commanded the 23rd Illinois, then at Jefferson City, "a regiment raised in Chicago and locally known as the Irish Brigade."

5. Maj. John K. Hall, Osage County Regt., Missouri Home Guard ("Soldiers' Records," MDH). Kelso also wrote that "Soon after I left Jefferson City, Major Hall, who had put me out of the Fair Grounds, was tried for some grave offense, and was degraded by having his straps taken off in the presence of the men. These facts I learned from what I regarded as a good authority. Thus my revenge came, but not, as I had intended that it should, by my own hand" (D mss 3: 220–21).

6. D mss 3: 221–22.

7. D mss 3: 220; Gerteis, *Civil War in Missouri*, 102–9. Kelso enlisted on Aug. 18, 1861, in Dallas Co., Mo. and was mustered with the official organization of the regiment (also called the "Lyon Legion") on Oct. 14, 1861, at Benton Barracks, St. Louis, Mo. ("Soldiers Records," MDH).

8. D mss 3: 225; Frederich F. Kiner, *One Year's Soldiering* (Lancaster, [Pa.]: E. H. Thomas, 1863), 11–12; [Jacob Gilbert Foman], *The Western Sanitary Commission: A Sketch of Its Origin, History, and Labors for the Sick and Wounded of the Western Armies* (St. Louis, Mo.: R. P. Studely & Co., 1864), 13–14. Kiner's regiment shared in the suffering: "Some time in December the measles broke out among the troops, and its ravages were very fatal among us" (Kiner, 13).

9. D mss 3: 226. Col. Sempronius H. "Pony" Boyd (1828–1894), 24th Reg. Infantry Volunteers ("Soldiers' Records," MDH). Boyd resigned his command April 18, 1863, to serve in the 38th Congress (March 4, 1863–March 3, 1865). Kelso would challenge and defeat him for the seat in the next cycle. Boyd would serve another term in Congress (1869–71) and finish his political career as President Benjamin Harrison's Minister Resident and Consul General to Siam. See *Biographical Directory of the United States Congress*, http://bioguide.congress.gov; Holcombe, *History of Greene County*, 743; *Pictorial and Genealogical Record of Greene County, Missouri* (Chicago: Goodspeed Publishing Co., 1893), 215–19. Maj. Gen. Samuel R. Curtis (1805–1866) graduated from West Point in 1831 and served as adjutant general of Ohio and colonel of the 3rd Regiment, Ohio Infantry during the War with Mexico. He practiced law and served in Congress (1857–1861). He began the war as colonel of the 2nd Regiment, Iowa Volunteer Infantry, and brigadier general of Volunteers in the spring of 1861. In Dec. 1861 he was put in command of the District of Southwest Missouri. After the March 1862 victory at Pea Ridge he was promoted to major general. In Sept. 1862 he became commander of the Department of Missouri. He was unable to work well with the conservative governor H. R. Gamble, and President Abraham Lincoln, who could not remove Gamble, instead removed Curtis in May 1863. Reassigned to the Department of Kansas in early 1864, he again defeated the Confederate army of Sterling Price in October. See *Biographical Directory of the United States Congress*, http://bioguide.congress.gov; William L. Shea, "Curtis, Samuel Ryan," *American National Biography* (www.anb.org) [hereafter, *ANB*]; and esp. Terry Lee Beckenbaugh, "The War of Politics: Samuel Ryan Curtis, Race, and the Political/ Military Establishment" (PhD diss., University of Arkansas, 2001).

10. M. Jeff. Thompson, Report, Oct. 15, 1861, *OR*, Ser. 1, Vol. 3, 225, and see 201–36). See also Gerteis, *Civil War in Missouri*, 27 (on Thompson), 112–16 (the expedition and battles). D mss 3: 243–44.

11. D mss 3: 245.

12. Ibid., 247.

13. *OR*, Ser. 1, Vol. 3, 225–30; Gerteis, *Civil War in Missouri*, 113–16.

14. D mss 3: 229–30.

15. Ibid., 230; Wood, *Civil War Springfield*, 52, 57–58.

16. D mss 3: 232–33.

17. Ibid., 236.

18. D mss 3: 241. Joseph W. McClurg (1818–1900) was a merchant in Lynn Creek, Camden Co., Mo. His business with his father-in-law and brother-in-law— McClurg, Murphy, Jones and Company—"became a major merchant-distributor of all kinds of trading goods throughout the upper Ozarks region." The census taker in 1860 estimated his personal property at $95,000, and recorded him as the owner of 6 slaves and the co-owner of 2 others. In 1861 he organized 17 companies as the Osage Regiment of Missouri Volunteers, in which he served as a colonel, and spent $8,000 to supply the regiment. Supporting emancipation, he freed his slaves in the fall of 1863. "[T]wice during the war, his business fell victim to raids from pro-Southern guerrillas, who attacked and burned his storehouses at Linn Creek." McClurg served three terms in Congress 1863–8 as a Radical Republican and was governor of Missouri, 1869–1871. See William E. Parrish, "McClurg, Joseph Washington," *ANB* (quotations); Floyd C. Shoemaker, ed., *Missouri, Day by Bay* (Columbia, Mo.: State Historical Society of Missouri, 1942–3), 1: 142–3; U.S. Federal Census; 1860 U.S. Federal Census Slave Schedules; "Soldiers' Records," MDH; Lynn Morrow, "Joseph Washington McClurg: Entrepreneur, Politician, Citizen," *MHR* 78 (Jan. 1984): 168–201.

19. D mss 3: 251.

20. On Kelso's complaint about his pay, see D mss 3: 241–42. Gen. Curtis died on Dec. 25, 1866. Kelso's service record for the 24th Reg. Infantry Volunteers notes that his "Date of discharge not available," although he mustered into the 14th Cavalry, Missouri State Militia on March 24, 1862. As an amendment to an appropriations bill, Congress approved "Arrears of pay and bounty" for Kelso on Mar. 2, 1889 (*List of Private Claims Brought before the Senate of the United States from the Commencement of the Forty-Seventh Congress to the Close of the Fifty-First Congress* [Washington, D.C.: Government Printing Office, 1895], Vol. 2, 354.) On Civil War espionage generally and McClellan, Burnside, and Hooker particularly, see Edwin C. Fishel, *The Secret War for the Union: The Untold Story of Military Intelligence in the Civil War* (Boston and New York, 1996); see also Edwin C. Fishel, "The Mythology of Civil War Intelligence," *Civil War History* 10, no. 4 (Dec. 1964): 344–67, and William B. Feis, "Neutralizing the Valley: The Role of

Military Intelligence in the Defeat of Jubal Early's Army of the Valley, 1864–1865," *Civil War History* 39, 3 (1993): 199–215.

21. On Frémont's Jessie Scouts, see Fishel, *Secret War for the Union*, 178, and William B. Feis, *Grant's Secret Service: The Intelligence War from Belmont to Appomattox* (Lincoln: University of Nebraska Press, 2002), 57. On Grant and espionage see Feis. On Halleck in Missouri see John F. Marszalek, *Commander of All Lincoln's Armies: A Life of General Henry A. Halleck* (Cambridge, Mass.: Belknap Press of Harvard University Press, 2004), 105–28; on Halleck and espionage, see Fishel, *Secret War for the Union*, 184–86, 215, 245; and see Henry W. Halleck, *International Law; or, Rules Regulating the Intercourse of States in Peace and War* (New York: D. Van Nostand, 1861), esp. 406, and Halleck, "Military Espionage," [probably written 1864], *American Journal of International Law* 5, no. 3 (July 1911): 590–603.

22. On three or four spies captured and a dozen or more turned back for every successful one, see Fishel, "Mythology," 363; on ten of thirty or so in the Shenandoah Valley: William Gilmore Beymer, *On Hazardous Service: Scouts and Spies of the North and South* (New York: Harper & Bros., 1912), 1; for Lorain Ruggles, see E. C. Downs, *Four Years a Scout and Spy: "General Bunker," one of Lieut. General Grant's Most Daring and Successful Scouts* (Zanesville, Ohio: Hugh Dunne, 1866), 399, a memoir by Lorain Ruggles, a corporal in the 20th Ohio Vol. Infantry, as told to Downs, his former company commander.

23. James Pike, *The Scout and Ranger: Being the Personal Adventures of Corporal Pike, of the Fourth Ohio Cavalry* (Cincinnati, Ohio: J. R. Hawley & Co., 1865), 391; Halleck, "Military Espionage"; H. B. Smith, *Between the Lines: Secret Service Stories Told Fifty Years After* (New York: Booz Brothers, 1911), 53; Feis, *Grant's Secret Service*, 16; Downs [Ruggles], *Four Years a Scout and Spy*, 135.

24. John Truesdale, *The Blue Coats, and How They Lived, Fought and Died for the Union* (Philadelphia: Jones Bros. & Co., 1867), 17 (quotation), 334 (John Morford); Pike, *Scout and Ranger*; Smith, *Between the Lines*. See also Solomon Woolworth, *The Mississippi Scout; or, A Detail of What the Writer Saw in a Scout Inside the Rebel Lines around Vicksburg in 1863* (Chicago, 1867), and George S. Jones, *Philip Henson, The Southern Union Spy* (St. Louis, Mo.: Nixon-Jones Printing Co., 1887), about a double agent who did not use a disguise. On spy narratives see Curtis Carroll Davis, "Companions of Crisis: The Spy Memoir as a Social Document," *Civil War History* 10, no. 4 (Dec. 1994): 385–400.

25. Downs [Ruggles], *Four Years A Scout and Spy*, 400, 12. On the confidence man see Johannes Dietrich Bergmann, "The Original Confidence Man," *American Quarterly* 21, no. 3 (Autumn 1969): 560–77; Karen Halttunen, *Confidence Men and Painted Women: A Study of Middle-Class Culture in America, 1830–1870* (New Haven, Conn.: Yale University Press, 1982); William E. Lenz, *Fast Talk and Flush Times: The Confidence Man as a Literary Convention* (Columbia: University of Missouri Press, 1985); Kenneth D. Pimple, "Melville's 'The Confidence-Man' and the Problem of Deception," *Western Folklore* 51, 1 (Jan. 1992): 33–50.

26. D mss 3: 241.

27. Ibid., 252. On hardtack see Scott Nelson and Carol Sheriff, *A People at War: Civilians and Soldiers in America's Civil War* (New York: Oxford University Press, 2007), 215.

28. D mss 3: 253-4.

29. Ibid., 254.

30. Ibid., 257–58.

31. Ibid., 258–59.

32. Ibid., 259–61. Proslavery Christians frequently referred to the following scriptural passages: Genesis 9:25–27; Genesis 17:12; Deuteronomy 20:10–11; 1 Corinthians 7:21; Romans 13: 1, 7; Colossians 3:22, 4:1; 1 Timothy 6: 1–2. See Mark A. Noll, *The Civil War as a Theological Crisis* (Chapel Hill: University of North Carolina Press, 2006), 34–35. See also John Patrick Daly, *When Slavery Was Called Freedom: Evangelicalism, Proslavery, and the Causes of the Civil War* (Lexington: University Press of Kentucky, 2002). On slavery and the U.S. Constitution, see: Art. I, Sec. 2, Para. 3; Art. I, Sec. 9, Para. 1; Art. I, Sec. 8, Para. 15; Art. IV, Sec. 2, Para. 3; Art. IV, Sec. 4; Art. V. See also Paul Finkelman "Garrison's Constitution: The Covenant with Death and How It was Made," *Prologue Magazine* 32 (Winter 2000), www.archives.gov, and James Oakes, *Freedom National: The Destruction of Slavery in the United States, 1861–1865* (New York: W. W. Norton & Co., 2013).

33. D mss 3: 261–62.

34. Ibid., 262–63.

35. Ibid., 258, 263–64.

36. Ibid., 264–66.

37. Ibid., 266.

38. Ibid., 268.

39. Ibid., 266–67; Holcombe, *History of Greene County*, 369–72; Gerteis, *Civil War in Missouri*, 109–23; Wood, *Civil War Springfield*, 77–78.

40. D mss 3: 270–71.

41. *OR*, Ser. I, Vol. 3, 569. See Nevins, *Frémont*, 523–25, 531–33; see also Parrish, *Turbulent Partnership*, 68. On Frémont's hundred days in Missouri see Nevins, *Frémont*, 473–549. See also Parrish, *Turbulent Partnership*, 48–76; Rolle, *John Charles Frémont*, 190–213; Connelly, *Schofield and the Politics of Generalship*, 23–40; and Boman, *Lincoln and Citizen's Rights*, 36–62. On Frémont's Body Guard see Gerteis, *Civil War in Missouri*, 118.

42. D mss 3: 272. Col. Thomas Roe Freeman's regiment of 700 men was camping about 30 miles south of Rolla on Oct. 30, 1861 (*OR*, Ser. 1, Vol. 3, 537, 557). The "notorious" Freeman (1829–1893) served as lieutenant, captain, and then colonel of the 1st Reg. Cavalry, McBride's Division; he was captured by Federal troops in Feb. 1862 (*OR*, Ser. 1, Vol. 8, 269), imprisoned for 8 months, and then exchanged in the fall of that year. He was then commissioned by the C.S.A. to organize a brigade (Freeman's

Brigade), which operated on the Arkansas-Missouri border by mid-1863. He sent out small squads of bushwhackers to rob stagecoaches and conducted raids with larger forces. Union army reports connect his brigade to "guerrillas and horse thieves" (*OR*, Ser. 1, Vol. 22, 548; see also 746). "Soldiers' Records," MDH; Nichols, *Guerrilla Warfare in Civil War Missouri*, Vol. 2, esp. 146–49, 242–45; James E. McGhee, *Guide to Missouri Confederate Units, 1861–1865* (Fayetteville: University of Arkansas Press, 2008), 111.

43. D mss 3: 274.
44. Ibid., 273.
45. Ibid., 274–75; William Dorsheimer, "Fremont's Hundred Days in Missouri," Part II, *Atlantic Monthly* 9 (Feb. 1862): 247–59, esp. 248.
46. Holcombe, *History of Greene County*, 372–83; Gerteis, *Civil War in Missouri*, 117–19; Wood, *Civil War Springfield*, 55–68.
47. William Dorsheimer, "Frémont's Hundred Days in Missouri, Part III," *Atlantic Monthly* 9 (March 1862): 372–85, esp. 375.
48. D mss 3: 266–67; "Our Southeast Missouri Correspondent," *New York Herald* (Nov. 7, 1861), 1. See also Chaffin, *Pathfinder*, 463–72. On Frémont's hundred days in Missouri see Nevins, *Frémont*, 473–549. See also Parrish, *Turbulent Partnership*, 48–76; Rolle, *John Charles Frémont*, 190–213; Connelly, *Schofield and the Politics of Generalship*, 23–40; and Boman, *Lincoln and Citizen's Rights*, 36–62.
49. D mss 3: 277; Gerteis, *Civil War in Missouri*, 119–25.
50. D mss 3: 278. Kelso does not name the neighbor, but circumstantial evidence indicates that it was White. In 1861, White, 50 years old and born in Virginia, lived with his wife and three sons, ages 20, 18, and 6 (1860 U.S. Census, Benton Township, Dallas County, Missouri, family no. 110). White is not, however, on the Sept. 1862 list of Dallas County rebels or rebel sympathizers (Missouri Provost Marshall Papers, Reel F1588, file 2133, MDH).
51. D mss 3: 283–84. Lebanon, Laclede County, was on the main wagon road to Springfield. See *History of Laclede, Camden, Dallas, Webster, Wright, Pulaski, Phelps and Dent Counties, Missouri* (Chicago: Goodspeed Publishing Co., 1889), 63–72. Lebanon was "a town so alternately plundered by both sides as early as the beginning of 1862 that it was entirely destitute of even the most common domestic goods"; see Bradbury, "Good Water & Wood," *MHR* 90 (Jan. 1996), 171. Confederate correspondence of Nov. 5, 1861, reported: "Three detachments of the Texas regiments had been near Springfield" (*OR*, Ser. 1, Vol. 3, 739).
52. D mss 3: 284–85.
53. Ibid., 286–87.
54. Ibid., 288.
55. Ibid., 288–290.
56. D mss 4: 290-1.
57. Ibid., 291-2.
58. Ibid., 294–96.

59. Ibid., 299-300; Curtis to Capt. J. C. Kelton, Rolla, Dec. 19, 1861, *OR*, Ser. 1, Vol. 8, 472. Smallpox was reported in some of the camps, including Kelso's, in mid-January ("From Rolla," *Daily Missouri Republican* [Jan. 17, 1862], 2). On Kelso and books, see Holcombe, *History of Greene County*, 477, and Britton, *Civil War on the Border*, 2: 205–206. On prisoner exchanges, see James M. McPherson, *Battle Cry of Freedom: The Civil War Era* (New York: Oxford University Press, 1988), 791.

60. D mss 4: 301-2.

61. Ibid., 303–4.

62. Ibid., 304-5.

63. Ibid., 304.

64. *OR*, Ser. 1, Vol. 8, 370–71, 515; Gerteis, *Civil War in Missouri*, 123–28. On rebel troops in mid-January 1862: "From Rolla," *Daily Missouri Republican*, Jan. 22, 1862, 2; see also Wood, *Civil War Springfield*, 79–81.

65. D mss 4: 308.

66. Ibid., 309–10. On Union spies being instructed to tell the truth if captured, see Fishel, *Secret War for the Union*, 286, 570.

67. D mss 4: 311.

68. Ibid., 311-12.

69. Ibid., 312–13.

70. Ibid., 313.

71. Ibid., 314–15.

72. Ibid., 316.

73. Ibid., 317.

74. On Union spies giving their information only to their commanding officers, see Fishel, *Secret War for the Union*, 290; Downs [Ruggles], *Four Years a Scout and Spy*, 48.

75. D mss 4: 319.

76. Ibid., 320–21; Curtis report, Camp at Copley, 18 miles in advance of Lebanon, February 10, 1862—5:00 p.m., *OR*, Ser. 1, Vol. 8, 59; Curtis to Capt. J. C. Kelton, Feb. 10, 1862, *OR*, Ser. 1, Vol. 8, 551; Curtis to Sigel, Rolla, Jan. 25, 1862, and Curtis to Kelton, Lebanon, Feb. 2, 1862, *OR*, Ser. 1, Vol. 8, 526, 541; Samuel Prentis Curtis, "The Army of the South-West, and the First Campaign in Arkansas," Chapter Second, *Annals of Iowa*, 4 [July 1866]: 673–88, esp. 678. See also William J. Shea and Earl J. Hess, *Pea Ridge, Civil War Campaign in the West* (Chapel Hill: University of North Carolina Press, 1992), 27.

77. D mss 4: 321-2.

78. Ibid., 321.

CHAPTER 7

1. D mss 4: 336–37.

2. See "Latest from Springfield," *Daily Missouri Republican* (Jan. 6, 1862): 2, and ibid.: "From Rolla" (Jan. 8): 2; "Affairs in the Southwest" and "From Rolla" (Jan.

10): 2; "From Rolla" (Jan. 11) 2; "From Rolla" (Jan. 13): 2, 3; "From Rolla" (Jan. 15): 2; "Help for Gen. Price" (Jan. 15): 3; "Blows to Fall" (Jan. 17): 2; "From Rolla" (Jan. 17): 2; "From Rolla" (Jan. 18): 1, 2; "From Rolla" (Jan. 19): 3; "Where's Price?" (Jan. 21): 2; "From Rolla" (Jan. 22): 2; "From Rolla" (Jan. 23): 2; "Important Correspondence. Letters between Gen. Halleck and Gen. Price" (Jan. 25): 1; "Southwest Missouri" (Jan. 26): 2; "From Rolla" (Jan. 29): 2; "From Rolla" (Jan. 30): 2; "From Rolla" (Feb. 1): 2; "From Rolla" (Feb. 4): 2; "From Rolla" (Feb. 6): 2; "Rolla, Feb. 5" (Feb. 6): 2 (Curtis arrives in Lebanon); "The News from the West" (Feb. 9): 2; "From Gen. Curtis' Command" (Feb. 10): 2; "From Rolla" (Feb. 12): 2; "News from the West" (Feb. 14): 2; "Special Dispatch . . . Rolla" (Feb. 14): 2; In the *[St. Louis] Missouri Democrat*, see "From Rolla" (Jan. 1, 1862): 2 , and "Latest News . . . From the West," 3; "Late from Price's Army" (Jan. 4): 2; "From the Southwest" (Jan. 9): 2; "From Rolla" (Jan. 10): 2; "One Day Later (from Lebanon)" (Jan. 7): 1; "From Rolla: Gen. Price Still at Springfield" (Jan. 12): 2; "From Rolla" (Jan. 14): 2; "From Rolla" (Jan. 15): 2; "News items—Camp Life" (Jan. 17): 2; "From Rolla: A Forward Movement" (Jan. 24): 2; "From Rolla" (Jan. 29): 2; "From Rolla" (Jan. 30): 3; "From Rolla" (Feb. 3): 2; "From Rolla" (Feb. 10): 2. See also Curtis correspondence and reports, and orders issued by Acting Assistant Adjutant General T. I. McKenny, *OR*, Ser. 1, Vol. 8, 58–59, 550–54. For a detailed narrative of the movements of both armies before the Battle of Pea Ridge (March 6–8, 1862), see also Shea and Hess, *Pea Ridge*, 27–61.

3. "Military Post in Southwest Missouri," *Daily Missouri Republican* (Jan. 1, 1862): 2; "The War," ibid. (Feb. 9, 1862): 2 (quotation); "The Rebellion Cut in Two," ibid. (Feb. 26, 1862): 2.

4. "From Rolla," *Daily Missouri Republican* (Jan. 24, 1862): 2, and see "From Rolla," ibid. (Jan. 18, 1862): 2; Matthews, *Souvenir of the Holland Company Home Guards*, 36.

5. "From Rolla," *Daily Missouri Republican* (Feb. 11, 1862): 2; Special Orders No. 75, issued for Gen. Curtis on Feb. 7 while the troops camped at Lebanon, *OR*, Ser. 1, Vol. 8, 548–49. On fresh beef and pork "abundant in the country," *OR*, Ser. 1, Vol. 8, 548, and see 549. For the soldier worried about starvation see Shea and Hess, *Pea Ridge*, 51 (quotation). D mss 4: 324–28, esp. 324.

6. "The News from the West," *Daily Missouri Republican* (Feb. 8, 1862): 2; "From Rolla," *Missouri Democrat* (Feb. 10, 1862): 2; *OR*, Ser. 1, Vol. 8, 58–59, 550–54; see also Lyman G. Bennett, "Route of the Army of the Southwest. Commanded by Major General Samuel R. Curtis . . . 1862," a volume of maps and cartographic sketches of Curtis's pursuit of Price, in Samuel R. Curtis Campaign Books, [not before 1862]—1865, Military History Collection, Kansas State Historical Society, Topeka Kan. The first map is a sketch of the skirmish at Pearson's Creek, upon which Bennett (?) gives the higher estimate of enemy casualties. Bennett was a corporal in the 36th Reg. Ill. Infantry who was following a few weeks behind Curtis's army, catching up right before the Battle of Pea Ridge. See also Bennett, Civil War Diary, Dec. 1861–April, 1862, R274, Western Historical Collection, State Historical Society of Missouri Research Center, Rolla, Mo. (MDH). The skirmish had taken

place right next to E. R. Danforth's farm. Danforth was wealthy and owned fifteen slaves, but it is not clear if he supported the Confederacy. See Holcombe, *History of Green County*, 207, 247, 265, 406, 602, 706, 903; Bennett, sketch of the skirmish at Pearson's Creek, "Route of the Army"; U.S. Federal Census; 1860 U.S. Federal Census—Slave Schedules. D mss. 4: 328–29.

7. "Springfield Retaken," *Daily Missouri Republican* (Feb. 15, 1862): 2; "Price's Army Routed," *Missouri Democrat* (Feb. 15, 1862): 2; *OR*, Ser. 1, Vol. 8, 59; Robert P. Matthews, of Phelps' regiment, 24th Mo. Infantry, quoted in Wood, *Civil War Springfield*, 82; D mss 3: 256, 4: 329.

8. *OR*, Ser. 1, Vol. 8, 59–61. See also "From Springfield," "The Pursuit of Price," "Springfield, Missouri," "Springfield, Missouri . . . 5:00 p.m.," "From Arkansas," *Daily Missouri Republican* (Feb. 23, 1862): 3, and ibid.: "From Springfield" (Feb. 24): 1; "The Pursuit of Price" (Feb. 27): 2; "Rebel Reports of the Battle of Sugar Creek, Arkansas," "From Gen. Curtis' Command," and "From Springfield" (Feb. 28): 1; "Late Southern News. Burning of Fayetteville, Arkansas" (March 1): 1; "The Army of the Southwest. Its Victorious March" and "Letter from Cross Hollows, Benton Co., Arkansas" (March 5): 2. In the *Missouri Democrat*: "Glorious News from the Southwest" (Feb. 17): 2; "Latest from Springfield" (Feb. 18): 2; "After Price," "Further Particularities," and "Second Dispatch" (Feb. 19): 2; "From Springfield, Mo." (Feb. 21): 1 and 2; "Good News from Curtis's Column" (Feb. 22): 2; "From Springfield, Mo." (Feb. 24): 1, and "Another Letter from Springfield," 3.

9. D mss 4: 330; *OR*, Ser. 1, Vol. 8, 562, 568, 570; "From Arkansas," *Daily Missouri Republican* (Feb., 23, 1862): 3; Henry Perrin Mann, Civil War diaries, 1862–1865, State Historical Society of Missouri, Rolla, R 455, entry for Fri. Feb. 21, typescript, 6. See also "From Curtis' Command," *Daily Missouri Republican* (Feb. 28, 1862): 2; "General Order No. 49," ibid. (March 1, 1862): 2 . In the *Missouri Democrat*: "Latest from Curtis's Columns" (Feb. 28): 2: Col. Boyd in Lebanon thinks the men were poisoned from drinking tainted stomach bitters left in a drug store.

10. "Letter from Cross Hollows, Benton Co., Arkansas," *Daily Missouri Republican* (March 5, 1862): 2; D mss 4: 331–32, 334; Gen. Curtis, in camp near Fayetteville, Ark. on March 1, 1862 (citizens' letter and his response), *OR*, Ser. 1, Vol. 8, 577–78. See also Mann, Civil War diaries, entry for Wed., Feb. 26, typescript, 7; *Missouri Democrat*, "From Arkansas" (March 5, 1862): 2 .

11. "From Rolla," *Daily Missouri Republican* (Feb. 12, 1862): 2, and see "From Rolla," ibid. (Feb. 4, p. 2 and Feb. 6, p. 2); T. I. McKenny, Special Orders No. 90, Sugar Creek, Ark., Feb. 18, 1862, *OR*, Ser. 1, Vol. 8, 560; D mss 4: 341.

12. Franc B. Wilkie, *The Iowa First: Letters from the War* (Dubuque, Iowa: Herald Book and Job Establishment, 1861), 78; Matthews, *Souvenir of the Holland Company Home Guards*, 45. On Federal soldiers dressing up in women's clothing to humiliate rebel women, see Lisa Tendrich Frank, "The Union War on Women," in Brian D. McKnight and Barton A. Meyers, eds., *The Guerrilla Hunters: Irregular Conflicts during the Civil War* (Baton Rouge: Louisiana State University Press,

2017), 171–91, esp. 179. Blevins, *History of the Ozarks*, Vol. 2: 122, notes that some Confederate plunderers in 1864 also dressed in "ladies' hats and wraps."

13. D mss 4: 342–44. In a passage not quoted, Kelso likens the man running with the butter churn to a character in George Washington Harris, "Parson Bullen's Lizards," in *Sut Lovingood. Yarns Spun by a "Nat'ral Born Durn'd Fool." Warped and Wove for Public Wear* (New York: Dick and Fitzgerald, 1867), 48–59.

14. D mss 4: 342. Kelso, writing in California in the spring of 1882, may have seen articles in the California papers such as "The Latest Pen Portrait of Oscar Wilde," *San Francisco Bulletin* (Feb. 21, 1882): 4, reprinted from the *New York Herald*. Wilde came to California in March: "Oscar Wilde: His First Appearance before a California Audience," *San Francisco Bulletin* (March 28, 1882): 2. See also Mary W. Blanchard, "The Soldier and the Aesthete: Homosexuality and Popular Culture in Gilded Age America," *Journal of American Studies* 30, no. 1 (April 1996): 25–47.

15. "February 17, 1862—Action at Sugar Creek, Ark.," *OR*, Ser. 1, Vol. 8, 61; Shea and Hess, *Pea Ridge*, 41–43, esp. 42 ("hornet's nest," from a Confederate's diary); D mss 4: 344-5.

16. Shea and Hess, *Pea Ridge*, 43–44 (Cummins quotation); D mss 347, 348.

17. D mss 4: 346–47.

18. From the *Daily Missouri Republican*: "More Union Victories" (Feb. 21, 1862): 2 (Sugar Creek); "Another Federal Victory!" (Feb. 22): 2 (Bentonville); "The Pursuit of Price," "Springfield, Missouri," "Springfield . . . 5:00 p.m.," and "From Arkansas" (Feb. 23): 3; "Rebel Report" (Feb. 28): 1; "From Gen. Curtis' Command" and "From Springfield" (Feb. 28): 2; "Late Southern News. Burning of Fayetteville" (March 1): 1; "Letter from Cross Hollows" (March 5): 2 (though dated Feb. 22 and reiterating what had been previously reported); "From Springfield" (March 7): 2. In the *Democrat*: "From Springfield, Mo." (Feb. 21); "Good News from Curtis's Column" (Feb. 22): 2; "From Springfield, Mo." (Feb. 24): 1, and "Another Letter from Springfield," 3; "Latest from Curtis's Column" (Feb. 28): 2; "From Arkansas: The Retreat and Pursuit of Price" (March 3): 2; "From Arkansas" (March 5): 2; "From Arkansas: Price on the Skedaddle" (March 10): 1.

19. "Great Battle at Sugar Creek," *Daily Missouri Republican* (March 11, 1862); "From Arkansas: The Battle of Sugar Creek," *Missouri Democrat* (March 12, 1862): 2. For the Battle of Pea Ridge, or Elkhorn Tavern, Ark., March 6–8, 1862, see *OR*, Ser. 1, Vol. 8, 189–330. There have been several studies of this battle; the best is Shea and Hess, *Pea Ridge*. For an assessment of human costs and strategic importance, see 270 (casualty numbers quoted here), 334 (regiment losses), and 308: "Pea Ridge reshaped the strategic balance in the West. . . . Curtis's victory at Pea Ridge was the turning point of Federal efforts to dominate the Trans-Mississippi."

20. *OR*, Ser. 1, Vol. 8, 562 (Curtis to Halleck, Feb. 22, 1862) and 568 (Halleck to Curtis, Feb. 26, 1862); Shea and Hess, *Pea Ridge*, 52; D mss 4: 348–51. Sgt. James H. Garrison, Co. F, 24 Reg. Inf. Vols. He would be discharged to accept a

commission as captain in Co. G, 8th Mo. Cavalry Vols. in Sept. 1862 ("Soldiers' Records," MDH).

21. D mss 4: 336–37, 349. The abandoned wagon was part of a train that had been attacked and burned by the enemy (Gen. Curtis's report, Feb. 27, 1862, *OR*, Ser. 1, Vol. 8, 74; and see 74–76). See also Shea and Hess, *Pea Ridge*, 54.

22. D mss 4: 368–69. Kelso recruited especially in King's Prairie, a township, and then a precinct of McDonald Township, in Barry Co., Mo. An 1888 county history describes a state militia of 92 men being formed sometime in 1862 before fall, Unionists who apparently had not been persuaded by Kelso's spring recruitment effort. See *History of Newton, Lawrence, Barry, and McDonald Counties, Missouri* (Chicago: Goodspeed Publishing Co., 1888), 639. A portion of Curtis's army had been sent back to Keetsville, including Kelso's 24th Missouri. Gen. Curtis to Capt. N. H. McClean, March 18, 1862 (*OR*, Ser. 1, Vol. 8, 624). See also Michael E. Banasik, ed., *Duty Honor and Country: The Civil War Experiences of Captain William P. Black, Thirty-Seventh Illinois Infantry* [Iowa City, Iowa: Camp Pope Bookshop, 2006], 88). Curtis's army, including the 4th Iowa Infantry, which had had a prominent role in the Battle of Pea Ridge, would soon push farther south to Helena, Arkansas.

23. *OR*, Ser. 1, Vol. 13: "Report of Brig. Gen. Egbert B. Brown," June 17, 1872, 90; "Report of Col. John M. Richardson," June 11, 1862, 90–92; "Report of Lieut. Col. James K. Mills," June 13, 1862," 92–94, and see "Reposts of Col. Stand Watie, Second Cherokee Mounted Rifles [Confederate]," 94–95. D mss 4: 381–85: 403.

24. D mss 4: 381. Col. John M. Richardson (1820–1889) after the war became a conservative and supported Pres. Andrew Johnson. See Holcombe, *History of Greene County*, 217, 248, 252, 257–59, 271–73, 410, 503–506; Malcolm G. McGregor, *The Biographical Record of Jasper County, Missouri* (Chicago, 1901), 67–68; "Soldiers' Records," MDH.

25. Cos. A, C, E, G, and Kelso's H, numbering 220 men, marched from Mt. Vernon to Neosho (40 miles), Wed.–Thurs., May 28–29, 1862 (*OR*, *Supplement*, Pt. II, Vol. 35, 771, 785). The force also included one company of the 10th Illinois Cavalry (*OR*, Ser. 1, Vol. 13, 92). Col. John Trousdale Coffee (1816–1890) commanded the 6th Mo. Cavalry of the Mo. State Guard ("Soldiers' Records," MDH), operating independently of Sterling Price's forces and from the Confederate army. A lawyer before the war, he had also served in the Mo. State House and Senate and was briefly a captain in the U.S. Army. See John N. Edwards, *Noted Guerrillas, or The Warfare on the Border* (St. Louis, Mo.: Bryan, Brand, and Co., 1877), 93, 100, 105; Nichols, *Guerrilla Warfare in Civil War Missouri*, 1: 37, 43, 81–82; Gerteis, *Civil War in Missouri*, 145–46. See also Emmett MacDonald, Letter to Thomas C. Hindman, Sept. 1, 1862 (attempts to recruit Coffee for the Confederacy), Peter Wellington Alexander Papers, Box 2, and Charges Filed against John T. Coffee, ca. Oct. 1862 (on his drunkenness and dereliction of duty), Wellington Papers, Box 10, Rare Book & Manuscript Library at Columbia University in the City

of New York, MDH. Stand Watie (1806–1871) was a leader of the Cherokee Nation and became a colonel of the 1st Reg., Cherokee Mounted Volunteers (CSA), principal chief of the Confederate Cherokees, and then a brigadier general for the Confederacy. See Kenny A. Franks, *Stand Watie and the Agony of the Cherokee Nation* (Memphis, Tenn.: Memphis State University Press, 1979), and Franks, "Watie, Stand," *ANB*. Shea and Hess, *Pea Ridge*, 296, 300 (Curtis and Confederates in Arkansas); D mss 4: 380.

26. Richardson's report, *OR*, Ser. I, Vol. 13, 91; D mss 4: 382–83.

27. Richardson's report, *OR*, Ser. I, Vol. 13, 92; D mss 4: 382, 384–5: 385.

28. D mss 4: 384, 5: 385–87.

29. Richardson's report, *OR*, Ser. I, Vol. 13, 92; D mss 4: 384, 5: 385–87.

30. Richardson's report, *OR*, Ser. I, Vol. 13, 91.

31. Richardson's report, *OR*, Ser. I, Vol. 13, 91.

32. D mss 5: 389–91.

33. D mss 5: 391–92.

34. D mss 5: 393–94; Sgt. Wesley S. Rice (b. 1834), Co. A, 14th MSM Cavalry ("Soldiers' Records," MDH; U.S. Federal Census).

35. D mss 5: 394–95.

36. D mss 5: 395–97.

37. D mss 5: 397–400; *History of Newton . . . Counties, Missouri*, 312 (Richardson's attempt to surrender); U.S. Federal Census, 1860 (Julian's age).

38. Reports of Col. Stand Watie," *OR*, Ser. I, Vol. 13, 94–95, esp. 95; D mss 5: 401.

39. Mills's Report, *OR*, Ser. 1, Vol. 13, 92–94.

40. Mills's Report, *OR*, Ser. 1, Vol. 13, 92–94.

41. D mss 5: 385 (Rick Johnson), 388–89. A Capt. Rick Johnson did command a company of Confederate irregulars in Missouri ("Soldiers' Records," MDH) but no ties to Neosho, Richardson, or this battle have been established. Milton Burch, writing from Neosho two years later on Aug. 5, 1864, identified the rebel Col. Rector Johnson as "formerly a citizen of this place" (*OR*, Ser. 1, Vol. 41, Pt. 1, 194). A Capt. M. R. Johnson who operated in southwestern Missouri and was killed by Federal troops in 1863 (Nichols, *Guerrilla Warfare*, 2: 280), might have been the M. R. Johnson listed in Neosho in the 1860 census. But again, no link of either Rector or M. R. to the Neosho skirmish or to Richardson has been established. Confederate Col. Stand Watie's June 1, 1862, report on the skirmish mentions only officers Col. [John T.] Coffee, Capt. R[obert]. C. Parks, and Capt. [Thomas R.] Livingston (*OR*, Ser. 1, Vol. 13, 94–95). None are linked to Neosho or Richardson. Robert C. Parks became a lieutenant colonel in the 1st Reg. Cherokee Mounted Volunteers, CSA (NPS Database); Livingston had been a miner and a brawler before the war (Nichols, *Guerrilla Warfare*, 1: 37).

42. D mss 5: 403; Brown's report, *OR*, Ser. I, Vol. 13, 90; *History of Newton . . . Counties, Missouri*, 311, claims that "Richardson was not allowed to command again," but in

fact he was commanding the post at Cassville by Nov. 1862 and led troops in battle again on Dec. 7, 1862 (*OR*, Ser. 1, Vol. 13, 360, and Vol. 22, Pt. 1, 86–78).

43. D mss 4: 370, 4: 373, 7: 13, 8: 33, 45; 5: 402, 8: 16; 7: 8 [522]; 9: 13; 7: 518. Kelso wrote that Susie destroyed most of his letters after their divorce.

44. D mss 9: 34–35.

45. D mss 4: 376; 8: 45–46.

46. D mss 4: 379, 382.

CHAPTER 8

1. D mss 5: 464–65.

2. D mss 5: 467–68.

3. "Report of Gen. John M. Scofield . . . of Operations in Missouri and Northwest Arkansas, April 10–Nov. 20, 1862," [no date], *OR*, Ser. 1, Vol. 13, 9. On the war in the Ozark region, see Blevins, *History of the Ozarks*, 2: 38–136, on Union counterinsurgents, 94–111.

4. On the EMM see Nichols, *Guerrilla Warfare*, 1: 103–105, 2: 57–58; on the guerrilla response to the Emancipation Proclamation, see Phillips, *The Rivers Ran Backward*, 249–50.

5. D mss 4: 375.

6. Halleck, General Orders No. 32, Dec. 22, 1861, and Halleck to McClellan, Dec. 26, 1861, *OR*, Ser. 1, Vol. 8, 462–64; C. W. Marsh, Asst. Adjutant-General [for Gen. Halleck], General Orders no. 18, *OR*, Ser. 1, Vol. 13, 402–3.

7. Nichols, *Guerrilla Warfare*, 2: 69, 105; 1: 13; 3: 391.

8. See Stiles, *Jesse James: Last Rebel of the Civil War*.

9. Nichols, *Guerrilla Warfare*, 2: 19; 3: 80; 2: 209, 223; 2: 120. On the prison roof collapse, see Charles F. Harris, "Catalyst for Terror: The Collapse of the Women's Prison in Kansas City," in William Garrett Piston, ed., *A Rough Business: Fighting the Civil War in Missouri* (Columbia, Mo.: State Historical Society of Missouri, 2012), 187–204.

10. Nichols, *Guerrilla Warfare*, 1: 11, 92–95, 145, 179, 205; 2: 96, 105, 107–9, 120, 175, 211–19, 285–86; 3: 130, 132, 136; 4: 174–77. On Quantrill see also Edward E. Leslie, *The Devil Knows How to Ride: The True Story of William Clarke Quantrill and His Confederate Raiders* (Cambridge, Mass.: De Capo Press, 1998 [orig. pub. 1996]), esp. 193–244 on the Lawrence massacre.

11. Nichols, *Guerrilla Warfare*, 1: 57; 2: 46, 175, 209, 223; 3: 138–40; 3: 234–35, 249, 253, 287, 295, 298, 311, 384; 4: 36, 89, 93, 109, 121, 127, 174, 201. See also Albert Castel and Tom Goodrich, *Bloody Bill Anderson: The Short, Savage Life of a Civil War Guerrilla* (Lawrence: University Press of Kansas, 1998).

12. Nichols, *Guerrilla Warfare*, 1: 7–9; Gen. Halleck to Sec. of War Stanton, March 25, 1862, *OR*, Ser. 1, Vol. 8, 641–42.

13. Brig. Gen. James Totten to Brig. Gen. John M. Schofield, April 15, 1862, *OR*, Ser. 1, Vol. 8, 663.

14. Nichols, *Guerrilla Warfare*, 1: 77; 2: 43, 146, 168, 170, 180, 187, 199, 276, 289, 300; 3: 33; 4: 35, 58, 128, 229.

15. Nichols, *Guerrilla Warfare*, 2: 199, 260, 261, 301; 4: 28–29, 95.

16. "An Act to Organize Bands of Partisan Rangers," *The Statutes at Large of the Confederate States of America* (Richmond, Va.: R. M. Smith, 1862), 48; Thomas C. Hindman, General Order 17, June 17, 1862, *OR* Ser. 1, Vol. 13, 835; Nichols, *Guerrilla Warfare*, 1: 43, 60; 3: 238; 4: 36, 41, 121, 174–77, 201. On Quantrill's band being mustered in, see Leslie, *The Devil Knows How to Ride*, 137.

17. On the Lieber Code: Francis Lieber, *Instructions for the Government of Armies of the United States, in the Field* (New York: D. van Nostrand, 1863), esp. 21–22; General Orders No. 100, April 24, 1863, *OR*, Ser. 3, Vol. 3, 148–64; James W. Erwin, *Guerrillas in Civil War Missouri* (Charleston, S.C.: History Press, 2012), 31–37; Harry S. Stout, *Upon the Altar of the Nation: A Moral History of the Civil War* (New York: Viking Press, 2006), 191–93.

18. D mss 3: 272. On irregulars: Nichols, *Guerrilla Warfare*, 1: 37, 110, 113, 176, 211–12. On "no quarter" becoming the de facto Confederate policy for dealing with Federal Black troops, see George S. Burkhardt, *Confederate Rage, Yankee Wrath: No Quarter in the Civil War* (Carbondale: Southern Illinois University Press, 2007).

19. D mss 5: 422, 434.

20. D mss 5: 424, 432-3.

21. D mss 7: 21–22.

22. D mss 7: 21–22.

23. D mss 7: 25–26.

24. D mss 5: 468–69. Joseph Hale Mooney, Co. C, 8th Mo. Inf. (Confederate), enlisted at Elma Springs, Ark., served as a private from Feb. 4 to Aug. 4, 1862, and then was promoted to captain; 2nd Lt. Reuben P. Mooney, Co. D, 14th MSM Cavalry, enlisted at Springfield, Mo. March 29, 1862, had been wounded in action Oct. 17, 1862, but had returned to the field ("Soldiers' Records," MDH). Joseph Hale Mooney lived in Texas Co., Mo. (*History of Laclede . . . Counties, Missouri*, 461). On Capt. Mooney see also Nichols, *Guerilla Warfare*, 1: 118. Reuben (b. 1823 in Tenn.) in 1860 lived in Linden, Christian Co., Mo. with his wife and nine children (U.S. Census).

25. D mss 5: 470–74.

26. D mss 5: 470–74; 6: 485. Capt. Burch's account of the Mooney affair, in his report of the expedition filed at Ozark, Mo., Dec. 18, 1862, *OR*, Ser. 1, Vol. 22, Pt. 1, 159–61, differed somewhat from Kelso's version. Kelso remembered the raid occurring in late November, but it was Dec. 12, 1862. Burch wrote that he sent Kelso and 8 men out to capture the pickets; they did so, but returned with 2 prisoners, not 6. But Burch went on to say that Kelso, continuing to lead the advance, then "by the most

excellent management, succeeded in capturing 7 or 8 rebels, who lived near the road, without giving any alarm to the country around." Burch reported taking only one other man besides Mooney at the captain's house, though Kelso remembered "several."

27. On Rude Arnold: In his official report, dated July 25, 1862, Kelso wrote that he led a detachment of 50 men on the evening of June 19 in the direction of Buffalo. By the next morning, they had 37 prisoners. On June 23, he sent Sgt. Baxter and a small party after "Capt. Thomas Lofton and his gang." In the resulting skirmish, Rude Arnold was killed (*OR*, Ser. 1, Vol. 13, 164–66). Jonas Rudisill ("Rude") Arnold Jr. (b. 1829, d. July 24, 1862) had lived in Benton Township, Dallas Co., Mo. with his wife, Mary, and their year-old baby in 1860. His father, Jonas Rudsill Arnold, Sr., was on the Sept. 1862 list of Dallas County rebels or rebel sympathizers. See U.S. Federal Census, 1860; Missouri Provost Marshall Papers, Reel F1588, files 2133 and 1236, MDH; www.findagrave.com #75652033 and #37707799.

28. D mss 5: 405: *OR*, Supplement, 785; John R. Kelso, Provost Marshal's Office, Ozark, Mo., to Maj. James H. Steger, Aug. 4, 1862, photocopy, John F. Bradbury Jr. Collection.

29. D mss 5: 407; Report of Capt. Milton Burch, Ozark, Mo., Aug. 5, 1862, *OR*, Ser. 1, Vol. 13, 196–99; Report of Col. Robert R. Lawther, Missouri Partisan Rangers (Confederate), Aug. 2, 1862 [report captured by Capt. Burch near Forsyth, Mo., Aug. 4, 1862], in ibid., 199–200.

30. D mss 5: 408; Burch Report, *OR*, Ser. 1, Vol. 13, 197.

31. D mss 5: 409–10; Burch Report, *OR*, Ser. 1, Vol. 13, 197.

32. Lawther's report, *OR*, Ser. 1, Vol. 13, 199–200.

33. Burch's account of the Battle of Forsyth, sent to Kelso, which Kelso copied into his autobiography, D mss 5: 411–17, esp. 415, 416; Burch's report, Aug. 5, 1862, *OR*, Ser. 1, Vol. 13, 199. Lawther was captured in Osage Co., Mo., Sept. 1, 1862, and after spending time in the Gratiot Street Prison in St. Louis and the Military Prison at Alton Illinois, was exchanged at Camp Chase, Ohio, on Jan. 31, 1863. He subsequently commanded the 10th Mo. Cavalry for the Confederacy. See "Roll of Prisoners Received at Military Prison, Alton, Illinois," in "Civil War Prisoner of War Records, 1861–1865," ancestry.com; *Memorial and Biographical History of Dallas County, Texas*, 754–55.

34. D mss 5: 419; Kelso, *Works*, 43.

35. D mss 5: 436.

36. D mss 5: 419–21. Kelso remembered the regiment's "adjutant" being forced to resign. According to the *Official Register of Missouri Troops for 1862* (St. Louis, Mo., 1863), 101–102, and the *Annual Report of the Adjutant General of Missouri for 1863* (Jefferson City, Mo., 1864), 207–208, however, it was the Quartermaster T. W. Moses (appointed Oct. 2, 1862) who resigned (Dec. 8, 1862), and not the Adjutant, Roland P. Wilcox.

37. D mss 5: 437–38. Tolbert's (or Talbot's or Talbert's) Barrens, also called Rapp's Barrens, Marion Co., Ark. (a prominent citizen was S. H. Tolbert), was later called Mountain Home, which is in what is now Baxter Co., Ark.

38. D mss 5: 440.

39. D mss 5: 440–41.

40. D mss 5: 441-2.

41. D mss 5: 443-4.

42. D mss 5: 450.

43. D mss 5: 451.

44. "Report of Maj. John C. Wilber," 14th MSM Cavalry, Oct. 20, 1862, *OR*, Ser. 1, Vol. 13, 317–18.

45. "Report of Capt. Milton Burch," Ozark, Mo., Nov. 13, 1862, *OR*, Ser. 1, Vol. 13, 356–58, esp. 357.

46. D mss 5: 455.

47. D mss 5: 457–58.

48. D mss 5: 460–61. Burch's account of the raid on Yandle's place, *OR*, Ser. 1, Vol. 13, 356–57, matches Kelso's except in its ultimate result. Because of the reporting soldier's mistake, according to Burch, they were only able to take two prisoners at Yandle's. On the expedition as a whole they did take 25 prisoners, but 23 of these were captured after the incident at Yandle's. There are 7 men named Yandle in the 19th Reg. Ark. Infantry [Confederate], none of them living in Carroll Co. at the time of the census two years earlier [NPS Database; U.S. Census]).

49. D mss 5: 465.

50. D mss 5: 476.

51. Report of Capt. Milton Burch, Ozark, Mo., Dec. 18, 1862, *OR*, Ser. 1, Vol. 22, Pt. 1, 159–61, esp. 160. Burch had started the expedition with 100 men but had sent 25 back with the prisoners and sent 34 to the other side of the White River to help cover their retreat.

52. D mss 5: 476.

53. D mss 5: 478–6: 478 [repeated page number].

54. D mss 6: 481.

55. D mss 6: 482.

56. D mss 6: 484.

57. Burch's Report, Dec. 18, 1862, *OR*, Ser. 1, Vol. 22, Pt. 1, 159–61; D mss 6: 485.

58. Gerteis, *Civil War in Missouri*, 147–49; "Battle of Newtonia (1862)," www.ozarkscivilwar.org/archives/336; Alvin M. Josephy, *The Civil War in the American West* (New York: Alfred A. Knopf, 1992), 362–66; D mss 7: 34–35.

CHAPTER 9

1. This chapter's account of the Battle of Springfield, and the events preceding it, is based on the dispatches and official reports of the Union and Confederate officers

involved in *OR*, Ser. 1, Vol. 22, 178–211; "The Battle of Springfield, Mo.," *New York Times* (Jan. 26, 1863): 2, by a reporter signing as "Kickapoo" who was at Fort. No. 4 during the attack; John N. Edwards, *Shelby and His Men: Or, the War in the West* (Cincinnati, Ohio: Miami Printing and Publishing Co., 1867), chaps. 8 and 9, by a Confederate major who was Col. Joseph Shelby's adjutant; Holcombe, *History of Greene County, Missouri*, 424–56, a detailed local history informed by interviews with some of the participants; and Kelso's autobiography, D mss 6: 486–510. See also Paul M. Robinett, "Marmaduke's Expedition into Missouri: "The Battles of Springfield and Hartville, January, 1863," *MHR* 58, no. 2 (Jan. 1964): 151–73; Elmo Ingenthron, *Borderland Rebellion: A History of the Civil War on the Missouri-Arkansas Border* (Branson, Mo.: Ozarks Mountaineer, [1989]), chap. 25; Frederick W. Goman, *Up from Arkansas: Marmaduke's First Missouri Raid, Including the Battles of Springfield and Hartville* (Springfield, Mo.: Wilson's Creek National Battlefield Foundation, 1999); Wood, *Civil War Springfield*, chaps. 10 and 11.

2. D mss 6: 486.
3. Holcombe, *History of Greene County*, 437; D mss 6: 487.
4. Holcombe in *History of Greene County* repeatedly refers to MacDonald as "Long-Haired"; William Garrett Piston and Thomas P. Sweeney in *Portraits of Conflict: A Photographic History of Missouri in the Civil War* (Fayetteville: University of Arkansas Press, 2009), 322, cite the "legend" of MacDonald's long hair, but note that "photographic and written evidence indicate that he started the war with long hair" (322).
5. Edwards, *Shelby and His Men*, 134.
6. Gen. Brown's reports to Gen. Curtis, Jan. 8, 1863, 10:00 a.m. and 11:50 p.m., *OR*, Ser. 1, Vol. 22, 179–80, 180–81. Goman, *Up from Arkansas*, 123, n. 26, notes that Brown's tally missed the 72nd EMM.
7. "The Battle of Springfield, Mo.," *New York Times* (Jan. 26, 1863).
8. Edwards, *Shelby and His Men*, 144; Piston and Sweeney, *Portraits of Conflict*, 72; "The Battle of Springfield, Mo.," *New York Times* (Jan. 26, 1863); *History of Greene County*, 357, 360–61, 454.
9. Gen. Brown's report to Gen. Curtis, Jan. 8, 1863 [probably about 11:00 a.m.], *OR*, Ser. 1, Vol. 22, 180.
10. "The Battle of Springfield, Mo.," *New York Times* (Jan. 26, 1863).
11. Ibid.; D mss 6: 490.
12. "The Battle of Springfield, Mo.," *New York Times* (Jan. 26, 1863); Edwards, *Shelby and His Men*, 139.
13. D mss 6: 491.
14. *History of Greene County*, 443–44.
15. Holcombe, *History of Greene County*, 443, 453. Janey Toney was the 28-yr.-old wife of carpenter Henry Toney (1860 U. S. Federal Census); David V. Whitney was a surgeon in Fourth MSM Cavalry.
16. Quotations from Burch's letter to Kelso in D mss 6: 494–95.

17. D mss 6: 492.

18. D mss 6: 493.

19. D mss 6: 495; Gen. Samuel R. Curtis dispatch to Gen. Brown, Jan. 8, 1863, 9:00 p.m., *OR*, Ser. 1, Vol. 22, 179.

20. Col. Crabb's report, Jan. 10, 1863, *OR*, Ser. 1, Vol. 22, 184–87, esp.186; Burch in Kelso, D mss 6: 495.

21. D mss 6: 496. Holcombe, *History of Greene County*, 445–46.

22. D mss 6: 49[7], 49[8] (Kelso misnumbered his pages; brackets indicate corrected numbers). On the soldiers sleeping next to smoldering houses and the quiet Confederate withdrawal, see also "Report of Col. Joseph O. Shelby, Missouri Cavalry (Confederate)," Jan. 31, 1863, *OR*, Ser. 1, Vol. 22, 199–205, esp. 202.

23. Kelso, "Auto-Biography," 795.

24. D mss 6: 49[8]–[499].

25. D mss 6: 499.

26. D mss 6: 500.

27. On the Confederates at Phelps's farm, see also Edwards, *Shelby and His Men*, 138.

28. D mss 6: 501.

29. D mss 6: 502.

30. D mss 6: 502.

31. D mss 6: 503; Edwards, *Shelby and His Men*, 134. Marmaduke commented on his men being "indifferently armed and equipped, thinly clad, many without shoes and horses . . . without baggage wagons or cooking utensils" (*OR*, Ser. 1, Vol. 22, 197–98); Gen. Shelby remarked on their "unshod and miserable horses" (*OR*, Ser. 1, Vol. 22, 204).

32. "Return of Casualties in the Union Forces Engaged at Springfield, Mo., January 8, 1863," *OR*, Ser. 1, Vol. 22, 181; "Return of Casualties in Marmaduke's Command, Jan. 2–11, 1862 [*sic.*, 1863]," *OR*, Ser. 1, Vol. 22, 199; Holcombe, *History of Green County*, 252; Goman, *Up from Arkansas*, 62; Wood, *Civil War Springfield*, 117.

33. D mss 6: 505; on the wagon train coming to Springfield, see Col. Crabb's report, *OR*, Ser. 1, Vol. 22, 187.

34. D mss 6: 506.

35. D mss 6: 509.

36. D mss 6: 507.

37. Kelso, "Auto-Biography," 798.

38. D mss 6: 509.

39. D mss 6: 510.

40. Report of Gen. Marmaduke, Feb. 1, 1863, *OR*, Ser. 1, Vol. 22, 197; "Report of Col. Joseph O. Shelby, Missouri Cavalry (Confederate)," Jan. 31, 1863, *OR*, Ser. 1, Vol. 22, 202–204.

41. On Porter as a recruiter see Nichols, *Guerrilla Warfare in Civil War Missouri*, 2: 12. For accounts of Marmaduke's 1863 raid (after the Battle of Springfield), see *OR*, Ser.

1, Vol. 22, 178–211, and Edwards, *Shelby and His Men*, chap. 9. See also Robinett, "Marmaduke's Expedition into Missouri," 151–73; Ingenthron, *Borderland Rebellion*, chap. 25; Goman, *Up from Arkansas*; Wood, *Civil War Springfield*, chap. 11.

42. Shelby's report, *OR*, Ser. 1, Vol. 22, 203; D mss 6: 510.

43. Edwards, *Shelby and His Men*, 145 ("gallant charge"); Maj.-Gen. Samuel R. Curtis dispatch to Gov. Gamble, Jan. 12, 1863, *OR*, Ser. 1, Vol. 22, 179. On the funeral in Springfield, see Holcombe, *History of Greene County*, 454–55; on Brown's injuries see Piston and Sweeney, *Portraits of Conflict*, 236.

44. Kelso, "Auto-Biography" in "Works," 800. On the damage to Springfield, see Holcombe, *History of Green County*, 440, 445, and "The Battle of Springfield, Mo.," *New York Times* (Jan. 26, 1863): 2; on the refugees see Wood, *Civil War Springfield*, 120.

45. D mss 6: 511.

46. D mss 6: 512. Kelso rendered "damned" as "d____d."

47. All quotations in this paragraph and the remainder of the chapter are from John R. Kelso Court Martial Case File, Springfield, Mo., Jan. 21, 1863, NN-2499, Record Group 153, Records of the Office of the Judge Advocate General (Army), National Archives and Records Administration, Washington, D.C. Kelso did not mention the court martial in his autobiography.

48. On the reorganization of the MSM, see *Organization and Status of Missouri Troops (Union and Confederate) In Service during the Civil War* (U.S. Record and Pension Office [War Department]: Washington D.C., 1902), 21–47; however, the (incomplete) reproduction of General Orders No. 5 of Feb. 2, 1863 (see 30–31) excludes the part about the reorganization of the 14th—instead see *OR*, Vol. 22, Pt. 2, 97–98, and *Annual Report of the Adjutant General of Missouri for 1863* (Jefferson City, Mo.: W. A. Curry, 1864), 195.

CHAPTER 10

1. D mss 8: 47–48. On Sedalia see I. MacDonald Demuth, *The History of Pettis County, Missouri, Including an Authentic History of Sedalia* (n. p., 1882), 399–461; see also Samuel Bannister Harding, *Life of George R. Smith, Founder of Sedalia, Missouri* (Sedalia, Mo.: privately printed, 1904), 279–379, and Rhonda Chalfant, "The Midland's Most Notorious: Prostitution in Sedalia, Missouri, 1867–1900" (PhD diss., University of Missouri–Columbia, 2005), 1–30.

2. D mss 8: 48.

3. Wiley Britton, *The Union Indian Brigade in the Civil War* (Kansas City, Mo.: Franklin Hudson Publishing Co., 1922), 225; Britton, *The Aftermath of the Civil War: Based on Investigations of War Claims* (Kansas City, Mo: Smith-Grieves Co., 1924), 232; Britton, *Memoirs of the Rebellion on the Border, 1863* (Chicago: Cushing, Thomas, & Co., 1882); Britton, *The Civil War on the Border*, 2 vols. (New York: G. P. Putnam's

Sons, 1899, 1904), 2: 204. Earlier versions of this and the next six paragraphs appeared in the introduction to *Bloody Engagements*.

4. Britton, *Civil War on the Border*, 2: 201, 202–3, 206.

5. Ibid., 73.

6. Ibid., 203, 206.

7. Ibid., 204; Holcombe, *History of Greene County*, 477.

8. "The Scout of the Ozarks: John R. Kelso's Mysterious and Bloody Career in Southwest Missouri," *St. Louis Republic* (June 18, 1893): 23.

9. Britton, *Civil War on the Border*, 2: 203; "The Scout of the Ozarks."

10. "The Scout of the Ozarks."

11. D mss 10: 5–6.

12. "The Scout of the Ozarks" references "Mart Hancock": Martin Hancock was a private on Co. F, 8th and 14th Reg. MSM Cavalry (NPS "Soldiers' Database"); Britton, *Civil War on the Border*, 2: 230, 202, 71.

13. Britton, *Aftermath of the Civil War*, 222; Britton, *Civil War on the Border*, 2: 204–5, 207; Holcombe, *History of Greene County*, 477; "The Scout of the Ozarks."

14. Britton, *Civil War on the Border*, 2: 207, 208.

15. D mss 7: 18–19.

16. Ibid., 19.

17. Ibid., 20.

18. Ibid., 21.

19. Britton, *Civil War on the Border*, 2: 197; D mss 7: 24–25.

20. D mss 7: 24–25.

21. D mss 7: 24–25. Wallace Finney, 27 years old, had been a miner in Granby, Newton Co., Mo. (1860 U.S. Federal Census, Granby, Newton Co., Mo., family no. 800). See also Nichols, *Guerrilla Warfare*, 1: 158, 169. Joel P. Hood was a 23-yr.-old government scout with the 8th MSM. Before the war he had been a law student in Jasper County, Mo. (1860 U.S. Census, North Folk, Jasper Co., Mo., family no. 420).

22. D mss 7: 516–17.

23. Ibid., 517.

24. Ibid., 518.

25. Ibid., 518–19.

26. Ibid., 520–21.

27. Ibid., 8 [522]. Kelso here switched from numbering from the previous books to numbering relevant to this book only.

28. Report of Capt. Ozias Ruark, Post Neosho, Mo., April 21, 1863, *OR*, Ser. 1, Vol. 22, Pt. 1, 314; Britton, *Civil War on the Border*, 2: 70–71.

29. D mss 8: 29.

30. D mss 7: 30.

31. Ibid., 32.

32. Ibid., 32–33.

33. D mss 8: 35–36.

34. D mss 9: 43–44.
35. D mss 7: 16–17.
36. Ibid.,17–18.
37. Ibid., 10; "The Scout of the Ozarks."
38. D mss 7: 10.
39. D mss 11: 50-2, 10: 9, 7: 515.
40. D mss 8: 38–39.
41. Ibid., 39–40.
42. Ibid., 22–24, 9: 1–5.
43. D mss 9: 22–23, 8: 43–45. Mathew M. Anderson (NPS Database).
44. D mss 6: 512 (Kelso and others spell it "Bolen"). On Bolin see Wellington Allen Reminiscence, 1885, C0692, State Historical Society of Missouri; Nichols, *Guerrilla Warfare in Civil War Missouri*, 2: 17; Larry Wood, "Alf Bolin: Just the Facts," Parts I and II, http://ozarks-history.blogspot.com; Ingenthron, *Borderland Rebellion*, 285–89, esp. 286; Blevins, *History of the Ozarks*, 2: 91–92. Maj. John C. Wilber of the 14th MSM Cavalry had encountered Bolin's gang in early August 1862, killing two of them (*OR*, Ser. 1, Vol. 13, 222–23, although transcribed as "Boler"). Kelso thought the head went on a pole in Ozark. Allen (spelling the name "Bowlin") said the head was carried in a box and identified in Ozark, but then sent to Springfield. Wood notes that a short newspaper item mentions the head on a pole in Springfield.
45. Holcombe, *History of Greene County*, 476–77; Jonathan Fairbanks, *Past and Present of Greene County, Missouri* (Indianapolis, Ind.: A. W. Bowen, 1915), 380; *Christian County [Missouri]: The First Hundred Years* ([n. p.]: 1959), 12; William Neville Collier, "Ozark and Vicinity," *White River Valley Historical Quarterly* 10 (Winter 1966): 14–24, esp. 19–20; Matthew J. Hernando, *Faces Like Devils: The Bald Knobber Vigilantes in the Ozarks* (Columbia: University of Missouri Press, 2016), 40. On Edwards and the success of Lost Cause propaganda more broadly, see: Stiles, *Jesse James*; Matthew Christopher Hurlbert, *The Ghosts of Guerrilla Memory: How Civil War Bushwhackers Became Gunslingers in the American West* (Athens: University of Georgia Press, 2016), 43–62; and Heather Cox Richardson, *How the South Won the Civil War: Oligarchy, Democracy, and the Continuing Fight for the Soul of America* (New York: Oxford University Press, 2020).
46. On Livingston see Nichols, *Guerrilla Warfare in Civil War Missouri*, 1: 37, 45, 112, 176, 179, 182; 2: 11, 86–88, 94, 100–102, 158, 161. For the engagements mentioned, see Maj. Edward B. Eno, Newtonia, Mo. March 4, 1863, *OR*, Ser. 1, Vol. 22, Pt. 1, 235–36 (Granby); Maj. T. R. Livingston (Confederate), Diamond Grove, Jasper Co., Mo., May 28, 1863, ibid., 321–22; "Scout to Newtonia," Reports of Lt. Col. Thomas Crittendon and Eno, May 13–18, 1863, ibid., 328–32; Col. W. W. Cloud, Springfield, Mo., to Maj. H. Z. Curtis, April 23, 1863, *OR*, Ser. 1, Vol. 22, Pt. 2, 246.
47. Maj. T. R. Livingston to Gen. Sterling Price, May 27, 1863, *OR*, Ser. 1, Vol. 22, Pt. 2, 849–50.

48. D mss 7: 34. *OR, Supplement,* Pt. 2, Vol. 35, 570: Co. M, 8th MSM Calvary, stationed at Newtonia May 30–July 20, 1863: during that time "engaged by order of Colonel [William F.] Cloud in operation against Livingston and other guerrillas." Nichols, *Guerrilla Warfare in Civil War Missouri,* 2: 163–64, drawing from Britton, *Civil War on the Border,* 2: 195, Britton, *Memoirs of the Rebellion,* 363–64, and *OR, Supplement,* Pt. 2, Vol. 35, 438, describes Houts skirmishing with Livingston's men on July 17–19, after Livingston's death on July 11 (for which see Nichols 2: 161), but Kelso is describing an (unsuccessful and unrecorded) expedition that occurred a month earlier. Pvt. William H. Anderson, Co. M, 8th MSM Calvary: "Killed by enemy on Turkey Creek, Mo. June 10, 1863" ("Soldiers' Records," MDH); Pvt. Joshua Black, Co. M. 8th MSM ("Soldiers' Records," MDH).

49. Nichols, *Guerrilla Warfare in Civil War Missouri,* 2: 107 ("nags").

50. D mss 7: 35. Private Levi N. Scott, Co. M. 8th MSM Cavalry (NPS Database).

51. D mss 7: 36. Sgt. John W. Grantham, Co. L, 8th MSM Cavalry ("Soldiers' Records" MDH).

52. D mss 7: 37.

53. Ibid., 39.

54. "The Scout of the Ozarks."

55. D mss 7: 39.

56. Ibid., 41–42. Francis Henderson, Co. M. 8th MSM Cavalry (in "Soldiers' Records," MDH and NPS Database, listed as a private).

57. D mss 7: 42–43. Private Albert Francis Smithson III was a 36-yr.-old father of six children, with a seventh born five weeks after Ab's death. Kelso took him to a doctor, where he lingered for five days and then died (U.S. Federal Census, McDowell, Barry Co., Mo., family no. 822; "Soldiers' Records," MDH; research by genealogist Barbara Hammons Davis, orig. posted at http://www.cwnorthandsouth.com/14thBioH88.htm). His nephew was Pvt. A. [Andrew] J. Smithson, also in Co. M, 8th MSM Cavalry ("Soldiers' Records," MDH).

58. D mss 7: 44.

59. Ibid., 46–47. *OR, Supplement,* Pt. 2, Vol. 35, p. 571: The 8th MSM Cavalry, Co. M, was stationed at Carthage, Mo., in Sept., killing 15 rebels; it marched to Springfield Oct. 6–10, except "a portion of this company [which] was ordered in the field and has been on the march ever since, after the enemy," until Nov. 11–13, when the company went to Neosho.

60. D mss 7: 47–48. Burch reported the pursuit of the bushwhackers who attacked the wagon train on Sept. 6, 1863, but left the assessment of his own casualties blank (*OR,* Ser. 1, Vol. 22, Pt. 1, 613). Brig. Gen. John McNeil, in a letter from Springfield to Col. Wm. F. Cloud, Sept. 8, 1863, refers to the same attack and mentions "several men killed and wounded" (*OR,* Ser. 1, Vol. 22, Pt. 2, 517). Perhaps "James Briggs" was James Bright, an 18-yr.-old private from Polk County in Co. M, 8th MSM Cavalry ("Soldiers' Records," MDH).

61. D mss 8: [1]. Kelso's injuries from the horse accident and the shotgun blast are detailed in over a dozen affidavits in John R. Kelso, Pension File, National Archives.

62. D mss 8: 5. The successful scout may be the Oct. 4, 1863, "Skirmish near Widow Wheeler's, southwest of Neosho," in Burch's report of Oct. 6. He describes a chase on the prairie where he and his 40 men (he mentions Hood, but not Baxter) killed 10 bushwhackers (*OR*, Ser. 1, Vol. 22, Pt. 1, 685–86). The extant reports concerning the Shelby raid and its aftermath are in *OR*, Ser. 1, Vol. 22, Pt. 1, 621–79; the relevant correspondence is in ibid., Pt. 2, 588–671, and see 681, 685. Gerteis ably summarizes the raid in *Civil War in Missouri*, 157–60.

63. Report of Capt. Charles B. McAfee, Springfield. Mo., Oct. 16, 1863, *OR*, Ser. 1, Vol. 22, Pt. 1, 656–57; Report of Capt. Milton Burch, Carthage, Mo., Oct. 6, 1863, in ibid., 685–86; D mss 8: 7.

64. D mss 8: 8–10; Col. John Edwards, Report, Buffalo, Mo., Oct. 12, 1863, *OR*, Ser. 1., Vol. 22, Pt. 1, 654–55; Brig. Gen. John McNeil, Report, Fort Smith, Nov. 1, 1863, in ibid., 650. A headstone for Joel P. Hood, "The Buckskin Scout," erected much later, in Dudham Cemetery, Sarcoxie, Mo., mistakenly lists his death a year later, in Oct., 1864 (findagrave.com/memorial/64594812/joel-p-hood).

65. [Petition of Lexington, Mo., Citizens against Gen. Brown, Sept. 9, 1864], *OR*, Ser. 1, Vol. 41, Pt. 3, 120; Report of Col. Joseph O. Shelby (Confederate), Nov. 4, 1863, *OR*, Ser. 1, Vol. 22, Pt. 1, 670; Report of Gen. E. B. Brown, Sedalia, Mo., Oct. 15, 1863, ibid., 625, quoting Col. John F. Phillips.

66. D mss 8:10; Brig. Gen. Jas. Totten, St. Louis, Mo., to Col. Quin Morton, commander of Linn Creek, Mo., Oct. 14, 1863, *OR*, Ser. 1, Vol. 22, Pt. 2, 653; Maj. Gen. J. M. Schofield, St. Louis, to Gen.-in-Chief H. W. Halleck [Washington, D.C.], in ibid., 642; Scofield to Totten, Oct. 16, in ibid., 659; Report of Brig. Gen. E. B. Brown, Jefferson City, Mo., Oct. 28, 1863, *OR*, Ser. 1, Vol. 22, Pt. 1, 626–29, esp. 628.

67. D mss 8: 11–12.

68. Ibid., 12–13; Maj. Austin A. King, Report, Humansville, Mo., Oct. 17, 1863, *OR*, Ser. 1, Vol. 22, Pt. 1, 655.

69. D mss 8: 12–15; Brig. Gen. John McNeil, Report, Fort Smith, Ark., Nov. 1, 1863, *OR* Ser. 1, Vol. 22, Pt. 1, 650–52, esp. 651; Col. Jo. O. Shelby, Report, Camp Price, Ark., Nov. 16, 1863, in ibid., 670–78, esp. 677. Shelby thought he was being attacked by a force of 3,000 out of Fayetteville led by Col. William F. Cloud rather than McNeil's nine hundred, who had chased him from Missouri.

70. D mss 8: 18. The rest of Co. M had marched from Carthage Oct. 6–10; Burch, Kelso, and the 14 arrived Nov. 11–13 (*OR, Supplement*, Pt. 2, Vol. 35, 571, 573).

71. D mss 8: 28–31. Kelso remembered this happening on Christmas night, though signaled some uncertainty about the day with the phrase "If I remember rightly" (D mss 8: 26). Burch's report about the incident with the bushwhackers in the tent, however, is dated Nov. 29, 1863, and it connects it to a different attack on bushwhacker houses (not the dance): Report of Capt. Milton Burch, Neosho, Mo.,

OR, Ser. 1, Vol. 22, Pt. 1, 761–63. Co. M, 8th MSM Cavalry, "Stationed at Neosho, Missouri, November–December 1863," *Supplement, OR*, Pt. 2, Vol. 35, 571.

72. D mss 8: 32. Kelso is working from Byron's *Childe Harold's Pilgrimage*, Canto iii, stanzas 21–30.

CHAPTER 11

1. "Hon. J. R. Kelso," *[St. Joseph, Mo.] Herald and Tribune* (Dec. 13, 1864): 2; "Sempronius H. Boyd," *Biographical Directory of the United States Congress* (bioguide.congress.gov); Holcombe, *History of Greene County*, 237–38, 476–78, 524, 743. On the Boyd family see also Blevins, *History of the Ozarks*, 2: 185–88.

2. Charles D. Drake, *Union and Anti-Slavery Speeches, Delivered during the Rebellion* (Cincinnati, Ohio: Applegate & Co., 1864), iv, 58–59; Gen. Henry W. Halleck, quoted in Parrish, *History of Missouri*, 3: 88. On conservative Unionism see Astor, *Rebels on the Border*, chaps. 3 and 4. Adam Arenson, in *The Great Heart of the Republic: St. Louis and the Cultural Civil War* (Cambridge, Mass.: Harvard University Press, 2013), describes Missouri as an incompatible combination of three regional visions: Northern, Southern, and Western (2, and see 133–64).

3. Parrish, *History of Missouri*, 3: 93–94.

4. Ibid., 88–114; William E. Parrish, *Missouri under Radical Rule* (Columbia: University of Missouri Press, 1965), 2–13.

5. "Call for a Mass State Convention," *[Jefferson City, Mo.] Missouri State Times* (August 8, 1863): 2; *Proceedings of the Missouri State Radical Emancipation and Union Convention, Convened at Jefferson City, Tuesday, September 1, 1863* [Jefferson City, Mo.?, 1863], 10, 2–4, 38.

6. S. H. Boyd, "Amnesty Proclamation," *CG*, 38th Congress, 1st Sess. (March 8, 1864), 952 (speech delivered March 5), and published in the *Democrat*: "Speech of the Hon. S. H. Boyd" (March 11, 1864): 2.

7. McPherson, *Battle Cry of Freedom*, 714; "Don't Forget the Main Issue," *[St. Louis, Mo.] Democrat* (April 29, 1864) 2. See also in the *Democrat*: "The Practical Question of Reconstruction" (Jan. 6, 1864): 2; "The Coalition Crumbling" (Jan. 19, 1864): 2; "A Conversation between a Conservative and a Radical on the Subject of Reconstruction" (Jan. 22, 1864): 2; "Progress on Principle" (Feb. 6, 1864): 2; "A Full Vote" (Feb. 18, 1864): 2; "The Issue in Missouri" (Feb. 20, 1864): 2; "The Future" (Feb. 23, 1864), 1; "War on the Conservatives—The Two Addresses" (March 1, 1864): 2; "The Political Situation in Missouri" (March 2, 1864): 1; "The President— The Man" (March 4, 1864): 1; "Leaders and Followers" (March 5, 1865): 2; "Party Complications" (March 21, 1864): 2; "Whose Is the Credit" (March 26, 1864): 2; "The Duty of Radical Men" (April 11, 1864): 2; "Missouri Democracy" (April 26, 1864): 2; "Missouri's Congressional Representation" (July 8, 1864): 2.

8. Kelso, "Speech Delivered at Mt. Vernon, Mo.," in "Works," 1–9, esp. 1, 9.

9. Boyd, "Amnesty Proclamation," 952–53; Kelso, "Speech at Mt. Vernon," 3.

10. Boyd, "Amnesty Proclamation," 952–53; Kelso, "Speech at Mt. Vernon," 3.

11. Kelso, "Speech at Mt. Vernon," 4; 1860 U.S. Census, Campbell Township, Greene County, Mo., and 1860 U.S. Census, Campbell Township, Greene County, Mo.— Slave Schedules: family no. 836: Marcus Boyd, farmer, had $13,600 in real estate, $15,000 in personal estate, and 13 slaves; S. H. Boyd, lawyer, had $5,000, $2,000, and 3 slaves. (S. H. Boyd is misidentified as "W. S." here, though the record—a Springfield lawyer born in Tennessee in 1828 and married to a woman named Margaret—certainly refers to Sempronius.)

12. "Familiar Letter to Col. S. H. Boyd," *[St. Louis, Mo.] Daily Missouri Republican* (April 8, 1864): 1; Kelso, "Speech at Mt. Vernon," 9. On Dec. 17, 1860, on the floor of the U.S. Senate, Sen. Benjamin Wade of Ohio had charged that Southerners "intend either to rule or ruin this Government" (*CG*, 36th Congress, 2nd Sess., Dec. 17, 186, 30, Pt. 1, 102).

13. Holcombe, *History of Greene County, Missouri*, 422–23; Kelso, "Speech at Mt. Vernon," 9.

14. On "negro equality" in the *[St. Louis, Mo.] Democrat* in early 1864, see: "Negro Equality" (Jan. 6, 1864): 1; "Two Kinds of Equality" (Jan. 9, 1864): 1; "The Conservatives and Their New Rival" (Jan. 13, 1864): 2; "The Latest News . . . From Washington" (Feb. 24, 1864): 1; "Miscegenation—Conservative Sincerity" (March 16, 1864): 2. In the *[St. Louis, Mo.] Republican*: "Negro Equality" (Jan. 19, 1864): 1; "Negro Equality" (Jan. 21, 1864): 3; "Negro Equality" (Feb. 23, 1863): 3; "New Abolition Platform" (April 21, 1864): 2. In the *[Jefferson City,] Missouri State Times*: "Mr. Barr, of Ray, on Negro Equality" (Feb. 20, 1864): 2.

15. *[St. Louis, Mo.] Republican*, Feb. 16, 1864): 3 (the debate was held on Thursday Feb. 11).

16. Samuel S. Cox, *Eight Years in Congress, from 1857–1865: Memoir and Speeches* (New York, 1865), 352–70; *Miscegenation: The Theory of the Blending of the Races, Applied to the American White Man and Negro* (New York, 1864) [orig. pub. 1863]. See Sidney Kaplan, "The Miscegenation Issue in the Election of 1864," *Journal of Negro History* 34, no. 3 (July 1949): 274–343. "Miscegenation" in the *[St. Louis, Mo.] Republican* during the first half of 1864: (Feb. 28): 2; (Feb. 17): 2; (March 2): 1; (March 25): 3; (April 7): 3; (April 13): 1; (June 5): 2; (June 6): 1; (June 15): 1; (June 23): 2. Other newspapers in the state such as the *St. Joseph Morning Herald*, the *Palmyra Spectator*, and the *[Weston] Border Times* denounced the pamphlet and the furor over it as ridiculous; the *[St. Louis] Democrat* mostly ignored it.

17. "Negro Equality. Extracts from the Speech of Mr. Allin, in the General Assembly," *[St. Louis, Mo.] Republican* (Feb. 23, 1864): 3.

18. Kelso, "Speech at Mt. Vernon," 5. On colonization 1863–4, see "The Latest News . . . The Blair Colonization Scheme Exploded," *[St. Louis, Mo.] Democrat* (March 22, 1864): 1; "The Deportation Bubble Burst," *Democrat* (March 28, 1864): 2; McPherson, *Battle Cry of Freedom*, 509; J. D. Lockett, "Abraham Lincoln

and Colonization: An Episode That Ends in Tragedy at L'Ille à Vache, Haiti, 1863–1864," *Journal of Black Studies* 21, no. 4 (June 1991): 428–44.

19. Kelso, "Speech at Mt. Vernon," 5–6.

20. Ibid., 6–7. An editorial in the *[St. Louis, Mo.] Democrat*, "The Deportation Bubble Burst" (March 28, 1864): 2, voiced a similar argument that Blacks and Whites would naturally separate once the artificial constraints of slavery were removed.

21. Drake, "Slavery's Destruction, the Union's Safety," speech delivered Feb. 22, 1864, in *Union and Antislavery Speeches*, 407–23, esp. 415–16. On Black suffrage see esp. Xi Wang, *The Trial of Democracy: Black Suffrage and Northern Republicans, 1860–1910* (Athens: University of Georgia Press, 1997); on Black suffrage in Missouri, see Margaret Leola Dwight, "Black Suffrage in Missouri, 1865–1877" (PhD diss., University of Missouri-Columbia, 1978), though the study begins its analysis, in chapter 2, only in late 1864.

22. "Speech of Hon. F. P. Blair," Feb. 27, 1864, *CG*, 38th Congress, 1st Sess., Pt. 4, Appendix, 46–49, esp. 46 ("Jacobin"); *CG*, 38th Congress, 1st Sess., Pt. 1, 1842–46, esp. 1843. See Wang, *Trial of Democracy*, 1–18. See also *CG*, 38th Congress, 1st Sess., Pt. 1: 712, 1107, 2239–49; Henry Wilson, *History of the Antislavery Measures of the Thirty-Seventh and Thirty-Eighth United States Congresses, 1861–1864* (Boston: Walker, Fuller & Co., 1865), 188, 335; "Negro Suffrage," *[St. Louis, Mo.] Republican* (March 6, 1864): 2; "Negro Suffrage," *Republican* (May 19, 1864): 2; "Progress from Worst to Better," *Liberator* 33, no. 35 (Aug. 28, 1863): 138; "Shorter Catechism of Negro Equality," *Liberator* 33, no. 27 (Sept. 11, 1863): 146; "Our Government and the Blacks," *Continental Monthly* 5, no. 4 (April 1864): 431–35; "The Progress toward Negro Equality, Negro Suffrage, and Miscegenation," *[Columbus, Ohio] Daily Ohio Statesman* (April 1, 1864): 2.

23. "Negro Equality," *[St. Louis, Mo.] Republican* (Jan. 21, 1864): 3; Kelso, "Speech at Mt. Vernon," 6.

24. Kelso, "Speech at Mt. Vernon," 8. On rebel disfranchisement see "Missouri Legislature Deferred Debates," *[St. Louis, Mo.] Republican* (Jan. 4, 1864): 3. On the test oath operating in Missouri after 1861, see Martha Kohl, "Enforcing a Vision of Community: The Role of the Test Oath in Missouri's Reconstruction," *Civil War History* 40, no. 4 (1994): 292–307; see also Parrish, *History of Missouri*, 64–68.

25. "From Colonel S. H. Boyd. To the Radical Voters of the Fourth Congressional District," *[St. Louis, Mo.] Democrat* (April 27, 1864): 4, reprinted from the *[Lebanon, Mo.] Union* of April 26.

26. In the *[St. Louis, Mo.] Democrat*: "From Springfield, Mo." (March 4, 1864): 2; "From Springfield, Mo." (March 19, 1864): 2; "Congressional" (Aug. 23, 1864): 2; "Congressional Nominations" (Aug. 26, 1864): 1; "A Word to Radical Unionists" (Aug. 26, 1864): 2.

27. In the *[St. Louis, Mo.] Democrat*: "From Springfield, Mo." (March 25, 1864): 2; "From Springfield, Mo." (April 30, 1864): 2.

28. In the *[St. Louis, Mo.] Democrat*: "Grand Ratification Meeting . . . Speech of Colonel S. H. Boyd" (July 26, 1864): 2; "Colonel S. H. Boyd" (July 27, 1864): 1.

29. D mss 9: 40; J. Willard Brown, *The Signal Corps, U.S.A., in the War of the Rebellion* (Boston, Mass.: U.S. Veteran Signal Corps, Assoc., 1896), 593–94, 681.

30. D mss 9: 40–41.

31. McPherson, *Battle Cry of Freedom*, 718–55; Long and Long, *Civil War Day by Day*, 474–549; Gerteis, *Civil War in Missouri*, 179–80; Nichols, *Guerrilla Warfare in Civil War Missouri*, 3: 56–303.

32. D mss 8: 34, 9: 34–35.

33. Burch report, Oct. 6, 1863, *OR*, Ser. 1, Vol. 22, 685; Burch report, May 14, 1864, *OR*, Ser. 1, Vol. 34, 921–22; Kelso report, June 2, 1864, *OR*, Ser. 1, Vol. 34, 957–58.

34. Kelso report, June 2, 1864, *OR*, Ser. 1, Vol. 34, 957–58.

35. D mss 9: 3.

36. Ibid., 2; Report of Maj. Lyman W. Brown, 11th Missouri Cavalry, Jan. 30, 1864, *OR*, Ser. 1, Vol. 34, 95 (attack on Sgt. Jones, reporting 12 killed).

37. D mss 9: 5–6.

38. Sgt. Joshua Ruark and Pvt. Robert Poag, both Co. L., 8th MSM Cavalry, "Soldiers Records," MDH. 1860 U.S. Census, Marion Township, Newton County, Missouri, family no. 574: John R. Good, a 26-yr.-old farmer, then living in with his wife Madaline (Madeline) and 2-yr.-old son John in the household of Harmon Middleton (age 63). The military records spell his name Goode and Kelso spells it Gude. Report of Capt. Henry D. Moore and Report of Capt. Ozias Ruark, both June 3, 1864, *OR*, Ser. 1, Vol. 34, Pt. 1, 966–67; D mss 9: 9–11. On this episode see also Nichols, *Guerrilla Warfare in Civil War Missouri*, 3: 190–91.

39. D mss 9: 7; Pvt. Levi N. Scott and Corp. Joseph M. McConnell, both Co. M, 8th MSM Cavalry, NPS Soldiers Database.

40. D mss 9: 8.

41. Ibid., 9.

42. D mss 9: 11; Ozias Ruark Diary, 1864–1865, Western Historical Manuscript Collection, Columbia Missouri, MDH, entry for June 2, 1864, p. 26; Ruark report, *OR*, Ser. 1, Vol. 34, Pt. 1, 967.

43. "William Cloe's Story," in Colleen Belk, comp., "Part One: Civil War Stories and Data of Southwest Missouri, and Tombstones" (Web City, Mo., n.d.), typescript, 14–15. (Thanks to Steve Weldon, Jasper County Archivist, Jasper Co., Mo. Records Center, Carthage, Mo., for giving me access to this document.)

44. "William Cloe's Story," 15; D mss 9: 10; Burch report, Aug. 5, 1864, *OR*, Ser. 1, Vol. 41, Pt. 1, 195; Ozias Ruark Diary, entry for Aug. 2, 1864, p. 38.

45. D mss 9: 11.

46. Ibid., 12.

47. Ibid., 13–15, 16; Gravely report (Baxter), Aug. 18, 1864, *OR*, Ser. 1, Vol. 41, Pt. 1, 198; Report of Brig. Gen. John B. Sanborn, Addenda: Itinerary of the District of Southwest Missouri, Aug. 13, 1864, *OR*, ibid., 193–94; Nichols, *Guerrilla Warfare*

in Civil War Missouri, 3: 197; *OR Supplement*, Pt. 2, Vol. 35, 572. The Granby miners had made a special appeal for military protection: "An Appeal from Southwest Missouri," *[St. Louis, Mo.] Democrat*, March 30, 1864, 1.

48. D mss 9: 27–28; *OR*, Ser. 1, Vol. 41, Pt. 1, 194–95.

49. D mss 9: 25–26.

50. Ibid., 28. For some reason, Burch reported for Hunter; his Aug. 5, 1864, report, *OR*, Ser. 1, Vol. 41, Pt. 1, 194–95, listed 3 killed, 9 missing, and 1 wounded severely; Brig. Gen. Sanborn's Aug. 13, 1864, summary, in ibid., 193, noted that 6 of Hunter's missing subsequently made it back to camp.

51. D mss 9: 30–32; Burch report, Aug. 9, 1864, *OR*, Ser. 1, Vol. 41, Pt. 1, 196–97.

52. D mss 9: 32; Burch report, Aug. 9, 1864, *OR*, Ser. 1, Vol. 41, Pt. 1, 197: 1 killed, 4 severely wounded (Kelso said one of these, Pvt. Joseph T. Howard, would die of his wounds), and 4 horses disabled. Pvt. Joseph T. Howard, Co. L, 8th MSM Cavalry, "Soldiers Records," MDH; Corp. Jonathan C. Thomas, Co. L, 8th MSM Cavalry, NPS Database.

53. D mss 9: 32–33.

54. Augusta and Joshua Miller, 1860 U.S. Census, Rutledge, McDonald Co., Mo., family no. 20. I have not been able to identify Lieutenant Gunter.

55. Thaddeus Stevens, *Speech . . . on the Bill to Raise Additional Soldiers . . . Feb. 2, 1863* ([Washington, D.C.]: Towers & Co., 1863), 3; Samuel Sullivan Cox, *Free Debate in Congress Threatened . . . April 6, 1864* [Washington, D.C., 1864], 11; Stephen E. Towne, *Surveillance and Spies in the Civil War: Exposing Confederate Conspiracies in America's Heartland* (Athens: Ohio University Press, 2015), 211. Scholars have come to vastly different conclusions about the significance of the KGC and similar secret societies in the Civil War. Frank L. Klement's *Dark Lanterns: Secret Political Societies, Conspiracies, and Treason Trials in the Civil War* (Baton Rouge: Louisiana State University Press, 1984) influenced a generation of scholarship. Klement forcefully argued that Bickley (like the founders of other similar societies) was a fantasist and a con man, and that the KGC was an amalgam "mostly of rumors, conjecture, and fancy" which politically-minded Union officers and Republican politicians used to create "a bogyman" for their "political gain" (33). Republicans, Klement argued, inflated, and distorted a few shards of evidence and then made up the rest for propaganda purposes in the fall 1864 elections. David C. Keehn, however, in *Knights of the Golden Circle: Secret Empire, Southern Secession, Civil War* (Baton Rouge: Louisiana State University Press, 2012), argues that Klement was looking in the wrong place (the Midwest) and at the wrong time (during the Civil War) for influence of the KGC. It was influential in the South in 1860–1861 during the push for secession. Towne's *Surveillance and Spies*, though, is a direct and persuasive challenge to Klement. With deep research in the National Archives, Towne shows that Union commanders and politicians did indeed have credible evidence of subversive secret societies operating in favor of the Confederacy in Border and Northern states. For a discussion of the ideology of the KGC, see also Mark A.

Lause, *A Secret Society History of the Civil War* (Urbana: University of Illinois Press, 2011), chaps. 3 and 6.

56. D mss 9: 38–39; Charles O. Perrine, *An Authentic Exposition of the K.G.C.* [Indianapolis, Ind., 1861], 48–49; Benn Pittman, *The Trials for Treason at Indianapolis* (Cincinnati, Ohio: Moore, Wilstach, & Baldwin, 1865), 170.

57. Christopher Columbus "Lum" Dawson, b. 1838, was in 1887 shot to death outside a saloon in Mt. Pleasant, Mo., by an escaped convict. 1860 U.S. Census, Carthage, Jasper Co., Mo., family no. 459 (C. C. Dawson) and no. 449 (A. M. Dawson); 1860 U.S. Census—Slave Schedules, Marion Township, Jasper County, Mo. (A. M. Dawson); "First Paper in Carthage," *Carthage [Mo.] Banner* (May 16, 1878): 3; Joel Thomas Livingston, *A History of Jasper County, Missouri* (Chicago, 1912), 1: 47; Kenneth E. Burchett, *The Battle of Carthage: First Trans-Mississippi Conflict of the Civil War* (Jefferson, N.C., 2013), 62–63; "Columbus Dawson," NPS "Soldiers' Database; "U.S. Civil War Draft Registration Records" (ancestry.com) from NARA, Consolidated Lists of Civil War Draft Registration Records; *Patriot* (May 10, 1866): 3; *[Carthage, Mo.] Weekly Banner* (Jan. 26, 1867): 2; 1870 U.S. Census, Campbell Township, Greene Co., Mo., family no. 630; *Cameron [Mo.] Sun*, Aug. 27, 1887): 2; *History and Directory of Cass County, Missouri* (Harrisonville, Mo.: Cass County Leader, 1908), 163. (Thanks to Dan Nelson for genealogical help on Dawson).

58. Sanderson's June 12, 1864, report to Gen. Rosecrans: *OR*, Ser. 2, Vol. 7, 228–29; "A Startling Revelation. An Immense Conspiracy Discovered," *[Jefferson City] Missouri State Times*, Aug. 13, 1864, 1, and other papers. For related articles in the *Democrat*, see "Rebel Secret Organization" (July 30, 1864): 1; "Another Revelation" (Aug. 1, 1864): 1; "The Alleged Conspiracy" (Aug. 1, 1864): 2; "Treason in Indiana" and "The Scheme of a Northwestern Republic" (Aug. 2, 1864): 2; "The Great Conspiracy," "The Conservative Press and Provost Marshal Sanderson," and "Not So Amusing" (Aug. 5, 1864): 1; "Owning Up at Last" (Aug. 5, 1864): 2; "The Second Great Conspiracy" (Aug. 6, 1864): 1; "The Democratic Conspiracy in Illinois" (Aug. 9, 1864): 2; "Secret Political Societies" (Aug. 11, 1864): 2; "The O.A.K. and the Democratic Party" (Aug. 12, 1864): 2; "Arrest of an O.A.K. Missionary" (Aug. 15, 1864): 2; "The Latest Explanation of the O.A.K. Developments" (Aug. 16, 1864): 2; "Important Revelations. O.A.K.'s in Earnest" (Aug. 20, 1864): 1; "Democratic Treason in Indiana" (Aug. 23, 1864): 1; "Treason in Indiana" (Aug. 24, 1864): 2; "Order of American Knights" (Aug. 25, 1864): 4.

59. Carrington, at the insistence of Indiana Gov. Oliver P. Morton, published a similar report in the *Indianapolis Daily Journal* on July 30, 1864 (Towne, *Surveillance and Spies*, 243). Working from Sanderson, Carrington, and other information Joseph Holt, Judge Advocate General, U.S. Army, filed a long report for Sec. of War Stanton on Oct. 8, 1864: *OR*, Ser. 2, Vol. 7, 930–53. The substance of these reports was republished in newspapers across the country and separately as pamphlets. See for example *Treason in Indiana Exposed* (Indianapolis, Ind.: Union State Central

Committee, 1864) (Carrington's report); *Report of the Judge Advocate General on "The Order of American Knights" alias "The Sons of Liberty"* (Washington, D.C.: Chronicle Print, 1864). Keehn in *Knights of the Golden Circle*, chap. 13, argues that while the Order of American Knights and the Sons of Liberty mostly supplanted the KGC after 1863, they did not evolve directly from the previous organization, having mostly different principles, rituals, and leadership.

60. On Price's 1864 invasion, see especially Kyle S. Sinisi, *The Last Hurrah: Sterling Price's Missouri Expedition of 1864* (Lanham, Md.: Rowman and Littlefield, 2015); Mark A. Lause, *Price's Lost Campaign: The 1864 Invasion of Missouri* (Columbia: University of Missouri Press, 2011); Mark A. Lause, *The Collapse of Price's Raid: The Beginning of the End in Civil War Missouri* (Columbia: University of Missouri Press, 2016); see also Charles D. Collins Jr., *Battlefield Atlas of Price's Missouri Expedition of 1864* (Fort Leavenworth, Kans.: Combat Studies Institute Press, 2016); Gerteis, *Civil War in Missouri*, 179–202. In the official records: "Price's Missouri Expedition," *OR*, Ser. 1, Vol. 41, Pt. 1, 303–729.

61. On Glasgow see Gerteis, *Civil War in Missouri*, 193–94.

62. On the battle at Fort Davidson (Pilot Knob) see Sinisi, *Last Hurrah*, 70–86; Lause, *Price's Lost Campaign*, 46–67; Gerteis, *Civil War in Missouri*, 182–88.

63. Lincoln on Rosecrans as a confused duck quoted in Lause, *Price's Lost Campaign*, 20. Sinisi argues that Price decided against marching against St. Louis (even though he continued in that direction) the morning after the Federals blew up Fort Davidson on Sept. 27 (*Last Hurrah*, 85); Lause argues that despite what the general reported later, Price probably did not give up on the plan to attack the city until Oct. 1 (*Price's Lost Campaign*, 112–43). To the 6,000 troops defending St. Louis, Sinisi adds "a hastily assembled conglomeration" of 4,400 men in the Enrolled Missouri Militia, 5,000 Home Guards, and five regiments of 100-day volunteers from Illinois (102). Lause argues that these numbers are inflated: the EMM available to Rosecrans "probably numbered no more than an indifferently armed and equipped 1,500 men" (95). On Rosecrans in Missouri see also William M. Lamers, *The Edge of Glory: A Biography of General William S. Rosecrans, U.S.A.* (New York: Harcourt, Brace, and World, 1961), 415–39.

64. Confederate Maj. John N. Edwards on Price as lion and guinea pig, quoted in Lause, *Price's Lost Campaign*, 4. Lause quotes a passage from the OAK circular on p. 20.

65. Lause, *Price's Lost Campaign*, 183: "The lesser standards of success for a raid recast almost any stolen farm wagon as an achievement." Gerteis, *Civil War in Missouri*, 196–97, gives the numbers of wagons and cattle; Sinisi, 176, says these numbers are inflated. Again, Lause and Sinisi differ on troop numbers. Sinisi, adhering to the numbers in the official report, puts the Jefferson City defenders at 8,200 (*Last Hurrah*, 103–104); Lause, analyzing the rolls to determine the actual number of fighters available, estimates 6,000 (*Price's Lost Campaign*, 162–65). For the range of estimates of the casualties at the Battle of Westport—fewer than 900 or more than 3,500?—see Sinisi, 258.

66. On the Battle of Westport, see Sinisi, *Last Hurrah*, 217–57, Lause, *Collapse of Price's Raid*, 75–139, and Gerteis, *Civil War in Missouri*, 198–201.

67. D mss 9: 41–44.

68. Ibid., 44–45.

69. Ibid., 45.

70. D mss 9: 45-46. On Lt. Robert H. Christian, "Old Grisly": *OR*, Ser. 1, Vol. 22, Pt. 2, 824; *OR* Ser. 1, Vol. 41, Pt. 1, 637–38, 669, and 824–25; "Honor to Whom Honor is Due," *Patriot* (Aug. 24, 1865): 2; *History of Newton, Lawrence, Barry, and McDonald Counties Missouri* (Chicago: Goodspeed Pub. Co., 1888), 262, 322; Larry Wood, *The Two Civil War Battles of Newtonia* (Charleston, S.C.: History Press, 2010), 116–17; Nichols, *Guerrilla Warfare in Civil War Missouri*, 2: 94–95 and 4: 28–29; Sinisi, *The Last Hurrah*, 311–12. Christian's long gray hair and beard made him appear older than he was: he was 34 at his death. 1850 U.S. Census, District 53, McDonald County, Mo., Family No. 57; 1860 U.S. Census, Richwoods, McDonald County, Mo., Family no. 411.

71. D mss 9: 46–47.

72. D mss 9: 49.

73. Ibid., 50, 54; Sinisi, *Last Hurrah*, 312; "Honor to Whom Honor is Due," *Patriot* (Aug. 24, 1865): 2.

74. D mss 9: 50–51.

75. Ibid., 51.

76. Ibid., 53. As Kelso notes, 30,000 men was an estimate of Price's force when it entered the state a month earlier. He probably had under 13,000 then, and half that by the time he reached Newtonia.

77. Sinisi, *Last Hurrah*, 313–21; Wood, *Two Civil War Battles of Newtonia*, 113–31; Lause, *Collapse of Price's Raid*, 170–83.

78. D mss 10: 3–4.

79. Ibid., 5–6. The official records merely note that on Oct. 29, 1864, "Lieutenant Colonel Brutsche attacked a body of rebels, killing a large number and taking a large number of prisoners" (*OR*, Ser. 1, Vol. 41, Pt. 1, 396).

80. D mss 10: 1–2.

81. Ibid., 6–7.

82. Long and Long, *Civil War Day by Day*, 646–47.

83. D mss 10: 11.

84. Ibid., 11; Castel and Goodrich, *Bloody Bill Anderson*, 47; Nichols, *Guerrilla Warfare*, 4: 257, 303.

CHAPTER 12

1. D mss 10: 21–22; George Alfred Townsend, *Washington Outside and Inside* (Cincinnati, Ohio: James Bets & Co., 1873), 137, 143; John B. Ellis, *The Sights and Secrets of the National Capitol: A Work Descriptive of Washington City in All Its Various Phases* (New York: U.S. Publishing Co., 1869), 21–24.

2. D mss 10: 22–23; Ellis, *Sights and Secrets of the National Capital*, 24.

3. D mss 10: 23–24; Ellis, *Sights and Secrets of the National Capital*, 443–45; Kathryn Allamong Jacob, *Capital Elites: High Society in Washington, D.C., after the Civil War* (Washington, D.C.: Smithsonian Institution Press, 1995), 54–55; "Congressional Record," *Washington, D.C. Daily National Intelligencer*, Dec. 8, 1865, 4.

4. *New-York Daily Tribune*, June 20, 1866, 7.

5. D mss 10: 12–13, 16; Townsend, *Washington Outside and Inside*, 154–55; John M. Barclay (comp.), *Constitution of the U.S. . . . Jefferson's Manual of Parliamentary Practice . . . and Barclay's Digest* (Washington, D.C., 1860–1861).

6. D mss 10: 13, 16.

7. Kelso, "Speech Delivered at Walnut Grove, Missouri, September 19, 1865," in "Works," 10–11. In a speech delivered at Rochester, N.Y., on Oct. 25, 1858, New York senator William Henry Seward had described the sectional dispute as "an irrepressible conflict." For a discussion in the Missouri press, see, for example, "The 'Irrepressible Conflict': Wm. H. Seward's Brutal and Bloody Manifesto," *[St. Louis, Mo.] Republican* (Oct. 22, 1859): 2.

8. Kelso, "Speech Delivered at Walnut Grove," 12–13; Andrew Johnson, Speech of Sep. 11, 1865, in John Savage, *The Life and Public Services of Andrew Johnson . . . Including His State Papers, Speeches, and Addresses* (New York: Derby and Miller, 1866), 405, previously published as "The President's Speech: How the States Are to Be Restored," *[St. Louis, Mo.] Republican* (Sept. 17, 1865): 1: "The South, true to her ancient instincts of frankness and manly honor, comes forth and expresses her willingness to abide the result of the decision [on the battlefield] in good faith"; Andrew Johnson, speech of April 3, 1865, in Frank More, ed., *Speeches of Andrew Johnson* (Boston, Mass.: Little, Brown, and Co., 1865), xlv: "I would say death is too easy a punishment. My notion is that treason must be made odious and traitors must be punished and impoverished, their social power broken, though they must be made to feel the penalty of their crime."

9. Kelso, "Speech Delivered at Walnut Grove," 14.

10. Ibid., 17–18.

11. Ibid., 18–19; Abraham Lincoln, quoted in John Hay's diary, in John G. Nicolay and John Hay, *Abraham Lincoln: A History* (New York: Century Co., 1890), 9: 121; "Reconstruction. Speech of the Hon. Thaddeus Stevens," *New York Tribune* (Sept. 11, 1865): 8. It is not clear whether or not Kelso read this speech before he wrote his own. The *[Jefferson City, Mo.] Missouri State Times* did not publish Stevens' speech until ten days after Kelso had delivered his: Sept. 29, 1865, 1.

12. Kelso, "Speech Delivered at Walnut Grove," 21, 24.

13. Ibid., 22–23, 27.

14. Ibid., 25.

15. D mss 10: 24; William H. Barnes, *History of the Thirty-Ninth Congress* (New York: Harper and Bros., 1868), 16, 26; Ellis, *Sights and Secrets*, 108–109; *CG*, 39th Congress, 1st Sess., Dec. 4, 1865, 3–7.

16. D mss 10: 17, 24.

17. *CG*, 39th Congress, 1st Sess., Dec. 4, 1865, 3–7; Barnes, *History of the Thirty-Ninth Congress*, 16–17.

18. *CG*, 40th Congress, 1st Sess., March 14, 1867, 100–101; on conservative radicals and radical radicals, see Michael Les Benedict, *A Compromise of Principle: Congressional Republicans and Reconstruction, 1863–1869* (New York: W. W. Norton, 1974), 21–58.

19. On Stevens: Ellis, *Sights and Secrets*, 141; Barnes, *History of the Thirty-Ninth Congress*, 24–25; Eric Foner, *Reconstruction: America's Unfinished Revolution, 1863–1877* (New York: Harper and Row, 1988), 229; Hans L. Trefousse, *Thaddeus Stevens: Nineteenth-Century Egalitarian* (Chapel Hill: University of North Carolina Press, 1997), 7, 137, 175, 229.

20. Thaddeus Stevens, "Reconstruction," *CG*, 39th Congress, 1st Sess., Dec. 18, 1865, 72–75, quotations on 72.

21. Ibid., 72–75, esp. 74.

22. Henry J. Raymond, "Reconstruction," *CG*, 39th Congress, 1st Sess., Dec. 21, 1865, 120–25. On Raymond see Benedict, *Compromise*, 113, 122, 127–28, 141–42.

23. Raymond, "Reconstruction," *CG*, 39th Congress, 1st Sess., Dec. 21, 1865, 120–25, esp. 125.

24. D mss 10: 25.

25. *CG*, 39th Congress, 1st Sess., Dec. 5, 1865, 9; Dec. 12, 1865, 31; 39th Congress, 1st Sess., House of Representatives, *Evidence in the Contested Election of Boyd vs. Kelso*, Misc. Doc. No. 92, ordered printed March 24, 1865.

26. *Evidence in the Contested Election*, 17, 23, 29, 133, 155.

27. D mss 10: 26.

28. Ellis, *Sights and Secrets*, 140–41.

29. U.S. Postal Service, *The United States Postal Service: An American History, 1775–2006* (Washington, D.C.: U. S. Postal Service, 2007); *CG*, 39th Congress, 1st Sess., Dec. 20, 1865, 100; Feb. 14, 1866, 836–37; Feb. 15, 1866, 853–55; March 26, 1866, 1656–60; July 11, 1866, 3744–47; July 12, 1866, 3766–68; "Mail Facilities for the Southwest," *[St. Louis, Mo.] Democrat* (March 1, 1866), supplement; "Letter from Mr. Kelso," *Patriot* (Feb. 1, 1866): 1.

30. Gerald Culliman, *The United States Postal Service* (New York: Praeger Pub., 1973), 54–88; Mary Clemmer Ames, *Ten Years in Washington: Life and Scenes in the National Capital as a Woman Sees Them* (Hartford, Conn.: A. D. Worthington, 1875), 386; Michael Les Benedict, *Impeachment and Trial of Andrew Johnson* (New York: W. W. Norton, 1973), 48–49; "Johnson's Policy in Phelps County," *[St. Louis, Mo.] Democrat* (Nov. 5, 1866): 2; [no title], *Patriot* (May 10, 1866): 2; Holcombe, *History of Greene County, Missouri*, 505–506. See also Lindsay Rogers, *The Postal Power of Congress: A Study in Constitutional Expansion* (Baltimore, Md.: Johns Hopkins University Press, 1916, rpt. 2006); Richard H. John, *Spreading the News: The American Postal System from Franklin to Morse* (Cambridge, Mass.: Harvard University Press, 1995); Winifred Gallagher, *How*

the Post Office Created America: A History (New York: Penguin Press, 2016), 143–51.

31. *CG*, 39th Congress, 2nd Sess., Jan. 7, 1867, 319. The debate ran from Wed., Jan. 10 through Thurs., Jan. 18. See *CG*, 39th Congress, 1st Sess., 173–311 (quotations: Boyer, 177; Rogers, 196–97; Chanler, 218; Johnson, 306–307.

32. *CG*, 39th Congress, 1st Sess., 173–311 (quotations: Farnsworth, 204–6; Kelley, 181, 186; Wilson, 173–75; Grinell, 223; Julian, 255–56).

33. *CG*, 39th Congress, 1st Sess., Jan. 17, 1866, 282; Jan. 28, 1867, 311.

34. "From Congressman Kelso," *[St. Louis, Mo.] Democrat* (Jan. 20, 1866): 3

35. Ibid.; *Boyd vs. Kelso*, 157.

36. "From Congressman Kelso," 3.

37. Ibid., 1 and 4; "Mr. Kelso's Circular," *Patriot* (Jan. 11, 1866): 2 (the circular itself was printed on the first page of this issue).

38. "Mr. Kelso's Circular," 2.

39. "Letter from Mr. Kelso," *Patriot* (Feb. 1, 1866): 1.

40. Ibid.; "Gems from the Journal," reprinted in the *Patriot* (March 8, 1866): 2. On Ingram and the *Patriot* see Holcombe, *History of Greene County, Missouri,* 479, 768, 762.

41. "From Cedar County," *Patriot* (Feb. 15, 1866): 1.

42. *CG*, 39th Congress, 1st Sess., Jan. 26, 1866, 446; Jan. 31, 1866, 537; Feb. 5, 1866, 645; "Missouri in the House," *[St. Louis, Mo.] Republican* (Feb. 10, 1866): 4.

43. Ellis, *Sights and Secrets of the National Capital*, 154; *CG*, 39th Congress, 1st Sess., Feb. 10, 1866, 781; D mss 10: 25. For an example of a speech heavy with citations, see William Lawrence, [no title], *CG*, 39th Congress, 1st Sess., Feb. 17, 1866, 904–10; for a conversational address, see J. H. D. Henderson, "Punishment of Traitors," *CG*, 39th Congress, 1st Sess., Feb. 7, 1866, 728–30.

44. John R. Kelso, "Reconstruction," 39th Congress, 1st Sess., Feb. 7, 1866, 730–33, esp. 730, 731.

45. Ibid., 731.

46. Ibid., 732.

47. Ibid., 732.

48. Ibid., 733.

49. Ibid., 732.

50. Ibid., 733; D mss 10: 25. See also John R. Kelso, *Reconstruction. Speech of Hon. John R. Kelso, of Missouri. Delivered in the House of Representatives, February 7, 1866* (Washington, D.C.: McGill & Witherow, 1866); John R. Kelso, "Reconstruction," *Patriot* (May 3, 1866): 1.

51. "Contested Election Cases," *New York Herald*, Feb. 6, 1866, 1. The *Herald* also reported that Kelso was being represented by John M. Richardson—the bumbling colonel who had led his "Mountain Rangers" to defeat at the Battle of Neosho in 1862. Despite Richardson being a lawyer who, as a former Missouri Secretary of State, would have known election law, this seems highly unlikely. A document in

Evidence in the Contested Election shows that by late January, Kelso had hired the firm of Lindenbower, McAfee & Phelps (154). House receives *Boyd vs. Kelso* evidence: *CG*, 39th Congress, 1st Sess., Dec. 12, 31; Feb. 6, 698; Feb.8, 755; March 2, 1147; March 12, 1333; March 26, 1652; April 17, 1866, 2008. Examples of contested election discussions on the floor: *CG*, 39th Congress, 1st Sess., Feb. 2, 1866, 610–14; Feb. 16, 1866, 887–95; Feb. 19, 1866, 923–30; Feb. 23, 1866, 991–1005; March 27, 1866, 1662. Testimony on the 17 nonresident soldiers: *Evidence in the Contested Election*, 145–46. Of the votes submitted by both sides from over forty military units, Kelso won 586 and Boyd 334. Boyd did somewhat better among troops stationed outside southwest Missouri. On the soldier vote as a campaign issue, see William E. Chandler, *The Soldier's Right to Vote. Who Opposes It? Who Favors It? Or, the Record of the McClellan Copperheads against Allowing the Soldier Who Fights, the Right to Vote While He Fights. Prepared for the Union Congressional Committee* (Washington, D.C.: Lemuel Towers, 1864); Oscar Osburn Winther, "The Soldier Vote in the Election of 1864," *New York History* 25, no. 4 (Oct. 1944): 440–58.

52. Benedict, *Compromise*, 147–50; 162–68; Foner, *Reconstruction*, 243–51; Allen C. Guelzo, *Reconstruction: A Concise History* (New York: Oxford University Press, 2018), 31–32.

53. Johnson's veto messages: *CG*, 39th Congress, 1st Sess., Feb. 19, 1866, 155–58; April 9, 1866, 1857–60. On the veto overrides: *CG*, 39th Congress, 1st Sess., April 9, 1866, 1861 (House); Benedict, *Compromise*, 157–58, 164–65.

54. *CG*, 39th Congress, 1st Sess., April 30, 1866, 2286–87; May 9, 1866, 2459.

55. *CG*, 39th Congress, 1st Sess., June 13, 1866, 2459. In the later Jim Crow era, however, the White South would both disenfranchise African Americans and maintain their states' full representation in Congress and the Electoral College.

56. *CG*, 39th Congress, 1st Sess., May 10, 1866, 2544–45, and see Benedict, *Compromise*, 183–84.

57. Foner, *Reconstruction*, 257–58; Gerard N. Magliocca, *American Founding Son: John Bingham and the Invention of the Fourteenth Amendment* (New York: New York University Press, 2013), 2, 121–24. It would be the foundation for transformational Supreme Court decisions on civil rights in the 1950s, reproductive rights in the 1970s, and marriage equality in the 2010s. Stevens, however, expected Congress, not the courts, to aggressively pursue equal rights (thanks to Michael Les Benedict for clarification on this point).

58. *Evidence in the Contested Election*, 1–8, 130–32.

59. Ibid., 17; 39th Congress, 1st Sess., House of Representatives, *Boyd vs. Kelso*, Report No. 88, ordered printed June 25, 1866, 1, 3, 4–5. The statute guiding (not exactly governing) the work of the Election Committee was passed in 1851: "An Act to Prescribe the Mode of Obtaining Evidence in Cases of Contested Elections," Feb. 19, 1851, *The Statutes at Large and Treaties of the United States of America*, Vol. 9, from Dec. 1, 1854, to March 3, 1851 (Boston, Mass., 1851), 568–70. See Henry C. Remnick, *The Powers in Congress in Respect to Membership and Elections* (privately

printed, 1929), 395–402. *CG*, 39th Congress, 1st Sess., June 25, 1866, 3399; *Patriot*, Supplement (June 28, 1866): 1.

60. D mss 10: 28; *CG*, 39th Congress, 1st Sess., July 13, 1866, 3793.

CHAPTER 13

1. D mss 10: 27, 29–30.

2. On the election of 1866 generally: Benedict, *Compromise*, 188–208; Foner, *Reconstruction*, 261–71. On the election in Missouri: Parrish, *Missouri Under Radical Rule*, 78–93; "Address of the Radical Union Executive Committee," *[St. Louis, Mo.] Democrat* (May 13, 1866): 2; "To the Radical Union Clubs," ibid. (June 20): 1. On the election in Missouri's fourth district: "From Springfield, Mo.," *[St. Louis, Mo.] Democrat* (Feb. 24, 1866): 1; "The Southwest Awake. The Voice of Greene County," ibid. (March 13, 1866): 3; "The Unionists of Dallas County. Where They Stand," ibid. (April 3, 1866): supplement, 1; "The Meeting Monday," *Patriot* (July 19, 1866): 2; "From Southwest Missouri," *[St. Louis, Mo.] Republican* (July 23, 1866): 4; "From Southwest Missouri," ibid. (July 27, 1866): 2.

3. On Gravely: "The Standard Bearer in the Fourth District. Sketch of His Life, Services, and Traits," *[St. Louis, Mo.] Democrat* (Oct. 18, 1866): 5; "Our Candidates," *Patriot* (Aug. 9, 1866): 2; "Gravely, Joseph Jackson," *Biographical Directory of the U.S. Congress*, http://bioguide.congress.gov; Benedict, *Compromise*, 359, 364. Reports from county caucuses: *Patriot* (July 5, 1866): 1 (Taney); July 19, 1866, 2 (Christian, Webster, Greene, Wright); Aug. 2, 1866, 2 (Jasper, Barry, Stone). Fourth District election: "Missouri Election Returns," *[St. Louis, Mo.] Republican* (Nov. 17, 1866): 2; *The [Carthage, Mo.] Weekly Banner* (Dec. 22, 1866): 1, estimated that Gravely had carried the district by 5,000 votes.

4. "From the Southwest. Gov. Fletcher at Springfield, Mo.," *[St. Louis, Mo.] Democrat* (July 17, 1866): 2; "From Laclede County," *Patriot* (July 19, 1866): 4; [no title], *Patriot* (May 10, 1866, 2; "The Hon. John R. Kelso, *Warrensburg Standard*, rpt. in the *Patriot* (July 19, 1866): 4; "From Illinois," *Patriot* (July 26, 1866): 1; "Hon. J. R. Kelso," ibid. (July 5, 1866): 2.

5. "From Southwest Missouri," *[St. Louis, Mo.] Republican* (July 27, 1866): 2; "The Meeting Monday," *Patriot* (July 19, 1866): 2.

6. "From Southwest Missouri," *[St. Louis, Mo.] Republican* (July 23, 1866): 4; D mss 10: 29; "The District Convention," *Patriot* (Aug. 2, 1866): 1; "Nomination for Congress," ibid., 2; "Letter from Colonel Boyd," ibid. (Aug. 9, 1866): 2.

7. "Should Johnson Be Impeached?" *[St. Louis, Mo.] Democrat* (Nov. 14, 1866): 2; "Springfield, Mo.," ibid. (Nov. 28, 1866): 1; "The Washington News," ibid. (Dec. 5, 1866): 1; Benedict, *Compromise*, 202, 204–206; Foner, *Reconstruction*, 264–65.

8. *The Southern Loyalists' Convention: Call for a Convention of Southern Unionists, to Meet at Independence Hall, Philadelphia, on Monday, the Third Day of September, 1866*, Tribune Tracts No. 2 (Philadelphia?, 1866); Benedict, *Compromise*, 210–11.

9. "To the Republican Members of Congress," *[St. Louis, Mo.] Democrat* (Jan. 7, 1867): 1. On Congress and the economy, see Benedict, *Compromise*, 49–54, 262–65. Kelso's votes on the money question: *CG*, 39th Cong., 1st Sess., Dec. 18, 1865, 75; March 16, 1866, 1467; 2nd Sess., Dec. 10, 1866, 49; Dec. 17, 1866, 150. There were also differences among radical Republicans on the tariff. The radical *[St. Louis, Mo.] Democrat* took a moderate position on tariffs ("Too Much Protection" [Feb. 19, 1867]: 2). Kelso voted for a mild tariff bill at the end of the first session (*CG*, 39th Cong., 1st Sess., July 10, 1866, 3725) and was criticized for it in the press ("From Southwest Missouri," *[St. Louis, Mo.] Republican* (July 27, 1866, 2). He voted against a tariff bill in the second session (*CG*, 39th Cong., 2nd Sess., Feb. 2, 1867, 1658). In later years, he would come to loathe protective tariffs of any sort.

10. Patrick W. Riddleberger, *1866: The Critical Year Revisited* (Carbondale: Southern Illinois University Press, 1979), 230–49; Trefousse, *Impeachment*, 50.

11. "Impeachment of the President," *New York Tribune* (Jan. 8, 1867): 4.

12. "Washington . . . Caucus of Radical Representatives," *New York Herald*, Dec. 3, 1866, 5; *CG*, 39th Cong., 2nd Sess., Dec. 17, 1866, 154; Trefousse, *Impeachment*, 54.

13. "Washington—The Republican Caucus," *New York Tribune* (Jan. 7. 1867): 4; "Congress," *[Concord] New Hampshire Patriot* (Jan. 9, 1867): 2.

14. "The News," *New York Herald* (Jan. 7, 1867): 4.

15. *CG*, 39th Cong., 2nd Sess., Jan. 7, 1867, 319.

16. *CG*, 39th Cong., 2nd Sess., Jan. 7, 1867, 319. For a garbled press account, see "Washington: Important Proceedings in Congress," *New York Herald* (Jan. 8, 1867): 3. The best historical account of the Loan-Kelso impeachment resolutions as a prelude to Ashley's (though it is just a brief synopsis) is probably Trefousse, *Impeachment*, 54.

17. "The Impeachment of the President," *New York Tribune* (Jan. 8, 1867): 4; "The Hon. Mr. Loan's Attack upon the President," *New York Herald* (Jan. 16, 1867): 4; "The Proposition for Impeachment," *Baltimore Sun* (Jan. 11, 1867): 2. The *Herald* article was written after Loan linked Johnson to the Lincoln assassination (see below).

18. *CG*, 39th Cong., 2nd Sess., Jan. 7, 1867, 319.

19. Ibid.; "Washington," *New York Tribune* (Jan. 8, 1867): 1.

20. *CG*, 39th Cong., 2nd Sess., Jan. 7, 1867, 320; "Washington," *New York Tribune* (Jan. 8, 1867): 1.

21. *CG*, 39th Cong., 2nd Sess., Jan. 7, 1867, 320; "The President's Impeachment—The Initial Step Taken in Congress," *New York Herald* (Jan. 8, 1867): 6.

22. *CG*, 39th Cong., 2nd Sess., Jan. 7, 1867, 320–21; Barclay, *Barclay's Digest*, 137; *CG*, 39th Cong., 2nd Sess., Jan. 7, 1867, 320; "The President's Impeachment—The Initial Step Taken in Congress," *New York Herald* (Jan. 8, 1867): 6.

23. *CG*, 39th Cong., 2nd Sess., Jan. 7, 1867, 321.

24. On Ashley as the "Great Impeacher," see for ex. [no title], *[New Haven, Conn.] Columbian Register* (Feb. 9, 1867): 2; "Ashley, the Impeacher," *New Orleans Times*

(Aug. 14, 1867): 4; "Ashley and Forney," *New York Herald* (Oct. 6, 1867): 6; "A Scheme Against Ohio," *[Macon, Ga.] Macon Weekly Telegraph* (Nov. 22, 1867): 5; "The Amiable Ashley," *[Concord] New Hampshire Patriot and State Gazette* (Dec. 11, 1867): 2. The *St. Louis Democrat*, in "Impeachment" (Jan. 16, 1867): 1, saluted Loan as "the first member of Congress to offer resolutions for the impeachment of the President." "Review of the Week. The Action of Congress" (Jan. 12, 1867): 2, misidentified Kelso as Kelley; "Night Dispatches," [Galveston, Tex.] *Flake's Bulletin* (Jan. 15, 1867): 5 ("Retzer").

25. *CG*, 39th Cong., 2nd Sess., Jan. 14, 443–44.
26. Ibid., 444–46.
27. Howard Means, *The Avenger Takes His Place: Andrew Johnson and the 45 Days That Changed the Nation* (Orlando, Fla.: Harcourt, 2006), 10–33; *Impeachment Investigation Testimonies Taken before the Judiciary Committee of the House of Representatives. Investigation of Charges against Andrew Johnson, Second Session, Thirty-Ninth Congress, and First Session, Fortieth Congress, 1867* (Washington, D.C.: Government Printing Office, 1867), 1194–207.
28. Criticism of Loan: "The Hon. Mr. Loan's Attack upon the President," *New York Herald* (Jan. 16, 1867): 4, and "Politicians Schooling the People," *Baltimore Sun* (Jan. 16, 1867): 2; both articles make the comparison to Stevens. "Speech of Mr. Loan," *[St. Louis, Mo.] Democrat* (Jan. 21, 1867): 1.
29. *CG*, 39th Cong., 2nd Sess., Jan. 28, 1867, 807–808; Feb. 4, 1867, 991.
30. *CG*, 39th Cong., 2nd Sess., Jan. 28, 1867, 761. The full text of Kelso's proposed amendment was printed in "Kelso's Resolution," *Patriot* (Feb. 14, 1867): 1.
31. "Kelso's Resolution," *Patriot* (Feb. 14, 1867): 1.
32. Ibid., 1; Foner, *Reconstruction*, 255–56; Trefousse, *Impeachment*, 88–89; Parrish, *Missouri under Radical Rule*, 274–77. For examples of women's suffrage being discussed on the House floor, see *CG*, 39th Cong., 1st Sess., Jan. 10, 15, 23, 24, 26, and Feb. 7, 1866, 177, 238, 380, 409, 449, 714; 2nd Sess., Jan. 15, 1867, 472. Kelso's colleague from Missouri, Thomas E. Noell, representing the state's third district, though a conservative on other issues (he jumped from the Republican to the Democratic party for the campaign of 1866), would offer a resolution against voter discrimination on the bases of sex a week after Kelso offered his resolution: *CG*, 39th Cong., 2nd Sess., Feb. 4, 1867, 991.
33. "Kelso's Resolution," *Patriot* (Feb. 14, 1867): 1.
34. Foner, *Reconstruction*, 144–48; Benedict, *Compromise*, 137–38, 257–58.
35. *CG*, 39th Cong., 2nd sess., Jan. 28, 1867, 761; "Kelso's Resolution," *Patriot* (Feb. 14, 1867): 1.
36. Benedict, *Compromise*, 225–57; 125–26.
37. Ibid., 227–28.
38. Ibid., 227–31.
39. *CG*, 39th Cong., 2nd Sess., Feb. 13, 1867, 1213–15.

40. David Donald, in *The Politics of Reconstruction, 1863–1867* (Baton Rouge: Louisiana State University Press, 1968), explained that it is difficult to find "objective criteria for separating" Republican congressmen into factional groupings and that no single vote could "serve as a clear-cut test of Radicalism" (28, 29). Examining the roll-call tabulations of every vote taken in the second session of the 39th Congress, however, he found six votes that revealed significant patterns of bloc voting, even if some of these votes, by themselves, were on "small and even procedural matters" (29–30). With these six votes he sorted the Republicans into five factions: Ultra-Radicals, Stevens Radicals, Moderates, and Conservatives. He listed Kelso as a Conservative (Appendix IV, 103). Kelso, however, happened to be absent or not voting for three of his six test votes. The other three votes all pertained to the choice between the Blaine amendment and the Stevens version of the military government bill on Feb. 13, 1867. Benedict, in *Compromise*, using more sophisticated statistical methods, sorted the members of the second session of the 39th Congress into six categories: Democrats and Johnson Conservatives, Conservative Republicans, Conservative Centrist Republicans, Stevens Radical Republicans, and Radicals Voting against Stevens to Open the Military Government Bill to Radical Amendment. He lists Kelso as a Conservative Centrist Republican (List 11, Group 2, p. 354). Of the four test votes he finds most indicative of Conservative Centrist Republicans, Kelso happened to be absent or not voting for three of them. His designation as a "conservative centrist" seems to rest on a single vote for the Blaine amendment on Feb. 13, 1867.

41. Benedict, *Compromise*, 231; Albert Castel, *The Presidency of Andrew Johnson* (Lawrence, Kans.: Regents Press of Kansas, 1979), 108–109.

42. *CG*, 39th Cong., 2nd Sess., Feb. 18, 1867, 1334–37; Benedict, *Compromise*, 232.

43. *CG*, 39th Cong., 2nd Sess., Feb. 12, 1867, 1177.

44. Ibid., 1213–15.

45. Ibid., 1315–40, 1399–1400 (Feb. 20, 1867, vote); Benedict, *Compromise*, 234–40; Foner, *Reconstruction*, 273–76.

46. Benedict, *Compromise*, 242–43; Foner, *Reconstruction*, 275–80.

47. "Reconstruction—A Victory," *[St. Louis, Mo.] Democrat* (Feb. 22, 1867): 2; "Well Done," ibid. (March 5, 1867): 1; "At Home Again," *Patriot* (March 14, 1867): 1.

48. D mss 11, inside cover.

49. Guelzo, *Reconstruction*, 113–14.

50. Lobbyists on the House floor: *CG*, 39th Cong., 1st Sess., June 25, 1866, 3403; 2nd Sess., Jan. 28, 1867, 808. Ellis, *Sights and Secrets of the National Capital*, 183–214; "More Corruption in Washington. Extraordinary Charges of Fraud against the Post Office Department," *Cincinnati Daily Gazette* (Dec. 21, 1868): 5; "Washington," *New York Herald* (Dec. 22, 1868): 1. See generally Mark Wahlgren Summers, *The Era of Good Stealings* (New York: Oxford University Press, 1993), 3–45. Postmaster General Randall explained away the post office corruption charges,

but was involved in a scheme to bribe senators during the Johnson impeachment (see Summers, 36–37).

51. D mss 10: 34–35.

52. Ibid., 35. On the Credit Mobilier scandal see Summers, *Era of Good Stealings*, 504, 226–27, 231–37; Richard White, "Information, Markets, and Corruption: Transcontinental Railroads in the Gilded Age," *Journal of American History* 90, no. 1 (June 2003): 19–43; Paul Kens, "The Credit Mobilier Scandal and the Supreme Court: Corporate Power, Corporate Person, and Government Control in the Mid-Nineteenth Century," *Journal of the Supreme Court* 34, no. 2 (2009): 170–82; Robert B. Mitchell, *Congress and the King of Frauds: Corruption and the Credit Mobilier Scandal at the Dawn of the Gilded Age* (Roseville, Minn.: Edinborough Press, 2018).

53. D mss 10: 26–27; Office of the Historian—Department of State, *Papers Relating to Foreign Affairs . . . to the First Session of the Thirty-Ninth Congress*, Correspondence: Sweden, https://history.state.gov/, documents, 192–219.

54. D mss 10: 27.

55. D mss 1: 27, 29–30.

56. Kelso, "Influences," in *Miscellaneous Writings*, 85–125; D mss 10: 27.

CHAPTER 14

1. D mss 11: [13], 20.

2. D mss 10: 30, 45; Holcombe, *History of Greene County, Missouri*, 741–74; Jonathan Fairbanks and Clyde Edwin Tuck, *Past and Present of Greene County, Missouri* (Indianapolis, Ind.: A. W. Bowen, 1915), 1: 211–13, 619.

3. Analysis of 1870 U.S. Census for Campbell Township (including Springfield), Greene County, Missouri (1,886 households, 1,417 property holders). By 1870, however, as discussed below, Kelso had moved to a different home 3.5 miles from downtown of Springfield (though still in Campbell Township).

4. "A Foul Murder," *Patriot* (Aug. 9, 1866): 2; Spencer P. Wright, 1860 U.S. Census, Benton Township, Webster County, Mo., family no. 327; "The Murder of Hiram Christian," *Patriot* (May 30, 1867): 2; Holcombe, *History of Greene County, Missouri*, 508–10. On continuing violence in the Ozarks after the war, see Blevins, *History of the Ozarks*, 2: 157–68.

5. D mss 11: 11.

6. D mss 10: 46–47; "Kelso Academy" [advertisement], *Patriot* (Aug. 1, 1867): 3. On the Board of Trustees: 1870 U.S. Census, Springfield, Campbell Township, Mo., family nos. 243 (Holland), 153 (Gilmore), 79 (Ingram), 211 (Vaughan), 244 (Sheppard); Holcombe, *History of Greene County, Missouri*, 479 (Ingram), 585 (Sheppard), 771 (Gilmore), 763 (Vaughan); Fairbanks and Tuck, *Past and Present of Greene County*, 2: 978, 1744–1748 (Holland); 1: 696 (Gilmore); 1: 359 (Sheppard); 1: 510 (Vaughan). In "Agricultural College," *Patriot* (Nov. 22, 1866): 3, the writer

discussed the plan to get a state agricultural college established at Springfield, and suggested that Kelso Academy, once incorporated, might be connected to it. Kelso was one of thirteen men calling for a meeting to discuss opening a college at Springfield ([no title], *Patriot* [July 25, 1867]: 3).

7. "Improvements in the City," *Patriot* (Sept. 20, 1866): 3: Kelso's college building was "fast approaching completion"; "Kelso Academy" [advertisement], *Patriot* (Nov. 1, 1866): 2; "Kelso Academy" [article], *Patriot* (Nov. 8, 1866): 3; "The Kelso Academy" [article], *Patriot* (Nov. 22, 1866): 3; "The Kelso Academy" [article], *Patriot* (March 21, 1867): 3; "Kelso Academy" [advertisement] (April 4, 1867): 2; "Kelso Academy" [advertisement], *Patriot* (July 25, 1867): 2. In his autobiography, D mss 10: 30, Kelso wrote that he rented the building to the public school district in 1866–67, which actually must have happened later, unless the public school met in the large new building and his Academy, taught by two teachers he had hired, met in one of the cottages. He also simplified the launch of the Academy by focusing only on the Sept. 1867 opening of the 1867–68 term.

8. "Kelso Academy" [advertisement], *Patriot* (July 25, 1867): 2.

9. Ibid.

10. D mss 10: 46; "First Annual Report of the Board of Education of the Public Schools of Springfield," *[Springfield, Mo.] Leader* (Aug. 20, 1868): 3 (hereafter, *Leader*), and see "Second Annual Report of the Public Schools of the City of Springfield," *Patriot* (Sept. 2, 1869): 3; "Our Public School," *Patriot* (Sept. 16, 1869): 3; "Our City Schools—A Word from the County Superintendent," *Patriot* (Dec. 23, 1869): 3.

11. Kelso, "To the Voters of the 4th Congressional District," *Patriot* (June 4, 1868): 2.

12. Parrish, *Missouri Under Radical Rule*, esp. 230–35; Andrew L. Slap, *The Doom of Reconstruction: The Liberal Republicans in the Civil War Era* (New York: Fordham University Press, 2006), 1–24; and see Samuel DeCanio, *Democracy and the Origins of the American Regulatory State* (New Haven, Conn.: Yale University Press, 2015), 78–87; Erik B. Alexander, "The Fate of Northern Democrats after the Civil War: Another Look at the Presidential Election of 1868," in Gary W. Gallagher and Rachel A. Sheldon, eds., *New Directions in Mid-Nineteenth-Century American Political History* (Charlottesville: University of Virginia Press, 2012), 188–205.

13. "Letter from the Hon. J. J. Gravely," *Patriot* (June 4, 1868): 9; J. P. Tracy, "A Card," *Patriot* (June 18, 1868): 2; "Capt. Kelso," *Patriot* (Sept. 24, 1868): 2.

14. "Kelso," *Leader* (June 11, 1868): 2; Kelso, "To the Voters of the 4th Congressional District," *Patriot* (June 4, 1868): 2; Kelso, "Reconstruction," *CG*, 39th Cong., 1st Sess., Feb. 7, 1866, 730–33.

15. Kelso, *Leader* (June 11, 1868): 2; Kelso, "To the Voters of the 4th Congressional District," *Patriot* (June 4, 1868): 2; "Kelso vs. Boyd," *Leader* (Sept. 24, 1868): 2.

16. "The Fourth Congressional District—Col. J. J. Gravely," *[Carthage, Mo.] Weekly Banner* (April 16, 1868): 2; "Col. J. J. Gravely for Congress in the 4th District," *[Bolivar, Mo.] Free Press* (June 25, 1868): 2.

17. "The Congressional Convention," *Patriot* (July 30, 1868): 2; "The Radical Convention," *Leader* (July 30, 1868): 3.

18. "The Congressional Convention," 2; "The Radical Convention," 3.

19. "The Congressional Convention," 2.

20. "The Radical Convention," 3 (on Boyd); "Radical County Convention. Hon. J. J. Gravely Vindicates his Course," *Leader* (Aug. 13, 1868): 3; D mss 11: 5, 7.

21. Thomas H. Coleman, *The Election of 1868: Democratic Effort to Regain Control* (New York: Octagon Books, 1971; orig. pub. 1933), 24–40.

22. *Official Proceedings of the National Democratic Convention, Held at New York, July 4–9, 1868* (Boston: Rockwell & Rollins, 1868), 58; *Proceedings of the National Union Republican Convention, Held at Chicago, May 20 and 21, 1868* (Chicago: Evening Journal Print, [1868]), 84; "Republican Convention," *Patriot* (July 16, 1868): 2; "The Congressional Convention," *Patriot* (July 30, 1868): 2. See also Coleman, *Election of 1868*, 24–40.

23. "Radical County Convention," 3; "From Springfield, Mo.," *[St. Louis, Mo.] Republican* (Aug. 14, 1868): 1.

24. D mss 11: 5. In the *Patriot*: "Colonel Gravely's Course" (Aug. 20, 1868): 2 (rpt. from the *[Neosho, Mo.] Tribune*); "The Congressional Canvass" (Aug. 20, 1868) (rpt. from the *[Bolivar, Mo.] Press*); "Enthusiastic Meeting in Old Christian" (Aug. 13, 1868): 2; "From Newton County" (Aug. 20, 1868): 2; "Radical Meeting in Polk" (Aug. 27, 1868): 3. In "Negro Suffrage—How to Deal with It" (July 2, 1868): 2, the *Patriot* urged that the suffrage question *not* be a test of party loyalty. See also "The Suffrage Question" (July 16, 1868): 1, and "Nigger Equality" (Sept. 10, 1868): 2.

25. "Kelso," *[Bolivar, Mo.] Free Press* (Sept. 24, 1868): 2. A Gravely-Kelso détente may have been engineered by Harrison J. Lindenbower, previously one of Gravely's staunchest advocates who became "the chief manager of the Kelso movement" ([No title], *Patriot* [March 25, 1869]: 2).

26. In the *Patriot*: "Southwestern Items" (Sept. 24, 1868): 1 (rpt. from *[Neosho, Mo.] Tribune*); "Your Kelso" (Sept. 17, 1868): 2; [no title] (Sept. 17, 1868): 2; "Capt. Kelso" (Sept. 24, 1868): 2; "The Gravely, Kelso & Co.'s Dicker with McAfee" (Oct. 1, 1868): 2 (rpt. from *[Mt. Vernon, Mo.] Fountain*); "Kelso" (Oct. 1, 1868): 2 (rpt. from *[Bolivar, Mo.] Free Press*).

27. In the *Leader*: "Hon. John R. Kelso" (Sept. 17, 1868): 2; "Boyd, Kelso, Fyan, Hendrick, Gilmore, and Baker" (Oct. 8, 1868): 2; "The Bondholder" (Sept. 24, 1868): 4; "Boyd and Kelso," 2; "New Radical Campaign Song" (Oct. 15, 1868): 4.

28. D mss 11: 4–5.

29. Ibid., 5–6. Mention of Kelso's September circular: [no title], *Patriot* (Sept. 17, 1868): 3; "Kelso vs. Boyd," *Leader* (Sept. 24, 1868): 2; "Kelso," *[Bolivar, Mo.] Free Press* (Sept. 24, 1868): 2; "Independent Candidate," *[Lebanon, Mo.] Chronicle*, rpt. in the *Patriot* (Oct. 1, 1868): 2. Kelso's itinerary: [no title], *Patriot* (Sept. 24, 1868): 3; "Public Speaking," *Patriot* (Oct. 8, 1868): 3. Poor attendance: "Kelso,"

Patriot (Oct. 22, 1868): 2; "From Barry County," *Patriot* (Oct. 29, 1868): 1; [no title], *[Mt. Vernon, Mo.] Fountain*, rpt. in the *Patriot* (Oct. 29, 1868): 2.

30. In the *Leader*: "Hon. John R. Kelso" (Sept. 17, 1868): 2; [no title] (Oct. 8, 1868): 2; "Kelso vs. Boyd" (Sept. 24, 1868): 2; "Boyd or Kelso" (Oct. 1, 1868): 2; "Boyd, Kelso, Fyan, Hendrick, Gilmore, and Baker" (Oct. 8, 1868). On the bonfire brawl: "Free Speech in Springfield," *Leader* (July 16), rpt. in *[St. Louis, Mo.] Republican* (July 25, 1868): 2.

31. Kelso, "To the Voters of the 4th Congressional District," *Patriot* (June 4, 1868): 2; "Kelso," *[Bolivar, Mo.] Free Press* (Sept. 24, 1868): 2; "Your Kelso," *Patriot* (Sept. 17, 1868): 2; [no title], *Patriot* (Sept. 24, 1868): 3; "Independent Candidate," *[Lebanon, Mo.] Chronicle*, rpt. in the *Patriot* (Oct. 1, 1868): 2; "From Barry County," *Patriot* (Oct. 29, 1868): 1; "John R. Kelso," *Free Press* (Oct. 15, 1868): 2.

32. "Capt. Kelso," *Patriot* (Sept. 24, 1868): 2; "Kelso," *[Bolivar, Mo.] Free Press* (Sept. 24, 1868): 2.

33. "Democracy Skunked in the Southwest," *Patriot* (Nov. 12, 1868): 2 (table of election results in the fourth congressional district, by county, preliminary returns); "Official Returns of the Congressional Vote in the 4th District," *Patriot* (Jan. 21, 1869): 2.

34. D mss 11: 7.

35. "The Protest of the Soreheads," *Patriot* (Aug. 4, 1870): 2, (and other short untitled articles on the same page); "The True Way," *Patriot* (Aug. 11, 1870): 2; "Remains of Sam Kneeland," *Leader* (Nov. 22, 1877): 2; Parrish, *Missouri under Radical Rule*, 279–324. On the Liberal Republicans nationally, see Heather Cox Richardson, *The Death of Reconstruction: Race, Labor, and Politics in the Post-Civil War North, 1865–1901* (Cambridge, Mass.: Harvard University Press, 2001), 101–5, 119–20; Slap, *Doom of Reconstruction*.

36. [No title] (announcement of suffrage meeting), *Leader* (Jan. 6, 1870): 3, and *Patriot*, 3.

37. "Sorosorial," *Leader* (Jan. 20, 1870): 3; "Card from Mrs. Mary Phelps," *Leader* (Sept. 24, 1868): 2. On Phelps: "One More Appeal to the Generous Citizens of St. Louis," *[St. Louis, Mo.] Republican* (Feb. 23, 1865), rpt. in Siddali, ed., *Missouri's War*, 152–54; *CG*, 39th Cong., 1st Sess., July 28, 1866, Appendix, 444; David Hopkins Jr., "A Lonely Wandering Refugee: Displaced Whites in the Trans-Mississippi West During the American Civil War, 1861–1869 (PhD diss., Wayne State University, 2015), 338–40; "The Orphan's Fair," *Patriot* (Nov. 2, 1865): 3; "The Orphan's Home," *Leader* (July 25, 1867): 3; "Gift Concert," *Leader* (Aug. 1, 1867): 3; L. P. Bennett and Mary C. Vaughan, *Woman's Work in the Civil War: A Record of Heroism, Patriotism, and Patience* (Philadelphia, Pa.: Zeigler, McCurdy, and Co., 1867), 520–21; "Jefferson City. Female Suffragists and Their Gallants," *[St. Louis, Mo.] Republican* (Feb. 4, 1869): 3; "Jefferson City. Lovely Ladies, Law and Logic," *Republican* (Feb. 5, 1869): 3; "Woman's Suffrage," *[Jefferson City, Mo.] People's Tribune* (Feb. 10, 1869): 2; "Woman's Suffrage. Convention at Mercantile Hall," *[St.*

Louis, Mo.] Republican (Oct. 7, 1869): 3; 1870 U.S. Census, Campbell Township, Greene County, Mo., family no. 1064; "The Body of General Lyon—How It was Buried," *Patriot* (Dec. 17, 1874): 1; "Death of Mrs. Mary Phelps," *Leader* (Jan. 31, 1878): 3; Holcombe, *History of Greene County, Missouri*, 822–23.

38. Monica Cook Morris, "The History of Woman Suffrage in Missouri," *MHR* 25, no. 1 (Oct. 1930): 67–82; Parrish, *Missouri Under Radical Rule*, 274–78; Mark H. Neill, "The Women's Rights Movement in Missouri," *Journal of the Missouri Bar* (March/April 2011): 114–19 (orig. pub. 1973); Ellen Carol DuBois, *Feminism and Suffrage: The Emergence of an Independent Women's Movement in America, 1848–1869* (Ithaca, N.Y.: Cornell University Press, 1978); Laura Staley, "Suffrage Movement in St. Louis during the 1870s," *Gateway Heritage* 3, no. 4 (Spring 1983): 34–41; Suzanne M. Marilley, *Woman Suffrage and the Origins of Liberal Feminism in the United States, 1820–1920* (Cambridge, Mass., 1996), 66–99. See also LeeAnn Whites, "A Tale of Two Minors: Women's Rights on the Border," in LeeAnn Whites, Mary C. Neth, and Gary R. Kremer, eds., *Women in Missouri History: In Search of Power and Influence* (Columbia: University of Missouri Press, 2004), 101–18; Jean Carnahan, *If These Walls Could Talk: The Story of Missouri's First Families* (Jefferson City: Missouri Mansion Preservation Inc., 1998), 37–47; Jerena East Giffen, *Mary, Mary, Quite . . .: The Life and Times of Mary Whitney Phelps, 1812–1878* (Peabody, Mass.: Giffen Enterprises, 2008).

39. "Woman's Rights and Wrongs," *Patriot* (Jan. 13, 1870): 3; "Sorosorial," *Leader* (Jan. 13, 1870): 3.

40. "The Sorosis," *Patriot* (Jan. 20, 1870): 3; "Sorosorial," *Leader* (Jan. 20, 1870): 3.

41. "Sorosorial," *Leader* (Feb. 3, 1870): 3. Mrs. Stephens could have been any one of four women of that name (1870 U.S. Census, Campbell Township, Greene County, Missouri, family nos. 122, 1119, 1120, 1357); Mrs. Eversoll was either Tabitha, 45, or one of her daughters-in-law: Augusta, 26, or Julia, 24 (family no. 1047).

42. Lydia Fuller, "Woman Suffrage in South Missouri," *Woman's Journal* 5 (1874): 204; Marilley, *Woman Suffrage*, 68–82.

43. Kelso, "Dangers that Threaten the People," delivered, extempore, at the Spiritualistic Camp-meeting at San Jose, Calif., June 7, 1885, in Kelso, "Miscellaneous Writings," 378.

44. Holcombe, *History of Greene County, Missouri*, 477; "Arrest of a Bloomer," and "Woman Suffrage. Convention at Mercantile Hall Yesterday," *[St. Louis, Mo.] Republican* (Oct. 7, 1869): 3; "Southwest Items," *Leader* (April 8, 1869): 2, and "Southwestern Items," *Patriot*, both reprinting an item from the *Marshfield Yeoman*. See also "The Reform Dress," *Leader* (Sept. 2, 1869): 1, rpt. from the *Revolution*, Susan B. Anthony's suffrage journal. On the Bloomer costume: Robert E. Riegel, "Women's Clothes and Women's Rights," *American Quarterly* 15, no. 3 (Autumn 1963): 310–401; Amy Kesselman, "The 'Freedom Suit': Feminism and Dress Reform in the United States, 1848–1875," *Gender and Society* 5, no. 4 (Dec. 1991): 495–510; "'We'll Fight for Nature-Light, Truth-Light and Sunlight, against

a World in Swaddling Clothes': Reconsidering the Aesthetic Dress Movement and Dress Reform in Nineteenth Century America," *Past Imperfect* 13 (2007): 108–33.

45. Holcombe, *History of Greene County, Missouri*, 477; D mss 10: 47.

46. D mss 10: 47; 1860 U.S. Census, Campbell Township, Greene Co., Mo., family no. 951 (Chandler). On "grass widows": John Russell Bartlett, *Dictionary of Americanisms* (Boston: Little, Brown, Mass., 1859), 2nd ed., 179; William L. Snyder, *The Geography of Marriage: or, Legal Perplexities of Wedlock in the United States* (New York: G. P. Putnam and Sons, 1889), 173. Carnahan, *If Walls Could Talk*, 42, and Giffen, *Mary, Mary, Quite*, 69–70, briefly mention Phelps's estrangement from her husband.

47. Kelso, "Marriage," in "Miscellaneous Writings," 128, 146–47, 160, 164, 165.

48. Kelso, "Marriage," in "Miscellaneous Writings," 170–72. See also Kelso, "Dangers that Threaten the People," in "Miscellaneous Writings," 383 ("free-love"). On "free love" see John C. Spurlock, *Free Love: Marriage and Middle Class Radicalism in America, 1825–1860* (New York: New York University Press, 1988); Martin Henry Blat, *Free Love and Anarchism: The Biography of Ezra Heywood* (Urbana: University of Illinois, 1989); Helen Lefkowitz Horowitz, *Rereading Sex: Battles Over Sexual Knowledge and Suppression in Nineteenth-Century America* (New York: Alfred A. Knopf, 2002); Joanne E. Passet, *Sex Radicals and the Quest for Women's Equality* (Urbana: University of Illinois Press, 2003); Wendy Hayden, "(R)Evolutionary Rhetorics: Science and Sexuality in Nineteenth-Century Free-Love Discourse," *Rhetoric Review* 10, no. 2 (2010): 111–28; Patricia Cline Cohen, "The 'Anti-Marriage Theory' of Thomas and Mary Gove Nichols," *Journal of the Early Republic* 34, no. 1 (Spring 2014): 1–20.

49. D mss 10: 48.

50. Ibid., 47; D mss 11: 27–28.

51. D mss 11: 28.

52. D mss 10: 46.

53. D mss 11: 8–9; Fairbanks and Tuck, *Past and Present of Greene County, Missouri*, 1: 358, 412.

54. "Select School," [advertisement], *Patriot* (Dec. 10, 1868): 2; see in the same issue the editor's endorsement on p. 2. The school opened on Jan. 11, 1869. D mss 11: 12–13, 23.

55. D mss 11: 11–[13]; Fairbanks and Tuck, *Past and Present of Greene County, Missouri*, 1: 619; "The Academy," *Leader* (March 9, 1871): 3; "A Convent," *Patriot* (Aug. 10, 1871): 3. Kelso's property was listed in the "Sale List of Delinquent Lands, for the Year 1869," *Patriot* (March 9, 1871): 1. Kelso's farm would be sold to pay his remaining debts: "Trustee's Sale," *Patriot* (Nov. 14, 1872): 4.

56. D mss 10: 47–48.

57. D mss 11:30–31; 1870 U.S. Census, Buffalo, Dallas County, Mo., family no. 21 (Hovey); [no title], *Patriot* (May 20, 1869): 2 (courthouse). Hovey was appointed architect and superintendent for the new courthouse in 1868; the completed building, costing $17,500, opened in June 1870. It was a two-story brick

building, 44 by 60 feet, with a large cupola. It would be featured in Thomas Hart Benton's painting, "County Politics," painted in 1965, apparently from a photograph, since the building had burned down ten years earlier. "Thomas Hart Benton and Dallas County, Missouri," Dallas County Historical Society, http://dallascountymohistory.weebly.com

58. D mss 11: 32.

59. Ibid., 28, 30, 32.

60. Ibid., 27.

61. Ibid., 18–19.

62. Ibid., 19–20.

63. Ibid., 20; "Died," *Patriot* (Sept. 8, 1870): 3 (Freddie's death notice); another item on the same page misidentifies Freddie as John R. Kelso Jr.

64. D mss 11: 21–22.

65. Ibid., 24.

66. Ibid., 25.

67. Ibid., 26; "Self Destruction: A Lad of Fourteen Years Deliberately Takes His Own Life," *Leader* (Sept. 22, 1870): 3; "A Young Lad Commits Suicide. A Sad Scene at His House. Verdict of the Coroner's Jury," *Patriot* (Sept. 22, 1870): 3. The newspaper accounts, working from the same coroner's report, misidentify the deceased as John R. Kelso Jr.

68. D mss 11: 22.

69. Ibid., 28.

CHAPTER 15

1. Architect of the Capitol, website, https://www.aoc.gov/art/other-paintings-and-murals/westward-course-empire-takes-its-way; Ellis, *Sights and Secrets of the National Capitol*, 106–7.

2. D mss 12: 2, 8–9.

3. D mss 11: 36, 37, 38, 40.

4. Ibid., 44–45.

5. D mss 12: 4.

6. Ibid., 4–5. Kelso mentions his "indomitable will" in another context, D mss 8: 7.

7. D mss 12: 9; "Colonel John R. Kelso," *Sacramento Daily Union* (May 9, 1872): 2; "Failed to Connect," ibid. (May 11, 1872): 2. See Peter Cherches, "Star Course: Popular Lectures and the Marketing of Celebrity in Nineteenth-Century America" (PhD diss., New York University, 1997); for a discussion of the celebrity lecture season in 1873–74, see esp. 139–55. On the culture of lecturing more generally, see Tom F. Wright, *Lecturing the Atlantic: Speech, Print, and the Anglo-American Commons* (New York: Oxford University Press, 2017), introduction and chap. 1.

8. "From Col. John R. Kelso," *Patriot* (Jan. 29, 1874): 3. Kelso visited the War Department in 1881, but at the time only government employees could get access to the military records (D mss 14: 22).

9. Kelso, "Influences," in "Miscellaneous Writings," 85–125, esp. 110, 114. See Charles E. Rosenberg, "The Bitter Fruit: Heredity, Disease, and Social Thought in Nineteenth-Century America," *Perspectives in American History*, Vol. 8 (Cambridge, Mass.: Harvard University, 1974), 189–235.

10. "Influences" in "Miscellaneous Writings," esp. 98–108.

11. D mss 14: 15–16; Timothy Gilfoyle, "'America's Greatest Criminal Barracks': The Tombs and the Experience of Criminal Justice in New York City, 1838–1897," *Journal of Urban History* 29, no. 5 (July 2003): 525–54.

12. "Marriage" in "Works," esp. 250.

13. D mss 11: 46.

14. Ibid., 53.

15. Ibid., 53, 56-7; I have not rendered his underlining in italics because it is unknown whether it was in the original letter. Missouri Divorce Records, http://thelibrary. springfield.missouri.org/lochist/records/d1873.htm; "Divorce," *Patriot* (Feb. 5, 1874): 3.

16. John R. Kelso, "The Lock of Hair," in "Works," 59, and "Miscellaneous Writings," 406; "Dost Thou Remember, Mima," in "Works," 48–49, and "To Mima" in "Miscellaneous Writings," 421; "To Adelia," in "Works," 56–57, and "Miscellaneous Writings," 262; "To the False Wife," in "Miscellaneous Writings," 56.

17. D mss 11: 27–28; "The Better Land," in "Works," 42, and "Miscellaneous Writings,", 6–7.

18. D mss 11: 20–21, 27-28.

19. Ibid., 29; "The Devil's Defense," in "Works," 63–125, esp. 86, 65–66.

20. "The Devil's Defense," in "Works," 82.

21. D mss 11: 29; "The Devil's Defense," in "Works," 91, 96, 123.

22. D mss 12: 14–15.

23. Ibid., 17, 28–29.

24. Ibid., 29–30.

25. Ibid., 25.

26. Ibid., 36.

27. D mss 11: 34–35, 12: 36; Wallace Finney [?], "Florella A. Kelso [Finney]," typescript, Trudie Sheffield Collection (privately held), written sometime after her death in 1940, probably by her son, and paraphrasing Florella's "autobiography," which I have not been able to locate. On Lynn A. Finney, see *A Memorial and Biographical History of the Counties of Merced, Stanislaus, Calaveras, Tuolumne and Mariposa, California* (Chicago: Lewis Pub. Co, 1892), 404. Lynn and Florella married on Sept. 8, 1873.

28. D mss 12: 18–22.

29. Ibid., 37–38. James Burney was the Stanislaus County School Superintendent from 1872–1876 (L. C. Branch, *History of Stanislaus County, California* [San Francisco, 1881], 253), and a trustee of the Methodist Episcopal Church (George H. Tinkham, *History of Stanislaus County* [Los Angeles: Historic Record Co., 1921], 114).

30. 1880 U.S. Census, Empire Township, Stanislaus Co., Calif., family no. 74; John R. Kelso, *Deity Analyzed in Six Lectures* (New York, 1883); John R. Kelso, *The Bible Analyzed in Twenty Lectures* (New York, 1884), vi, [9]. An edition of *Deity Analyzed* along with *The Devil's Defense* was advertised for sale a year earlier (*Boston Investigator*, April 19, 1882), but no copies seem to have survived.

31. Albert Post, *Popular Freethought in America, 1825–1860* (New York: Columbia University Press, 1943), 76; Kelso, "Thomas Paine," in "Miscellaneous Writings," 184–209, esp. 185, 191, 197, 208; "Invocation to Paine," ibid., 210–11.

32. Orvin Larson, *American Infidel: Robert G. Ingersoll: A Biography* (New York: Citadel Press, 1962), esp. 129; Kelso, "Thomas Paine," in "Miscellaneous Writings," 184; Nancy Prattler, "Petaluma Letter," *Sonoma Democrat* (June 1881): 2. On Ingersoll see also Paul Stob, "Religious Conflict and Intellectual Agency: Robert Ingersoll's Contributions to American Thought and Culture," *Rhetoric and Public Affairs* 16, no. 4 (2013): 719–52; Susan Jacoby, *The Great Agnostic: Robert Ingersoll and American Freethought* (New Haven, Conn.: Yale University Press, 2014).

33. Marshall G. Brown and Gordon Stein, eds., *Freethought in the United States: A Descriptive Bibliography* (Westport, Conn.: Greenwood Press., 1978), 47–61. See Sidney Warren, *American Freethought, 1860–1914* (New York: Columbia University Press, 1943); James Turner, *Without God, Without Creed: The Origins of Unbelief in America* (Baltimore, Md.: Johns Hopkins University Press, 1985); Evelyn A. Kirkley, *Rational Mothers and Infidel Gentlemen: Gender and American Atheism, 1865–1915* (Syracuse, N.Y.: Syracuse University Press, 2000); Leigh Eric Schmidt, *Village Atheists: How America's Unbelievers Made Their Way in a Godly Nation* (Princeton, N.J.: Princeton University Press, 2016).

34. [Masthead], *Truth Seeker* (Jan. 1874), 1: "Devoted to Science, Morals, Free Thought, Free Discussion, Liberalism, Sexual Equality, Labor Reform, Progression, Free Education, and Whatever Tends to Emancipate and Elevate the Human Race," and "Opposed to Priestcraft, Ecclesiasticism, Dogmas, Creeds, False Theology, Superstition, Bigotry, Ignorance, Monopolies, Aristocracies, Privileged Classes, Tyranny, Oppression, and Everything That Degrades or Burdens Mankind Mentally or Physically." On the *Boston Investigator*, see Grasso, *Skepticism and American Faith*, 331–46; On Bennett and the *Truth Seeker*, see George A. MacDonald, *Fifty Years of Freethought: Being the Story of The Truth Seeker, with the Natural History of Its Third Editor* (New York: Truth Seeker Co., 1929). The *Investigator* had one agent in Missouri (St. Louis) and six in California (including one in Stockton) by 1870 (Jan. 5, 1870, 288). Freethought lecturer B. F. Underwood "found quite a large number of intelligent and earnest Freethinkers" at Modesto in the summer of 1873 ("A Letter from B. F. Underwood," *Investigator* [July 30, 1873]: 2).

35. On the Deists see especially James A. Herrick, *The Radical Rhetoric of the English Deists: The Discourse of Skepticism, 1680–1750* (Columbia: University of South Carolina Press, 1997). On Spinoza and the radical Enlightenment, see esp. Roy A. Warrisville and Walter Sundberg, *The Bible in Modern Culture: Theology and Historical-Critical Method from Spinoza to Käsemann* (Grand Rapids, Mich.: Wm. B. Eerdmanns Pub. Co., 1995); Jonathan I. Israel, *Radical Enlightenment: Philosophy and the Making of Modernity, 1650–1750* (New York: Oxford University Press, 2001). Spinoza was in effect reviving the stance of Epicurus (341–270 BCE), who contended that religion was primarily about priests manipulating people by institutionalizing dogmas and rituals that exploited a superstitious fear of the gods.

36. This paragraph greatly simplifies a rich and complicated history. On the Enlightenment see esp. Peter Gay, *The Enlightenment: An Interpretation*, Vol. 1, *The Rise of Modern Paganism* (New York: Alfred A. Knopf, 1966), and Vol. 2, *The Science of Freedom* (New York: Alfred A. Knopf, 1969); Henry F. May, *The Enlightenment in America* (New York: Oxford University Press, 1976); Roy S. Porter and Mikuláš Teich, eds., *The Enlightenment in National Context* (Cambridge: Cambridge University Press, 1981); Samuel Fleischacker, *What Is Enlightenment?* (London: Routledge, 2013); and Caroline Winterer, *American Enlightenments: Pursuing Happiness in the Age of Reason* (New Haven, Conn.: Yale University Press, 2016). On biblical criticism see esp. Hans Frei, *The Eclipse of Biblical Narrative: A Study in Eighteenth and Nineteenth Century Hermeneutics* (New Haven, Conn.: Yale University Press, 1974); R. E. Clements, "The Study of the Old Testament," in Ninian Smart et al., eds., *Nineteenth Century Religious Thought in the West*, Vol. 3, (Cambridge: Cambridge University Press, 1985), 109–41; J. C. O'Neill, "The Study of the New Testament," ibid., 144–67; Nigel M. de S. Cameron, *Biblical Higher Criticism and the Defense of Infallibilism in Nineteenth-Century Britain* (Lewiston, N.Y.: E. Mellen Press, 1987); John Rogerson, *Old Testament Criticism in the Nineteenth Century: England and Germany* (London: SPCK and Fortress Press, 1985); William Baird, *History of New Testament Research, Vol. 1: From Deism to Tübingen* (Minneapolis, Minn.: Fortress Press, 1992); Harrisville and Sundberg, *The Bible in Modern Culture* (1995).

37. Francis Ellingwood Abbot, editor of the *Index*, critic of the *Investigator*: "Communication," *Index* (July 8, 1871): 215; "Communications," *Index* (Aug. 5, 1871): 247. Horace Seaver, editor of the *Boston Investigator*, "A Popular Book" (Sept. 6, 1871): 6. [Masthead], *Investigator* (April 28, 1875): 1. A rare discussion of relatively recent biblical scholarship in the *Investigator*: W. Henry Burr, "Abstract of Colenso's Argument," *Investigator* (March 9, 1870): 353; March 16, 1870, 362; March 28, 1870, 369; Oct. 26, 1870, 177. The scholarly burden in the *Investigator* for the first half of the decade was carried mostly by Margaret Chappellsmith, who started an essay series, "Doubt as to 'the Historical Evidence of Jesus' Not Extravagant" (Sept. 6, 1871): 1, and concluded it with no. 60 (Nov. 18, 1874): 1, and then started a new series, "Did Christianity Originate in Astronomical Allegory?"

(Dec. 23, 1874): 1. A writer signing as "Antichrist" in the second half of the decade also had scholarly aspirations ("The Resurrection of Christ" [Feb. 24, 1875]: 1, through "Life of Simon Kepha, Alias St. Peter" [Feb. 4, 1880]: 1). On complaints that biblical scholarship was boring: W. H. Rundle, "God and the Bible" (Nov. 4, 1874): 2; "The Bible—We Must Continue to Oppose Its Influence" (Dec. 16, 1874): 2. Examples of common sense critiques of the Bible appear in nearly every issue of the *Investigator*. See, for ex., "The Bible Not Inspired, No. 1" (June 22, 1870): 57; "The Exodus from Egypt" (Jan. 27, 1875): 1; "How the Gospels Were Written" (April 14, 1880): 1.

38. On biblical scholarship in nineteenth-century America: Jerry Wayne Brown, *The Rise of Biblical Criticism in America, 1800–1870: The New England Scholars* (Middletown, Conn.: Wesleyan University Press, 1969); Philip F. Gura, *The Wisdom of Words: Language, Theology, and Literature in the New England Renaissance* (Middletown, Conn.: Wesleyan University Press, 1981); Richard Grusin, *Transcendentalist Hermeneutics: Institutional Authority and the Higher Criticism of the Bible* (Durham, N.C.: Duke University Press, 1991); Michael Kamen, "The Science of the Bible in Nineteenth-Century America: From 'Common Sense' to Controversy, 1820–1900" (PhD diss., Notre Dame University, 2004); Elisabeth Hurth, *Between Faith and Unbelief: American Transcendentalists and the Challenge of Atheism* (Leiden: Brill, 2007); Grasso, *Skepticism and American Faith*, chap. 8. On Common Sense philosophy in America see D. H. Meyer, *The Instructed Conscience: The Shaping of the American National Ethic* (Philadelphia: University of Pennsylvania Press, 1972); Mark A. Noll, *America's God: From Jonathan Edwards to Abraham Lincoln* (New York: Oxford University Press, 2002), 93–113, 367–85; E. Brooks Holifield, *Theology in America: Christian Thought from the Age of the Puritans to the Civil War* (New Haven, Conn.: Yale University Press, 2003), 174–80.

39. Kelso, *Deity Analyzed*, 14, 36. On Draper and White, see Warren, *American Freethought*, 59–65; on Draper see James C. Ungureanu, "Rethinking the Historical 'Conflict' between Science and Religion," *Biologos*, https://biologos.org/articles/rethinking-the-historical-conflict-between-science-and-religion.

40. Kelso, *Deity Analyzed*, 190, 275.

41. Kelso, *Bible Analyzed*, 104.

42. Ibid., 11.

43. Robert Cooper, *The Infidel's Text-Book* (Boston: J. P. Mendum, 1846; orig. pub. Hull, England, 1846) [iii]. Cooper quoted the Hilkiah and Ezra arguments from Thomas Cooper, *The Fabrication of the Pentateuch Proved* (Granville, Middletown, N.J.: George H. Evans, 1840; orig. pub. anon. 1829); T. Cooper got the Hilkiah argument from C. F. Volney, *New Researches on Ancient History* (London: W. Lewis, 1819; orig. pub. in French, 1814), esp. 76–86, and the Ezra argument from Baruch de Spinoza, *A Treatise Partly Theological, Partly Political* (London: London and

Westminster, 1737; orig. pub. in Latin as *Tractatus Theologico-Politicus* [1670]), esp. 194–228, who was expanding upon suggestions by Ibn Ezra (1089–1167 CE).

44. Branch, *History of Stanislaus County*, esp. 109–112.

45. Ibid., 10; D mss 12: 25, 27–28.

46. Branch, *History of Stanislaus County*, 231, 233, 240; Tinkham, *History of Stanislaus County*, 129–30; "Centennial Poem," delivered at Modesto, Calif., July 4, 1876, in "Miscellaneous Writings," 434–41; "Grand Centennial Celebration in Modesto," *Modesto Herald* (July 6, 1876), 5; "Fourth of July Poem," read at Modesto, Calif., July 4, 1884, ibid., 387–90. On the *Herald*, see Branch, *History of Stanislaus County*, 121, and Tinkham, *History of Stanislaus County*, 121; on Kelso's involvement with the paper see Elias, *Stories of Stanislaus*, 284; D mss 12: 43. *Modesto Herald* editorials, summer 1877: "Republican Primaries" and "A Warning" (June 14): 4; "Mr. Harp's Letter" and "The Millennium" (June 21): 4; "Beware of It" (June 28): 4; "The Ticket" (July 5): 4; "Mr. Harp's Letter" and "Wants to Know, You Know" (July 12): 4; "Walden! Walden! Walden!" (July 19): 4; "What Is It That Troubles You" and "Ward's Letter" (July 26): 4; "Dead Ducks" (Aug. 2): 4; "Subsidy vs. Senator" (Aug. 9): 4; "A Specimen Brick," "The Little Tweed Ring in Our County," and "The Tweed Ring and the Court House Ring" (Aug. 16): 4; "A Warning," "Chance to Explain," "The Big Tweed and the Little Tweed," and "The People vs. the Ring" (Aug. 23): 4. All the editorials are unsigned, and Kelso did not save any of his political writings and speeches from this period. On the attack on Kelso's military record, in the *Herald*: "That Record" (Aug. 16, 1877): 4, and [no title] (Sept. 6, 1877): 4.

47. "Another Version," *Stanislaus County Weekly News* (Aug. 31): 1. McGrath in his letter refers to the Confederates as "our side"; he served in the (Confederate) State Guard ("Soldiers' Database," MDH). The retraction to the attack on Kelso's military record: "An Issue," *Stanislaus County Weekly News* (Sept. 7, 1877): 2. For election results: "Election Results," *Stanislaus County Weekly News* (Sept. 7, 1877): 2; "The Election," *Herald* (Sept. 13, 1877): 5: Kelso got 38% of the vote, and received one vote more (487) than the lowest total for a Republican candidate (486 for County Treasurer).

48. D mss 12: 38; 12: 44–45; "New Constitution Party State Convention, Third Day," *Sacramento Daily Union* (June 28, 1879): 1; "Democratic Rally," *San Jose Herald* (Sept. 10, 1880): 3.

49. *Modesto Herald*, quoted in Tinkham, *History of Stanislaus County*, 144; earlier articles by Elias quoted in Tinkham, 101, and Elias, *Stories of Stanislaus*, 293; Tinkham, 139; [No title], *[Grass Valley, Calif.] Morning Union* (May 4, 1884): 3, reprinted from the *Stockton Herald*. See also Elias, *Stories of Stanislaus*, 296.

50. Elias, *Stories of Stanislaus*, 298–99; Tinkham, *History of Stanislaus County*, 145. See also "News of the Morning," *Sacramento Daily Union* (Aug. 16, 1879): 2; "Coast Items," *[Healdsburg, Calif.] Russian River Flag* (Aug. 21, 1879): 1; [no title], *[San*

Francisco] Pacific Rural Press (Aug. 23, 1879): 121; "The Chinese Must Go," *Santa Barbara Weekly Press* (Aug. 23, 1879): 1.

51. "The Modesto Vigilantes," *[San Francisco, Calif.] Daily Alta California* (Aug. 28, 1879): 1, quoting the *Stanislaus News*; Elias, *Stories of Stanislaus*, 304–305.

52. Elias, *Stories of Stanislaus*, 307 (quotation); Tinkham, *History of Stanislaus County*, 143.

53. Elias, *Stories of Stanislaus*, 310; Tinkham, *History of Stanislaus County*, 147–48.

54. Elias, *Stories of Stanislaus*, 311–12; Tinkham, *History of Stanislaus County*, 148; "San Joaquin Valley Regulators. A Saloon-Keeper Near Modesto Shot by Armed Men," *San Francisco Bulletin* (March 21, 1884): 5.

55. Elias, *Stories of Stanislaus*, 313–14; Tinkham, *History of Stanislaus County*, 148–49 (quotations). See also "San Joaquin Regulators. A List of Persons Ordered to Leave Modesto," *San Francisco Bulletin* (March 24, 1884): 1; "Murderous Regulators," *[Grass Valley, Calif.] Morning Union* (March 25, 1884): 1; "Modesto Regulators," *Mariposa Gazette* (March 29, 1884): 2.

56. "Mob Government," *[San Francisco, Calif.] Daily Alta California* (March 23, 1884): 3; the *[Grass Valley, Calif.] Morning Union* reprinted and endorsed pieces in the *Stockton Herald* (May 4, 1844): 3; [no title] (April 26, 1884): 1; "A Mob Law Community" (March 29, 1884): 2; and see the *Union*, [no title] (May 9, 1884): 2. On the young men from good families: [no title], *Morning Union* (April 2, 1884): 2; "Sad Indeed," *Santa Cruz Sentinel* (May 1, 1884): 4, rpt. from *Merced Argus*. Elias, *Stories of Stanislaus*, 303; Tinkham, *History of Stanislaus County*, 149.

57. Elias, *Stories of Stanislaus*, 326; Tinkham, *History of Stanislaus County*, 102, 140. See also "Excitement in Modesto," *Sacramento Daily Union* (July 10, 1884): 1.

58. D mss 12: 40–42; 13: 36–38; "The State Normal School," *[San Francisco, Calif.] Daily Alta California* (May 24, 1878): 1; *California, County Birth, Marriage, and Death Records, 1849–1980*, ancestry.com, Ransom McCapes and Martha S. Kelso, Aug. 9, 1883 (marriage); Martha Susan McCapes, "Declaration for Remarried Widow's Pension," Nov. 1, 1916, John R. Kelso, Pension File, National Archives (divorce).

59. D mss 13: 37–38.

60. Ibid., 38, 40–41.

61. Ibid., 44.

62. Ibid., 47, 48.

CHAPTER 16

1. D mss 13: 1–4; [no title], *Boston Investigator* (April 6, 1881): 6; "The Liberal League," *Boston Investigator* (April 27, 1881): 1; Correspondence, *Boston Investigator* (June 8, 1881): 5; [no title], *Truth Seeker* (May 14, 1881): 315; "A New Lecturer in the Field," *Truth Seeker* (May 28, 1881): 347. On the National Liberal League, see Warren, *American Freethought*, 30, 34–35, 162–67, 176–78.

2. D mss 13: 4–13; "Letter from Colonel John R. Kelso," *Truth Seeker* (July 2, 1881): 423; John R. Kelso, "Mirage," *Boston Investigator* (June 15, 1881): 1; "A Note from Col. Kelso," *Truth Seeker* (Nov. 19, 1881): 749.

3. D mss 13: 34, 59; "Brief Notes," *Boston Investigator* (July 20, 1881): 6; "Col. John R. Kelso," *Boston Investigator* (July 27, 1881): 1; "Letter from John R. Kelso," *Truth Seeker* (July 23, 1881): 467.

4. D mss 13: 57–58; "A Fright at the Fair," *St. Louis Globe-Democrat* (Sept. 15, 1881): 1.

5. D mss 13: 66, 64; "The Liberal Congress," *Boston Investigator* (Oct. 12, 1881): 6; "The National Liberal League Congress," *Boston Investigator* (Oct. 19, 1881): 1; "Report of the Fifth Annual Congress of the National Liberal League," *Truth Seeker* (Oct. 15, 1881): 660–61 (Kelso mentioned 661).

6. D mss 14: 3, 18; John R. Kelso, *The Real Blasphemers* (New York: D. M. Bennett, Liberal and Scientific Publishing House, Office of the *Truth Seeker*, [1883]); Macdonald, *Fifty Years of Freethought*, 301–302.

7. D mss 14: 7, 17–18.

8. Ibid., 3, 8–10, 14; Stephen Pearl Andrews, *The Primary Synopsis of Universology and Alwato: The New Scientific Universal Language* (New York: D. Thomas, 1871), 186–87. On Andrews see Madeleine B. Stern, *The Pantarch: A Biography of Stephen Pearl Andrews* (Austin: University of Texas Press, 1968).

9. John R. Kelso, *The Universe Analyzed* (New York: The Truth Seeker Co., [1887]), [vii].

10. Ibid., 141, facing 156, viii.

11. Jenny M. Parker, *Rochester: A Story Historical* (Rochester, N.Y.: Scranton, Wetmore, & Co., 1884), 245, 270; D. M. Dewey, *History of the Strange Sounds or Rappings, Heard in Rochester and Western New York . . . Which are Supposed by Many to Be Communications from the Spirit World* (Rochester, N.Y.: D. M. Dewey, 1850), esp. 49–50. See Caitlin Powalski, "Radical Transmissions: Isaac and Amy Post, Spiritualism, and Progressive Reform in Nineteenth-Century Rochester," *Rochester History* 71, no. 2 (Fall 2009): 1–25; Nancy A. Hewitt, *Radical Friend: Amy Kirby Post and Her Activist Worlds* (Chapel Hill: University of North Carolina Press, 2018), esp. 140–41, 154–55. 285. The Posts were supporters of Frederick Douglass, and Amy signed the Seneca Falls "Declaration of Sentiments." Isaac became a medium who communicated messages from the spirits of Benjamin Franklin, George Washington, and John C. Calhoun, among others; see Isaac Post, *Voices from the Spirit World, Being Communications from Many Spirits* (Rochester, N.Y.: Charles H. McDonnell, 1852). On Spiritualism see R. Laurence Moore, *In Search of White Crows: Spiritualism, Parapsychology, and American Culture* (New York: Oxford University Press, 1977); Ann Braude, *Radical Spirits: Spiritualism and Women's Rights in Nineteenth-Century America* (Boston, Mass.: Beacon Press, 1989); Bret E. Carroll, *Spiritualism in Antebellum America* (Bloomington: Indiana University Press, 1997); Taves, *Fits, Trances, and Visions*, 119–250; Robert S. Cox, *Body and Soul: A Sympathetic History of American Spiritualism* (Charlottesville: University

of Virginia Press, 2003); Molly McGarry, *Ghosts of Futures Past: Spiritualism and the Cultural Politics of Nineteenth-Century America* (Berkeley: University of California Press, 2008); Mark A. Lause, *Free Spirits: Spiritualism, Republicanism, and Radicalism in the Civil War Era* (Urbana: University of Illinois Press, 2016).

12. John R. Kelso, "Spiritualism," in "Works," 125–219; John R. Kelso, *Spiritualism Sustained in Five Lectures* (New York: Truth Seeker Office, [1886]), 8.

13. Kelso, "Spiritualism," in "Works," 125; "Spiritualism," *Patriot* (June 15, 1871): 3; [no title], *Patriot* (July 6, 1871): 3; Ebenezer V. Wilson, *The Truths of Spiritualism: Immortality Proved beyond a Doubt* (Chicago: Hazlitt & Reed, 1876). Fishback was a former Universalist minister who had become an itinerant spiritualist lecturer; see John Benedict Buescher, *The Other Side of Salvation: Spiritualism and the Nineteenth-Century Religious Experience* (Boston, Mass.: Skinner House Books, 2004), 121–22; Frederick W. Evans, *Spiritualism on Trial: Containing the Arguments of the Rev. F. W. Evans in the Debate on Spiritualism between him and Mr. A. J. Fishback, held in Osceola, Iowa, Commencing Nov. 18, and closing Nov. 28, 1874* (Cincinnati, Ohio: Hitchcock & Walden, 1875).

14. D mss 1: 14; 11: 23, 46; 14: 54.

15. D mss 14: 26, 27. Full names of Tilden and Van Auken from *Polk's Rochester (Monroe County, N.Y.) City Directory* (Rochester, N.Y.: Sampson and Murdock Co., [1884], 505, 512.

16. D mss 14: 34, 38–39.

17. Ibid., 39.

18. Ibid., 42–43.

19. Kelso, "Auto-Biography," in "Works," 668, 800.

20. D mss 13: 24–25; 11: 23. Eighteenth-century aesthetic theory, which delineated beautiful, picturesque, and sublime scenes (and their corresponding emotional states), was domesticated in nineteenth-century travel guides. Speechless, rapturous awe before natural wonders—illustrating the viewer's refined sensibility and appreciation of the sublime—had become a trope in the guide books by midcentury. See Will B. Mackintosh, *Selling the Sights: The Invention of the Tourist in American Culture* (New York: New York University Press, 2019), 96–98, 107.

21. David W. Blight, *Race and Reunion: The Civil War in American Memory* (Cambridge, Mass. Belknap Press of Harvard University Press, 2001), 140–210, esp. 150, 170, 187, 207. For challenges to Blight's thesis that Union veterans focused on White reconciliation and "whitewashed" their memories of the war, see Andre Flesche, "'Shoulder to Shoulder as Comrades Tried': Black and White Union Veterans and Civil War Memory," *Civil War History* 51, no. 2 (June 2005): 175–201; Caroline Janney, *Remembering the Civil War: Reunion and the Limits of Reconciliation* (Chapel Hill: University of North Carolina Press, 2013); Casey, *New Men*.

22. Randall Fuller, Review of *Bloody Engagements: John R. Kelso's Civil War* in *Common-Place: The Interactive Journal of Early American Life* 18, no. 1 (2018), www.common-place.org.

23. D mss 4: 288–90, 293–94.

24. D mss 12: 43; 14: 47–48, 51; Dr. L. Tenney, Eureka Magnetic Clothing, listed in *Williams' Cincinnati Directory* (Cincinnati, Ohio: Williams Directory Co., 1883), 1176; [Advertisement], "Dr. Liebig's Wonderful German Invigorator," *Daily Alta [San Francisco] California* (Nov. 22, 1884): 3.

25. D mss 14: 54. On Mrs. Reynolds in the spring of 1885 in the *[San Jose, Calif.] Evening News*: "Elsie and Henry" (March 7): 3; "Spiritualism. Trotting Out Ghosts for Silver Coin" (March 28): 3; "Ghost Makers" (March 30): 3; "Spirits Again" (April 18): 3; "Who Laughs Now" (May 13): 3; "The Spirits. Elsie Reynolds in Trouble" (May 14): 3; "Elsie Dear. The Ghost Maker Is in Town Again" (June 5): 3; "Elsie Reynolds. Grabbing a Spirit in a Chemise" (June 10): 3; "It Won't Wash" (June 11): 2; and see "Pacific Coast Brevities," *San Francisco Bulletin* (May 13, 1865): 1. On her later career, see, for ex., [Advertisement], Materializing Séances with Mrs. Elsie Reynolds, *San Francisco Call* (July 27, 1913): 53. On the Fox sisters: "Spiritualism's Down Fall. Mrs. Kane, Its Founder, Publicly Confesses it to be a Fraud," *New York Herald* (Oct. 22, 1888): 2; see also David Chapin, *Exploring Other Worlds: Margaret Fox, Elisha Kent Kane, and the Antebellum Culture of Curiosity* (Amherst: University of Massachusetts Press, 2004), 31–53.

26. D mss 14: 54. On the spiritualist camp meeting: [no title], *Sonoma Democrat* (May 16, 1885): 2 (notice); Julia Schlesinger, *Workers in the Vineyard: A Review of the Progress of Spiritualism* (San Francisco: [s. n.], 1896), 25–26.

27. Kelso, *Spiritualism Sustained*, 153, 157, 207; Kelso "Spiritualism Sustained," in "Works," 138; Carroll, *Spiritualism in Antebellum America*, 66.

28. Kelso, *Spiritualism Sustained*, 172, 174, 227. On atheistic spiritualists, or those agnostic on the question of a personal God, see Moore, *In Search of White Crows*, 52–53.

CHAPTER 17

1. Kelso, "Marriage," in *Miscellaneous Writings*, 177–78; D mss 14: 74.

2. D mss 14: 52, 55.

3. Ibid., 56; "Sandstone Ranch Album," Longmont Museum, www.longmontcolorado. gov ("dynamic and progressive," referring to Julia); Samuel P. Putnam, "American Secular Union—News and Notes," *Boston Investigator* (Aug. 18, 1886): 3; *Portrait and Biographical Record of Denver and Vicinity, Colorado* (Chicago: Chapman Pub. Co., 1898), 951–52; 1870 U.S. Census, Blackberry, Kane Co. Ill., family no. 176; 1880 U. S. Census, [no town], Weld County, Colo., family no. 4; John W. Cook and James V. McHugh, *A History of the Illinois State Normal University* (Normal, Ill., 1882), 71; Illinois State University, *Semi-Centennial History of the Illinois State Normal University, 1857–1907* [Normal? Ill.: ca. 1907], 257; Deed of Trust, Feb. 5, 1877, Emmet F. Turner and Etta S. Dunbar, Morse H. Coffin, trustee, Office of the Clerk and Recorder, Boulder Co., Colo.; Contract, Sept. 4, 1877, Denver Pacific

Railway and Telegraph Co. and Etta S. Dunbar, Office of the Clerk and Recorder, Weld Co., Colo.; Deed, Aug. 8, 1884, Gould and Russell, trustees for Union Pacific Railway Co., and Etta S. Dunbar, Office of the Clerk and Recorder, Weld Co., Colo.; Chattel Mortgage, June 23, 1885, J. D. Heinrich and Etta S. Dunbar, Office of the Clerk and Recorder, Weld Co., Colo. (piano).

4. D mss 14: 53.

5. Ibid., 56; Dean F. Krakel, *South Platte Country: A History of Old Weld County, Colorado, 1739–1900* (Laramie, Wyo.: Powder River Publishers, 1954), 204–53; [Anon.], *Portrait and Biographical Record of Denver and Vicinity, Colorado* (Chicago: Chapman Pub. Co., 1898), 951. Coffin wrote letters reminiscing about his pioneer days, published in the *Longmont Ledger*: July 12, 19, 26, and Aug. 2, 9, 16, 1907; June 18, 25, and July 2, 9, 1909; Feb. 17, 1911.

6. D mss 14: 56; Kelso, Pension File, National Archives: Etta D. Kelso, "Neighbor's Affidavit," Nov. 16, 1888.

7. Ibid., 63.

8. Ibid., 74; John. R. Kelso and Etta S. Dunbar, Marriage Certificate, Sept. 5, 1885, Denver, Colo., *Marriage Records. Colorado Marriages*, Colorado State Archives, in *Colorado County Marriage Records and State Index*, ancestry.com.

9. John R. Kelso, "That Marriage. To the Outraged Citizens of Valley Falls, Kansas, Letter 1, cont.," *Lucifer the Light-Bearer* (Oct. 22, 1886): 2; John R. Kelso, "That Marriage. To the Outraged Citizens of Valley Falls, Kansas, Letter 1," *Lucifer the Light-Bearer* (Oct. 15, 1886): 3; John R. Kelso, *Autonomistic Marriage: As Viewed from the Standpoint of Law, Justice and Morality, to the "Outraged" Christians of Valley Falls, Kansas* (Valley Falls, Kans.: M. Harman and Son, [1887]). Kelso in the *Boston Investigator* on polygamy: "Does the Bible Teach Polygamy?" (Aug. 30, 1882): 1; "Mormonism" (Nov. 28, 1883): 1; "Mormonism, concluded" (Dec. 5, 1883): 1; "Mormonism" (May 7, 1884): 3; "The Mormons" (Dec. 18, 1885): 1; "The Mormons" (April 8, 1885): 3; "The Mormons, concluded" (April 22, 1885; "From a Mormon Woman" (July 15, 1885): 3. Editors' responses follow the letters. See also in the *Investigator*: Charles F. Blackburn, "Mr. Kelso—Mormons Defended" (Nov. 12, 1884): 1; Joseph Lee, "Anti-Mormonism" (Nov. 19, 1884); L. Hutchinson, "Anti-Mormonism" (Nov. 19, 1884): 5; J. S., "A Few Thoughts" (Nov. 26, 1884): 1; A Lawyer, "A Constitutional Question" (April 29, 1885): 6.

10. Kelso, "The Mormons," *Boston Investigator* (April 8, 1885): 3.

11. Annie Musser Sheets, "Sentiments of an Intelligent Man. What Prof. Kelso Thinks of the Victims of Anti-Mormon Prosecutions, and How He Thinks They Should Act. His Intercepted Letters," [Salt Lake City, Utah] *Deseret News* (Oct. 14, 1885): 610.

12. Kelso, "Marriage," in "Miscellaneous Writings," 177–78; D mss 14: 74; Samuel P. Putnam, "American Secular Union—News and Notes," *Boston Investigator* (Aug. 18, 1886): 3, and March 16, 1887): 3.

13. Kelso, Pension File, National Archives: John R. Kelso, "Declaration for the Increase of an Invalid Pension," March 27, 1886; John R. Kelso, "Form of Application for Increase of Invalid Pension," April 29, 1886; "Examining Surgeon's Certificate," Nov. 4, 1865; Milton Burch, letter, Sept. 2, 1866; E. S. Robinson, letter, Dec. 10, 1866; "Claim for an Invalid Pension—Proof Exhibited," Jan. 7, 1867; Kelso, "Application for an Increase of Invalid Pension Under Act of June 6, 1866," March 13, 1869; "Claim for an Invalid Pension—Proof Exhibited," Sept. 6, 1869; "Claim for an Invalid Pension—Proof Exhibited," Nov. 26, 1869; Kelso, "Application for an Increase of Invalid Pension Under Act of June 6, 1866," July 6, 1871; Kelso, "Brief Claim to [Increase] Invalid Pension," Sept. [?], 1871; Kelso, "Declaration for Increase of Invalid Pension," Oct. 24, 1874; "Invalid Increase," notecard, Dec., 21, 1876; "Invalid Increase," notecard, Feb. 27, 1877; Kelso, "Declaration for the Increase of an Invalid Pension," Nov. 8, 1877; "Claim for an Invalid Pension—Proof Exhibited," Sept. 6, 1879; "[Increase] Invalid Pension," Nov. 4, 1879.

14. Kelso, Pension File, National Archives: Kelso, [Affidavit], March 1, 1880; "Increase—Invalid Pension," March 15, 1880.

15. Kelso, Pension File, National Archives: Kelso, "General Affidavit," July 31, 1886.

16. Kelso, Pension File, National Archives: Etta D. Kelso, "Neighbor's Affidavit," Nov. 16, 1888.

17. Kelso, Pension File, National Archives: Milton Burch, "Affidavit to Origin of Disability," Aug. 8, 1866; Andrew J. Smithson, [Affidavit], July 2, 1886; Ozias Ruark, [Affidavit], July 5, 1886; Peter F. Hutchison, [Affidavit], July 10, 1886; Levi N. Scott, "General Affidavit," July 29, 1886; Elias Chapman, "General Affidavit," Aug. 15, 1886; Peter Humphrey, "General Affidavit," Aug. 21, 1886; Andrew Smithson, letter, Nov. 12, 1888; Milton Burch, letter, Dec. 1888; Peter Humphrey, letter, Aug. 4, 1889.

18. Kelso, Pension File, National Archives: Samuel Gibson, "Neighbor's Affidavit," Sept. 22, 1886; J. D. Harp, letter, Oct. 12, 1888; Jared E. Smith, "General Affidavit," Nov. 30, 1888; Kelso, "General Affidavit," Dec. 18, 1888; E. D. Ott, "Neighbor's Affidavit," Dec. 24, 1888.

19. Kelso, Pension File, National Archives: John Rice, "Neighbor's Affidavit," Nov. 10, 1888; Georgiana Rice, "Neighbor's Affidavit," Nov. 10, 1888; Florella A. Finney, "Neighbor's Affidavit," Nov. 16, 1888. *A Treatise on the Practice of the Pension Bureau* (Washington, D.C.: Government Printing Office, 1898), 13: "It is important that claims for pension be established by witnesses who are not relatives of claimants, but testimony of relatives who are [financially] disinterested will be accepted."

20. Chapter 234, 42 Congress, Session 3, "An Act to Revise, Consolidate, and Amend the Laws Relating to Pensions," *U.S. Statures at Large*, 17, no. Main Section (1873), 566–77; *A Treatise on the Practice of the Pension Bureau*; Claire Prechtel-Kluskens, "'A Reasonable Degree of Promptitude': Civil War Pension Application Processing, 1861–1885," *Prologue Magazine* 42, no. 1 (Spring 2010), www.archives.gov.

21. *Treatise on the Practice of the Pension Bureau.*

22. *Treatise on the Practice of the Pension Bureau*, 46, 28, 122–25; Kelso, Pension File, National Archives: Wm. E. McLeash, Department of the Interior, Bureau of Pensions, to Peter Humphrey, Oct. 12, 1888 [request for further information; similar requests must have been sent to Smithson and Burch]; Forms to secure affidavits as to the character of witnesses Smithson, Burch, and Humphreys, Oct. 12, 1888; Notecards, Oct. 12 and 13, 1888, request to Adj. Gen. for report on absence or presence of Scott, Hutchison, Humphrey, Burch, and Ruark, on or about Sept. 7, 1863.

23. William Henry Glasson, *History of Military Pension Legislation in the United States* (New York: Oxford University Press, 1900); William Henry Glasson, *Federal Military Pensions in the United States* (New York: Oxford University Press, 1918); Theda Skocpol, "America's First Social Security System: The Expansion of Benefits for Civil War Veterans," *Political Science Quarterly* 108, no. 1 (Spring 1993), 85–116. See also Brian Matthew Jordan, *Marching Home: Union Veterans and Their Unending Civil War* (New York: Liveright Pub. Corp., 2014).

24. Kelso, Pension File, National Archives: Kelso, "Affidavit of Claimant," Oct. 20, 1888; Kelso, "General Affidavit," Dec. 18, 1888.

25. Roberts Bartholow, *Spermatorrhoea: Its Causes, Symptoms, Results, and Treatment*, 4th ed., rev. (New York: W. Wood & Co., 1879), 22, 34, 75; W. H. Ranking, "Observations on Spermatorrhea: Or the Involuntary Discharge of Seminal Fluid," *Provincial Medical Journal and Retrospect of the Medical Sciences* 7, no. 159 (Oct. 14, 1843): 26–29 and 7, 162 (Nov. 4, 1843): 93–95; Claude Francois Lallemand, *A Practical Treatise on the Causes, Symptoms, and Treatment of Spermatorrhea* (Philadelphia: Blanchard and Lea, 1853), orig. pub. 1848; Abram Edmund Small, *Causes That Operate to Produce the Premature Decline of Manhood and the Best Means of Obviating Their Effects* (Chicago: Clindinning & Co., [1873]). See Ellen Bayuk Rosenman, "Body Doubles: The Spermatorrhea Panic," *Journal of the History of Sexuality* 12, no. 3 (July 2003): 365–99; Elizabeth Stephens, "Pathologizing Leaky Male Bodies: Spermatorrhea in Nineteenth-Century British Medicine and Popular Anatomical Museums," *Journal of the History of Sexuality* 17, no. 3 (Sept. 2008): 421–38.

26. Kelso, Pension File, National Archives: Form 3-111 [Medical Exam Certificate], Oct. 31, 1888; Form 3-146, "Invalid Pension: Reissue to Allow Additional Disability," April 7, 1890.

27. On the Haymarket affair, see esp. Timothy Messer-Kruse, *The Trial of the Haymarket Anarchists: Terrorism and Justice in the Gilded Age* (New York: Palgrave Macmillan, 2011), and Messer-Kruse, *The Haymarket Conspiracy: Transatlantic Anarchist Networks* (Urbana: University of Illinois Press, 2012); see also Paul Avrich, *The Haymarket Tragedy* (Princeton, N.J.: Princeton University Press, 1984) and Bruce C. Nelson, *Beyond the Martyrs: A Social History of Chicago's Anarchists, 1870–1900* (New Brunswick, N.J.: Rutgers University Press, 1988).

28. "Bombs and Blood," *[Denver, Colo.] Rocky Mountain News* (May 5, 1886): 1; "Government," "General Intelligence," "The Bloodshed and Rioting in Chicago,"

and "Anarchy," *Boston Investigator* (May 12, 1886): 4, 7, 6; "The Outcome of Christian Teaching," *Truth Seeker* (May 15, 1886): 312.

29. Moses Harman in *Lucifer the Light-Bearer* kept up a running commentary on anarchism, but see esp. "The Logic of Freethought" (Feb. 26, 1886): 2, and "Propaganda in Deed" (April 19, 1886): 2; On Haymarket see "The Chicago Riots" (May 7, 1886): 2; on Harman see William O. Reichert, *Partisans of Freedom: A Study in American Anarchism* (Bowling Green, Ohio: Bowling Green University Popular Press, 1976), 301–14.

30. The *[Denver, Colo.] Labor Enquirer* denounced the biased coverage in the capitalist press. It argued that the police provoked the violence, the anarchists had nothing to do with it, the bomb-thrower was a lone "idiot," and the farcical, corrupt trial, violating law and the fundamental principles of the Declaration of Independence, produced no evidence to convict. See (all 1886): "Its Lessons" (May 15): 1; "The Usual Lies" (May 15): 2; "Rattled" (May 22): 1; "Responsibility" (May 22): 2; "Anarchism" (June 12): 1; "The Chicago Trial" (July 24): 2; "The Anarchist Trial" (Aug. 14): 2, 3; "Parson's Speech" (Aug. 21): 1 and 2; "A Powerful Orator" (Aug. 21): 3; "Bribing the Jury" (Aug. 28): 3; "History of a Crime" (Sept. 11): 1; "The Bomb" (Oct. 23): 1. John and Etta visited the Denver *Labor Enquirer* offices ("Personal," *Labor Enquirer* [Feb. 25, 1888]: 2). In a postscript to his essay "The Anarchists," dated Oct. 13, 1886, in "Miscellaneous Writings," 331–59, Kelso wrote that he sent the piece to *Arbiter Zeitung*, the leading radical German-language newspaper in Chicago, but by "an unfortunate misdirection, the manuscript of this article was lost for several months. It finally returned to me through the Dead Letter Office at Washington." He wrote that it was finally published the following spring, 1887, in that paper, but I have not been able to find it. It was published in the *Chicago Labor Enquirer* and republished in the *Denver Labor Enquirer* as "The Law and the 'Anarchists'" (Oct. 8, 1887): 1, 5, 8 (thanks to D. L. Trainor for this reference). The headline describes Kelso as a "constitutional lawyer." The essay was also published as a pamphlet (see ad, ibid. [Jan. 14, 1888]: 3). The version in "Miscellaneous Writings," cited here, "contains a good many changes and additions" (359).

31. D mss 14: 27; John R. Kelso, "Our Great Non-needy and Non-Deserving U.S. Paupers," in "Miscellaneous Writings," 301–406, dated March 16, 1886, pub. in *Truth Seeker* (April 17, 1886): 242–43.

32. Edwin J, Shellhous, *The New Republic, Founded on the Natural and Inalienable Rights of Man* (San Francisco: Bacon & Co., 1883). For a review see "The New Republic," *San Francisco Daily Evening Bulletin* (Oct. 20, 1883): 1. Kelso's copy of the book, still owned by descendants, is inscribed with his name and "1884." I am presuming that he read it.

33. Kelso, "The Anarchists," 331, 346.

34. Ibid., 358–59.

35. Dyer D. Lum, *A Concise History of the Great Trial of the Chicago Anarchists in 1886* (Chicago: Socialistic Pub. Co., [1887]), 174. On Lum see Reichert, *Partisans*

of Freedom, 236–44, and esp. Frank H. Brooks, "Anarchism, Revolution, and Labor in the Thought of Dyer D. Lum: 'Events are the True Schoolmasters'" (PhD diss., Cornell University, 1988), and Frank H. Brooks, "Ideology, Strategy, and Organization: Dyer Lum and the American Anarchist Movement," *Labor History* 34, no. 1 (Winter 1993): 57–83. On Lum's *Concise History* as propaganda and William Dean Howells' reaction, see Messer-Kruse, *Trial of the Haymarket Anarchists*, 153–55. Kelso also read Gen. Matthew M. Trumbull's two pamphlets, *Was It a Fair Trial?* (Chicago? 1887) and *The Trial of the Judgment* (Chicago: Health and Home Pub. Co., 1888). Trumbull was a close friend of Samuel Fielden, one of the defendants. For the revisionist narrative of the Haymarket affair, see Messer-Kruse, *Trial of the Haymarket Anarchists* and *Haymarket Conspiracy*; the previous standard work was Avrich, *Haymarket Tragedy*.

36. John R. Kelso, "Our Martyrs," delivered before the Rocky Mountain Social League at Denver, Colorado, Nov. 10, 1889, in "Miscellaneous Writings," 459–91, esp. 459, 471.

37. Kelso, "Our Martyrs," 469, 465; Lum, *Concise History*, [ii].

38. On Proudhon see Benjamin Tucker, "State Socialism and Anarchism: How Far They Agree, and Where They Differ," in Frank H. Brooks, ed., *The Individualist Anarchists: An Anthology of* Liberty *(1881–1908)* (New Brunswick, N.J.: Transaction Publishers, 1994), 86, orig. in *Liberty* (March 10, 1888); Kelso, *Government Analyzed*, 14–15; Tucker in Brooks, "Anarchism, Revolution, and Labor," 173. Kelso frequently argued with recourse to etymology, so he had not necessarily read Proudhon. On anarchism generally see April Carter, *The Political Theory of Anarchism* (London: Routledge & Keegan Paul, 1971). On American Anarchist thought in the 1880s see esp. Reichert, *Partisans of Freedom*; Nelson, *Beyond the Martyrs* chap. 7; Brooks, "Anarchism, Revolution, and Labor"; see also David DeLeon, *The American as Anarchist: Reflections on Indigenous Radicalism* (Baltimore, Md.: Johns Hopkins University Press, 1978).

39. Kelso, *Government Analyzed*, 4, 40, 106, 6.

40. Ibid., 31, 57.

41. Ibid., 70, 62–63.

42. On border state slaveholders' rejection of Lincoln's offer of compensated emancipation in 1862, see McPherson, *Battle Cry of Freedom*, 498–99, 502–4.

43. Kelso, *Government Analyzed*, 297–98.

44. Ibid., 299.

45. Ibid., 47–49.

46. Ibid., 47–49.

47. Ibid., 300; "Government Analyzed," *Lucifer the Light Bearer* (May 20, 1892): 1.

48. [Book review of *Government Analyzed*], *Freethinkers' Magazine* (Jan. 1893), 62; Victor Yarros, "A Book Analyzed," *Liberty* (Dec. 3, 1892): 2–3.

49. Yarros, "A Book Analyzed," esp. 2; Benjamin Tucker, "On Picket Duty," *Liberty* (Dec. 3, 1892): 1.

50. Benjamin Tucker, "State Socialism and Anarchism: How Far They Agree and Wherein They Differ," *Liberty* (March 10, 1888): 2–3, 6, in Brooks, ed., *Individualist Anarchists*, 77–89, esp. 78; Lizzie M. Holmes, "Pity for Our Quaking Victims," *Liberty* (July 26, 1890): 3, in Brooks, ed., *Individualist Anarchists*, 259–60, esp. 259; Victor Yarros, "Methods and Results," *Liberty* (Dec. 13, 1890): 4–5, in Brooks, ed. *Individualist Anarchists*, 251–53, esp. 251; Victor Yarros, "Corollaries," *Liberty* (Jan. 14, 1893): 2–3, esp. 2. On "Tucker the Terrible," see Reichert, *Partisans of Freedom*, 141–70.

51. Yarros, "A Book Analyzed," 2. Moses Harman, in "A Case of Bighead," *Lucifer the Light Bearer* (Jan. 27, 1893): 2, thought that Yarros was pedantically objecting to Kelso saying that government had been "invented" to enslave the masses, but this was merely a play on words. Kelso spent many pages describing how coercive government probably evolved from stronger primates dominating the herd to an extension of patriarchal power over families to various forms of oligarchy.

52. [Book review of *Government Analyzed*], *American Journal of Eugenics* (March/ April, 1909), 36–37, esp. 37; Kelso, *Government Analyzed*, 484; Yarros, "A Book Analyzed," 3. At his last speech Kelso called himself both a "Democrat" and an "Anarchist"—another contradiction Yarros would have found absurd ("Why Heaven Failed," *Rocky Mountain News* [Nov. 17, 1890]: 6). Although it is hard to distinguish Kelso's hand from Etta's, a case might be made that he was more individualistic and she more communitarian; that he was more inclined to strip away social artifice to let natural laws do their work, recurring to the logic of Adam Smith's laissez-faire economics, while she leaned more toward the "unfoldment" of moral evolution, inspired by Herbert Spencer's sociology; that while he predicted violent revolution, she seemed more hopeful for peaceful progress.

53. Kelso, *Government Analyzed*, 275–76, 35.

54. On the strategies for advancing anarchism by the individualist anarchists of *Liberty*, see Brooks, ed., *Individualist Anarchists*, 247–314.

55. Book review of *Government Analyzed*, in *American Journal of Eugenics* (March/ April, 1909): 36–37, esp. 36.

56. "Philosophical Anarchists," *[Denver, Colo.] Rocky Mountain News* (Nov. 16, 1890): 7; "Why Heaven Failed," *Rocky Mountain News* (Nov. 17, 1890): 6; John R. Kelso, "The Kingdom of Heaven, or, The Teachings for which Our Comrades Suffered Martyrdom," delivered before the Rocky Mountain Social League, Denver, Colorado, November 16, 1890, in "Miscellaneous Writings," 492–519, esp. 507, 508.

57. Kelso, The Kingdom of Heaven," 509–10.

58. Kelso, *The Bible Analyzed*, chapters 3, 4, 19, and 20; on Jesus as a "tramp," see esp. pp. 725–26; Kelso, "The Kingdom of Heaven," in "Miscellaneous Writings," 511–18.

59. Kelso, "The Kingdom of Heaven," in "Miscellaneous Writings," 519.

60. Ibid., 519; Kelso, "The Anarchists," in "Miscellaneous Writings," 356, 359.

CONCLUSION

1. Kelso, Pension File, National Archives: Etta Dunbar Kelso, "Widow's Declaration for Pension," July 3, 1891; Etta D. Kelso, "Neighbor's Affidavit," Nov. 16, 1888; Dr. D. N. Stradley, "Affidavit to Date and Cause of Soldier's Death," May 7, 1891; Dr. D. N. Stradley, "Affidavit to Date and Cause of Soldier's Death," May 29, 1897.

2. D mss 7: 43–44; Milton Burch, letter, Dec., 1888, Kelso Pension File, National Archives. His newspaper obituary, like Dr. Stradley's two pension affidavits, stated the cause as stomach cancer: "Local," *Idaho Springs News* (Jan. 30, 1891): 4.

3. The Weld Co., Colo., County Clerk's Office found no property listed for Kelso at his death (Weld County Deputy County Clerk, "General Affidavit," June 22, 1897, Kelso Pension File, National Archives); Advertisement for *Government Analyzed*, in *American Journal of Eugenics* (Nov./Dec. 1908): 326 (Harman's successor publication to *Lucifer*); Britton, *The Aftermath of the Civil War*, 222–23; Florella Finney, letter, Dieu collection; Joe Dieu reminiscence, Nov. 2016 (portrait). Family members have a few of the books he owned, his military document case, his sword, and his Liberal League ceremonial cane. Kelso thought Susie had sold his big shotgun, but she gave it to her son John Jr. A grandson shot turkeys with it; a great grandson held it in the 1960s, but then it disappeared (Rhiannon and John Jeffrey Kelso reminiscence, Dec. 2019).

4. 1900 U.S. Census, Highland Lake, Weld Co., Colo., family no. 40; 1910 U.S. Census, St. Vrain, Weld Co., Colo, family no. 30; "Coffin-Paulus," *Longmont Ledger* (March 3, 1899): 3. Kelso, Pension File, National Archives: Etta D. Kelso, "Widow's Declaration for Pension," July 3, 1891; Etta D. Kelso, "Declaration for Widow's Pension," Aug. 23, 1891; George E. Smith, "General Affidavit," May 29, 1897; Etta D. Kelso, "General Affidavit," May 29, 1897; Samuel A. Pole, "General Affidavit," May 20, 1897; Florella A. Finney, "General Affidavit," June 18, 1897; Deputy Clerk, Weld Co., CO, "General Affidavit," June 22, 1897; J. J. Burke, "General Affidavit," July 22, 1897; Morse and Julia Coffin, "General Affidavit," Nov. 18, 1903; Etta D. Kelso, "General Affidavit," Dec. 11, 1903; Morse and Julia Coffin, "General Affidavit," Dec. 14, 1903; "Widow's Pension," Feb. 3, 1904. Etta's social calls were sometimes recorded in the local papers: "Personal Points," *Loveland Leader* (March 10, 1893): 1; "Home News," *Longmont Ledger* (June 16, 1899): 3; "Pleasant View Ridge," *Longmont Ledger* (April 6, 1900): 5; "Friday," *Longmont Ledger* (July 27, 1900): 3; "Rooseveld," *Longmont Ledger* (Sept. 21, 1900): 3; "Liberty Hall," *Longmont Ledger* (Sept. 6, 1901): 2; "Home News," *Longmont Ledger* (May 23, 1902); "Home News," *Longmont Ledger* (Sept. 5, 1902): 2; "Home News," *Longmont Ledger* (Feb. 6, 1903): 5; "Liberty Hall," *Longmont Ledger* (Feb. 13, 1903): 2; "Mount Zion," *Greeley Tribune* (April 2, 1903): 2; "Home News," *Longmont Ledger* (March 5, 1909): 5. On the Fisher affair: "Mrs. Etta D. Kelso in Trouble," *Longmont Ledger* (Aug. 12, 1910): 1; "Decision for Mrs. Kelso," *Longmont Ledger* (April 7, 1911): 1; Arthur J. Cramp, *Nostrums and Quakery: Articles on the Nostrum Evil and Quackery Reprinted from the Journal of*

the American Medical Association, vol. 3 (Chicago: Press of the AMA, 1936), 87; George B. Fisher, *Murdering God Is the Science of Obtaining Health; with a Blending of Foods, Drinks, Brain, Lung and Stomach Gymnastics, Massaging and Percussion* (Denver: J. D. Young, 1905–6); "Letters Testamentary," Nov. 7, 1910 (Etta declared mentally incompetent), Office of the Clerk and Recorder, Weld Co., Colo. Etta Dunbar Kelso, 1837–1923, Mountain View Cemetery, Longmont, CO, findagrave. com; "Sandstone Ranch Album," Longmont Museum, www.longmontcolorado. gov. Several of Etta's paintings still hang on the walls of Sandstone Ranch.

5. Kelso, Pension Pile, National Archives: Martha S[usan] McCapes, "Declaration for Remarried Widow's Pension," Nov. 1, 1916; Martha S. McCapes, letter, May 3, 1917; "Remarried Widow's Pension," May 18, 1917. California Death Index, 1905–1939, ancestry.com; Mary Adelia Lynch, 1880 U.S. Census, Monroe, Daviess Co., Mo., family no. 124; D mss 14: 43, and see 2: 165; Missouri Death Certificates, 1910–1962, ancestry.com.

6. D mss 14: 42, 14: 50, 11: 18; 1900 U. S. Census, District 0012, Township 5, Fresno Co., Calif., family no, 4; 1910 U.S. Census, Township 9, Santa Barbara, Calif., family no. 132 (as John E. Kelso); 1920 U.S. Census, Betteravia, Santa Barbara, Calif., family no. 109; 1930 U.S. Census, Pacific Grove, Monterey, Calif., family no. 130 (as John H. Kelso); Gordon Chappell, et al, *Kelso Depot Historic Structure Report: An Oasis for Railroads in the Mojave* (Washington, D.C.: U.S. Dept. of the Interior, National Park Service,1998), 37–38; Rhiannon Kelso and John Jeffrey Kelso reminiscence, Dec. 2019. Thanks to Kris Stoever and Rhiannon Kelso for genealogical help on JRK Jr. A railroad depot and later a very small town in California's Mojave Desert was named Kelso after railroad workers, wanting a name for the place, pulled his out of a hat. Why John Jr. changed his name is unclear, but descendants remember a story about him wanting to differentiate himself from a "horse thief" of the same name. "Horse thief" did not necessarily refer to an actual stealer of horses: it was a "familiar epithet . . . sometimes employed as a label for one's wartime or political enemies" (Blevins, *History of the Ozarks*, 2: 173; and see Jonathan Green, *Cassell's Dictionary of Slang* [London: Cassell, 2004], 743: "horse thief" was slang in the early 20th c. U.S. for a dishonest person).

7. D mss 14: 49, 11: 18; "Iantha A. Kelso (Mrs. W. R. Cooke)," *Historical Sketch of the State Normal School at San Jose, California* (Sacramento, Calif.: J. D. Young, 1889), 195; 1900 U. S. Census, Township 5, Fresno, Calif., family no. 214; Iantha Cooke, California Voter Registrations, 1900–1968, Alameda, Calif., 1940, ancestry.com; Find A Grave index, ancestry.com.

8. D mss 3: 238, 4: 295, 11:18; 1900 U. S. Census, District 0053, Modesto, Stanislaus County, Calif., family no. 35; 1940 U. S. Census, Modesto, Stanislaus County, Calif., house no. 199; California Death Index, 1940–1997, ancestry.com.

9. Kelso, "Thomas Paine," in "Miscellaneous Writings," 184–85.

10. Kelso, Preface, "Miscellaneous Writings," 5.

11. D mss 14: 38–9.

12. John R. Kelso, "Dangers that Threaten the People, Delivered, Extempore, at the Spiritualistic Camp-meeting at San Jose, Cal. June 7th, 1885," in Kelso, "Miscellaneous Writings," 381–82.

13. Florella A. Finney, inserted note in D mss 14: after final page.

Index

For the benefit of digital users, indexed terms that span two pages (e.g., 52–53) may, on occasion, appear on only one of those pages.